The Moral Property of Women

The
Moral
Property
of Women

A History of
Birth Control Politics
in America

LINDA GORDON

LCCC LIBRARY

University of Illinois Press
Urbana and Chicago

This book is a substantially revised and updated edition of
Woman's Body, Woman's Right: Birth Control in America
(Grossman Publishers, 1976; 2d ed., Penguin Books, 1990).

♾ This book is printed on acid-free paper.

Library of Congress Cataloging-in-Publication Data
Gordon, Linda.
The moral property of women : a history of birth control
politics in America / Linda Gordon. — 3d ed.
p.   cm.
Includes bibliographical references and index.
ISBN 0-252-02764-7 (cloth : alk. paper)
1. Birth control—United States—History.
I. Title: History of birth control politics in America.
II. Gordon, Linda. Woman's body, woman's right.
III. Title.
HQ766.5.U5G66   2002
363.9'6'0973—dc21   2002001551

Contents

Preface

In 1988 the French minister of health overruled a large pharmaceutical company and ordered the abortion drug RU-486 (mifepristone) placed on the market, declaring that it was "the moral property of women." When I heard the phrase, I realized that it was an exact statement of the ethical premise of this book and a much better title for it than the one I used in 1976, which has become rather hackneyed.

When I began this book in the early 1970s, I had the advantage of Norman E. Himes's exhaustive medical history of contraception published in 1936 (extensively cited in the early part of this book). But the basic arguments of my book—that birth control history was a fundamental part of the history of industrial and postindustrial society and specifically of women's emancipation and radical transformations of gender systems —came from the newly developing women's history. That birth control is women's "moral property" is not a given of God or nature but a creation of historical conflict, of politics, and specifically of feminism. This "property," like all property and like rights, has been and remains the object of political conflict.

This is a work of *longue durée* history, that is, an interpretation of several centuries of the politics of reproduction control. In creating this revised and updated edition, I have not tried to detail the extensive and intricate conflicts over reproductive rights that swirled around us in the United States in 2002. I stuck instead to my original purpose: to put contemporary reproduction control issues in a 200-year-long historical context. My goal is to enable readers of this book to relate "voluntary motherhood" advocates of the 1870s to "pro-choice" activists of the 1970s, to compare today's "right-to-life" advocates to abortion opponents of a century ago, and to connect the impact of the oral contraceptive pill to that of the diaphragm. Most important, I want to continue the story of the changing meanings and political significance of birth control into the twenty-first century.

I did not think it would work simply to add more chapters, as I had done for the 1990 edition. New developments do not simply attach to an old story, they change the way we understand the old story. Furthermore, I wanted to keep this book at a reasonable length. So I determined to add only the broadest of generalizations about the developments of the past three decades. This approach seemed appropriate because, while there have been excellent new studies of aspects of birth control history and contemporary reproductive rights conflicts, no new work has attempted to place the politics of birth control as a whole in the longer historical context with which this book is concerned.

So *The Moral Property of Women* involved much rethinking and rewriting. I added new material, subtracted some old material, revised previous interpretations, and appraised how new studies have changed our understanding of the past. Since I finished the first edition of this book—in the mid-1970s—I have gone on to other topics and many excellent scholars have focused on recent reproduction control issues. I have used this new scholarship only sparingly. I did not wish to give the appearance of trying to improve my imperfect book on the basis of other people's work.

The fundamental arguments of this book remain what they were when the first edition appeared in 1976: that conflicts about reproductive rights are political conflicts; that even what appear to be technological developments and neutral social scientific surveys must always be understood in political context; and that political contexts include particularly prominently the gender system as well as class and race structures. In the first edition of *Woman's Body, Woman's Right* I identified three major moments in the development of modern U.S. reproduction control politics: "voluntary motherhood," the first political claim that control over reproduction and sexual activity was a woman's right; "birth control," at first the slogan for a radical reform movement, a movement powerful enough that its slogan became generic; and "family planning," which captured the integration of reproduction control into a new family norm. I situated these in relation to three more conservative perspectives on reproduction control—neo-Malthusianism, eugenics, and population control.

Organizing the book around these changing programs rested on a theoretical premise that was almost as important as the substantive historical periodization. This was the recognition that a historical account could not presume that reproduction control was a transhistorical behavior with a fixed set of purposes, then modified by different methods and widening use. Rather, I argued that the purposes and meanings of these attempts to control reproduction were created and re-created differently in different contexts and historical periods. The languages of different reproduction control programs—neo-

Malthusianism, voluntary motherhood, Planned Parenthood, race suicide, birth control, population control, control over one's own body, for example— were not merely different slogans for the same thing but helped construct different activities, purposes, and meanings; the language was itself insepara- ble from the creation of those different meanings and the political struggles that arose around them.

Rejecting the idea that there are fixed, essential categories that can be differently interpreted is today often identified with post-structuralism, and historians benefit from this theorizing of how human beings create meanings through language. I am less comfortable with readings of history that deny the existence of a "real" past and reduce both historical sources and historiogra- phy to an endlessly pluralistic play among an infinite number of possible per- spectives. By contrast, I argue here that in different historical periods there are specifiable hegemonic and resistant meanings and purposes to reproduc- tion control; that these meanings are socially and politically, not individually, constituted; and that they express the (unstable) balances of political power between different social groups.

Evidence of that shifting balance of political power is visible in the shift- ing reputation of this book. When *Woman's Body, Woman's Right* appeared in 1976 it was praised by feminists but harshly criticized by mainstream aca- demic reviewers and by the journal of the Planned Parenthood establishment, *Family Planning Perspectives.*[1] They resisted my conclusion that social move- ments had been influential in the legitimation and development of contracep- tion. They also disliked the indeterminism of my critical perspective, my re- jection of a narrative that assumed (a) the inevitability of development in certain directions—for example, toward the medicalization of birth control and its assimilation to population control ideas—and (b) steady progress due to enlightened leadership. But in the intervening quarter century, feminist ap- proaches—that is, an understanding of gender as a fundamental power rela- tion—have become widespread even as the backlash against feminism has also gained strength. The result has been a convergence of interests between fem- inist and mainstream family planning organizations. From a historian's perspec- tive it is remarkable how quickly the negative judgments of *Woman's Body, Woman's Right* were revised. This transformation has to do not with the book itself but with the rapid cultural change that gave rise to and then surround- ed this book.

Once again, language offers a way to encapsulate such changes. When I wrote *Woman's Body, Woman's Right,* words such as "sexism," "sexual harass- ment," and "Ms." were newly invented, not part of popular or academic vo- cabularies. It was then unconventional, even illegitimate, to discuss birth con- trol in a college classroom, let alone a secondary or primary school. Planned

Parenthood was nervous that feminists and abortion rights advocates would make birth control disreputable. Today it is part of a feminist lobby for reproductive rights. This convergence was, of course, due not only to feminist gains but also to the antifeminist backlash. The rise of Christian Coalition–type conservatism and its alliance with traditional Republicans such as the Bushes posed threats great enough to narrow the gap between feminists and family planners, as it became clear that the legality and funding, not only of abortion, but even of contraceptive services, were threatened.[2]

A subcategory of that larger cultural change has been the rapid growth of the field of women's history. A smaller first wave of women's historians, associated with the first wave of feminism, had been suppressed by lack of academic recognition and was virtually invisible at the time of my education. Now I am but one member of a large national and international network of women's historians who have reshaped many earlier historical understandings. *Woman's Body, Woman's Right* was deeply influenced by the call of these historians for a reconceptualization of women's social roles as active as well as passive; for an end to what came to be called "victim history"; and for an understanding that if we were to represent women's influence as well as their powerlessness, we would have to think critically about women's contributions and avoid hagiography. The rapid sophistication of the new women's history is one reason that my critique of Margaret Sanger, for example, received with hostility by her partisans then, is now considered commonplace.

Given the extraordinarily rapid and rich growth of a gender-conscious history, I had to be highly selective in rewriting this book. Here is what is different in *The Moral Property of Women:* The old chapters 1, 2, and 3 have been rewritten and combined in the new chapters 1 and 2. I rethought and rewrote chapter 8, "Birth Control and Social Revolution." Chapters 3–7 and 9–11 retain substantially the same arguments and material, with some cuts and some new material integrated. What follows after that is new: chapter 12 on birth control and public policy; chapter 13 on the all-consuming abortion debates of the last third of the twentieth century; chapter 14 on the concentric circles of reproduction control arguments that move out from abortion—arguments about contraception, sterilization, teenage pregnancy and childbearing, stem cell research. I also rewrote the conclusion and added an appendix of selected recent scholarship on the history of reproduction control.

Acknowledgments

This book is the granddaughter of one originally published in 1976, so it is itself a piece of historiographical evidence for future historians. In their interest, I have organized these acknowledgments of my vast intellectual debts in historical periods.

Regarding the 1976 edition: The interpretations offered in this book depend on virtually everything I have learned about history and gender and sexual politics. While the immediate labor on it is mine, congealed in it, invisible to most readers, is the labor of many others. I can mention only those to whom my debt is quite specific. I am grateful to those who read and criticized part or all of the draft: Ros Baxandall, Frank Brodhead, Mari Jo and Paul Buhle, Nancy Chodorow, Michele Clark, Ellen DuBois, Elinor Langer, Charles Rosenberg, Sheila Rowbotham, Kathryn Kish Sklar, Carroll Smith-Rosenberg, Marilyn Webb, and Peter Weiler. Allen Hunter read virtually the entire manuscript, demanding clarity, proof, and precision in many places; although I was not always able to meet his demands, their existence as goals greatly improved what I was able to accomplish. Ellen DuBois, Elinor Langer, Martin Legassick, and Rabbi Saul Spiro generously contributed useful source materials. Discussions with my Bread and Roses consciousness-raising group, my students at the University of Massachusetts at Boston, my Marxist-feminist conference group, the *Radical America* editorial board, and the Marxist Institute for a New History, as well as with Ros Baxandall, Elizabeth Ewen, Stuart Ewen, Susan Reverby, and Meredith Schwarz greatly elevated my thinking. During the years of working on this book, I benefited from the support and confidence of friends, especially Wini Breines, Michele Clark, Margery Davies, Ann Froines, David Hunt, Allen Hunter, and Danny Schechter. Susan Siens typed a great deal of this manuscript beautifully. My editor, Ellen Posner, and my copy editor, Caroline Lalire, helped me to clarify my thoughts. In the 1960s, thanks to Ellen Walker, I spent some time with Dr. Lena Levine, and I vividly remember her warmth and intelligence. Had she been alive when I turned to birth control as a historian, I suspect that my interpretation of her pioneering sex counseling work would have been greatly strengthened through discussion with her.

Regarding the 1990 edition: I am grateful to the Vilas Associates and the Graduate School of the University of Wisconsin at Madison for awards that helped me work on the revision. My main intellectual debt is to Rosalind Pollack Petchesky, whose *Abortion and Woman's Choice,* published in 1984, remains the most sophisticated interpretation of recent reproduction control politics; I have been influenced by her interpretations probably more than I realize. I am particularly indebted to Allen Hunter, Judith Walzer Leavitt, Nancy MacLean, Rosalind Petchesky, Norma Swenson, and Nadine Taub, who read all the new material, offered detailed comments, and saved me from some errors. Susan Stanford Friedman helped me say more exactly what I wanted to in the preface to the second edition. Vicki Alexander, Ros Baxandall, Elizabeth Fee, Ruth Hubbard, Carole Joffe, and Barbara Katz Rothman made thoughtful suggestions. Norma Swenson of the Boston Women's Health Book Collective gave me not only a long evening but also her vast store of knowledge and understanding. Jan Brin, Judy Norsigian, and Esther Rome of the Collective went out of their way to help me; I am grateful to the whole Collective, even those I've never met, for the wonderful archive of material they have created. I am indebted to Byllye Avery, Vicki Alexander, and Larry Bumpass for telephone consultation and to Bob Buchanan, Marie Laberge, Chris Sullivan, and Susan Traverso for research help. My editor, Lori Lipsky, graciously offered not only editorial but even some research assistance. Many of those named in my earlier acknowledgments are still parts of my intellectual life, and I am now also indebted to some newer friends and colleagues, particularly those in the history department and the Women's Studies Program at the University of Wisconsin at Madison. I have particularly learned a great deal about the meanings of reproduction from Judy Leavitt and Susan Friedman. I am grateful to Nancy Miller for beginning my education about the meanings of infertility several years ago. My discussion of the teenage pregnancy problem was influenced by Martha Fineman, Sara S. McLanahan, and Ann Orloff. In less direct but equally important ways I learned from several colleagues and friends who have let me try out my opinions, listen to how they think about the world, or simply benefit from their energy and kindness: Ed and Susan Friedman, Dirk and Nancy Hartog, Larry Hirschfeld, Judy and Lewis Leavitt, Gerda Lerner, Nellie McKay, Ann Stoler, and Erik and Marcia Wright.

2002 acknowledgments: Again my intellectual and personal debts are extensive. I want particularly to thank Suzanne Desan, Liz and Stuart Ewen,

Barbara Forrest, Susan and Ed Friedman, Heinz Klug, Judy and Lewis Leavitt, Gerda Lerner, Gay Seidman, and Erik and Marcia Wright. I continue to learn a great deal regarding this material from Ros Baxandall and Allen Hunter, and I am once again grateful. Special thanks to Tracey Deutsch and Micki McElya for extremely thoughtful assistance; to Dorothea Browder and Sarah Costello for indexing; to Rebecca Wind of the Alan Guttmacher Institute and Suzanne Grossman of the Center for Reproductive Law and Policy for last-minute help; and to Theresa L. Sears for editing *extraordinaire*.

The Moral Property of Women

Introduction

Birth Control, the Moral Property of Women

This book offers a general history of birth control politics in the United States. It stresses the unity and development of political thinking about birth control during the past two centuries. It shows that the campaign for birth control was so broad that at times during its history it constituted a grassroots social movement and that it was frequently a controversy involving fundamental and embattled ethical and political values.

The acceptability of birth control has always depended on a morality that separates sex from reproduction. In the nineteenth century, when the birth control movement began, such a separation was widely considered immoral. The eventual widespread public acceptance of birth control required a major reorientation of sexual values. This book tells that story from the point of view of those at the center of the conflict, namely, women seeking sexual and reproductive self-determination.

The Moral Property of Women surveys this movement in its largest sense: its ideas, its constituency, the motivations and needs of its advocates and its opponents. It is a movement with a continuous history from the mid-nineteenth century, when feminists attacked unwanted pregnancies in the name of sacred female chastity, through the early twentieth century, when contraception hastened the breakdown of traditional standards of chastity, to the end of the twentieth century, when birth control was again intensely controversial. The movement began in the 1870s as a campaign for "voluntary motherhood," the slogan for a program that condemned contraception and proposed long periods of sexual abstinence for married couples as the remedy for unwanted children. The most recent expressions of that movement grew from the revival of feminism in the late 1960s and 1970s and produced, notably, a campaign for the legalization of abortion and promotion of contraception on a mass scale by governments all around the world. Clearly, such large changes not only reflect but have also nurtured parallel changes in sexual attitudes and practices.

From the Introduction to the First Edition

This book argues that birth control has always been primarily an issue of politics, not of technology. Effective forms of birth control were used in nearly all ancient societies; in the modern world, restrictive sexual standards forced birth control underground. The re-emergence of birth control as a respectable practice in the twentieth century was a process of changing sexual standards, largely produced by the women's rights movement and the rejection of Victorian prudery.

As a piece of history, this book rests within two new fields—women's history and the history of sexuality. In comparison with work done in historical fields where there are strong, tested methodologies, a study about women and/or about sex will necessarily be naïve.

The weakness and newness of these fields are related. The lack of adequate history about sexual behavior and attitudes is a result of the inattention to women in history, because sex itself cannot be comprehended except as a facet of the relations between the two sexes. (This is because sex has been primarily, though not exclusively, defined in terms of relations between men and women.) The relations between the sexes cannot, in turn, be analyzed productively except with an understanding of the subordination of women and their resistance and accommodation to it. Not having incorporated an analysis of this subordination, no historical tradition can yet produce sophisticated work on human sexual behavior.

It seemed to me, thinking that we must start somewhere, that a major factor in the development of women's sexuality was birth control. My premise was that birth control represented the single most important factor in the material basis of women's emancipation in the course of the past hundred years—that contraception promised the final elimination of women's only significant biological disadvantage. (The capacity to reproduce is not a disadvantage, but lack of control over it is.) So I began to study birth control—and rather quickly had to question my original premise. It is true that the technology of contraception provided women with a valuable tool, but why did the technology develop when it did? And why did some women seize it more eagerly than others? I discovered that there is a complex, mutual, causal relationship between birth control and women's status. Birth control has been as much a symptom as a cause of larger social changes in the relations between sexes.

My mistake in seeing birth control as only cause, never result, was characteristic both of my academic training and of the early phases of second-wave feminist analysis. Although sympathetic to the people on the bottom, influenced by the new "history from the bottom up," I had been accustomed to view the fate of the poor as determined by the power of the rich. The working class, for example, appeared solely as the creation of the capitalist class. So in our frustration over women's roles, many feminists of my generation at first saw ourselves as victims of male supremacy, battling a discriminatory system and an ideology of femininity created by men for their benefit. The complexities of the birth control question illustrated the inadequacy of that whole approach. The suppression of birth control, I learned, was partly a means of enforcing male supremacy but also partly a self-protection for women, a means of enforcing men's responsibility for their sexual behavior. Indeed, all the cultural aspects of womanhood were created and re-created jointly, though not always amicably, by men and by women who were resisting and accommodating their own subjection. The major institutions of sex and reproduction, such as family and codes of morality, were established as much by women's activity as by men's.

The suppression and then the legalization of birth control were developments in the relations between the sexes and the changing social and economic organization of society. Since I could not describe these processes by looking at birth control alone, I had to broaden this book and make it more complex. It is about birth control, sexuality, and women. But it is about women as subjects, women trying to create the conditions of their lives. This book is about social movements for birth control, sexual freedom, and feminism.[1]

Introduction 2002

It is tricky to demarcate the moments when advocating birth control became a social movement. How does one distinguish between those who struggled to control their own childbearing and those who fought for reproductive rights as a matter of justice? Most social movements involve self-interest. Workers often strike "only" for higher wages, yet their activism forms a social movement when they struggle collectively. So I would say that birth control became a social movement when individuals banded together to develop collective strategies. Many began from an ideology of feminism or of sexual freedom or of civil liberties, while others began with no ideology beyond a conviction that the prohibition on birth control was unjust. When the birth control movement developed ideologies, these ideologies often arose from aspirations and motives that had already propelled people into political action. For many these ideologies formulated and articulated what was already present in their actions.

The birth control movement passed through four distinct stages, each characterized by a different slogan for reproduction control. The first was "voluntary motherhood," a slogan advanced by feminists in the second half of the nineteenth century. It expressed exactly the emphasis on choice, freedom, and autonomy for women around which the women's rights movement was unified. Voluntary motherhood became a basic plank in the feminist platform, more universally endorsed than woman suffrage and, arguably, reaching farther to describe and change the plight of women than any other single issue. Stage two, approximately 1910–20, produced the term "birth control." It represented not only a new concept but a new organizational phase, with separate birth control leagues initially created by feminists who were influenced by the large socialist movement of the time. It stood not only for women's autonomy but for transforming the gender and class order through empowering the powerless, primarily identified as the poor and the female sex. (Although "birth control" was originally associated with this specific, radical movement, it has since become the accepted generic term for reproductive control, so that I have no choice but to use it in both senses in this book.)

From 1920 through approximately 1970, the movement evolved away from the radicalism of its second stage into a liberal reform movement. This third stage produced a new slogan, "planned parenthood," in the 1940s, though the new content had been developed in the 1930s. With the revival of feminism in the late 1960s, a fourth stage began, associated first with the concept "reproductive rights." In the 1970s, 1980s, and 1990s, a new and largely Christian Right made an attack on abortion rights one of its leading issues, possibly its flagship campaign. As a result, the antiabortion slogan "right to life" became equally characteristic.

The Moral Property of Women offers a narrative and analysis of these four stages and their accompanying slogans. Part 1 introduces reproduction control before the birth control movement began. Part 2 examines the campaign for birth control in the context of nineteenth-century feminism and early twentieth-century radicalism. Part 3 covers the political legitimation of contraception in the period 1920–70. Finally, part 4 addresses the intense reproductive rights controversies that emerged from second-wave feminism and the opposition to it in the late twentieth century.

PART 1

From Folk Medicine to Prohibition to Resistance

1   *The Prehistory of Birth Control*

Although birth control is very old, the movement for the right to control reproduction is young. About two centuries ago, when the movement began, birth control had been morally and religiously stigmatized in many parts of the world, so illicit that information on the subject was whispered, or written and distributed surreptitiously. Birth control advocates in the United States served jail terms for violation of obscenity laws. Moreover, reproductive rights advocates were often dissenters in other dimensions as well—trade unionists, socialists, feminists, for example. As a result, the modern birth control movement has at various times included campaigns for women's rights, economic justice, freedom of speech, freedom of the press, and the extension of democracy. To understand these struggles we must first understand something about the nature and sources of the censoring ideology.

People have tried to control reproduction in virtually all known societies, and not simply as private matters. These attempts were always acknowledged and socially regulated in some way. Although it is customary to speak of "natural" birth control, as opposed to commercially manufactured methods, and although many long for the simplicity of what is conceived as "natural" sexual and family life, in fact there is no "natural" when it comes to human society. Social control—rules, prohibitions, stigma, and moral condemnation—has always characterized human sexuality. Birth control also has consequences, of course, for population size, a crucial issue for human communities. Birth control affects the size of families, also a matter crucial to well-being. And it bears, too, on the role of women. Women's status cannot be correlated on a one-to-one basis with any particular system of sexual or reproductive regulation. But if the connections between social patterns of sexual activity and female activity are complex, they are nonetheless close. Systems of sexual control change as women's status changes; they both reflect and affect each other. There has been an especially strong connection between the subjection of women and the prohibition on birth control: the latter has been a means of enforcing the former. Inversely, there has been a strong connection between women's emancipation and their ability to control reproduction.

Still, birth control was widely practiced in pre-agricultural and nomadic societies (by means of methods examined below). Small families were particularly important to nomadic societies, where families and entire clans had to pack up their belongings and children and regularly travel long distances, often on foot. Not surprisingly, they practiced rudimentary forms of contraception as well as abortion and infanticide—always, of course, regulated by the community.

The development of agriculture seems to have produced a revolutionary change in reproduction control practices. Sedentary farming life made it possible to accumulate personal property, the capacity of agriculture to absorb labor made larger families an asset, and the capacity of agriculture to produce a surplus made larger populations supportable. Among the peasant majorities throughout the world, children typically contributed more to the family economy than they cost. At the same time, high mortality, especially among infants, meant that women had to give birth to more children than the family needed. Thus agricultural societies often produced ideologies that entirely banned birth control.

In the past five centuries further social changes made a lower birth rate economically advantageous in the more developed parts of the world. These changes included improved diet and sanitation, and thus a decline in the death rate, particularly the infant mortality rate. Even before medical progress, however, which was mainly a nineteenth- and twentieth-century phenomenon, economic developments radically undercut the value of large families. A money economy, the high costs of living for city dwellers, and the decreasing relative economic contribution of children reversed the traditional family economy and made children cost more than they could contribute. Some social groups were affected by these changes before others, perhaps the earliest being professionals living on salaries and coping with the high cost of education required to let their children inherit their status. Gradually, urbanization produced a decline in the birth rate among all classes.

Nevertheless, the new small family standard did not immediately or thoroughly subvert the prohibition on birth control. Ideologies about sex, women, gender, and motherhood had a powerful hold. The three modern Western religions—Judaism, Christianity, and Islam—all condemned at least some aspects of reproduction control, and these condemnations reinforced, and were reinforced by, their subordination of women. All three excluded women from core aspects of religious practice and status, and Christianity in particular distrusted sexual pleasure. So anti–birth control standards outlived whatever economic function they once had. When these standards began to weaken, they did so not only because a high birth rate was no longer necessary but also because of transformations of sexual and gender norms through the emancipation and employment of women and the development of a more individualist culture with a more positive appraisal of sexual pleasure.

As often happens with large-scale social change, however, these transformations produced reaction as well as accommodation. The resultant "Victorian" political culture of sex and gender, named for the queen who ruled the British Empire through much of the nineteenth century, dominated the industrial world. This was the particular form of sexual repression that pro–birth control campaigners had to contend with, and it had complex meanings for reproduction control. Far from relaxing the Christian suspicion of sex, it intensified and secularized these norms and applied them more stringently to women than to men. Physicians and other secular moral authorities joined men of the cloth in preaching maternity and domesticity as women's destiny and true desire, thus labeling those with different or additional aspirations as unwomanly. But the same culture gave rise to a powerful feminist movement, a movement ironically the strongest in the United States where Victorian prudery was also the most intense. So hegemonic was this ideology that it framed even the arguments of the opposition: Victorian radicals and conservatives alike typically acceded to the notion that women were purer than men and that the only worthy purpose of sexual activity was reproduction. Many feminists agreed.

Yet the essence of Victorian sexual respectability was hypocrisy. Victorian sexual norms preached the debilitating effects of sexual activity and the bracing effects of self-denial and chastity, but the Victorians simultaneously created a gigantic prostitution industry, and it was not unusual for "respectable" men to patronize it. The typical directive of prudery was to hide sex, that is, never to speak of what was widely practiced and to impose silence even about readily observable human experiences such as pregnancy. Birth control was one of those unmentionables. As a system of sexual politics, prudery forced birth control knowledge underground and may even have produced a decline in knowledge of reproduction control methods.

This hypocrisy operated a double standard: the "fair sex" was to be protected from dirty matters such as money, politics, and sex. Delicacy, fragility, paleness, softness were the official feminine qualities. But this conception of femininity—of the female gender—was a class and a race phenomenon. Women who worked at housework or on farms or in factories could not (and often would not) be delicate, fragile, pale, or soft. The Victorian normative emphasis on female respectability, accessible only to privileged women, expelled from "true" womanliness the majority of women, namely, slaves, peasants, farmers, the working class, and the colonized.

With respect to birth control, these gender norms are puzzling, since the physical processes of reproductive sex, pregnancy, childbirth, and breast-feeding are hardly dainty and require considerable strength and stamina. Their integration into this new gender system was accomplished through a mystification of "motherhood," which, like prudery itself, was produced both by opponents and advocates of women's rights. Commercial and industrial production undermined fathers' authority by making individuals economically "independent" in the wage-labor market, and conservatives began to exhibit anxiety that women would forsake their maternal destiny. The Victorian romance with the self-sacrificing mother was in part a public relations campaign to confine women. Simultaneously, relationships outside the family, especially for city dwellers, became less permanent and less reliable, unlike the community patterns of mutual dependency that had prevailed in precapitalist society. Motherhood came symbolically to represent loyalty, community, solidity in a world in which "all that is solid melts into air."

These changes spelled greater freedom for many individuals, especially those once subordinated to a master, such as wives, children, unmarried women, apprentices—although not for slaves and colonized peoples. But even in the world of the free, these changes had a down side: they carried the potential for loneliness and disorientation among individuals and a resultant social instability that alarmed many nineteenth-century working people, especially those who had recently migrated or immigrated from nonindustrial areas.

The disintegration of the economic unity of family life in no way ended its function as a social institution. On the one hand, families remained the primary means of socializing children into adult personalities appropriate to the demands of industrial capitalism. Authoritarianism and willingness to accept external controls over basic life processes such as work, learning, and sex were among the lessons children learned in their families, and restriction of sexual activity to marriage was an important means of enforcing these controls. On the other hand, families were called upon to absorb the heavy strains that the economy placed upon individuals. The traditional sexual division of labor within the family meant that women had to carry the bulk of this new psychological burden.

Both these familial functions contributed to an intensification of the cult of motherhood, embedding motherliness into the very definition of femininity. Maternal virtues justified and idealized the restriction of sex within marriage. The maternal tenderings of wives were now expected to extend beyond their children to their husbands, to turn their homes into soothing, comforting, challengeless escapes[1] for men returning from exhausting workdays of cutthroat competition and constant vigilance to buy cheap and sell dear, or of grinding physical labor and rigid external control. Women provided compensatory services as against the hidden and not so hidden injuries of a capitalist economy. In this way, the cult of motherhood was not merely an intrafamily ideology but carried on important ideological work throughout the society. For many in the upper class, women's tasks included supervising servants; wives' services were thus subtle, often symbolic, both their subservience (to husbands) and their authority (over servants) strengthening their husbands' class consciousness. In the working class, wives' and daughters' subordination helped construct a virile masculinity that created cross-class unity among men. It also provided real, not illusory or only symbolic, privileges for working-class men that many of them enthusiastically defended. Finally, it offered working-class women a sense of dignity that their forcible removal from access to productive labor threatened to erode.

In justifying this further specialization of the sexes in the division of labor, nineteenth-century ideologists of motherhood offered the view that the two sexes were not only different in all things but nearly opposite. It became unfashionable among the educated to say outright that women were inferior. (By contrast, a forthright male supremacist refrain had dominated most discussions of the sexes, both religious and secular, before the late eighteenth century.) Victorian ideology maintained that the spheres of men and women were separate but equal. Women, although allegedly inferior in intellectual, artistic, economic, and physical aptitude, were labeled morally superior as a result of their innate capacity for motherliness. This alleged superiority then justified narrow constraints on women's choices lest they be sullied.

The theory of the oppositeness of the sexes was particularly marked in matters of sex. Sex drive became, supposedly, a uniquely masculine trait. Some authorities flatly denied that women had sex drives—the maternal instinct was the female analogue of sex drive, according to this theory. Female chastity was no longer just a man's right but now also a woman's destiny, as a naturally asexual being; men were asked merely to moderate the extremes of their powerful sexual urges. Although purity was raised to first place among women's desired virtues, the virtues of a significant number of poor women were sacrificed, through prostitution, to the maintenance of male supremacy. The motherhood ideology also defined the context in which sexuality was allowable for women: the only justifiable purpose of sexual intercourse for "respectable" women was reproduction.[2] The label "prostitute" was sometimes applied to any women who engaged in sex outside of marriage.

A more complex matter is the degree of success of the ideologues in making their proposed norms work in practice. There is increasing historical evidence that many women were resistant to Victorian sexual indoctrination.[3] Furthermore, the mask of prudery virtually required hypocrisy, and many men and women behaved and felt differently in private than in public. Still, few could remain unaffected by these powerful norms. The euphemistic avoidance of direct discussion of sexual matters made sex appear as a dirty fact of life, unavoidable but unpleasant, like excretion. Advice books urged excluding sex from consciousness as well as from behavior. Women's purity of mind and body would determine not only their fate in the hereafter but also their marriageability on earth. Prudery was not merely an ideological system—the sanctions on women who deviated were material and often permanent, such as spinsterhood, desertion, economic ruin, disease, and death.

The repression[4] of female sexuality expressed itself physically as well as psychologically. Many women learned unease with their own bodies. Many women never undressed, even when alone, and bathed under their shifts; when they submitted sexually to their husbands, they remained clothed. For many women sexual intercourse was such a quick act of penetration that they never became aroused. People never exposed to sexual stimulation may indeed have had truncated, underdeveloped sex drives. Ill health also contributed to lessening sexual energy. Lack of exercise and confinement indoors made women of the privileged classes physically weak; terrible working and living conditions made poor women unhealthy in other, more serious ways. Among fashionable women, heavy corseting may have caused serious and permanent internal damage. The official approach to pregnancy ("confinement" it was called, and confinement it was, for the sight of a pregnant woman was indecent in "respectable" circles) prohibited exercise and social activity, while poor women were deprived of the rest they needed. Little could be more effective in depressing sexual interest than the fear of painful and dangerous pregnancies and childbirths.

Victorian constraints also interfered with the communication of birth control remedies from one generation to the next. And prudery hardly encouraged the ingenuity and experimentation required for developing home-remedy birth control techniques.

So the factors working against birth control were intensifying for the first three quarters of the nineteenth century. Although the rights of women were in many respects greater by the nineteenth century than they had ever been before in the Western world, the prohibition on birth control and on open discussion of sexual matters had rarely been more severe. After a nationwide "social purity" campaign, resulting in dozens of state laws prohibiting abortion, an 1873 federal law prohibited any form of birth control. Using the authority of the postal service, this Comstock law forbade sending obscene matter through the U.S. mail and specifically defined any discussion of birth control—even abstract philosophical discussion—as obscene.[5]

But we must recall once again that this repression was primarily a response to growing rebellion against the Victorian sexual system. That rebellion, as we shall see, was closely connected to the feminist movement that arose in the 1840s. The two rebellions had common causes and were related just as the two forms of repression—the repression of sex and the subjugation of women—were related. Moreover, this discursive and legal repression would have been unnecessary if birth control technology had been unknown.

The Folklore of Birth Control

There is a prevalent myth, in our technological society, that birth control technology came to us with modern medicine. This is far from the truth, as modern medicine did almost nothing prior to the 1950s to improve on birth control devices that were literally more than a millennium old. It is important to look at this heritage of traditional birth control if we are to understand the birth control movement, for that movement took its strength from women's understanding of the suppression of actual possibilities.

Birth control was not invented by scientists or doctors. It is a part of folk culture, and women's folklore in particular, in nearly all societies. Even though women rarely had a formal or absolute right to decide unilaterally when to bear children and when not to, women's birth control practice was usually respectable. At other times it was practiced illegally, its technology passed on by an underground of midwives and wisewomen.

An extensive folklore of birth control was handed down from generation to generation in most traditional societies. Some of these practices have remained so unchanged that, for example, vaginal sponges sold in the 1990s were virtually identical to those used several thousand years before Christ. The variety of attempts to prevent conception, and the creativity behind them, tells us something about how much people wanted control over reproduction. New inventions, after all, do not fall from the sky. They are developed by practice—through trial and error—in response to people's needs. A cataloging of the extent, variety, and ingenuity of these practices is eloquent testimony to the intensity of women's concern.

Differences in birth control methods have social significance, in part because some techniques are more amenable to being used independently and even secretly by women, some give full control to men, while others are more likely to be used cooperatively. A list of birth control methods might look like this: infanticide; abortion; sterilization; withdrawal by the male (*coitus inter-*

ruptus); suppositories designed to form an impenetrable coating over the cervix; diaphragms, caps, or other devices, which are inserted into the vagina over the cervix and withdrawn after intercourse; intrauterine devices; internal medicines—potions or pills; douching and other forms of action after intercourse designed to kill or drive out the sperm; condoms; and varieties of the rhythm methods, based on calculating the woman's fertile period and abstaining from intercourse during it.[6] All these techniques were practiced in the ancient world and in modern preindustrial societies. Indeed, until modern hormonal chemicals there were no essentially new birth control devices, only improvements of the old.

People have been designing homemade contraceptive formulas and performing homemade abortions for years. These folk techniques cannot compete with today's methods for effectiveness and safety, but when they were developed they were extraordinary achievements. On a societal level, even a small percentage of effectiveness produces an impact on the birth rate. Today women want 100 percent certainty that their pregnancies will be voluntary, a reasonable and practicable desire. But the development of that desire was itself produced by its historic possibility. Lacking that kind of effective contraception, women in preindustrial societies did not form such high expectations.

For our purposes, however, birth control attempts in preindustrial societies are significant whether or not they worked. They are evidence not only of the desire to control reproduction but also of the conviction that it is proper to do so and of the aspiration to do so. Today we need to combine the sophistication of modern chemistry and medicine with the attitude of these women and men of long ago, who believed that birth control was their responsibility and took responsibility for experimenting and judging what was best for themselves.

What we know today of the traditional use of these techniques represents only a fraction of what once existed. We have only sparse observations, and what information we have often comes from foreign travelers, merchants, even colonizers/invaders of other cultures who are hardly sensitive to their social organization, let alone the private culture of women. Anthropologists produce more reliable information, but they too are often handicapped by their cultural insensitivity and, when male, by their sex. Some of our information comes from the written records of ancient societies; but these records, too, were often based on the impressions of historians whose limitations were not dissimilar from those of modern anthropologists. What follows is only a sample drawn from inadequate information—a double handicap. But the sample serves a specific end: to demystify the technology of birth control.

In preindustrial societies one solution to periodic overpopulation or overburdened mothers was infanticide, the killing of newborn babies. The anthropologist Ralph Linton argued that infanticide met the needs of primitive groups more efficiently than contraception.[7] Contraception, at the level of technology available in most preindustrial societies, resulted in hit-or-miss population limitation. Infanticide provided not only precise population control but also control of the size and spacing of individual families.

Although women had the most to gain from reproduction control, infanticide was nevertheless frequently a direct expression of male supremacy. Not only have male babies been more valued, but female children were sometimes so valueless, despised, and even burdensome that a portion of them were systematically killed.

In these societies, infanticide was most distinctly not murder (assuming that "murder" refers to illegitimate, illegal killing). Infanticide was legal and respectable, fully distinguished in law and in custom from criminal homicide, even from justifiable homicide. Just as the Right to Life movement argues that a fetus is as much a living being as an infant, so in infanticide-practicing society it seemed that a newborn baby was no more a living being than a fetus. Certainly societies that have permitted infanticide have not defined newborn infants as human.

Nor was it just the "primitives" whose moral codes permitted infanticide. Both approval and condemnation are found in preliterate as well as highly advanced societies. Aristotle and Plato recommended infanticide for eugenic reasons.[8] The Romans legislated against infanticide, perhaps because, in conformity with their imperialist policies, they sought to expand their population, whereas the Greeks preferred to curb or stabilize theirs.[9] Nevertheless, infanticide persisted throughout the Roman period as a widespread and rarely prosecuted crime. Tacitus, the Roman historian, found it odd and foolish that the Jews did not practice infanticide.[10] For the Christians, the emphasis on the eternal life of the soul in heaven or hell redefined the moral issue. The sin of infanticide became not just a matter of human life but of the potential damnation of an immortal soul if it passed out of the body before baptism. It followed from this that killing a newborn child was a worse sin than killing a baptized adult.[11] But even Christianity was for a long time unable to secure full conformity to its commandments in this area, and throughout the Middle Ages, in Christian Europe, infanticide by exposure was not unusual.[12]

Are we, today, at a higher stage of moral development than these classical worthies or medieval sinners? Perhaps, but the fact that we have developed better methods of birth control makes it a bit too easy for us to claim superiority. Moreover, ignorance and shame still give rise to occasional infanticide in the United States.

Abortion has always been far more prevalent than infanticide. One antiabortion argument is that abortion violates some age-old and God-given "natural law," but the historical evidence dissolves that illusion. Almost all preindustrial societies accepted abortion. The ancient Jewish metaphor calls the fetus part of the mother as the fruit is a part of the tree till it ripens and falls; the Islamic metaphor holds that the welfare of the trunk is more vital than that of the branches. One anthropological collection of tribal studies, the Human Relations Area Files, found that 62 percent, or 125 of 200 groups, used abortion. Considering that anthropologists often didn't ask, or couldn't find out, about abortion, that is almost certainly an underestimate.[13]

The high incidence of abortions did not mean that they were easy. Women accepted the pain and danger of abortion in the same manner that they accepted the pain and danger of childbirth, with the assumption that both were necessary for their own and their communities' health and welfare. Over the centuries there developed a varied technology of abortion—magical and mechanical, external and internal. When abortions became illegal, these techniques merely went underground. In fact, there is striking continuity between abortion techniques used in ancient societies and those used in modern "home-remedy"[14] abortions. These methods remain prevalent among the poor throughout the world; in communities deprived of access to professional medical care, dependence on folk medicine continues.

One standard method of attempting to induce abortion, ancient and modern, was the potion, or abortifacient. In modern usage, only 7 to 14 percent of reportedly successful abortions resulted from internal medicine (before RU-486).[15] With few exceptions these recipes were part of a folk culture of herbal medicine. Recipes ranged from teas made of common herbs—such as marjoram, thyme, parsley, rosemary, ginger, and lavender—to exotic and elaborate concoctions such as a paste of mashed ants, foam from camels' mouths, and tail hairs of the black-tailed deer dissolved in bear fat.[16] The basic principle behind these various brews is that, to the degree they are effective at all, they are indirectly effective. None of them specifically aims at the fetus or its uterine support system. Rather, they so irritate or poison the body or the digestive system that they cause rejection of the fetus as a side effect. Some of the herbs commonly used may in fact be mild emmenagogues, stimulating the onset of menstruation and thus appearing to cause abortion. Hence the following description of the properties of basil from a seventeenth-century English herbal: "To conclude. It expelleth both birth and afterbirth; and as it helps the deficiency of Venus in one kind, so it spoils all her actions in another."[17]

Abortions performed by inserting an object into the uterus were more effective. These procedures were done frequently, and with great success, in preindustrial societies. For example, this instruction from the Persian physician Abu Bekr Muhammed ibn Zakariya Al-Razi in the tenth century: "If these methods [contraceptives he has prescribed] do not succeed . . . there is no help for it but that she insert into her womb a probe or a stick cut into the shape of a probe, especially good being the root of the mallow. One end of the probe should be made fast to the thigh with a thread that it may go in no further. Leave it there . . . until the menses do appear and the woman is cleansed."[18] Or this ingenious technique observed in Greenland:

> Certain Eskimo tribes use a thinly carved rib of walrus which is sharpened as a knife on one end, while the opposite end is made dull and rounded. The sharp end is covered with a rolled cover made of walrus skin, which is opened on both ends, and the length of which corresponds to the cutting part of the piece of bone. A long thread made of the sinews of reindeer is fastened to the upper as well as lower end of the cover. When this probe is being placed in the vagina, the sharp part is covered with the leather covering. After it has been inserted far enough, the thread fastened on the lower end of the covering is gently tugged. The sharp end thus being bared, a half turn is given the probe together with a thrust upwards and inwards, which punctures the uterus.[19] Before withdrawing the instrument, the upper thread of the covering is pulled in order to cover the sharp end, thus preventing further injury to the genital organs.[20]

In modern times this operation is performed with knitting needles, crochet hooks, nail files, nutcrackers, knives, hatpins, umbrella ribs, and pieces of wire; or with a catheter (a rubber tube), when more-professional equipment is available. The physiological event, the irritation of the uterus causing it to reject embryo and placenta, can also be created by the injection of a chemical into the uterus, such as potassium soap. Ancient prescriptions of this type called for the use of tar, cinnamon on a tampon of linen, or even pepper.[21]

Other abortion experts sought to destroy the fetus by external means, instructing women to engage in rigorous exercise: lifting heavy objects, climbing trees, taking hot baths, jumping from high places, shaking. Early twentieth-century Jewish women on the Lower East Side of New York City attempted to abort themselves by sitting over a pot of steam, preferably from hot stewed onions—a technique identical with one prescribed in an eighth-century Sanskrit source. Some ancient techniques are significantly more dangerous. We have reports of abortions performed by pouring hot water or hot ashes on the belly of the pregnant woman, having her bitten by large ants, grasping the uterus through the abdominal wall and twisting it until the fetus is detached.[22]

Despite the great pain involved, some women successfully aborted themselves, though most enlisted an experienced helper, typically a specialist. Sometimes the providers were exclusively or mainly abortionists, as in ancient Rome, where they were called *sagae* (probably the root word for the French *sage-femme,* or midwife). In the harem of the sultan of Turkey the official abortionist, called the "bloody midwife," was one of the sultan's own wives. Frequently, too, the providers were not only abortionists but general medical providers for women—we might call them folk gynecologists.[23]

Birth control before conception, if it can be done, is less painful and safer than birth control after conception. But contraception, as we call it today, was not easy to arrange in the premodern world. Effective contraception required at least a rudimentary understanding of the process of conception. Moreover, it usually required forethought, and an antagonistic male could sabotage a woman's attempts to contracept. Developing contraceptive techniques that work required a scientific trial-and-error process of study that was difficult in earlier times, given the lack of privacy and the superstition that frequently surrounded sexual intercourse. Considering these obstacles, the contraceptive knowledge accumulated in the ancient world is impressive.

Some of that ancient technology was lost over the centuries, often due to religious and moral suppression of birth control. The better methods, which required more preparation, were probably the first to disappear. But the suppression was never complete. When the first birth control clinics opened in Europe and America in the early twentieth century, their records showed that the majority of women coming to the clinics for the first time had used contraception previously.[24]

In traditional reproduction control attempts, little or no distinction was made between abortion and contraception; reproduction seemed a process with no sharply differentiated stages prior to birth. So many of the same potions described above as abortifacients were also used at an earlier stage. Magical as well as medical, potions were often concocted of symbolically sterile ingredients, as teas made from fruitless plants.[25] Despite almost universal failure to prevent conception through taking internal medicine, the same recipes used in ancient societies and in medieval Europe continued in use in the modern world.

The single most common contraceptive method in history, throughout the world, is *coitus interruptus,* or withdrawal—the male withdrawing his penis before ejaculation so that his semen is deposited outside the vagina. Unlike potions, this can be an effective method. Withdrawal was traditionally used in Africa, in Australasia, throughout Islamic society, and in Europe. Judaism and Roman Catholicism both condemned the practice, but in medieval Europe its practice was common enough to be frequently attacked in the canonical writings as a "vice against nature," one of the several species of lust. A related contraceptive practice is *coitus obstructus,* recommended in several ancient Sanskrit texts (and, as we shall see in chapter 2, by nineteenth-century American reformers): "If one, at the time of sexual enjoyment, presses firmly with the finger on the fore part of the testicle, turns his mind to other things, and holds his breath while doing so . . ."[26]

These practices are dependent on considerable male will and skill. Women's analogous methods were physical exertions—such as jumping and running—designed to expel semen from the body after intercourse or to prevent it from reaching the uterus. Sneezing was recommended by the physicians of ancient Greece, by rabbis, and, as late as 1868, in an anonymous birth control pamphlet. These were not particularly effective techniques, and the more canny ancient doctors advised combining them with additional precautions. A common myth was that a woman's passivity during intercourse would make her less likely to conceive. The converse myth—that for intercourse to be fruitful the woman must be active—reveals an understandable association between passion and fertility. By the Middle Ages, Christian influence had succeeded in reversing this folk belief: too much female passion ought to be avoided, for it would make intercourse sterile.

Douching, which could have been effective, was apparently not widespread. Spermicidal substances, such as citrus fruit juice, were identified but used in less effective ways. The ancient Greek physician Aëtios knew the spermicidal properties of vinegar, but instead of recommending it to women as a douche, he suggested applying it to the penis. In the nineteenth century attempts to kill sperm by bathing the penis in some spermicidal lotion remained common, judging by the recipes for such lotions in home-remedy books. For example, "Take bichloride of mercury, 25 parts; milk of almonds, 400 parts; alcohol, 100 parts; rose-water, 1000 parts. Immerse the glands in a little of the mixture, as before, and be particular to open the orifice of the urethra so as to admit the contact of the fluid. This may be used as often as convenient, until the orifice of the urethra feels tender on voiding the urine. Infallible, if used in proper time."[27] Douching would have been less painful, and some nineteenth-century household management books recommended it and offered recipes for the liquid.[28]

The most effective traditional contraceptive techniques were various sorts of pessaries, which aimed to block the cervix. Pessaries were particularly effective when combined with spermicides. Numerous ancient formulas for pessaries have been recently discovered, tested, and found effective, such as ancient Egyptian recipes using crocodile dung or a mixture of honey and natron (natural sodium carbonate) or a natural gum. Although none of the substances is strongly spermicidal, all are of a consistency that, at body temperature, would form an impenetrable covering over the cervix. Islamic medical writings offer thirteen different prescriptions for pessaries. Both Islamic and Sanskrit sources suggest rock salt, a good spermicide. An Indian work of the first century B.C. suggests rock salt dipped in oil, which is even better, since the oil would retard the motility of sperm and clog the cervix. Oil inside the vagina is one of the most continuous practices in folk contraception. Aristotle suggested oil of cedar or olive oil. Women of the U.S. Midwest in the twentieth century have used lard. Marie Stopes, an English birth control champion of the early twentieth century, reported high effectiveness rates with the use of oil and nothing else.[29]

Another form of pessary was a solid object used to occlude the cervix. This type of contraceptive was also widespread in preindustrial societies, such as Africa, where women used plugs of chopped grass or cloth. On Easter Island women used algae or seaweed. Japanese prostitutes used balls of bamboo tissue paper, Islamic and Greek women used wool, and Slovak women used linen rags. Geography ruled, and women used what they could get. The most effective natural cervical cap—the sponge—was first used by people who lived by the sea and was the most effective contraceptive in use until the development of the rubber diaphragm. If properly used, a sponge will not only block the cervix but will also absorb semen and can be saturated with a spermicidal fluid. Sponges were promoted by birth control clinics as late as 1930, and a study done in New York at that time found a 50 percent success rate among women using sponges even without medical advice.[30]

As to condoms, many tropical peoples used coverings for the penis for a variety of purposes, such as protection against tropical disease or insect bites, as marks of rank, as amulets, or merely as decoration. A linen sheath was promoted as a specifically anti–venereal disease precaution by the Italian anatomist Fallopius (discoverer of the "Fallopian tubes"), an early authority on syphilis, in 1564. In the eighteenth century these devices were being made of animal membrane, thus waterproof and effective as a contraceptive. By this time, sheaths for the penis were widespread, often given to men by prostitutes, and they had acquired a wealth of charming nicknames and euphemisms: the English riding coat, assurance caps, the French letter, bladder policies, instruments of safety, condoms, cundums, and, of course, prophylactics. Through the mid-nineteenth century, books of home remedies gave instructions for making condoms, as for example:

> Take the caecum of the sheep; soak it first in water, turn it on both sides, then repeat the operation in a weak ley of soda, which must be changed every four or five hours, for five or six successive times; then remove the mucous membrane with the nail; sulphur, wash in clean water, and then in soap and water; rinse, inflate and dry. Next cut it to the required length, and attach a piece of ribbon to the open end. Used to prevent infection or pregnancy. The different qualities consist in extra pains being taken in the above process, and in polishing, scenting, &c.[31]

A few groups used internal condoms for women: in one location women inserted into their vaginas seed pods about five inches long with one end cut off.

Occasionally ancient peoples tried to practice a rhythm method. To do so successfully they would have needed either an exact knowledge of the physiology of contraception or a sophisticated observation of a large number of cases—neither of which was likely. (A precise and commonly accepted identification of the fertile period of the human female was not made until 1924.) So these practices were often faulty: for example, East African Nandi women and the great Greek gynecologist Soranus agreed that avoiding intercourse for a few days after menstruation would prevent conception. A somewhat more effective—and very widespread—practice was prolonging the suckling of infants, which reduces fertility to some degree.

Midwives in Java performed external manipulations that caused the uterus to tip, or become retroflexed, thus preventing conception. This procedure was usually done after either abortion or childbirth. An anthropologist visiting Java in 1897 found 50 percent of the women with retroflexed uteruses, but the midwives told him that they could restore the uterus to its normal position by massage whenever a woman wanted a child.

The most ambitious forms of contraception practiced in the preindustrial world were surgical sterilizations, which were unusually invasive. Some groups of Australians performed surgery in which the cervix was cut and forced to heal in an open position.[32] Others did ovariectomies (removal of the ovaries). Of less clear intent was subincision of males, in which the urethra was surgically opened at the base of the penis so that both urine and semen emerged at a point just on top of the testicles. Subincision did not entirely prevent conception, and there is no clear evidence that it was performed with any population control intent, but it did make conception less likely with each act of intercourse.

The wide array of birth control techniques used in preindustrial societies discloses something vital to understanding the modern birth control movement: that the burden of involuntary childbearing was not the result of *lack* of technology but of the *suppression* of technology. This means that childbearing cannot be considered the cause, or at least not the simple, exclusive cause, of women's subject status, because efforts—sometimes successful—to transcend the biological, and thereby to reshape some of the operations of gender, were present in the earliest known human societies.

2   *The Criminals*

The widespread popular knowledge of birth control techniques, combined with the private nature of sexual intercourse, made birth control difficult to suppress. Long before the emergence of an organized social movement for birth control, individuals, couples, and groups defied the birth control prohibition. The prohibition never did what it was intended to do. It did not successfully make birth control taboo or even sinful; indeed, many people continued to consider it appropriate, advisable behavior. Rather, the prohibition forced people underground in their search for reproductive control. It transformed traditional behavior into criminal behavior and thereby attached to birth control some of the characteristics of all criminal activity: it raised the cost and lowered the quality. Before we can appreciate the significance of the birth control movement we must take a look at the experience of ordinary women and sometimes men who were forced to become criminals as they practiced birth control.

The American fertility rate has been declining since 1800. In a period of concern about overpopulation, it is worth dwelling on that fact. The average fertility rate in the United States was 7.04 per 1,000 women in 1800, 3.56 in 1900, and 2.0 in 2000.[1] America in the eighteenth century had one of the highest birth rates in the world and was legendary in Europe for its fertility, but by the end of the nineteenth century only France had a lower birth rate than the United States.[2]

Another way to understand these changes is in terms of family size. In the late eighteenth century women usually gave birth to eight children.[3] By 1900 the average family had three. Of course, this does not mean that the size of actual families changed that much in one century. Infant and general mortality rates were high enough that even when women had on average eight live births, the average household size in 1790 was only 5.7 persons, a bit more than double the size of average households in 2000, when it was 2.6.[4] Yet in a study of birth control it is the larger change, the change in birth rate, that concerns us. It would be even better if we could obtain figures on the pregnancy rate, for that would give us a better estimate of reproduction control and help us to distinguish contraception from abortion and infanticide. Just as the infant mortality rate was high in the nineteenth century, so was the rate of miscarriage, and many women had to endure several unsuccessful pregnancies. Since the vast majority of women married, and since the proportion of women marrying increased well into the twentieth century (with the highest proportion—95.2 percent—counted in 1965), celibacy was unlikely to have caused the birth-rate decline.[5] Rather, birth control was responsible.[6]

This fertility decline continued steadily despite the prohibition of all reproduction control technologies by state and federal governments between the 1840s and 1890s. That contradiction suggests something of the desire to control reproduction.

Some forms of reproduction control used in the modern United States were, unfortunately, similar to traditional ones. The stigma on illegitimacy sometimes drove unmarried women to infanticide. The pioneering women's historian Julia Spruill, writing in the 1930s, found three cases of infanticide reported in the *Maryland Gazette* on one day in 1761. It was, of course, difficult to prove whether a child had been murdered or stillborn, and the legislation dealing with this problem—making it a crime to conceal a child's death—suggests that the problem was large. Women convicted were usually hanged.[7]

That women took such risks hints at their desperation. Unlike abortion, infanticide was primarily a crime of very poor women whose desperation came from the terrible conditions of female poverty. An 1806 infanticide trial tells a poignant and not unusual story. Elizabeth Valpy, alone in Boston, worked as a maid for a Dr. Jarvis and became pregnant, allegedly by a black indentured servant, William Hardy, of the same household. Discovering her pregnancy, she asked her employer for medicines for abortion and he provided them, but they did not work. So the doctor turned her out of the house. She demanded that Hardy provide for her and her child-to-be. He rented lodgings for her in a "low" neighborhood in South Boston, where she gave birth to a girl, completely white. The child was found drowned twenty-three days later. Valpy claimed that Hardy had killed it after taking it from her, saying he would bring the baby to a wet nurse so she, Valpy, could go out to work. A jury acquitted him for lack of evidence, and there was not enough evidence to charge her either, though she was widely suspected. We cannot know the truth about who was the murderer. But what matters in this story is to understand the situation. Neither Valpy nor Hardy alone could raise a child while earning a living; and their color difference probably contributed to their not marrying. The trial was particularly brutal for Valpy, as witness after witness was brought in to defend Hardy by testifying to Valpy's loose character and moral viciousness. But this double standard rested on racial as well as gender norms: although rhetorically defending the black Hardy, the court damned the white Valpy as a "foul, degraded harlot" for having been intimate with a black man.[8]

In the mid-nineteenth century, infanticide was still a regular occurrence in the United States.[9] Observers suspected that the huge amounts of laudanum being sold were used not just to quiet crying children but also to kill infants painlessly.[10] Fifteen-year-old Mary Turtlot, for instance, working as a domestic for a well-to-do farm family in Warren County, New York, became pregnant by a son of the family; her pregnancy discovered, she was discharged. The son gave her the address of a New York City abortionist, which he got from a cousin living in the city. Arriving there penniless, she persuaded the doctor to take her in as a domestic in return for his medical help. She remained there until her arrest, after the police found a seven-day-old child dead in the house.[11] Poor women like this, trapped by a double standard about sexual sin, became murderers.

Abortion was much more common than infanticide, however, practiced most often by the married and frequent in all classes.[12] In 1862, when the wife of a Confederate general, William Dorsey Pender, wrote him that she was, unfortunately, pregnant, he wrote her pious phrases about "God's will" but also sent her pills that his camp surgeon had thought might "relieve" her.[13] An unmarried woman schoolteacher in South Hadley, Massachusetts, writing in 1859 to her parents in Derry, New Hampshire, shows familiarity with abortion as a common event: "Alphens' wife has been up here with her mother all summer. Poor Alphens he has got so poor that he cant keep house so he sent his wife to live on his father all winter—her poor health was caused by getting rid of a child as I suppose Alphens didn't feel able to maintain another one you must not say anything as I have only guessed it she was very large when she came here and in a short time she shrank to her normal size."[14] Elisa Adams, the author of this letter, was a rural, upper-middle-class, respectable young woman with strong family and community ties, not a poor, lonely immigrant girl in a big city, like Elizabeth Valpy. If Elisa Adams knew that women, including married women, had abortions, we must conclude that the phenomenon was not uncommon. In 1871 Dr. Martin Luther Holbrook wrote that American women were "addicted" to the wicked practice and that it was especially widespread in New England,[15] where the decline in the birth rate was most pronounced. One antiabortion propagandist, in a style clearly intended to repel and frighten, wrote: "Nowadays, if a baby accidentally finds a lodgement in the uterus, it may perchance have a knitting-needle stuck in its eyes before it has any."[16]

In 1871 the *New York Times* called abortion "The Evil of the Age." The *Times* estimated that there were two hundred full-time abortionists in New York City, not including doctors who performed abortions occasionally.[17] It may be that tens of thousands of abortions were done in New York City alone in the 1870s, one judge estimating, probably exaggeratedly, one hundred thousand a year in the 1890s.[18] In 1904 a physician estimated six to ten thousand a year in Chicago.[19] In the 1890s doctors were estimating two million abortions a year in the United States—they, too, were probably exaggerating, but the numbers represented their anxiety.[20] In 1921, when statistics on these matters were more reliable, a Stanford University study calculated that one out of every 1.7 to 2.3 pregnancies ended in abortion, of which at least 50 percent were illegal.[21] Among a thousand women who went to a birth control clinic in the Bronx, New York, in 1931–32, 35 percent had had at least one illegal abortion, a proportion that applied to Catholics as well as Protestants and Jews.[22]

Part of the reason for Elisa Adams's matter-of-factness about abortion was that it was at least as safe and successful as childbirth.[23] In 1881 the Michigan Board of Health estimated one hundred thousand abortions a year in the United States, with just six thousand deaths, or a 6 percent mortality rate. There is some misunderstanding about abortion safety today because the campaign for legalized abortion has understandably emphasized the dangers of illegal abortion. In fact, illegal abortions in this country have an impressive safety record. The Kinsey investigators, for example, were impressed with the safety and skill of the abortions they surveyed. Studies of maternal mortality in the late 1920s and early 1930s found that 13–14 percent resulted from illegal abortion (meaning, of course, that 86–87 percent resulted from childbirth).[24] Legal abortion has made that ratio even more uneven today in the United States, when eleven times more women die in childbirth than from abortions.[25]

This does not mean that abortions were pleasant. They were painful and frightening, and anxiety was worse because they were "gotten in sin" and, often, in isolation. The physical risk was heightened by the illegality, just as it is today. Women facing childbirth also feared death, but the fear of dying alone, humiliated, and disreputable from an abortion was considerable. Women's fear was heightened because illegal abortions were typically made public only if they ended in disaster: if the aborted woman either died or became very ill. But illegality made abortion more dangerous in fact as well as in impression, as the secrecy made it harder for abortionists and clients to get medical help when they needed it.

The criminalization of abortion also increased women's anxiety. Before the nineteenth century, few people considered abortion wrong if performed in the first few months of pregnancy. The first modern legislation banning abortion altogether did not originate in Catholic canon law, as is widely believed, but in the secular law of England in 1803. Until then the Protestant churches had gone along with the Catholic tradition that before "quickening"—the moment at which the fetus was believed to gain life—abortion was permissible.[26] U.S. courts upheld this interpretation until at least 1845. The Catholic Church was a follower, not a leader, in restricting abortion, only legislating to prohibit it in 1869, well after most states in the United States of America had outlawed all abortions during the Civil War period.[27] Throughout the nineteenth century, most American women seemed to share the belief that before quickening, taking action to "bring on menstruation" was in no way reprehensible.[28]

Criminalization probably weakened that certainty, but it was contradicted by the plentiful public advertisements for abortifacients. Newspapers printed many ads like this one: "Portuguese Female Pills, not to be used during pregnancy for they will cause miscarriage."[29] The denomination "French" indicated a contraceptive device (a "French letter" was a condom), while "Portuguese" denoted an abortifacient. Another standard euphemism for abortion was "relief" or "removing obstacles": "A Great and Sure Remedy for Married Ladies—The Portuguese Female Pills always give immediate relief. . . . Price $5."[30] Many such ads were actually offering emmenagogues, often called "Female Regulators," to stimulate menstruation when it was late or irregular. Thus, they did not even have to mention the euphemisms for abortion.[31] In the 1830s one abortionist, known as Madame Restell, brought herself fame and fortune through a veritable abortatorium in a Fifth Avenue brownstone. As she bragged in her own advertisement, "Madame Restell, as is well known, was for thirty years Female Physician in the two principal female hospitals in Europe—those of Vienna and Paris—where, favored by her great experience and opportunities, she attained that celebrity in those great discoveries in medical science so specially adapted to the female frame."[32]

Abortifacients were by no means completely commercialized. Use of folk remedies remained common. Even men knew about them or how to get them. Stories of men dosing their pregnant girlfriends with abortifacients come from all periods of American history. In Maryland in 1652, Susanna Warren, a single woman made pregnant by "prominent citizen" Captain Mitchell, said that he prepared for her a "'potion of Phisick,' put it in an egg, and forced her to take it." It didn't work and she brought charges against him.[33] Slaves commonly practiced abortion. An antebellum doctor found abortion four times as frequent among blacks as among whites, noting that "all country practitioners are aware of the frequent complaints of planters from this subject."[34] Though the doctor may have been underestimating the prevalence of abortion among whites, abortion among slaves was undoubtedly not only a tool of self-preservation but also a form of resistance.

One way to get a picture of a nineteenth-century abortion is to examine a particular case. The transcript of the trial of Dr. William Graves of Lowell, Massachusetts, in 1837 for the murder of Mary Anne Wilson of Greenfield, New Hampshire, offers us such a view.[35]

Testimony of Dr. James S. Burt: Sometime in May latter part, 1837, I was in Greenfield and was called to see Mrs. Wilson. She said she was in a family way and wished to get relieved of her burden. I told her I had rather not give medicine for that purpose, that it would injure health or life. She said she had sent to Lowell for medicine and got a box of pills for that purpose. . . . she brought forward the box—I examined it there were about two or three dozen common sized pills—she said it had been full. I told her she was injuring her health by doing so, and she had better not take any more of them— I also advised her to see the young man who had done it, tell him her situation and he would do the thing that was right. She said she had, but he seemed to be bashful or ugly and wouldn't do anything. I asked her how long she had been in this situation and she said about 4 months. . . . she said then she would go to Lowell, for she was informed there was a physician there who would perform this operation with safety. I asked her how she came by her news or information and she said she heard it from good authority and that it could be performed without danger and that in 4 or 5 days, she could go about her daily employ. I then told her this is a folly—it will endanger your life, your health at any rate, and I advise you not to go—it may be done, but not without danger. I then said death is your portion if you do go, in my opinion, and you had better not go. . . .

Testimony of Elizabeth Bean: I am a sister of Mary Anne Wilson. . . . I opened her trunk when it came back from Lowell—in it was a little slip of paper on which was written "Dr. Graves, Hurd street, No. 7." (The witness produces the paper.) It was folded together and fastened with a needle. . . . She had been married and was a widow. She had been a widow 4 years next January. . . . [She roomed in a house in which also] lived Mr. Isaac Pollard and one child of her own, 3 years old last June. . . . It was understood in the family that Mrs. Wilson was courted by Mr. Pollard . . . for 2 years. . . .

Testimony of N. H. G. Welton [stage driver]: I left a lady at Dr Graves's last summer. . . . I left her just at twilight. I rang the bell for Dr Graves; he was not in; but just that moment he came up, and I said Dr, here is a lady to see you. . . . I heard the Dr say as I left them, "well, well, walk in and I will see."

Testimony of Lucinda Sanborn: I have lived at Dr Graves's for nearly 1½ years, and my business is to take charge of the house and doing the whole of the work. . . . The Monday before her death in the evening she was not so well, and Monday night she became very sick, and the abortion took place. She had severe pain in her back and bowels. . . . The abortion took place while she was in bed; we took her off, laid her onto another bed and removed the sheet. . . . We raked open the ashes in the fireplace and put the contents of the sheet into it and covered them up. . . . There was something that looked like a child which we found on the sheet. The after birth was with it. This was never removed from the fireplace; it was rather chilly, and I built up a small fire afterwards.

Testimony of Dr. Hanover Dickey, Jr.: I lived at Dr Graves's from June 17 to August 19, and boarded in the family. . . . I have previously studied with Dr Graves. . . . I chose to go into that room from curiousity. . . . I went in and found the . . . lady there on the bed. . . . She said she thought herself 3 months or more advanced in pregnancy. . . . She said she did not know but she should have been freed the night before from her embarrassment. I don't know as she used the word embarrassment, but something referring to her pregnancy. . . . I saw her again Saturday, August 19 forenoon . . .—her hair was not adjusted—everything betokened suffering—her general appearance, dress and countenance—great suffering—mental and bodily.

Mary Anne Wilson died on August 24, after three weeks alone in Dr. Graves's house, without communication from her parents, sisters, child, or lover. After Wilson's death, Graves hired some Lowell men to bring her in her coffin to Greenfield and turn her over to Pollard. He told her family that she had died in Boston of a "cholera morbus." But when her relatives initiated an investigation, having found Graves's address—in Pollard's writing—in her trunk, Pollard disappeared.

Consider Mary Anne Wilson's situation: widowed four years, supporting herself and a child with millinery work, "courted" by a boarder for two years but unable or unwilling to obtain his support for her child-to-be. Hardly a promiscuous woman, she paid very heavily for her "sin." William Graves was convicted. It seems he did a lot of "business" with people who lived "on the Appleton Corporation"—that is, the Lowell mills. We do not know his sentence.

We have more information about the commercialization of abortion in the later nineteenth century because the *New York Times* embarked on a series of investigative reports about it. The professional abortionists who advertised in the papers were often medical imposters—that is, they lacked medical degrees, though many "doctors" did too, having purchased their degrees from diploma mills. Frequently abortionists used several aliases, sometimes to avoid old prosecutions, sometimes to operate several establishments simultaneously under different names. Sometimes the advertisements would feature a woman's name, as a woman seeking help would be more likely to approach another woman, although the abortionist might be male. These two ads ran simultaneously in the *New York Herald:* "Madame Grindle, Female Physician, guaranteeing relief to all female complaints" and "Ladies' Physician—Dr. H. D. Grindle, professor of midwifery . . . guarantees certain relief to ladies in trouble, with or without medicine; sure relief to the most anxious patient at one interview; elegant rooms for ladies requiring nursing."[36]

The Grindles, who catered to an upper-class clientele, asked $300.00 for an abortion,[37] the equivalent of $3,941.89 in 2000 dollars. But the abortion industry was stratified, and standards of cost and treatment varied enormously. Some ads offered abortafacients for $5.00. Dr. Kemp, of Twenty-third Street at Seventh Avenue, just around the corner from the Grindles, charged $10.00 and promised to return half if the abortion wasn't successful; and, indeed, he did return $5.00 to one patient, twenty-year-old Anna Livingston.[38] Some physicians kept an expensive office for rich ladies and a cheaper one for poor women. Some of the disapproval of Madame Restell had a class dimension: once, she was almost imprisoned but "her lawyer stayed proceedings by a bill of exceptions, and now she rides over one of her judges, tosses up her beautiful head, and says in effect, 'behold the triumph of virtue!' Instead of a linsey woolsey petticoat . . . she is gloriously attired in rich silks and laces, towers above her sex in a splendid carriage, snaps her fingers at the law and all its pains and penalties, and cries out for more victims and more gold."[39]

Not all abortionists were disreputable. Dr. Graves, of the 1837 Lowell trial, had the best credentials available at that time. Dr. Cutter, tried for abortion in Newark, New Jersey, in the 1870s, was "one of the best known of the younger physicians in the State."[40] Nearly every physician writing or speaking on the topic would admit to being frequently asked for abortions. Clearly not all refused—at least not all the time; even those who normally refused were undoubtedly sometimes prevailed upon by old patients and friends.

Such was the demand that not even occasional convictions suppressed abortionists' practices. Consider the case of Dr. Henry G. McGonegal. In 1888 he allegedly aborted Annie Goodwin, a young working woman living with her married sister on 126th Street in New York City. She went to stay with a Mrs. Shaw, washerwoman, of 105th Street, and died there a few days later, her burial permit produced by Dr. McGonegal. Witnesses were able to place her in his office. An autopsy proved an abortion had been performed, and McGonegal was convicted.[41] Four years later McGonegal, then seventy years old and free on appeal, was arrested again, this time in association with quite a different social class. Now he was alleged to have had the aid of Dr. Marian A. Dale, a graduate of the New York Women's Medical College, forty-four years old, who boarded with McGonegal and shared his practice. Together they had called

on Mrs. Louisa Webb, the daughter of an old and respected family of Ravens-
wood, on Long Island, mother of one, temporarily staying with her parents.
Shortly after their visit she gave birth to a stillborn child and became very ill.
Her wealthy parents pressed charges against McGonegal and Dale and also
against her husband, Frank Webb, as accomplice. (Frank Webb was of a lower social class than his wife—he worked as a Pinkerton at Homestead.)[42]

When the medical establishment undertook a campaign against abortion
in the second half of the nineteenth century, its very vehemence served as a
further indication of the prevalence of illegal abortions. In 1857 the American Medical Association (AMA) initiated a formal investigation of the frequency of abortion. Seven years later the AMA offered a prize for the best popular
antiabortion tract. Medical attacks on abortion grew in number and virulence
until, by the 1870s, both professional and popular journals were virtually saturated with the issue. Physicians bemoaned the widespread lay acceptance of
abortion before quickening; in order to break that sympathy, they adopted a
new vocabulary that described abortion in terms designed to shock and repel,
such as "antenatal infanticide."[43] Physicians attempted to frighten women away
from abortion by emphasizing its dangers. Their common assertion that there
was *no* safe abortion may have betrayed ignorance, but more likely it was an
exaggeration justified by what they believed was a higher moral purpose.[44] Yet
occasionally even antiabortion doctors allowed the truth to slip out, revealing
despite themselves why their campaign remained ineffective. "It is such a simple and comparatively safe matter for a skillful and aseptic operator to inter-
rupt an undesirable pregnancy at an early date," wrote Dr. A. L. Benedict of
Buffalo, New York, an opponent of abortion, "that the natural temptation is
to comply with the request."[45]

For most of history, abortion had been a primary form of birth control. But
in the nineteenth century many were using abortion as a fallback when contraception failed, pointing to a revival of contraceptive use. Here, the author
of an 1888 antiabortion tract offered a fictional composite case study of a young
couple's path to the abortionist:

> So the young people are married. . . . they have freely given their friends to
> understand that it will not be convenient, for the present at least, for them to
> be troubled with children. They do not yet think it would be quite right to
> interfere with Nature when she has begun to create a human life, but they are
> prepared to prevent her from beginning the work. . . . They feel free to arrange
> for using all their time, vitality, and means in other ways; perhaps they plan a
> two or three years' course of travel and study in Europe, including a course of
> lectures and study for the wife. . . . By and by the wife is irregular. . . . What
> can it mean? It certainly cannot mean conception, for they have taken the strict-
> est precautions!

They now consult—not a physician; it isn't worth while to do that—but some young married pair of their acquaintance who have had more experience than they. . . . [They] learn some points which delicacy and shame had before kept back, and they finally decide to take the next step, and try if a jolting ride or a hot bath will not correct the difficulty. Nothing further than this has been suggested to them, and they still assure themselves that it is not a case of pregnancy.

But after a week or two more they are persuaded to try some "correcting pills" or other infamous nostrum which our leading dailies freely advertise under one or another thin disguise. . . . besides, the medicine was not bought, it was a gift from the box of the more experienced friend.[46]

The author, a physician, replicated the standard medical and moral condemnation in equating contraception with the wife's unconventional activities. He equated her course of lectures and the young couple's desire for adventure and intellectual growth with frivolity; he could not accept the postponement of children. He also pointed out some truths: that the couple in question was likely to be well-to-do (as opposed to the single pregnant woman who was more likely to be poor). And he saw that in the actual experience of women, abortion was becoming a follow-up to unsuccessful contraception.

In women's experience the continuity between abortion and contraception was natural. The present view of abortion as more iniquitous than contraception developed only in the past hundred years, as we shall see in later chapters. Both forms of reproduction control increased steadily throughout the nineteenth century.[47] Contemporary writers consistently attributed the falling birth rate to birth control.[48] Birth control clinics collected statistics on the previous birth control practices of clients and found widespread contraceptive use even among those who had received no previous professional help. In a Newark clinic in 1933, 91.5 percent of patients had used birth control prior to the clinic visit; a New York City clinic in 1934 found that 93.3 percent had used birth control previously, not counting abstinence.[49] *Coitus interruptus* was the most common pre–medical consultation technique.[50] Doctors argued that it was dangerous, causing nervousness and, ultimately, impotence, and their censure supplies further evidence of its practice.[51]

Simultaneously, less-conservative sex reformers were advocating not only withdrawal but *coitus reservatus*, that is, sexual intercourse with the male avoiding ejaculation altogether.[52] These iconoclastic ideas remained confined to small groups, and their proposals demanded a suppression of gratification by the male that would not seem destined for great popularity. Yet some people practiced it, and quite successfully. One woman wrote to Margaret Sanger in 1917 about the effect on her husband of "Karezza," the label given to *coitus reservatus* by the nineteenth-century feminist physician Alice Stockham:

For two years we had no children purposely because we were both nervous wrecks from over work. . . . all this was the result of a copy of Mrs. Stockham's "Karezza" falling into our hands before marriage. People of intellect, will and conscience—despise waste of any kind—to waste the most vital power in the universe (and concentration of vital fluid means untold force) seems most criminal to me. . . . My husband arises at 5 A.M., works till 7 P.M., does the work of any five men I could name, and is as fresh at night as when he starts out in the morning.[53]

Thousands of copies of Stockham's book, and equal numbers of others like it, circulated in the nineteenth century.

The rhythm method was also widely discussed in the nineteenth century by doctors and sex moralists, and it had the advantage that almost all found it acceptable. One must assume that it was widely attempted, but whether to consider it an actual birth control method is problematic since people continued ignorant of the female fertility cycle. Observing other mammals, as "primitive" peoples had done, they believed that human ovulation occurred either during menstruation or just before it.[54] This calendar coincided with the conventional taboo on intercourse during menstruation, but it did little to prevent conception.

But a thriving nineteenth-century market provided contraceptive devices that did work. Deterred only fractionally by the federal prohibition on birth control passed in 1873 (the Comstock law), hundreds of small entrepreneurs hand-manufactured gadgets of animal gut, rubber, metal, and chemicals to prevent conception. Even reputable public pharmaceutical and rubber companies produced items marketed for treatment of disease but bought overwhelmingly for their contraceptive effect.[55]

Condoms were second in popularity to male withdrawal, according to the clinic studies of the 1920s and 1930s. Typically, 25 to 50 percent of the patients interviewed had used condoms. Slaughterhouse workers made them in large quantities until the 1850s, when the vulcanization of rubber, which made it resistant both to melting and cracking, transformed the condom business. Condoms became easy to make,[56] and the price dropped steadily. Imported skins in the 1830s were as much as $1.00 a piece ($15.50 in 2000 dollars); in the 1850s and 1860s they cost $3.00–6.00 a dozen; and by the mid-1930s they were $1.00 a dozen ($12.50 in 2000 dollars).[57] Then, after World War I, increased public worry about venereal disease acquired by soldiers and sailors subverted the prudish rejection of condoms. With the introduction of latex, condoms became thinner and cheaper yet, and their sales increased enormously.[58]

Among women, douching was the most widely used method of contraception, although lack of privacy and running water probably limited this practice to relatively prosperous women.[59] Syringes also improved because of new rubber-production processes, and they had the advantage of having respectable uses. Used for enemas and for routine cleansing—both procedures having become medically fashionable in the nineteenth century—syringes could be advertised openly. And they were, constantly. Particularly in magazines of the popular health movement, but also in women's magazines, general magazines, and newspapers, syringe advertisements were standard, many of them with pictures of the instrument.

Before the Comstock law, syringe ads openly presented their contraceptive function—for example, to be used with "infecundating powders" and "anticonception compounds." Madame Restell's appeals to women were uninhibited, even poetic:

> Important to married females—Madame Restell's Preventive Powders. These valuable powders have been universally adopted in Europe, but France in particular, for upwards of thirty years, as well as by thousands in this country as being the only mild, safe and efficacious remedy for married ladies whose health forbids a too rapid increase of family. . . .
>
> Her acquaintance with the physiology and anatomy of the female frame enabled her—by tracing the decline and ill health of married females scarce in the meridian of life, and the consequent rapid and often apparently inexplicable causes which consign many a fond mother to a premature grave, to their true source—to arrive at a knowledge of the primary cause of female indisposition—especially of married females—which in 1808 led to the discovery of her celebrated Preventive Powders. Their adoption has been the means of preserving not only the health but even the life of many an affectionate wife and fond mother.
>
> Is it not wise and virtuous to prevent evils to which we are subject by simple and healthy means within our control? Every dispassionate, virtuous and enlightened mind will unhesitatingly answer in the affirmative. This is all that Madame Restell recommends, or ever recommended. Price five dollars a package, accompanied with full and particular directions.[60]

There was competition among purveyors. Dr. Frederick Hollick charged that most douches were ineffective and potentially injurious to the vagina; the right substance, he explained, "is both scarce and difficult to obtain, so that it is not likely to come into general use. . . . Those who really *need* information as to the means of *Preventing Conception* may address Dr. Hollick, Box #__."[61] D. M. Bennett, a freethinker himself persecuted under the censorship laws, wrote in 1878, "There is probably not a druggist in the United States who has not sold female syringes."[62]

Many advertisers and vendors of syringes were prosecuted for obscenity under the Comstock law. Comstock employed entrapment to secure the culprits: he would write under a false name asking for a syringe and then arrest whoever sent it. Thus, for example, on May 9, 1878, Dr. Sara Chase was arrested and held on $1,500 bail at the Tombs (a New York City prison) for having sold two female syringes. The charges against her read in part, ". . . by the syringes which she recommends and sells, she places it in the power of wives to prevent conception."[63] One of the prosecutions of the free-love anarchist Ezra Heywood, the most important propagandist of planned conception of the 1870s, was for advertising a syringe. Heywood used his various trials as a platform from which to argue, from his singularly feminist point of view, the right of women to reproductive self-determination, and he made the syringe a symbol of that right. He later wrote: "The advertisement . . . had one sole, exclusive purpose, viz.: the proclamation of an opinion, the assertion of Woman's Natural Right to ownership of and control over her own body-self—a right inseparable from Women's intelligent existence; a right unquestionable, precious, inalienable, real—beyond words to express."[64] Ironically, what he sold was called the "Comstock Syringe for Preventing Conception, sent prepaid on receipt of price, $10."[65] Noting the irony that the syringe was called Comstock, Heywood wrote: "To name a really good thing 'Comstock' has a sly, sinister, wily look, indicating vicious purpose; in deference to its N.Y. venders, who gave it that name, the Publishers of *The Word* inserted an advertisement . . . which will hereafter appear as 'The Vaginal Syringe'; for its intelligent humane and worthy mission should no longer be libelled by forced association with the pious scamp who thinks Congress gives him legal right of way to and control over every American Woman's Womb."[66]

But Heywood's rhetoric was atypical. After the Comstock law passed, ads became euphemistic, usually claiming only a hygienic purpose for the goods, although the hints were quite clear to those familiar with the discourse of the time:

THE FOUNTAIN SYRINGE

The most philosophic of all instruments of the kind ever devised. The cheapest, most effect [sic] and most durable in the market. The *sina qua non* [sic] to hygienic practice. A thousand times more effect than pills or powders, and without the slightest danger to any person under any circumstances.[67]

Dr. Edward Baxter advertised a zinc preparation he had invented as a remedy for leucorrhoea[68] and "other female weaknesses," inserting the caution that "special care should be taken not to use the remedy after certain exposure has taken place, as its use would almost certainly prevent conception."[69]

These advertisements listed a range of prices, appealing to clients across a class spectrum, although there is no evidence that the more expensive were superior. Class privilege in birth control use was most evident with intravaginal contraceptive methods, for these more often required a physician's help.[70] IUDs, or pessaries,[71] were plentiful, in part because they could be prescribed for the correction of cervical and uterine irregularities and in part because physicians promoted them. Already in 1864 a report at a medical conference listed 123 designs for IUDs. A parody from the *New York Medical Journal* of 1867 leaves no doubt that many doctors were prescribing and even inserting such devices:

A RAID ON THE UTERUS

A distinguished surgeon in New York City, twenty-five years ago, said when Dupuytren's operation for relaxation of the *sphincter ani* was in vogue, every young man who came from Paris found every other individual's anus too large, and proceeded to pucker it up. . . . It seems to me that just such a raid is being made upon the uterus at this time. . . . Had Dame Nature foreseen this, she would have made it iron-clad. . . . The *Transactions* of the National Medical Association for 1864 has figured one hundred and twenty-three different kinds of pessaries, embracing every variety, from a simple plug to a patent threshing machine, which can only be worn with the largest hoops. . . . Pessaries, I suppose, are sometimes useful, but there are more than there is any necessity for. I do think that this filling the vagina with such traps, making a Chinese toy-shop of it, is outrageous.[72]

There were also "soluble pessaries," later called suppositories, for example:

THE FAMILY LIMIT.
SOLUBLE PESSARY

This check is one of the cleanest, safest, and most convenient methods extant. It requires no preparation before, or trouble afterwards. It entirely obviates the inconvenience entailed by the use of the enema. Post free, $\frac{1}{6}$ per doz. Preventive sheaths 2/-per doz. post free.[73]

Recipes for homemade suppositories circulated commonly throughout the nineteenth and earlier twentieth centuries. A formula from a young woman's papers around 1920 hardly differed from an early nineteenth-century one: "Acid citric—6 grains; Acid boracic—1 dram; Cocoa butter—90 grains "[74] Such formulas were often made up by druggists at the request of customers. Women had rather high success rates with suppositories, according to the early clinic surveys; one study showed a success rate of 54.4 percent, approximately the same as that with the condom and topped only by the 71.9 percent success rate of pessaries.[75]

Sponges might have been the most effective means of contraception, but they were the least used.[76] The reason for this is unclear, since, as one doctor commented in 1898, "The little sponge in a silk net with string attached is a familiar sight in drug stores."[77] Others argued that sponges decreased female sexual pleasure,[78] one doctor writing that the "ejaculation and contact of the sperm with the uterine neck, constitutes for the woman the crisis of the genital function, by appeasing the venereal orgasm and calming the voluptuous emotions" and that perhaps the semen itself has special properties needed by the womb.[79] (Thus the official medical expertise of the time regarding women's sexual experience.)

Although many doctors ceaselessly attacked contraception, others, equally respectable, sometimes revealed their cynicism about the ideals of purity that they preached. One amusing case was exposed by the freethinker D. M. Bennett, who, retaliating for his prosecution under the Comstock law, found in an advertisement for Vaseline the following statement by a physician: "Physicians are frequently applied [to] to produce abortion. . . . In some cases of this kind prevention is better than cure, and I am inclined to think, from some experiments, that *vaseline, charged with four or five grains of salicylic acid,* will destroy spermatozoa, without injury to the uterus or vagina." Vaseline was maufactured by the Samuel Colgate Company, and Samuel Colgate was head of the New York Society for the Suppression of Vice, one of the main backers of Comstock's crusade. The ad gave the Colgate Company's return address.[80]

Inconsistencies like these pointed to a class double standard surrounding enforcement of the prohibition on contraception. "The 'regular'[81] aristocratic physicians," Bennett charged, "may prevent conceptions, produce abortions, or do anything else they choose, and your agent [Comstock] will not disturb them. I have never heard of Comstock bringing a charge against a regular physician or a regular druggist. Druggists may import and sell contraband French goods with perfect impunity. . . . He is not anxious to attack the fraternity of druggists; they are too strong and could raise too much money to successfully oppose him."[82]

There were, indeed, class differences in nineteenth-century birth control. The well-to-do had access to more effective contraceptives, whereas poor women were more likely to rely on abortion as a primary form of birth control. Many other variables affected the distribution of contraceptive use: location, religion, ethnic group, community networks, the availability of sympathetic doctors and/or druggists. But these differences were marginal in comparison to what they became by the 1920s, when women with social and economic standing could obtain diaphragms.[83] Like the general differential in medical care, nineteenth-century class privilege in birth control was moderated by the fact that the best available methods were not very good. In many areas of medicine the "regular" doctors of the nineteenth century were offering remedies inferior to those of traditional folk healers, and the birth control views of the "regulars" were particularly backward.

In the nineteenth century, then, cross-class similarities in women's experiences were greater than differences. Although infanticide was practiced predominantly among the very poor, the number of infanticides was tiny compared with the prevalence of other birth control methods. Efforts to secure abortion and contraception made up a shared female experience. The abortion techniques of upper-class doctors were not much safer than those of working-class midwives. The most commonly used contraceptives—douches and withdrawal—were accessible to most women. The desire for spaced motherhood and smaller families existed in every class, a desire often so intense that women would take great risks to accomplish it. The shared female experience included not only the biology of reproduction but also the social structure that made child-raising the responsibility of women.

But when a birth control movement began, that unity among women dissolved. Even when the movement seemed to focus on a single issue—the legalization of birth control—it was actually saturated with broader ideas about everything from family size to gender to education. From the first attempts at arguing for the legalization of birth control, advocates developed ideologies for their cause that reflected their identities and aspirations—and, no matter how radical or transgressive, were also shaped by the values hegemonic in their society. We will see, for example, how the first feminists' arguments for birth control worked *within* the conservative gender ideology of their age. Part of what has made birth control so controversial for two centuries is that it cannot easily be isolated from a wide range of other personal and public values.

3   *Prudent Sex*

Even as women were risking their lives and their reputations to control their childbearing, small groups of little-known radicals were publicly challenging the prohibition on birth control. In the United States the first challenges came from socialists, called "utopian socialists" by Marxists who applied that derogatory term as a criticism of these socialists' alleged lack of strategic thought about how to transform society. At the time, in the 1840s, 1850s, and 1860s, the more religious of these groups were often called "perfectionists," also pejoratively, by more-orthodox Christians who accused them of the heresy of attempting to create perfection here on earth. Several perfectionist groups established rural communes where they practiced reproduction control. Although they attracted very few members, their influence was greater than their size, especially on the women's rights advocates who several decades later began to agitate on the question of reproduction control.

The American perfectionists and utopian socialists, oddly enough, got their birth control ideas primarily from British Malthusians and neo-Malthusians, groups that were distinctly antiperfectionist. The Malthusian tradition was, in fact, markedly pessimistic and skeptical about any except minimal reforms. Despite the geographical and emotional distance of British Malthusianism from American radicals, it is important that we grasp its contributions to the American birth control movement.

Malthusianism

In Britain in the nineteenth century, population growth and the possibility of its control became for the first time a public controversy. The development of a secular, capitalist "science" of economics helped move population growth from the category of ineluctable natural events to a category of events open to human manipulation. Modernity was creating a contradiction between sexual prudery and fears of overpopulation.

The political theory of the new industrial-capitalist order had a Radical and a Liberal version by the late eighteenth century. "Radical" defined a vision of a democratic and somewhat egalitarian society—that is, among its white male members—with an optimistic, even perfectionist view of the future. The Liberal tradition, by contrast, was more pessimistic. By the early nineteenth century Liberals had absorbed much of the cynicism of the Hobbesian conservatives, a cynicism appropriate to them now that they represented a dominant class. Liberals speculated that inequality and widespread poverty were inevitable and necessary to the maintenance of a high culture. Their laissez-faire economics was often but a rewording of natural-law arguments against tampering with the ordained order.

This political division carried into the population issue. The response to Malthus was divided doubly, between Radical and Liberal attitudes toward social control and between concern for sexual control and concern for population control. These differences made the Malthusian controversy complex.[1]

Malthus's ideas on population were part of his work as a political economist of the developing industrial-capitalist system, which he defended primarily against its mercantilist opponents. Malthus was a Liberal, and the economic forms he defended, such as the transformation of the nation's men into wage laborers, were attacked more from the Right than from the Left.[2] Yet as his ideas developed, Malthus identified with the capitalist class and equated its welfare with the welfare of his nation. He argued that it was impossible "to remove the want of the lower classes of society. . . . the pressure of distress on this part of a community is an evil so deeply seated, that no human ingenuity can reach it."[3] An opponent of the existing British Poor Laws (legislation providing support for the needy), he wrote in the second edition of his *Essay on Population.*

> A man who is born into the world already possessed, if he cannot get subsistence from his parents on whom he has a just demand, and if the society do not want his labor, has no claim of *right* to the smallest of good, and, in fact, has no business to be where he is. At nature's mighty feast there is no vacant cover for him. She tells him to be gone, and will quickly execute her own or-

ders, if he do not work upon the compassion of some of her guests. If these guests get up and make room for him, other intruders immediately appear demanding the same favor.[4]

In his attacks on the traditional right of subsistence recognized in the Poor Laws, Malthus was helping the British bourgeoisie to weaken local traditions of welfare and community responsibility and thereby create a working class that would be defenseless against incorporation into industry. His work was ultimately influential in securing the passage of the Poor Law of 1834, a measure reflecting the interests of the industrial capitalists almost exclusively: it abolished "outdoor relief," forcing the poor to enter workhouses or, as their only alternative, to take low-paying factory jobs.[5] The 1834 law has been called Malthusian, and certainly Malthus supplied the original (and tenacious) theory that welfare provisions themselves contribute to overpopulation by encouraging reproduction among the poor.[6]

The most important contribution of Malthusian population theory to that line of political thought lay in its assumptions, not in its calculations or policy recommendations. Malthus's formula that population increases geometrically and subsistence arithmetically does not stand up.[7] His prediction that deliberate birth limitation could not work was already being proven false in France, where birth rates had been falling for many decades.[8] More durable, however, was the idea that overpopulation itself is the major cause of poverty. Indeed, this idea became the kernel of Malthusianism. It made "natural" disasters such as war and famine take on social meaning: they were population regulators whether so intended or not. In the particular historical period in which Malthus offered his interpretation of population and poverty, the theory justified employers' interests in offering the lowest possible wages. Indeed, the theory presented the capitalist system of forcing laborers into jobs at subsistence wages as somehow inevitable, as being determined by natural laws such as those that seemed to govern reproduction. Malthusian population theory tended to draw attention away from the organization of labor and the distribution of resources as well as from the traditional social regulation of reproduction. Periodic overpopulation was presented as universal. Malthus did not notice, or did not care to mention, that the rich did not suffer from overpopulation and famine.

By denying a class (or gender or race) analysis of poverty, Malthusian theory denied the validity of the struggle for political democracy as a strategy for change. Demands made of the rich by the poor were illegitimate; only through self-help and sexual restraint could the poor help themselves. Malthus saw this sexual restraint as doubly valuable: not only would it reduce population, but it would also stimulate industriousness. (Malthus operated on the basis of a crude theory of sublimation and on the assumption that the frustration of the sex urge would induce men to put more energy into their work.) Yet at the same time Malthus was suspicious of sexual restraint, as of all forms of birth control, not merely out of religious scruples, but because of his primary concern for the development of a profitable labor market: "Prudential habits with regard to marriage, carried to considerable extent among the labouring class of a country mainly dependent upon manufactures and commerce, might injure it."[9] As Marx pointed out, Malthus in fact understood overpopulation as a product of the economic system, of the "trinity of capitalistic production: over-production, over-population, over-consumption," though he did not articulate this understanding.[10]

Two assumptions, then, were central to Malthusianism: that overpopulation causes poverty and that individual failings in the form of lack of restraint cause overpopulation. These two assumptions were equally central to neo-Malthusianism and reveal the historical connection that gives the two "isms" the same name. In birth control history Malthusianism and neo-Malthusianism were in opposition. Malthus was opposed to contraception, which he considered a vice. "Neo-Malthusianism," to the contrary, was the term applied to early advocacy of contraception. Both shared the view that overpopulation caused poverty, and it was on that premise that the neo-Malthusians concluded that population control could prevent poverty. Both also shared the recommendation of individual self-help through self-restraint, as opposed to collective political struggle for reform, as a remedy for poverty.

Neo-Malthusianism

Neo-Malthusianism originated as the Radical version of Malthusian population theory. More optimistic than the pessimistic Malthus, the neo-Malthusians believed not only that population could be controlled but that its control could provide a key to the creation of a good society. It is sometimes said that they turned Malthus on his head. But they only reversed his religious opposition to contraception; they did not reverse his basic assumptions.

Nevertheless, the neo-Malthusians differed substantially from the Liberals. They not only accepted contraception, but their anticlericalism, antimysticism, and even, in some cases, anti-Christianity made the Radicals more prepared to challenge both the conservative interpretation that Providence determined family size and the Liberal one that only restraint could do so. Also associated with Radicalism was a positive, even adulatory, attitude toward science and technology that inclined them favorably toward contraception. Perhaps most important was the Radicals' greater acceptance of the scientific attitude that nature could be controlled and manipulated by human effort.

Surely it was this urge that led the neo-Malthusians, when they encountered some traditional contraceptive formulas, to recommend them enthusiastically to the poor as a cure for their poverty.[11]

With respect to birth control, a major difference between the neo-Malthusians and the Malthusians was the former's rejection of sexual prudery.[12] They were willing not only to accept the implications of conception-free intercourse but also to support publication and public discussion of contraceptive methods, matters considered offensive to taste as well as to morals by most Liberals. Hence, Radicals also differed from Malthusians in their concern to defend freedom of speech and of the press.

Although its libertarian views were important, neo-Malthusianism was essentially a campaign to promote contraception in the hope that smaller families might ameliorate poverty. It began as a particular interpretation of Malthusian theory and later became the dominant interpretation. As it developed, its differences from Malthus's original meaning increased. When neo-Malthusians began radical agitation in the 1820s and 1830s, they did not challenge the framework of capitalist and class relations. Nevertheless, they were responding to a period of strong working-class resistance to the oppressive conditions of industrialization in Britain. The notorious massacre of demonstrators at Peterloo in 1819 was a signpost of that unrest. In the 1820s and 1830s, Britain experienced the first attempts at mass unionization. The development of the Grand National Consolidated Trades Union—an attempt at a national industrial workers' organization—brought militant syndicalist ideas and threats of general strike to the public. Whereas some advocated increased repression as a means of preventing social upheaval, others, equally worried, searched for peaceful solutions. Neo-Malthusianism appealed to the latter.

Leading this appeal was Francis Place, the most prominent neo-Malthusian of the 1820s. An artisan tailor, he had amassed enough money by 1816 to retire at the age of forty-five and continue full-time his work in Radical electoral politics. His political work was derivative of an older tradition of artisanal, individualist reformism, oriented to self-help. He was distant from and even hostile to the industrial working class and had never even visited the industrial north of England. He did not take into account massive structural unemployment and doubted the existence of undeserved poverty. He wanted to instruct workers "in the great truth, that it is themselves, and themselves only, who have the means to better their own condition, to increase their own respectability."[13] The content of his radicalism was political democracy for Englishmen within electoral representative institutions; in his economic thought he did not deviate from classical capitalist theory; and his social thought was directed to helping the poor without fundamental redistribution of wealth. Thus, he focused his efforts for many years on providing education for the working class. The goal of public education was to make the workers better workers and to afford a tiny proportion of them the opportunity—through excelling in their work, by the standards of the employing class—to leave their class and reach a higher social status. Place worked for the repeal of the Combination Laws, which had banned unions, but only because he thought these laws stirred up class conflict: "They made them hate their employers. . . . And they made them hate those of their own class who refused to join them." He believed labor unions suppressed workers' individual striving.[14]

In 1823 Place wrote and published four anonymous handbills urging contraception as a means of self-help for the working class.[15] In them he recommended the use of a sponge, attached to a thread, inserted in the vagina before intercourse.

> With mankind and healthy married people, sexual intercourse is as unavoidable, as it is wholesome and virtuous. But it is by no means desirable, it is indeed, a continued torture, that a married woman should be incessantly breeding or bringing forth children, often unhealthy, and born with a certainty of death in infancy and nothing but the patients [*sic*] of pain: as often born where there are not the means of wholesome support: and, what is still worse, where the mother is of a delicate frame, and never can produce healthy children, conception is to her nothing but torture.[16]

Even in these short leaflets, Place made clear the Malthusian basis of his economic theory in the form of the classic wages-fund theory. "It is a great truth," he wrote, "often told and never denied, that when there are too many working people in any trade or manufacture, they are worse paid then they ought to be paid, and are compelled to work more hours than they ought to work."[17] It is not my purpose here to evaluate Place's economics on its merits but merely to point out its social implications. For example, in his handbills Place also implied that large families were the cause of child labor and that small families could end it. His argument was that the working class was the cause of much of its own misery and was responsible for helping itself. Self-help is the common theme in all of Place's political work.

Place's handbills won him a few enthusiastic followers but never a general popularity. The response of most working-class Radicals to Place's propaganda was, to the contrary, negative. Anti-Malthusianism was already established in working-class thought by the 1820s.[18] *The Black Dwarf,* a working-class newspaper especially popular among miners, attacked Place's proposals. It argued in 1823 that the population of "drones," who ate without working, ought to be checked rather than cut back the number of working bees to leave more honey for the drones.[19] Early Chartists, who fought to extend democratic political rights to working-class men, considered Place's campaign as reactionary, politically indistinguishable from Malthusianism. The *Trades Newspaper and Mechanics Weekly Journal,* which Place had helped establish, denounced his theories as not in the best interests of the working people and not touching on their real grievances.[20] But prudery and sexism were also influential in the working-class press, which charged Place and his supporters with stimulating prostitution, destroying the chastity of women, and licensing unnatural acts.

The working-class opposition to neo-Malthusianism might have looked different had women of that class been heard. These early nineteenth-century workers' publications and organizations in Britain were thoroughly dominated by men. Place was more progressive than his detractors in his awareness and concern with the problems of working-class women. Furthermore, he never claimed that population control was a panacea. Later, neo-Malthusianism began to claim increasingly grandiose benefits from population reduction, which culminated in mid-twentieth-century advocacy of population control as a cure for poverty and underdevelopment; but Place, by contrast, continued to devote his energies to a wide range of reforms in what he saw as the interest of the urban poor.

Nevertheless, Place offered contraception encapsulated in an ideology that denounced workers' struggles and accepted the class system. His recommendation was flawed, even as an individual remedy, for no single small family could benefit from higher wages, even on Place's wages fund theory, unless all or many workers similarly limited their families. It is no wonder that many industrial workers rejected this inherent "blame the victim" logic.

Unable to compete with the campaign for the suffrage reform bill of 1832 and with the Chartist movement, contraception propaganda claimed the attention of Radicals only sporadically in the first half of the nineteenth century. And the evidence of birth rates suggests that the impact of the publication of contraceptive information was small. Only the revival of neo-Malthusianism in the 1870s correlated with a marked birth-rate decline in England, and that was among the professional and business classes.[21] It is not clear that the neo-Malthusians' political decision to aim their propaganda at the working class was ever successful. Rather, their major contribution seems to have been the creation of a new political culture in which, after much controversy and some legal struggle, contraception again became a fit topic for public discussion. Despite its intentions, British neo-Malthusianism was ultimately most effective as a sexual reform movement, a challenge to Victorian standards of propriety.

Perfectionism

The same could be said of American neo-Malthusianism—that it was most influential as a challenge to the Victorian sexual system. In its development, however, American neo-Malthusianism followed a different trajectory. Spread largely through the influence of the English reformer Robert Owen, it was adopted by utopian socialists such as his son, Robert Dale Owen, and Frances Wright and by religious utopians such as John Humphrey Noyes. These socialists tried to put contraception into practice within alternative socialist communities. They saw a more revolutionary potential in contraception than had the British neo-Malthusians and communicated this new interpretation of contraception to others.

In abbreviated form, the intellectual flow of Malthusian ideas to the United States might look like this: Malthus to radical democratic neo-Malthusians; through Owen to U.S. utopian socialists; through the cluster of reformers and radicals in the United States in the 1840s to the women's rights movement.

In the 1820s the United States was less industrialized than Britain, and as a result American reformers were less concerned with the problems of a large working class and agricultural impoverishment. The continuing small farm basis of American society drew many reformers into an attempt to reject industrialism either by struggling to retain a society based on independent farm and artisanal families as economic units or by creating transfamily units of collective life. From the 1820s to the Civil War, American radicals explored a variety of reform programs akin to one another in their hostility to industrial capitalism. Religious revivals, vegetarianism and other health cults, and communitarian socialism were prominent among them. Reformers in all three types of movements promoted reproduction control. Although their first birth control ideas were close to early British neo-Malthusian thinking, the optimistic mode of radical thought in the United States transformed them, ending by rejecting the pessimistic and conservative outlook of their Malthusian origins.

Robert Owen, a socialist industrialist from New Lanark, Scotland, may have been a supporter of Place's neo-Malthusian ideas; his son, Robert Dale Owen, moved to the United States and become a major advocate of contraception through his New York paper *The Free Enquirer*.[22] Dale Owen's coeditor, the feminist Frances Wright, also supported those ideas in Nashoba, her utopian colony in Tennessee, and influenced the women's rights movement.[23] Dale Owen's tracts, produced just a few years after Place's work, had already begun a major transformation of the neo-Malthusian idea. Arguing for reproduction control on the grounds of women's right to self-determination, he attacked the fear that contraception would stimulate license as an example of an invidious sexual double standard. He also attacked celibacy, sexual repression, and sexual ignorance. He insisted that the fundamental economic problem was not overpopulation but maldistribution of wealth and oppression of the poor. Population excess was relative, not just to the means of subsistence, but also to the system of control over the means of subsistence. Population control measures would alleviate certain local pockets of poverty temporarily, but poverty would always reproduce itself under capitalism.[24] Thus Dale Owen's anticapitalism and feminism placed neo-Malthusian ideas in a different context. There was far less altruism, condescension, or individual uplift in his ideas and far more concern to transform the whole society. Later reformers who incorporated contraceptive ideas into their theory and practice moved still farther in this direction.

Religious groups shared this impulse. In its original sense, American "perfectionism" referred to the belief of a group of upstate New York and western New England Christian revivalists in the 1830s that human beings could, through conversion, become perfect while still on earth. The leading exponent of religious perfectionism was John Humphrey Noyes, who founded a utopian colony at Oneida, New York, in the 1840s. For him and his followers, retiring to a new community allowed the rejection of worldliness and the creation of a perfect society. His purpose in forming a separate, deliberate socialist community was identical with that of many secular communitarians. His perfectionism was a religious version of revolutionary utopianism, as exemplified by anarchists such as William Godwin and his followers in the United States.

In early nineteenth-century America, all radicalism was imbued with perfectionism. The perfectionist tendency rejected the skepticism of the Old World, a skepticism engendered by the solidity of caste and class distinction, the seeming eternalness of human suffering, and the "lessons" of industrialization—that economic progress had to be bought with the misery of the many. In the United States many factors were different: the availability of land, the sense of starting with an open if not empty slate, the absence of an aristocracy, and the promise of great social mobility combined to produce a more optimistic view of the potential of human society. Utopianism seemed practicable.

Perfectionists, in their enthusiasm, often dreamed up panaceas, that is, they identified individual reforms as carrying the potential for total cure of social ills. The skepticism of the old-world tradition carried with it a view of social ills as insolubly complex, whereas new-world optimism tended toward oversimplification. Characteristic of all the early nineteenth-century reformers was the belief that a single level of change might bring the utopia into being. As Sylvester Graham recommended a whole grain and fruit diet, as Mary Gove Nichols recommended therapeutic baths, as Noyes recommended a new religion—each as a cure-all—so some thought that reproduction control could solve all the problems of humanity. There was something about the hope for perfection on earth that made it difficult for reformers to encompass many variables in their analyses of problems, to contemplate the complex clusters of factors that produce social change.

Two aspects of the perfectionist application of reproductive control schemes are worth discussing here, as both created traditions of thought that continued into the twentieth century. One was the notion to use contraceptive techniques to effect qualitative as well as quantitative control over human reproduction—a system later called "eugenics." A second was the notion that conception could be prevented by changing the nature of sexual intercourse itself and that this transformation would bring into being, along with reproduction control and sexual liberation, perfectly contented individuals—and, through them, a perfectly tuned society. Both theories involved a rejection of mechanical or chemical contraception in favor of self-control in sexual activity and therefore involved whole theories of sexuality and human relations. For this reason, they were of importance for future feminist birth control thought.

Both eugenic and sexual aspects of the perfectionist approach to reproduction control are well exemplified in the communitarian writings and practice of John Humphrey Noyes, first at Putney, Vermont, and from the late 1840s at the Oneida Community in upstate New York. Noyes imposed on his followers a sexual system that he called "male continence." Under this regimen, men refrained from ejaculation altogether. The system rejected *coitus interruptus* as well as propagative intercourse; intercourse including ejaculation was permitted only when it had been decided in advance that conception was desirable. Male continence allowed a system of multiple sexual partners, and Noyes prohibited monogamous marriage entirely. More than a system of preventing conception, male continence was a higher form of sex, and sex was considered the highest expression of love. Expanding and deepening human sexual experience was part of perfection here on earth, Noyes insisted, just as he argued that sexual intercourse went on in heaven too.[25]

Although male continence challenged male preferences in intercourse, to say the least, it was in theory neither antisexual nor antimale. Supporters believed that it need not involve any form of physical frustration. By learning to constrict the seminal ducts—a task considered by Noyesians to be easy once learned—the male could experience orgasm without ejaculation.[26] Nor did male continence abolish male supremacy and heterosexuality as the norm of sexual expression. In Noyes's community, sexual relations could be had between any individual man and woman. But Noyes did not tolerate homosexual relations or group sex, and men always did the asking. Furthermore, in exalting the benefits of suppressing ejaculation, only male sexual pleasure was considered.

What was it, then, that made male continence an allegedly superior form of sexual intercourse? The answer lay in a theory of human energy frequently called "animal magnetism" by its nineteenth-century believers; at other times they used electrical metaphors, or hydraulic ones. The operative assumption was that the body's energy was of finite quantity and, normally, in a closed circuit; the loss of semen was weakening to the system and was not a loss readily recouped. The loss of semen caused by regular intercourse produced many afflictions, ranging from nervous anxiety to general lassitude to specific ailments. By contrast, intercourse without the loss of semen was highly beneficial. It produced an interchange of magnetic or electrical influences between a man and a woman that was the physiological correlate of love and that contributed good health and energy to both persons. One variation of magnetic sexual theory, "sedular absorption," had it that the reabsorption of semen into the male's system added to his mental, physical, and sexual strength. Even those who did not posit any particular salubrious effect from seminal fluid itself argued that the control acquired and exercised in refraining from ejaculation strengthened character and raised up the sexual experience until it gained the spiritual level of art or religious communion.[27]

Magnetation theorists saw themselves as "transcending" the "propagative plane" and reaching toward more-intense sexual experience: "Physical propagation is but the vestibule of sex use."[28] They were in some ways sexual connoisseurs, but in an antihedonist, radical mode, and saw sexual stimulation in itself as wholesome. Indeed, magnetation theorists made an important contribution to ultimate popular rejection of Victorian prudery through their distinction between "amative" and "propagative" aspects of sexual intercourse— acclaiming the former and charging that the latter was often misused. This view rested on distinguishing between amative and propagative physical organs, thus separating sexual feeling from propagative desire. Thus, they recognized women's sex drive as separate from the maternal drive. Furthermore, their insistence on the healthfulness of sexual stimulation applied to both sexes, and the control they required of men helped to challenge the double standard. Avoiding ejaculation meant that men should be able to continue intercourse for longer periods of time. Male-continence advocates harped on this as a feature of their system that brought special delight to women, and their publications were regularly full of glowing testimonials from women about how much they liked it. For example:

> Since my husband became acquainted with this new theory he has endeared himself to me a hundredfold; and although our so-called "honeymoon" was passed five years ago, it was no more real and far less lasting then the ecstatic, the unspeakable happiness which is now continually mine. My prosaic and sometimes indifferent husband has changed by a heavenly magic into an ardent and entrancing lover, for whose coming I watch with all the tender raptures of a schoolgirl. His very step sends a thrill through me, for I know that my beloved will clasp me in his arms and cover me with kisses.[29]

Male-continence advocates did not exhibit much concern with women's sexuality. They identified the vagina, not the clitoris, as the female "amative" organ. In describing the process of the interchange of energies, they thought only of the friction of intercourse and did not consider other variations of sexual stimulation as capable of producing the desired effect. Magnetation theorists continued, as did Noyes, within a male-centered definition of "the sexual act." Indeed, their use of that phrase, still common today, expressed their confidence that there was but one normal sexual form, namely, heterosexual intercourse. So this perfectionist sexual system promised little perfection for women, inasmuch as it did not directly threaten the male power to define what appropriate sex was. Nevertheless, in its system-building quality it expressed the utopian urge to leave the existing society behind and start anew, and it looked to sex not merely as a reform but, foreshadowing Wilhelm Reich, as a panacea. In this respect it helped legitimate other radicalisms, different in content but similar in the condemnation of the status quo as wholly corrupt.

That tendency was greatly strengthened by its association with various eugenic theories and schemes, forms of human reproductive engineering expected to lead to perfection. Perfectionist eugenic ideas were expounded by all the American birth control advocates, including the most rationalist of them. Robert Dale Owen wrote: "I may seem an enthusiast—but so let me seem then—when I express my conviction, that there is no greater physical disparity between the dullest, shaggiest race of dwarf draught horses, and the fiery-spirited and silken-haired Arabian, than between man degenerate as he is, and man perfected as he might be; and though mental cultivation in this counts for much, yet organic melioration is an influential—an *indispensable*—accessory."[30] Dale Owen, Charles Knowlton, and others emphasized the prevention of hereditary diseases through the use of birth control.[31] But these perfectionist utopians also created what they saw as an even grander eugenic experiment, trying not only to weed out bad hereditary traits from human stock but also to breed deliberately for positive traits. Such a scheme had occurred to many—as exemplified in Henry Ward Beecher's comment that the surest way for a man to improve himself would be to choose his own grandparents. But other scruples against birth control prevented all but those who took sexually radical positions from attempting to put such thoughts into practice.

The sexual ideology of the Oneida Community made such an experiment possible.[32] Although Oneida gained a contemporary reputation for promiscuity, in fact its sexual relations were tightly controlled. Rules governed everything: the couples that might form, the places they could go, their allotted time together. Permanent couples were not permitted, and multiple sexual partners were encouraged, though women, at least in principle, were guaranteed the right to refuse a partner. All the members of the community were said to be married to each other collectively—Noyes called it "complex marriage"—and indeed they were all socially and economically committed to one another. Organized social pressure disciplined men who had not mastered the technique of continence, and few unwanted children were born. The desired children were produced with the intervention of Noyes and a committee who examined applicants for parenthood and assigned them to mates with whom they could produce desirable children.

Through a eugenic system he labeled "stirpiculture," Noyes planned not only to expand but to improve the quality of the Oneida Community through breeding ever more perfect members. Nothing could have been a better expression of the perfectionist impulse than the notion of applying human intelligence to breeding a better race. Unlike later eugenists, the Oneidans had no precise theory of genetics and paid as much attention to upbringing as to breeding. Their communist alternative to the nuclear family extended to child-raising as well as sexual relations, and they reared the "stirps" communally, their private hours with their mothers rigorously restricted. They sought to create human beings who were spiritually, religiously, and emotionally perfect.

It is a long way between these schemes and British neo-Malthusianism. The antiscientific, utopian, and even mystical attitudes of the American perfectionists seem remote from Malthus and Place. The American radicals, by and large, opposed contraception whereas their British counterparts accepted it. The Americans had an anti-industrial and antitechnological bias that made them suspicious of contraception; the Americans also, in their unorthodox way, were more moralistic and antihedonistic in their sexual attitudes. Furthermore, the large land area and later industrialization in the United States meant that overpopulation did not seem a threat. The American descendants of British neo-Malthusians did not adhere to Malthusian economics or its contraceptive recommendations. What the Americans shared with the neo-Malthusians was an enthusiasm for reproduction control as a means of creating larger social change. Reproduction control was a path to a new order, an instrumental and utilitarian tool, only secondarily a matter of increasing individual freedom. (Indeed, some collectivist utopians considered themselves opposed to individualism and had no commitment to expanding individual rights.) In this they were part of the population control tradition.

But the American perfectionists' modification of neo-Malthusian ideology made them more favorable to women's rights. The optimism and utopianism of the American reform community nourished the women's rights aspirations of female reformers even as it developed their organizational skills. When organized feminism began in the United States, it was not simply a reaction to the discrimination against women in reform movements such as abolition but also a logical development of the idea, often absorbed from male reform mentors, that a perfect society could be created. Within this general reform climate, specific ideas about women's rights drew specifically from the sex radicalism of American perfectionists.

In the conditions of early Victorian America, any rebellion against sexual prudery had to contain at least a glimmer of recognition of female sexuality. The essence of prudery was not blanket sexual repression but a sexual distortion based on deepening the male-female distinction to an extent that sexualized the entire universe. Contemporary critics of prudery believed that the distortion they hated had created oversexualization more than undersexualization. We will see in the next chapter how they constructed their arguments, but let us note their conclusion now: that the suppression of women was a necessary basis and key prop of the whole Victorian sexual system. In demanding the end of censorship on sexual discussion, the legalization of divorce, the abolition of prostitution, and the spiritualization of sexual relationships, the sex radicals believed that these objectives could not be achieved with women in bondage.

The perfectionist birth controllers, almost all men, were sometimes frightened by the logical trajectories of their own ideas. They were worried by the accusation that birth control would destroy female chastity and took care to answer such objections at length. (They were unconcerned at the possible loss of male chastity, by contrast.) John Humphrey Noyes took care to institutionalize his sexual experiments within rigidly male-supremacist lines. Frances Wright became a spokesperson for Robert Dale Owen's birth control views, but her own unconventional sexual behavior left her defenseless against vicious, misogynistic attacks and ultimately destroyed her effectiveness as an advocate. Yet Dale Owen seems to have realized that the direction of his sexual thought was inherently appealing to women. In 1830, shortly after having published *Moral Physiology,* he noticed a high proportion of favorable responses from women. He wrote that he had always expected that women would appreciate his views more than men, "inasmuch as their minds are less contaminated and their moral feelings stronger." Dale Owen went on to say that he could hardly urge women to endanger themselves by making their birth control views public, that women could not easily oppose any dominant prejudice until they had political equality. Nevertheless, he added, "I know that we men are always more inclined to push ourselves forward and monopolize whatever we can; but it is not always those that are the most forward, who best deserve the situations they assume. There are many things which women could teach us better than men, if they would but overcome their diffidence, and turn their minds to it."[33]

Dale Owen's request was answered. The women's rights movement of the 1840s stimulated the discussion of sexual issues among women, and women began to express their views on birth control with a remarkable lack of diffidence considering the heavy condemnation they received. From the beginnings of women's rights agitation, women talked among themselves about their unhappiness with the prevailing sexual system. By the 1870s they had gained sufficient clarity about their critique of the system, and sufficient confidence in their movement, to raise publicly a birth control demand, which they called "voluntary motherhood." As we turn to examine it now, we will see how deeply that demand—voluntary motherhood—was influenced by perfectionism.

PART 2

Birth Control and Women's Rights

4   *Voluntary Motherhood*

By the 1870s the women's rights movement in the United States, although divided among different organizations, ideologies, and strategic choices, had developed a remarkably coherent credo on some major questions—marriage, suffrage, education, employment opportunity, for example. On no question did the feminists agree so clearly as on birth control. The slogan they used—"voluntary motherhood"—was an exact expression of their ideology, incorporating both a political critique of the status quo, as *involuntary* motherhood, and a solution.

The feminists who advocated voluntary motherhood fell into three general groups: suffragists (divided among two national organizations and many local groups), moral reformers (in causes such as temperance, social purity, church auxiliaries, and women's professional and service clubs), and members of small free-love groups. The political distance between some of these was so great—as between the socially conservative churchwomen and the usually atheistic and anarchistic free-lovers—that their relative unity as voluntary motherhood advocates was the more remarkable.

Free-love groups in the 1870s were the closest successors to the perfectionist reform groups of the first half of the nineteenth century. The free-love movement was always closely related to free thought, or agnosticism, and was characterized by a passionate resentment of the Christian established churches, especially of their power to dictate laws and create restrictive social and cultural norms in a supposedly secular state. Advocates called themselves free-lovers as a means of describing their opposition to legal and clerical marriage, which, they believed, stifled love. Free-love groups were small, sectarian, and usually male dominated, despite their ideological feminism. They never coalesced into a large or national organization. They were, in some ways, radical modernists but in other ways conservatives, the dying remnants of preindustrial utopian reform. Because their self-definition was built around their iconoclasm and isolation from the masses, they were able to offer intellectual leadership in formulating the shocking arguments that birth control in the nineteenth century required.[1]

The suffragists and moral reformers, by contrast, concerned with winning mass support, became increasingly committed to social respectability; as a result, they did not generally stray far beyond prevalent standards of propriety in discussing sexual matters publicly. Indeed, as the century progressed the social gap between respectable reformers and the free-lovers grew. Whereas in the 1860s and 1870s the great feminist theoreticians, such as Elizabeth Cady Stanton, were intellectually close to the free-lovers, and at least one notorious feminist, Victoria Woodhull, was for several years a member of both the suffragist and the free-love camps, the leading suffragists of the 1890s and the early twentieth century increasingly narrowed their platform. But even the quest for legitimacy did not stifle these feminists completely, and many of them said in private writings—in letters and diaries—what they were unwilling to utter in public. Free-lovers and suffragists represented, on sexual issues such as birth control, the left and right wings of feminism.

The similarities between free-lovers and suffragists on the question of voluntary motherhood should be understood, then, not as minimizing the political distance between them but as showing how their analyses of the social meaning of reproduction for women were converging. The sources of that convergence, the common ground of their feminism, were their contradictory attractions to modernism and tradition. Most were educated Yankees from professional, farm, or commercial families responding to severe threats to the stability, if not dominance, of their class positions. Both groups were alarmed at the consequences of rapid industrialization—the emergence of great capitalists and a clearly defined financial oligarchy, the increased immigration that provided cheap labor and further threatened the dignity and economic security of the white elite. They feared and resented the loss of their independence, and many would have undone the wage-labor system entirely had they been able. Both free-lovers and suffragists welcomed the decline in patriarchal power within families that followed industrialization, but they worried, too, about the possible disintegration of the family and the loosening of sexual morality. They saw reproduction in the context of these larger social changes and in the context of a movement for women's emancipation; and they saw that movement as an answer to some of these large social problems. They hoped that giving political power to women would help to reinforce the family, make the government more just and the economy less monopolistic, and provide moral leadership in private life. In all these wishes there was something traditional as well as something progressive. Their voluntary motherhood ideas reflected this duality.

Since today we bring to our concept of birth control a medical understanding, it is important to stress at the outset that voluntary motherhood promoters disapproved of contraceptive devices. Ezra Heywood, free-love patriarch and martyr, thought "artificial" methods "unnatural, injurious, or offensive."[2] Tennessee Claflin, feminist, spiritualist, and sister of Victoria Woodhull, wrote that the "washes, teas, tonics and various sorts of appliances known to the initiated" were a "standing reproach upon, and a permanent indictment against, American women. . . . No woman should ever hold sexual relations with any man from the possible consequences of which she might desire to escape."[3] *Woodhull and Claflin's Weekly* editorialized: "The means they [women] resort to for . . . prevention is sufficient to disgust every natural man."[4]

Their arguments reflected a romantic yearning for the "natural," rather pastorally conceived, which was typical of many nineteenth-century reform movements. Women's arguments against contraception also featured an underlying fear of the promiscuity that it could permit, a fear associated less with anxiety about their personal virtue and more with anxiety about other women—"fallen women"—who might undermine a husband's fidelity. Perhaps most passionately, voluntary motherhood advocates feared contraception as a means by which men could exploit, even rape, women with impunity.

To today's readers it might seem that a principle of voluntary motherhood that rejects contraception is a principle so theoretical as to create little real impact. What gave it substance was that it was accompanied by another, potentially explosive conceptual change: the reacceptance of female sexuality. Both free-lovers and suffragists staked their claims here on the traditional grounds of the "natural." Free-lovers argued, for example, that celibacy was unnatural and dangerous—for men and women alike. "Pen cannot record, nor lips express, the enervating, debauching effect of celibate life upon young men and women."[5] Asserting the existence, legitimacy, and worthiness of a female sex drive was one of the free-lovers' most important contributions to sexual reform. It was a logical correlate of their argument for things "natural" and their appeal for integration of body and soul.

Women's rights advocates also began, timidly, to argue for the existence of female sexuality. Isabella Beecher Hooker wrote to her daughter: "Multitudes of women in all the ages who have scarce known what sexual desire is—being wholly absorbed in the passion of maternity—have sacrificed themselves to the beloved husbands as unto God—and yet these men, full of their human passion and defending it as righteous & God-sent lose all confidence in womanhood when a woman here and there betrays her similar nature & gives herself soul & body to the man she adores."[6] Alice Stockham, a spiritualist and feminist physician, lauded sexual desire in men and women as "the prophecy of attainment." She urged that couples avoid reaching sexual "satiety" with each other in order to keep their sexual desire alive, for she considered desire both pleasant and healthful.[7] Elizabeth Cady Stanton, commenting in her diary in 1883 on the Walt Whitman poem "There Is a Woman Waiting for Me," wrote, ". . . he speaks as if the female must be forced to the creative act, apparently ignorant of the fact that a healthy woman has as much passion as a man, that she needs nothing stronger than the law of attraction to draw her to the male."[8] Still, she loved Whitman—largely because of that openness about sex that made him the free-lovers' favorite poet.

According to the system of ideas then dominant among preachers of purity, women, lacking sex drives, submitted to sexual intercourse in order to please their husbands and to conceive children. There was an inconsistency in this view, however, even among these moral authorities, expressed in the contradiction that women naturally lacked a sex drive but also needed protection from exposure to sexuality lest they "fall" and become depraved, lustful monsters. This ambivalence stemmed, no doubt, from a lack of certainty about the reality of the sexless woman, which was, after all, a construct laid only thinly on top of an earlier conception of woman as highly sexed, even insatiably so, that prevailed until the late eighteenth century. Victorian ambivalence on this question is nowhere more tellingly revealed than in the writings of physicians, who viewed woman's sexual organs as the source of her essence, both physical and psychological, and blamed most mental derangements on disorders of these organs.[9] Indeed, they saw it as part of the nature of things, as Rousseau had written, that men were male only part of the time, but women were female always.[10] Whether the discourse deemed women highly sexed or asexual, it identified women with sex. In a system that limited women's opportunities to make other contributions to culture, this should not be surprising. Indeed, females were frequently called "the sex" in the nineteenth century.

Experts employed the concept of the maternal instinct to make Victorian sexual attitudes more consistent. In many nineteenth-century writings we find the idea that the maternal instinct was the female analogue to the male sex instinct, as if the two instincts were seated in analogous parts of the brain, or soul. Thus, to suggest, as these feminists did, that women might have the capacity to be sexual subjects rather than objects, feeling impulses of their own, tended to weaken the claim that the maternal instinct was always dominant. In the fearful imagination of the self-appointed protectors of family values and womanly innocence, the possibility that women might desire sexual contact not for the sake of pregnancy—that they might even desire it at a time when they positively did not want pregnancy—opened a door to denying that women were governed by maternal instinct.

Most of the feminists did not want to open that door either. Indeed, nineteenth-century women's rights advocates commonly used the presumed special motherly nature and sexual purity of women as an argument for increasing their freedom and status. It is no wonder that many of them chose to speak their subversive speculations about the sexual nature of women privately, or at least softly. Even the outspoken free-lovers hedged. Lois Waisbrooker and Dora Forster, writing for a free-love journal in the 1890s, argued that although men and women both had an "amative" instinct, it was much stronger in men, and women—only women—also had a reproductive, or "generative," instinct. "I suppose it must be universally conceded that men make the better lovers," Forster wrote. She thought that it might be possible that "the jealousy and tyranny of men have operated to suppress amativeness in women, by constantly sweeping strongly sexual women from the paths of life into infamy and sterility and death," but also that the suppression, if it existed, had been permanently inculcated into woman's character.[11]

Modern birth control ideas rest on accepting female sexuality. Modern birth control—that is, contraception—is supposed to permit sexual intercourse as often as desired without the risk of pregnancy. Despite the protestations of sex counselors that there are no norms for how often people should engage in intercourse, the popular view has always had such norms. Most people in the mid-twentieth century thought that "normal" couples indulged several times a week. Given this concept of sexual rhythms, and the accompanying concept of the purpose of birth control, the free-lovers' rejection of artificial contraception and "unnatural" sex seems to eliminate the possibility of birth control at all. Nineteenth-century sexual reformers, however, had different sexual norms. They did not seek to make an infinite number of sterile sexual encounters possible. They wanted to make it possible for women to avoid pregnancy if they badly needed to do so for physical or psychological reasons, but they did not believe that it was essential for women to be able to indulge in sexual intercourse under those circumstances.

In short, for birth control they recommended periodic or permanent abstinence, and the tradition of magnetation theories of sex among the perfectionists made this seem a reasonable, moderate procedure. The proponents of voluntary motherhood had in mind two distinct contexts for abstinence. One was the mutual decision of a couple; the other was the unilateral decision of a woman. Let us consider them one at a time.

Abstinence chosen by a couple meant self-imposed celibacy, either continuous or through a form of rhythm method. Some medical observers had correctly plotted a woman's fertility cycle, but the majority of physicians, accepting a logic of analogy from lower mammals rather than direct observation of humans, had got it wrong. (It was not until the 1920s that the ovulation cycle was correctly plotted and the 1930s before it was generally understood among American doctors.) Ezra Heywood, for example, recommended avoiding intercourse from six to eight days before menstruation until ten to twelve days after it.[12] Careful use of the calendar could also provide control over the sex of a child, Heywood believed: conception in the first half of the menstrual cycle would produce girls, in the second half, boys.[13]

Some voluntary motherhood advocates explored another form of abstinence—male continence, or avoidance of ejaculation. Heywood, for example, endorsed the Oneida system, but was repelled by John Humphrey Noyes's authoritarian leadership and his ban on monogamous relationships.[14] Stockham developed a more woman-centered approach to male continence, which she termed "Karezza," in which it was necessary for the woman as well as the man to avoid climax.[15]

Any of these systems required self-control, and free-lovers (like conservative moral reformers) passionately preached sexual self-control. This credo came to them mainly from the thought of the utopian communitarians of the early nineteenth century, and Heywood developed it further. Beginning with the assumption that people's "natural" instincts, left untrammeled, would automatically create a harmonic, peaceful, ecological society—an optimism deriving from liberal philosophical faith in the innate goodness of humankind—Heywood applied it to sexuality, arguing that the natural sexual instinct was innately moderated and self-regulating. He also denied the social necessity of sublimation. On one level, Heywood's theory may seem inadequate as a psychology, since it cannot explain phenomena such as repression and the fact that adults have greater self-control than children. As a social critique, however, it had explanatory power. It argued that the society and its attendant repressions had distorted the animal's natural self-regulating mechanism and thereby created excessive and obsessive sex drives. It offered a social, evolutionary explanation for phenomena usually described in psychological terms and held out the hope that they could be changed.

Heywood's theory of self-regulation was essentially the same as Wilhelm Reich's theory of sex-economy, but Heywood went beyond Reich in providing a weapon against one of the ideological defenses of male supremacy. Self-regulation as a goal undercut the prevalent attitude that male lust was an uncontrollable urge, an attitude that functioned as a justification for rape specifically and for male sexual irresponsibility generally. We have to get away from the tradition of "man's necessities and woman's obedience to them," Stockham wrote."[16] The idea that men's desires are irrepressible was the other face of the idea that women's desires are nonexistent. Together they created a seamless fence that imprisoned woman, making it her exclusive responsibility to say no and making pregnancy her God-given, exclusive burden if she didn't, while denying her both artificial contraception and the personal and political power to reject male sexual demands.

Heywood developed his theory of natural sexual self-regulation in answer to the common anti-free-love argument that the removal of social regulation of sexuality would lead to unhealthy promiscuity: ". . . in the distorted popular view, Free Love tends to unrestrained licentiousness, to open the flood gates of passion and remove all barriers in its desolating course; but it means just the opposite; it means the *utilization of animalism,* and the triumph of Reason, Knowledge, and Continence."[17] He applied the theory of self-regulation to the problem of birth control only as an afterthought, perhaps when women's concerns with that problem reached him. Ideally, he believed, the amount of sexual intercourse that men and women desired would be exactly commensurate with the number of children that were wanted. Since sexual repression had had the boomerang effect of intensifying human sex drives far beyond "natural" levels, effecting birth control now would require the development of the inner self-control to contain and repress sexual urges. But Heywood expected that in time sexual moderation would come naturally.

Heywood's analysis, published in the mid-1870s, was concerned primarily with excessive sex drives in men. Charlotte Perkins Gilman, one of the leading theoreticians of the suffrage movement, reinterpreted that analysis two decades later to emphasize its effects on women. The economic dependence of woman on man, in Gilman's analysis, made her sexual attractiveness necessary not only for winning a mate but also as a means of gaining a livelihood. This is the case with no other animal. In the human female it had produced "excessive modification to sex," emphasizing weak qualities characterized by humans as "feminine." Gilman made an analogy to the milk cow, bred to produce far more milk than she would need for her calves. But Gilman agreed entirely with Heywood about the effects of exaggerated sex distinction on the male, producing excessive sex energy and its excessive indulgence to an extent that was debilitating to the whole species. Like Heywood she believed that the path of progressive social evolution ran toward monogamy and toward reducing the promiscuous sex instinct.[18]

A second context for abstinence was the right of the wife unilaterally to refuse her husband. This principle was at the heart of voluntary motherhood. It was a key substantive demand in the mid-nineteenth century, when both law and practice made sexual submission to her husband a wife's duty. A woman's right to refuse was the fundamental condition of birth control—and of her independence and personal integrity.

In their crusade for this right of refusal, the voices of free-lovers and suffragists were in unison. Heywood demanded "Woman's Natural Right to ownership and control over her own body-self—a right inseparable from Woman's
intelligent existence."[19] Paulina Wright Davis, at the National Woman Suffrage
Association in 1871, attacked the law "which makes obligatory the rendering
of marital rights and compulsory maternity." When, as a result of her statement,
she was accused of being a free-lover, she accepted the label.[20] Isabella Beecher
Hooker wrote her daughter in 1869 advising her to avoid pregnancy until "you
are prepared in body and soul to receive and cherish the little one."[21] Elizabeth Cady Stanton characteristically used the same concept as Heywood's, that
of woman owning her own body. Once asked by a magazine what she meant
by it, she replied: ". . . womanhood is the primal fact, wifehood and motherhood its incidents. . . . must the heyday of her existence be wholly devoted to
the one animal function of bearing children? Shall there be no limit to this but
woman's capacity to endure the fearful strain on her life?"[22]

The insistence on women's right to refuse often took the form of attacks
on men for their lusts and their violence in attempting to satisfy them. In feminist complaints against the unequal marriage laws, loudest among them was
the charge that the laws legalized rape.[23] Woodhull raged, "I will tell the world,
so long as I have a tongue and the strength to move it, of all the infernal misery hidden behind this horrible thing called marriage, though the Young Men's
Christian Association sentence me to prison a year for every word. I have seen
horrors beside which stone walls and iron bars are heaven."[24] Angela Heywood,
wife of the free-love leader, wrote bluntly: "Man so lost to himself and woman as to invoke legal *violence* in these scared nearings, *should have solemn
meeting with, and look serious at his own penis until he is able to be lord and
master of it, rather than it should longer rule, lord and master, of him and of
the victims he deflowers.*"[25] Suffragists spoke more delicately, but no less bitterly. Feminists campaigned against prostitution, which they attributed to the
double standard. Their proposed remedy was that men conform to the purity
standards required of women.[26]

A variant of this concern was a campaign against "sexual abuses," which
in Victorian euphemistic language could mean deviant sexual practices or
excessive sexual demands but not necessarily violence or prostitution. The free-
lovers in particular turned to this cause because it gave them an opportunity
to attack marriage. The "sexual abuses" question was one of the most frequent
subjects of correspondence in free-love periodicals. For example, a letter from
Mrs. Theresa Hughes of Pittsburgh: ". . . a girl of sixteen, full of life and health
when she became a wife . . . She was a slave in every sense of the word, mentally and sexually, never was she free from his brutal outrages, morning, noon
and night, up almost to the very hour her baby was born, and before she was

again strong enough to move about. . . . Often did her experience last an hour or two, and one night she will never forget, the outrage lasted exactly four hours."[27] Or from Lucinda Chandler, a well-known moral reformer:

> This useless sense gratification has demoralized generation after generation, till monstrosities of disorder are common. Moral education, and healthful training will be requisite for some generations, even after we have equitable economics, and free access to Nature's gifts. The young man of whom I knew who threatened his bride of a week with a sharp knife in his hand, to compel her to perform the office of "sucker," would no doubt have had the same disposition though no soul on the planet had a want unsatisfied or lacked a natural right.[28]

From an anonymous woman in Los Angeles: "I am nearly wrecked and ruined by . . . nightly intercourse, which is often repeated in the morning. This and nothing else was the cause of my miscarriage—he went to work like a man a-mowing, and instead of a pleasure as it might have been, it was most intense torture."[29]

Clearly, there was hostility toward sex here. Though several historians have observed that many feminists hated sex, they have failed to perceive that feminists' hostility and fear derived from the fact that they were women, not that they were feminists. Women in the nineteenth century were urged to repress their own sexual feelings, to view sex as a reproductive and wifely duty. But they also resented what they had experienced, which was not an abstraction but a particular, historical kind of sexual encounter: intercourse dominated by and defined by the man in conformity with his desires and in disregard of what might bring pleasure to a woman.

Furthermore, sexual intercourse brought physical danger. Pregnancy, childbirth, and abortions were risky and painful experiences in the nineteenth century, and venereal diseases were frequently communicated to women by their husbands. Elmina Slenker, a free-lover and novelist, wrote, "I'm getting a host of stories (truths) about women so starved sexually as to use their dogs for relief, and finally I have come to the belief that a CLEAN dog is better than a drinking, tobacco-smelling, venereally diseased man!"[30]

Sex-hating women were not simply misinformed or priggish or neurotic. They were often responding rationally to their material reality. Denied the knowledge of sexual possibilities other than those dictated by the rhythms of male orgasm, they typically had two choices: passive and frequently pleasureless submission, with high risk of undesirable consequences, or rebellious refusal. In that context abstinence to ensure voluntary motherhood was a most significant feminist demand. There was a medical superstition that women could not conceive unless they felt sexually aroused; it is understandable, then, that Alice Stockham, for example, proposed deliberate sexual coldness as a form of birth control.[31]

This antisexual feeling should hardly be surprising. What is remarkable is that some women recognized that it was not sex itself but their husbands' style of making love that repelled them. One of the women who complained about her treatment went on to say, "I am undeveloped sexually, never having desires in that direction; still, with a husband who had any love or kind feelings for me and one less selfish it *might* have been different, but he cared nothing for the torture to *me* as long as *he* was gratified."[32]

Slenker, the toughest and most crusty of all the "sex-haters," dared to explore and take seriously her own longings, thereby revealing herself to be a sex-lover in disguise. As the editor of the *Water-Cure Journal* and a regular contributor to the *Free Love Journal,* she expounded a theory she called "Dianaism," or "Non-Procreative Love" (sometimes also called "Diana-love" and "Alpha-abstinence").[33] It meant free sexual contact of all sorts except intercourse. "We want the sexes to love more than they do; we want them to love openly, frankly, earnestly; to enjoy the caress, the embrace, the glance, the voice, the presence & the very step of the beloved. We oppose no form or act of love between any man & woman. Fill the world as full of genuine sex love as you can . . . but forbear to rush in where generations yet unborn may suffer for your unthinking, uncaring, unheeding actions."[34] Comparing this recommendation to the more usual physical means of avoiding conception, *coitus interruptus* and male continence, reveals how radical it was. The definition of sex as heterosexual intercourse has been one of the oldest and most universal cultural norms. Slenker's alienation from existing sexual possibilities led her to explore alternatives with a bravery and a freedom from religious and psychological taboos extraordinary for a nineteenth-century Quaker reformer.

In the nineteenth century neither free-lovers nor suffragists ever relinquished their hostility to contraception. Free speech, however, was always an overriding concern.[35] As a protest, Ezra Heywood published some advertisements for a vaginal syringe, an instrument whose use for contraception he personally deplored, or so he continued to assure his readers.[36] Those advertisements led to his prosecution for obscenity, and he defended himself with characteristic flair by making his position more radical than ever before.

Contraception was moral, Heywood argued, when it was used by women as the only means of defending their rights, including the right to voluntary motherhood. He would have agreed that contraception was women's "moral property." Although "artificial means of preventing conception are not generally patronized by Free Lovers," he wrote, reserving for his own followers the highest moral ground, still he recognized that not all women were lucky enough to have free-lovers for their sex partners. "Since Comstockism makes male will, passion and power absolute to *impose* conception, I stand with women to resent it. The man who would legislate to choke a woman's vagina with semen, who would force a woman to retain his seed, bear children when her own reason and conscience oppose it, would waylay her, seize her by the throat and rape her person."[37] His wife enthusiastically pushed this political line. "Is it 'proper,' 'polite,'" Angela Heywood wrote, "for men, real *he* men, to go to Washington to say, by penal law, fines and imprisonment, whether woman may continue her natural right to wash, rinse, or wipe out her own vaginal body opening—as well as legislate when she may blow her nose, dry her eyes, or nurse her babe. . . . Whatever she may have been pleased to receive, from man's own, is his gift and her property. Women do not like rape, and have a right to resist its results."[38] Her outspokenness, even vulgarity in the ears of most of her contemporaries, came from a substantive, not merely a stylistic, sexual radicalism. Not even the heavy taboos and revulsion against abortion stopped her: "To cut a child up in woman, procure abortion, is a most fearful, tragic deed; but *even that* does not call for man's arbitrary jurisdiction over woman's womb."[39]

It is unclear whether Angela Heywood was actually arguing for legalized abortion; if so, she was alone among nineteenth-century sexual reformers in saying it out loud. Other feminists and free-lovers condemned abortion and argued that the necessity of stopping its widespread practice was a key reason for instituting voluntary motherhood by other means. The difference on the abortion question between sex radicals and sexual conservatives was in their analysis of its causes and remedies. While "regular" physicians and preachers sermonized on the sinfulness of women who had abortions,[40] the sex radicals pronounced abortions themselves undeserved punishment and women who underwent them helpless victims. Victoria Woodhull and Tennessee Claflin wrote about Madame Restell's notorious abortion "factory" in New York City without moralizing, arguing that only voluntary conception would put it out of business.[41] Elizabeth Cady Stanton also sympathized with women who had abortions and used the abortion problem as an example of women being victimized by laws made without their consent.[42]

Despite stylistic differences, which came from differences in goals, nineteenth-century American free-love and women's rights advocates shared a basic perspective toward birth control: they opposed contraception and abortion but endorsed voluntary motherhood achieved through periodic abstinence; they believed that women should always have the right to decide when to bear a child; they believed that women and men both had natural sex drives and that it was not wrong to indulge those drives without the intention of conceiving children. The two groups also shared the same appraisal of the social and political significance of birth control. Most of them were favorably inclined toward neo-Malthusian reasoning (at least until the 1890s, when the prevailing concern shifted to the problem of underpopulation rather than overpopulation).[43] They were also interested in controlling conception for eugenic purposes. Beyond their mutual hostility toward the hypocrisy of the sexual double standard, they shared a general sense that men had become oversexed and that sex had been transformed into something disagreeably violent.

And their commitment to voluntary motherhood expressed their larger commitment to women's rights. Stanton thought voluntary motherhood so central that on her lecture tours in 1871 she held separate afternoon meetings for *women only* (an unfamiliar practice at the time) and talked "the gospel of fewer children & a healthy, happy maternity."[44] She wrote: "What radical thoughts I then and there put into their heads & as they feel untrammelled, these thoughts are permanently lodged there! That is all I ask."[45] Only Ezra Heywood had gone so far as to defend a particular contraceptive device—the syringe. But the principle of women's right to choose was accepted in the most conservative parts of the women's rights movement. At the First Congress of the Association for the Advancement of Women, in 1873, a whole session was devoted to the theme "Enlightened Motherhood," which had voluntary motherhood as part of its meaning.[46]

The general conviction of the women's rights community that women had a right to choose when to be pregnant was so strong by the end of the nineteenth century that it seems odd that they were unable to overcome their scruples against artificial contraception. The basis for this reluctance was that effective contraception would separate sexuality from reproduction too completely. Permitting sexual intercourse to take place regularly, even frequently, without the risk of pregnancy seemed to nineteenth-century middle-class women to be an attack on the family. In the mid-Victorian sexual system, men usually conducted their sexual philandering with prostitutes; accordingly, prostitution, far from being a threat to the family system, was a part of it—indeed, an important support of it. Moreover, many believed that prostitutes had special knowledge of effective birth control techniques, and this strengthened the association of contraception with sexual immorality. It did not seem, even to the most sexually liberal, that contraception could be legitimized to any extent, even for the purposes of family planning for married couples, without licensing extramarital and commercial sex. Contraception was therefore a potential threat to a woman's marriage. The fact that contraception was not morally acceptable to respectable women was, from a woman's point of view, an obstacle to male infidelity that they did not wish to give up.

The fact that sexual intercourse often led to conception seemed also a guarantee that men would marry in the first place. In the nineteenth century, women needed marriage more than men. Lacking economic or social independence, women needed husbands for support and status. The prospect of dissolving the cement of nuclear families was frightening, and in many cases children, and even the prospect of children, provided that cement. Men's responsibilities for children were an important pressure for marital stability. Women might also depend on their children to provide them with meaningful work. The belief that motherhood was a woman's fulfillment had a material basis: parenthood was often the most creative, challenging, and rewarding activity in a woman's life.

Legal, efficient birth control would have increased men's freedom to indulge in extramarital sex without greatly increasing women's freedom to do so even had they wanted to. The double standard of the Victorian sexual and family system, which had made men's sexual freedom irresponsible and oppressive to women, left most feminists convinced that increasing, rather than releasing, the taboos against extramarital sex was in their interest, and they threw their support behind social purity campaigns.

In short, we must discard the twentieth-century association of birth control with a trend toward sexual freedom. The voluntary motherhood advocates of the 1870s aimed to enforce their sexual morality. Achieving voluntary motherhood by a method that would have encouraged sexual license contradicted the felt interests and ethical commitments of the very group that formed the main social basis for the cause—middle-class women. Separating these women from the early twentieth-century feminists, with their interest in sexual freedom, were nearly four decades of significant social and economic changes and a general weakening of the ideology of the "Lady." The ideal of the free-lovers—responsible, open sexual encounters between equal partners—was impossible because men and women were not equal. A man was a man whether faithful to his wife or not. But women's sexual activities divided them into two categories—wife or prostitute. These categories were not mere ideas but were enforced in reality by severe social and economic sanctions. The fact that so many, indeed most, free-lovers in practice led faithful, monogamous, and legally married lives is not insignificant in this regard. It suggests that they understood that free love was an ideal not to be realized in that time.

As voluntary motherhood was an ideology intended to encourage sexual purity, so it was also a pro-motherhood ideology. Far from debunking motherhood, voluntary motherhood advocates consistently continued the Victorian mystification and sentimentalization of the mother. It is true that at the end of the nineteenth century an increasing number of feminists and elite women—that is, still a relatively small group—were choosing not to marry or become mothers. This behavior derived from their increasing interest in professional work and social activism and the difficulty of doing such work as a wife and mother, given the norm of domesticity, the disapproval and uncooperativeness of husbands, and the lack of social provisions for child care. Voluntary motherhood advocates shared the general belief that mothers of young children ought not to work outside their homes but should make mothering their full-time occupation. Suffragists argued both to make professions open to women and to ennoble the task of mothering; in fact, they often insisted on increased rights and opportunities for women *because* they were mothers.

The free-lovers were equally pro-motherhood but wanted to separate motherhood from legal marriage, devising pro-motherhood arguments to bolster their case against marriage. Mismated couples, held together by marriage laws, made bad parents and produced inferior offspring, free-lovers said.[47] In 1870 *Woodhull and Claflin's Weekly* editorialized, "Our marital system is the greatest obstacle to the regeneration of the race."[48]

This concern with eugenics was characteristic of nearly all feminists of the late nineteenth century. At the time, eugenics was an implication of evolutionary theory, used by many social reformers to buttress their arguments that improvement of the human condition was possible. Eugenics had not yet become a movement in itself. Feminists used eugenic arguments as if aware that arguments based solely on women's rights had not enough power to conquer conservative and religious scruples about reproduction. So they combined eugenics and feminism to produce evocative, romantic visions of perfect motherhood. "Where boundless love prevails, the mother who produces an inferior child will be dishonored and unhappy . . . and she who produces superior children will feel proportionately pleased. When woman attains this position, she will consider superior offspring a necessity and be apt to procreate only with superior men."[49] Free-lovers and suffragists alike used the cult of motherhood to argue for making it voluntary. Involuntary motherhood, wrote Harriot Stanton Blatch, daughter of Elizabeth Cady Stanton and a prominent suffragist in her own right, is a prostitution of the maternal instinct.[50] The free-lover Rachel Campbell cried out that motherhood was being "ground to dust under the misrule of masculine ignorance and superstition."[51]

Not only did feminists consider motherhood an exalted, sacred profession, and a profession exclusively woman's responsibility, but they often believed that a woman who avoided motherhood had chosen a distinctly less noble path. In arguing for the enlargement of woman's sphere, feminists haltingly began to envisage combining motherhood with other activities but never rejected motherhood. Woodhull and Claflin wrote:

> Tis true that the special and distinctive feature of woman is that of bearing children, and that upon the exercise of her function in this regard the perpetuity of race depends. It is also true that those who pass through life failing in this special feature of their mission cannot be said to have lived to the best

purposes of woman's life. But while maternity should always be considered the most holy of all the functions woman is capable of, it should not be lost sight of in devotion to this, that there are as various spheres of usefulness outside of this for woman as there are for man outside of the marriage relation.[52]

For these reformers, birth control should not necessarily open the possibility of childlessness. Rather, they wanted it to give women leverage to win more recognition and dignity. Dora Forster saw in the fears of underpopulation a weapon of blackmail for women (in an echo of Lysistrata or a birth strike): "I hope the scarcity of children will go on until maternity is honored at least as much as the trials and hardships of soldiers campaigning in wartime. It will then be worth while to supply the nation with a sufficiency of children. . . . every civilized nation, having lost the power to enslave woman as mother, will be compelled to recognize her voluntary exercise of that function as by far the most important service of any class of citizens."[53] Lois Waisbrooker, a feminist novelist and moral reformer, wrote: "Oh, women of the world, arise in your strength and demand that all which stands in the path of true motherhood shall by removed from your path."[54] Helen Hamilton Gardener based a plea for women's education entirely on the argument that society needed educated mothers to produce able sons (not children, *sons*): "Harvard and Yale, not to mention Columbia, may continue to put a protective tariff on the brains of young men: but so long as they must get those brains from the proscribed sex, just so long will male brains remain an 'infant industry' and continue to need this protection. Stupid mothers never did and stupid mothers never will furnish this world with brilliant sons."[55]

Clinging to the cult of motherhood was part of a larger conservatism shared by free-lovers and suffragists—namely, acceptance of the Victorian gender system. Even the free-lovers rejected only one factor—legal marriage—of the many conventions that defined woman's place in the family. They did not challenge conventional conceptions of woman's passivity and limited sphere of concern.[56] In their struggles for equality women's rights advocates never suggested that men should share responsibility for child-raising, housekeeping, nursing, or cooking. When Victoria Woodhull in the 1870s and Charlotte Perkins Gilman in the first decade of the twentieth century suggested socialized child care, they assumed that only women would do the work.[57] Most feminists wanted economic independence for women, but most were reluctant to recommend achieving this by turning women loose and helpless into the economic world to compete with men.[58] This preference was conditioned by an attitude hostile to the egoistic spirit of capitalism; but since the attitude was not transformed into a political position, it often appeared in the guise of expressing women's failings rather than the system's faults.

Failing to distinguish, or even to indicate awareness of a possible distinction, between women's learned passivity and their equally learned distaste for competition and open aggression, these feminists also followed the standard Victorian rationalization of its gender system, namely, the idea that women were morally superior. Thus the timidity and self-effacement that were the marks of women's powerlessness became innate virtues. Angela Heywood, for example, praised women's greater ability for self-control and, in an attribution no doubt intended to jar and titillate the reader, branded men inferior on account of their lack of sexual temperance. She also identified men's refusal to accept women as human beings as a mark of men's incapacity: ". . . man has not yet achieved himself to realize and meet a PERSON in woman."[59] This feminist and maternalist trope—that women's powers are superior and men's lack of discipline an incapacity—was rhetorically stirring. But she omitted to mention the power and privilege to exploit women that the supposed "incapacity" gave men.

This omission reveals a false consciousness characteristic of the cult of motherhood, a consciousness that ignored or denied the privileges men received from women's exclusive responsibility for parenthood. For the "motherhood" of the feminists' writings was not merely the biological process of gestation and birth but a whole package of social, economic, and cultural functions. Although some nineteenth-century feminists had studied and thought deeply about the historical and anthropological origins of woman's social status, they nevertheless agreed with the biological-determinist point of view that woman's parental capacities had become implanted at the level of instinct, the famous "maternal instinct." That concept rested on the assumption that the qualities parenthood requires—capacities for tenderness, self-control and patience, tolerance for tedium and detail, emotional supportiveness, dependability and warmth—were not only instinctive but sex-linked. The concept of the maternal instinct thus also involved a definition of the normal instinctual structure of the male that excluded these capacities, or included them only to an inferior degree; it also carried the implication that women who did not exercise these capacities, presumably through motherhood, remained unfulfilled, untrue to their destinies.

Belief in the maternal instinct reinforced a putatively "natural," spiritual connection for women between sex and reproduction and thereby limited the development of birth control ideas. But the limits were set by the entire social context of women's lives, not by the intellectual timidity of their ideas. For women's "control over their own bodies" to lead to a rejection of motherhood as the *primary* vocation and measure of social worth required the existence of attractive alternative vocations and sources of worthiness. The women's rights advocates of the 1870s and 1880s were fighting for those other opportunities, but a significant change in this direction had come only to a few privileged women, and most women had no such opportunities. Thus voluntary motherhood in this period remained almost exclusively a tool for women to strengthen their positions within conventional marriages and families, not to reject them.

5   *Social Purity and Eugenics*

The social purity movement sought to abolish prostitution and other sexual philandering. That the movement also contributed to the acceptance of birth control in this country may, therefore, seem odd. Social purity really meant sexual purity ("social" was the standard Victorian euphemism for "sexual") and that meant confining sex within marriage and moderating its indulgence even there. Contraception, by removing the "risk" of illegitimate pregnancies and even of venereal disease from nonmarital affairs, undermined some of the props of that sexual morality. Social purity advocates were unequivocally opposed to contraception. But so too, as we have seen, were most sex radicals—free-lovers, utopians, and feminists.

Because few nineteenth-century reformers advocated or even accepted the separation of sexuality from reproduction, there was remarkable unity among sex radicals and sex conservatives on the issue of birth control. Indeed, the attempt to use categories such as "radical" and "conservative" with regard to sexual issues becomes questionable on close examination. Just as many interpreters of the sexual reform program of the nineteenth-century feminists focused on their "prudery," applying twentieth-century attitudes to it and missing its political content, so the program of the social purity advocates has been shallowly interpreted.

The birth control ideas of social purity advocates were remarkably feminist. Social purity was a direct continuation of one line of voluntary motherhood thought: the use of eugenic arguments to support women's control over their reproductive capacities. The eugenic propaganda of the social purity movement is a neglected part of American intellectual history, inasmuch as two decades later eugenics became one of the most influential fads in American culture, both academic and popular. Social purity advocates began the attempt to use eugenic logic to increase women's power and dignity; yet, ultimately, eugenic thought did more harm than good to feminism and voluntary motherhood.

Social Purity

The social purity agenda had intellectual roots in early temperance and moral reform, in abolitionism, in left-wing Protestantism, and in utopian radicalism. Like many of these earlier nineteenth-century causes, social purity had a double-edged political blade: liberal in its commitment to legal equality for all persons and to a single standard of morality, yet conservative in its desire to enforce rural, Calvinistic moral values on the whole society. Energized by the women entering organized reform activity and threatened by the specter of "regulated" prostitution, the movement first formed in opposition to the legalization of prostitution. That danger having been averted, in the 1880s social purity reformers began to campaign for lowering the age of consent, prosecuting customers of prostitutes as well as the prostitutes themselves, reforming prostitutes, providing police matrons, sexually segregating prisons, stopping abortion, censoring pornography, and spreading purity education.[1]

This list of issues suggests that the attraction of the social purity cause for women was not peripheral but fundamental. The closer we look, the harder it is to distinguish social purity groups from feminist ones. Feminists from very disparate groups were advocates of most major social purity issues—women committed to such varied causes as suffrage, free love, and temperance, for example.[2]

They had in common a current of fear and hostility toward sexuality. Their frequent attacks on "lust" and "sexual excess" have made them appear as sex haters to many twentieth-century readers, including historians. Here is Clara Cleghorne Hoffman of the National Women's Christian Temperance Union (NWCTU) addressing the International Council of Women in 1888:

> In thousands of homes everything seems to be perfectly pure, perfectly moral . . . and yet . . . hundreds go forth from these homes to swell the ranks of recognized prostitution, while thousands more go forth into the ranks of legalized prostitution under the perfectly respectable mantle of marriage. The fires of passion and lust lurk in these homes like the covered fires of Lucknow, only needing the occasion, only needing the temptation, to burst forth into

flame, carrying death and destruction to every pure, and true and lovely attribute of heart and soul.[3]

One historian has defined that view as "pansexual," observing that sex drives seemed to sex haters to be omnipresent and ever present and that social progress depended upon sublimating these drives.[4] That interpretation leaves many feminist social purity ideas unexplained, however, because it assumes a Freudian view of sexuality. Social purity advocates did believe that sex drives could interfere with work discipline and subvert the necessary societal commitment to hard work, competition, and social status earned by worldly success. But that belief, which dates back at least to early Puritanism, is not the same as a Freudian theory, which postulates that the sex drive is identical with the "life force," that it is the *only* creative drive of human beings. This distinction is important because without it the singular contribution of feminism to social purity thought is lost. Feminists believed that men had developed excessive sex drives, which contributed to the subjection of women and hence limited the development of the whole civilization. From this feminists drew the inference that excessive sex drive had to be *eliminated*, not merely checked or sublimated, in order to create a pure and sexually equal society. This goal did not seem to them unrealistic.

Social purity grew from a "new abolitionism" directed against prostitution to a holistic reform movement intent upon transforming the consciousness, changing the basic "needs" (to use a twentieth-century term), of society. Social purity advocates considered that transformation possible precisely because they believed that the current set of "human needs" was itself a social product, not a biological instinct.

If there is such a thing as "natural" human sexual behavior, we do not and cannot know what it is; sexual behavior is always culturally regulated. For women, normal "sex" in the nineteenth century meant a form of intercourse dictated primarily by male desires and typified by the mutually dependent institutions of marriage and prostitution. In both, sex carried the risks of venereal disease, unwanted conception, and dangerous and painful parturition or abortion. Throughout every reform movement that touched on the "social" question, including the free-love movement, feminist influence tended to coincide with an attack on "excessiveness" in sex. But this did not mean that the authors of these attacks hated sex absolutely. Rather, they were concerned to make women's risks calculated, to create some limitations on men's unilateral right to define every sexual encounter.

This feminist orientation was not the only one within social purity, which was a complex movement, really a coalition. Differences were sharp on some issues, such as censorship. Toward the common end of abolishing sexual sin, some social purity reformers considered it necessary to free society from pornography, while others promoted sex education and speaking candidly. Another important issue of division within social purity was the proper place of women. Despite the general commitment to a single sexual standard of conduct, many social purity advocates opposed woman suffrage as well as employment opportunities and higher education for women. By contrast, there was a distinctly feminist strain within social purity, composed mostly of women,[5] whose writings and speeches were as militant as anything the suffrage movement produced. Voluntary motherhood itself was not a controversial issue, and almost all the social purity advocates endorsed it in principle. But the feminists within the movement were more passionate in their demands for voluntary motherhood, gave it higher priority, and, most important, were more inclined to support deviations from standard notions of proper sex.

When social purity reformers endorsed voluntary motherhood, they altered the customary feminist rhetoric slightly. Free-love and women's rights advocates often argued that voluntary motherhood was a woman's right. Social purity advocates often spoke more religiously. Sin, wrote Lady Henry Somerset in 1895, begins with the unwelcome child.[6] Belle Mix began an official pamphlet of the National Purity Association by quoting Saint Paul and went on to say, "Enslaved motherhood is the curse of civilization."[7] Whereas the antisexual attitudes of the Christian founders had been directed mainly against women, the social purity imprecations were typically turned against men. Elizabeth Lisle Saxon, vice-president of the National Woman Suffrage Association for Tennessee, speaking on social purity in 1888, said, "For two thousand years we have preached Christ and practiced Moses, in all our dealings with woman— stoning her to death and letting the man go free."[8] Mix went on, in her pamphlet, to praise the "rebellion of woman against the lustful domination of man."[9]

Hereditarian Thought

Nearly everyone who supported voluntary motherhood was concerned with the welfare of children, and nearly all thought that unwanted or unwisely spaced children might suffer. In the 1890s these concerns were usually expressed in the language and logic of eugenics. Birth control advocates had used eugenic arguments since early in the century to argue the advantages of reproduction control.[10] As a form of simple hereditarian thought, eugenics is as old as humanity. The resemblance of children to their parents has produced a folklore of heredity in every culture, from "Tuesday's child is full of grace" to astrology to taboos against incest. Hereditarian thought in the nineteenth century was still largely folkloric in that it had not yet distinguished accurately between hereditary and nonhereditary characteristics. It was employed primarily in an optimistic, perfectionist vein to demonstrate the possibilities of improvement of the human condition; it did not distinguish environmental from reproductive control. The looseness and flexibility of this pre-Mendelian hereditarian thought continued throughout the nineteenth century, permitting eugenics to be used to fit the biases of any of its users—that is, the threat of bad heredity could be used to enforce any moral code. But in another respect hereditarian thought changed drastically after the 1870s, becoming associated with a social and political pessimism used to justify the miseries and inequalities of the status quo. Still lacking a sound genetic base, eugenic thought emphasized heredity in opposition to environmentalist schools of thought. In medicine, law, sociology, criminology, psychology—in nearly every social science—hereditarian arguments explained social problems in terms of individual biological inferiority and doubted the efficacy of social reforms to solve those problems. At the end of the century an upsurge in nativism produced a self-conscious eugenics movement dedicated to maintaining the supremacy of the northern European–Americans.

It is important to bear in mind this trajectory of hereditarian thought in order to place the social purity advocates along its continuum. Using hereditarian arguments, they remained in the perfectionist vein of American reformism. Eugenics helped them integrate their grievances into a unified program for reform; if vice was itself hereditary, once abolished it would be gone forever. Thus, for example, Benjamin Flower wrote that bad heredity created lust which created prostitution; if prostitutes could be prevented from bearing children, their ranks would not be replenished.[11]

Beyond suggesting birth control as a means of abolishing existing vice, the same people also suggested that involuntary motherhood produced vice. It would be hard to find a single piece of writing on voluntary motherhood between 1890 and 1910 that did not assert that unwanted children were likely to be morally and/or physically defective. Frequently, the eugenic argument for voluntary motherhood assumed rhetorically the point of view of the child (a device similar to the "rights of the fetus" propaganda of the 1970s abortion opponents). Moses Harman, a free-lover, wrote The Right to Be Born Well,[12] and Margaret Deland, a popular writer, wrote of "the right of children not to be born."[13]

Free-love advocates—that is, opponents of marriage—used eugenic arguments to defend their more daring sexual proposals. Lillian Harman, for example, justified divorce with eugenic logic: "[the] state has barred the way of evolution, has rendered natural selection of the best human characteristics impossible, by holding together the mismated."[14] Tennessee Claflin and Victoria Woodhull argued as early as 1870 that the entire marital system was an "obstacle to the regeneration of the race."[15] Many sex radicals thought that illegitimate children were usually superior as they were the children of love.[16]

But even conservative social purity advocates argued that love between parents made children superior and that the offspring of unloving couples were likely to be defective.[17]

These judgments were based on a misconception that permeated all eugenic thinking from 1890 until at least 1910—namely, belief in the inheritability of acquired characteristics.[18] On this basis, for example, Dr. George Napheys, an early voluntary motherhood advocate, argued in 1869 that the mood of the woman at the time of intercourse "has much power in the formation of the foetus, both in modifying its physical constitution and in determining the character and temperament of its mind." Able to speak about sexual matters with impunity in the years before the federal antiobscenity statute, Napheys quoted Shakespeare that a "dull, stale, tired bed" would create a "tribe of fops" and quoted Montaigne to the effect that prolonged continence before conception would create especially gifted children.[19] Many writers, both lay and medical, endorsed the notion that the circumstances and mood of the intercourse itself could affect the child's character.[20] Nearly all the books of guidance for pregnant women taught that "mental impressions" received by women during pregnancy would be transmitted to the fetus and argued that pregnant women should therefore be protected from all disturbances.[21]

Several specific applications of this genetic theory served to reinforce particular causes of the social purity advocates. One was discussion of the hereditary damage caused by drinking. There was perhaps no social question on which there was such unanimity among reformers—feminists of all kinds, social purity advocates both feminist and antifeminist, free-lovers, and conservative Christian moralists—as the question of alcohol. All agreed that parental drinking, during or after conception, could cause severe genetic damage to the child and that intemperance was itself hereditary.[22] The argument that alcohol was a "race poison" was standard in both temperance and prohibition movements.[23]

It is possible to identify several common bases for the opposition to alcohol, each of which bears on the voluntary motherhood question as well. Reformers reviled drunkenness as a state in which humanity was "lowered" beneath any possibility of spiritual aspirations or attainments. Voluntary motherhood through continence represented precisely a spiritual ideal, a victory of self-control. Alcohol not only lessened self-control, it stimulated lust. Social purity advocates preferred that sexual feelings be an expression of the "highest" spiritual love. Their antialcohol tirades expressed a longing for "purity," an ideal that contained both sexual and cultural meanings and was essentially pastoral, related to a preurban, preindustrial way of life. The traditionalist strain in antialcohol sentiment should not be overstated or taken to mean that temperance was simply an elitest campaign. Another strain in temperance was widespread among the working class and poor—woman's resentment of the saloon as both a symbol and a weapon of male supremacy. In the nineteenth century, working-class men drank in saloons, not at home; most saloons were exclusively male preserves.[24] Men's regular absences from their homes were oppressive to the women who were confined there and, perhaps worse, could exhaust the family budget. A husband's drunken presence at home, however, might lead to physical and psychological mistreatment of his wife and children. Drunkenness certainly made husbands less sensitive to the need for family limitation and to their wives' personal happiness.

These attitudes came together in another cause in which eugenic arguments loomed large: the attacks on "sexual abuse." A key motif of social purity in the 1890s was that sexual immorality was just as bad—nay, worse—inside marriage as outside it. Even conservative social purity advocates echoed the free-love and feminist criticism that marriage should not license rape. They charged that husbands' excessive sexual demands on their wives were a serious social problem[25] and criticized the brutality of husbands insistent on "vindicating" their "manhood" on their wedding night.[26]

Sex radicals differed from respectable social purity advocates in their language and frankness, not in their message. "I know of one case where a man when his wife was so near her confinement that he did not care to enforce his claim in the natural way, forced her to relieve him by making a 'sucker' of her and she would vomit with the disgust and nausea thus caused," wrote Lois Waisbrooker, a freethinker and free-love novelist, in 1890.[27] Behind this story lay the assumption, also universal among social purity advocates, that sexual intercourse during pregnancy was immoral and would produce terrible consequences for the child. A woman during gestation should be "set apart to holy and sacred uses," wrote Clara Cleghorne Hoffman of the NWCTU.[28] The result of the indignity that Waisbrooker and others reported, following eugenic logic, was that "the child was a poor sickly thing that seemed so disgusted with food that they could hardly get enough down to keep it alive."[29]

What social purity advocates defined as sexual abuse or sexual excess was in part determined by prudish sexual standards and in part by their discomfort with the separation of reproduction from sexuality. By their definition, both abuse and excess included any situation in which the woman was unwilling— a view uniquely feminist and crucial to voluntary motherhood. Antifeminist as some of the social purity advocates may have been in their condemnation of woman's higher education, political rights, or employment outside the home, they could not countenance the doctrine that a woman owed sexual obedience to her husband. In this respect, their desire to check male lust imbued the entire social purity movement with some important feminist convictions.

The addition of hereditarian thought to this set of attitudes could be used to make them even more feminist. For example, Dr. Joseph Greer, writing in 1902, reprinted a letter allegedly sent to him by a patient:

> I was married when only sixteen. . . . He was twenty-two; strong, healthy, and with large sexual demands. . . . I thought him exacting and selfish, and he thought me unaccommodating and capricious. . . . If I refused, his great, strong fingers would sink into my flesh and force would compel submission. . . . He meant to be a good husband and thought he was. He gave me "a good home," and I did not have to work, and all he asked was what marriage is supposed to secure to every husband. He did not intend to be unreasonable and thought and said, "The sooner you do as I say the sooner we will have peace." I thought so too, and tried hard to be an obedient wife. I would resolve not to resist again, but the Scotch blood was strong; there was too much freedom in my nature, and before I knew it I was fighting away "tooth and nail." As a result I would be bruised and beaten, and perhaps made sick and have a doctor before I got over it. Two little babies were literally killed before they were born, and the one that did live I have seen often in convulsions from "sexual vice," either a transmitted tendency or a birthmark due to the infernal nastiness I was forced to witness during pregnancy. When at last I watched his little life go out, I knew that he was spared a life of imbecility or idiocy, and I could not mourn.[30]

This letter illustrates an important point about the propaganda against sexual excess: that the men accused were not allegedly monstrous but normal. Eliza Bisbee Duffey, who insinuated feminist ideas into her dozens of marriage and household guidance books for women, wrote that forty-nine out of fifty men had sexually abused their wives.[31] Many of these social purity advocates offered a social analysis of men's lustfulness as something learned. Furthermore, the attack on men's lust in the name of social purity often included an assertion of women's suppressed sexual instinct. Dr. Elizabeth Blackwell wrote of the "radical physiological error" that "men are much more powerfully swayed by this instinct of sex, than are women."[32]

In the 1870s, free-lovers had developed the hypothesis that the excessive sex drive of the human male was the dialectical result of the repression and attempted rejection of sexuality in Christian society.[33] In the 1890s, social purity advocates, though hostile to free love, repeated similar views. The excessively sexual male might be normal as an individual in relation to his society, but the whole human species was aberrant: "The Satyr (male or female) who cannot see one of the opposite sex without the production of physical excitement, is not strong, but irritable; the nature is diseased."[34] Every woman's struggle for the right to refuse her own husband came to be seen as part of an evolutionary process, a process in this case conceived as restoring a previous "natural man." Bad hereditary consequences provided social purity advocates with reasons for checking male sexual selfishness that were more persuasive than the mere principle of women's integrity.

What is more, the problem—the oversexing of the male—was blamed on societal male supremacy. Some of the social purity advocates explained the sexual "diseasedness" of the society in terms of the subjection of women. The gynocentric theories of Charlotte Perkins Gilman and Lester Frank Ward were the culmination of this line of thought.[35] Gilman believed that the passing of the power to choose a mate from the woman to the man was a major cause of the hereditary decline in the human race—a theory shared by many other social purity advocates.[36] And, of course, the social purity campaigners charged that the double standard functioned in a dangerously dysgenic manner.[37] Ward even repeated the hypothesis of some feminists that the subjection of women to the excessive sexual demands of men had produced monthly menstruation as an evolutionary mutation, undesirable in his view, away from the more infrequent rhythm common among lower mammals.[38]

A Feminist Eugenics?

Eugenic thinking thus provided empirical arguments for previously abstract contentions that the status of women was an indicator of civilization. The polemical function of eugenic arguments for feminists was to give teeth to their moralism, to provide a punishment with which to threaten those who would ignore or despise women's demands for equality and a single standard of morality. Helen Hamilton Gardener, speaking in 1893 before the World Congress of Representative Women, called maternity "an awful power" that "strikes back at the race, with a blind, fierce, far-reaching force, in revenge for its subject status."[39] Here she was apparently referring to genetic deterioration; elsewhere her threat could equally have been carried out through children's imitativeness: the "pretended subservience but resentful acquiescence of wives helps to account for the mendacity of their offspring."[40] Speakers at the National Purity Congress in 1894 declared prostitution to be a simple consequence of the double standard and the double standard to be the chief obstacle to race progress. The physical and spiritual uncleanness of fathers made their offspring inferior.[41] "Race progress," to those fledgling eugenists, was another name for the "civilization" concept they had argued before; race was not understood as a specifically biological term. The suffragist Harriot Stanton Blatch argued in 1891 that the three primary conditions for "race progress" were voluntary maternity, including financial independence for women, broader education for women, and assurance of women's sole authority over their children.[42]

When that line of thought was followed to its limit, eugenic logic could prove that women's subjection was the specific cause of all the social suffering in the world: ". . . towards her own emancipation from all slaveries, economic dependence on man included . . . in order that she may worthily fulfill her function of motherhood; in order that she shall no longer be compelled to become the unwilling creator and builder of mental and moral dwarfs and imbeciles—in order that she may no longer be compelled to help supply the gallows, the prison, the poorhouse, the house of ill-fame, with birth-predestined victims."[43] Moses Harman, a leading early eugenist as well as a free-lover, blamed the development of American imperialism partly on women's subordination. In a 1908 article he combined populist and feminist arguments (in a manner characteristic of midwestern social purity advocates) to list the four major causes of imperialism as (1) concentration of the ownership of land, (2) an undemocratic monetary system, (3) the subjection of women and the consequent development of a slave-owning mentality in man, and (4) denial of women's control over reproduction and the consequent increase in the number of degenerate offspring.[44] In point 3, Harman connected the individual male consciousness in a male-supremacist system with the racial and cultural sense of superiority that underlay and justified imperialist policies. In this feminist eugenic logic, women's subjection had corrupted men, who in turn passed on that corruption, physical and mental, to successive generations.

We are now in a position to understand one of the important peculiarities of the thought of these early eugenists: They believed that the independence of women would automatically produce a eugenic effect. Some thought education might be needed first: "If a girl were brought up with any rational knowledge of herself and of the pains and perils as well as the pleasures of maternity, the dangers of indiscriminate procreation in her case would be reduced to a minimum."[45] But others, such as Blatch, thought women were natural eugenists: "In contrast to this, the man's commercial view of race production, stands the women's intuition backed by reason: She asks, first, will the child be welcome? second, what will be its inheritance of physical, mental, and moral character? third, can the child be provided for in life?" When the first and second questions are answered in the affirmative, the third problem would take care of itself.[46]

Such confidence in the automatic and immediate benefits of women's emancipation reflected a dominant nineteenth-century view that, in the competitive world created by capitalism, women had somehow remained unsullied by individualism. Women represented pure, selfless good, as opposed to the egocentrism developed as a survival instinct by men. Essentially the view of the sentimental "cult of true womanhood," it was used by feminists to argue that women should have the opportunity to make public contributions through the exercise of virtues they had developed as their survival instincts—namely, tenderness, self-effacement, and the expression of emotion.[47] The qualities of virtuous womanhood were almost fully contained in the concept of motherhood. The nineteenth-century view did not distinguish between biological and social motherhood because it considered the social (and cultural and economic) work of motherhood to be dictated by biological instinct.[48]

In this usage, the maternal instinct and its realization, motherhood, expressed a whole female politics. The lack of distinction between hereditary and learned characteristics, even in the "expert" genetics of that day, left feminist eugenists free to develop an all-encompassing view of women's contribution to humanity. They used eugenic ideas to place *both* hereditary and environmental concerns in opposition to an earlier view of reproduction that attached little prestige or skill to childbearing or child-raising.[49] They were trying to make motherhood a profession—Gilman called it "child-culture."[50] It was a "profession" that combined genetics and child psychology. In her presidential address to the National Council of Women in 1891, Frances Willard spoke of "scientific motherhood," referring to heredity, prenatal and postnatal psychology, and health.[51]

In this new rhetoric the reformers were, of course, revising and in some sense undermining their own argument that women were "natural" eugenists. Gilman argued for "unnatural motherhood," charging that what women had done naturally for so many centuries was insufficient.[52] Feminists used the newfound importance of child-raising to win gains for women. In a plea for women's education, Gardener wrote: ". . . so long as the laws of heredity last no man can give free brains to his children if their mother is the victim of superstition and priestcraft."[53]

Stepping even further away from the earlier nineteenth-century view of the moral superiority of the woman/mother, feminist eugenists attacked the selflessness and emotional generosity that was hitherto the very essence of the sentimental ideal of womanhood. The submissiveness of women, in social as well as sexual matters, was itself dysgenic, they declared. Self-sacrifice in women is a violation of duty to unborn children, charged a National Purity Association pamphlet.[54] In one of her widely read books of short stories, published in 1890, Gardener wrote: ". . . so long as motherhood is serfhood, just so long will this world be populated with a race easy to subjugate, weak to resist oppression, criminal in its instincts of cruelty toward those in its power and humble and subservient towards authority and domination."[55] Sexual surrender to one's husband was identified with political surrender to tyranny; voluntary motherhood was the correlate of political independence. Eliza Duffey wrote that self-denial and surrender to one's husband's selfishness were the worst things to do for one's unborn child.[56] Women's self-abnegation only fostered selfishness in others, and "unreasonable and unreasoning patience is a sin."[57]

There were practical purposes in these arguments, of course. Feminist eugenists used the importance of a skilled motherhood to argue for women's education.[58] Along with most social purity advocates they also demanded sex education.[59] They argued against the diluted education that was conventionally supposed to prepare women for motherhood, saying that it left them with no wisdom to pass on to their children.[60] And, of course, they insisted that a wise and eugenic motherhood had to be voluntary.

As a general motif, the eugenic arguments for birth control of the 1890s were pro-motherhood, as they had been in the first voluntary motherhood statements of the 1870s. Feminist eugenists wanted to make motherhood better, not challenge its place as the number one career of women. In the development of this argument, these feminists changed the concept of motherhood, emphasizing its social and cultural and de-emphasizing its biological aspects. They hoped that in so doing they might win popular acceptance of the voluntary motherhood principle within the conventional view of women's place as primarily in the home.

In that attempt they failed. Every eugenic argument was in the long run more effective in the hands of antifeminists than feminists. Motherhood was "proved" to be weakened, rather than strengthened, by higher education for women; those who argued that work outside the home devitalized motherhood had the best of the debate against those who supported job opportunities for women. By the turn of the century, widespread familiarity with certain rather superficial but provocative statistics—that educated, upper-class women were having fewer children than uneducated, poor women—had turned the voluntary motherhood argument on its head and produced the "race-suicide" argument, to the effect that voluntary motherhood was lowering the quality of the nation's population.

So powerful seemed these "proofs" that many erstwhile feminists followed their own eugenic arguments to extremely antifeminist conclusions. Some feminist social purity advocates, for example, endorsed the race-suicide fear of the first decade of the twentieth century, criticizing women for not having enough children, arguing that higher education and professional employment for privileged women were enticing the most able women away from motherhood.[61] The old arguments got turned around. Anna Garlin Spencer, attacking sexual vice, cited as one of its destructive consequences the "lamentable" fall in the birth rate.[62] Elizabeth Blackwell condemned the English divorce law for its double standard, citing "the very grave National danger of teaching men to repudiate fatherhood, and accustoming women to despise motherhood and shrink from the trouble involved."[63] Even free-lovers such as Moses Harman used the argument in antifeminist ways, arguing that this generation of women were not yet worthy of freedom, that they should learn "honorable maternity" first.[64] The much-jailed free-lover also endorsed Theodore Roosevelt's attack on women's "selfishness" in preferring small families.[65] The maternal instinct thus became a means for manipulating women.

Was it that eugenic ideas had a logic of their own, leading inexorably in an antifeminist direction? One might argue this by pointing to the later discrediting of Lamarckian in favor of Mendelian genetics. The effect of this change was to transform eugenics into a strictly hereditarian social theory in which environmental changes such as female education, respect for women, and sexual independence of wives had no intergenerational consequences. But eugenics was never, despite its pretensions, a strict translation of genetic theory into social theory. Indeed, no such strict translations are possible. Eugenists could have responded to Mendelian genetics by going entirely in the other direction, toward child psychology and public health. Eugenic ideas were always the tools of politics, and political needs defined these ideas.

Eugenics became predominantly antifeminist and anti–birth control because antifeminists seized control of some of the basic eugenic concepts. It is not as if the antifeminist side won the debate about women's employment and education because of the superiority of their arguments. They won because of the greater effectiveness of their organization and propaganda and the greater sympathy of the influential public with their point of view. In using eugenic arguments, feminists had tried to win more political and social power for women with the support of dominant institutions and professions—churches, schools, and medicine, for example. To do this they had to seek change without challenging their social place as mothers and housewives, using the argument developed in the first half of the nineteenth century that reforms such as voluntary motherhood would enhance their effectiveness in these roles. The same thing is true of social purity ideas. Although an important part of the antisexual orientation of social purity came from women's resentment of their sexual subjection to men, social purity advocates always defended the conventional male-headed nuclear family, resisting any critique of the restrictions it imposed on women. The social purity view had always raised up motherhood into a cult; eugenics merely gave this elevation a scientific basis.

The radical potential of eugenics and social purity, their usefulness for advancing women's control over reproduction, reached a limit by the end of the nineteenth century. Feminist propaganda for fewer children, children only when wanted, and the right to refuse or even to redefine sexual intercourse, which had steadily intensifed since the 1870s, had created a backlash.

By the early twentieth century, feminist reformers were increasingly impressed by the negative aspects of the motherhood cult. The new feminists diverged from social purity advocates on sexual and family issues such as divorce. More important, as eugenic-hereditarian thought entered the mainstream, it became more conservative and feminists came to doubt its usefulness. Some became convinced that emphasizing women's innate differences from men supported male dominance rather than the advancement of women. The pretense that those differences made the sexes different but equal was wearing thin. As long as one group had all the political power, theories of innate differences functioned most effectively as arguments for the status quo. (As women gained political power in the twentieth century, they revived and influentially deployed difference assumptions again.)

Eugenic thought had always contained the assumption that reproduction was not just a function but the purpose, in some teleological sense, of a woman's life. Furthermore, as eugenics moved toward greater emphasis on heredity as opposed to environment, it moved away from an emphasis on woman's labor and skill as a mother and back toward a view of her as a breeder, of her motherly function as part of nature. It was not just that the cult of motherhood was itself limiting but also that feminist attempts to make it more prestigious and to qualify it as skilled labor failed. As an ideology, motherhood was becoming more animal-like and less human. The ideology elevated biological reproduction from a precondition of human striving and achievement to the goal of human life itself. This is evident in the eugenic rhetoric of "improving the race." The idea that the human "race"—in the sense of "species"—was in genetic decline reversed a humanist orientation that measured human progress in terms of culture. Similarly, when "race" meant "white" or "black," this sociobiological logic rooted white racial supremacy in evolution rather than politics, another step away from enlightenment humanism. But humanism was the intellectual tradition that had given birth to feminism, and feminism as then conceived could not survive without it. The two kinds of race talk flowed together into a "race suicide" campaign, which became a direct attack on women's rights.

6　*Race Suicide*

In March 1905 the president of the United States attacked birth control. Theodore Roosevelt condemned the tendency toward smaller families as decadent, a sign of moral disease. Like others who worried about "race suicide," he specifically attacked women, branding those who avoided having children as "criminal against the race . . . the object of contemptuous abhorrence by healthy people."[1]

Although Roosevelt did not invent the term "race suicide," it quickly became the popular label for his ideas. The weight and publicity naturally given to the views of the president, and a president so newsworthy, made birth control a public national controversy, and Roosevelt became one of the chief spokesmen for the race-suicide alarm. This sharpened and broadened attack on birth control, coming from such high places, necessitated stronger defenses of it than ever before. Placed on the defensive, feminists and voluntary motherhood advocates revealed their motivations and ideology more openly than they had before. Roosevelt's bombast led many hitherto cautious suffragists to speak out publicly for birth control for the first time. At the same time the race-suicide theorists expressed more clearly what they thought birth control threatened.

The race-suicide controversy, which lasted from about 1905 to 1910, was not only illuminating but influential for the future of birth control. While it forced conservative feminists to incorporate the demand for birth control into their programs, it simultaneously narrowed the appeal of birth control to educated and prosperous women. The outspoken feminist defense of birth control and the narrow class terms in which it was argued were connected and mutually reinforcing. To show this connection we must consider both the arguments for birth control and the evidence about its use. The race-suicide alarm did not emerge out of the imagination of Roosevelt or any other social conservative but from the meanings they ascribed to actual changes in the birth rate, family structure, and sexual practice. Contemporary perceptions of these changes were not always accurate, of course. But both sides of the dispute recognized that fundamental changes were affecting a significant minority of the U.S. population and that small families and birth control use were not a temporary aberration but a secular trend, possibly even a new norm.

The Threat to the Race

By the early twentieth century several different reactions to demographic changes and birth control use had been subsumed under the loaded term "race suicide." One was an objection to the practice of birth control because it was sinful. Another was an objection to family limitation on the grounds that the nation needed a steadily growing population and large, stable families. A third was the fear that the northern European stock, which displayed the lowest birth rates, would be overwhelmed, numerically and hence politically, by immigrants, nonwhites, and the poor. Fourth, there was the view that birth control represented a rebellion of women against their primary social duty—motherhood. These four strands were never entirely distinct and tended to reinforce one another. Sin and small families weakened social cohesiveness and moral fiber, which encouraged and enabled women to stray from their proper sphere—home and children. Women's wanderings weakened the family, which in turn led women to stray further, in a vicious cycle of social degeneration. The upper classes, who believed themselves destined for political and economic leadership, saw this degeneration as weakening their position vis-à-vis those who continued to reproduce in larger numbers. The situation was culturally and morally fatal because, proportionately, the most valuable sectors of the citizenry were shrinking and the least valuable were expanding.

The fear of race suicide was at least four decades old by the time of Roosevelt's imprecations. Anxiety about immigrants and the poor reproducing faster than the elite had been current since before the Civil War.[2] Physicians in particular noticed these demographic patterns. Nathan Allen, a New England doctor, reported with concern that in 1860 the foreign-born population of Massachusetts produced more children than the native-born inhabitants and that in 1877 a full 77 percent of the births in all New England were, ominously, Catholic.[3] Another physician wrote that the birth rate was declining in "our most intelligent communities."[4] Medical journals carried many similar articles of warning.[5]

In 1891 Francis Amasa Walker, a noted academic economist, made the first comprehensive statistical case against race suicide. As superintendent of the 1870 and 1880 U.S. censuses, Walker had observed a declining birth rate among white native-born Americans and a steadily high birth rate among the foreign-born. He concluded that there was a direct relationship between immigration and the falling birth rate among the native-born: observing the poverty and wretchedness of the immigrants, and the necessity of competition with these "unkempt" newcomers for employment, the native-born shrank from bringing children into the world.[6] A decade later in his book *Poverty*, Robert Hunter drew the logical, if extreme, conclusion from Walker's figures that continued immigration, combined with a continuation of the current trend in the native-born birth rate, would result in the complete substitution of one kind of people for another throughout the United States. Hunter also pushed his analysis of census figures in another direction by showing the class differential in the birth rate among native-born Americans. The poor, he feared, would crowd out the rich.[7]

As U.S. enthusiams for overseas expansion grew at the turn of the century, the differential birth rate took on international implications. The demographer-sociologist Edward A. Ross saw parallels between U.S. problems and those of other imperial powers. "In South Africa," he wrote, "the whites stand aghast at the rabbit-like increase of the blacks." He feared that our "more fecund rivals" would outstrip us in "colonizing the waste places" and that our prosperity would likely be "darkened by the pressing-in of hunger-bitten hordes."[8]

Simultaneously, other social critics emphasized more domestic aspects of the race-suicide problem—notably, women's avoidance of their proper role. But the criticism of women, unlike nativist and racist fears, was primarily directed at relatively privileged women. For example, higher education for women was a favorite target. Attacked by antifeminists since its inception, on the grounds that it unfitted women for motherhood, demographic statistics now added to these charges the weight of quantification. College-educated women married less often, married later, and had fewer children than their less privileged sisters.[9] By 1917 only half of all the graduates of women's colleges in the United States were married.[10]

There was some evidence that the more intellectual the schooling, the lower the birth rate: for example, in 1909 only 16.5 percent of the Radcliffe class of 1900 were married.[11] The birth rate went down among married college graduates too, showing that birth control was a contributing factor. One writer calculated in 1904 that the average number of children of married alumnae was 1.8.[12] Of course the birth rate for male college graduates was low too: for example, in 1902 the president of Harvard had done his part to raise the anxiety level about race suicide with his pronouncement that Harvard graduates were not even replenishing their own numbers, with only 75 percent marrying, 25 percent of those childless, and an average of only two children for the rest. But the corresponding female birth rates were even lower.[13]

Race-suicide talk similarly condemned women's work outside the home.[14] Antifeminists frequently argued that college education and employment reduced women's health and therefore their biological fertility.[15] (Though the heavy labor that many working-class women did might have produced this effect, the professional work and educational experience of the prosperous women whose birth rates were decreasing probably did not.)

Recognizing the likelihood that the birth-rate reductions had voluntary causes, the race-suicide alarmists attacked the practice of birth control specifically. They accused women of selfishness and self-indulgence in avoiding their "duty," thus revealing their own recognition that childbearing and child-raising could be arduous, thankless tasks. The implications of these charges were that women were unilaterally avoiding conception, presumably by using birth control devices without the complicity of their husbands, or by refusing themselves sexually to their husbands, or by bamboozling their husbands into accepting their "selfishness." A doctor defined the problem as woman's "social ambition" for a "false social position" and "attainment of luxury."[16] In any of those cases, the source was the same: the newfangled independence of women. Roosevelt wrote: ". . . a desire to be 'independent'—that is, to live one's life purely according to one's own desires . . . in no sense substitutes for the fundamental virtues, for the practice of the strong, racial qualities without which there can be no strong races."[17] Clearly the definition of "strong, racial qualities" reflected the social and political values of the definer. A physician active in the attack on birth control lamented that the two groups of women who did not breed were those with the best minds (intellectuals) and those with the best bodies (prostitutes).[18]

These views obviously reflected a double standard. The very attitudes that were attacked in women—social ambition, desire for wealth—were applauded in men. Individualist, self-aggrandizing, and materialist values were the norm in the world of men—that is, in politics and the economy. In the world of women these values were unnatural and sinful. In order to preserve the "race," nature had ordained not only a division of labor but an ultimate division of values as well, one that required of women absolute selflessness. The anti-individualism of the attack on women is noticeable in the relative infrequency of "right-to-life" arguments about unborn children, despite the common conflating of contraception with abortion.[19]

A variant of the objection to women leaving their sphere was a fear that home and family would be subverted. Roosevelt spoke of this passionately, declaring that "the whole fabric of society rests upon the home."[20] He associated the ideal home with a large family. Six children were the minimum number for people of "normal stock"; those of better stock should have more.[21] William S. Rossiter, chief clerk of the U.S. Census, thought that the large family had been one of the key sources of the "finer elements of American character."[22]

Many strands of race-suicide thought—belief in large families, women's domesticity, nativism and racism, both domestic and international—were unified in the minds of the believers. They were parts of an organic worldview, made aggressive because it was on the defensive. Both the defensiveness of the viewpoint and the convergence of different attitudes within it are particularly clear in Roosevelt's own thought. Roosevelt is doubly important here, as a representative of race-suicide thought and as a powerful influence on it. His intellectual development is a microcosm of the tendency of white supremacy and male supremacy to reinforce each other against threats.

The young Roosevelt had been in favor of women's emancipation. His senior essay at Harvard in 1880 was titled "The Practicability of Equalizing Men and Women Before the Law"; his biographer, Henry F. Pringle, quoted some extraordinary passages from it.

> ". . . even as the world now is, it is not only feasible but advisable to make women equal to men before the law. . . . A son should have no more right to any inheritance than a daughter. . . . Especially as regards the laws relating to marriage, there should be the most absolute equality preserved between the two sexes. I do not think the woman should assume the man's name. The man should have no more right over the person or property of his wife than she has over the person or property of her husband. . . . I would have the word 'obey' used not more by the wife than the husband."[23]

These views were quite advanced for the day, and it is possible that they represented the temporary influence of his fianceé at the time, Alice Lee, because shortly afterward, as a New York State assemblyman, he was not an active partisan of woman suffrage.[24] Still, the first instances in which he expressed fears for the birth rate were during his campaign to justify the seizure of the Philippines by the United States.[25] He wrote then to Henry Cabot Lodge: "'Did I write you of my delight at meeting one Hiram Tower, his wife and his seventeen children?'"[26] For Roosevelt, virile men, womanly women, and large families were necessary conditions for the world supremacy of white Americans.

When, as president, Roosevelt began his series of direct attacks on birth control, he sounded the then-fashionable eugenic rhetoric about the importance of building the "race." (Eugenic rhetoric of this period and Roosevelt's personal rhetoric were often ambiguous in their use of the word "race"—it could mean the human race or the white race. The trope was powerful precisely because it connoted both meanings simultaneously, encouraging a tendency to identify the human race with the white race.) In January 1905, he attacked both the low birth rate and the increased divorce rate as leading to race suicide.[27] In March 1905, addressing the National Congress of Mothers, he repeatedly condemned the selfishness, self-indulgence, and "viciousness, coldness, shallow-heartedness" of a woman who would seek to avoid her reproductive obligation, comparing it to a soldier's duty.[28] If women failed in this regard, "no material prosperity, no business growth" could save the race, he declared.[29] In Roosevelt's authoritarian image of society, it was clear where women belonged, and heightened militarism and imperialist passion required tightening their bonds.

Feminist Self-Defense

The race-suicide attacks forced pro–birth control feminists to reject the cult of motherhood, which they had previously shared with more conventional women. By focusing not simply on the principle of voluntary versus involuntary childbearing—a principle abstract enough to be theoretically acceptable to many—but on small versus large families, race-suicide theorists forced feminists to address the issue of whether women ought to devote themselves exclusively to child-raising. Prior to the race-suicide controversy, that issue had been avoided because voluntary motherhood advocates had argued for birth control on the grounds that it would produce a better motherhood and a purer race. Suffragists had emphasized the nobility of motherhood as a symbol for a female selflessness with which they argued the political expediency of women's rights.[30] The desire for respectability led them to lean on the "motherhood" refrain, for they perceived that motherhood was the only social position in which all women could command respect. There was no form of special pleading that American feminists found so hard to reject as that of motherhood—that is, female parenthood mystified and spiritualized, defined as the ineluctable destiny and fulfillment of womankind.

Roosevelt's public attacks made the continued use of this line of argument uncomfortable for a newer generation of feminists. Race-suicide propagandists included even the most conservative goals of feminism—such as suffrage—in a generalized condemnation of women leaving their domestic sphere. Many women felt themselves personally attacked as well, in an era when many educated women were seeking careers and remaining single. Roosevelt's attacks reverberated in widespread popular recognition of new values and practices and stimulated a wave of criticism against feminists, spinsters, childless women, and even mothers of small families. The hysteria lasted many years. For example, when the feminist Catherine Waugh McCulloch denounced the race-suicide scare in 1911, she received obscene and threatening postcards.[31] The birth rate had been falling steadily for many decades, birth control devices and abortions were widely, if disguisedly, advertised, and smaller families were visible in most middle-class neighborhoods.[32] Roosevelt did not invent the race-suicide hysteria. But as president he put it into the forefront of public concern.

Even such a broad attack did not produce a unified response. The motherhood mystique was familiar, and most feminists clung to it. A few took the side of the race-suicide alarmists and remonstrated with other women to do their duty. Julia Ward Howe was representative of that view. She offered, in defense of her sex, the observation that lack of money and the growing expenses of child-raising were partly responsible; but she believed that this in turn was because people were selfish, cared too much for personal and not enough for civic success. Sacrifice was necessary. "It is the sense of this duty which gives especial dignity to parentage," she wrote.[33] Motherhood would guarantee to a woman an "unlimited part in the future of her race":

> She has learned the sweetness of self-sacrifice. . . . Now let us for a moment contrast this picture with that of a woman who is never weaned from the intense personality of her start in life. . . . She may win personal distinction and high fame. She may surely deserve them, but she will be in danger of following the false way which begins and ends in self. If the fates deny her marriage, or leave it bare of offspring, let her win to arms some motherless child. . . . I would not exaggerate even so great a blessing as that of maternity. Many women in our days have a gift and callings which detain them far from the pains and pleasures of the nursery. . . . I should be the last to undervalue their labor and their reward. But to young mothers not yet weaned from the vanity of girlhood I would say: "If this great blessing of maternity shall visit you . . . do not whine at its fatigues and troubles."[34]

Howe and others like her accepted the double standard: they did not challenge the selfishness of men who avoided children.

Other feminists, probably the majority, accepted race-suicide assumptions but reinterpreted the evidence so as to shift the blame. Thus Ida Husted Harper, a leading suffragist, responded to these fears by charging that men, not women, were responsible for smaller families.[35] Elsie Clews Parsons, a feminist anthropologist, blamed the problem on legal and social policies that forced women to choose between motherhood and other interesting, useful work. She was angered specifically by a ruling of the New York State Board of Education against married women teachers.[36] Parsons and many others agreed that small families were a misfortune.[37]

Some feminists accepted the eugenic logic of the race-suicide theory but argued for different correctives. The quality of offspring and the racial health of the nation remained their primary concerns. But they asserted, for example, that the most careful studies showed that educated women were healthier, not weaker.[38] They also raised the now customary eugenic bogeys: that unwanted children would be likely to be inferior and/or neglected; that children also had a right not to be born if they would be weak or deprived or defective; that only a voluntary and intelligent motherhood in a marriage of equals was capable of producing good citizens.[39] Martha Bensley, later to become active in a national birth control organization, argued in 1905 that perhaps it was just as well that the very best and the very worst human specimens did not reproduce, pointing out that children did not necessarily inherit the pre-eminence of extraordinary parents.[40] A 1904 article signed by "An Alumna" ventured the suggestion that the low marriage rate among university alumnae might be eliminating potentially unhappy marriages.[41]

Putting the eugenic arguments to their own uses, other feminists argued that smaller families were healthier. The phrase "fewer but better" became common.[42] Ida Husted Harper attacked large families, charging prolific parents with weakening the race by producing deprived children, sending them to work instead of school, and eventually filling the poorhouses. As to the command, "Multiply and replenish the earth," she wrote, we have only men's word for it, handed down to us by the "masculine hierarchy" of the churches.[43] Other feminists criticized the hypocrisy of the race-suicide moralists who ignored the poverty and sufferings of children already born. The Reverend Anna Howard Shaw, a suffragist leader, pointed to the *true* race suicide caused by disease, food adulteration, impure water, filthy cities, poor schools, child labor, and drunkenness.[44] Socialists and anarchists also took this line of reasoning and in addition charged that the call for large families was conditioned by the capitalists' desire to fill their factories and armies.[45] Susan B. Anthony went so far as to introduce the threat of overcrowding, an unfamiliar idea in an era when birth-rate decline was the general fear.[46]

Other feminists rejected the entire eugenic framework and argued instead on the basis of women's right to self-determination. But their line of argument remained abstract; they did not discuss small families or childlessness. Charlotte Perkins Gilman stormed: "All this talk, for and against and about babies, is by men. One would think the men bore the babies, nursed the babies, reared the babies. . . . The women bear and rear the children. The men kill them. Then they say: 'We are running short of children—make some more.'"[47] Catherine McCulloch thought that it was "unbecoming for men to talk about this subject and make demands upon women. . . . The question of having children should rest entirely with women."[48] Ellen Key, a much published and influential European voice in this country, also argued that the declining birth rate was a consequence of the devaluation of mothering. The challenge and rewards of motherhood, she said, had not grown commensurately with women's expectations.[49] Even before Roosevelt's fulminations, Moses Harman had written that the birth-rate decline represented a strike by women: "If they cannot get employment as mothers on their own terms, if they cannot have children without putting their necks under the yoke of marital bondage, they will not have children at all."[50] Harman's interpretation of "marital bondage" came from his conviction that all state regulation of private relationships was wrong. But with a broader interpretation, marital bondage—including the material conditions that limited women and especially mothers—was acknowledged throughout the feminist community. Parsons attacked the system that forced women to choose between motherhood and other work—a system enforced by law, custom, and lack of opportunity. Refusing motherhood was indeed a strike against those conditions.

The concept of a birth strike was widely known. Educated women knew of Lysistrata as a sex strike, and Gilman's anger at raising children to feed men's armies was a common theme, particularly provoked by Roosevelt's imperialist policies. A modern version of *Lysistrata* entitled *The Strike of a Sex*, by George Noyes Miller, an English neo-Malthusian, circulated in the United States in the 1890s.[51] In Miller's fantasy the women of an entire community leave their husbands until the men adopt "Zugassent's Discovery," or "Karezza"—that is, the avoidance of ejaculation, or male continence. However militant the birth strike discussion, it still used refusal of motherhood as a lever to gain something else, a lever that could be relinquished when the end was won. In birth strike logic, birth control was a temporary expedient, not a permanent change in the female condition.

The most radical response to the race-suicide attack was one that reinterpreted woman's role and "duty" altogether. Offered tentatively, and in language far less militant than Gilman's, the defense of small families and childlessness directly challenged motherhood as a life's work. Harper argued in 1901 that motherhood represented a huge sacrifice of other kinds of talents and might not be the right choice for every woman. Some marriages *ought* to remain childless, she wrote.[52] In 1905 another woman, who signed herself "A Childless Wife," wrote that she believed herself to be more useful to society without children than as a mother because she made a social contribution through her profession.[53]

Though the challenge to motherhood was the minority position among feminists, it was newsworthy and frightening because it implied profound changes in social values. To the extent that it challenged motherhood but not marriage, it tended to separate sexuality from reproduction and implicitly defended sexual activity for its own sake. It chipped away at the emphasis on differences between the sexes, differences often comforting to both men and women. When Roosevelt called childless women "selfish," he was calling up a powerful bogey; this was the ultimate kind of selfishness because it involved in the contemporary understanding a betrayal of the entire human race for the sake of self. Feminists who refused to accede to this condemnation were implicitly condemning all those women who had accepted maternal selflessness as their source of self-esteem. And, indeed, some such women sensed this condemnation and resented it, feeling that their labors as full-time mothers were being discounted.[54]

This reaction became particularly heated because the issue was increasingly posed as motherhood versus career. Feminists responding to race-suicide attacks often focused on the question of professions for women. The "Childless Wife," as we have seen, justified her childlessness by her profession. Harper wrote that women *ought* to work.[55]

The "work" that these spokeswomen had in mind—professional jobs—was available only to educated upper- and middle-class women. Because they were taking a utilitarian line—that childbearing might not be the best way for women to serve society—they had to focus on jobs that commanded respect. This argument must have lacked persuasiveness with working-class women. By and large the jobs that were available to working-class women were not preferable to full-time mothering and housewifery, and married working-class women usually took jobs out of necessity. This does not, of course, imply that working-class women had no interest in winning acceptance for birth control and smaller families. From what we know of the prevalence of abortion among working-class married women, their concern was great, as was their willingness to take risks to have fewer children. Even without outside employment as a desirable alternative, the labor of mothering could be made far less oppressive with fewer and more widely spaced children.

But the race-suicide controversy occurred primarily on terms set by middle-class white feminists defending their interest in activity outside their homes. The situation of women who worked for wages because their families needed the money was obliterated in this discourse. As a result, the controversy had the effect, at least temporarily, of making it difficult for nonelite women to construct an understanding of birth control as their own, of moving birth control farther from working-class and other poor people than it had been several decades earlier. Women dedicated to improving the lot of the working class, especially those in the Socialist party, were silent during this controversy. *The Socialist Woman* and *The Progressive Woman*, Socialist party women's journals published monthly beginning in 1907, said nothing at all about birth control during this controversy despite their strong calls for women's rights on issues such as equal work and equal wages. In her 1912 book, *The Sorrows of Cupid,* which covered many other problems of sex and marital relations, Kate Richards O'Hare, a leader of the Socialist party women's movement, ignored the birth control question. She accepted the Rooseveltian premise that the shrinking family was a misfortune and blamed it on working-class poverty, ignoring the fact that the lowest birth rates were among the wealthy. Instead, she defended working-class women against charges that they had lost the maternal instinct.[56] None of the women active in the socialist movement in this period, though many of them were very feminist, believed that birth control was an urgent concern for working-class women.[57]

The Root of the Problem

What caused so-called race suicide? Effective remedies to social problems must address themselves to root causes, and the race-suicide theorists naturally argued their proposals in those terms. Two causal theories prevailed at the time, and still do. One was the view that feminism was the culprit; the other was an economic explanation.

Those who attacked the "independence" and "selfishness" of women saw such attributes as the individual reflection of a vicious doctrine that violated nature. In refusal of motherhood it seemed that personal and ideological feminism were joined: women's unnatural and inauthentic yearnings threatened the entire race. Something about the feminist movement had communicated that particular threat to its enemies from its very inception. In 1867 an anti-Reconstruction writer saw it as a regional phenomenon because women's rights agitation at that time was largely confined to the northeastern United States:

> The anti-offspring practice has been carried in New England and wherever New England ideas prevail. It is the esoteric, the interior doctrine of the woman's rights movement. These female reformers see that if they are to act the part of men in the world, they must not be burdened with the care of young children. So they have resolved to marry, but to limit, in certain ways well understood in France [which was well known to have a falling birth rate] the number of their offspring. . . . in proportion as women's rights ideas prevail, are parents becoming ashamed of large families. It is not that the New England women are unable to bear as many children as formerly, but that they will not.[58]

This view reveals one kind of effect the women's rights movement was having, but it is not necessarily an accurate description of the movement. Opponents of the movement commonly exaggerated its influence. Catherine Beecher wrote in 1871 that "this woman movement is one which is uniting . . .

all the antagonisms that are warring on the family state. Spiritualism, free love, free divorce, the vicious indulgences consequent on regulated civilization, the worldliness which tempts men and women to avoid large families, often by sinful methods, thus making the ignorant masses the chief supply of the future ruling majorities."[59] Here was the entire race-suicide nightmare, foreseen thirty years before Roosevelt discovered it, and the blame laid squarely upon the women's rights movement. Though the movement in the early twentieth century did not in fact advocate birth control or rejection of the family, its opponents perceived its influence in the reproductive behavior of even non-feminist women. The small-family norm was a concession, they believed, to a rebellion of women. One historian used the phrase "domestic feminism" to refer to an alteration in the balance of power within the family in favor of women and attributed the birth-rate decline to it.[60]

An alternative explanation for the race-suicide phenomenon was economic, and it was the prevalent theory among contemporaries. Writers noticed that children had been an asset in agricultural societies, whereas industrialization and urbanization made large families no longer economically advantageous.[61] The journalist Lydia Kingsmill Commander interviewed thirty-eight physicians practicing in the New York City area about "the causes of the prevalence and popularity of the small family" and found uniformly economic explanations. Here are some of their observations:

> Children are an expensive luxury. They cost a lot to raise; they are late in getting to work, because of the long training they must have; and few parents get anything back from them. . . . What I mean is that nowadays raising children is all outlay, financially speaking

> . . . the secret of success in the new world is education and years of training. The fittest to survive in our civilization are the trained and educated. Brain rules, not brawn. This is the American idea, and it involves small families, for so much cannot be given to a large number.

And the reverse:

> The large families of Italians are easily understood when we realize that almost nothing is spent raising the children, and they begin to work almost as soon as they can walk. You will find that newsboys and bootblacks always come from large families. . . . The Italians are just like animals. They produce as freely and naturally and they expect their children to look out for themselves almost as early as animals do.

> These people [German, Irish, and English poor on the East Side] look upon their children as a sort of insurance. The man has just a certain number of years

to work. Then rheumatism, consumption, an accident or some such trouble attacks him, and he cannot work full time. . . . By this time his children are getting old enough to "earn a couple of cents," and the family pulls through. A large family is an advantage to people of that type.[62]

There were no independent women avoiding maternal responsibilities in these vignettes. Indeed, several articles showed us women who wanted more children but felt that their husbands could not afford them.[63] The historians Joseph and Olive Banks have offered a similar economic explanation of the birthrate decline in England, their study finding that married women's fertility was associated with the class position of their husbands, not with feminist ideas.[64]

Which theory was right? What did cause "race suicide?" The second question was made more difficult by asking the first. Seeking an either/or explanation, choosing between feminism and new economic needs among urban people, observers overlooked the connections between the two phenomena. Just as city dwellers, particularly educated professionals, had new values and a lifestyle more favorable to women's equality than peasants had,[65] so feminism both in principle and in practice had an economic basis. To put it another way: to answer the question, What caused the decline of fertility? by saying "women" or "feminism" merely raises other questions: What caused feminism? What changed women?

Feminism itself grew from the economic transformations that made smaller families more economical. A closer look at the birth rates of women college graduates shows this. First, female college students in these early years of women's higher education (roughly, the last quarter of the nineteenth century) were upwardly mobile, genderwise. Education represented for them a challenge; they went to college carrying the burden of proof of their abilities, often over the objections of those who felt their education would be wasted. Frequently the students were feminists themselves. For these women, to ask whether the cause of their low marriage and birth rates was feminism or the economy would be to introduce a false distinction. Second, among female college students— even among students from the same college—birth rates varied according to class in the same way that they did in society as a whole. And third, a high proportion of females in college themselves came from small families and had already been influenced by attitudes favorable to small families.[66]

Smaller families were both cause and effect of feminism. Women's desire for more leisure to use in the areas now open to them (charity work, club and reform activism, jobs) made fewer children preferable. And their husbands' economic calculations produced the same view of desirable family size. These "new middle-class" husbands, satisfied with smaller families, were also less concerned with other ostentatious displays of wealth. More and more they identified professional and educational attainment as signs of status.[67] This made them ask different things of their wives as well as their children. The phenomenon of educated and ambitious women remaining unmarried, characteristic of the late nineteenth century, began to change quickly in the twentieth century. Women who were educated, experienced, even mentally energetic were increasingly acceptable as wives to educated men.[68]

A man (or could it have been a woman?) who signed himself "Paterfamilias," writing in 1903, gave vivid expression to the juxtaposition of feminist and economic sentiment for smaller families. Insisting that his *main* reason for opposition to Roosevelt's large-family sentimentality was his recollection of the oppression large families meant for women in earlier America, he spoke frankly of his personal economic calculations.

> I have four children. . . . It happens that we are able to care for four, not quite in the style in which two could have been maintained, but to all intents and purposes quite well enough for them, and sufficiently well for us to maintain our social position, which is very dear to us, though to some such a statement may seem folly. If a time should come when we had to give up our present style of living (which, practically, means our friends, since in that event we would not and could not continue present relations with them), I would consider it, perhaps, the most serious day of my life. So far as can be judged at present, the only thing that might threaten such an event would be the appearance say of a couple of more children. I presume there are those who will think that this is an ignoble statement; but it is not only true, but it is true of about every family of which I have any personal acquaintance, except in those rather numerous instances where there are no children at all.

About his ambitions for his children, "Paterfamilias" was equally blunt: "[If a young man] is to be anything more than a hewer of wood and a drawer of water, it must needs be that he become fitted for the race in the best manner possible. Perhaps his best chance will be with the great corporations where only experts are wanted in the paying positions."[69] This writer's understanding of the future of reproduction was exactly coincident with his understanding of the future economy.

"Paterfamilias" was not alone. Many important establishment spokesmen supported the small-family trend and refused to take alarm at race suicide. *World's Work,* an early twentieth-century business journal, editorialized that the birth-rate decline might be a good thing, implying more appreciation of the individual child.[70] This psychology—appreciation of the individual child— is the correlate of the economics "Paterfamilias" outlined, of increasing expenditure on each individual child. *Harper's Weekly* editorialized in 1903 against race suicide when Harvard president Charles W. Eliot reported his fears of

Harvard's inability to replenish itself from among its peers,[71] but four months later its editorial line shifted to support the idea of spawning only the children that one could afford to raise well.[72]

The economic and the feminist explanations for the decline of the birth rate are inextricably connected. The economic reorganization that made smaller families more economical also made upper- and middle-class women eager for broader horizons, which in turn made them desire smaller families. The changes were in fact gradual, the product of the entire course of American economic development. The race-suicide alarm was a response to the transformation of an entire society, and the alarm tells us as much about the old values as about the new. It was a conservative response, as hostile to the new, professional values of "Paterfamilias" as to feminism. These conservatives were both genuinely threatened by social changes and simultaneously overreacting to them, imagining a challenge to white male hegemony far greater than that actually posed by changes in birth rates. It will be easier to distinguish between what was really happening and what the race-suicide theorists thought was happening if we review, briefly, the actual demographic and family changes of the period.

The most fundamental perception of the race-suicide theorists still stands as correct: women in the nineteenth century bore progressively fewer children. At the beginning of the twentieth century only France, notorious home of contraception and other vices, had a lower fertility rate than America.[73]

A second perception was equally valid: that the decline in fertility was deliberate. Nearly all those involved in the race-suicide controversy, on all sides, asserted or assumed that birth control practices were widespread.[74] Physicians, who were probably in the best position to judge in the era before sex behavior surveys, reported the same.[75] The demographers agreed.[76]

A third belief of race-suicide theorists is more controversial today: that the fertility rate was much lower among "respectable" white people than among people of color, immigrants, the working class, and the "underclass." This judgment is controversial because it depends on how one defines population categories. For example, although the immigrant birth rate remained relatively high in relation to the birth rate among the native-born privileged class, a little-noticed fact is that blacks had the greatest birth-rate decline of all. Despite a discourse about the danger of a huge black population increase, in fact the black population of the South was increasing more slowly than the white population. In 1870 there were 5 million blacks in the South and in 1910, 8.7 million; in that same period the white southern population increased from 8.6 million to 20.5 million. Even Dr. John Billings, director of the Census Bureau's Division of Vital Statistics and publicizer of race-suicide dangers, pointed out this decrease in the black birth rate, although he then attempted to account for it by inaccuracy in census statistics.[77] Though new immigrants had, on the whole, higher birth rates than native-born Americans, the birth rate of all immigrants fell in relation to their length of residence in the country. Furthermore, the urban and rural birth rates declined in approximately equal ratios.[78] Whereas effective contraceptive practices were common in the middle and upper classes, abortion was common in all classes—with a high maternal mortality rate, to be sure, but effective in lowering the birth rate nonetheless.[79] By stressing or suppressing the birth-rate statistics of certain social groups over others, one could arrive at a picture of the race-suicide "problem" that could prove any of a number of theories of its causes, economic, ethnic, feminist, and religious.

It is true that the birth rate fell first among educated, professional people. Where the women of that class had lower fertility rates than the men, it was of course because they were less likely to marry; but it is not obvious that the reasons for remaining unmarried were identical with the reasons for having fewer children. (In fact, some unmarried women in this era adopted children.) The assumption of contemporaries that the phenomena of spinsterhood and small families had identical causes reflected their own bias about the proper role of women and the identity of marriage and reproduction.

A fourth belief shared by most race-suicide theorists—that there had been a sharp decline in birth rates in the *late* nineteenth century—was wrong. On the one hand, birth rates had been declining steadily and gradually since 1810, the differential between classes and ethnic groups remaining reasonably constant. On the other hand, from as early as 1905 the gap in birth rates between classes and ethnic groups began closing: birth rates among college graduates actually rose, and other birth rates fell until at least 1965.[80]

Re-evaluating these race-suicide tenets demonstrates several things about the historical trajectory of change. Although shifts of the greatest magnitude were taking place, they had been occurring for so long that it would be hard to attribute them to the influence of an organized feminist movement. The birth-rate differential was in fact only a lag. The race-suicide alarm was due partly to the impact of immigration—the sudden and massive introduction of people from rural and preindustrial situations. The societal changes that make large families no longer advantageous—the high cost of education, food, and rent, and the end of productive child labor—took time, often a whole generation, before they produced new family values. Parents' willingness to accept small families required their understanding that children would not provide them security in their old age, either because their children would be unwilling or unable to do so or, later, because their security would come from other sources. Meanwhile, new industrial workers utilized preindustrial family patterns to meet new economic needs, patterns such as extended families and the contributions of working children to the parental income. In most new economic situations, people try at first to use old values and social patterns in new ways and surrender them only after long resistance. The notion that children represented wealth and security was a particularly tenacious conviction. Naturally, those who had most to gain from giving up the large-family life-style—such as the upwardly mobile and the professionals—made that change first.

These changes appeared to contemporaries to be more sudden than they were because gradual and incremental social change sometimes appears to take qualitative leaps when previously exceptional patterns become new norms. The illusion of suddenness led some to search for acute causes; the birth-rate differential led some to anticipate a continuing divergence among different social groups in population patterns. Race-suicide theorists believed the small-family trend would produce social disaster if it was not stopped. But even at the time, a few social critics found perspectives from which to appreciate both the long-term origins of the changes and their inevitability, and some even equated them with progress.

In short, some people argued that there was no race suicide. The socialist eugenist Scott Nearing wrote that the "race murderers" were really race saviors, since birth control was establishing a new equilibrium between birth rates and declining death rates.[81] A "brilliant and thoughtful Hebrew lawyer of Boston," probably Louis Brandeis writing under the pseudonym Joseph Lorren, argued that although the birth rate was inevitably falling as a result of "the advance of civilization," the fact that children lived longer and that social childhood was extended more than compensated for the decline.[82] Another writer thought it odd that the "suicide" of the rich was feared when the far greater problem was continued high mortality among children of the poor.[83]

These dissident voices agreed that important demographic changes were taking place but perceived that "race suicide" represenated a particular spin on those changes, deflecting attention from alternative meanings. Indeed, "race suicide" was worse than a spin—it was a red herring. It was a way of refusing to accept the implications of democracy without clearly rejecting democracy. It provided a focus for distress among business and professional classes about the growth of working-class and nonwhite groups and about shifts in family and gender patterns produced by industrialization and the feminist movement. Since traditional religious and moral scruples, and belief that the economic system needed population growth, would not allow seeking remedy by urging birth control upon the poor, the alarmists turned in the other direction and asked prosperous women to restore upper-class families to a competitive size. Women became the scapegoats.

Blaming prosperous women for the declining birth rate was the reverse side of blaming immigrant groups for keeping their birth rate high. The race-suicide theorists saw fertility and family changes holistically. A physician writing about inadequate reproduction among women of the "better class" put many things together: "The family idea is, indeed, drifting into individualism. . . . Now [woman] has weaned herself from the hearthstone, and her chief end is self. Pray! What has brought about these changes? By the invention of the sewing-machine, by the introduction of ready-made clothing, and by that damnable sin—the avoidance of offspring, our women are no longer compelled to stay at home—the home-tether is broken. . . . [The sin of avoiding offspring] comes from fashion, from cowardice, from indolent wealth and shiftless poverty."[84] Poor women *and* rich women were to blame, in the view of race-suicide theorists. Hostile to the social disruptions of industrial society but misunderstanding the dynamics of capitalist industrialism, race-suicide theorists turned from blaming the working class to blaming *all* women for the social evils of the whole economic system.

The race-suicide propagandists did not succeed. Few women responded to Roosevelt's castigations by giving up their birth control devices. On the contrary, the lasting result of the race-suicide controversy was that many feminists and professional women previously silent on the subject now committed themselves publicly and lastingly to birth control. Furthermore, the birth control case they put forward was more woman-centered than any since the first timid voluntary motherhood assertions of the 1870s. They wanted women to have options other than full-time motherhood—at least those women who could afford it.

The qualification is as important as the basic demand, however. Although the race-suicide controversy released a strong feminist endorsement of birth control, it also brought to the forefront those issues that most separated feminists from the working class and the poor. This happened in two ways. First, the feminists were increasingly emphasizing birth control as a route to careers and higher education—goals out of reach of the poor with or without birth control. In the context of the whole feminist movement, the race-suicide episode was an additional factor identifying feminism almost exclusively with the aspirations of the more privileged women of the society. Second, the pro–birth control feminists began to popularize the idea that poor people had a moral obligation to restrict the size of their families, because large families created a drain on the taxes and charity expenditures of the wealthy and because poor children were less likely to be "superior." Though the idea that birth control was an attack on the working class and immigrants was not new, this episode supplied more solid evidence for it than ever before and popularized the fear. Consider this letter to the editor of a pro–birth control journal in 1907:

Dear Doctor . . . I want to say that I am surprised to here a Man of your supposed intelligence to ask in sincerity if it would not be better to criminally limit
the off spring of the Poor, what would you gain by adding crime to poverty? it
has never been held a crime (even in N.Y.) to bee Poor. . . . Human life is more
than money, is a man justified in killing his own children be cause his business
failes? then the history of our country and the history of the Human race would
read verry diferent if we was to exclude from its pages all the workes of our
grate men who was born in obscure poverty we would cut out the workes of
the immortal Lincolen.[85]

Such defensiveness and suspicion toward birth control is still common, and
one of its historical sources is here in the race-suicide controversy.

7   *Continence or Indulgence*

Early in the twentieth century, simultaneously with the race-suicide controversy but less public, another dispute raged over the implications of birth control. Confined primarily to the pages of medical journals, it concerned the moral and physical healthfulness of continence. In more contemporary language, was doing without sex harmful?

The question arose because of the principle of voluntary motherhood. At the turn of the century, the major respectable form of birth control—as opposed to the birth control people actually used—was sexual abstinence. This could mean, and many physicians and moralists explicitly prescribed, abstinence from one conception until the time another conception was desirable and possible. It could alternatively mean abstinence during the periods when a woman was likely to be fertile—the rhythm method. But the exact female ovulation cycle had not yet been successfully calculated, and medical opinion was mounting, no doubt based on women's sad experiences, that the rhythm method did not work.[1] "Continence" came to refer specifically to abstinence for the purpose of birth control.

Whether continence was harmful depended, of course, on one's view of the nature of the sex drive. The two most frequently argued positions were extremes: sex was an absolute physiological necessity, like food, or a dispensable item, like liquor. Another axis of disagreement was whether the sex drive was the same in both sexes or entirely different in men and women. In short, the arguments about birth control in this period led to basic questions about sexuality.

Many of the participants in these discussions were physicians. Looking back, this perhaps seems natural, as birth control today seems so much a medical issue. If one were to have looked into the future from the year 1870, however, voluntary motherhood did not seem at all a medical matter. Furthermore, most doctors in the nineteenth century had been opposed to birth control of any sort. So before focusing on the continence-versus-indulgence debate of 1910 and thereafter, we must trace the role of medicine in the spread of birth control.

In the nineteenth century the leaders of the American medical profession had been reluctant, to say the least, to accept birth control. Instead, they frequently identified contraception with quackery and immorality. As Norman E. Himes, the noted historian of birth control technology, remarked, "One way to gain a reputation for supermorality . . . was to condemn birth control in portentous tones with much moral exhortation to purity, and in violent language."[2] Physicians had obtained a monopoly on the treatment of upper- and middle-class women's diseases and pregnancies in part by forcing out midwives and popular healers, who had been the social repository of birth control knowledge; they also constructed syndromes of diseases that explained away their patients' depressions and resentments and helped make physical fragility, weakness, sickliness, and consequent hypochondria part of the convention of bourgeois femininity.[3] Birth control, part of the growing self-assertion of women generally, particularly annoyed many doctors.

Indeed, much of the medical establishment responded hysterically to voluntary motherhood, denouncing birth control on the basis of expertise. In the face of easily available evidence to the contrary, some asserted to the public, and presumably to their patients, that there was no method of contraception that worked. H. S. Pomeroy, writing in 1888, was typical: "It is surprising to what an extent the laity believe that medical science knows how to control the birth-rate. Just here let me say that I know of but one prescription which is both safe and sure—namely, *that the sexes shall remain apart.* So thoroughly do I believe this to be a secret which Nature has kept to herself, that I should be inclined to question the ability or the honesty of any one professing to understand it so as to be able safely and surely to regulate the matter of reproduction."[4] In the same book Pomeroy revealed his awareness of the widespread use of "prevention" throughout the population, but his moralism overwhelmed his scientific curiosity.

Since the 1860s doctors had been writing popular books and articles attacking birth control.[5] They commonly asserted that contraception was physically harmful, and the harm was often described as a mortal threat. For example, in 1880 a Michigan doctor, Eliza Barton Lyman, wrote in *The Coming Woman; or, The Royal Road to Perfection* that contraception led to hardening of the uterus.[6] Medical journals also carried dire warnings, such as Edward J. Ill's admonition in 1899 that contraceptive practices led to permanent sterility.[7]

Like many lay people, physicians did not clearly distinguish between birth control and abortion.[8] At other times they called birth control "onanism" (since it was fruitless intercourse, or "wasting seed"), thus associating its condemnation with the Bible. Women who used birth control were brutally maligned— "Legitimate prostitutes," according to Ill, who noted that "the depth of moral degeneracy in such cases can only be imagined."[9] In 1888 Dr. Thomas E. McArdle branded sexual intercourse with the use of contraceptives "marital masturbation."[10] Abbot Kinney, in a popular 1893 antiabortion tract, wrote: "Sexual intercourse, unhallowed by the creation of the child, is lust. . . . wife without children is a mere sewer to pass off the unfruitful and degraded passions and lust of one man."[11]

Such misogyny was usually accompanied by a defense of the double standard. Kinney, transforming common moralistic views into physiological language, wrote that nature had created the hymen as a sign of woman's purity, because purity was so much more important for women than for men.[12] But so extreme was the physicians' fear of voluntary motherhood that many condemned even sexual abstinence for women. Kinney was among several who charged that not having children was in itself unhealthy: a woman still childless at twenty-five would have a "continuous tendency to degeneracy and atrophy of the reproductive organs."[13]

Not all doctors shared these repressive attitudes. Medicine was far from homogeneous during the nineteenth century. Indeed, the creation of uniform standards and education for doctors was the focus of a significant upheaval among doctors, for healing had traditionally been a craft, a skilled labor, performed with as much personal variation and latitude as other artisanal crafts. Furthermore, the craft of healing had once, centuries before, been dominated by women. The growth of male hegemony in medicine developed concurrently with the prestige of medicine. Doctors worked to establish their profession, like a church, differentiating a group of "regular" doctors from "irregulars," standardizing education in European techniques, including "heroic" medicine—for example, bleeding, surgery, and powerful emetics. Eventually they won establishment through a state licensing system. In the course of this campaign the regulars attempted to discredit the older, folk tradition of healing by identifying it with quackery, implying that it was not only universally ineffectual but universally dishonest as well.[14]

Victory did not come quickly or easily to the new professionals, however. They faced the stubborn attachment of traditionally minded people to the older healing practices; and in the eighteenth century this came to include the conviction that, especially in gynecological and obstetrical matters, women ought not to be attended by men. Then in the 1830s the young medical profession met direct rebellion. A popular health movement began to refashion and reassert older traditions, expressing in part a new class hostility toward the emergence of powerful professional elites.[15] Describing that peculiar combination of rebellion and traditionalism in the movement, the medical historian Joseph F. Kett wrote that popular health campaigners "saw their movement as wresting medicine from the doctors and completing the great revolution which, beginning with the Reformation, freed government from the lawyers and despots and religion from the priests."[16]

Begun by a few charismatic individual reformers, such as Sylvester Graham and Samuel Thomson, the movement spun off many local groups, either followers of one or another of these medical prophets or originators of their own medical systems for health and happiness. Many of these were women's groups—"Ladies' Physiological Reform Societies."[17] The popular health movement emphasized preventive hygiene, having good reason to distrust the uncertain cures of that period. Many "natural" cures became associated with the movement—for example, water cures, homeopathy, animal magnetism, physical culture, and herbal medicines. By mid-century many irregulars were creating their own sectarian medical schools and awarding their own degrees, and as the century progressed the medical sects became increasingly dogmatic and narrow. The word "irregular" was used to describe everyone from herbalists to osteopaths, from partisans of popular health principles to shysters.

As the regulars established their medical approach as the correct one, their success was not always the public's gain. Ignorant of germ theory and with only rudimentary understandings of physiology, the regular physicians of that period often relied upon harsh drugs, bleedings, and surgery for cures that were frequently dangerous and/or ineffective. The herbal medicines that the regulars condemned as fraudulent often contained substances now recognized as genuinely valuable. The hygienic recommendations of the sectarians—frequent bathing; whole-grain cereals; more vegetable and less animal foods; loose, warm clothing; fresh air and exercise; avoidance of tobacco and alcohol—were sometimes more sound than the book-learned methods of the regulars.

Two important aspects of this popular health movement are at the center of our concern. One is that it produced some of the first frank medical tracts about birth control in the United States. The second, closely connected to the first, is that the movement was often feminist: in the preponderance of women in the movement, in its challenge to the conventional medical version of a restrictive definition of women's place, and in its assertion of the right of women to become doctors and the propriety of their doing so. In 1847 the *Boston Medical Surgical Journal* estimated that ninety-nine out of a hundred patients of the "quacks" were women.[18] Many groups in the popular health movement specifically directed their appeals to women, considering them the primary victims of the violent methods of the regulars. It was these sectarians who pioneered a new approach to pregnancy, attacking the tradition that required hiding it from public view, proscribed physical exercise, and insisted on protection from the slightest psychological stimulation. Ironically, although some irregulars fought prudery by encouraging education about sex, pregnancy, and childbirth, they often asserted that it was improper for men to be gynecologists or obstetricians. In part that view disguised their real purpose, which was to assert women's right to work in medicine. "'We cannot deny that women possess superior capacities for the science of medicine,'" one medical reformer wrote.[19]

But prudishness was not a disguise for feminism; it was an integral part of much feminist thought of the time. Furthermore, the antagonism toward male doctors had a basis in women's desire to protect themselves. In the late twentieth century the women's liberation movement began to bring to light the fact that women had often been humiliated in medical examinations by men—at worst by sexual molestation and more commonly by arrogance and disregard of women's own feelings, minds, and physiological self-understanding. In the nineteenth century women's powerlessness in such situations might well have been even greater.

The issue of birth control cannot be separated from the question of power. For its opponents, particularly its male opponents, birth control was a symbol of and a basis for female power. It was also a symbol of the power of irregulars. The two fears reinforced each other. Preventive hygiene programs combined with birth control and abortion formulas and female midwifery in threatening to restore women to their traditional roles as healers. As Kett put it, the irregulars "replaced the infirmary with the family."[20] One way they did this was through writing medical manuals aimed at the public, particularly wives and mothers, offering them help and confidence to do their own diagnoses and treatment.

It would be wrong, however, simply to reverse the establishment view and make the irregulars into progressive reformers. They had among them quite a few dishonest, avaricious, and ignoble men, as the regulars did. Many were quacks, especially in the field of birth control, selling pills, douche powders, and other nostrums that they must have known were ineffective. When their abortion patients sickened or died, regular and sectarian doctors alike frequently tried to conceal their role, even if it meant leaving a woman to die alone. The fact that the popular health movement advanced some useful health reforms did not automatically give its practitioners integrity. Nevertheless, their different situations —needing larger practices, since they could not charge as much as the regulars, being accustomed to seeing themselves as less prestigious, and being closer to communities of poor people—may have made the irregulars do more for the birth control cause than the regulars. Certainly the irregulars were more active as publicists of birth control. The popular health movement stimulated the publication of books of health and hygiene for the public, many with birth control information, and the authors included both honest sectarians and unscrupulous quacks.

An example of the latter is A. M. Mauriceau, a charlatan who described himself as a "professor of Diseases of Women," with offices at 129 Liberty Street, New York City. In his 1847 book, *The Married Woman's Private Medical Companion,* he used the rhetoric of the popular health movement, claiming that he wanted to "extend to every female, whether wife, mother or daughter, such information as will best qualify her to judge of her own maladies, and, having ascertained their existence, apply the proper remedies."[21] In 1871, he and his wife were practicing abortionists. A *New York Times* reporter who had investigated the couple and been explicitly promised a sure, safe abortion, wrote that the Mauriceaus spent sixty thousand dollars a year on advertising their business.[22] *The Married Woman's Private Medical Companion* sold well and may have been as big a financial success as the abortion business. Yet its contraceptive information was vague—"'The principle . . . is to neutralize the fecunding properties in semen,'" probably referring to a douche or suppository[23]—making it necessary for a patient to see the doctor to get more explicit directions.

In the same time period, and by way of contrast, irregulars published health manuals full of sound and useful advice, both general and contraceptive. Books of the 1850s recommended condoms, douche powders, withdrawal, the rhythm method, and vaginal sponges.[24] One of the more influential of these early works was Frederick Hollick's *The Marriage Guide,* published in 1860. Hollick regularly lectured on "physiological science" to women's groups. It was probably this activity, as much as the content of his book, that led some whom he branded "Medical *Old Fogies*" to attempt, unsuccessfully, to suppress his book.[25] By no means open-minded about contraception, Hollick condemned withdrawal as physiologically harmful; considered douching ineffective unless done with spermicides, in which case it could injure the vagina; and objected to condoms for their desensitizing effect on the male. Process of elimination suggests that he gave out some kind of pessary or suppository.[26] His philosophical defense of birth control was strong:

> It may appear to some persons . . . that there is danger in making such facts as these known, because, they say, young persons knowing that there are times when they can indulge with safety [he has just discussed the female fertility cycle] will be led to do so. . . . It seems to me also that it is forming a very low

and degrading opinion of young persons, especially of females, to suppose that they are only kept from indulgence by fear of the consequences. If their virtue is solely dependent upon this, it is scarcely deserving of the name.[27]

This supportive and respectful attitude toward women pervaded Hollick's work and that of many irregulars in these publications. They often rejected the double standard and many of them harped on the importance of sexual pleasure for women. They were more opportunist than feminist; as with regular physicians, the irregulars' sexual ideology served professional interests and business pressures. The irregulars were primarily doctors to women, especially women of poor or modest income and class. The health and hygiene books aimed at female buyers, both because they dealt with female medical problems and because mothers continued to be the primary source of medical care for their families. The success of these manuals, with their birth control formulas and their relatively enlightened views of sexuality, suggests the existence of women's demand for such information.

In the second half of the nineteenth century the popular health movement diminished in size and popularity. Medical sectarianism and hygienic and medical fads lost their political content. The irregulars no longer organized popular health groups, no longer spoke politically against the monopolization of medicine by a self-regulating profession, and lost their association with women's rights. Quackery continued, however, as a business. The manufacture and sale of patent medicines, home health manuals, health spas, and various health gadgets (electrical belts, special baths, posture supports, and so forth) flourished. In 1873 the Comstock law prohibited the interstate mailing of obscene material, and it specifically defined birth control as obscene. Selling contraceptives became dangerous just as the movement of irregulars lost its motivation for taking risks. These factors set back the spread of contraceptive information but by no means stopped it.

Some exceptional doctors resisted the commercialization of irregular medicine and challenged the censorship laws. Most important of this group in the late nineteenth century were the three doctors Foote, father Edward Bliss, son Edward Bond, and daughter-in-law Mary Bond. The Footes differed from other pro–birth control doctors in that they were conscious, articulate social reformers. Because their contribution was so great and their reforming style so typical of late nineteenth-century medical reformers, it seems useful to describe their work in some detail.

Born into a poor family in 1829, Edward Bliss Foote worked as a printer's devil and then a journalist before attending medical school in Philadelphia. In 1858, two years after his graduation, he published a popular medical guide.

Still very much a follower of traditional medicine, he prescribed herbal po-tions, electricity cures, inhalations, and baths.[28] His early sympathies with spiritualism and phrenology gave way later in his life to liberal Unitarianism and evolutionism. Always a civil libertarian, he spent many years fighting the Comstock law. Comstock meant for Foote not only obscurantism but also di-rect personal oppression, since Foote had built his career as a writer and re-former in part on public advocacy of the prevention of conception and free speech about sexual matters. Having been able to express himself relatively freely for at least fifteen years before the Comstock law was enacted, he found its passage a maddening obstacle to his work.

Foote's writings on birth control and sex emphasized women's rights. An ardent feminist in the tradition of the popular health movement, he was ar-rested for violating the Comstock law, which only confirmed him in his defiance: "It is my conscientious conviction that every married woman should have it within her power to decide for herself just when and just how often she will receive the germ of a new offspring."[29] Quoting from *Revolution,* Susan B. Anthony and Elizabeth Cady Stanton's newspaper, he also gave a descrip-tion of female infanticide in China as a lesson in the consequences of prohib-iting birth control.[30]

In Foote's time medicine was an open and competitive field, and he ran his medical office like a high-profit factory. He advertised constantly: for ex-ample, "'Dr. E. B. Foote and His Assistants May be Consulted daily from 9 A.M. to 6 P.M. (excepting Sundays) in the English or German Languages.'"[31] He established his own publishing company to put out his books and claimed to be an inventor as well as a purveyor of contraception: "The first reliable means for the use of the wife was an invention of my office, having been im-perfectly suggested by an associate physician and developed by myself some 15 years ago. Application was made at that time for a patent (!), which was refused on the ground that it was a question in the mind of the Commission-er whether the invention was not one which might be employed for immoral purposes. Without the protection of a patent it was, as might have been ex-pected, extensively counterfeited."[32] His son later described it as "the best mechanical means yet devised, though commonly described as a 'French' ar-ticle."[33] Since Foote could hardly claim to have invented the "French letter," or condom, he was probably referring to a pessary of some sort.[34]

Foote's establishment, at Lexington Avenue and Twenty-eighth Street in New York City, contained a small pharmaceutical factory where thousands of dollars' worth of medicinal roots and plants were processed into patent medi-cines. "'The floor below the laboratory,'" wrote the *New York Independent,* "'is occupied by the stenographers . . . who are employed in attending, under the direct dictation of the Doctor, to the immense correspondence, which often exceeds one hundred letters per day. . . . The Doctor has originated and perfected a series of questions relating to the physical conditions of invalids. These questions are so thorough and complete that when they are answered by patients at a distance, the Doctor is able to make a complete diagnosis and prescribe for his patients with about the same facility that he could do were they present.'"[35]

One kind of advice Foote sent out to these correspondence cases was contraceptive. In 1876 he was arrested for having sent such a letter in response to a decoy inquiry sent by one of Comstock's agents. (Entrapment was a standard and frequent Comstock technique.) The pamphlet he sent "was set up in pearl type, so as to make it only thirty-two pages of about the size of a letter envelope, in which it was invariably sent *sealed, under letter postage.* . . . The pamphlet took strong grounds against producing miscarriage or abortion." Foote may have believed that the Comstock law would never be enforced against physicians, but he was convicted and fined $3,000.[36] Foote's prosecution had, and was intended to have, a chilling effect upon other pro–birth control doctors. Although actual dissemination and use of contraception probably did not fall off, birth control education did.

Foote occupied a unique position: an irregular who in his later life won the respect of the established profession. His son, Edward Bond Foote, became a respected, if liberal, regular doctor, also active as a civil libertarian (particularly in the field of sexual matters as founder of the Free Speech League and a campaigner for the repeal of the Comstock law). He, too, argued for birth control as a woman's right to the "control of her person."[37] Dr. Mary Bond Foote, his wife, was a lecturer and crusader for birth control, women's equality, and welfare legislation.[38] By the early twentieth century the Footes seemed unusual because traditions of the popular health movement had been forgotten. Feminists in the medical profession were oddities then.

The Footes stand in contrast to most regular physicians, who did little to advance the birth control cause or contraceptive technology. The regulars seldom tried to educate women about their sexual and reproductive systems; rather, they often contributed to developing and maintaining fears and mystification. Equally important, while many doctors did give birth control help and even abortions to individual patients, they publicly attacked birth control. There was no necessary contradiction between doing this and "helping" individual patients who found themselves in difficult situations—precisely *because* most of the doctors concerned were humanitarian and principled. They disapproved of birth control on high principles of morality and health; but they could understand that in exceptional cases the principles had to be flexible. Indeed, part of the doctors' anti–birth control propaganda was a response to their awareness of increased birth control use. At another level, their stance on birth control came from a new perception of their own place in society as doctors, a sense of responsibility and privilege as guardians of sexual morality and arbiters of situations in which exceptions might be appropriate.

Doctors were the new ecclesiastics. Especially in the increased concern of the entire medical profession for the diseases of women, many of them believed to be genital in origin, the line between physiology and morality became fuzzy. In 1908, Robert Latou Dickinson, later to become president of the American Gynecological Society, wrote: "Our high function as confessors and advisers of the saintly half of the race, and the imperative need, at times, of one step within the Holy of Holies, is impossible without intimate speech, gentle, reverent, direct."[39] Religion was an "unrecognized branch of higher physiology," wrote another doctor of the same era.[40] Throughout the whole society in the nineteenth century, an overwhelming concern with sex, specifically with the difficult but urgent necessity of checking the anarchic sex drive, showed in the narrowing of previously general moral terms—such as "virtue," "propriety," "decency," "modesty," "delicacy," and "purity"—to exclusively sexual meanings.[41] Using the increase of physiological knowledge, medicine replaced the church as the authority on sex, and that authority simultaneously aided the new medical establishment in distinguishing itself from the irregulars of the popular healing tradition.

For many doctors, playing churchmen merely required translation of ecclesiastical into medical language. What had been sin became physically injurious. In an earlier chapter I commented on the concept of vice as including sin but also carrying the connotation of physical destructiveness. We can now see that concept as transitional, between a purely metaphysical morality and a purely "empirical" commitment to science. Thus, in the late nineteenth and early twentieth centuries physicians began to write and speak about "hygiene," by which they meant sexual morality. Schools gave classes in hygiene. "Social hygiene" meant the control of venereal disease. And somewhat later, "feminine hygiene" became a euphemism for contraceptive douches. Injuries supposedly caused by contraception, such as venereal disease, were just punishments for sin. Augustus Kinsley Gardner, a Boston gynecologist and moralist, wrote—in a single sentence—that condoms degraded love and produced lesions.[42] The lesions or other physical debilitations were "God's little allies" in promoting chastity.[43] It was almost as if doctors felt a subconscious satisfaction, a justification, when their patients developed infections. (This discourse obviously resembles that of social conservatives about AIDS.)

The victory of the regulars in establishing control over medical practice in the United States naturally supported this high sense of moral leadership. In the first two decades of the twentieth century, aided by the influence of German medical science, money from the Carnegie Corporation, a system of accreditation of medical schools, and the wide powers ceded to the American Medical Association (AMA), the regulars drove midwives and lay healers out of business. Reforms spurred by the AMA improved the standard of health care available to some—prosperous—Americans. Medical re-examination of birth control followed these reforms, for doctors were gaining a sense of their own responsibility as guardians of sexual morality. Their debates about the healthfulness or harmfulness of sexual continence were translations of deep moral concern, and their words betrayed their sense of self-importance. As is the case with most ideologists, their self-evaluation was exaggerated. The major breakthroughs in public acceptance of birth control came from broad social change and public policy—the continued underground spread of birth control knowledge and the campaign against venereal disease during World War I—not from elite discourse. Still, those debates shed light on social changes. The doctors' search for a convincing moral affirmation of plentiful sexual intercourse was like a flag marking still-invisible subterranean upheavals.

Just as medicine in America was influenced by German science, which reached this country largely through American medical students studying in Germany, so contraceptive information came here from a less prudish Europe. A birth control clinic was established in 1882 in the Netherlands. In France, socialists had organized a clandestine birth control conference in 1900. In Germany, too, contraception was widely practiced, and it was a common observation that a veritable birth strike was taking place, so rapidly had smaller families become the norm there. Although the legitimacy of birth control was contested in Europe as in America,[44] by 1900 the United States seemed backward in this field, and some physicians wanted to catch up.

In 1912 Abraham Jacobi, president of the AMA and known to many as the father of pediatrics, broke with the conservative mainstream. One of the country's most distinguished physicians and medical reformers, he spoke in his presidential address against war, for a campaign for industrial health, and for required venereal disease tests before marriage. He specifically endorsed birth control, calling particular attention to the injustice of its prohibition while the well-to-do already had access to contraception.[45]

Jacobi's address had an impact. Yet it was more a product than a cause, more a culmination than a beginning, of the revival of medical birth control activism. Jacobi was influenced by his revolutionary background as a youth in the German upheaval of 1848 and by his feminist wife, Dr. Mary Putnam Jacobi. Yet he was "organized" into his support for birth control, as were many others, by the remarkable William Josephus Robinson, who had been editing two pro–birth control journals since 1903, the *Medico-Pharmaceutical Critic and Guide* and the *American Journal of Urology*. Starting with his first pamphlet in 1904, Robinson wrote at least two dozen books on sex and birth control before his death in 1936. Probably no doctor in America has been as influential in winning support for birth control and in defining its future development toward contraception.

Like Foote before him, Robinson combined something of the tradition of the popular health movement with the most advanced scientific medicine, especially from Germany. He served as president of the Berlin Anglo-American Society and was a member of the Internationale Gesellschaft für Sexualforschung (International Association for Sex Research). A civil libertarian, remarkably free of anxiety about his own respectability, Robinson was never a free-lover, though he published free-love writings and, more important, respected their thought. He took over some of the ideas of the irregular doctors—for example, he recommended nudity inside one's own house for health reasons, believing that the skin needs light.[46] Yet he frequently attacked quacks and midwives.[47] His style was restrained, lacking the pugnaciousness and righteousness of the sex radicals (and political radicals), though he often went after the conservatives of the medical profession for their hypocrisy on sexual questions.[48]

Like so many doctors before and after him, Robinson received numerous requests for contraceptive information. In his journal he announced that he would send such information to other doctors only.[49] But since he later, in a privately printed and circulated memoir, admitted to having done abortions ("cleaned out uteruses"),[50] it seems likely that he also gave birth control information to patients. Certainly he knew that many other doctors did so. He tirelessly argued the case for birth control, which he considered to be "the most important problem affecting the welfare of humanity."[51] Robinson often gave his reasons in lists, claiming every conceivable benefit from birth control: women's health, children's health, reduction of abortion, happy marriages, improving the overall human stock, reducing sexual "neurasthenia" caused by *coitus interruptus* and worry, population control, family planning. Later he became one of those single-minded devotees of the cause who sometimes presented birth control as a panacea. The tendency to see it that way was characteristic of those who came to it without another overriding ideology, such as feminism or Malthusianism.

In most of the early history of American birth control agitation, advocates had approached birth control with a larger radical social ideology. The voluntary motherhood proponents were feminists, envisioning a new order of sexual power relations; the free-lovers were anarchists; and the utopians were religious socialists. The Malthusians were equally ideological. For Robinson, sex reform itself was the overriding concern, the key to a better society, and birth control was the key to sexual liberation. Unlike his predecessors, but like many of his successors, in the birth control movement, Robinson was a single-issue reformer. He fought for birth control under different guises, flexibly redesigning his arguments to fit current social trends and crises. During the Theodore Roosevelt administration, he wrote and published on the race-suicide question. In the 1920s he turned to eugenics. In between he denounced continence as the only means of reproduction control.

Until the 1880s sexual reformers almost unanimously condemned contraception and supported continence. In 1881, Edward Bliss Foote reopened the issue, pointing out the inefficiency of continence as a means of ensuring voluntary parenthood. He argued, first, that only the "most intelligent and conscientious" would be able to maintain continence, and thus the paupers and criminals would continue producing unwanted children; second, that continence could be physiologically damaging, since the sexual organs lost their power through inaction; and third, that sexual intercourse was in itself good and healthful and did not need reproduction to justify it. Some feminist reformers sharply criticized these ideas but maintained a civil and respectful discourse by printing their attacks in his own magazine, the *Health Monthly*. Foote was not so far distant from their point of view anyway, for his defense of sex was couched in spiritualist terms. Every individual had an animal magnetism, and each person's was different; the exchange of these magnetic forces through social contact was invigorating, physically and mentally, and was at its most perfect in the act of sexual intercourse.[52] For him, as for the feminists, sex had to be justified by some higher purpose.

In the last decades of the nineteenth century a few more doctors repeated that continence was not the best solution and might even be injurious, and in the first decade of the twentieth century that opinion was aggressively asserted. The doctors' debate on the subject was nowhere better capsulized than in Robinson's *Medico-Pharmaceutical Critic and Guide*. This magazine, more like a popular health journal than a contemporary professional journal, published letters and articles from subscribers, and many laypersons were among its readers. Robinson, consciously or unconsciously, worked out many of his ideas through this discourse with others before presenting them in his books.

The development of the continence debate is revealing. In 1904 and 1905, public birth control discussions were almost all couched in terms of the problem of small or large families, terms prompted by the race-suicide controversy. In January 1906, Robinson asserted that safe "contracepts" existed and their use was justifiable.[53] In the next months many responses and amplifications from other doctors focused on spelling out the medical indications for contraception. In 1911 Robinson began to report his findings that whereas periodic continence seemed to produce no ill effects, prolonged abstinence had a tendency to cause relative impotence and premature ejaculation,[54] thus opening up a discussion of continence as a form of birth control.

The responses to Robinson's editorials made the *Critic and Guide* a compendium of the sexual attitudes in the liberal parts of the medical profession.

In addition to various evaluations of the strength of the sex drive, there emerged a sharp disagreement on the double standard, for in his attack on continence Robinson had spoken of its dangers for the male but not the female. He thought the difficulties of continence were mainly felt by men and defended this potential deviation from the single standard by asserting that he wished to eschew moralism and to be practical.[55] Another doctor reiterated the belief that continence was particularly hard on men and pointed out that in any case women suffered no physiological loss of potency from continence.[56] Some argued for it physiologically, such as Dr. Warbasse, who pointed out that it all depended on what was meant by the term "continence." True continence, he wrote, would have to mean not just abstention from coitus but also from all stimuli that "result in libidinous turgescence of the organs of copulation"; if this were done, there should be no special difficulties for men.[57] Feminists responded as well, one writer complaining that "women with imperative sexual desire are classed as Nymphomaniacs. Should not men with imperative sexual desires be classed as Satyromaniacs?"[58]

The question of the double standard inevitably led to a related question, that of sexual monogamy itself, since sex without fear of conception could remove an important risk from promiscuity. Almost all the sexual reform movements of the nineteenth century, especially those with a feminist orientation, had been unanimous in their commitment to the principles of monogamy and marital fidelity, and this commitment was one reason they preferred abstinence to contraception as a form of birth control. Now, in the early twentieth century, some social radicals were reconsidering the monogamy principle. Beginning in the 1890s, the remaining free-love journals began exploring "varietism" in love,[59] and these latter-day free-lovers contributed frequently to Robinson's journal. Edwin C. Walker wrote that "the proponents of the single standard have been handicapped from the beginning of the race by the needless burden they took upon themselves. They essayed the impossible task of bringing all men into and holding them in the narrow groove of monogamy."[60] Dr. James F. Morton, a free-love physician, also objected to Robinson's acceptance of a double standard but added that the "recognition of equality between the sexes is no guarantee that new fetters are to be put on the male, when the more natural sequence would seem to be the removal of the shackles with which the female has so long been bound."[61]

Endorsement of "varietism" at this time was limited to those who considered themselves sex radicals. But their position, as related to the birth control issue, differed only in degree from that favoring "indulgence." With one partner or several, the sacrifice of the principle of continence would force birth control advocates to look to contraception.

So serious was the threat that a veritable lobby for continence was organized to combat weakening moral standards. A rash of sex education books for young men, with venereal disease as a primary concern, appeared in the years 1890–1920, the vast majority of them preaching continence.[62] Under the aegis of the YMCA, Dr. M. J. Exner got 358 of America's "leading medical authorities and foremost physicians" to sign the following declaration:

> In view of the individual and social dangers which spring from the widespread belief that continence may be detrimental to health, and of the fact that municipal toleration of prostitution is sometimes defended on the ground that sexual indulgence is necessary, we, the undersigned, members of the medical profession, testify to our belief that continence has not been shown to be detrimental to health or vitality; that there is no evidence of its being inconsistent with the highest physical, mental and moral efficiency; and that it offers the only sure reliance for sexual health outside of marriage.[63]

This declaration shows what had changed. First, its interpretation of continence contrasts with the use of the term just a few decades earlier: now, remarkably, confining intercourse within marriage was enough to satisfy the requirements of continence. Second, the defensiveness of the declaration contrasts similarly with the statements of doctors of the late nineteenth century who warned that frequent intercourse, in or out of marriage, was debilitating; here Exner and his allies were trying to reassure their readers that continence was not debilitating. The doctors were no longer merely attacking sexual indulgence. Instead, they had to defend virtue against the charge that it was unhealthy.

Among doctors, then, early twentieth-century controversies focused on three issues: continence versus indulgence, monogamy versus variety, and the problem of venereal disease—all of them central to the future development of birth control. The medical participants in these discussions shared one important assumption—indeed, the assumption that made their discussion possible—namely, the need for a moral position on these questions. Robinson's tentative request for sticking to science was dismissed out of hand by the great majority of doctors, who did not believe that they should abdicate their responsibility for moral leadership in sexual matters.[64] No one doubted that there should be a general moral policy on contraception and that doctors should decide it. The pro–birth control doctors were operating out of the same professional self-image as the medical opponents of contraception. Thus, despite the reluctance of many of its members, the medical profession was to become the first established moral authority in the United States to endorse the separation of sex from reproduction through contraception. Because of the birth control question, doctors played a significant role in the changed sexual attitudes and practices that have been called a "sexual revolution."

From the vantage point of physicians, the old sexual standards included, as we have seen, a double standard of accepted sexual behavior for men and women but also an ideal of continence for both. Continence meant abstinence from sex outside of marriage and limited indulgence within marriage. An ideal at the very core of the whole sexual morality, continence represented not only a form of birth control but a virtue in itself. Continence was a form of self-control, and self-control to the Victorian middle class represented one of the highest human ideals. This was a strenuous self-control, perhaps more accurately described as self-repression. (The hegemony of this model of virtue can be seen in its acceptance even by the archenemies of the Victorian morality, the free-lovers. In questioning the right of an external authority to regulate individual behavior, they preferred to see morality enforced by the individual upon him- or herself; they were thus in the very vanguard of the self-control ideology.) Doctors contributed their own expertise to the general sentiment for self-control in criticisms of masturbation, abortion, and sexual excess in marriage. Repression of one's bodily urges led, like other forms of self-control, to spiritual awakening and strength of character. There was something beneficial not only in avoiding the bad effects of vice but in the very process of self-denial.

When the birth control issue revived in the early twentieth century, a reorientation was evident among physicians. Now, even those opposed to contraception rejected self-control as an ideal. This rejection underlay not only new sexual practices but also a new image of the ideal human character. Strength of character was no longer judged by the ability to postpone gratification. The ability to enjoy sensuous things was tolerated, encouraged, even romanticized. Contraception provided a material basis for this, making one form of self-denial dysfunctional. But contraception did not cause the change; indeed, there were no significant technological improvements of importance in this period.

Several historians have compared the nineteenth-century ideology of self-control and the saving of semen with the saving and reinvestment of money.[65] Without arguing that each nineteenth-century male regarded his penis as a bank, we can be sure that businessmen saw a connection between habits of personal self-control and economic industriousness. In this discursive system, sexual self-repression built character, which was then usable in other trying situations. There was much hypocrisy among men but somewhat less among women for whom sexual self-denial was an official requirement of respectability.

By the early twentieth century, economic and social transformation rendered the repressive view of sexuality less functional. The self-denying, reinvesting, "inner-directed" character structure fit less well with the new society than the indulgent, consumerist, "other-directed" personality type. Individual and corporate success and the solutions to economic problems no longer derived from industrious and penurious habits but rather from consumption and indulgence in immediate gratification. The new society needed citizens who spent rather than saved, in the phallic as well as the commercial sense. The new discourse accepting sexual activity (of the correct kind, of course) as healthy arose with men as its subject, but some women seized these ideas— which had been advanced by radicals for years—for themselves.

Physicians were well suited to play a leading role in rejecting the self-control values for a fuller acceptance of frequent sexual indulgence. As doctors, they were more aware than most people of the prevalence of sexual indulgence beneath the hypocritical obeisance to chastity. As men, which most of them were, they experienced the pleasures of that indulgence without the direct physical risks and burdens that women carried as a consequence. And their professional status and life-style made the more relaxed sexual standards seem appropriate. European training was common among prestigious U.S. physicians, and the general revival of interest in European medicine produced a cosmopolitan influence throughout the profession. Undergraduate education also contributed a broadening influence and brought young doctors-in-training into sympathy for liberal arts thought. Medicine was transmuting from a craft to a high form of learning, service, and even leadership. Like lawyers and professors, twentieth-century physicians felt increasingly detached from the competitive, materialistic standards of success that had dominated the late nineteenth-century prosperous classes. The professional identity involved helping and leading more than saving, investment, or striking hard bargains. A moral system of repressing gratification or enjoyment was unnecessary to their own motivation for work and achievement, and they were prepared to explore more tolerant and permissive moral standards. Of course, there was no simple correlation between joining the medical profession and accepting "a sexual revolution," and myriad individual factors explained the positions of individual doctors. The process of questioning, then rejecting, the strictures of the system of self-control was an intense and often painful one, which only a minority experienced. But the influence of this minority, its professional status and outlook, is unmistakable in its arguments and through them, as we shall see later, on the whole birth control movement.

Far from rebelling against moralism or authority, pro–birth control physicians tended to replace one prescriptive moral system with another. Influenced by European sex theorists, they argued for birth control by accepting free sexual expression as healthy. They began to suggest that sexual restraint, repressing a "need," was damaging to the total human psyche. As self-control once led to salvation, now it led to damnation—ill health, neurasthenia, debilitation (the same evils once attributed to masturbation and sexual excess).

Of course, this was still the minority position in the early twentieth century. The majority of physicians, from the most conservative to the most radical in sexual matters, retained a preference for moderation. The content of moderation, however, shifted radically. In the mid-nineteenth century moderate doctors thought it reasonable for sexual intercourse to take place only when conception was desired; by the early twentieth century they found twice a week to be a reasonable rhythm. The major change in this measurement of moderation resulted from a whole new view of good character, one that no longer saw the libido as antagonistic to the needs of civilization and social discipline.

The doctors' conception of this newly acceptable libido was entirely male. Their acceptance of greater sexual permissiveness went along with backing away from commitment to the single standard. The repressions of the nineteenth century had been primarily directed against male philandering; for women, moral, religious, and medical imprecations against sexual indulgence were less necessary, so serious were the social, biological, economic, and psychological risks, not to mention the frequent lack of pleasure in sex, that kept women from yielding to temptation or from experiencing temptation in the first place. Not only was the impulse that needed rescuing from repression primarily a male one, but the repression itself had been supported by many women's interest groups. It was partly empirical observation that led some of the anticontinence advocates to pronounce the single standard "impractical."

Thus the sexual reform views of twentieth-century doctors expressed an important historical shift in the views of moral leaders. In the nineteenth century, progressive sexual thought—advocacy of sex education, healthy diet, exercise, an open and nonprudish attitude toward reproductive functions— had been associated with feminism. The few female doctors were always in the forefront of these campaigns, and the more numerous male doctors involved were favorable to feminist causes. In the early twentieth century, those who attacked the ideal of continence were frequently hostile to feminism, sometimes pillorying feminists as sexually frustrated women who got that way by denying their true destinies.

The mid-twentieth-century understanding of Victorian prudery often associated it with ladylikeness, indeed, with a female elite standard imposed upon male society. But in fact prudery was a historical moment in a struggle between women's attempts to defend their interest in familial fidelity and men's attempts to preserve their traditional sexual privileges. The latter won, and the resulting unstable compromise rested on a fundamental hypocrisy in men's behavior. Understanding this, feminists and profeminists led the attack on prudery, analyzing it not as a female system but as a part of women's oppression. By the early twentieth century, the partial victories of this attack on prudery had forced a reorientation. Having succeeded in demolishing many sexual taboos, the feminists did not succeed in imposing a sexual single standard. Rather, they saw public acceptance of male sexual indulgence arrive without a reorientation of the social order that could provide women equivalent freedom, independence, and power.

It is for this reason that some leading feminists were hostile to sexual permissiveness in the pre–World War I period. Charlotte Perkins Gilman, the most important feminist theoretician at this time, clung to the belief that the oversexing of men was a creation of male supremacy and that women's interests lay in the restoration of a society of chastity with less energy devoted to sex.[66] This was her position even about monogamous sexual relations. She would have considered "varietism" abhorrent, for monogamy seemed to her the only organization of sexuality worthy of being called human.

Gilman's antagonism to sexual "indulgence" was traditionalist, but it was also a defense of women's interests as she saw them. As the sexual revolution affected the actual sexual behavior of millions of Americans between 1910 and 1930, both aspects of this feminist response were overwhelmed; and the defeat of this anti–sexual revolution orientation, as part of the decline of the whole feminist movement, was the inevitable death of a worldview outmoded by social and economic changes as well as a setback for women. As we will see later in this book, many of Gilman's fears about the antiwoman aspects of the New Morality were confirmed. And even in these early years before massive social changes were evident, women close enough to the disputes to be aware of these permissive ideas often feared and criticized them.

Even within the free-love movement there emerged a woman-centered opposition to the advocacy of indulgence and varietism. A woman from Brooklyn, New York, wrote in a free-love journal in 1897 that "sexual freedom, in the present stage of its development, means greater slavery for the average woman who embraces it. So long has she been the tool and slave of man, sexually, that she needs protection from herself."[67] In many such letters women argued that they could not become sexually free and equal to men merely by a change in law or mores. They saw sexual freedom not as liberating or progressive at all but as *reactionary,* a returning to the double standard and license of the eighteenth century. A decade later, when these issues reached out beyond the small free-love circles into conventional communities, a woman from Missouri wrote to William Robinson:

> I see that some of you doctors say, that the sexual instinct in man is imperative and should be gratified. Others say it is a natural function and that a moderate indulgence is beneficial, while too much is harmful. Still others argue that perfect continence is the right thing, tho nearly all will admit that it is almost an impossibility for most men to live that way. . . .

You doctors understand these things from a man's point of view, because you know the passions you have to overcome yourselves, and you understand it scientifically, but do you think you understand the woman's feelings and the place which these qualities in man force her to occupy? Do you realize that the spirit of possession and jealousy she has, must have been handed down to her thruout countless ages perhaps? And isn't the training of the ordinary so called respectable girl of this country such that she grows up believing that she must keep herself clean and chaste sexually; that somewhere in the world there is a man who will one day claim her for his wife from among all the other women of the world: that he will expect and demand that she has been continent in sexual affairs. . . . Is it any wonder then that when she grows older and wiser as to the true state of the husband's feelings in these matters, that she feels deceived. . . . if he is honest enough with her to admit after several years of married life that she does not thoroly gratify him sexually, and that his nature demands and cries out for this relation with other females, what is the wife to do? . . .

There is one thing that I cannot understand any more than some of the others. Why has man himself in the ages preceding this allowed the social conditions we now have to gradually grow up? Why has not some custom been maintained whereby he could have had this gratification in a lawful and legal way? Why have men themselves made bigamy a crime, and punish those who commit adultery?

If the women had been raised by polygamous parents, had the men always been allowed to have had many wives, or kept mistresses openly and publicly, there is no doubt but what women could now have looked on these things much more liberally than they do.[68]

This woman was probably not a feminist. She was humble before the doctors, pleading that she was too weak, too unprepared to deal with marital infidelity. Her expressions of respect for doctors held no sarcasm. Nevertheless, she rejected a logic that blamed women themselves for their inability to welcome sexual "freedom." She thought that, somehow, men were to blame.

8   *Birth Control and*
Social Revolution

A Sexual Revolution?

After about 1910 a radical shift in sexual attitudes became visible among leading American intellectuals and reformers, influenced by European sexual theorists. Although there were American traditions of sex radicalism, they were rather unsystematic. Most were sectarian proposals for sexual reform, few of them encompassing entire social analyses. The Europeans, by contrast, offered more empirical, "scientific" investigations of sexual behavior through psychology and anthropology. Or, like Edward Carpenter and Ellen Key, they continued in the old, utopian style but with social movements behind them (such as Fabian socialism and feminism), unlike the tiny sectarian groups of the American sex reformers.

The greatest "scientific" influence on sexual liberation thought in the United States was that of Sigmund Freud, though it was an influence largely based on misinterpretations of his work. The complexity, the pessimism, and the radicalism of Freud's work almost never penetrated the United States, and even in Europe much shallower interpretations of Freud soon began to dominate. Although Freudian psychology was in its essence an unraveling of the effects of repression, Freud was inclined to view repression as the inevitable cost of human progress, or at least as part of a total system that could be altered only by changing its fundamental structures of power. This tragic view of the human condition could be said to endorse sexual repression, as did nineteenth-century Victorian moralists and physicians.[1] American sex radicals, by contrast, transformed Freud's ideas into support for a campaign against sexual repression. They argued that Freud's psychological studies showed the inevitable "return" of repressed sex drives in destructive forms, thus mobilizing Freud's authority against continence as a practical route to voluntary parenthood. Still uneasy with a straightforwardly hedonist position toward sex—that is, that pleasure was a good in itself—American reformers preferred the notion of sex as an irresistible drive, dangerous to interfere with.[2]

The critique of sexual repression was part of a growing attack on hierarchy, authoritarianism, and all forms of social repression. Feminism, the critique of male tyranny, was thus a kindred social ideology, and the European sex theorists were usually profeminist. Havelock Ellis, Edward Carpenter, and Ellen Key, three major spokespeople for the "New Morality," all considered sexual liberation to be primarily dependent on women's sexual liberation, which in turn required women's independence and opportunity to seek full, creative lives. Carpenter, like the free-lovers before him, perceived male supremacy behind much of the brutality of civilization—"men so fatuous that it actually does not hurt them to see the streets crammed with prostitutes by night, or the parks by day with the semi-lifeless bodies of tramps; men, to whom it seems quite natural that our marriage and social institutions should lumber along over the bodies of women, as our commercial institutions grind over the bodies of the poor and our 'imperial' enterprise over the bodies of barbarian races"[3]—and thought that only sexual equality could correct these grotesque injustices. Like many of the sex radicals of his era, Carpenter was anticapitalist. He was convinced that women could not win equality under the "commercial system," with its "barter and sale of human labor and human love for gain." It seemed to him that the women's cause was the cause of all the oppressed and that freedom for women required communism.[4] Ellis and Key also believed in women's right to economic independence. But they doubted that total equality was likely or desirable. All believed that women's biologically specialized function—childbearing—was their destiny as well. Arguing that pregnancy and nursing would inevitably prevent women from ever achieving intellectual and economic equality with men, Ellis and Key also insisted that avoidance of the maternal function was unhealthy and abnormal, itself a form of repression. Key believed it was the obligation of every woman to have three or four children and to devote ten years of her life exclusively to child-raising.[5]

Such limited feminism reflected the limitations of this body of sexual theory. Hostile to all repression, or so they thought, these sex radicals imagined a "natural" human existence in which there was no necessity for repression at all. Ellis wrote: "The poet sang of 'Nature red in tooth and claw.' But we realize today that—if we are to adopt the conventional distinction—it is . . . Nature rather than Man that comes before us as the exalting and civilizing element in the world's life. Men—the men we thought the most civilized in the world—are to-day over a great part of the earth rending each other hideously by means of the most terrible weapons that intelligence can devise."[6]

Ellis, Key, and Carpenter came from pre-Marxist romantic socialist and feminist movements. Their program, calling for return to the natural, was no program at all, of course, but a fantasy. Antagonistic equally to class struggle and sex struggle, they were against capitalism and both male domination but counted on a cooperative socialism to which people of all classes and both sexes would be persuaded. Their ideas reached the United States first through intellectuals with similar backgrounds, but many of the latter were being transformed by an entirely different kind of socialist movement—a large movement with a broad base, including many working-class men and women. In the years before World War I, almost all American intellectuals seeking progressive social change were drawn into some kind of relationship to that movement, and this meant that sex reform ideas would be tested against the needs of many working-class men and women. European sex radicalism entered the American birth control movement through this filter and was changed in the process from a utopian, abstract libertarianism to a program offering immediate material aid to women and demanding of the state freedom to discuss, explore, and distribute contraception.

The enthusiasm of the birth controllers in this period came from their conviction that birth control was an idea whose time had come. They observed and sensed social changes that led to mass acceptance of contraception and demands for reproductive self-determination. The most immediate of these changes were the shrinking birth rate, smaller families, increased use of contraception, and increased public acknowledgment of birth control use. An example of the many signs that birth control was here to stay was the publicity given to two 1916 court cases, one in New York City and one in Cleveland, in which women accused of theft were released by sympathetic judges. Both defendants argued that they had stolen to feed their children. The first got a suspended sentence and the second was acquitted; both judges argued in their opinions, delivered from the bench, for spreading birth control information among the poor.[7]

Behind this attitude was an acceptance, even among birth control opponents, of the fact that the practice was unstoppable. Public opinion spiraled: the more evidence of birth control use became public, the more birth control became acceptable. A second factor, evident in the judges' opinions, was what we might call a neo-race-suicide view: the prosperous would use birth control anyway, so keeping it from the poor was socially destructive. A third and probably most important factor was a generally more positive attitude toward sex itself.

Some historians have argued that there was a sexual revolution of sorts in the early twentieth century. Whether these changes in sexual behavior and attitudes constituted a revolution or not, they created a new concept of birth control. Birth control now meant reproductive self-determination along with unlimited sexual indulgence. This new definition—quite different from that of voluntary motherhood—understood sexual activity and reproduction as two separately justified human activities. Either might be considered immoral under certain circumstances, but they need not be connected. The eventual mass acceptance of this new morality required the conviction not only that sexual indulgence without the risk of pregnancy was a good thing but also that fear of illegitimacy was not necessary to maintain an acceptable public morality. This new morality could challenge the weight of tradition, law, and Christianity because it conformed to the needs or strong wishes of many people and because social changes had made the traditional morality uncomfortable. Sex philosophers like Ellis were influential only with people already uncomfortable with Victorian restrictiveness; physicians who challenged the healthfulness of continence were reflecting rather than creating social changes. Free love was no longer a utopian ideal, as it had been in the nineteenth century. It was being practiced among intellectuals, radicals, bohemians, professionals, and even office workers in big cities. Unmarried people spent the night together, even lived together; unmarried women took lovers whom they were not even engaged to, often many consecutively, occasionally more than one at a time; a few experimented with peyote and marijuana; women drank and smoked with men; sex was discussed in mixed groups; and all these things were done without disguise.

For a long time historians associated this "sexual revolution" with the flappers, jazz, and speakeasies of the 1920s and only more recently discovered that these cultural changes began in earnest before World War I.[8] The reason for the original chronological mistake was that greater sexual latitude became a mass commercial phenomenon in the 1920s, and new forms of sexual behavior were both "sold" through the mass media as fashionable and used to sell other products through modern advertising.

Before the war the sexual revolution was very different. It was not only not commercialized but often anticommercial. Confined to small groups of urban sophisticates, it was a process of self-conscious and ideological experimentation. Two of its most important locales were Greenwich Village and Harlem. Harlem was almost exclusively white until 1900, but thereafter African Americans began moving in, both to take advantage of its well-built housing and because racism was driving them out of other neighborhoods and parts of the country. By 1930 Harlem was home to two hundred thousand blacks. The black bohemianism associated with the Harlem Renaissance of the 1920s had actually moved into Harlem before the war. At the same time, bohemians took over Greenwich Village by replacing the Italian immigrants who had dominated the neighborhood. The white bohemians have unsurprisingly garnered more historical renown, in part because few historians were interested in African American history until recently and in part because the Village residents were so much more prosperous. The Village became the semiofficial center of bohemianism with the decision to move the Liberal Club there in 1913. The move was a self-conscious attempt to create a community for radical intellectuals: "artists and writers had always lived here—but in tiny groups and cliques, mutually indifferent, or secretly suspicious of each other. . . . how would the new invaders . . . university people, students and professors, the social workers, the newspaper men and women . . . ever get acquainted with those shy and timid aborigines, the artist folk? . . . 'Why . . . shouldn't intelligent people to-day have the same chance to know each other that the church and the tavern gave their grandparents?'"[9]

White and black bohemians shared that rejection of grandparents' communities and embrace of urban modernism but for somewhat different reasons.[10] A disproportionate number of black intellectuals were immigrants from the rural South or the rural West Indies. Among the pioneers of the Great Migration, many came to New York precisely because they wanted the big city's freedom. Yet they did not relinquish traditional values any more than other immigrant groups did, and although there are few studies of this group prior to the 1920s, we can surmise that the new Harlemites continued the black tradition of respect (at least greater than among whites) for female independence and nonlegal marriage. In this respect they shared with whites a rejection of nineteenth-century family norms as unnecessarily constricting. Josephine Herbst wrote: "If a fine martial spirit existed between the sexes, it was a tonic and a splendor after so much sticky intermingling and backboneless worship of the family and domesticated bliss."[11] For some the discomfort in the old forms had created conscious ethical rejection of the traditional values; others perceived themselves as simply "enjoying life" a little before "settling down." Settling down, of course, meant different things to bohemians of different classes. For blacks, job discrimintion and educational deprivation was so great that a family wage was a rarity. White bohemians were more often in rebellion against a bourgeois norm that dictated marriage structured with the man the sole wage earner and the woman a full-time, housebound wife and mother.

Though men and women were both in rebellion against the family, among whites the rebellions of the two sexes took different forms. White men were often rejecting economic responsibilities and business careers for the chance to be footloose and pursue less lucrative but more passionate vocations as artists, intellectuals, reformers, or even revolutionaries. Their sexual rebellion was less intense than women's, for the double standard had already permitted a certain amount of philandering without overly harsh consequences. In sexual activity, women's rebellion was sharper, for the traditional norms had given them no sexual latitude whatever. Even pro-feminist Victorian standards had prescribed that a woman could have sexual relations with only one man in her lifetime, and if she wanted to limit her pregnancies, she could have sex with him only occasionally. A culture that was re-evaluating sex as a positive human experience made such limitations intolerable.

Changes in women's sexual behavior constituted the very essence of the sexual revolution. That fact has been obscured in general by the tendency of most historians to place men at the center of all large changes and more specifically by the Kinsey and other reports on sexual behavior that drew attention to changes among both sexes. But in the first decades of the twentieth century *the* significant change was that women were claiming some small part of the sexual freedom men had long enjoyed. Contemporary observers were clear about that fact. V. F. Calverton associated the "New Morality" with the "New Woman." Samuel Schmalhausen spoke of the "strange sexual awakening of woman."[12] Attacks on illicit sexuality were especially concerned with adolescent females.[13] The basis for the decline in prostitution between 1910 and 1920 was not the conversion of men to purity; it was the conversion of women to "indulgence." Sex studies done in the 1920s showed a tendency toward convergence between male and female rates of nonmarital sexual intercourse. Though men and women were both becoming more likely to have nonmarital sex, the change for women was proportionally greater. Most significant, men were more likely to have sex with the women they would later marry, thus making virginity a less universal requirement for a marriage partner, while the men's rate of intercourse with women other than future spouses remained almost stationary.[14]

We can never know (fortunately for human privacy) whether and how much sexual activity increased in this period, but a few sex and demographic studies—virtually all of whites exclusively—have given us some clues and bits of relevant data. For example, the premarital pregnancy rate probably fell significantly between 1800 and 1880 and then picked up again.[15] A 1925 sex study found that of middle-class married New York City women, 30 out of 50 of those born after 1890 had had nonmarital sex, whereas only 17 out of 50 born before 1890 had.[16] A study done in the 1930s asked 777 college-educated women about premarital sexual intercourse. It found that women born between 1890 and 1899 (women, therefore, coming to sexual maturity between 1910 and 1920) had twice as high a percentage of premarital intercourse as those born before 1890:[17]

Birth Date	Percent Experiencing Premarital Coitus
pre-1890	13.5
1890–1899	26
1900–1909	48.8
1910 on	68.3

A Kinsey study found the same doubling percentage for women born after 1900:[18]

Birth Date	Percent Experiencing Premarital Coitus
pre-1900	26.6
1900–1909	51.3
1910–1919	56.1
1920–1929	51.2

One of the few early twentieth-century sex studies to collect data on homosexuality suggests that the sexual revolution was exclusively heterosexual: lesbian activity did not seem to increase for women born after 1890.[19] This finding is based on a very small sample—2,200 college-educated women—but it is supported by evidence of the prevalence of intense emotional relationships between women in the nineteenth century. Partly because they did not define physical expressions of affection between women as sexual, nineteenth-century women felt free to hug and kiss and sleep in beds together; they wrote and spoke to each other in words of passionate endearment.[20] We will never know how many women actually had genital sexual contact with one another, but we do know that they had opportunities to engage in lovemaking. General and imprecise as this observation may be, it is extremely significant, since we are describing not just changes in frequency of sex but a transformation of ideology and emotional experience of love and sex as well, so that we must look not just at intercourse but whole relationships. With that perspective, we notice that the sexual revolution was not a general loosening of sexual taboos but only of those on nonmarital heterosexual activity. Indeed, so specifically heterosexual was this change that it tended to intensify taboos on homosexual activity and did much to break patterns of emotional dependence and intensity among women. Greater freedom of emotional and sexual expression with men made women view their time spent with women friends as somehow childish in comparison, or at least less sophisticated and less adventurous. In other words, the sexual revolution produced a social as well as sexual emphasis on heterosexuality.

Women's gains from these changes were by no means clear and unequivocal. Their new sexual license exempted them from some of the immediate penalties of sexual surrender to men. It did not, however, make them men's equals, sexually or in any other way, and it did not give them the power to claim what they really wanted for themselves sexually. Economically, socially, and politically, sexually "free" women were often as powerless as conventional women (with the exception of those who were able to have "careers"). As with all women, their survival and success largely depended on pleasing men; those in bohemian communities merely had new male demands to meet. Floyd Dell, a Village commentator, recognized how bohemian men used philosophical principles of sexual liberation to coerce women:

> girls wanted to be married, not only for conventional reasons, but also because sexual relations outside marriage aroused in them feelings of guilt which made them miserable. . . . The . . . spiritual hocus-pocus which sufficed instead of a wedding-ring to give a girl a good conscience, seemed to consist in quotations and arguments from Edward Carpenter, Havelock Ellis, and other modern prophets, arguments designed to show that love without marriage was infinitely superior to the other kind, and that its immediate indulgence brought the world, night by night, a little nearer to freedom and Utopia.[21]

Over and over in memoirs as well as in contemporary comments from these prewar bohemian days, we hear the lament of women who felt used and ultimately weakened by the new sexual freedom. The contemporary historian Caroline Ware analyzed it thus: Men could "fit the facts of freedom and experimentation . . . into the tradition of the double standard . . . which remained an essential part of their attitude. . . . The very girls whom men persuaded to sleep with them by a learned discourse later became objects of their contempt, and their conversation when no women were present would have done credit to any similar bourgeois group."[22] Meridel LeSueur, who arrived in the Village in 1916 at age sixteen, recalled that "free sex nearly ruined men." She was like many young immigrants there, vulnerable because of her desperate desire to be a writer. Theodore Dreiser chased her at a party, and when she steadfastly refused him sexually, he told her that she would never be a writer unless she got rid of her prudery.[23] Samuel Schmalhausen, a chief spokesman for the sexual revolution, saw these problems: "His [man's] most crafty technique for the diminution of her personality is the quasi-comradely exploitation of her sexuality—which he can now rationalize as a simple behavior of perfect equals."[24]

One cannot, after all, separate sexual behavior from people's experience of love. Bohemian men as well as women usually associated their affairs with love. They fell in love over and over; or, alternatively, they were endlessly unsure of their capacity to love. The ideology and practice of love was changing along with that of sex. In the late eighteenth and early nineteenth centuries, another sexual revolution—the birth of prudery—had also carried with it a transformation of love. Love became then pre-eminently a spiritual union, as free of lust as it was possible to make it. Ironically, it was the nineteenth-century sex radicals—free-lovers and spiritualists—who carried that desexualized definition of love to its extreme. They wanted even to desexualize sex, arguing through analogies to magnetism and electricity that the most important purpose of sexual union was the exchange of spiritual energies. Dialectically, this had enabled them to put sex back into an honorable place within love. Now, twentieth-century sex radicals were making sex the very center of love. As love became more sexualized, its imagery divorced from the ideal of purity, it also became more transient—or, more accurately, its transience became acceptable. The bohemians were fascinated with the disappearance and the fragility of love, with its rarity. They were quick to see everyday human relationships as imperfect. "All the women I have been close to . . . have been in a way cripples, of broken beauty. With them I have often felt a profound sympathy and a nearness, because they were cripples like me. I could not, however, really love them, for it seems to me that complete beauty only can be completely loved."[25] Expressions like this, by the novelist and Village-dweller Hutchins Hapgood, were common in this period. In effect, they defined love out of the existence of most people for most of their lives. Love came to describe a moment's emotion. John Reed's telegram of rejection of Mabel Dodge from Paris read, "'J'aime X.L. Pardonnez-moi et sois [*sic*] heureuse' (I love X.L. Forgive me and be happy)."[26]

For women, it had been precisely the function of the family to protect them against the transience of love. Only men could afford that kind of transience. For women, economic and social discrimination and responsibility for children meant that desertion by men left them vulnerable. Sexual freedom made birth control important for women; the possible impermanence of love made birth control an absolute necessity. It was not a solution to the problem of sexual inequality, but it was a small help.

In all this rapid change, women's frequent unhappiness and men's frequent opportunism were perhaps inevitable. The sexual revolution, like real revolutions, brought suffering, which often accompanies the destruction of older social institutions. And like many rebels, the bohemians were excessive. Their sexual behavior was often promiscuous. Max Eastman called this period the adolescence of the twentieth century.[27] Like adolescents, the bohemians were fickle and extremist, overstating their rejection of their parents' values. Many of them drew back after a few years of experimentation, sometimes to more moderate positions and sometimes all the way to traditionalism. Some of this drawing back was part of the process of change, a naturally uneven process at best. A larger part of it was the product of a general rightward turn in the society in the 1920s. The traditionalism that recurred then, however, was not a full return to nineteenth-century norms. On the contrary, the sexual freedom claimed by bohemians in the prewar period began, in the 1920s, to be extended to masses of urban and even small-town Americans. The difference was that the bohemians had been rebels and the children of the flapper era were conforming to new conventions.

To understand this difference we must take note of the political and social context of bohemianism. The bohemians were often newcomers to the big cities, but among the whites, few were from poor or working-class backgrounds— Emma Goldman and Margaret Sanger stood out as exceptions. Most were from prosperous, native-born professional or business families. Floyd Dell remarked that they were usually the children of important men in their hometowns, often college educated; often too they were in flight from marriages and careers laid out for them by their successful parents.[28] Their well-to-do backgrounds gave them both the freedom to experiment and the safety net to retreat into as they aged. Neither the black Harlemites nor the whites who were drawn into the sexual revolution in the 1920s possessed that privilege.

But despite the rather upper-class base of white bohemianism, their political influence gained shape and impact from the working-class militancy in the prewar period. The Villagers were especially influenced by the revolutionary union, the Industrial Workers of the World (IWW), and by mass industrial strikes. In a period of class struggle, the bohemians' own struggles against cultural repression and bourgeois values seemed to them a part of the working class's fight against capitalism. Their exploration of sexual freedom, odd forms of dressing, modern dance, and even drugs seemed to them a part of a process of reaching toward a nonauthoritarian, democratic society. Many Villagers supported the Women's Trade Union League. Revolutionaries like Bill Haywood and Emma Goldman were featured guests at parties. Even the wealthy Mabel Dodge, in her always white, beautifully draped gowns, helped organize a mass rally for the Paterson strikers in Madison Square Garden. And Dodge and her crowd did not see these efforts as philanthrophy. Rather, a sense of unity with a sharp class struggle, a struggle in which it seemed that the working class was bound to be victorious, gave the bohemians the optimism and sense of purpose they needed to create a cohesive community.

In both Harlem and the Village, socialist ideology was hegemonic among these radicals. The Harlem "New Crowd Negroes" were disdainful not just of the equally racist white Republicans and Democrats but also of the conservative "Old Crowd" black elders, such as Booker T. Washington's man in New York, the Republican Charles Anderson, and Tammany's man, Ferdinand Q. Morton.[29] From Harlem's soapboxes on Lenox and Seventh Avenues, the speeches were overwhelmingly socialist. They denounced the capitalist and imperialist world war and discussed the relevance of socialist ideas to race oppression.[30] After World War I, both W. E. B. Du Bois and *The Messenger*, Harlem's major newspaper, edited by A. Philip Randolph and Chandler Owen, were supporting birth control.[31] In the Village, even the seemingly frivolous and self-centered bohemians identified with the Socialist party and contributed to its projects.

And these New Yorkers did not live only in their small villages. African American artists and intellectuals came downtown regularly, to salons, to lectures, to meetings. Whites ventured uptown less often but increasingly, mainly to hear music.

Women were present and visible in all these scenes. Women's rebellion was not only the essence of the sexual revolution; it contributed substantially to the strength of the bohemian/socialist community as well. Hutchins Hapgood wrote, "When the world began to change, the restlessness of women was the main cause of the development called Greenwich Village, which existed not only in New York but all over the country."[32] This should not be construed to suggest that bohemianism was dominated by women or feminist views; on the contrary, men often used women's rebellion for their own purposes. But it was the motion among women, the risks they took themselves, that placed them in vulnerable positions. The rejection of marriage, of the traditional family, of propriety in dress and behavior—the whole gamut of rejections that marked the bohemians' radicalism—began because women offered themselves to men and to a larger social and political community without the usual protections of these institutions. Understood even less by most historians has been the dependence of the great strikes of the prewar period on women. Although the IWW in the West had been primarily a male, even a masculinist, movement, it made its impact in the East through its willingness to support massive workers' uprisings in female-dominated industries. In the Paterson, New Jersey, silk mill strike of 1913, the New York shirtwaist strike of 1909, and the Lawrence textile mill strike of 1912, women constituted from nearly half to the overwhelming majority of workers; and in incident after incident women proved themselves the more militant and persevering of strikers. Political leadership remained almost exclusively in the hands of men (to the disadvantage of the working class as a whole, one might add). But, again, it was women's action in stepping, sometimes forcibly, out of traditional restrictions that made possible the class unity that gave the strikes such great strength.

Working women's activism rested on a consumer economy that was rapidly drawing young women into the wage-labor force. In 1870, 1.9 million women were employed; in 1890, 4 million. By 1910 the number had doubled.[33] Over the long run probably no single factor did more to change the sexual behavior of unmarried women than employment, especially when it meant living away from home. Protecting the morals of unmarried working girls in the big cities became a major worry for social workers, reformers, and moralists; they built boardinghouses and YWCAs and attempted to attract the young women into supervised living. But the greatest charm of the big cities for young women was privacy, and the YWCAs reported over and over that women preferred private apartments if they could get them.[34]

Open neighborhoods in these as in other ways, Greenwich Village and Harlem attracted many such young workers. Landlords allowed groups of women to share small apartments. The old Village bohemians even complained about the influx of "green" working women.[35] Once in the big cities, young women often outnumbered single men. They usually worked in sexually segregated occupations, where they did not quickly find husbands. In this period employed women were still overwhelmingly single: nationally, only about 5 percent of wives worked for money outside their homes. Of course, this percentage was much higher among lone mothers and the poor, and in these groups domestic service remained the major wage-earning opportunity for women.

For white women, by contrast, clerical work expanded more rapidly than any other kind of employment after 1880. In 1880 women numbered only 4 percent of clerical workers; in 1890 they numbered 21 percent; by 1920, 50 percent.[36] The working conditions in offices differed greatly from those in factories. Typists and secretaries often had close contact with men. Their subculture emphasized dressing well, and although they were poorly paid they earned more than almost all factory workers. Many young secretaries spent so much of their salaries on clothes that they literally had to skip eating for periods of time; urban employed women also frequently spent a large portion of their earnings for the luxury of an apartment and the relative privacy it afforded. Even without overspending, many independent women workers had to count on being taken out to dinner several nights a week in order to make ends meet.[37] The other side of these new circumstances was the disappearance of many traditional restraints. Not only were parents absent, but so were close, prying neighbors. Church and school influences were distant. Even older brothers and sisters, who had once helped sanction traditional moral values, could no longer do so. Big cities generally provided physical and social privacy in ways that small towns never had, for the married or unmarried. At the same time the old-fashioned view of independent working women as not quite respectable persisted and combined with the male double standard to make these women morally suspect.

Inextricably related to the increased privacy for sexual activity among unmarried women was the decline of prostitution. During and after World War I, a nationwide campaign by reformers for the suppression of red-light districts—that is, tolerated prostitution—was nearly universally successful. This success was both a consequence of these sexual changes and a contributory cause of them, and it added to the pressure for birth control. For men, the unacceptableness of hiring prostitutes, and the acceptableness of lovemaking with unmarried women for free, grew together and reinforced each other. Prostitutes had access to birth control information and devices through their own underground; for the new sexual system to work, other women needed access to the same information. Campaigners against prostitution counseled early marriage. But to make early marriage an economic possibility, in an era when husbands were still expected to support their wives, contraception was a necessary component.

Another important factor in the increased acceptability of contraception was the scourge of venereal disease and the campaign against it. V.D. had, of course, been a serious problem in the United States throughout the nineteenth century. Widespread prostitution meant that many women were infected by their husbands, and for feminists and voluntary motherhood advocates this injustice loomed large in their attack on the double standard. Medical investigation of the consequences of syphilis and gonorrhea showed that they were even worse than had been previously understood,[38] and in the early twentieth century some physicians began educational campaigns for their prevention. Soldiers had always spread V.D., even in peacetime; World War I worsened the problem considerably. Between September 1917 and February 1919 more than 280,000 cases of V.D. were reported in the U.S. Army and the U.S. Navy.[39] In 1914 one expert estimated exaggeratedly that more than half the men of the country had had gonorrhea.[40] The main reason for the spread of V.D. among the armed forces was, of course, the proliferation of prostitution near bases and in ports, much of it tolerated by military authorities.

Before the Great War the anti-V.D. campaign was tied to antiprostitution work, indeed, to the social purity movement; its key recommendations were abolition of prostitution (or, occasionally, the licensing and inspection of prostitutes)[41] and continence propaganda.[42] So serious was the problem that one well-known social purity writer urged soldiers to masturbate if they could not manage continence![43] Then, in 1909, the compound 606, or Salvarsan, was shown to be effective in destroying syphilis spirochetes. As early as 1912 a war department general order required that soldiers take postexposure chemical prophylactic treatment against V.D.[44] Condoms—far more effective than chemical treatment—had been available for centuries, rubber condoms since the mid-nineteenth century, and they were omnipresent in many of the ports and bases where American GIs were located. But moralists rejected condoms because they had to be given out before the fact to be useful, thus allegedly encouraging intercourse, and they had a clear contraceptive capability besides. But a significant percentage of the 4 million men who served in World War I learned how to use them.[45] Demobilization then sent many veterans in search of condoms on the domestic market. V. F. Calverton's study of Baltimore found that 2–3 million condoms were sold annually before the war and 6.25 million by the mid-1920s. Furthermore, he believed that half of those buying them were unmarried.[46]

Were the moralistic opponents of condoms right? Did contraception actually encourage nonmarital sex? Katherine Bement Davis's 1929 sex study established a correlation (though based on a small sample) between knowledge of contraception and premarital sex.[47] But the causality was probably mutual: the availability of contraceptives licensed sexual activity and the new acceptability of sexual activity licensed contraception. The war merely accelerated long-term tendencies.

We can get a sense of the social change by noticing what its opponents thought. Social purity advocates had been growing steadily more defensive since 1910. Even their gratification at the victory over prostitution was ruined by their sense of an impending corruption that would be even worse. They described the decline of sexual morality in the vocabulary of crisis and revolution. They had a sense of emergency, of values crumbling so rapidly that they must be shored up quickly or be lost forever.[48]

The Pioneers

The movement that first coalesced around the term "birth control," coined by Margaret Sanger in 1915, was composed of people fighting for their own immediate needs, and for that reason it had an intensely personal dimension for its participants. The fact that the birth controllers often stood to gain immediately in their personal lives from legalization of birth control did not narrow their vision but strengthened their commitment. They united their personal experience and emotional understanding with political thought and action. They created a politics based on women's shared experience that, for a brief period, united women across class and race groups. At the same time, the birth controllers transcended women's immediate needs. They were not seeking incremental improvements in their sex lives or medical care; rather, they viewed birth control not as primarily a sexual or medical reform but as a social issue with broad implications. They wanted to transform the nature of women's rights—indeed, of human rights—to include free sexual expression and reproductive self-determination.

They used birth control to make a revolutionary demand, not a reform proposal. They did not want just to limit or schedule pregnancies but to change the world. They believed that birth control could alleviate much human misery and fundamentally alter social and political power relations, thereby creating greater sexual and class equality. In this they shared the voluntary motherhood analysis—that involuntary motherhood was a major prop of women's subjection—and added a radical version of a neo-Malthusian analysis that overlarge families weakened the working class in its struggle with the capitalist class. They also demanded sexual freedom.

The birth controllers were putting forward these demands at a time when American radicalism was at top strength and breadth. Indeed, the birth control movement that began in 1914 was part of a general upswing in activism. Joining that resistance, birth controllers appealed for support, particularly to women and to working-class and poor people in general, because they believed that lack of control over reproduction helped perpetuate an undemocratic distribution of power.

Their strategy was to bring the women's rights, civil liberties, and labor movements together. The leading birth controllers between 1914 and 1920 were feminists, socialists, and liberals, and they wanted to unite their respective goals and constituencies. Many of them came to the birth control cause from multi-issue reform or revolutionary movements, ranging from the suffrage organizations to the IWW. Few were themselves members of the working class, although some important leaders—Margaret Sanger is only one—had working-class origins. Nationally, the leadership was all white. But their experience of the common oppression of women in sexual and reproductive matters convinced them that they could transcend class and race differences and create a movement in the interest of the least-privileged women. They failed in this grand intention, but that does not mean that their analysis and strategy were completely wrong or that their experiences are useless to us today.

By 1914 the radical movement in the United States was unified to a large extent in the Socialist party (SP). From 10,000 members in 1901, the party grew to include 118,000 members in 1912. Its voting strength was many times greater—almost 6 percent of the total in 1912—and by 1912 it had elected twelve hundred public officials and regularly published more than three hundred periodicals.[49] No other political party in American history ever fought as consistently for women's rights (such as suffrage, employment opportunities, legal rights).[50] Especially after 1910, many feminists joined the SP and began agitating for a more feminist program, working in women's committees in many SP locals and socialist woman suffrage societies. They got a few women elected to the National Executive Committee.[51]

The party's conception of what women's rights were, however, accepted the conventional definition of woman's proper sphere and activities—home, motherhood, housework, and husband care. The SP as a whole did not support birth control or any other reforms that threatened to alter or even question traditional sex roles and division of labor. In clinging to their conventional views of the family, socialists often cited as their authority the early Marxist

view that drawing women out of their homes was one of the evils of capitalism that socialism would put right. The radicals in the SP, more inclined to
reject the conventions, were concerned even more exclusively than the rest
of the party with class struggle in the workplace and consequently saw questions of domestic relations as a distraction. The party's women's journal, *Socialist Woman,* published in Girard, Kansas, did not include a single article
before 1914 that discussed the principle of voluntary motherhood. (Indeed,
even when the journal's editors received a letter asking them to take up the
question, they declined to publish it.)[52] Socialist women concerned with sexual issues, even regular contributors to party periodicals, published their writings on birth control elsewhere.[53]

Despite its great influence in the birth control movement, the Socialist
party *never* formally endorsed birth control. Indeed, before 1912 the issue was
never the subject of major debate within the party, so great was the pressure
not to create internal divisions. The rejection of anything but the most limited feminist goals by the SP majority reflected a larger split in the whole U.S.
radical and reform community between socialism and the women's movement.
That split deepened in the early twentieth century. Previously, almost all supporters of birth control had been socialists of one sort or another. Voluntary
motherhood advocates of the 1870s had been critical of capitalist values and
social organization, as had utopian communitarians who practiced birth control; many American feminists by the end of the nineteenth century had concluded that women's emancipation would require a higher level of economic
justice than capitalism could provide; and most European sex radicals were
socialists. But as Marxian "scientific" socialism began to dominate, and the
organized socialist movement gained a working-class constituency, emphasis
on class differences and class struggle squeezed out sex equality as a program.
Many socialist feminists, although thoroughly anticapitalist, refused to follow
socialist theory into a denial of their own experience of sex oppression. Meanwhile, within the Marxist organizations the emphasis on unions and organizing at the workplace left men without pressing reasons to appeal to women,
most of whom remained outside the labor force. Arrogance and disrespectful
attitudes toward women were widespread among socialist men. Thus, anyone
trying to formulate a socialist *and* feminist theory about the importance of birth
control faced serious difficulties: a conservative and elite woman suffrage
movement and a rather blindly antifeminist Socialist party.

Despite its limitations, the existence of the SP was one of the most important conditions for the emergence of the birth control movement in the second decade of the twentieth century, in that the SP brought together almost
all radicals and reformers concerned with working-class welfare. Without this
opportunity to reach and to learn from working-class women, sex radicals might

have continued to pursue sterile, theoretical formulations, contributing at most to a bohemian life-style among urban intellectuals. By contrast, the sexual conservatism of the party's male leadership could not contain the growing restlessness produced among women by their changed circumstances.

Some midwestern socialists still cherished some of the feminist traditions of pre-Marxian socialism. For instance, Virginia Butterfield, in *Parental Rights and Economic Wrongs,* published in Chicago in 1906, argued that birth control was a form of self-defense against capitalism. In agricultural society children were a form of wealth and birth control was economically unnecessary, she argued, but under conditions of industrialism, birth control arose because capitalism's system of unjust distribution made people poor. Ideally, she believed, socialism would again make birth control unnecessary and would restore the "natural equilibrium of the sexes" by allowing men to earn enough so that all women could stay at home—the restoration of a natural condition that would end marital unhappiness and the necessity for divorce.[54] Until then, however, women's refusal to bear children under conditions of oppression was a form of rebellion. Indeed, since procreation was one of the highest forms of human labor, birth control became, for Butterfield, a form of workers' control.[55] Many socialists turned their attention to the prohibition on birth control and asked, Whom does it serve? Many concluded that the ruling class kept birth control from the working class in the interest of continued exploitation. One reason was war—a large population of underlings was needed for cannon fodder.[56] Another was that capitalists used a reserve army of labor to keep wages down.[57] To the charge that birth control might weaken the working class by decreasing its size, they pointed to historical events in which an underclass—a lumpen proletariat—had played an antirevolutionary role.[58]

The limitations of these analyses reflected the general limitations of socialist theory regarding women. The debate about whether the working class would benefit from increasing or shrinking its size implicitly ignored women's needs and desires.

A few U.S. radicals, Margaret Sanger and Emma Goldman among them, were able to advance beyond this partly because they were influenced by European developments. In Protestant countries with mass working-class socialist parties, there were by now many birth control clinics. In Germany, birth control had been an important issue in the Social Democratic party since early in the century, and the demands of party rank-and-file women had forced the leadership to quit opposing it.[59] Both Goldman and Sanger, attracted more by anarchism than by the Social Democratic parties, were at first less impressed by the clinics than by the theories of sexual freedom, but they transformed these ideas into an action program, a program of sex education.

In this era sex education was not merely action but militant action because it involved breaking the law. The Comstock law still barred "obscene" materials from the mails, and most noneuphemistic sex discussion—such as naming the human genitalia—was categorized as obscene. Defying such laws was a form of what the IWW called direct action, acting directly against state and capitalist power, not petitioning or negotiating but taking what was needed. Women needed sex education. Feminists and sexual freedom advocates agreed that women's ignorance of their bodies was debilitating and that deference to conventions about what was good for "ladies" to know deepened their passivity and political fearfulness.

In the United States a campaign of sex education formed a bridge between pro–birth control ideas and an organized movement for birth control. Sex manuals had been plentiful since the mid-nineteenth century, but their style had begun to change in the early twentieth century. Even conservative writers, while remaining moralistic, introduced detailed physiological descriptions and sometimes drawings of reproductive anatomy.[60] Midwestern socialists and feminists of Virginia Butterfield's tradition had written dozens of sex education books in the first decades of the twentieth century.[61] Somewhat later, demands for sex education appeared within the Socialist party itself. One particularly effective spokeswoman and practitioner of sex and birth control education was Antoinette Konikow, a Russian immigrant physician. A founding member of the SP and later one of the five members of its Women's Commission, she practiced medicine in Boston after her graduation from Tufts Medical School in 1902; and although Boston was then, as now, an overwhelmingly Catholic city, with little support even within its radical community for sexual unconventionality, she was outspoken for birth control and probably provided abortions.[62] Konikow wrote for the *New York Call,* a daily socialist newspaper, arguing that sex education was an important task for socialists.[63] Dr. William J. Robinson also wrote for the *Call* on sex hygiene; he and Konikow were the first to focus their sex education articles on birth control.[64]

The most notorious for speaking out on sexual questions was Emma Goldman. More than any other person, she fused into a single ideology the many currents that mingled in American sex radicalism. She had connections with European anarchism, syndicalism, and socialism; with American utopian anarchists and free-lovers such as Moses Harman; with American feminism; and with dissident doctors such as Robinson.[65] In 1900, Goldman had attended the secret neo-Malthusian conference in Paris and had even smuggled some contraceptive devices into the United States.[66] She exerted substantial influence on other radicals as a role model and a practitioner of the New Morality. Her pupils included Margaret Sanger, who later tried to hide that influence. Always needing recognition and fearing rivals for power and importance, Sanger underestimated Goldman's contribution to birth control in her later writings. She met Goldman when Goldman was a magnetic and dominating figure nationally and she was an insecure young woman lacking a cause and a political identity. Sanger still clung to more-conservative sexual ideas, and Goldman must have been shocking to her, at the least.[67] But Sanger was an extraordinary student whose drive and charisma soon made her a greater force than her teacher.

When Sanger moved to New York City in 1911 and searched for work, her background as a nurse made it natural for her to take an interest in sex education. At about the same time she became an organizer for the Women's Commission of the Socialist party (with a small salary), secretary of the Harlem Socialist Suffrage Society, and a writer for the *New York Call*, the SP daily. Becoming proficient at speaking and writing, she got such enthusiastic responses when her topics were health and sex that she began to specialize in these areas.

Still, Sanger was disappointed in her more "orthodox" socialist organizing, working with striking laundry workers and trying to garner support for a legislative campaign for a wages-and-hours bill. She resigned as an organizer in January 1912.[68] But her dissatisfaction with SP work did not at first push her more deeply into sex education activities; rather, she was drawn, as were so many radical intellectuals at the time, toward the greater militancy of the IWW, with its direct action tactics. When the strike of Lawrence, Massachusetts, textile workers, endorsed by the IWW, broke out in January 1912, Sanger became involved in support work for the strikers, which she continued until June 1912.[69]

Sanger resumed her articles in the *Call* in November 1912 with the series "What Every Girl Should Know." It was more daring than the first series, which had been called "What Every Mother Should Know" and had been designed to help mothers tell their children about sex and reproduction, largely through analogy to flowers and animals.[70] The second series spoke more fully of human physiology, especially the female sexual and reproductive apparatus, and argued that the "procreative act" was something natural, clean, and healthful.[71] But when Sanger turned to the problem of venereal disease, which had for decades been discussed in public only with euphemisms such as the "social problem" and "congenital taint," the U.S. Post Office could take no more, declaring the article unmailable under the Comstock law. The *Call* responded by printing the headline of the column—"What Every Girl Should Know"—and in a big box underneath it the words "NOTHING, by order of the Post-Office Department."[72] (The Post Office ban was lifted two weeks later on orders from Washington and the full article appeared in the *Call* on March 2, 1913. In one of the finer ironies produced by the rapid changes in attitudes of those years, that same article was reprinted—without credit to the author—by the government and distributed among U.S. troops during World War I.)[73]

Up until this time, Sanger had not discussed birth control in writing. Her sex education work was again interrupted by a more urgent demand for her services—the Paterson silk workers' strike that had begun in February 1913. The workers asked the IWW for help, and "Big Bill" Haywood sent Sanger and Jessie Ashley (a socialist feminist lawyer who was later active in birth control issues) to New Jersey to organize picket lines.[74] Sanger worked there until the strike failed that summer. She did not write anything further on sexual hygiene in 1913 and in October sailed for Europe with her husband and children. In Paris she began the first stage of her research into birth control, a practical phase. Not yet interested in sexual theory, she spoke with her neighbors, with the French syndicalists that Haywood (also then in Paris) introduced her to, and with druggists, midwives, and doctors. She collected contraceptive formulas. She discovered that birth control was respectable, widely practiced, and almost traditional in France. Women told her that they had learned about contraception from their mothers.[75] In fact, U.S. birth control advocates such as William J. Robinson had been publishing articles about the low birth rate and widespread contraceptive use in France for years.[76] But all this was new and thrilling to Sanger in 1913. For the rest of her life birth control was to be her exclusive passion.

What were the sources of this decision of Sanger's? Years later she herself portrayed it as a rather sudden conversion and attributed it to an incident that had happened a year earlier in her work as a visiting nurse: an encounter with a poor Jewish family in which a beloved wife died from one pregnancy too many.[77] She also wrote that before going to Paris she had spent a year in New York libraries and the Library of Congress futilely searching for contraceptive information[78] and that Haywood urged her to go to France to learn.[79] There can be no doubt that she was hearing about birth control frequently and that it had the basic approval of people she respected. Even in the Paterson strike it was in the air. Elizabeth Gurley Flynn recalled a meeting for women strikers at which Carlo Tresca, an IWW organizer, "made some remarks about shorter hours, people being less tired, more time to spend together and jokingly he said: 'More babies.' The women did not look amused. When Haywood interrupted and said: 'No, Carlo, we believe in birth control—a few babies, well cared for!' they burst into laughter and applause."[80]

One key difference between Sanger and her radical friends who saw the importance of birth control was that she was dissatisfied with her role as a socialist organizer and was searching for something more like a career. Biographers have commented on Sanger's drive and ambition. Among men, in most situations, that kind of drive would have seemed so admirable that it would have been praised and would not have stimulated the criticism Sanger received. She instinctively understood that the recognition she needed required a special cause, a specialization. As a nurse, she felt comfortable building on expertise and experience she already had.

But the reason she chose contraception rather than venereal disease or sex education was her recognition of the potential historical and political impact of birth control. Most American socialists at this time, primarily oriented to class relations, saw birth control in neo-Malthusian terms, that is, in terms of economics. They were concerned to help raise the standard of living of workers and thus increase their freedom to take political control over their own lives. Measured against this goal, birth control was at most an ameliorative reform. Seen in terms of sexual politics, however, birth control was revolutionary because it could free women entirely from the major burden that differentiated them from men and made them dependent on men. Sanger gained this perspective in Europe from sexual liberation theorists such as Havelock Ellis. Ellis tutored Sanger, literally. His idealism about the potential beauty and expressiveness of human sexuality and his rage at the damage caused by sexual repression fired Sanger with a sense of the overwhelming importance, urgency, and profundity of the issue of birth control, a sense lacking in most other American radicals.

The entire future course of birth control in the United States was influenced by Sanger's European education. Yet the curiosity that led her to her research in Europe would almost certainly have led someone else there if she had been diverted. Sanger's European trips took place in the midst of a flurry of activity for sexual change in the United States that began before her influence was great and would inevitably have led to a birth control campaign before long. Sanger was stimulated by it and returned to lead it, but at first she was part of a social movement and not its sole inventor.[81]

In 1937, when the first general history of contraception was published, Dr. Benjamin L. Reitman, once Emma Goldman's comrade and lover, wrote a letter of protest to its author, charging that the book had suppressed the radical origins of the birth control movement. It was a passionate and amusing letter, and largely correct:

> My Dear Himes.
> You made me weep.
> Because your article
> On the history
>   Of Birth Control
> was inaccurate
>   Superficial
>   "Highschoolish"
> And you gave no evidence
> Of attempting
> To learn the facts.

You delved into history.
    But failed to get data from the living.
    Moses Harmon[82]
Was the true father of American Birth Control
His grand Children are living
And have lots of splendid material. . . .
You "muffed" all the fine material
In the early Socialist, Anarchist & I.W.W. literature.
The tremendous amount of Free Love literature
Passed you by.
There are several hundred pamphlets
On B.C. that you evidently know nothing about.
The technique of B.C. propaganda
In America is a Mystery to you. . . .
I mean your prejudice against the RADICALS
Is so great that you COULD not give them credit
    Emma Goldman
More than any one person in America
Popularized B.C.
She was Margaret Sanger's INSPIRATION
No that ain't the word.
Margaret imitated her and denied her.
Emma was the first person in America
To lecture on Birth Control
in one hundred Cities. . . .
The physicians, Social Scientists, Clergy & etc.
Became interested in B.C.
Only after the Radicals had "broken" the ground.
And gone to jail.
The inclosed pamphlet
Was distributed by the millions.
Free.
    In hundreds of Cities in America
It went through many many editions
Was copied and recopied. . . .
The decline in the Birth Rate
Was influenced by this pamphlet
More than any other one piece of literature.
    Including Margaret's "Family Limitation" . . .
    B.L.R.
    Was arrested
      For distributing the pamphlet
    In New York City (60 days)
    Rochester, N.Y. (freed)

Cleveland, Ohio (six months)
         He was picked up by the police in many cities
But was let go.
Big Bill Shatoff
         Who was an I.W.W. Organizer
Translated the pamphlet
Into Jewish and most all
         Of the Radical Jews had copies.
In the early days of the Communists' activity
In Russia this pamphlet
Had a tremendous circulation in Russia . . .
GET THIS INTO YOUR HEAD.
This was all done as part of the radical propaganda.
ANTI WAR
ANTI MARRIAGE
         ANTI CHILDREN BY ACCIDENT . . .
I see no hope for your Medical Scientific group to make any real
Contribution to history or°°°°   Enough for today
                                             Ben L. Reitman[83]

Allowing for nostalgia, loyalty to Goldman, and the pique of a radical who saw "his" movement taken over by nonradicals, the essence of Reitman's claims is nevertheless correct. Himes defended himself by pointing out that he had written a *medical* history of contraception and was primarily concerned with those who made medical and technological contributions. Nevertheless, it is true that historians and biographers have overlooked or underestimated the radical roots of the American birth control movement. Sanger herself contributed to that distortion. She was ignorant, in the early years of her career, of the free-love and feminist roots of birth control propaganda, and, although she came to the birth control cause through the SP, later she sought to diminish the socialists' participation in the movement when she wrote and spoke about it.[84]

After about 1910, Goldman regularly included a birth control speech on her tour offerings. In it she placed birth control in the context of women's rights and opposition to conventional legal marriage. Like all radicals of her era, she used eugenic arguments: "Woman no longer wants to be a party to the production of a race of sickly, feeble, decrepit, wretched human beings. Instead she desires fewer and better children." She also spoke about homosexuality, criticizing social ostracism of the "inverts," as homosexuals were commonly called at that time. Her sexual and feminist theories were integrated into her whole politics. "To me anarchism was not a mere theory for a distant future; it was a living influence to free us from inhibitions . . . and from the destructive barriers that separate man from man."[85] Reitman was himself a birth control campaigner, not a mere companion to Goldman, and he did indeed, as he claimed, serve sixty days shoveling coal on Blackwell's Island and six months in an Ohio workhouse for distributing birth control leaflets.[86]

Goldman and Reitman distributed a small, four-page pamphlet called *Why and How the Poor Should Not Have Many Children,* which may have been written by Goldman or Reitman, or possibly by William J. Robinson. It described condoms, instructing the user to check them for leaks by blowing them up like a balloon, and recommended rubber cervical caps and diaphragms (also called pessaries or womb veils; in the early twentieth century there was no standard nomenclature for these various devices), which could be bought in drugstores, though the pamphlet urged that users be fitted by a physician for reliability. The pamphlet also suggested three contraceptive methods that could be homemade: suppositories, douches, and a cotton ball dipped in borated Vaseline. (It advised against relying on the rhythm method, which it nonetheless described, unfortunately defining the safe period as the two weeks between menstrual periods.) The political argument of the pamphlet was brief: although normal people love and want children, society is a "wretched place" for poor children, who are not only a burden to their mothers and families, but also "glut the labor market, tend to lower wages, and are a menace to the welfare of the working class. . . . If you think that the teaching of the prevention of conception will help working men and women, spread the glad tidings."[87] American sex radicals, despite their militant rhetoric, had not so far defied law and convention by publishing such explicit contraceptive advice. Goldman and Reitman's ideas about birth control were not new, but their sense of its political importance and their willingness to take risks to spread it were.

The first radicals since the free-lovers to act in defiance of the law, Goldman and her associates were not able to make birth control a mass cause. Goldman's connections made her seem the right person for that task. But she was an extremist and, as a result, was often isolated. Partly because she took outrageous positions and partly because she was personally individualist and egocentric, Goldman left most of her admirers behind. She did not work well with other women, and her male followers were usually skeptical about the importance of sexual and women's rights issues.

Though she began later, Sanger was more effective as an organizer for birth control. She drew supporters, at first, through assuming a role in which she was more convincing than Goldman: that of victim. Early in her career, people frequently commented on Sanger's apparent fragility and vulnerability; only as they came to know her did her stamina, tenacity, and personal power impress them. Intellectuals repelled by the abrasive style of Goldman and her comrades could adore Sanger. Max Eastman, for example, hailed Sanger as a hero in *The Masses* but refused to speak at a Carnegie Hall meeting to welcome Goldman out of jail after she had served sixty days for distributing birth control pamphlets because, he said, he would not appear with Reitman: "Reitman was a white-fleshed, waxy-looking doctor, who thought it was radical to shock people with crude allusions to their sexual physiology."[88] Nevertheless, Sanger's debut as a birth control activist was tactically and substantively within the pattern plotted out by Goldman and the IWW. Sanger began with provocative, illegal action and then, once arrested, organized support for her defense.

The key difference between Sanger's and Goldman's strategies in 1914 was that Sanger became a single-issue exponent. The path that led the Sanger-inspired birth control movement away from the Left thus began with her first actions, though they may not have been consciously intended in that direction. When Sanger's divergence from the organized Left led to total separation, it was as much because the Left had rejected birth control as because Sanger and her followers had rejected the Left. Nevertheless, the roots of the split can be found at the beginnings of the birth control movement itself.

Sanger returned from Paris to New York in December 1913, deeply influenced by her discovery that birth control was widely accepted in Europe. She did not return to Socialist party work but decided instead to publish an independent, feminist paper. *The Woman Rebel*, which appeared seven times in 1914 before it was suppressed by the Post Office, emphasized birth control but was not a single-issue journal. For example: "The marriage bed is the most degenerating influence of the social order, as to life, in all of its forms—biological, psychological, sociological—for man, woman and child."[89] Although concerned with the whole gamut of injustices that the capitalist system created, *The Woman Rebel* focused mainly on women. Yet it sharply attacked the non-Socialist suffrage movement and various "bourgeois feminists." For example, of Katherine Bement Davis, then New York City commissioner of corrections (and later, ironically, a sociologist of sexual behavior who worked with Sanger on several sex education projects), *The Woman Rebel* wrote: "We have no respect for the type of so called 'modern' and 'advanced' woman who becomes a willing and efficient slave of the present system, the woman who curries favors of capitalists and politicians in order to gain power and the cheap and fulsome praise of cheaper and more fulsome newspapers."[90] Also characteristic of the journal was a supermilitancy, surpassing Goldman in its rhetorical support of violence. An editorial asked women to send rifles instead of messages of solidarity to striking miners in Colorado.[91] It was an article in the July issue entitled "A Defense of Assassination" that led the Post Office to declare the journal unmailable, although when Sanger was indicted, two counts of obscenity were also brought against her.[92]

The Woman Rebel did not represent a tendency in American feminism or socialism at this time. It was, rather, a singular, unrepeated attempt by Sanger to combine her IWW-influenced commitment to direct action with her deepened feminism and sense of the radical potential of birth control. At any rate, it did not last long—and its sudden demise may well have been in part Sanger's intention. She claimed that she wanted to be arrested in order to force a legal definition of "obscenity."[93] Or, she may have recognized the journal's lack of political viability.

Nevertheless, *The Woman Rebel* had given Sanger space and stimulus for further political exploration. She was able to correspond with leading European and American feminists in the name of a publication; she discovered the pro–birth control tradition among many quasi-religious groups such as spiritualists and theosophists. She coined the term "birth control." When prevented from mailing the journal, Sanger drafted a detailed birth control pamphlet, *Family Limitation*, and got IWW member Bill Shatoff to print a hundred thousand copies. She got a few hundred dollars to pay for it from a free-speech lawyer who administered a fund left by Edward Bond Foote (Sanger called him "A certain Dr. Foote," again illustrating her ignorance of the American birth control tradition).[94] She arranged for *Family Limitation* to be sent out by IWW comrades on receipt of a prearranged signal from her, thereby releasing the provocative information it contained after she was already in jail.[95] This would make an effective climax to her work, for *The Woman Rebel* was never able to print actual contraceptive information. The pamphlet not only recommended and explained a variety of contraceptive methods—douches, condoms, pessaries, sponges, and vaginal suppositories—but even gave a suggestion for an abortifacient. While promising that birth control would make abortion unnecessary, Sanger nevertheless defended women's rights to abortion, something she was unable to do at any later time. In this period her attitude toward sexual issues was consistent with her general militance. Still using IWW anarcho-syndicalist rhetoric, she wrote that "the working class can use direct action by refusing to supply the market with children to be exploited, by refusing to populate the earth with slaves."[96]

When her case came to trial, however, Sanger changed her strategy. Fearing that she would lose publicity because of the dominance of war news, and perhaps also that juries would be unsympathetic at this time, she decided to flee, traveling to London via Canada under an assumed name.[97] In the United States the illegal pamphlets were mailed out as she had planned. With them went a letter asking that the pamphlets be passed on to "poor working men and women who are overburdened with large families. . . . Thousands of women in the cotton states bearing twelve to sixteen children request me to send them this pamphlet. Thousands of women facing the tortures of abortion . . . Three hundred thousand mothers who lose their babies every year from poverty and neglect . . . Are the cries of these women to be stifled? Are the old archaic laws to be respected above motherhood, womanhood! The mothers of America answer no. The women of America answer no!"[98]

Sanger remained in Europe from October 1914 to October 1915. There she further studied the history, philosophy, technology, and practice of birth control, working in archives and libraries and visiting clinics and doctors in Holland, France, and England. Havelock Ellis directed and encouraged her work in a relationship made more intense and nourishing to her because it was a love affair.[99] Ellis had sympathy for neither revolution nor the working class. His influence in diminishing Sanger's attraction to the revolutionary Left was communicated to her not only through his political views but also through the life-style and charm of the British neo-Malthusians she met through him.[100] After she returned to the United States, she never resumed the revolutionary posture she had held beforehand. In this second trip to Europe, the basic outlines of Sanger's entire future work took shape. She committed herself to birth control as a single issue. She would offer feminist or pro-working-class arguments for birth control when they were helpful, along with many other arguments, but she never again saw her identity as mainly within a socialist, or even a generally radical, movement. For all its rhetoric, *The Woman Rebel* had already been a step away from the radical community.

Sanger's reputed radicalism hereafter became more specifically the sex radicalism she learned from Ellis and his circle. This was not the hedonistic sex-for-enjoyment ideology of the mid-twentieth century. Sanger's sexual views always remained within the romantic school of thought that had reached her from the European sex radicals and American free-lovers. Her orientation was always to treat sexual activity as a form of communication, expressing love through extrasensory impulses. In their desire to rescue sexuality from its degraded reputation under the reign of prudery, Sanger and her sex-romantic followers virtually reversed the Victorian view of sexuality: from an animal passion it became a spiritual one, at least potentially. There were degrees of development of one's sexual nature that were presumably determined by more than technical expertise. The stages of development represented depth of communication and emotional intensity, which in turn reflected men's consideration of women. (This consideration was necessary because Sanger did not argue for women's equal assertiveness in sexual encounters.)

In Sanger's own sex manual, published in 1926, she entitled intercourse "sex communion," the use of a religious term revealing her tendency to spiritualize the sexual act: "At the flight, body, mind and soul are brought together into the closest unity. 'No more are they twain, but one flesh,' in the words of the Bible." She went on to write that "sex-communion should be considered as a true union of souls, not merely a physical function for the momentary relief of the sexual organs. Unless the psychic and spiritual desires are fulfilled, the relationship has been woefully deficient and the participants degraded and dissatisfied. . . . the sexual embrace not only satisfies but elevates both participants. The physical demands are harnessed for the expression of love."[101] Sanger's work in sex education helped to alleviate the guilt of married couples and to give women an ideology with which to encourage men to be considerate and proceed more slowly. Still, her type of sex education did not challenge the conventional Victorian structure of sex relations, which were confined to the nuclear family and rested on male assertiveness and female passivity.

Sanger's politics tended not toward a socialist, and certainly not toward a Marxist, feminism but rather toward a mystique about womanliness, the successor to nineteenth-century feminist notions of the moral superiority of women (a precursor of what came to be known in the 1970s as "cultural feminism").[102] Sanger believed in the "feminine spirit," the motive power of woman's nature. It was this spirit, coming from within, rather than social relations that drove women to revolt.[103] She thought of women as fundamentally different from men.

A Grassroots Movement

Meanwhile, before Sanger returned to the United States, a decentralized birth control movement appeared in the eastern, midwestern and western parts of the country. It was stimulated by word of Sanger's indictment, which was carried in newspapers in such distant places as Pittsfield, Massachusetts, and Reno, Nevada. Some of these papers described Sanger as an IWW editor. Local socialist groups were distributing Sanger's and other birth control leaflets.[104] Local birth control organizations were established in several places in 1915 before Sanger's return and her first speaking tour.[105] These came out of women's Socialist party groups and IWW locals. In many places people had been introduced by Goldman to Sanger's pamphlet, Sanger's name, and sometimes *The Woman Rebel*, just as Goldman would later raise money for Sanger's defense on her speaking tours.[106] Elizabeth Gurley Flynn spoke about birth control in the Northwest and pledged local IWW and other anarchist support if Sanger would go on a speaking tour there.[107] Socialists saw Sanger as one of their own and flooded her with letters of support and, inevitably, advice. Eugene V. Debs was one of the first to write, promising the support of a "pretty good-sized bunch of revolutionists."[108] Goldman, in her bossy way, wanted to take Sanger under her wing, not only recommending a tactical plan for Sanger's trial, but suggesting that Sanger "hold out until I come back the 23rd of this month. Then go away with me for 2 weeks to Lakewood or some place . . . we'd both gain much and I would help you find yourself."[109] Others, such as Kate Richards O'Hare, Rose

Pastor Stokes, Georgia Kotsch, Caroline Nelson, Rockwell Kent, Alexander Berkman, William J. Robinson, Jessie Ashley, and many lesser-known socialist organizers, sent her messages of support and spoke on her behalf.[110] Liberals supported her too: for example, *The New Republic* published several editorials in her favor after March 1915.[111] In May 1915, birth control supporters held a large meeting at the New York Academy of Medicine to urge the establishment of public birth control clinics, and many prominent reformers spoke there.[112] But in March 1915, when a group of liberals organized the National Birth Control League (NBCL)—which, despite its name, was never more than a New York City group—they would not support Sanger or any law-defying tactics. (They also excluded Goldman and other radicals.)[113] To the end of 1915 at least, those who supported Sanger and engaged in local birth control organizing everywhere except New York City were socialists.

In September 1915, Margaret Sanger's estranged husband, William, was tried for distributing her *Family Limitation* pamphlet. He had been entrapped by a Post Office agent who requested a copy[114] and was convicted in a dramatic trial in which he defended himself. The audience was filled with radicals, who shouted at the judge until he ordered the police to clear the courtroom. Messages of support came from many parts of the country. From Portland, Oregon, a strong IWW city and a site of birth control fervor, came a handwritten petition:

1. A woman has the right to control her own body even to the extent of deciding when she will become a mother.
2. Unwelcome or unfit children ought not to be born into the world.
3. Motherhood is dignified and noble only when it is desired and a joy. . . .
4. Scientific knowledge of sex-physiology can never be classified as impure or obscene. Those who do so classify it, proclaim only the impurity of their own minds.

The first signer added after his name: "The industrial system which needs children as food for powder or factories may desire unlimited propagation, but the masses who suffer in poverty have no right to add sufferers to the already too many competing for bread."[115] In these phrases were summarized fifty years of different birth control arguments as they had reached the grass roots in the United States: women's rights, hereditarian social thought, social purity transformed by a faith in science and human dignity, and neo-Malthusianism. It was such communications that made William Sanger believe his trial a great success, making "birth control a household word."[116] The responses that flowed in to the Sangers showed that the concept of birth control, if not the term, was already widely known and supported. It was as if people had been waiting for a leader to ask them for help.

Margaret Sanger returned from London soon after her husband's trial. Seeking support for the trial she herself faced, she found that her husband's confrontational conduct at his trial had aroused many strong opinions as to how she should conduct her own. The flurry of letters offering to tell her how to run the trial emerged from gallant but male chauvinist assumptions that she was in need of help. Most of her friends urged her not to follow her husband's example (pleading not guilty and acting as his own lawyer) but to plead guilty and use a lawyer.[117] Goldman begged her to resist those counsels, branding that line of defense cowardly.[118] One of her medical "supporters" preached to her about her duty to her children, which raised Goldman's ire, if not Sanger's.[119] In the end, Sanger stood firm in her plan to plead not guilty.

But Sanger also developed her own tactics. Her public relations activities in the fall of 1915 combined militance with shrewd politics. She held a "distinguished guests only" dinner at the Brevoort Hotel and in her speech gave an apologia for her militant tactics, explaining that her methods had been unorthodox merely to secure publicity.[120] Instead of devoting time to preparing her defense, she worked on publicity; and the steady growth of public support led to the government's dismissal of the charges against her on February 18, 1916.[121] On April 1, Sanger left for a three-and-a-half month speaking tour across the country. By its conclusion she was nationally famous. Newspaper coverage of her speeches was copious and often enthusiastic. Her occasional misadventures were usually transformed into successes: refused halls in Akron and Chicago, arrested and jailed in Portland, Oregon, and locked out in St. Louis due to pressure by the Catholic Church, she responded like a seasoned political campaigner, turning always from defense to offense. She made birth control a free speech as well as a sexual freedom issue and won support from important liberal civil libertarians.[122] She also sought to establish effective coalitions of liberal and radical groups for birth control.

At this time the grassroots work for birth control was being done by Leftists. In Cleveland, the first major city to organize a birth control group and a place where the birth control campaign was later to be especially successful,[123] workers' groups sponsored Sanger's tremendously successful speeches and led the birth control movement. In St. Paul, the Women's Socialist Club led that city's birth control movement.[124] Agnes Inglis, a socialist activist, organized a group in Ann Arbor, Michigan.[125] Even the relatively staid Massachusetts Birth Control League was led by socialists.[126] In small towns as well as big cities, socialists were organizing for birth control.[127] Although Sanger varied her appeals to particular audiences, she made several sharp attacks on the conservatism of privileged groups. When the snobbish Chicago Women's Club canceled her speaking engagement, she attacked it, saying she did not care to speak to a "sophisticated" audience anyway. "I want to talk to the women of the stock yards, the women of the factories—they are the victims of a system or lack of system that cries out for corrections. I am interested in birth control among working women chiefly."[128]

By 1916, the birth control movement in the United States was radical and large. Birth control as a political demand had demonstrated an ability to involve not only educated but also working-class women in a participatory social movement. Elizabeth Gurley Flynn wrote to Sanger that she had found everywhere in the country the "greatest possible interest" in birth control and that "one girl told me the women in the stockyards District [Chicago] kissed her hands when she distributed [Sanger's birth control pamphlet]."[129] Flynn recalled that when she visited a Tampa, Florida, cigar factory in 1913 she had observed *el lector*[130] reading aloud to the Spanish-speaking workers from a pamphlet on birth control.[131] Letters from women all over the country came pouring in not only to Sanger but also to others who were identified in newspapers as birth control activists, letters asking for contraceptive information and thanking them for their efforts. Often the writers were fearful: "I nearly had nervous prostration after I had mailed you my letter asking for that 'information.'"[132] "Please send me one of your Papers on birth control, I have had seven children and cannot afford any more. Please don't give my name to the Papers."[133] They poured out the difficulties of their lives, with their most intimate sexual problems and most externally caused economic problems intermingled—as they indeed always are in real life.

"I was married at the age of eighteen. Now I am married for seven years and I have four children. . . . I am a little over twenty-four and already skinny, yellow and so funny looking and I want to hold my husband's love. . . . He tried to help me but somehow I got caught anyway and a baby came. We didn't have any money to get rid of it and now when I look on her little innocent, red face I am glad I didn't kill it. . . . When you was in Chicago I wanted to go to see you but I had no nice clothes and I knew I would make you feel ashamed if I went dressed shabbily."

"I have six children, am forty-one years old . . . have reason to believe my husband has a venereal disease. . . . To all of my pleadings my husband turns a deaf ear. He beats me, curses me and deserts us for weeks at a time when I refuse intercourse. . . . The place we call home is only a hovel. . . . I must live with him to get his support until my youngest children are older (youngest is eighteen months . . .) but to live with him I must indulge him sexually and whatever protection I get I must provide myself."[134]

Many of the letters expressed exasperation at the class injustice behind the fact that they were deprived of birth control information: "Tell me how it is the wealthier class of people can get information like that and those that really need it, can't?"[135] Many others plunged immediately into political action, like Mrs. Lulu MacClure Clarke of St. Louis, who wrote to Sanger:

> I have been through suffrage wrangles all my adult life, in backwoods com-
> munities and [among] the vicious of a city and I know how very chivalrous
> indeed men can be when any new freedom is asked for by women, and this is
> harder for them to swallow. . . . I cannot help financially, altho I would like to.
> We are just working people, but I am writing to various friends about it and
> tonight I mailed a letter to the Post-Dispatch of my city. . . . But even if wom-
> en cant help much, don't know how to speak in public or write for the press,
> etc., yet they are awakening up all over the nation and waiting for someone to
> lead the way. I think—in fact, I know—there is a well-spring of gratitude to
> you—that they think you are fighting for them and they wait hoping and pray-
> ing. . . . I am glad you have a husband who is a help and not a hindrance. Tell
> him I send him my heartiest goodwill and best wishes. If there is anything that
> you think I could do, please let me know. And oh, Please dont give up or get
> discouraged.[136]

Direct Action

Not only was there a potentially large movement here, but its proponents were ready for action. What they wanted personally, the *minimum* demand, was to be given information in defiance of the law. Beyond that, women in many places quickly moved to a strategy that logically followed—namely, opening illegal birth control clinics to share that illegal information with others. There was a practical reason for this: the best contraceptive—a vaginal diaphragm—required a private fitting. Sanger was already convinced of the efficacy of "direct action." She gained support for this plan on her national tour.[137] In many ways that tour was as much a learning experience for her as a teaching experience for her audience. In Ann Arbor, Inglis had a de facto clinic functioning before Sanger returned to New York.[138] In St. Paul, socialist women announced plans for a clinic in June.[139] Sanger herself dreamed of a "glorious 'chain' of clinics" throughout the country.[140]

Returning to New York City in July 1916, Sanger organized a clinic of her own in the Brownsville section of Brooklyn. Brownsville was then a Jewish and Italian immigrant neighborhood, an extremely poor slum. Sanger worked with her sister, Ethel Byrne, also a nurse, and Fania Mindell, whom Sanger had recruited in Chicago. The three women rented an apartment and gave out to every family in the district a handbill printed in English, Yiddish, and Italian. They were not prepared to fit women with contraceptives but only to "give the principles of contraception, show a cervical pessary to the women, explain that if they had had two children they should have one size and if more a larger one."[141] Women were lined up outside when the clinic opened on October 16, and as many Catholics came as Jews. When Sanger asked one Catholic woman what she would say to the priest at confession, the woman replied, "'It's none of his business. My husband has a weak heart and works only four days a week. He gets twelve dollars, and we can barely live on it now. We have enough children.'"[142] Most of the neighbors were friendly and supportive. The baker gave them free doughnuts and the landlady brought them tea. After nine days the clinic had 464 case histories of women on file.[143]

Then, inevitably, one of the patients turned out to be a policewoman. She seemed prosperous, which made Fania Mindell suspect her, but she was not turned away. The next day the woman returned as Officer Margaret White-hurst, arrested Sanger, Byrne, and Mindell, and confiscated all the equipment and case histories. Tried separately, Byrne was sentenced to thirty days on Blackwell's Island and immediately announced her intention to go on a hunger strike, which British suffragists were making into an international symbol of feminist resistance. Like the British suffragists, Byrne was force-fed via tubes through the nose; the lack of adequate nutrition and the brutality of the force-feeding left her so weakened that she required a year to recuperate.[144] At Sanger's trial, women who had visited the clinic were called to testify for the prosecution. Although they ensured her conviction by giving evidence that they had indeed received contraceptive advice without medical indication, politically they helped the birth control cause by their testimonials to the misery of involuntary pregnancy.[145] Sanger also was sentenced to thirty days on Blackwell's Island but conducted herself cooperatively. When she was released on March 6, her friends met her singing "The Marseillaise."[146] (Mindell's conviction was overturned on appeal.)[147]

During this period, many activists were arrested and jailed for their birth control activities—at least twenty besides Sanger on federal charges alone. Carlo Tresca, an Italian American anarchist, was sentenced to a year and a day for advertising a book called *L'Arte di non fare i figli* (The art of not making children) in his radical labor paper *Il Martello*. (American Civil Liberties Union intervention got his sentence commuted after he served just four months.)[148] Emma Goldman was also jailed for giving out contraceptive information. There was, of course, class injustice in arrest, convictions, and sentences.[149] Jessie Ashley, Ida Rauh Eastman, Bolton Hall, and Rose Pastor Stokes gave out birth control pamphlets publicly at mass meetings at Carnegie Hall; although Ashley, Eastman, and Hall were arrested, Stokes—a millionaire's wife—was not.[150] Carl Rave, an IWW longshoreman, was jailed in San Mateo, California, for three months for selling Sanger's *Family Limitation*. He pointed out that Professor Holmes of the University of California (probably a eugenist) proclaimed the need for compulsory birth control on the front page of the papers with impunity.[151] Others took risks as abortionists, though none was prosecuted on such charges. In addition to Antoinette Konikow, a Boston physician, these included Dr. Marie Equi in Portland, Oregon, a socialist (and later lover of Elizabeth Gurley Flynn) who later served ten months in San Quentin for making an anticonscription speech.

Police and prison guards were often hostile and violent toward birth control advocates, especially the women, for their support of what seemed to violate every male fantasy about what women should be like. The detective arresting Agnes Smedley in 1918 told her that "he wished he had me in the south; that there 'I would be strung up to the first lamp post'; I would be lynched. I tried to tell him that he was on the wrong side of the trenches," Smedley recalled, but he only threatened her again.[152]

Legal persecution always promoted publicity but sometimes also produced concrete victories. Birth control prisoners often propagandized their sister prisoners. Smedley wrote from the Tombs (a New York City prison) that "Kitty, Mollie Steiner, and I have wonderful meetings when we can dodge in some corner or hall. Kitty is turning the place into a birth-control branch. And she has held a meeting. And her friends are writing out demanding that their parents and friends vote Socialism!"[153]

Commitment to action was strong among these birth controllers. True, ideology mattered to them. As socialists, they believed that working-class strength was the key to political progress. As feminists, they wanted the equality of women. As socialist feminists, they believed that the subjugation of women supported capitalism directly by creating profit and indirectly by depriving the socialist movement of half its potential constituency and allowed socialist men to cling to privileges that corrupted. But they wanted most urgently to improve the lives of poor people in the present and did not try to fob them off with promises of a postrevolutionary paradise. Their task in trying to reach working-class women was made more difficult by their own class origins. Most of the leadership of this movement came from prosperous, white professional, even capitalist, backgrounds. Their superior confidence and articulateness often made them better talkers than listeners. But their humanitarianism, their desire to eliminate material misery, was shared by those among them of "lower" origins—such as Stokes, Goldman, Equi, and Sanger. It was also a conscious tactical choice, a rejection of the myth that greater misery makes workers more revolutionary.

Similarly, the plan to organize politically on an issue so private and so removed from industrial production was a choice, based on experience. Sanger had been struck by the strongly positive reaction among socialist constituencies to her writing and speaking on sexual hygiene. Elizabeth Gurley Flynn and Ella Reeve Bloor had worked with women, sometimes women who were not wage earners themselves but workers' wives, in many strike situations and had perceived the deep connections between family support and workers' militancy. William J. Robinson had been receiving for over a decade the kind of personal letters that began flooding in to Sanger and the birth control organizations after 1915—letters attesting to the mutually reinforcing nature of sexual, economic, and political helplessness. A systematic evaluation of five thousand such letters sent to Sanger after the publication of her book *Woman and the New Race* in 1920 showed that they were overwhelmingly from working-class and poor women. The most common occupation given for husbands was "laborer," the most common salary was fifteen dollars per week. One-third of the women were themselves wage earners, as compared to the overall national average of 23 percent in 1920. Eighty percent of the writers had married before the age of twenty and averaged five children.[154] These organizers thought birth control could improve the economic situations and family stability of the poor and give women in particular more free choice and greater alternatives. Focusing on the connection between the sexual and economic oppression of working-class women was a strategy for organizing.

Socialist feminist birth controllers in the prewar years developed educational propaganda that used birth control as a political issue. For example, Rose Pastor Stokes wrote a didactic script, "Shall the Parents Decide?," that tried to capture the revolutionary impact birth control could have. In it a factory owner, who has already attacked birth control for its threat to deprive him of cheap labor, fires his worker, Mrs. Jones, for coming in late. Mrs. Jones is burdened with many children to take care of and was late because of her grief over the death of one of her children. Helen, another worker in the plant, is incensed at the firing and organizes a wildcat strike to demand Mrs. Jones's job back. The owner orders his friend the police chief to arrest Helen, but Helen sneaks out a back door, with the help of her mother, because she is scheduled to speak at a birth control rally. Accidentally meeting the owner's ex-mistress, Helen offers her emotional support and a political analysis of her unhappy position. When the factory owner tries to buy off his mistress with money, she gives it to Helen for her bail.[155] These themes—women's solidarity and women's sexual exploitation—were both important in the writings of many of these early birth controllers. Sanger had written a short story in 1912, before becoming a birth control advocate, about a young nurse whose first employer tries to rape her. It concludes with a plea for working girls to stick together and defend one another.[156]

From their earliest efforts, however, these organizers learned that the task before them would not be easy. As early as June 1915 Caroline Nelson spelled out in a letter to Sanger the difficulties she had already encountered:

It seems strange, but it is almost impossible to interest the workers in this . . . So that our League here consists mostly of professional people. . . . I myself think that if the Leagues are ever to amount to anything, they must send trained nurses into the workers' districts, who speak the language of the district, whatever that may be. . . . I still hold that it would be beneficial to change the name. You know the workers are so afraid of being suspected of immorality, and they love the word—Moral—with an affection worthy of something better than it stands for today. That is why I cling to the name of—New Moral. After all, what we must do is to catch the worker's wife and daughter. . . . Dilettante Birth Control Leagues may help as the workers take their morals from the upper class, but they will not go far, they will not reach down to the bottom. . . . Yes, dear Margaret, this is the mere beginning of working women to do our work. The working men have gone around in a vicious circle, until today they are engaged in the very lawful occupation of killing each other, and where they are not killing each other they are running around begging for a job to feed their starved families. All this, after seventy-five years of revolutionary propaganda and scientific economy and academic discussion that the working woman had [no] interest in, chiefly because they were not practical, and did not touch her life, and the radical woman is chiefly an echo of the radical man, even in the sex question.[157]

Nelson's frank appraisal of the difficulties did not diminish her commitment. Indeed, her analysis led to the conclusion that there was no choice but to continue to fight for birth control, for she seemed convinced that unless working-class women could be aroused to leadership the entire cause of socialism would be doomed. Nelson had developed in her thinking from two years previously when she still saw birth control primarily in socialist neo-Malthusian terms: the rich have birth control but try to keep it from the working class.[158] By 1915 she saw birth control not merely as an economic device but as fundamental to women's liberation. Thus, like many other birth control activists, and despite membership in the Socialist party, she also looked to the woman suffrage movement for approval and support of her work. Though successful to an extent—the first to be interested in birth control did indeed come from the ranks of the SP and even of the National American Woman Suffrage Association—she also met with disapproval and even opposition from both sources.

Opposition and Setbacks

Suffragists and antifeminist socialists often disapproved of birth control, usually for very different reasons, occasionally for similar ones. Their common reasons expressed the deepest fears regarding the social implications of birth control.

Many suffragists were simply timid. In 1915, Sanger and Elsie Clews Parsons tried and failed to get fifty well-known women to state publicly that they not only believed in birth control but practiced it. "I was told to wait," Sanger said, "until we got the vote, I was told to wait until I became better known."[159] Some suffragists accepted race-suicide fears and worried about the dysgenic effects of birth control. Often they clung to the view that motherhood was a woman's vital source of dignity in a world that all too often denied it to her. In 1917 Anna May Wood, president of the D.C. Federation of Women's Clubs, declared that she opposed birth control because "motherhood glorifies Womanhood and . . . any teaching that would tend to take from each woman the desire for motherhood is not ennobling the race."[160] Others thought contraception would destroy the family. "Men no longer feel the 'urge' to marriage," wrote Dr. Eliza Mosher, editor of the *Medical Woman's Journal*, in 1925. "They can get on without wife and home and children, with much less expense and with all sexual gratifications desired without untoward consequences, and this largely through birth control education. . . . contraceptives are carried about, even by some high school boys and girls, just as they carry 'hip flasks.'"[161] Suffragists also feared sexual promiscuity, often for women' sake. They believed that marriage and monogamy were a woman's hard-won protection against the merciless selfishness of men. They were in favor of the voluntary motherhood principle, of course, but suspicious of contraception. They clung to notions that the human race had become oversexed, that sexual intercourse ought to be for reproduction, and that too much sexual activity was physically and spiritually weakening. The characteristic nineteenth-century suspicion of sexual pleasure itself shone through sometimes, as in this letter from a California feminist, Alice Park. She had just finished reading a sex book recommended by Mary Ware Dennett of the Voluntary Parenthood League (VPL), which succeeded the NBCL, and was furious:

> . . . of all the androcentric-inherited bias and self-opinionated pronouncements—this is the very top notch. Sex books are most of them in this class. But they do tend to move along from the dark ages to a degree. . . . I am always expecting a good one to be born. Intercourse every night and morning and sometimes noon—with satisfaction to both parties—PRAISED. Handling the clitoris—advised. Intercourse to advanced years hoped for—benefits recited. Intercourse in pregnancy—frequent etc. Really I can't remember in Forel or any other author—even the much quoted Martin Luther—anything approaching this. . . . it will certainly be liked by those whose wish is father to the thought of more and more intercourse until life would consist of nothing else.[162]

No doubt many older feminists shared these attitudes. But for others a commitment to women's rights made them reluctant to reject the birth control movement entirely. Park continued to argue for inserting into some VPL literature that "intercourse may be wisely and healthily limited."[163] Carrie Chapman Catt declined to give her name as a sponsor to the American Birth Control League (Sanger's organization, founded in 1921) but wanted to be sure that Sanger understood the ambivalence of her position:

> . . . pleased be assured that I am no opponent even though I do not stand by your side. . . . in my judgement you claim too much as the result of one thing. Most reformers do that. Your reform is too narrow to appeal to me and too sordid. When the advocacy of contraception is combined with as strong a propaganda for continence (not to prevent conception but in the interest of common decency), it will find me a more willing sponsor. That is, a million years of male control over the sustenance of women has made them sex slaves, which has produced two results: an oversexualizing of women and an oversexualizing of men. . . . There will come some gains even from the program you advocate—and some increase in immorality through safety. The gains will slightly overtop the losses however, so I am no enemy of you and yours.[164]

While Catt was repeating what Charlotte Perkins Gilman had written twenty years earlier, Gilman herself was defending her views against new kinds of attacks—from the New Morality spokespeople. She argued that it was not "Puritanism" to say that gluttony was unhealthy, in sex as in other indulgences. And she was suspicious of contraception: "While men talk of sex, they mean only intercourse; for a woman it means the whole process of reproduction, love and mating."[165] Gilman continued to view the ideology of sexual freedom as merely a renovation of male supremacy. What she had witnessed of the sexual revolution in practice bore out her fears. She was not arguing that sexual "liberation" was an exploitive male conspiracy but only that social power was indivisible, and unless it was shared among women and men in all areas, men would simply weave individual reforms into the fabric of sexism. Freud was popular, she charged, because he justified and legitimized man's "misuse of the female. . . . It was natural enough that the mind of man should evolve a philosophy of sex calculated to meet his desires."[166] Still, Gilman could not, any more than Catt, reject the birth control demand entirely. For Gilman it was always highest priority to increase the range of women's choice. She consistently defended legalized birth control; and in 1932, at the age of seventy-two, she testified for it before Congress.[167] Her persistent fears of sexual permissiveness were founded not on timidity but on an insightful assessment of the continuing general suppression of women. What had changed in the society that made these attitudes now seem to be cranky, old-fashioned prudery?

The fact is that very little had changed. More women were in the work force, receiving their own pay envelopes, but they were still underpaid and forced into the worst jobs. They had won the vote, in the middle of the birth control agitation, just as many socialist feminist women had concluded that it would give them little real power anyway. What seems odd, in fact, is that so many feminists of sexual liberation persuasion had somehow imagined that the assertion of female sexuality could erase deeply rooted male supremacy in the culture and in the economy. Did they believe that power relations ceased to exist in beds, that men shed their culturally determined attitudes and expectations at the bedroom door? Even the most socialist of these birth controllers, those who well understood that women's powerlessness was the product of a total economic and social discrimination, failed to recognize the infiltration of sexism into sex itself. They thought of the risks of sexual intercourse in terms of its consequences—involuntary pregnancy, venereal disease, the physical and economic dependency of pregnant women—but forgot the risks of sexual intercourse itself. A classic argument of the nineteenth-century feminists had been that in marriage women sold themselves, as sexual as well as house servants, in return for security and that, consequently, withholding sexual favors was one of the few powers that women had, a form of strike. The logic of sexual liberation made such withholding reprehensible, even selfish. The provision of good contraception often made the situation even more difficult for women, depriving them of an excuse for saying no. There was nothing inherent in sexual freedom that challenged the double standard, and, in fact, the double standard was easily adapted to allow the manipulation of women in new ways.

The socialist feminist birth controllers of the second decade of the early twentieth century would have readily admitted that they had barely scratched the surface toward uprooting male supremacy. The most likely explanation for their inconsistency is that they believed that involuntary pregnancy and sexual repression were not symptoms but causes of women's subjection. They understood women to be only victims. They did not understand that women's resistance as well as men's pressure had created the sexual and family system that was now being transformed and that many women as well as men had cause to fear and regret that transformation. Carrie Chapman Catt was right— they claimed too much as the result of one thing. It is not necessary to accept Gilman's view that humanity had become oversexed in order to question whether sexual reform alone could fundamentally change women's status.

Within the socialist movement, objections to birth control came from a different source. Many socialists found any concentration on women's problems dangerous because it deflected attention from the main issue of the class struggle, namely, wage slavery. Although claiming that capitalism was the cause of the "sex problem"—by which they meant both sex inequality and sexual immorality—many socialists nevertheless did not think that political agitation around sexual issues could effectively attack capitalism. Socialism would take care of these problems after the revolution. Sanger complained that socialists were forever telling her to wait, just as the feminists had: "'Wait until women have more education. Wait until we secure equal distribution of wealth.' Wait for this and wait for that. Wait! Wait! Wait!"[168] Antoinette Konikow challenged this attitude too: "Socialists cannot persist in sitting on the fence wisely and monotonously repeating: 'Socialism will change that.' They must go ahead and begin to shift things, ready for the change, or someone else will take their place in the onward movement of the world as far as the sex question is concerned."[169] By contrast, Rose Pastor Stokes, who became a communist in the 1920s as Sanger became a liberal reformer, adopted the "wait until the revolution" view after World War I. She drafted a letter to Sanger in 1925:

> At this time, when the greatest of all wars is preparing, when the contending capitalist groups will need cannon-fodder as never before in their destructive history, it is to my mind certain that no amount of agitation and earnest effort will force the desired [birth control] legislation upon the capitalist governments.
>   It is my conviction that by working for the abolition of capitalism, for the establishment of Soviet Governments we bring nearer the triumph of the [birth control] cause. . . . Those Soviet Governments would themselves hasten to pass B.C. legislation (as Russia is doing today) in the interests of the race and the mothers of the race.[170]

It was not that socialists did not care about women's liberation. Although most SP members supported the principle of voluntary motherhood, many believed that under socialism, prosperity would make women want to have as many children as came naturally. At the same time they supported the division of labor that made women solely responsible for reproduction and men solely responsible for production. In these views they were at one with the liberal feminists who wanted to retain the "sacredness" of motherhood and who believed that industrialism was destroying it. The socialists' version of this longing for an imaginary preindustrial family paradise was based on the Marxian tenet that capitalism and the bourgeoisie had destroyed the family. They disavowed projects for communal living and other family alterations that would have freed women to leave their homes. As the SP leader and Wisconsin congressman Victor Berger summarized this viewpoint, under socialism "women will not only be restored to the home, but enabled to *form* a home."[171] Sanger complained about such views after a difficult confrontation with some Fresno socialist men: ". . . the fact that women shall not desire to be breeders under a Socialist Republic no more than she wants to be today is difficult for them to see. There is harder work to do among the 'dyed in the wool' radical than with the average person. He has Marxian blinders on his eyes and will not see."[172]

Some socialists also clung to sex-hating attitudes. The following letter to Rose Pastor Stokes in 1916, when she was a birth control activist, from New York Socialist party comrades is typical of that view:

> We have full confidence in your sincerity and devotion to the cause of freedom, but, Dear Comrade, we consider it a waste of time and energy on such a tom-fullary [*sic*] as the B.C.L. venture. . . . We believe in one standard of morality, but, we are not willing to bring down the females to that low standard that men set, but we do want to help pull the men to the women's standard, but, again the B.C.L. propaganda can not and will not do. You know or you ought to know that, the generative organs as well as any other organ of the human body has its own particular function to perform, and that of the generative organ in particular is for perpetuation, and nothing else. . . . We hold . . . that the desire of sexual interrelation is the unconscious desire for "parenthood and perpetuation," and rather than destroy the fruit of that unconscious desire, it would be more expedient to deny one self that very desire.[173]

When Sanger published her sex hygiene articles in the *New York Call*, many readers protested. "I for one condemn the idea where a mother should show through the columns of a newspaper her nakedness to her children," Mrs. L.B. of Greenpoint, a Brooklyn neighborhood, wrote.[174] Caroline Nelson had met these attitudes since 1915: ". . . while they want to get the information in secret, they cannot discuss it in public without giggling and blushing and this holds good to our very learned radical men, or at least some of them. . . . I must say with great shame to our labor editors that the capitalist editors in many instances have been much more liberal and sensible on this question than they have, which shows that our class is not yet out of the woods of gullibility with its sewage minds, and sewage minds are not clear instruments of thinking."[175]

These antisexual attitudes were hard to separate from outright male chauvinism. Most socialists were not prepared to acknowledge the existence of sexism within the working class. They often disguised their defense of male privilege with criticisms of population control as a capitalist plot. One typical letter writer argued: "Will you kindly question yourself and see that it is better to relieve the poor than to bring more destruction. Naturally we all appreciate the fact that we would be free from having children, but it only brings a more adulterous [*sic*] generation and gives married women a freedom to wander more into the sin of the world."[176]

Some socialist leaders opposed birth control propaganda because they hoped that eschewing sexual radicalism would make their economic radicalism more palatable. That is, socialist economics combined with defense of family, home, and motherhood would presumably make a wider appeal to the American public. Here again, socialist tactical thinking was not so different from that of suffragists who also wished to avoid association with antifamily doctrines. Both socialism and suffragism had been charged with advocating free love in the late nineteenth and early twentieth centuries; both socialism and suffragism had defended themselves by condemning free love.[177]

The free-love charge was a constant thorn in the sides of birth controllers. Sanger was frequently accused of "free loveism" but always denied it.[178] Yet the origins of birth control as a women's movement *were* in free love. Some socialists not only recognized this but thought it best to accept that legacy, trying perhaps to redefine it. Those who took this view were inclined to the perception that the youth who were involved in sexual rebellion might be an important socialist constituency.[179] Others believed that refusing to face the necessity for fundamental change in family and sexual norms would ultimately betray the interests of women. Josephine Conger-Kaneko of the Socialist party argued that women and the whole party had to give up "bourgeois respectability" in order to make a thoroughgoing women's rights struggle.[180]

But most Socialist party members feared being forced back into isolation by attacks from the Right branding them as immoral. They felt this danger acutely now because changes in sexual behavior had made free love a real threat and because the sexual revolution meant increased sexual activity among women, which threatened to rob men not only of the pleasures of exclusive privilege but the security of women's dependency on marriage. Birth control was an easy focus for all this fear, and attacks from the Right were strong enough to prevent birth control from becoming an official program of either the Socialist party or any national women's rights organization.

At the same time, the socialist and women's rights movements weakened, and the political shift greatly affected the future course of birth control. The decline of the women's rights movement was, ironically, hastened by its one victory—namely, woman suffrage. The NAWSA had mobilized a powerful lobby, its work orchestrated by an excellent politician, Carrie Chapman Catt, and focused on the single issue of suffrage. But the narrowing focus of women's rights had diminished the movement's breadth and the victory then made some supporters doubt the need for further mobilization. The sexual revolution itself contributed to the conservative political mood, making it easy to malign publicly active women as unattractive and bitter. Greatly expanded commodity production and advertising appealed to women consumers as housewives, mothers, and beauty objects but rarely as citizens or workers. A false sense of prosperity also made it more unfashionable to be a malcontent.

Within the remnant women's organizations, the controversy over an equal rights amendment to the U.S. Constitution, introduced in Congress in 1923, pushed self-identified feminists farther into a minority corner, as the majority of progressive women activists opposed the amendment for fear of jeopardizing protective labor legislation for women. This conflict set up an apparent opposition between feminism and progressive labor reform.

Organized feminism was also weakened by antisocialist repression after the Great War. So virulent was the patriotic hysteria that any views critical of American society appeared disloyal. Many feminists and some socialists supported the war effort, but this did not help the reputation of their causes, especially since other feminists and socialists spoke against the war. Patriotism led to jingoism, not only against Germans but to some extent against all non-WASP immigrants. Many radicals, including Emma Goldman, were deported. Dr. William J. Robinson, a pacifist, was ostracized in his profession. Dr. Marie Equi was jailed. There were many local persecutions and even lynchings of antiwar radicals. Conservative men of power, long anxious for a tool to check the increasing strength of their enemies, stimulated and guided antiradical hysteria to a systematic and effective attack on socialist leaders and organizations.

Once under attack, the socialist movement could not respond effectively because it was divided by prowar versus antiwar politics. After November 1917, another division—based on attitudes toward the Russian Revolution—rapidly led to a final split. The Russian Revolution and civil war helped antisocialists brand socialist ideas as alien and violent. Meanwhile the postwar reaction against the Left escalated antifeminism. (For example, in 1923 representatives of the U.S. Army began to circulate the notorious "spider web" chart, a foreshadowing of McCarthyism purporting to illustrate a web of subversion that was encroaching on America. Feminists and progressive women's organizations were prominent on the chart.)

Thus, two separate factors pushed the birth control movement away from the organized Left: attacks on birth control by leftists and even some feminists and the independent decline of socialism and feminism. As a result the many socialists and feminists who were committed to birth control were unable to sustain a movement with the broad worldview and constituency of their movements of origin. Organizational connections with such groups as the Socialist party, the Industrial Workers of the World, the National American Woman Suffrage Association, the working women's suffrage leagues, and the Women's Trade Union League could have brought political experience and discipline into the birth control movement. Organizational estrangement from such groups and their constituencies made the task of building a broad-based coalition difficult.

Birth control as an issue also presented problems to new organizers. It required efforts to change the law, litigate test cases, strategize direct action and, not least, provide birth control information and devices. Outside of utopian communities and ill-fated workers' cooperatives, the American Left had had little experience with the provision of services through counterinstitutions such as birth control clinics. Fundamentally, birth control advocates were confused and ambivalent. They couldn't decide whether the practice of birth control or the illegal agitation for birth control would do the most to change society and, in the end, were unable to set their own priorities for political action.

PART 3

From Women's Rights
to Family Planning

9   *Professionalization*

The socialists and sex radicals who began the birth control movement before World War I were amateurs. With few exceptions, they had no professional or socially recognized expertise in sexology, public health, demography, or any related fields. (If they were professionals at anything, it was radical agitation.) They fought for birth control because they conceived it to be in their own interest but also because they believed it would reduce suffering and contribute to social justice. The intellectual work that had influenced them most in their birth control views was political philosophy and radical ethics. Birth control was, for them, pre-eminently a political and moral issue.

But after the war, the birth control cause changed rather rapidly. The local birth control leagues lost their momentum. Birth control became an increasingly centralized and professional campaign, commanded from New York City by Margaret Sanger's American Birth Control League (ABCL) and Mary Ware Dennett's Voluntary Parenthood League (VPL). The strategies that dominated—opening clinics and lobbying for legislation—required large sums of money, and the power of the wealthy in the organizations increased accordingly. People accustomed to working in respectable, even elegant, charity organizations joined the movement. Birth control leagues began to sponsor balls and expensive white-tie dinners. Simultaneously, the weakening of organized feminism and the Left deprived the birth control movement of leadership that might have created alternative tactics and strategies. The new constituency wanted to be rid of birth control's early associations with bohemianism, socialism, free love, and illegality. In efforts to break those associations, birth control organizers in the 1920s often condemned and publicly disassociated themselves from radicals.

The background to this new timidity was an anticommunist, anti-immigrant reaction that followed World War I, in part a reaction to the Russian Revolution, that took hold through the entrance of professionals into the birth control cause on a large scale. This was not the only important development in the birth control cause in the 1920s, but it was the single most influential one. But the professionals did not usually drive out grassroots activists (though this did happen in a few places); rather, they joined, even rescued, a cause that radicals had deserted.

The reason for this desertion was that the male-dominated Left saw birth control as a side issue rather than a central demand, as something requiring less than a fundamental change in society. Distinguishing between fundamental and superficial change, between revolution and reform, was characteristic of those influenced by a Marxist analysis of society. Marxists argued that certain aspects of social reality determined others, and the prevalent Marxist interpretation placed matters of sexual and reproductive relations in the "superstructure," determined, among other cultural phenomena, by the "base" (economic relations). Disagreement with this analysis lay at the center of the conflicts we have seen between feminist and nonfeminist socialists in the World War I era. Feminists were concluding that changes in sexual and reproduction patterns would in fact produce far-reaching changes, not only in family life, but also in social identity and consciousness and even in class composition, changes that could not be dismissed as "superstructure" and therefore not as primary or urgent.

The resistance of most male socialists to seeing birth control as a fundamental issue, along with the rigidity of the dominant socialist ideologies, led many feminists into coalitions with more-conservative reformers, for whom birth control was not part of a larger struggle for justice but a singular, self-contained cause. Doctors saw it as a health measure, and for them, human health was naturally a fundamental, not a superficial, condition of social progress. Eugenists' hereditarian views led them to consider reproduction the fundamental condition of social progress. Members of both groups, once converted to the birth control cause, devoted themselves to it with passion and perseverance.

Professionals entering the birth control movement brought with them a unique self-image and consciousness that made their reform work an integral part of their careers. They believed, by and large, that they worked not only to earn a living but simultaneously to help humanity and improve society. Since they saw the content of their work as well as its wage-earning function as important, they often combined paid work with volunteer activities as a unified whole. The professional attitude toward work was also a product of being paid not hourly wages but a weekly, monthly, or yearly salary; higher professionals often also had the privilege of determining their own work schedules. Furthermore, many of the professionals active in the birth control movement—and particularly doctors—were not wage workers at all but self-employed. For both kinds of professionals—employed and self-employed—participation in reform activities, if respectable enough, could add to their prestige.

The desire to make a contribution to civilization led many professionals to go beyond their places of employment to seek wider social influence. For many professionals, seeking political influence seemed to be a contribution rather than an indulgence because they believed society needed them. Especially in the early twentieth century, many professionals felt that their superior intelligence and education entitled them to a larger share of political leadership than their numbers in the population would automatically create in a democracy. Their ideal society was a meritocracy. Edward L. Thorndike, a eugenist educator, wrote in 1920 that "'the argument for democracy is not that it gives power to men without distinction, but that it gives greater freedom for ability and character to attain power.'"[1] Henry Goddard, who introduced intelligence test into the U.S. educational system, thought that democracy was "a method for arriving at a truly benevolent aristocracy."[2]

Behind this politics was the Progressive-era conviction that superior intelligence and education were coincident with superior political virtue. Professional psychologists in the 1920s were engaged in developing intelligence tests, and the bias of these tests was simultaneously hereditarian and meritocratic: the tests measured the ability to solve the kinds of problems urban professionals met with the kinds of solutions urban professionals would approve. Indeed, the Stanford-Binet test, for years the standard, classified intelligence in terms of what was "required" for five occupational groupings, with the professions placed in the top rank. (The others were semiprofessional work, skilled labor, semiskilled labor, and unskilled labor, in descending order.)[3]

Professionals did not assume that intellectual superiority came entirely from innate ability. On the contrary, they perceived that rigorous training, general knowledge, and tested methodologies had given them skills unavailable to the masses. They did not see their monopolization of this expertise and knowledge as special privilege because they were committed to equal opportunity. They did not usually perceive the effective social and economic barriers that kept most people from these opportunities. But they never doubted that their expertise and knowledge were useful guides for social policy. Because they had confidence in the universality, objectivity, and social value of the expertise they possessed, they did not hesitate to build professional organizations, institutions, and programs of self-licensing that excluded others from their privilege and influence.

The original social basis for the professionals' confidence in their uncorruptible dedication to rationality and expertise was their economic independence. The professions had traditionally been independent businesses, selling services, not hourly labor. By the twentieth century, professionals' sense of themselves as independent and therefore loyal only to self-defined standards of truth was a mystique held over from a previous era, no longer supported by reality. The professionals of the 1920s were literally a different class from the professionals of a century before. Not only was a decreasing proportion of them self-employed (by 1940 only 16 percent),[4] but all of them were increasingly dependent on funds, research direction, and political priorities set by corporate foundations and government. They helped transform the birth control movement from a radical, decentralized, unruly social movement to a reform that helped to stabilize, rationalize, and centralize foundation-directed social planning.

Professionals in the birth control movement sought to solve by objective study what had previously been ethical and political questions. In order to lend their support or even their names to a cause, they needed to be satisfied that it was honest, that its strategies were carefully developed, and that its tactics were appropriate to their dignity. They distrusted leaders who did not share their own values, skills, and social status. Their influence transformed birth control leagues from participatory, membership associations into staff organizations.

Had the professionals merely changed the structure and methods of the birth control movement their influence would not have been transformative. But structure and methods in social movements cannot be separated from goals. Despite their posture as reformers who sought changes for the benefit of the whole society, and particularly for the less fortunate in it, in fact professional men brought to the birth control movement their own political beliefs and social needs. Molded by different training and practice but also by class origin and individual experiences, these beliefs were by no means identical among professionals, even within one profession. But leading professionals did share a common set of values, with meritocracy at its root. Simply put, they believed that some individuals were more valuable to society than others. Whether environmentalists or hereditarians or both, they doubted that superior individuals were equally distributed within all classes and ethnic groups and believed that scientific study could determine where talent was most likely to occur. Birth control appealed to them as a means of lowering birth rates *selectively* among those groups less likely to produce babies of great merit.

Professionals also saw themselves as social benefactors, eager not just to legalize birth control but also to install it as social policy. Their commitment to individual liberty was tempered by their recognition that some people were wiser than others, that good social policy would not necessarily result from allowing each individual to make private decisions about such matters as birth control. Furthermore, many professionals (doctors, social workers, clergy, educators, and psychologists, for example) were placed by their jobs in position as moral authorities and teachers. Having accepted meritocratic values, they naturally taught them to others.

Many saw some of their clients as part of the social problems they desired to fix. Such a view strongly influenced the relationship of many doctors to their women patients, of social workers to their clients, and of ministers to their congregation. Eugenists particularly, with their analysis of social problems as hereditary, tended to see people as the problem. This view diverged sharply from a more democratic view that saw people as *having* problems, many of which were caused by social inequality; professionals often preferred to solve problems by restraining the autonomy of individuals in the interest of what they saw as wise social policy. Thus, for example, many doctors were willing to prescribe contraceptives for individual women whom they judged to be justified in limiting conceptions while opposing the general legalization of birth control. The professional's tendency was to trust his or her own judgment, even about others' lives. They feared that a democracy that allocated equal power to all, regardless of educational or intellectual qualifications, might produce unfortunate political decisions. Goddard wrote in 1920: "'The disturbing fear is that the masses—the seventy or even eighty-six million—will take matters into their own hands.'" Rather they should be directed by the four million of superior intelligence.[5] This elitism also reflected an effort to reassure themselves of their differences from the "masses." Indeed, professional reformers usually yearned for more influence and bemoaned the fact that they were not listened to. Their sense of the necessity of controlling the policies of a movement such as birth control came from both their sense of superior worth and their suspicion that they were being ignored.

These values were less common among women, even the wives of professionals. Although wives shared the class prestige and status of their husbands, they did not generally see themselves as contributing expertise to the birth control or any other social movement. They were essentially amateurs. The college education that most of them received did not automatically lead to a career but gave them skills and self-confidence, which they applied to running local and national birth control organizations. The minority of women who were practicing professionals shared, of course, many of the attitudes of their male peers—sometimes more strongly, because their sense of personal uniqueness and therefore merit was greater, and sometimes more tentatively, because of their identification with other women and their inferior status in their pro-

fessions. But on the whole the professionalization of the birth control movement produced a division of labor along sexual as well as class lines. The amateurs, mostly women, became the staff and organizers of the birth control
groups; the professionals, mostly men, functioned as directors and consultants,
influencing policy without sharing in the actual organizational work.

One group of professionals who joined and influenced the birth control
campaign was exclusively male: the clergy. Among Protestants and Jews a growing revisionism, antifundamentalist or Reform in orientation, allowed many
religious leaders to accept reform solutions to social problems and to view
moral decisions as individual matters. Churches with prosperous congrega-
tions most frequently endorsed birth control,[6] because of the more professional
orientation of their ministers and of their members. Perhaps the most common theme among pro–birth control religious leaders was concern for the
health of the family. In their role as counselors, ministers, and rabbis they were
aware of growing family instability. In clerical acceptance of freer sexuality and
contraception, a key hypothesis was that sexual repression caused the instability. Without challenging gender, churchmen began to emphasize the importance of good sexual relations within marriage.[7] They altered the nineteenth-century religious antisexual view, as the historian David Kennedy put
it, by "understanding . . . sex as an instrumentality for the preservation of
marriage." But these pro–birth control ecclesiastics were a minority, though
a prestigious one. Winning over the greater part of organized religion took
several decades. The Catholic Church, meanwhile, remained firm in its opposition to contraception.[8]

Direct exposure to the acute problems of poor women also drew social
workers to birth control, as, for example, Alice Hamilton, who "discovered" it
while working at Hull-House (a settlement house established by Jane Addams
in Chicago).[9] But the professional status of social workers was more an aspiration than a reality at this time, and as a result social workers came to support birth control only slowly in the 1920s. Influenced by conservative postwar
pressures, they distanced themselves from controversial political involvement.
Seeking the prestige that had been denied them because of their traditional
amateur status and domination by the female sex, social workers in the 1920s
were after professional recognition and respectability above all. The more
progressive social work activists made the strategic decision to avoid shady
sexual matters such as birth control in favor of a maternalist welfare program.[10]
On Sanger's national tour in 1916, the Hull-House staff told her they were "not
interested." (She, in turn, denounced "charitable institutions" for using "well
intentioned palliatives," much like quack doctors "treating a cancer by burn-
ing off the top" while disease spreads underneath.)[11] When the Women's Trade
Union League brought other reformers into support of women's strikes, so-

cial workers remained aloof. Sanger and the ABCL actively cultivated social workers and did win some influential supporters and semisupporters, such as Julia Lathrop, president of the National Conference of Social Work.[12] But it would take the social crisis of the depression to win over the profession as a whole.

The professionals who exerted the greatest influence on the 1920s birth control movement were doctors and eugenists. The latter group did not constitute a professional occupation in itself, although private foundations began in the 1920s to make it possible for an increasing number of scholars to work full-time on eugenic research. The eugenists were largely university academics in various fields—genetics, demography, economics, psychology, and sociology in particular. Scholarly eugenic organizations brought them together and gave them a collective consciousness as strong as that among doctors.

Sanger's leadership was an important factor in facilitating, even encouraging, the professionalization of the birth control movement. Despite her origins in multi-issue socialist feminist agitation, by the 1920s her approach was distinguished by her willingness to make it her full-time, single cause. From her return from Europe to face trial for *The Woman Rebel* in 1915, until her trial for the illegal Brownsville clinic in 1917, an ambiguous political posture helped Sanger retain the support of many disparate political groups. She simultaneously pursued direct action and defiance of the law and, keeping a low profile on her radical ideas, organized financial and public relations support from wealthy reformers. At the same time she was preparing an organizational structure to make birth control an influential mainstream cause.

In the fall of 1916, while working on the Brownsville clinic, Sanger founded the *Birth Control Review* and recruited Frederick Blossom, a professional charity fund-raiser from Cleveland, to come to New York as its paid editor and manager.[13] In December she founded the New York Birth Control League (NYBCL) as a rival to Dennett's National Birth Control League (NBCL) and asked Blossom to work in that organization as well. Sanger and Blossom had an ugly disagreement in 1917 that led to their split. Whoever was in the right— and it seems likely that both of them acted badly—the quarrel demonstrated Sanger's drive for control and separated her still further from the radical movement. Blossom quit when he could not have his way and took the records and small bank account of the *Review* with him, which prompted Sanger to bring legal charges against him. Socialists in the NYBCL became infuriated when Sanger turned to the "capitalist state" to solve her quarrel, and their investigation committee condemned Sanger and exonerated Blossom, a member of the Socialist party. But Blossom's subsequent behavior led the Industrial Workers of the World (IWW) to conduct another investigation, in 1922, that wound up condemning Blossom for the break with Sanger.[14]

Whatever the actual issues involved, Sanger did not quail before the disapproval of her former socialist comrades. Ironically, some of them had defended Sanger's personal control on the grounds that she was trying to create a movement with radical politics, which should not be diluted. Dennett's NBCL excluded people identified with the Left and avoided militant tactics like civil disobedience, and Sanger's radical reputation had arisen partly in being distinguished from Dennett. But even before the break with Blossom and his socialist supporters, Sanger had begun to move in another direction, though it was not widely perceived as such at the time.

While planning for her Brownsville clinic, Sanger sought a doctor to prescribe and fit contraceptives. New York State law at the time would have permitted her to legalize the clinic by putting it under a physician's supervision, which was an important part of her motivation. Section 1142 of the New York State Penal Code made it a misdemeanor to give out any contraceptive information, but section 1145 allowed lawfully practicing physicians to prescribe devices for the cure and prevention of disease. Sanger knew that this provision was intended to allow only the prescription of prophylactic measures against venereal disease, and she wanted to challenge and broaden its interpretation. But she also seemed convinced that contraception required the attendance of a physician. Since she was a nurse herself, it seems odd that she should have doubted that a nurse could fit a diaphragm as well as a doctor. Her earliest medical tutor, Dr. Johannes Rutgers of Holland, had taught her to fit a diaphragm; she herself fitted some of his patients while in The Hague. She had observed Rutgers training midwives in contraceptive techniques so that they could start birth control clinics elsewhere.[15] Nevertheless, Sanger argued to the end of her career—even after laws no longer stood in her way—that every applicant for birth control should see a doctor. After the forcible closure of her clinic, she again sought medical support for her work. As early as January 11, 1917, a year before she was brought to trial for the Brownsville clinic, the NYBCL's model law reform permitted only physicians to give out birth control information.[16] The NBCL, despite its more respectable image, was fighting for a more thoroughgoing reform: a bill that simply removed birth control from any definition of obscenity.

Sanger's leadership was particularly responsible for making birth control a medical issue in the United States. In the 1920s she also courted another group of professionals—the demographers, geneticists, and other academics who led the eugenics movement. In promoting professionals to increasing importance in the birth control movement, she encouraged a trend that would have happened without her. She was hardly responsible for the decline of the feminist movement, although her individualist and dominating style did not help to build solidarity with surviving feminist groups. She was hardly responsible for the repression, division, and shrinking of the socialist movement, although her alliances with conservative professionals were spurred by the refusal of male-dominated socialism to incorporate birth control and women's rights issues into their programs. Still, the weakening of both socialist and feminist movements created a political power vacuum into which Sanger moved. But she could not fill that vacuum—she needed help.

Doctors

Despite the efforts of pro–birth control doctors in attacking sexual continence, most physicians in the early 1920s remained opposed to contraception. The predominant position among prestigious doctors was not merely disapproval but revulsion so hysterical that it prevented them from accepting evidence. As late as 1925, Morris Fishbein, editor of the *Journal of the American Medical Association,* asserted that there were no safe and effective birth control methods.[17] In 1926, Frederick McCann wrote that birth control had an insidious influence on the female, causing many ailments; and although "biology teaches" that the primary purpose of the sexual act is to reproduce, the seminal fluid also has a necessary and healthful effect on the female.[18] Many doctors believed that they had a social and moral responsibility to fight the social degeneration that birth control represented. The sexual values underlying their opposition were often extremely conservative, as George Kosmak, a prominent gynecologist, noted: ". . . fear of conception has been an important factor in the virtue of many unmarried girls, and . . . many boys are likewise kept straight by this means. . . . the freedom with which this matter is now discussed . . . must have an unfortunate effect on the morals of our young people. It is particularly important . . . to keep such knowledge from our girls and boys, whose minds and bodies are not in a receptive frame for such information."[19] Kosmak went on to attack the birth controllers for their affiliations with anarchism and quackery. Although he acknowledged that physicians should have the right to prescribe contraception in those extraordinary cases in which it was necessary to save a life, he reasserted that sexual abstinence ought to be the means of avoiding not only unwanted children but also deleterious sexual excess.

Running throughout Kosmak's attack was a stream of elitism. Sharing eugenic assumptions about innate inequalities in the population, he did not, however, buy the race-suicide argument that overbreeding among the "inferior" was a danger.

> . . . those classes of our social system who are placed in a certain position by wealth or mental attainments, require for their upkeep and regeneration the

influx of individuals from the strata which are ordinarily regarded as of a lower plane. . . . it is necessary for the general welfare and the maintenance of an
economic balance that we have a class of the population that shall be characterized by "quantity" rather than by "quality." In other words, we need the
"hewers of wood and the drawers of water," and I can only repeat the question that I have already proposed to our good friends who believe in small families, that if the "quantity" factor in our population were diminished as the result
of their efforts, would they be willing to perform certain laborious tasks themselves which they now relegate to their supposed inferiors. Might I ask whether
the estimable lady who considered it an honor to be arrested as a martyr to
the principles advocated by Mrs. Sanger, would be willing to dispose of her
own garbage at the river front rather than have one of the "quantity" delegat-
ed to this task for her?

Kosmak's concern to guard accustomed privilege also applied to the particular prerogatives of his profession and reflected the professional ideology
that expertise should decide social values.

. . . the pamphlets which have received the stamp of authority by this self-con-
stituted band of reformers . . . are not scientific and in most instances have been
compiled by non-scientific persons. . . . Efforts to impress the public with their
scientific character need hardly be dignified by further professional comment,
and yet they are a source of such potential danger that as physicians we must
lend our assistance in doing away with what is essentially indecent and obscene. . . . Shall we permit the prescribing of contraceptive measures and drugs,
many of which are potentially dangerous, by non-medical persons, when we
have so jealously guarded our legal rights as physicians against Christian Scientists, osteopaths, chiropractors, naturopaths and others who have attempted to invade the field of medical practice by a short cut without sufficient preliminary training such as is considered essential for the equipment of every
medical man? Will we not by mere acquiescence favor the establishment of
another school of practice, the "contraceptionists," . . . if as physicians we do
not raise our voices against the propaganda which is spreading like a slimy
monster into our homes, our firesides, and among our young people?

In guarding his profession's jurisdiction, Kosmak resembled a craft unionist;
in his sense of responsibility for morality, his point of view was uniquely professional. The sexual values that the anti–birth control doctors cherished were
not so different from Victorian values: that the major function of women and
of sexual intercourse was reproduction of the species; that the male sex drive
was naturally greater than the female, an imbalance unfortunately but probably inevitably absorbed by prostitution; that female chastity was necessary to
protect the family and its descent; that female chastity must be enforced with

severe social and legal sanctions, among which fear of pregnancy functioned effectively and naturally.

But other physicians, arguing for a higher valuation of human sexuality as an activity in itself, had gained support by 1920—and not only among radicals. A leading spokesman for this point of view, the gynecologist Robert Latou Dickinson had been using his medical expertise to comment on social problems for several decades. In 1902 he had written on masturbation, urging a less hysterical view of its dangers;[20] earlier, he had defended women's bicycling against those who argued that it might foster masturbation.[21] He believed that mutual sexual satisfaction was essential to a happy marriage, and as early as 1908 he was giving instruction in contraception as premarital advice to his private patients.[22] Dickinson encouraged his colleagues in obstetrics and gynecology to take greater initiatives as marriage and sex counselors, and in his 1920 address as president of the American Gynecological Society he recommended that the group also take an interest in "sociological" problems. Although he disliked the radical and unscientific association of the birth control movement, unlike Kosmak he preferred to respond not by ignoring the movement but by disciplining it, and he thus urged his colleagues to that strategy as early as 1916.[23]

Sensitive to the difficulties of pulling his recalcitrant colleagues into a more liberal view of contraception, Dickinson began his campaign with a typical professional gambit. In 1923 he organized a medical group to study contraception, with the aim of producing the first scientific and objective evaluation of its effectiveness and safety. He used the threat of radicalism to win support for the plan. "May I ask you . . . whether you will lend a hand toward removing the Birth Control Clinic from the propaganda influence of the American Birth Control League," he wrote to a potential supporter in 1925.[24] So firm was Dickinson's insistence that the group would merely study, without preformed opinion, that he was able to get Kosmak himself to serve on the committee. He obtained financial support from Gertrude Minturn Pinchot, who had been the first president of the NBCL until she was alienated by the movement's radicalism, and a qualified endorsement from the New York Obstetrical Society.

Dickinson's Committee on Maternal Health (CMH), as his research project was called, was a rejoinder to Margaret Sanger's persevering efforts, begun in 1921, to open and maintain a birth control clinic that would serve also as a center for the medical study of contraception; the women who received contraception at the clinic would be research subjects. Named the Clinical Research Bureau, it opened in January 1923 with a woman physician as its supervisor. However, Dorothy Bocker was not a gynecologist but a former Georgia public health officer—in other words, she did not have professionally elite credentials.

Furthermore, Sanger had insisted on considering social and economic (as well as medical) problems as sufficient indications for prescribing contraception. Thus, because of Sanger's alternative, many doctors, while remaining suspicious of birth control, supported Dickinson's endeavor as a lesser evil.

At first Dickinson's group was hostile toward the Sanger clinic. They tried—and failed—to get Sanger and Bocker to accept the supervision of a panel of medical men. In 1925 Dickinson wrote a report scathingly critical of Bocker's scientific work.[25] But several factors intervened to lessen the hostility and even bridge the gap between Sanger's Clinical Research Bureau and Dickinson's Committee on Maternal Health. One was the fact that the CMH clinic had a difficult time attracting enough patients with medical indications for contraception. Its insistence on avoiding publicity and open endorsement of birth control made women reluctant to try the clinic, anticipating rejection and/or moralistic condemnation of their desire for contraception. Furthermore, it had difficulty obtaining diaphragms, which had to be smuggled into the country. By 1926 its three years of work had produced only 124 incomplete case histories. Meanwhile, Sanger's clinic saw 1,655 patients in 1925 alone, with an average of three visits each.[26]

Another factor conducive to rapprochement between the two clinics was Sanger's conciliatory attitude toward Dickinson and other influential doctors. Her organization, the American Birth Control League, had been courting medical endorsement since its establishment in 1921. The ABCL accumulated massive medical mailing lists, for example, and sent out reprints of pro–birth control articles from medical journals.[27] Sanger's wealthy second husband paid a $10,000 yearly salary to a doctor, James F. Cooper, to tour the country speaking to medical groups on behalf of the ABCL.[28] Although even he was not immune from attacks as a quack,[29] Cooper commanded the attention of male physicians as no woman agitator could ever have done. And his prestige was enhanced when he shared the speakers' platform with prestigious European physicians at the International Neo-Malthusian and Birth Control Conference held in New York in 1925 under ABCL auspices. Indeed, the prestige of the Europeans—whose medical establishment was far more enlightened on the birth control question than the Americans'—was sufficient to entice the president of the American Medical Association (AMA), William A. Pusey, to offer a lukewarm endorsement of birth control at that conference.[30] The ABCL kept exhaustive files, not only of letters but also from their clipping service, on every physician who appeared even mildly favorable to birth control; by 1927 those files contained 5,484 names.[31] Thousands of people all over the country wrote to the ABCL asking for help, and they were asked for the names of doctors near them so that the ABCL could then write to the doctors asking whether "it is your custom to give contraceptive advice in your regular course of practice, to those patients who in your judgment need it." The names of doctors who responded positively were then sent to people in their vicinity who were seeking contraception.[32]

In 1925, in response to criticism from the Dickinson group, Sanger decided against a defensive reaction and instead asked the Committee on Maternal Health to take over and run her clinic, hoping in return to obtain a license from the State Board of Charities. Dickinson demanded the removal of all propagandistic literature and posters, to which Sanger agreed. The scheme failed anyway because Sanger's radical reputation and opposition from the Catholic Church led the State Board to refuse the license. For his part, Dickinson made his professional influence clear and useful to Sanger by procuring for her a $10,000 grant from the Rockefeller-backed Bureau of Social Hygiene.

Undoubtedly, the largest single factor drawing doctors into the birth control movement was Sanger's support for a "doctors only" type of birth control legislation. She had apparently been strongly influenced by Judge Crane's 1918 decision in her Brownsville clinic trial. He had upheld her conviction under the New York State obscenity law but had suggested the possibility of broadly interpreting section 1145, which made an exception for physicians prescribing contraception for the cure or prevention of disease, to define "disease" as any pathological bodily change. Since then Sanger and the ABCL had worked, on both state and federal levels, for legislation that would simply strike out all restrictions on doctors' rights to prescribe contraception, giving them unlimited discretion. The ABCL also proposed an amendment to the Comstock law that would exempt from restriction all medical and scientific journals, all items prescribed by physicians, and all items imported by manufacturers, wholesalers, or retail druggists doing business with licensed physicians.[33]

Meanwhile, Mary Ware Dennett and her colleagues in the Voluntary Parenthood League continued to campaign for an "open bill" removing all restrictions from the discussion of contraception, that is, decriminalization rather than medical regulation. The VPL's objections to the doctors-only bill were well founded. The league's president, Myra P. Gallert, wrote: "Yes, of course we believe in medical advice for the individual, but again how about the large mass of women who cannot reach even a clinic? . . . Mrs. Sanger's own pamphlet on methods finds its way through the American mails . . . and *it is not a physician's compilation.* . . . Mrs. Sanger herself testified 'that the Clinical Research Department of the American Birth Control League teaches methods so simple that once learned, any mother who is intelligent enough to keep a nursing bottle clean, can use them.'"[34] Dennett argued that the doctors-only bill left "the whole subject . . . still in the category of crime and indecency."[35] Not only did it accept the definition of sexuality without reproduction as obscene, but it also removed the technique of contraception from a woman's control. If women could not have direct access to birth control information, they would have to get their information from doctors along with censorship at worst and moral guidance at best. Tactically, the doctors' bill also had serious repercussions. As Antoinette Konikow wrote, the very advantage that its supporters liked—that it would make birth control seem safely controlled—was its worst feature "because it emasculates enthusiasm. To the uninformed the exemption seems hardly worth fighting for."[36] The very substance of the politics doctors brought to the birth control movement tended to squash lay participation in the movement.

Many doctors, of course, believed that they had an ethical duty to oppose an open bill. Sharing the views expressed by Kosmak in 1917, their sense of professional responsibility and importance led them to anticipate all sorts of moral and physiological disasters should contraceptive information and devices be generally available. Strategically, Dickinson feared that an open bill would increase religious opposition to birth control legalization.[37] Sanger's opposition to Dennett's bill combined condescension, conservatism, and compromising practicality. "I have come to realize," she wrote to Dennett supporter James Field in 1923, "that the more ignorant classes, with whom we are chiefly concerned, are so liable to misunderstand any written instruction that the Cause of Birth Control would be harmed rather than helped, by spreading abroad unauthoritative literature." Sanger wrote to Dennett that "clean repeal" was impossible because it would have to mean removing abortion from the obscenity category as well, something which Sanger knew could never win and which she probably did not personally accept. "You," she wrote to Dennett, "are interested in an abstract idea. . . . I am interested in women, in their lives."[38]

The effect of concentrating on a doctors-only bill can be seen by examining the work of a local birth control league. (Although there are many differences in the histories of the local leagues, I emphasize here certain developments that were common to most of them while illustrating them with specifics from the Massachusetts case.) A birth control group had emerged in Boston in 1916 with the arrest of a young male agitator, a Fabian socialist, for giving a police agent the pamphlet *Why and How the Poor Should Not Have Many Children.* Supporters of the accused, Van Kleeck Allison, organized a defense committee that later became the Birth Control League of Massachusetts (BCLM). League members were, from the beginning, a coalition of radicals (Allison's fellow Fabians and members of local Socialist party groups) and liberals (social workers and eugenic reformers in particular). As elsewhere, no doctors—with the exception of the revolutionary socialist Antoinette Konikow—were conspicuous in the movement in its first years.[39] Some were attracted to the cause by civil libertarian principles, as was the Reverend Paul Blanshard, who took the stance that the right to speak out on birth control should be defended even by those who opposed birth control itself.[40] More commonly, BCLM members argued the neo-Malthusianism prevalent among Socialist party birth controllers. Ella Westcott, a settlement house worker, argued from her observation of the poor struggling with overlarge families and resorting to dangerous abortion attempts, since they were denied access to safe and effective contraception. Simultaneously, some of the upper-class reformers talked of using birth control to restrict reproduction among the "unfit."[41]

Despite the variety of its membership, the BCLM agreed in 1916 and 1917 on tactics designed to make birth control a public issue and a popular cause. The league tried and often succeeded in getting publicity in the popular press, sponsoring mass meetings and public debates and contacting nine hundred women's clubs around the state to recruit supporters. BCLM members accepted support from all quarters and featured speakers as far to the left as Frederick Blossom, of Sanger's *Birth Control Review,* and Theodore Schroeder, of the Free Speech League of America, a group associated with Emma Goldman.[42] From the beginning, however, some of the socialists in the BCLM experienced tension between campaigning for freedom and justice in the long run and using the support of elites to win immediate gains. Influential eugenists, mostly Harvard professors, were quickly attracted to the cause. One of them, Charles Birtwell, proposed in 1917 to replace the league with a eugenic organization that would be "so big and supported by so many people of influence that the authorities would never think of attacking us."[43] Cerise Carman Jack, a Harvard faculty wife of radical leanings, expressed her conflicts about the tension between her radical ideas and her desire to win. "It is the same old and fundamental question," she wrote Birtwell, "that everyone who has any independence of mind encounters as soon as he tries to support a really radical movement by the contributions of the conservative. . . . The Settlements have . . . found it out and have become . . . crystalized around activities of a non-creative sort; the politician has found it out and is for the most part content to lose his soul in the game. . . . [But] half-baked radicals . . . [tend to] have nothing to do with any movement that savors of popularity and . . . think that all reforms must be approached by the narrow path of martyrdom."[44]

Unable to resolve that problem, many radicals throughout the country lost interest in birth control in favor of what then seemed more pressing issues: the Great War, the Russian Revolution, and repression against the Left. Cerise Carman Jack was typical when she decided in 1918 that the most important and strategic direction for her political efforts should be defense work against political repression. Birth control could wait; in her opinion it would "come so spontaneously wherever the radicals get control of the government, just as the war has brought suffrage . . . now is the time to work for the fundamentals and not for reform measures."[45]

In Massachusetts, as in many places, the immediate effect of the defection of radicals and the entrance of professionals into the birth control leagues was a period of inactivity. In 1918 birth control supporters among high professionals were still in the minority. Most doctors, lawyers, ministers, and professors found birth control too radical and improper a subject for public discussion; besides, they feared race suicide. But in the 1920s quiet though steady concentration on a doctors-only bill by remaining birth control activists transformed medical opinion. Despite Massachusetts's special problem of Catholic political power, the MBCL got twelve hundred doctors to endorse its bill.[46] The principle of doctors' rights even led the league to defend the ultraradical Konikow, who regularly lectured on sex hygiene to women, demonstrating contraceptives as she discussed birth control. She was arrested for this on February 9, 1928, and appealed for help to the by-then defunct MBCL. Rising to her defense in fact rehabilitated the league under its former president, Blanche Ames. Konikow was a difficult test case for the league to accept: a Bolshevik and regular contributor to revolutionary socialist periodicals, she was most inelegant in appearance and, as we have seen, was rumored to be an abortionist.[47] Nevertheless, the principle at stake was too important for the doctors to ignore: the prosecution of any physician under the obscenity statutes would have set a dangerous precedent for all physicians. The Emergency Defense Committee formed for Konikow worked out an extremely narrow line of defense: that she was not exhibiting contraceptive devices within the meaning of the law but was using them to illustrate a scientific lecture and warn against possible injuries to health.[48] This line worked and Konikow was acquitted.

The verdict stimulated renewed birth control activity and a new BCLM nucleus drew together with the goal of persuading doctors to support birth control and passing a doctors-only bill in Massachusetts. A new board was chosen, and ten of the sixteen new members were physicians. The lobbying activities took all the league's time, and it lost all public visibility. Konikow herself was extremely critical of this policy. She saw that commitment to it required maintaining a low profile and specifically meant giving up the project of a clinic. She argued, in fact, that opening a clinic would in the long run do more to bring the medical profession around than a long, slow legislative lobbying campaign.[49]

Konikow's criticisms angered the BCLM leaders. Possibly in retaliation, they refused to lend her their mailing list of fifteen hundred names to publicize her new book, *The Physicians' Manual of Birth Control*. (She had been given not only a mailing list but also a letter of endorsement by Dennett and the Voluntary Parenthood League.) Konikow's angry protests described an organization entirely different from the original local birth control leagues: "... the relations between the Executive Board [of the BCLM] and the membership are so distant that the members do not know what the official policy of the organization is."[50]

As Konikow had predicted, one of the consequences of this new kind of organization was failure. While the BCLM had narrowed, the Catholic opposition retained mass support. The BCLM had become less a participatory organization than a professionals' lobbying group. Yet, no matter how decorous and conservative the league's arguments for birth control, it could not escape red-baiting and scurrilous attacks. Cardinal O'Connell said that the bill was a "'direct threat . . . towards increasing impurity and unchastity not only in our married life but . . . among our unmarried people.'" The chief of obstetrics at a Catholic hospital said that the bill had "'the essence and odor that comes from that putrid and diseased river that has its headquarters in Russia.'" Another opponent charged that this was a campaign supported by Moscow gold.[51] A broad opposition defeated the bill. Even non-Catholic attackers recognized the radical potential of birth control, particularly the removal of one of the main sanctions for female chastity—namely, involuntary pregnancy. Even had birth control never had its reputation "damaged" by association with socialists, anarchists, and free-lovers, its content still could not be disguised. This was the weak point in the conservative strategy of the BCLM, even measured against its own goals. Birth control was subversive of conventional morality in its *substance,* and no form of persuasion could fool those who liked the conventional morality. The sexual meanings of birth control could not be disguised by describing it as a medical tool.

Although the Catholic Church played a particularly large role in Massachusetts, doctors-only bills were defeated in every state in which they were proposed, even in states without large Catholic populations.[52] Indeed, the BCLM's pattern of development was repeated in many local birth control leagues. After the radical originators of the movements left for other causes that seemed to them more pressing (or, in a few instances, were pushed out by professionals and conservatives), the birth control leagues sank into lower levels of activity. The impact of professionals—particularly doctors—on birth control as a social movement was to depress it, to take it out of the mass consciousness as a social issue, even as contraceptive information continued to be disseminated. Furthermore, the doctors did not prove successful in the 1920s in winning even the legislative and legal gains they had defined as their goals. Although some birth control organizers, such as Cerise Carman Jack of the BCLM, felt torn between focusing on social justice issues and immediate gains, in fact there is doubt that the surrender produced any greater effectiveness at all.

The Massachusetts example, though typical of the national struggle for legislation legalizing birth control, was not representative of birth control clinics nationally. By 1930 there were fifty-five clinics in twenty-three cities in twelve states.[53] In Chicago, a birth control clinic was denied a license by the city health commissioner, but the Illinois Birth Control League secured a court order overruling the commissioner and granting a license. Judge Harry M. Fisher's 1924 decision in this case marked out important legal precedents. His opinion held that the project was a clinic under the meaning of the law; that there existed contraceptive methods not injurious to health; that the actions of the health commissioner (who had cited biblical passages in his letter of refusal to license) amounted to enforcing religious doctrines, an illegal use of power; that the obscenity statutes only sought to repress "promiscuous" distribution of contraceptive information; that "where reasonable minds differ courts should hesitate to condemn."[54]

As the clinic movement mushroomed around the country, conflict continued about how and by whom the clinics should be controlled. In New York, Sanger still resisted relinquishing personal control of her clinic to the medical profession. No doubt part of her resistance stemmed from her loss of control over the ABCL and the *Birth Control Review* by 1929, leaving the clinic as her only institution. But part of her resistance also came from disagreement with the doctors' insistence on requiring medical indications for the prescription of contraceptive devices. Her Clinical Research Bureau consistently stretched the definition of appropriate indications; and if an appropriate medical problem that justified contraception could not be found, a patient was often referred to private doctors, for whom prescribing contraceptives would be less dangerous.[55] Sanger was willing to avoid an open challenge to the law on the question of indications, but she was not willing to allow close medical supervision to deprive physically healthy women of access to contraception.

Throughout her career Sanger retained a critical view of medical control. As late as 1940 she wrote to Dr. Clarence Gamble, "I am absolutely against our educational or propaganda or organizational work being in the hands of the medicos. . . . Being a medico yourself you will know exactly what I mean because you are not strictly medical."[56] Yet nationally her work had the impact of supporting medical control. The only actual birth control help the ABCL ever offered individuals was referral to sympathetic physicians. At ABCL-sponsored birth control conferences, nonmedical people were excluded from the sessions that discussed contraceptive technique.[57] The Voluntary Parenthood League protested this policy, but the VPL was among those excluded from these sessions.[58] Some local birth control groups also resisted these policies. Caroline Nelson, for example, the IWW birth controller of the prewar period who was still active in California, complained in 1930 of "nothing more nor less than an effort to get the laymen out of the field to leave it to the doctors."

Now we have this Conference called by Margaret Sanger, who wants the dissemination of the information limited to doctors, which means that every doctor can demand the arrest and prosecution of every layman who hands it on. Fine! The whole proposition has been evolved outside the medical profession. They have tried with all their professional sneers to hold it back, and refused to include it in their medical curriculum. Now when they find that they can't hold it back, they want to appropriate it and police the layman.[59]

But Sanger's dominion over the national conferences, lobbying efforts, and publicity was complete, and the increasing medical control was not checked.

So completely has birth control become identified with the medical profession that it is sometimes difficult for us today to imagine how it could have been otherwise. A 1960s population control expert whose international experiences gives him a perspective on the limitations of a medical approach to birth control described Sanger's impact like this: "Partly because of the medical orientation of Margaret Sanger, and primarily because of legal difficulties under which the movement in this country has labored, a very strong medical bias dominates the movement in the United States. Among other things it has meant a concern with 'maximum protection' . . . the clinical system . . . examination rooms, case histories and white coats. It has also meant a highly conservative attitude toward abortion, sterilization, publicity and non-medical personnel."[60] Among the other effects of medical domination were narrow indications for birth control and conservative attitudes about motherhood, sex education, and sexual morality.

But Sanger continued to face the problem that without medical supervision her clinics were illegal and vulnerable. She continued to seek a license in New York. When she withdrew the clinic from the auspices of the ABCL in 1928, she once again approached Dickinson, requesting that he find her a medical director whose prestige might help obtain a license. Dickinson in response demanded that the clinic be turned over to a medical authority, suggesting New York Hospital. Sanger was convinced that such an affiliation would hamstring her work and refused. Then, in April 1929, police raided the clinic. As at Brownsville thirteen years earlier, a plainclothes policewoman asked for and was supplied with contraceptives. She even returned for a checkup, to make sure her diaphragm was fitted properly, and then returned five days later with a detachment of police, who arrested three nurses and two physicians and confiscated the clinic's medical records. The last action was, however, a tactical mistake on the part of the police, for it united the medical profession behind Sanger and in defense of confidential medical records. Furthermore, the individual policewoman had been a poor choice because the clinic doctors had found that she had pelvic abnormalities that provided a medical indication for giving her a diaphragm. So the case was thrown out of court. (Some time later the policewoman returned to the clinic, off duty, to seek treatment for her pelvic disorders.)[61]

This episode improved relations between Sanger and the doctors who supported birth control, and Dickinson made a last attempt to persuade Sanger to give up the clinic—this time to the New York Academy of Medicine rather than a hospital. Sanger was probably closer to acceding now than she had ever been—and might have done so had it not been for countervailing pressure she was getting from another group of professionals, eugenists. Though easily as conservative as the doctors in terms of the feminist or sexual freedom implications of birth control, eugenists were solidly in Sanger's camp on the issue of indications. They could not be content with a medical interpretation of contraception, that is, that its function was to prevent pathologies in mothers, because they sought a large-scale impact from birth control: they wanted to improve the quality of the whole population, not just protect the health of women. They were also fighting a turf battle with physicians. Eugenists had been among the earliest nonradicals to support birth control, and some of them had spoken out for it publicly even before the war. They perceived doctors as joining the cause after it was safe to do so and then trying to take it over from its originators.[62] Though politically conservative, eugenists' intensity of commitment to their reform panacea—selective breeding—allowed them to accept Sanger's militant rhetoric and her willingness to challenge and stretch the law. At the same time, the eugenists influenced not only Sanger but the whole birth control movement.

Eugenists

Eugenic ideas had attracted reformers of all varieties for nearly a century. Nineteenth-century eugenics, as we have seen, did not oppose environmentalism to hereditarianism. The early eugenists believed that individual improvements acquired through an improved environment could be transmitted to offspring, just as corrupt social relations would produce physically and mentally deformed individuals. The scientific discrediting of the theory of the inheritance of acquired characteristics required more restricted understandings of what eugenics could accomplish. As Sanger described it, "eugenics, which had started long before my time, had once been defined as including free love and prevention of conception. . . . Recently it had cropped up again in the form of selective breeding."[63] This new eugenics sought to reproduce the entire American population in the image of those who dominated it politically and economically. It was not a reform program but a defense against the growth of democracy. Its essential argument—that the "unfit," the criminal, and the poor were the products of congenital "deformities"—suited the desire of upper-class eugenics supporters to justify their own monopoly on power, privilege, and wealth.

New genetic theories promised reliable methods of prediction, and therefore control, of the transmittal of some identifiable physical traits, and they stimulated scientific research into human genetics. The first eugenics organizations were research centers, such as the Eugenics Record Office and the Station for Experimental Evolution. As eugenics enthusiasts developed specific political and social proposals for action, they established organizations to spread the gospel and lobby for legislation. The first of these was the Eugenics Section of the American Breeders Association, set up in 1910; in 1913 human breeding became the main focus of the association, which changed its name to the American Genetic Association. Several other organizations were established in the next decade.[64]

The personnel of these organizations consisted largely of professional men, particularly university professors, but their professionalism was by no means identical to that of doctors. Whereas doctors remained largely self-employed, teachers were one of the first groups to become salaried workers. Their reduction to employee status brought pronounced discomfort, especially among university professors who sought to preserve their prestige and status. In the 1920s professors and university administrators complained bitterly over their lack of recognition and their inability to attract recruits of the highest quality.[65] The new eugenics attracted those frustrated by their loss of status. Eugenics provided them with an ideology that defended their superiority and sought to increase their prestige through mobilizing anxiety about continued democratization. As more Americans sent their children to colleges and universities, professors increased in number and declined in status. Their longing for full-time research opportunities was one reason that professors welcomed the intervention of large corporate foundations into American education.

Corporate foundations changed the content and structure of higher education in the twentieth century, and their impact supported the eugenics movement. The foundations, of course, were not the first channel for business influence on educational institutions. Business gifts to education grew rapidly after the Civil War, and between 1872 and 1905 business gifts were already the largest single source of income for colleges.[66] But the development of foundations magnified these contributions so much that they created a qualitative change in the direction of academia and its research agenda. Between 1893 and 1913 education received 43 percent of foundation gifts. Furthermore, these gifts were directed increasingly to the elite schools (between 1902 and 1934, 73 percent of the gifts went to just twenty institutions). The Carnegie and Rockefeller foundations in particular were responsible for far-reaching changes not only in university curriculum but, through the reshaping of university admissions requirements, in secondary education as well. Foundations helped to unify universities and businesses, drawing businessmen onto university boards of trustees and professors onto the boards of foundations.

In no academic field was the coalition between corporate capital and scholarship developed more fully than in eugenics. In the 1920s eugenics was a required course in many American colleges and universities.[67] The widespread adoption of eugenics as a scholarly field represented the capitulation of higher education to a fad, allowing the eugenists' skills to become a commodity for sale to the highest bidder. The backers of eugenic research and writing included the wealthiest families in the country. The Eugenics Record Office was established by Mrs. E. H. Harriman. The Station for Experimental Evolution was paid for by Andrew Carnegie.[68] Henry Fairfield Osborn, a gentleman scholar and founder of the New York Museum of Natural History, was a main financial backer of the eugenics societies; in the late 1920s, Frederick Osborn, nephew of Henry Fairfield, assumed leadership in the cause and financed a research program for the Eugenics Research Association.[69]

The cause carried with it for many years some of its historic aura of progressivism, an aura that disguised its increasingly conservative content. Liberals could welcome some eugenic reforms, such as requiring syphilis tests before marriage. Moreover, the eugenists' apocalyptic warnings (for example, "race suicide" and "menace to civilization") and perfectionist visions ("a world of supermen") alienated conservative and religious people who objected to this hubris, and this opposition tended to rally progressives to the eugenics camp. Furthermore, in the programs and logic of many eugenists, heredity and environment continued to be imprecisely distinguished; and as a result, some socialists, feminists, and sex radicals remained loyal to a "popular eugenics" tradition that offered proposals based on the inheritance of acquired characteristics. These popular eugenists endorsed programs for the prevention of birth defects and included demands for prenatal medical care for women under the aegis of eugenics.

After World War I, however, academic eugenists consistently avoided all except strictly hereditarian interpretations of eugenics. In these hereditarian assumptions,[70] they stood in opposition to the tradition of social reform in America. Eugenists justified social and economic inequalities as biological. Their journals featured articles about "aristogenic" families, as if the existence of several noted gentlemen in the same family proved the superiority of their genes. Their definitions of what was socially worthy used their own professional and upper-class standards of success. These biases can be seen particularly clearly in their emphasis on intelligence. Standard eugenic concepts of inferiority—such as "degeneracy"—consistently equated lack of intelligence with viciousness and intelligence with goodness. "Among the 1000 leading American men of science," the eugenist Paul Popenoe wrote, "there is not one son of a day laborer. It takes 48,000 unskilled laborers to produce one man distinguished enough to get in *Who's Who,* while the same number of Congregational ministers produces 6000 persons eminent enough to be included."[71] The eugenists wanted to rid society of all who could be classified as disabled.

Aristogenic stock was missing not only from the working class as a whole, but also from nonwhites in particular. Here is an explanation of the problem from a standard eugenics textbook first published by Bobbs-Merrill in 1916:

> From the rate at which immigrants are increasing it is obvious that our very life-blood is at stake. For our own protection we must face the question of what types or races should be ruled out. . . . many students of heredity feel that there is great hazard in the mongrelizing of distinctly unrelated races. . . . However, it is certain that under existing social conditions in our own country only the most worthless and vicious of the white race will tend in any considerable numbers to mate with the negro and the result cannot but mean deterioration on the whole for either race.[72]

Consider, too, the following—also typical—passage from *Revolt against Civilization: The Menace of the Under Man* by Lothrop Stoddard, one of the most widely respected eugenists: "But what about the inferiors? Hitherto we have not analyzed their attitude. We have seen that they are incapable of either creating or furthering civilization, and are thus a negative hindrance to progress. But the inferiors are not mere negative factors in civilized life; they are also positive—in an inverse destructive sense. The inferior elements are, instinctively or consciously, the enemies of civilization. And they are its enemies, not by chance, but because they are more or less uncivilizable."[73]

The eugenics movement began campaigning for immigration restriction before World War I[74] and contributed to the growth of racist fears and hatreds. In 1928 the Committee on Selective Immigration of the American Eugenics Society recommended that future immigration be restricted to whites.[75] The movement also supported the enactment of antimiscegenation laws throughout the South,[76] and southern racists used the academic prestige of eugenics to further segregation.[77]

Like other social Darwinists, eugenists were enamored of the process of natural selection, as they understood it, and the survival of the fittest, which they believed it produced. They romanticized the "health" of animal and premodern societies in which, supposedly, nothing interfered with these processes. On this point, however, eugenists were caught in a contradiction: the logic of their argument led to a laissez-faire ideology, but the reforms they sought required intervention not only into social policy (such as immigration restriction) but into one of the most intimate aspects of human life—reproduction. The contradiction had been bequeathed them, so to speak, by race-suicide discourse, the immediate predecessor of eugenics. Race-suicide advocates had wanted to stop dysgenic population tendencies by encouraging those of "better stock" to refrain from using birth control and to have large families; in the 1920s eugenists merely added another proposal—to discourage reproduction among those of "inferior stock." They called this two-part program "positive" and "negative" eugenics, encouraging and discouraging reproduction in different social groups.

When they turned their attention to positive eugenics, most eugenists were antagonistic to birth control. To appreciate this conflict fully, we must remember that the eugenists were concerned not only with the inadequate reproduction of the "superior" but also with a declining birth rate in general.[78] As late as 1940 demographers worried that the net reproduction rate of the United States was below the replacement level.[79] Many eugenists clung to mercantilist notions that a healthy economy should have a steadily growing population. In the area of negative eugenics, they approved of birth limitation, of course, but preferred to see it enforced more permanently, through sterilization and the prohibition of dysgenic marriages.

The feminist content of birth control practice and propaganda was especially obnoxious to the eugenists. They endorsed the race-suicide critique of the growing "independence" of women and propagandized for the protection of the family and against divorce.[80] The most common eugenic position was virulently antifeminist, viewing women primarily as breeders.[81] As one eugenist wrote in 1917, "in my view, women exist primarily for racial ends. The tendency to exempt the more refined of them from the pains and anxieties of child bearing and motherhood, although arising out of a very attractive feeling of consideration for the weaker individuals of the race, is not, admirable as it seems, in essence a moral one."[82]

Although most eugenists were opposed to birth control, some were not, and all saw that they had certain common interests with the birth controllers. Some believed that though sterilization would be necessary in extreme cases, birth control could be taught to and practiced by the masses. Especially the younger eugenists and the demographer-sociologists (demography was not at this time a distinct discipline) were convinced that the trend toward smaller families was irrevocable and that the only way to counteract its dysgenic tendency was to make it universal. Finally, they shared with birth controllers an interest in sex education and freedom of speech on sex issues.

If these factors contributed to close the gap between eugenists and birth controllers, the attitudes of the leading birth controllers contributed even more. Whereas eugenists by and large opposed birth control, birth controllers did not make the reverse judgment. On the contrary, many birth control supporters agreed with eugenic goals and felt that their cause could benefit from the popularity of eugenics.

For many birth controllers, identification with eugenic goals arose from familiarity with the nineteenth-century radical eugenic tradition. They did not immediately apprehend how eugenics had been intellectually transformed by the adoption of exclusively hereditarian assumptions or politically transformed by its newly conservative goals. Some leftists were critical of the eugenics' elitism—for example, the socialist Henry Bergen, who wrote in 1920: "Unfortunately eugenists are impelled by their education and their associations and by the unconscious but not less potent influences of the material and social interests of their class to look upon our present environment . . . as a constant factor, which not only cannot be changed but ought not to be changed."[83] But most socialists continued to believe in the importance of inherited characteristics. Thus the British birth controller and socialist Eden Paul wrote in 1917 that the "socialist tendency is to overrate the importance of environment, great as this undoubtedly is."[84] And the IWW birth control organizer Caroline Nelson wrote in the *Birth Control Review:* "We no longer believe that the child comes into the world psychologically blank, but with an ancestral soul that potentially contains the strength or weakness of the past."[85]

Nelson was not ignoring environmental influences; rather, she clung to the older eugenic view of the confluence of environmental and hereditary factors. The problem was that in admitting any place to hereditary factors at all, radicals made it difficult to argue that the deepest existing inequalities were environmentally produced. This was particularly noticeable with respect to racial or ethnic differences, where the white Left shared its prejudices with the Right. In the same article in which Bergen identified the class function of eugenics, he endorsed the goal of using eugenic programs to improve the white race.[86] In a socialist collection of essays on birth control published in 1917, we find passages like this:

> Taking the coloured population in 1910 as ten millions; it would in 1930 be twenty millions; in 1950, forty millions; in 1970, eighty millions; and 1990, one hundred and sixty millions. A general prohibition of white immigration would thus, within the space of about eighty years, suffice to transform the union into a negro realm. Now although individual members of the Afro-American race have been able, when educated by whites, to attain the highest levels of European civilisation, negroes as a whole have not hitherto proved competent to maintain a lofty civilisation. The condition of affairs in the black republic of Haiti gives some justification for the fear that negro dominance would be disastrous.[87]

Like other leftists, many feminist birth controllers harbored racist and ethnocentric attitudes. Like most middle-class reformers, the feminists also had a reservoir of anti-working-class attitudes. The American feminist movement had its own tradition of elitism, in the style of Elizabeth Cady Stanton's proposal for suffrage only for the educated.[88] Many feminists had been active in the temperance movement and saw immigrants and working-class men as drunken undesirables. Anti-Catholicism in particular, stimulated by Catholic opposition to prohibition and women's rights, had been an undercurrent in the women's rights movement for decades. Southern feminists used the fear of the black vote as an argument for female suffrage and the national woman suffrage organizations accepted this strategy. Birth control reformers were not attracted to eugenics *because* they were racists; rather, they had interests in common with eugenists and had no strong tradition of antiracism on which to base a critique of eugenics.

Sanger, too, had always argued the "racial" values of birth control, but as time progressed she gave less attention to feminist arguments and more to eugenic ones. "More children from the fit, less from the unfit—that is the chief issue of birth control," she wrote in 1919.[89] In *Woman and the New Race,* published in 1920, she put together statistics about immigrants, their high birth rates, low literacy rates, and so forth, in a manner designed to stimulate racist fears.[90] In *The Pivot of Civilization,* published in 1922, she urged applying stockbreeding techniques to society in order to avoid giving aid to "good-for-nothings" at the expense of the "good" and warned that the masses of the illiterate and "degenerate" might well destroy "our way of life."[91]

Sanger developed favorite eugenic subthemes as well, such as the cost to society of supporting the "unfit" in public institutions and the waste of charitable funds that merely put bandages on sores rather than cured diseases. Society is divided into three demographic groups, she argued: the wealthy, who already practiced birth control; the intelligent and responsible, who wanted birth control; and the reckless and irresponsible, including "the pauper element dependent entirely upon the normal and fit members of society."[92] Later, in the 1920s, Sanger shifted her analysis of these social divisions, citing a "Princeton University authority" who had classified the U.S. population as consisting of twenty million intellectual persons, twenty-five million mediocre, forty-five million subnormal, and fifteen million feeble-minded.[93] By the early 1930s, the overtones of her rhetoric had become decidedly racist and virulent. In 1932 she recommended the sterilization or segregation by sex of "the whole dysgenic population."[94] She complained that the government, which was properly concerned with the quality of immigrants, lacked concern for the quality of its native-born population.[95]

Eugenics became a constant, even a dominant, theme at birth control conferences. In 1921, at the organizational conferences of the American Birth Control League, many eugenists spoke and exhibited charts showing the dysgenic heritage of the infamous Jukes and Kallikak families. In 1922 Sanger went to London for the Fifth International Neo-Malthusian and Birth Control Conference as its only female honored guest. Yet not a single panel was devoted to birth control as a woman's right, nor did Sanger raise this point of view. In 1925 she brought the Sixth International Conference to New York under the sponsorship of the ABCL. ABCL control made the tone more eugenic and less neo-Malthusian, but there was no increase in concern with women's rights. Not a single session was chaired by a woman, and only about one in ten speakers was a woman. Of the eleven conference sessions, four focused specifically on eugenics; none looked at women's problems.[96]

Meanwhile, ABCL's own propaganda began to focus more on eugenics at the expense of women's rights. The introductory brochure used during the 1920s listed first among ABCL activities publishing and distributing literature and conducting lectures "on the disgenic [sic] effect of careless breeding." The program of the ABCL included a sterilization demand and called for "racial progress."[97]

The ABCL's *Birth Control Review* had reflected the influence of eugenics from its inception in 1917. Although eugenists of the older, radical tradition dominated in its first years, the periodical also printed without editorial comment a eugenic anti–birth control argument, virtually a race-suicide argument, in its very first issue.[98] By 1920 the *Review* was openly publishing racist articles.[99] In 1923 it editorialized in favor of immigration restriction on a racial basis[100] and lamented "The Cost to the State of the Socially Unfit."[101] It printed Havelock Ellis's favorable review of Lothrop Stoddard's *The Rising Tide of Color against White World-Supremacy.*[102] Stoddard was, at the time, on the board of directors of the American Birth Control League, as was Clarence C. Little, president of the Third Race Betterment Conference and future president of the University of Michigan. Little justified birth control as an antidote to the "melting pot," a means of preserving the purity of "Yankee stock."[103] Also closely involved with the ABCL and writing regularly for the *Review* was Guy Irving Burch, a director of the American Eugenics Society and a leader in the American Coalition of Patriotic Societies. Burch supported birth control, he wrote, because he had long worked to "'prevent the American people from being replaced by alien or Negro stock, whether it be by immigration or by overly high birth rates among others in this country.'"[104] A content analysis of the *Birth Control Review* showed that by the late 1920s only 4.9 percent of its articles in that decade had any concern with women's self-determination.[105]

Conflicts continued, of course, between birth controllers and eugenists.

One of the most common sprang from the tendency of the former group to argue for birth control as if it were a panacea or at least a total solution to the problem of the "unfit." Edward East, for example, wrote to Margaret Sanger in 1925 to point out that "there will be many children of no value whatever to the community no matter what laws are passed and no matter what educational propaganda is put forth. . . . No matter what you say Birth Control is only a part of a eugenical program."[106] At other times Sanger's continued commitment to civil disobedience as a tactic alarmed the eugenists. As late as 1932 she quoted in a newsletter what some congressman had told her, off the record: "You'll never get this bill passed in Congress; get yourself arrested again, that's the only way to get the law changed."[107] Sanger's tactical militancy aside, she rarely clashed with eugenists about political goals. She kep her concern for women's emancipation under wraps.

In becoming converts to eugenics, birth controllers did not disavow feminism explicitly, but they found it not useful because of the general rightward turn in the country's political climate. Had they had a deeper understanding of racism, sexism, or class privilege embedded in alleged meritocracy, they might have been less comfortable with eugenic ideas. But eugenic ideas *were* useful. Eugenists gave them support they never got from the Left. The men who dominated the socialist movement did not perceive birth control as a fundamental matter of justice or freedom, and their theory categorized it as peripheral to the struggle of the working class. Eugenists, by contrast, once they caught on to the idea of urging birth control upon the poor rather than condemning it among the rich, were prepared to offer valuable support.

As academics and sexual theorists, eugenists were often concerned with matters of free speech, and in the early years of birth control many eugenists offered legal defense work when birth controllers were prosecuted. In Massachusetts, for example, Harvard professor Edward East aided in the defense of Van Kleeck Allison in 1916. Other academic eugenists supported birth control propaganda and clinics. University of Chicago professor James Field worked with a clinic organizing project as early as 1914, and the University of Michigan's president, Clarence C. Little, was an early member and activist in the Detroit Birth Control League.[108] In planning the First National Birth Control Conference for November 1921, Sanger had tried to recruit support from academics and scientists in particular. She won endorsement from economists and sociologists such as Irving Fisher, Edward A. Ross, Ellsworth Huntington, Warren Thompson, F. H. Giddings, Thomas Nixon Carver, and Raymond Pearl—all eugenists.[109] At a final session at Town Hall, Lothrop Stoddard helped her take the podium in defiance of a police ban. By exposing these professors to arbitrary suppressions of free speech, Sanger drew them into a deeper commitment to the cause, even to condoning civil disobedience.

As a means of increasing her exposure in academic circles, she conducted a university speaking tour in 1925, including stops at Yale, Bryn Mawr, Harvard, Tufts, Columbia, and Chicago.[110]

Sanger's efforts to win over academics gained additional support from British neo-Malthusians, including some of great prestige, such as Harold Cox, Member of Parliament and editor of the *Edinburgh Review*. Different economic and social conditions meant that the British upper classes were concerned with overpopulation when Americans were still worried about underpopulation. Despite this difference, British neo-Malthusians and American eugenists shared many attitudes and ideas. They represented the same classes, by and large; they were concerned not to let unbalanced population growth alter the social and political stability of their respective societies. Cox came to the United States in 1921 to deliver the keynote speech at the First National Birth Control Conference. At the Sixth International Neo-Malthusian and Birth Control Conference in 1925, Charles Vickery, a British neo-Malthusian, delivered the presidential address, and eugenists such as Edward East, Raymond Pearl, and Henry Pratt Fairchild—as well as firm opponents of birth control such as the demographer Louis Dublin—shared platforms with the neo-Malthusians.

By thus presenting at least the appearance of openness to her critics, Sanger won the respect of many academics. Two years later she organized, almost single-handledly, the First World Population Conference in Geneva. Again she brought American eugenists to confer with European neo-Malthusians. So great was her conviction that she needed the unity of these two groups that she submitted to the humiliation of having her name removed from the conference program by its chairman, Sir Bernard Mallet (formerly Registrar General of Great Britain and president of the Royal Statistical Society). "The names of the workers should not be included on scientific programs," Mallet said. Not surprisingly, the "workers" were all female and nonprofessionals. Another delegate told Sanger that Sir Bernard had been warned by Sir Eric Drummond that "these distinguished scientists would be the laughingstock of all Europe if it were known that a woman had brought them together." Sanger not only accepted the snub but took it upon herself to persuade the other women to do so as well.[111]

Just as Sanger accepted a back seat here, ABCL women in general lost their leadership positions to men (although women members remained in the majority). This takeover was a manifestation, of course, of the increasing influence of professionals.

The men, however, were not united. Although doctors and eugenists could mesh their concerns for individual and racial health in propaganda, they did not see eye to eye on the practice of the clinics. Particularly as regards indications, as we have seen, the doctors wanted to preserve stringent medical justifications for prescribing contraceptives, whereas eugenists and many lay birth controllers wanted to use contraception to ameliorate social, psychological, and economic problems as well. Eugenists were eager to use birth control clinics to collect data on family patterns, birth control use, changing attitudes, sexual behavior, and genetic history and, therefore, opposed medical supervision of clinics because it threatened to interfere with their data collection.[112] Many eugenists, such as Lewis Terman and Edward Thorndike, led in the development of improved quantitative and statistical techniques in the social sciences. For their part, the foundations generously funded such statistical studies.[113]

Most birth control clinics appreciated the eugenists' support for disseminating contraceptives in the absence of medical indications. The clinics also approved of eugenists' research interests. Many clinics conducted inquiries into the hereditary histories of their patients and presumably advised the women as to the desirability of having children.[114] In 1925, responding to suggestions from her eugenist supporters, Sanger redesigned the template for her clinical records to show the nationality, heredity, religion, occupation, and even trade union affiliation of patients.[115] In 1929 the Harvard eugenist Edward East wrote to Sanger, "I suppose it would be a delicate matter, but it would be a very interesting thing, from the standpoint of science, if your clinical records . . . show the amount of racial intermixture in the patient. Perhaps, without embarrassing questions, it would be possible to make a judgment as to whether the person was more or less pure black, mulatto, quadroon, etc." Sanger agreed, anticipating no difficulties, "as already colored patients coming to our Clinic have been willing to talk."[116] (The eugenists' passion for race categorization did not prevent them from accepting inexact measurements, such as "judgment.") A review of the work of seventy birth control clinics in Britain and the United States, published in 1930, proudly demonstrated that they reached a disproportionately large number of working-class women and claimed a eugenic effect from doing so.[117]

Of course, birth controllers also influenced eugenists. Sanger described the relationship thus: ". . . eugenics without birth control seemed to me a house built upon sands. It could not stand against the furious winds of economic pressure which had buffeted into partial or total helplessness a tremendous proportion of the human race. The eugenists wanted to shift the birth-control emphasis from less children for the poor to more children for the rich. We went back of that and sought first to stop the multiplication of the unfit."[118] In that one paragraph is condensed the transformation of birth control politics: the poor, "buffeted into partial or total helplessness" by economic pressure, are rechristened the unfit.

With such an attitude toward the poor, it is not surprising that clinics encountered difficulties in teaching working-class women to use birth control properly. Some such women were unteachable, Sanger and several other birth control leaders agreed. They particularly had trouble with "the affectionate, unreflecting type known to housing experts, who, though living in one room with several children, will keep a St. Bernard dog." For these women, sterilization was recommended.[119] The birth control workers' snobbery also manifested itself in their attitude toward working-class men. They projected an image of these husbands as uncontrolled, uncontrollable, sex-hungry, violent sexual aggressors with no regard or respect for their wives, who would never agree to contraception. Certainly the reasons such men might have for hostility toward birth control clinics were not taken seriously.[120]

Medical supervision of the clinics had created similar problems in reaching the poor with birth control, and Sanger and other clinic partisans ultimately saw more usefulness in eugenics than in medicine. Furthermore, the eugenists could not exercise the kind of direct control over clinics that the doctors could and were thus willing to share control with birth controllers such as Sanger. If Sanger and her colleagues ultimately chose to work with the eugenists, it was because it seemed to them the only realistic option. They would have preferred cooperative relationships with both eugenists and medical doctors; and perhaps, had this been possible, they might have retained more direct power in their own hands by playing off the two groups of professionals against each other. As it happened, the ideological disagreements and the jurisdictional rivalry of the two professions prevented this.

Ultimately, the rivalry held back the clinic movement. Although contraception became widespread in the 1930s, most middle-class people continued to get help from private doctors and most working-class and rural people, by contrast, did not get help at all. The latter problem was, of course, part of the general unequal distribution of medical care. Seen as a branch of medical care, birth control clinics broke with the private medical system in the United States, and their failure was part of a general failure of American medicine to provide for the poor.

The failure of the birth control clinics was also part of the failure of the United States to provide public medical insurance. Increasingly, the clinics were operated by groups of professional and well-to-do people for the poor. They were charities, not self-help organizations. Eugenic and neo-Malthusian logic had convinced many of these educated people that this particular charity was very much in their own interest, that without population limitation the poor and uneducated would become a destabilizing force. The clinics did not spread widely because the people who had become the backbone of the cause did not need them. Members of the ABCL got their birth control from private doctors. The attitude of many doctors toward their private patients continued, well into the mid-twentieth century, to parallel that of many elite nineteenth-century doctors: although they opposed the "promiscuous" and "indiscriminate" dissemination of contraception, they did not question their own discrimination and thought it important that private doctors should be able to make exceptions to the policies they supported as general rules. Well-to-do women were able to secure diaphragms without medical indications from doctors, including those who opposed clinics run on the same principles. The discretionary right of the individual doctor was a privilege as cherished by the profession as that of privacy—and the latter, of course, protected the former.

Birth controllers used eugenics but then discarded it. Eugenics was the driving ideology transforming a charity into a political cause. The passion behind eugenics led even conservatives to condone law-breaking and brought money into the birth control clinics.[121] Then the decline of eugenics deprived the clinics of some of their support. But soon the birth control cause no longer needed eugenics, as small families and reproduction control became normalized. Meanwhile, American eugenics was seriously tarnished by Nazi eugenic policies, which identified eugenics with fascist ideology and practice. Furthermore, scientific criticisms of Galtonian genetics stripped away some of the academic respectability that had clothed eugenic racism. Although some leading eugenists continued to function as a conservative sect, they lost much of their professional following in the 1930s. Some eugenists tried to reinterpret their credo in "value free" ways, discussing the decline in the quality of the population without using the word "eugenics."[122] In 1933, the *Journal of Heredity* disassociated itself from eugenics, declaring it was prepared "to give favorable consideration to analyses that might demonstrate fundamental unsoundness in present eugenic efforts."[123] (An indirect, but nonetheless damaging, admission of its earlier bias.)

Part of the reason that professionals could defect was that they had someplace else to go. Birth control had become a movement that could do much of the eugenists' work for them. Henry Pratt Fairchild, president of the American Eugenics Society, told the annual meeting of the Birth Control Federation (successor to the ABCL) in 1940: "One of the outstanding features of the present conference is the practically universal acceptance of the fact that these two great movements [eugenics and birth control] have now come to such a thorough understanding and have drawn so close together as to be almost indistinguishable."[124] A number of eugenists joined birth control organizations, partly because they were unemployed specialists needing jobs and new sources of recognition. But they were also genuinely concerned with a problem—race deterioration—and looking for ways to solve it. Important changes in birth control organizations made the eugenists comfortable in them, notably the new emphasis on making birth control a matter of public policy, not just private right.

Eugenics in the early and mid-twentieth century was a type of population control, a type of neo-Malthusianism. The former had been concerned with quantity and quality, whereas the latter had restricted its focus to quantity. But both aimed to manipulate reproduction on a large scale in order to control a society's development. Neither spoke of women's or even individuals' rights; on the contrary, both argued that individuals did not have those rights if they interfered with the best interests of the whole society. The loss of a women's rights emphasis left the birth control movement, as we have seen, without a guiding ideology, open to any justification that increased its importance beyond that of many other charities and minor ameliorative reforms.

National Organization

The influence of the professional birth controllers also transformed the nature and constituency of the birth control organizations themselves. In the pre–World War I period, the birth control leagues were local, tied together by a loose sense of common purpose and a few traveling speakers and organizers. By the mid-1920s one organization—the American Birth Control League—could claim national scope and hegemony. The ABCL, created in 1921 by Sanger and her protégé, Frederick Blossom, lasted until 1938; by 1927, at its peak, it had thirty-seven thousand dues-paying members from every state,[125] many of them brought into the ABCL through a bit of mild coercion, since the organization refused to send out birth control information except to members (to reduce the "free rider" effect). Although supporting itself through membership dues, the ABCL was primarily a staff organization and a centralized one. Policies and projects were decided and executed by a paid staff and national officers; local birth control groups were affiliates, but there was no structure providing for their participation in decision making.

The ABCL achieved national dominance largely through the contribution of its professional supporters. It was the center of most national lobbying and litigation, and most professional research and local clinics in the 1920s were affiliated with it in some way. Affiliated branches and projects were required to remit to the national organization 50 percent of the contributions they received and 25 percent of the dues they collected, in return for which the ABCL supplied birth control literature at minimum cost, trained organizers and speakers, and provided technical assistance in the establishment of clinics.[126] Individuals could join the ABCL itself, rather than a local affiliate. The ABCL built the respectability of birth control through national and international conferences and publicity campaigns, using prestigious professionals to promote the cause.[127] Throughout the 1920s, Sanger used the ABCL's rising prominence to proselytize for birth control. Her occasional controversial statements helped her grab media attention for the cause, although her publicity hunger also antagonized many of the ABCL staff, from whom she became estranged by the 1930s.

We can grasp the structure and direction of the ABCL more clearly by comparing it with the rival national birth control organization, the Voluntary Parenthood League, organized by the suffragist and civil libertarian Mary Ware Dennett. The VPL was the successor to the first American birth control organization, the National Birth Control League, initiated in March 1915 while Sanger was in Europe. Never reaching beyond New York City, the NBCL died in 1919, weakened by the war's impact in deflecting reform energies to other causes. Dennett had disapproved of Sanger's style and tactics since her revolutionary bravado in *The Woman Rebel* in 1914. So in 1919 Dennett created the VPL, dedicated to lobbying, in order to compete with Sanger, and for a time the VPL even published a paper rivaling the ABCL's *Birth Control Review*.[128] In 1923 and 1924 it introduced federal bills decriminalizing birth control, but they did not get reported out of committee. Between 1925 and 1927 the VPL gradually collapsed. Its appeal was limited by its exclusive focus on legislative lobbying, while birth control clinics were more visible, more newsworthy, and more capable of stimulating and absorbing local reform energies.

However, the VPL cannot be characterized simply as more conservative than the ABCL. The differences between the two groups were complex, based on personal rivalries between the leaders as often as on principle. But in this, as in all politics, personal conflicts did not reduce the importance of political differences. Dennett, always a liberal feminist, had never even flirted with radicalism. Perhaps for that reason she remained committed to fighting for the legalization of birth control on free speech grounds, whereas Sanger's early exposure to radical critiques of liberal civil liberties theory made her prefer arguments for the importance of birth control to social justice and practical compromises that would bring it closer. Dennett and her organizations opposed the doctors-only bills because they would leave birth control within the realm of the legally obscene and deny the general public access to contraceptive information. Indeed, Dennett fought the whole concept of legal obscenity, a challenge Sanger never made. Perhaps for this reason, too, Dennett disliked the phrase "birth control." Her choice, "voluntary parenthood," was a rephrasing of the nineteenth-century "voluntary motherhood," which emphasized individual rights. Prosecuted for distributing her pamphlet *The Sex Side of Life* in the late 1920s, Dennett was defended by the American Civil Liberties Union and strengthened her association with civil libertarians, while Sanger drew closer to doctors and eugenists.[129]

Dennett's emphasis on free speech brought her support from liberals but left her and her followers on the fringes of the most important currents in social thought. Not that she was uninterested in the practical case for birth control; on the contrary, she shared most of Sanger's and the ABCL's ideology. Dennett and the VPL propaganda defended sex without reproduction. Contraception was a good thing because sex itself was a good thing—if infused with love and "idealism."[130] Like Sanger, Dennett wrote on sex education.[131] She sought, before Sanger did, to disassociate the movement from the political Left. Dennett counted many rich, amateur reformers among her group, as did Sanger—who had organized society women into a Committee of 100 to defend her in 1916. However, such women did not significantly influence Dennett's or Sanger's birth control tendencies. It was Sanger's courting of doctors and eugenists that moved the ABCL away from both the Left and liberalism, away from both socialist-feminist impulses and civil liberties arguments toward an integrated population program for the whole society.

In attracting professionals, the ABCL had to overcome the taint of radicalism that clung to Sanger for decades. Though it is often hard to shake such reputations, Sanger had particular difficulty doing so because her personal style was combative. And she had, after all, been arrested for deliberately defying the law, whereas Dennett's organizations had never endorsed civil disobedience. Indeed, the NBCL and VPL at first even avoided litigation and limited themselves solely to advocating legislation. Meanwhile Sanger, long after she quieted her socialist and feminist ideas, refused to commit herself to staying within the law. No matter how she changed the content of her speeches, she was identified by most who knew her as a radical, at least until the end of the 1920s. Many doctors considered her untrustworthy even after she had campaigned for years for a doctors-only bill.

Sanger's clinic strategy provided a continuing basis for this suspicion. The successful operation of birth control clinics in the 1920s required at least bending the law, and the clinics' decisions about who should be given contraceptives required some dissembling in most cases. Certainly the application of the law was always open to interpretation, and Sanger had thought for many years to win the latitude the clinics needed through widening existing legal loopholes that gave doctors discretion in cases where pregnancy could be dangerous to a woman's health. But Sanger wanted that discretion used generously and found that doctors often preferred to employ it restrictively. Her refusal to give up tactics of civil disobedience was a major cause of her failure to get the unequivocal support of the medical profession for these clinics.

Sanger's commitment to civil disobedience in defending her clinics recalls an important distinction between militant tactics and radical goals, which are often confused. There were many historical precedents for Sanger's combination of militancy and pragmatic compromise. In both Britain and the United States the most militant suffragists were the more conservative in their social and political goals. Earlier, the Anti-Saloon League, despite its window-smashing tactics, had less far-reaching goals than the Women's Christian Temperance Union, whose tactics consisted mainly of education and consciousness-raising. Sanger herself often chose militance because it brought her publicity. Sexual reform by definition required shock tactics, for a part of the problem was that sexual matters were considered best not discussed at all. But law-breaking and convention-defying tactics did not necessarily indicate a challenge to existing relations of power.

Before the war, militant tactics had been associated with a radical content. Influenced by IWW direct-action ideas, birth controllers believed that people could take their lives into their own hands: reject laws over which they had no control by distributing contraceptives and contraceptive information, hold mass meetings in defiance of prohibitions, court arrest, conduct political trials. The war brought a sharp break in this activity. Most birth control leagues died between 1917 and 1919 and were re-established in the 1920s. This rupture produced sharp changes in constituency and policy. Before the war the local leagues were distributing contraceptive information, publicizing the virtues of birth control, holding mass meetings, planning and operating birth control clinics, and preparing legal defenses. After the war the mass meetings and illegal distribution of contraceptive information virtually disappeared. Birth controllers denied that their clinics were a form of civil disobedience to support their claim that the clinics were legal under medical discretionary powers. Arguing that contraception would check the massive illegal abortion trade, birth controllers convinced themselves that they were fighting crime, not perpetrating it.

Increasingly the ABCL organized its local affiliates as upper-class women's clubs, even high-society charity groups. In 1926, league organizing in Philadelphia was focused mainly on women of the Main Line, a group of extremely wealthy suburbs.[132] In Grand Rapids, Michigan, Mrs. C. C. Edmonds, of 1414 Wealthy St., S.E., was collecting "influential people" for a local group.[133] New York meetings were held in the Bryn Mawr Club.[134] These details pile up, drawing an unmistakable picture of an organization of privileged women.

The new respectability of the birth control movement shaped the constituency of the ABCL. In 1927 questionnaires were mailed to a random one-fifth (7,800) of ABCL members; of these, 964 were completed.[135] This sample may have tended to raise the apparent class level of the members, as more-educated people were more likely to reply, but the results are significant even if we allow for that. Politically the membership was slightly more Republican than the whole country, the men more inclined to be Republican than the women.[136] (The Republican party was the party most associated with progressive middle-class reform at this time.) One-third of the members lived in cities of more than fifty thousand people, 43 percent within five hundred miles of New York City, although this proportion had declined from 60 percent in 1922, suggesting increasing spread of birth control interest and knowledge. But half the membership came from population centers of less than twenty-five hundred, many of them suburbs. ABCL techniques in procuring members, however, require a reinterpretation of this phenomenon. Throughout the 1920s, league responses to letters of inquiry about birth control either explicitly or implicitly told writers that they could not receive information unless they joined the ABCL. "The information that you desire can only be given to League members," read a form letter signed by Sanger.[137] Thus big-city dwellers, more likely to have access to clinics or local birth control organizations, had less incentive to join the national organization, so ABCL membership could not be said to be representative of the overall distribution of people interested in birth control as a cause.

The average age of the members was thirty, the mean age thirty-five, suggesting that they were mostly of childbearing age but not newlyweds—in fact, the average member had been married five years and had two children. (Compare this, for example, to the figures given in chapter 8 for the women writing to Sanger and others asking for birth control help who had an average of five children and 80 percent of whom had married before the age of twenty.) Nor was there a significant proportion of immigrants, as there might have been among urban working-class people: the members were seven-eighths native-born, and of those 74 percent had native-born parents; of the foreign-born, over half were from Canada and Northern Europe. The survey director assumed, although he did not specifically ask, that the members were all white. Ninety percent were Protestants; Jews and Catholics numbered 5 percent each. The low percentage of Jews, a group once disproportionately well represented in the movement, reflects the more small-town and prosperous social base of the organization.

The questionnaires also asked the members what other organizations they belonged to, and these figures also demonstrate a respectable, prosperous white Protestant base. The other organization they must often belonged to was the Red Cross—one-third of the respondents checked this. Urban males tended to belong to Rotary or Kiwanis clubs, whereas 19 percent of rural males belonged to the Anti-Saloon League. Urban women most often belonged to local women's clubs (23 percent), and 10 percent of them belonged to the League of Women Voters. Rural women, naturally, did not belong to many organizations at all. A much higher percentage of men than women were Socialists—7.3 percent as compared with 3.3 percent. Since party affiliations were not correlated with other indices, we have no way of knowing what other characteristics might have distinguished this rather high proportion of Socialist party members from other ABCL members. Certainly the fact that a higher proportion of men than women were Socialists indicates not only the imbalance within the party but the male attitude toward birth control, for men on the whole still perceived this as a women's issue. Only 17 percent of the sample was male and 83 percent female.

Although men were not the major constituents of the American Birth Control League, those that were had higher social status than the women. Forty-nine percent of male members were professionals; of the remaining 51 percent, 11 percent worked in a trade, 8 percent did clerical work, 10 percent did agricultural work, and 14 percent did industrial work. Of course, a very high percentage—86 percent—of the women were housewives. But the husbands of female members also had a distinctly lower class status than male members: for example, only 19 percent of members' husbands were professionals. Education revealed the same general high status of male ABCL members: 47 percent were college graduates compared to 14 percent of females. (The questionnaire did not ask for the educational level of members' husbands.)

While men comprised just 17 percent of the membership, they made up 25 percent of the financial backers and a majority of the National Council. Of the council members, 36 percent were listed in Who's Who: nine clergymen, nineteen scientists, twenty physicians, and twenty-one other professionals. Ten female members of the council also had husbands listed in Who's Who.

The survey revealed an organization of predominantly white Protestant middle-class people, a high proportion from suburbs or small towns. It was also an organization with a very high proportion of male leaders, in light of the number of male members, and with a percentage of professionals among its male members far in excess of the nationwide percentage of professionals. The survey's findings were confirmed by the practice and propaganda of the ABCL, which also reflected the powerful influence of professional men in the organization. Symbolically, the ABCL listed its National Council members by profession: scientists (virtually all of these identifiable as eugenists), physicians, "other professionals," and "lay" members. The women on the council, of course, were almost all in the "lay" category, where they accounted for thirty-six of forty members. Not surprisingly, the women did all the work, both as staff members on the national and local organizations and as volunteers. The men typically served as professional volunteer consultants.

Professionals had the influence they did for several reasons. First, most professionals were gaining prestige at this time. Relative prosperity in the urban North was rapidly expanding the career opportunities for educated men, and they, in turn, pushed successfully for political reforms that increased their political power. Second, professionals had created a coherent social perspective that crossed disciplinary lines and gave them a collective influence greater than that of their individual numbers. Third, they were establishing their separate professions as controlled, standardized, and sometimes even licensed guilds. The exclusionary boundaries they patrolled were, ironically, a function of—and a reaction to—their declining independence. By the 1920s academics, social workers, scientists, and to a lesser extent doctors and lawyers were in a dependent relationship with the corporate industrial leadership of the country. Fourth, this dependence nevertheless gave leading professionals limited access to major resources—including foundation and government grants and contracts, private and governmental service programs—the manipulation of which in turn gave them influence in the organizations they joined.

These same factors also shaped their reform efforts. Professionals sought to improve society on the basis of what they believed were independent, objective criteria of justice. They had few doubts in the independence and objectivity of their judgment; if they perceived that they rarely challenged the existing class, race, and sex hierarchy, then they concluded it was because the hierarchy was advantageous and just. When they supported birth control, they did so in part to improve the lives of others, including those at the socioeconomic bottom—even though they thought that those on the bottom would, by and large, remain on the bottom. Professionals might work hard and devotedly to raise up the lower classes, but they did not envisage social leveling. Certainly, few of them thought that women's social roles and functions should be fundamentally altered relative to men.

The only check on professional influence would have been a continuation of a popular birth control movement based on a coalition of many groups that stood to gain from legal reproduction control. But the movements that might have been at the heart of such a coalition, movements of people who wanted birth control for themselves rather than for others, were losing steam and, in many cases, reeling from direct attack. The union movement lost ground in the 1920s, having been severely beaten in the repressive period that followed World War I. The organized Left was not only crushed by antisedition legislation and deportations but also divided in response to the Russian Revolution. And these groups were dominated by men, their leadership mostly hostile to or uninterested in birth control.

The women's rights networks also suffered from the hysterical attacks on the Left after World War I, but on the whole the weakening of the feminist birth control movement derived less from repression and more from internal contradictions. Early twentieth-century feminism's vision of a new sexual and gender order was threatening to many women, including many women's rights advocates. Separating sex from reproduction did not automatically spell liberation for all women. Although most supported access to contraception, most also remained suspicious and even alarmed by the sexual revolution that seemed to be licensing sex outside of marriage, overemphasizing sex altogether, and pulling women out of domesticity. In addition, the birth controllers increasingly saw their cause as a charity rather than a social movement.

Because so many post–World War I birth control activists were either "career women" or, more commonly, nonemployed prosperous wives (often of professionals) with the time to do volunteer work, they were reaping the benefits of a social emancipation that applied only to their class. They could hire help with housework or child care; they could get effective contraceptives in privacy; they enjoyed social acceptance for their work in the public arena, including public speaking, traveling alone, supervising others. But they had not experienced the raising of expectations that was to influence their daughters and granddaughters, expectations that made continued inequality with men galling and led to a revival of feminism a half-century later. Distant from the working-class and rural poor, and lacking a personal sense of urgency, they did not build the grassroots base that could have made them a significant influence. When public opinion began to be studied in the 1930s, working-class women appeared favorable to birth control. But as opinion polls of the 1960s and 1970s showed, support for women's rights does not necessarily carry over into identification with or desire to participate in feminist organizations. Most women wanted contraception to be available, but they perceived it, as the birth control leadership was offering it to them, as a commodity to be rationed out by experts; few saw it as part of a process of democratization that required broad participation. Thus the American Birth Control League's volunteers and supporters had already, by the mid-1920s, adopted goals and methods similar to those of the professionals who came after them, and thus the transition would be smooth.

10   *Depression*

The Great Depression of the 1930s had a mixed impact on the development of birth control. The staggering economy frightened many middle- and upper-class Americans into practicing family limitation and accepting it morally and sexually. Despite economic hardships, however, the movement for birth control did not grow. It remained a campaign run and staffed primarily by professional men, wealthy women, and middle-class reformers who felt little affinity with the powerful progressive social movements of the era. Notably, birth controllers were indifferent to the labor movement just as the labor movement remained suspicious of birth control, considering it both too radical and too conservative—radical in its sexual and gender implications and conservative in its neo-Malthusian and eugenic assumptions.

Instead, birth controllers turned to the government and tried to install contraception in New Deal welfare programs. In this effort their approach to social problems underwent a gradual but important change. The economic crisis changed the dominant ideology that explained social problems, such as poverty, by discrediting eugenic theories of hereditary inferiority and substituting environmentalist views. Applied to birth control, this shift placed less emphasis on reducing the population of the inferior and more on helping the underprivileged through family planning. Historically speaking, it was a shift back toward neo-Malthusianism and away from eugenics.

Despite rejecting hereditarian ideas, the birth controllers remained in some ways more conservative than the New Dealers whose help they sought, in that their dominant analysis of poor people's need for birth control blamed the victims. Many birth controllers adopted the ideas of "social pathologists" who argued, in the late 1920s and 1930s, that the major sources of social problems lay in the disabilities, albeit environmentally caused, of individuals.[1] Flowing from this analysis were recommendations for helping the poor by increasing the individual's ability to compete for jobs through education, socialization to middle-class norms of propriety, and reduction of family size. The goal was to move certain individuals up in the class structure. But unlike the New Dealers, the birth controllers did not think structurally, did not ask what created poverty and inequality in the first place and what role reproductive practices played.

At its depths the depression rendered this individual self-help approach useless and discredited and compelled a set of massive, structural remedies. The emergency relief programs did not assume that lack of skills was the cause of unemployment. Similarly, birth control advocates could not argue that large families were the cause of the extensive impoverishment around them. But the New Deal's massive remedies were temporary, because the predominant view among New Dealers was that the economic system was sick, not permanently disabled. Its return to "health" with World War II produced a return to individual/self-help solutions. What is surprising was the extent to which victim blaming prevailed among birth controllers during the depression. On the whole the transformation from hereditarian to environmentalist analyses of the relation between birth rates and economic status had few consequences. The "environment" was scrutinized in terms of influences on each individual, not in terms of systemic relations of power.

At the same time the sex and gender content of birth control seemed as radical and controversial as ever. Although high unemployment might logically have induced policymakers to promote birth control widely, continuing anxiety about its morality and potential to disrupt the gender order blocked any such promotion. No matter what the economic stress, birth control could not escape its radical sex and gender reputation.

Depression Eugenics

Giving up eugenic ideas proved difficult, for they had served the birth controllers well. But loyalty to the old eugenic assumptions was weakened by international political developments: As news of the Nazis slowly filtered into the United States, their eugenic policies—forced sterilizations and subsidies to large "Aryan" families—became identified with totalitarianism. Furthermore, the experience of sudden, massive unemployment and economic ruin weakened social Darwinist views of American economic justice. Even those who had taken prosperity for granted in the 1920s began to doubt in the 1930s that being of "good stock" was a guarantee of success, even in the long run. Those who had long been poor saw themselves joined by many others, and both groups suspected that their economic problems were not due to personal—hereditary or moral—failings.

Nevertheless, eugenists stubbornly continued to promote Malthusian and hereditarian explanations of the economic collapse. Birth-rate differentials "proved" that the "excess" people were mostly among the poorest. These calculations disguised assumptions that excess population caused poverty and that those in poverty somehow deserved to be there. In April 1933 a total of 4,445,338 families were collecting funds from the Federal Emergency Relief Administration (FERA), and early studies estimated that they had a birth rate 50 to 60 percent higher, on average, than those not on relief.[2] By 1935 "relief babies" had become a public scandal. Taxpayers' money was not only being used to support the poor but to produce more of them—at least this was the implicit charge being made in a variety of political arenas, from *Time* magazine to the *Birth Control Review*.[3]

The "relief babies" logic was not new. Margaret Sanger used that refrain frequently in the 1920s, arguing that birth control would cut public costs and thus taxes. "We are a nation of business men and women," she said, and as such we should use good business methods and cut overhead.[4] Nor was it new that public dependents had higher birth rates than the average.[5] But the sheer magnitude of unemployment in the 1930s gave the allegations urgency they had not had before. Previously, race-suicide arguments—namely, that the "best stock" would be overwhelmed by the faster breeding of the "unfit"—had threatened the future, not the present, and lacked persuasiveness with those who did not consider themselves of the best stock. During the depression, however, the problem of "relief babies" threatened to hit people immediately, in the pocketbook, and to hit everyone.

Birth controllers seized upon the relief crisis with gusto. "You are absolutely right that the economic situation is our greatest ally," one woman physician wrote to the president of the American Birth Control League (ABCL) in 1935. "The most sensitive nerve center in which to hit the public is their pocketbook. Sick poor mothers and the high mothers' death rate leave them cold."[6] Clarence C. Little, pro–birth control eugenist and former president of the University of Michigan, demanded birth control as an end to the "present tendency that pays money to non-productive and idle persons."[7] Another planner proposed a legal limitation of families to two children, with penalties for more, as a cure for unemployment.[8] To make her point, Sanger plotted escalating relief expenditures on a graph, which she displayed during her speeches.[9] James Bossard, a sociologist and social work expert, asked whether "those who are aided by society owe anything to society in return." The answer—their debt to society—was to control their fertility.[10]

At its 1935 annual meeting the ABCL unanimously resolved that:

> Whereas, the cost of public relief in the United States is now over 125 million dollars a month, and
> Whereas, scientific research has shown that families on relief have about 50% more children than similar families not on relief, and
> Whereas, these children add to the burdens both of their already over-burdened parents and of the taxpayers,
> Therefore, be it resolved that the American Birth Control League unite with the American Eugenics Society in formulating and securing the adoption of the most effective plans for providing that as a matter of routine, all families on relief shall be informed where they may best obtain medical advice in a strictly legal fashion as to the limitations of families by methods in accordance with their religious convictions.[11]

As they had done for decades, birth controllers used hereditarian arguments to make their case. To Eleanor Dwight Jones, president of the ABCL, it was obvious that the relief babies were of the "unfit" and that "social unfitness is, by and large, hereditary."[12] Despite the dimensions of the economic crisis, one birth control leader argued that "the man who shows no judgment about the number of children he sires is likely to be the man who loses his job in a crisis, perhaps because he lacks judgment all along the line."[13] Paul Popenoe, a pro–birth control eugenist, tried to make his views "objective" through IQ measurements proving that welfare children and their mothers were less intelligent.[14]

The eugenists were especially enraged that the birth rates of those on relief did not decline and in some cases went up. Between 1929 and 1932 the birth rate among families whose economic status dropped from moderate to poor was higher than that of families who continued in moderate circumstances. This phenomenon, seen as an irrationality, was proof of inferiority to the measurers.[15] Not only the birth rate but also the marriage rate, which was falling among the more prosperous, sometimes rose among poor immigrants and blacks.[16]

Although birth controllers saw these problems as evidence of the importance of contraception, not all drew the same conclusion. The alliance that Sanger had created with professionals was shaky in several areas. Many still found birth control too radical and objected to its capacity for licensing illicit sexuality and its interference with the divine or natural law of sex and reproduction. Underpopulation was still a common fear among those who gauged social health by nineteenth-century trends of steady population expansion.

Some physicians were anxious to preserve their exclusive control over reproductive medicine and felt threatened by the birth controllers' recommendation of contraception as a social and economic reform as well as a medical prophylactic. Many eugenists continued to fear the dysgenic effect of the rapid spread of contraception among the upper classes while the poor continued to produce large families.

Indeed, the first years of the Great Depression not only intensified the eugenists' attack on birth control but seemed, temporarily, to weaken the relative influence of the pro–birth control eugenists. In 1932 Henry Fairfield Osborn, a veritable dean of eugenics, delivered a major attack on birth control at the Third International Congress of Eugenics in New York. "BIRTH CONTROL PERIL TO RACE SAYS OSBORN," the *New York Times* headlined.[17] According to Osborn, "The country which has birth control in its most radical form is Russia, where it is connected with a great deal of sexual promiscuity. . . . Let us therefore consider birth control as one of the more or less radical departures from fundamental principles of our present social structure, not only in the religious but the ethical and moral fields." He criticized the feminist as well as the "dysgenic" component of birth control from a social Darwinist perspective. Although birth controllers said their aim was to free women of suffering, in Osborn's view they failed to realize that "women's share in the hard struggle for the existence of the race is a very essential element. . . . To relieve the animal or plant organism of its struggle for existence pressure is an extremely dangerous experiment, for . . . the struggle for existence is the *sine qua non* of every great human or animal quality."[18] Few eugenists condemned the birth control movement as totally as Osborn did, but many continued to press for "positive eugenics" programs in addition: that is, they wanted to encourage more reproduction among the "best stock." The eugenists considered themselves ahead of the birth controllers in projecting a whole population policy, not just a single reform.

The ABCL responded to Osborn with fury, arguing quite correctly that although contraception could give people the means to avoid reproducing, it was necessary to look elsewhere for their motivations—namely, to the "quality of our lives." The birth controllers challenged none of Osborn's basic assumptions, however: his eugenic categories (the "fit" and the "unfit"), his assumption that a growing population was desirable, his concept of "promiscuity," his facts about the Soviet Union.[19] Indeed, the ABCL began to argue that birth control was a flexible tool that would provide greater human choice and control over reproduction in every direction. Birth control clinics began to offer infertility therapy to couples who wanted children but had been unable to conceive.[20] Increasingly, the clinics' propaganda was directed toward "child spacing" rather than smaller families.[21]

Meanwhile, the early 1930s produced a number of demographic studies with conclusions potentially damaging to the birth control cause. Without challenging their assumptions, the birth controllers could not easily defeat their eugenic accusations. The development of statistical techniques in demography made possible ever finer breakdowns of census information, and foundation money paid for ambitious data-gathering projects. The questions these demographers asked of their informants, and of their data, once gathered, were influenced by eugenic fears, so the studies concentrated on birth-rate differentials. Furthermore, they usually did not conduct analysis over time, so their apprehension of historical trends was minimal. For example, surveys emphasized the differential birth rate—lower among prosperous, educated, white, native-born people—and often ignored the tendency, now several decades old, for the birth rates of the rich and poor to converge. Thus, Frank Lorimer reported in 1932 that the professional classes had a "replacement rate" of only 76 percent whereas unskilled workers had a rate of 117 percent.[22] In 1930, Edgar Sydenstricker and Frank Notestein published their study of differential fertility, which showed an "inverse" ratio of birth rate to class status. They listed the number of children per one hundred wives for the following classes.[23]

Urban		Rural	
Professional	129	Owners	247
Business	140	Renters	275
Skilled	179	Laborers	299
Unskilled	223		

Notestein also knew, and pointed out in a private discussion of the eugenic effort of contraception, that birth rates were declining fastest among groups previously most fertile.[24] Joseph Folsom, a sociologist with socialist leanings, pointed out that a look at the European experience showed a clear trend toward reducing the differential birth rate to zero.[25] But these trends were not usually integrated into the popularized versions of demographic alarms.[26]

Eugenists denied that birth control could be a solution. For one thing, the poor were morally irresponsible, possibly even vicious, and would not control their fertility. Eugenists sang the old chorus that accused welfare recipients of having children deliberately to get the added relief payments—even as little as $1.15 a week.[27] The Metropolitan Life Insurance Company reported that relief was the cause of the birth-rate increase.[28] A second argument was that the poor could not learn to use birth control properly; and in an era when the vaginal diaphragm was the only effective women's contraception, this hypothesis carried considerable weight. This had been longtime birth control skeptic Raymond Pearl's position in the 1920s,[29] and it was reiterated by many other scholars in the 1930s. Some recognized the need for the development of simpler and also cheaper methods of contraception.[30] But many merely repeated, thoughtlessly and uncritically, the various eugenic formulas. A common rhetorical device was a confusion of the rather large overall birth-rate differential between the urbanized and prosperous and the rural or newly urban poor with the numerically much smaller problem of reproduction among those with handicaps. In their attacks the eugenists frequently described the problem as if the poor and fertile were all feebleminded. As Dr. T. R. Robie expressed it: "I feel that I come from a very superior community because there one has the privilege of owning a garden. But from having this garden, I know how much faster weeds can grow than roses. There has been nothing said tonight about a way to stop the undesirables from overrunning us. . . . We talk about education, yet how can we educate feeble-minded mothers not to have children? We have got to look further."[31] Such views were all the more ill founded since there was not much evidence that most of the defects the eugenists feared—feeblemindedness and insanity, for example—were, in fact, hereditary; worse, many of their categories of undesirability did not describe objective congenital handicaps at all but merely characterized antisocial behavior, as in the concept of "degeneracy."

The fact that the vaginal diaphragm was the object of this skepticism is important, for the diaphragm was a "rich-folks contraceptive." It was difficult to use without privacy, running water, and a full explanation and fitting, luxuries not available to most Americans. The diaphragm was the most effective available contraceptive in the 1930s and certainly ought to have been offered to every birth control client. But simpler female methods, such as a vaginal sponge moistened with some spermicidal substance, had significant effectiveness rates and ought to have been made available as alternatives. In Miami, Florida, the maverick birth controller Dr. Lydia Allen DeVilbiss used the sponge method very successfully when combined with home instruction.[32] Unlike Sanger, DeVilbiss was openly racist, and her project was one of many sponsored by southern states to reduce the black population. Convinced that black women were of lower intelligence than whites, DeVilbiss systematically prescribed different devices for whites and blacks.[33] Such racist practices were not uncommon in birth control clinics, as we shall see later in this chapter, but DeVilbiss's experimentation with easier contraception for poor people could have been pursued in a nonracist way. The ABCL rejected DeVilbiss's experiments, not because of opposition to her racism, but because it did not find her work medically reputable.[34]

It is surprising, too, that birth controllers did not pay more attention to the advantages of the lowly condom—cheap, disposable, easy, quick, and pocket-sized. The condom had a lower effectiveness rate than the properly used diaphragm but a much higher effectiveness rate than the improperly used or misused diaphragm.[35] Of course, one reason for neglect of the condom was fear of licensing sexual immorality. The condom was well suited to be, as it indeed became, the chief contraceptive for "sinners." It was easy to get and required no doctors or special instructions. Indeed it is *because* the diaphragm was a medical device, requiring fitting and instruction in a clinic, that its distribution could be controlled. Until the late 1960s most birth control clinics would not aid unmarried women; and most women, married or not, had no access to clinics. The struggle over medical versus social and economic justifications for contraceptive prescriptions reflected not merely a fear for population size but also for the potentially immoral consequences of contraception.

That the birth control clinics aimed their appeal almost exclusively at women was a legacy of their early feminist heritage. But by the 1930s the birth controllers had virtually ceased expressing any concern with the women's rights aspects of birth control. It is all the more ironic and unfair, then, that birth controllers did not question the assumption that women should take the sole responsibility for contraception. This assumption also contributed to their failures, for they were asking women to take on this responsibility without arguing that it was specifically in their best interests.

The fact is that birth control clinics often failed to offer women the support and counseling they needed to include a diaphragm regimen in their sex lives. For example, the more common reason given by clinic patients for their failure to continue using birth control was "problems in marital adjustment."[36] There was a significant gap between women's exposure to contraception and their successful practice of it. For example, studies of several clinics showed that a mere two years after clinic visits, only 43–45 percent of women were still using any part of the clinical birth control methods they had learned.[37]

But the eugenists' argument that poor women could not practice contraception was not supported by the evidence.[38] Although studies showed higher effectiveness rates among the rich and well educated, they also showed significant effectiveness among the poor and very poor.[39] There were many reasons for the higher contraceptive effectiveness among more prosperous women: better facilities at home; husbands who also wanted to limit their families; possibly less moral or religious shame about sex; better instruction and medical advice. Women who obtained birth control devices from private doctors were likely to get more personal attention, and better-educated women, whether at private doctors' offices or clinics, were more likely to articulate their questions, doubts, and misunderstandings. Sharp differences in contraceptive effectiveness rates even within groups of the same class, religion, and ethnic origin suggested the importance of the kind of instruction women received and of incalculable personal and local factors.

The eugenic conclusion that the poor were stupid and immoral provided ammunition during the depression for a renewed campaign for sterilization. "Birth control or contraception cannot be depended upon to save us from the children of the very groups whom we are most eager to restrict," said Rabbi Sidney Goldstein at a eugenics conference in 1936.[40] The eugenics movement had introduced state laws for the compulsory sterilization of "degenerates" as part of a program that most progressives supported. Birth controllers had also supported sterilization for the feebleminded and others clearly unable to use contraception.[41] By 1915, thirteen states already had compulsory sterilization laws; by 1932, twenty-seven states. But sterilization proponents were discouraged that only 12,145 people had been sterilized under these laws.[42] With the help of the Human Betterment Foundation, established in 1928, eugenists stepped up their campaign for sterilization. Popenoe, one of the leading eugenists and sterilization advocates, estimated that, based on IQ testing, ten million Americans ought to be sterilized.[43] Another theme in sterilization propaganda was the waste of taxpayers' money in providing public institutional care and other "charity" for the "socially inadequate"; some even cited the economic loss of the wages that institutionalized patients did not earn.[44] The sterilization campaign identified economic dependence with hereditary feeblemindedness or worse. In the context of an alarm about relief babies, it reinforced fears that those with high birth rates were incompetent to use birth control.

To these objections to birth control—that the poor couldn't (and wouldn't) use it and the rich used it too much—the response of the birth controllers was to show that the poor not only wanted birth control but were capable of using it. Today there is little room for doubt about that proposition. One proof was in the mounting evidence that birth rates were falling fastest in those groups with remaining high birth rates, especially as a response to urbanization. Another could be seen in the public opinion polls about ideal family size. For example, a 1939 report on birth control among professionals cited 3.2 children as the ideal average, but a poll by the *Ladies' Home Journal,* with a less elite readership, produced almost identical results, 3.3 children as the overall ideal average.[45] (Studies done in the 1950s and 1960s have shown that poor people usually have more "excess" children—in terms of their own preferences—than higher-income people.[46] There is no reason to doubt that the same held true in the 1930s.)

A third kind of evidence was in the enthusiastic response of working-class people to birth control clinics.[47] The many women who did not return for follow-up visits and did not continue to use contraception properly had reasons other than lack of motivation, studies showed. These included unpleasant experiences at the clinics, hostile social pressure from husbands, relatives, and priests, and difficulties in using contraceptives. Furthermore, a large falling off in contraceptive use after the initial clinical visit was characteristic of women of all classes.[48] Social workers consistently reported both high interest in contraception among working-class women and problems in using it. For example, "In the follow-up work of the . . . cases which I have just completed I find many patients have used the method a short time or not at all. Some became confused as to technique, others lost confidence. Often they did not return to the clinic because of lack of carfare." Women were surprised when clinical workers took an interest in them, a surprise obviously based on long experience of disinterest. "Invariably, when I put on my coat to go," wrote one birth control caseworker, "the patients comment, 'how nice of Mrs. Sanger to send some one, I didn't know the clinic was so interested in us.'"[49] Birth control casework—visiting women in their own homes—was extremely rare in the United States. Clinical workers and observers always recognized its value but could not usually secure the funding for it.[50]

Money was always a problem for birth control clinics. In the first years few doctors had been willing to associate with a cause so risqué, and its growing respectability had not yet brought in funds on a scale grand enough to pay clinic doctors the salaries they could command elsewhere. Birth control clinics were not yet receiving large foundation grants.[51] So, despite the influx of professionals into the movement, the actual operation of local clinics, except for a few high-powered projects in New York and Baltimore, was still mainly in the hands of volunteer women. Financing them took hundreds of thousands of woman-hours of work. Just as it became most urgent to reach the poor, the Great Depression made raising funds more difficult and left the poor unable to pay for services.

The New Deal and Birth Control

Both sides of the depression's impact—lack of funds and eagerness to spread birth control among relief clients—contributed to a new tactic in the strategy of birth controllers: selling social workers on the importance of birth control. The increase in the number of caseworkers, as relief and other public assistance programs grew, made that group grow in importance as a channel for the cause. Social workers were likely converts because of the orientation toward service that led them to their profession in the first place and because of their direct and sometimes painful exposure to poverty in their jobs. Responding to their own common sense and to direct requests from clients, caseworkers pestered their supervisors and the birth control organizations with requests for contraceptive information and the authorization to pass it along to their clients. At social work conventions, American Birth Control League booths were flooded with questions—on techniques, locations of clinics, names of helpful doctors, speakers on birth control, and so forth. At the 1935

National Conference of Social Work, one-fifth of those attending registered at the ABCL booth.[52]

ABCL leaders were delighted. Emily Vaughn wrote in the *Birth Control Review* that "a major blessing may be pulled out of a major depression"—recognition that "prevention is better than cure."[53] Both in their professional organizations and at their agencies, social workers were heavily leafleted. The ABCL organized three or four panels at most social work conferences throughout the 1930s. In December 1935, the ABCL staged a mass meeting at Carnegie Hall to demand that relief agencies give out birth control information; speakers included Eduard Lindeman, a leading academic of the social work profession.[54]

Some birth control advocates, still oriented toward eugenics, criticized welfare services, charging that philanthropy without birth control was dysgenic. These charges often reflected conservative social values. Speaking at an ABCL panel at a 1932 social work conference, Frank H. Hankins, a sociologist and economist, argued: "Suppose now we take a look at the extreme environmentalist view of the causes of poverty . . . that the ills of poverty as well as . . . delinquency, crime, prostitution, venereal disease . . . are due almost entirely to the circumstances in which individuals grow up. . . . Certainly one cannot subscribe to the absurd extremes to which the environmentalist view has been pushed. . . . The restriction of the fertility of the less successful elements in modern society constitutes an important relief measure."[55] Sometimes the birth controllers' line amounted to a direct attack on relief programs, charging that they led to the "survival and increase of the unfit."[56] Indeed, some eugenists who spoke for the birth control cause were opponents of any kind of welfare programs,[57] and some birth controllers attacked the New Deal specifically. Margaret Sanger wrote in 1935: "As long as the procreative instinct is allowed to run reckless riot through our social structure . . . as long as the New Deal and our paternalistic Administration refuse to recognize this truism, grandiose schemes for security may eventually turn into subsidies for the perpetuation of the irresponsible classes of society."[58]

By and large, birth controllers were favorable toward the New Deal. Most were political liberals, and furthermore, as professionals, many stood to benefit from the expansion of state-provided services. Sanger attacked the New Deal because she was so single-minded about birth control and so antagonized by the Roosevelt administration's timidity and the president's personal ambivalence about birth control. The "underconsumption" theory of the cause of the depression, which influenced Roosevelt's "brain trust," had incorporated the *under*population theory promoted most vociferously by Louis I. Dublin, a demographer and statistician for the Metropolitan Life Insurance Company.[59] Sanger also suspected Roosevelt of caving in to Catholic pressure against birth control.[60] But despite the existence of good reasons to criticize the New Deal, the attacks coming from the birth controllers aided the right-wing antiwelfarist opposition to the liberal Roosevelt administration rather than the liberal or radical criticism of the inadequacy of New Deal programs. The birth controllers frequently pitted welfare funding against birth control funding, rather than arguing for both.

Public relief programs did indeed drag their feet on incorporating birth control services. In 1934 the ABCL sent a caseworker to the South in response to appeals from relief administrators, and she found them unanimously enthusiastic about birth control. (The caseworker did not seem aware of the possibility of racist motives in this enthusiasm.)[61] But they were not authorized to do anything. A 1935 survey of local administrators of the Federal Emergency Relief Administration showed no one willing to admit for the record that he or she gave out birth control advice.[62] An attempt to establish a birth control clinic as a Works Progress Administration project failed.[63] Key officials such as Harry Hopkins (head of FERA), Ray Lyman Wilbur (interior secretary), Katherine Lenroot (head of the Children's Bureau), and Thomas Parran (surgeon general of the Public Health Service) all refused to support birth control publicly, even in principle. Administrators of private charities shared their reluctance.

This continuing timidity about birth control put individual social workers in a difficult position. They never knew when their discretionary judgment might be respected, or when they would be reprimanded or even punished for what their supervisors tacitly accepted.[64] As long as officials chose to hedge, to protect themselves from political attack, social workers would be the scapegoats, as one journalist pointed out:

> . . . the social worker is merely a liaison officer . . . between the ruled and the rulers. . . . In general it seems neither just, pertinent nor useful to attack social workers for their failure to come out forthrightly and officially for the expansion of contraceptive service. . . . Unofficially, social workers . . . are not merely convinced, they are acting; they are everywhere and increasingly referring relief cases to the available clinics, sometimes at the very risk of their professional careers and their jobs.[65]

Behind official recalcitrance was, in some cases, strong opposition from the Catholic Church, which made politicians with Catholic constituencies especially fearful of the issue (these politicians included Roosevelt, of course).[66] Another source of official reluctance was the continuing radical reputation of the cause. In 1930, and again in 1937, a public relations consulting firm hired by the ABCL reported that birth control was being held back as a cause by Sanger's radical reputation.[67] Government officials expressed distaste for the term "birth control." Interior secretary Wilbur told the eugenist and birth controller Henry Pratt Fairchild that the notion of birth control was far too controversial for the government and that another name for it could not disguise what it was as long as Margaret Sanger was associated with it.[68] Dr. Lydia Allen DeVilbiss, while trying to organize birth control clinics in Florida, wrote to the ABCL in 1935 that the name "'birth control' . . . is still a red rag to the masses."[69] Furthermore, eugenic and underpopulation fears among welfare bureaucrats and social workers continued to support antagonism toward birth control.[70]

A partial defeat of official skepticism came about in part to popular pressure and in part to the realization that birth control among the prosperous classes was here to stay. Propaganda urging the "fit" to have more children had been repeated since the 1870s, and with great intensity in the first years of the twentieth century, but had made no impact whatsoever. Upper-class birth rates fell steadily and reached a new low during the depression. Furthermore, demographers and eugenists increasingly realized that repression of the organized birth control movement would not solve the problem. Since the well-to-do obtained contraceptives from private doctors, there was no practicable way to stop them. The clinics showed that a high percentage of women attempted some form of birth control before seeking clinical advice and that the higher the class of the clinic patients, the more often they had used birth control previously. As Dr. Regine Stix commented in 1937, "It wasn't the birth controllers who taught people to use contraception." Furthermore, "The things in general use, other than those prescribed by doctors, are extremely effective. The least effective method used cut the pregnancy rate in half."[71] The depression experience demonstrated more clearly than before that the key reason for smaller families was mainly economic self-interest—a motivation difficult to challenge in the American economic system.

Another factor, both consequence and cause of the "birth control is here to stay" phenomenon, was the commercialization of contraception. By the 1930s the manufacture of contraceptives was a large industry, retailing through millions of outlets. In 1936 the fifteen chief manufacturers of condoms were producing one and a half million a day at an average price of one dollar a dozen.[72] A survey done in Florida during 1932 showed condoms being sold in 376 kinds of places other than drug stores—including gas stations, garages, restaurants, barber shops, newsstands, and grocery stores.[73] One survey indicated that about $25,000,000 was spent on condoms in 1936;[74] another showed $436,000 spent on "feminine hygiene products" (i.e., douches) in 1933, the nadir of the depression, even though advertising expenditures were off by more than 20 percent.[75]

The contraceptive industry of the 1930s was an extreme example of commercial exploitation of popular ignorance. Although federal laws prohibited the mailing of contraceptive information, euphemisms such as "feminine hygiene" or "the intimate side of a woman's life" made possible the advertisement of products that were not only ineffective but potentially dangerous. The major danger was from chemical douches, which frequently created vaginal irritations. Lysol was such a product, advertised in *McCall's* in July 1933:

THE MOST FREQUENT ETERNAL TRIANGLE

A HUSBAND	A WIFE

AND HER

FEARS

Fewer marriages would flounder around in a maze of misunderstanding and unhappiness if more wives knew and practiced regular marriage hygiene. Without it, some minor physical irregularity plants in a woman's mind the fear of a major crisis.[76]

A variety of over-the-counter vaginal tablets and suppositories claimed to produce a shield across the cervix, but most were ineffective.[77] Preying particularly on women who were denied access to better information, some firms employed door-to-door peddlers who made fraudulent claims, offering, for example, diaphragms without fittings or proper instruction. One firm told women that the diaphragms could be exchanged at the nearest birth control clinic if they didn't fit. Another firm sent saleswomen to the very poor with an intrauterine device almost certain to be dangerous if inserted by oneself. One common racket was to sell two products in which the second allegedly made up for the failure of the first. The B-X Monthly Relief Compound, for example, promised to bring "'soothing, satisfying Glorious Relief,'" with the B-X Special Multi-Strength Treatment recommended if the purchaser complained that the first compound didn't work.[78]

Many advertisements for these products were manipulative, even brutal: "'She was a lovely creature before she married. . . . But since her marriage she seems forever worried, nervous and irritable. . . . Poor girl, she doesn't know that she's headed for the divorce court. . . . And yet, that tragedy could be so easily avoided, if *she only knew.*'"[79] Others simply lied, as in this ad for Hygeen vaginal tablets:

"Some time ago a group of prominent English physicians, thoroughly alarmed at the increasing variety and nature of various feminine hygiene products offered to the public—set about to determine which one was the safest and most effective. . . .

"So this group of English physicians under the auspices of the English Medical Society, had the Oxford University, Department of Anatomy and Zoology, determine under Dr. John R. Baker . . .

"THE RESULT OF THIS MOST THOROUGH INVESTIGATION REVEALED THIS SAME HYGEEN TABLET HOLDS FIRST PLACE AMONG ALL THE PRODUCTS INVESTIGATED."

In truth, there was no English Medical Society and the investigation was a complete fabrication. The tablets consisted of baking soda, tartaric acid, sand, starch, and a small amount of an organic chlorinated product, not an effective spermicide.[80]

Although contraceptives still could not be legally moved across state lines, the ban was no more effective than Prohibition had been to the sale and consumption of liquor. In fact, the prohibition of birth control probably raised its price. Manufacturers' and retail profits on the sale of contraceptives were enormous in comparison to those on other pharmaceutical items. For the three leading brands of condoms in the late 1930s (Ramses, Sheiks, and Trojans), the average gross retail profit was 72.5 percent, the average wholesale profit was 33.3 percent, and the manufacturer's average markup was 120 percent. Profits were equally high on diaphragms and spermicidal jelly products. For example:

Average Diaphragm	Molded	Dipped
Cost to manufacture	$ .25	$ .18
Price to wholesaler	$1.20	$ .60
Price to druggist or doctor	$1.50	$ .75
Price to consumer	$3.00–$5.00	$1.50–$2.50

Average 3-oz. Tube of Spermicidal Jelly	
Cost to manufacture	$ .11
Price to wholesaler	$ .40
Price to druggist or doctor	$ .60
Price to consumer	$1.00 and up

These were not the prices of fly-by-night, small-time operators but of the largest pharmaceutical houses and druggists.[81]

Despite high profits, the increasing commercial success of birth control contributed to its ultimate legalization. The toleration of euphemisms in advertising while the noncommercial discussion of contraception in popular journals remained illegal was a galling injustice that the birth controllers continually attacked. The fact that the "patent medicine" contraceptives were not only ineffective but often dangerous strengthened the unity of birth control organizers with the medical profession.

The birth controllers' reaction against commercialization was not to combat it with demands for public sex education but to lobby for doctors' privileges. Margaret Sanger argued not only against commercialization but against all "indiscriminate dissemination of birth control."[82] Furthermore, in the cam-

paign against commercialization the biggest drug companies—frequently referred to by birth controllers as the "reputable" companies—tended to support the restriction of sales to doctors. Their size made them reluctant to face
legal difficulties, whereas smaller, transient companies sought quicker profits.[83]
The more professional orientation of the larger firms found them discriminated
against in some avenues. For example, one large pharmaceutical house wanted to run an advertisement in a women's magazine urging women to consult
their doctors for contraceptive advice; no magazine would take the ad, even
those that regularly ran euphemistic ads for feminine hygiene products.[84] But
the fact is that private doctors and scholarly medical journals were free to
prescribe and discuss contraception. Although a legal basis for prosecuting
doctors existed under most state, if not federal, laws, no such prosecutions were
attempted and most doctors felt safe to do what they believed was medically
proper within the confines of their private practices.[85]

The more serious obstacles to birth control were not legal but social and
economic. Despite the fact that a 1937 poll showed 79 percent of U.S. wom-
en believed in birth control,[86] those who did not have regular access to private doctors were effectively deprived of contraceptive information, as birth
control clinics served only a negligible fraction of the population. By contrast,
the professional and upper classes did get the information they needed. Had
this not been the case, Sanger might have been able to mobilize a more effective lobbying campaign.

Despite a brilliant organizing effort, Sanger's National Committee for
Federal Legislation on Birth Control (NCFLBC) failed to push any legislation through the Congress. A doctors-only bill was reported out of the Senate
Judiciary Committee in 1934 but was quashed when Senator Pat McCarran,
of anticommunist fame, demanded that it be held over for reconsideration in
the next session. Sanger's efforts did, however, make possible a victory in the
courts in 1938. A test case had been designed to provide for litigation against
customs officials, who had tended to enforce bans on "obscene materials" more
rigidly than the U.S. Post Office. Sanger arranged to have a package of pessaries mailed to Dr. Hannah Stone of the New York Clinical Research Bureau
from Japan, and U.S. Customs seized the shipment. Holding against the government on appeal, Judge Augustus Hand used medical testimony in his opinion, arguing that in 1873, at the time of passage of the Comstock law, information on contraception was poor and that Congress would not have
considered contraception immoral had it understood all the facts.[87]

This decision removed all federal legal bans on birth control. But it did
not touch state legislation against birth control, and it did not solve the moral, social, and economic problems associated with obtaining birth control in
the United States. Furthermore, the federal decision was narrowly based.

Sanger's work in lobbying and testifying at the Senate hearings on her bill had brought to the attention of public leaders the pro–birth control opinion in the medical profession. This sense that birth control had been endorsed by the "experts" informed the judge's opinion. Indeed, it declared birth control not obscene *because* it was a medical tool but avoided any discussion of changing sexual morality or women's rights. The birth control movement had won its first federal victory by purporting to represent the medical profession. As a result, nonmedical birth control programs gained little from the decision. The progress of projects such as birth control education for relief recipients depended more on the balance of pressure applied to New Deal administrators.

In the final analysis, judges, doctors, government administrators, and pharmaceutical houses entering the contraceptive business were persuaded by the growth not only in public approval but also in demand for birth control. The top-down birth control programs of the New Deal were responses to bottom-up pressures. Just as all New Deal measures were both stabilization programs and concessions to demands, so were birth control measures.

The popular demand for birth control would have been much stronger, naturally, had women been more organized during the Great Depression. Still, both clinics and private doctors felt the pressure.[88] Clinic workers in Bangor, Maine, reported that one woman, a mother of seven, arrived at the clinic on a bitter winter day in 1937, having walked five miles in only a thin coat. They had to warm and feed her before she could see a doctor.[89] One birth control clinic worker in Brooklyn told about her visit to a working-class woman who, after a brief discussion about birth control, asked to be excused for a few minutes; when she returned, she had six more women with her and said, "They want to know about birth control."[90] In Paterson, New Jersey, a Working Women's Council organized to establish a birth control clinic. Mill workers were active in the initial efforts. The council invited a woman from the Montclair, New Jersey, ABCL clinic to speak, and she stressed the need to work quietly and avoid newspaper publicity in order not to provoke opposition. A social worker at the meeting reported that a "poorly dressed" woman had jumped up and in "scanty English she said, 'We want publicity; we expect opposition; we will fight it; we want to reach the women like myself.'"[91]

Letters continued to pour in to Sanger and the ABCL asking for help. Birth control was a subject of discussion in many local papers. When a woman's page columnist for the Columbus, Ohio, *Citizen* published Sanger's address as a source for birth control information, Sanger received more than five hundred letters in just a few days, including these two:

> "I have 8 children and the oldest is 14. My husband works on relief, because his job is shut down. . . . Please tell me the secret about birth control. When

you write about it, please write to me in plain words because I don't know what it means in big words."

"I am a farmer's wife in the drouth area and we have not had a crop for four years. My husband worked on the WPA, but now all the farmers have been layed off, so we are very hard up. . . . It spoils married life to be worried all the time over having more babies."[92]

Such letters confirmed what the polls had shown since the early 1920s: support for birth control was surprisingly high even in rural and small-town communities that seemed very conservative on other issues. The high proportion of mail from rural areas reflected in part the inaccessibility of local birth control advice. Furthermore, the most powerful organized opposition to birth control came from the Catholic Church, relatively weak in rural areas and strongest in large working-class parishes. Catholic women at this time consistently used birth control less and attended clinics less than Jewish or Protestant women; nevertheless, many working-class Catholic women used contraceptives. A report on a New York City clinic with a predominantly poor Italian Catholic clientele showed 63.5 percent had used birth control before coming to the clinic, as compared with approximately 90 percent of Protestant clients in a Harlem clinic. Other studies reported comparable statistics.[93]

The interest of working-class women, even Catholics, in birth control did not represent a rebellion against a traditional family role. As letters and interviews showed, women wanted control over pregnancies to improve and make easier their traditional home work, not to escape it. The increase in birth control use during the depression was not caused, as it had been in past decades among professional women, by the search for more education and better employment. Yet the desire for birth control came overwhelmingly from women, not men, and was not quite identical with the so-called economic motives that were discussed earlier. For working-class as opposed to more prosperous women, reducing family size and extending the gaps between children was not just a matter of budgeting resources but also parenting better and in a less alienated fashion; in other words, having more control over the conditions of housework and child care and being able to do the jobs well. It was a motivation not entirely different from that of an artisan or skilled worker who would rather do a good job than a poor one.

Many women viewed their childbearing capacity as a form of social labor, and some, like so many other workers in the depression, conceived of a strike as an appropriate tactic—in which case birth control became their weapon. In 1937 twenty housewives from New York's Lower East Side picketed city hall against delays in the construction of promised public housing and declared that they would have no more babies until their demands were met.[94] Women's activism on this as on many other issues of survival escalated in the depression, in part because high unemployment was reducing male, and thereby increasing female, familial power.

Some New Dealers and social workers supported and encouraged the birth control demands of working-class women. Social workers convinced settlement houses in New York City to provide contraceptive services.[95] In Connecticut, social workers organized a mobile contraceptive clinic, using a van to reach housebound women.[96] New Deal admirers of the Soviet Union sometimes urged emulation of its birth control policies.[97] But even pro–birth control caseworkers often remained condescending, following a neo-Malthusian principle in promoting birth control to their clients as a tool against poverty. For them, birth control became mainly a welfare program and only secondarily a human right.

Many caseworkers also tended to see their clients not as *having* problems but as *being* problems. No matter how environmentalist their analysis of the genesis of problems, they still saw them as embedded within the individual. It was as if social inferiority, now that it was no longer considered hereditary, was randomly distributed; the problems were in people themselves—their diseases and deficiencies—not in patterns of deprivation produced by the social structure. By contrast, the depression was revealing to many that inequality was a deep-rooted structural feature of the economy, which produced and reproduced poverty not only through periodic recessions but even in times of prosperity. Upward mobility was actually quite a rare event in the modern industrial economy; some proportion of the population would always be poor, disadvantaged, underprivileged, and it would usually be those whose parents were poor, disadvantaged, underprivileged. Birth control was unlikely to alter those structures.

Perhaps the worst case of ignoring such deep structure in New Deal–era birth control propaganda was the denial—through silence—that reproduction was particularly a woman's problem. The NCFLBC program, for example, listed four reasons for birth control: to help family spacing, to decrease poverty, to stop illegal abortions, and to eliminate mental and physical deficiency.[98] ABCL documents similarly omitted any mention of women's rights; for example, a 1934 pamphlet listed eight necessities for family health, in this order: prevention of venereal disease; complete elimination of abortion; reduction of maternal and infant mortality; sex education; early marriage (quite a difference from the anti–early marriage policies that dominated from the 1960s onward); prevention of conception for unhealthy, exhausted, or economically unprepared women; sterilization of the insane and feebleminded; good marital sexual adjustment.[99] For women, birth control was presented as a remedial aid in the case of abnormal personal problems: "unhealthy, exhausted or economically unprepared." The truth is, of course, that women's problems were not abnormal and personal but normal and social; that women needed birth control as a standard practice, not a cure for a disability, and particularly because they were almost always those charged with the responsibility for children, while they also had far less earning power than the men of their class. The birth controllers presented contraception antihistorically, as a new invention that could improve social welfare, ignoring birth control's capacity to affect the class, race, and sex balance of power. Failing to discuss, for example, the intrafamily and marital dynamics that could be affected by birth control was almost tantamount to dishonesty. The silence about sex discrimination actually made it more difficult to convince women of the importance, and potential, of birth control.

This "blame the victim" sociology helped to continue the professionalization of birth control. Viewing individuals as the problem was a way for social workers and bureaucrats to retain control of the service programs they offered. Welfare programs placed birth control in the context of social worker–client relations, thereby discouraging mass participation in the cause. Already in the 1920s the influx of professionals had moved birth control organizationally away from local leagues with amateur participation toward national staff organizations. That tendency continued in the 1930s. Margaret Sanger left the American Birth Control League altogether and put her energies into the NCFLBC, which, as a lobbying organization, had less room for membership participation than ever before. Indeed, the NCFLBC did not even have members; participation was limited to subscribing to its newsletter.

Sanger was not only passionate but also a dynamo of energy and daring (chutzpah to those who resented her) with an extremely sharp learning curve. She had taught herself by now to conduct a big-time lobbying operation. In one of her first actions with the new organization, Sanger hired a prestigious New York public relations firm to advise her on tactics.[100] She became, with her lieutenants, an expert Washington "pol." She accumulated endorsements from organizations claiming to represent twenty million voters;[101] she attempted to attach pro–birth control amendments as riders to relief bills (using the high birth rates of relief recipients as justification); she organized state-by-state pressure applied to any legislator who seemed even potentially winnable. Ultimately she failed, and no federal legislation for birth control was passed (although she managed to smother in committee H.R. 5370, in 1935, which would have made the receipt of contraceptive information illegal), But it is hard to imagine that any other leader could have achieved more in the absence of a women's movement.

Lobbying became a permanent part of the new-style birth control cause.[102] This kind of work required money, and Sanger also devoted increasing effort to fund-raising among the rich. Winning over upper-class women was part of the legislative strategy, for while the labor power in the movement remained primarily that of amateur women, their class status was all the more important. In a 1935 magazine article entitled "Birth Control Goes Suave," one reporter described the new birth control movement:

> Evidence that the cause has reached the dignity of a grown-up movement was offered at the recent banquet of the National Committee on Federal Legislation for Birth Control in the Hotel Mayflower in Washington. Limousines drew to the door in a prosperous relay, debouching a confident and well-bred crowd. Women predominated, society-page cameras clicked. Significant was the cordiality between dinner guests and the occasional Congressman they encountered among the potted palms. . . . No one expressed anger or impatience at the snail's pace methods necessary for doing business with our government. No one was *gauche* enough to recall the naive and impolite methods once used, when birth control leaders courted arrest and forced test cases on embarrassed magistrates. . . . Margaret Sanger's movement had tacitly announced that it was ready to play ball. . . .
>
> Women of the type now appearing in the birth control movement have had social training in drawing-room diplomacy, and they carry their tact with them into legislative halls. They are deft at fund-raising—their childhood friends are the heads of corporations, the publishers of newspapers. . . . Many a man . . . will reach for his checkbook when the appeal comes from his hostess of the week before. The owner of a radio station or a magazine chain, inaccessible to most callers, listens politely to the plea of a woman who heads the membership committee of the Junior League, which his daughter would like to join.[103]

The Washington committee in the winter of 1934 included Mrs. J. Borden Harriman, Mrs. John F. Dryden, Mrs. Harold L. Ickes, Mrs. Mary Roberts Rinehart, Mrs. Frederic A. Delano, Mrs. Eugene Meyer, Mrs. Dean Acheson, and Mrs. Dwight Clark; sponsors elsewhere in the country included Mrs. E. Marshall Field, Mrs. Thomas W. Lamont, Miss Anne Morgan, Mrs. Narcissa Cox Vanderlip, Mrs. George Thomas Palmer, Mrs. Victor Du Pont, Mrs. George LeBoutillier, Mrs. Elizabeth Hook, and Mrs. Thomas Hepburn.

The fund-raising events were sometimes so snobbish that they antagonized professionals. For example, Harry Hansen, *New York World Telegram* literary editor, wrote to Sanger: "Your formal invitation to the H. G. Wells dinner [held at the Waldorf-Astoria] looks to me like one of those Big Business Rackets. Hence I withdraw my name from your so-called reception committee."[104] So involved was Sanger with this pretentious style that she did not defend herself on the reasonable grounds that she was trying to raise money. Rather, she tried to convince Hansen that he belonged on the reception committee because of his literary merit: "You were asked to be on the Reception Committee not because I wanted $10.00 from you or wanted your financial support at all. There will be many literary people on the Reception Committee invited to the Dinner to sit at the speakers' table. There will be others—bankers and other persons who can pay and who . . . find it cheap at that. I do not know whether you attended the Tagore or Einstein dinners at which there were cover charges of $25.00 and $100.00 respectively."[105]

For Sanger this style of organizing had become a strategy more than a tactic. She believed that alliances with the wealthy and powerful could replace the broad mobilization that had started the movement. She did not, for example, try to mobilize masses of women to go to Washington to testify that birth control was their right; rather, she relied on society women and male experts to convince legislators that birth control was good for what ailed the country. While traveling, she ignored local birth control organizations that did not acknowledge her national leadership and the political line she laid down and excluded them from conferences. Her relations with co-workers were those of master and apprentice or employer and employee, and her apprentices and employees were frequently discontented. The files of her Clinical Research Bureau in New York City held many letters of complaint from workers, torn because they believed in the cause they were working for yet resentful that they were being treated like proletarians. Workers were poorly paid, allowed no participation in decision making, and deprived of information that would allow them an overview of their work—turning their work, in fact, into alienated labor or piecework. When they complained of speedups, Sanger insisted that they were not working as fast as they could. Often workers were fired without notice or explanation.[106]

The ABCL's organizational style did not differ fundamentally from Sanger's. It too concentrated on getting endorsements from the rich and prestigious and neglected education and the development of local chapters. ABCL president Eleanor Dwight Jones usually argued that reducing the population of the "unfit" was the main task of the movement.[107] The ABCL and Sanger's Clinical Research Bureau merged in 1938 into the Birth Control Federation of America (BCFA), and the new organization committed itself to "professionalizing" its work. New policies included the introduction of time sheets for the staff for the purpose of clocking working hours and evaluating the amount of time spent on particular activities, thus enabling a cost-benefit analysis of the work. In efforts clearly designed to check decentralization, the BCFA prohibited staff members from undertaking any work without clearing it with the national director and ordered elected board members to do so as well before making suggestions to local leagues.[108]

Birth Control and Government: Race and Class Politics

The top-down organization of birth control, both in politics and procedures, was strengthened by its integration into programs of governmental social welfare agencies. During the Great Depression, small-scale birth control programs developed in state, and occasionally city, public health programs; federal relief programs; and population control programs in Puerto Rico. Let us consider each in turn.

The first state to offer birth control services through its public health program was North Carolina in 1937, followed soon by South Carolina, Virginia, Georgia, Mississippi, Alabama, and Florida.[109] Despite control by health officials, birth control was offered to women for economic and social as well as medical reasons. On the whole, contraceptive advice was offered only to indigent mothers; others were directed to physicians.[110]

That these pioneering states were all southern was no coincidence. They were not the leading but, by and large, the most backward states in terms of social service programs. Their innovation in government-sponsored birth control was conditioned by the absence of large Catholic constituencies but, more important, by racism. A generally high southern birth rate was even higher among blacks. Black families, both urban and rural, were among those hardest hit in the South by the depression; they were the first fired, the first evicted, the first foreclosed. Like other poor people, they did not respond to economic pressure by lowering their birth rates, so the depression added to white fears of being overpopulated by blacks. The North Carolina public health officer responsible for the birth control program described his simple technique for convincing recalcitrant country health officers that birth control clinics were needed: Check your vital statistics, he would suggest, confident that they would discover a high proportion of black births and that they would then come around.[111] Miami set up separate birth control clinics for whites and black workers, but the separate-but-equal pretense broke down quickly when blacks, given autonomy in their clinic, ignored the "advice" of the white directors. A furious Dr. Lydia Allen DeVilbiss took away the black clinic's funding: "Our colored clinic did not turn out the way we thought it would so it should not be mentioned this time [on the ABCL list of affiliated clinics]. We shall likely have to re-organize it. I wonder if southern darkies can ever be entrusted with such a clinic. Our experience causes us to doubt their ability to work except under white supervision."[112] State leagues affiliated with the ABCL, later with the Planned Parenthood Federation of America, remained segregated into the 1940s.[113]

Racist use of eugenic rhetoric and theory was several decades old. Eugenics had provided justifications for antimiscegenation laws passed early in the twentieth century.[114] At first, echoing the conservative eugenists, Virginia officials in the mid-1920s thought that birth control was inimical to their maintenance of a racist society. An official of the State Board of Health wrote to the ABCL:

> I believe that Mrs. Margaret Sangster [*sic*] and her group have done far more to ruin the future of our country than all other methods combined, unless it be the amalgamation of the white and negro races, now rapidly in progress. The evidence which I have is that the universal adoption of the methods advocated by you has done much to increase immorality among the unmarried, who have no fear of consequences. . . . You may now be securing the adoption of such measures by the feeble-minded and lower type, but I very much doubt it. You have, however, met with overwhelming success among the higher type. . . . [This] will mean their ultimate deterioration, just as it occurred in Rome.[115]

But by the 1930s the same Virginia authorities promoted birth control. Methods changed, but goals did not: they had become convinced that the "lower type" would accept contraception and the "higher type" would never give it up.

Although racism in the South was built on segregation, it survived on the exploitation and impoverishment of a large proportion of whites as well and the continuing arrogance of "good" southern families toward "white trash." The demographic characteristics of southern blacks—high birth rates that were not lowered by increasing economic pressure—also described poor southern whites, though to a slightly lesser degree, and state programs tried to bring birth control to them as well. North Carolina, for example, persuaded several large textile mills, which employed mostly whites, to distribute slips in payroll envelopes telling workers that company nurses would provide contraceptive information.[116] (One might wonder at the efficacy of introducing birth control propaganda to workers through their employers.)

Racism, class inequality, and eugenic beliefs combined to produce a view of southern population and health problems as overreproduction of the "unfit." The unfit included all forms of undesirable inferiorities. "In a study of 1500 women admitted to the obstetrical wards . . . 39 percent of the whites and 70 percent of the negroes were found to be feeble-minded or at least of a mental age of only seven years or less," argued the Miami Mothers Health Clinic, which was later supported by the city health department and the Public Health Nursing Service.[117] A fund-raising letter read:

> Dear Friend and Taxpayer, You were taxed in round numbers TWO MILLION DOLLARS for the care of pauper, indigent sick and the criminal classes in Dade County for 1933. . . .
> 500 indigent mothers in Dade County have been instructed in eugenic birth regulations.[118]

Racism, then as now, is not a southern problem. Indeed, the tendency to project it exclusively upon the South has been a sign of northern denial. In 1939 the BCFA, with the cooperation of southern state public health officials, designed a "Negro Project," arguing that southern poverty was a major national problem and one that could be ameliorated through birth-rate reduction. "The mass of Negroes, particularly in the South, still breed carelessly and disastrously," argued the project proposal, "with the result that the increase among Negroes, even more than among whites, is from that portion of the population least intelligent and fit, and least able to rear children properly."[119] Despite the pretense of concern with the unfit *among* blacks, this statement was immediately followed by a chart showing the overall increase of the black as opposed to the white population. The eugenic disguise fell off to reveal overt white supremacy. "Public health statistics," the proposal continued, "merely hint at the primitive state of civilization in which most Negroes in the South live."

The project would hire three or four "colored Ministers, preferably with social-service backgrounds, and with engaging personalities" to travel throughout the South and propagandize for birth control, since "the most successful educational approach to the Negro is through a religious appeal." As Sanger wrote in a private letter, "We do not want word to go out that we want to exterminate the Negro population and the minister is the man who can straighten out that idea if it ever occurs to any of their more rebellious members."[120] The ministers would enlist the aid of black physicians—who were expected to offer their services gratis—and attempt to organize a "Negro Birth Control Committee" in each community. Sanger genuinely wanted this to be a project for black uplift, and she meant to avoid the substance as well as the appearance of trying to reduce the black population. But neither she nor her sponsors were willing to relinquish control, not even to handpicked local blacks. Clarence Gamble, author of the proposal and negotiator of its eventual funding by Mary Lasker, wrote in a private memo: "*Colored Steering Committee.* There is great danger that we will fail because the Negroes think it a plan for extermination. Hence lets appear to let the colored run it as we appeared to let south do the conference at Atlanta."[121]

The relationship between these projects and the local doctors was equally illuminating as to the BCFA mode of operation. Since doctors would not, at first, be paid, the proposal allowed them to compensate themselves at the expense of their patients by providing physicians a "limited supply of free material which they are at liberty to charge a private patient for, but which must be given without charge to an indigent patient." Eventually, Sanger and Lasker revised the project to include hiring a doctor. Gamble agreed to "a subsidy to a local colored doctor to put his weight behind the new regime,"[122] though he preferred to spend BCFA funds on education only, through the ministers. When the project became operational, Gamble clashed with South Carolina's public health director: Gamble did not want his funds "diluted with a lot of general health work," whereas Director Seibels thought that general health work was essential to the program.[123] Gamble's principle was adherence to the narrowest, single-issue orientation. Though he himself did not believe that birth control alone could solve problems of poverty and discrimination, that was the educational content of the project.

African American clients of the southern clinics were by no means controlled or duped by the birth control organizers, however. In North Carolina, as virtually everywhere clinics opened, some women eagerly sought contraceptive advice and materials. They attempted to negotiate with clinic staff about what kind of contraceptives they wanted, complained when those they were offered had unpleasant side effects, and spread to one another the news of their experiences with contraceptives. They were entirely willing to ignore the racist aspects of the program for their own purposes.[124] Despite the support of African American professionals in the community, however, none of the southern black clinics became permanent, though they had more success where they hired black nurses.[125]

In both content and organization, the BCFA's "Negro Project" functioned to stabilize existing social relations, working through conservative community leaders such as ministers and doctors. It failed to challenge the commercial relationship of doctors to patients by paying doctors to work with the poor. From New York the BCFA sought support for the project by writing to everyone in the Colored Who's Who.[126] Birth control propaganda in the South was removed from any politics that might have given it a democratic meaning: women's rights, civil rights, or any social analysis of southern poverty.

Lack of a larger analysis doomed even well-meaning birth controllers to the perpetuation of elitist attitudes in all their work, not only in projects specifically aimed at blacks. An ABCL fieldworker wrote about the southern women she encountered: "They are almost child-like in their faith in the clinic workers and what can be done for them." She was outraged at their poverty—"It is difficult to believe that so much poverty and misery can exist in such a playground as Miami with all its wealth and gaiety"—but quick to find solutions in the puny efforts being made: "However, during the Season generous donations are made for hospitalization and contraceptive work. . . . With laws no longer hindering and a method which is simple and obtainable everywhere under-privileged mothers can at last be free from over-frequent child bearing and establish for themselves and their children a decent standard of living."[127] With such an analysis a woman's failure to establish a decent standard of living must be due to her stupidity or irresponsibility.

The sympathetic but condescending attitudes of this birth control worker were common among caseworkers and public health nurses in federal as well as local programs. As the depression continued, a few federal agencies had begun surreptitiously funding birth control work. In the late 1930s a confidential memo in Sanger's files listed two federal birth control projects funded by the Farm Security Administration, which hired public health nurses to bring contraceptive information to poor farm women and to the California migrant labor camps.[128] In addition to these authorized programs, many caseworkers were directing clients to private clinics and doctors for contraceptive advice. Acting without explicit authorization, such caseworkers also lacked training in dealing with sexual issues. Furthermore, they were usually educated people coming into contact for the first time with the illiterate, demoralized, and resentful poor. No doubt many of the latter did not receive the social workers with welcome and trust, just as the social workers did not always avoid a moralizing attitude toward the poverty, din, dirt, and fatalism with which their clients often lived.[129]

Many caseworkers were supportive, but sometimes even the most sympathetic responded to the extremely poor with a blinding condescension, as in the report of this woman who visited a migrant worker's family in California:

> One of my first cases was a family reported to our agency for neglect of children. . . . It was a sort of improvised commune, which the poor and migratory had found for themselves. Here they could unload the dilapidated Fords and turn the children loose. The luxuries of the place included one water faucet, serving the colony of thirteen tents—apparently the only sanitary convenience.
>
> I found the family I sought established in two tents, the pots and pans hanging in a row along a tent beam, the washing steaming over a stove made from an old oil can. Five scrawny children hung about. Two of them, I learned, were registered in school, but were temporarily on vacation for lack of shoes. Three were babies, one obviously defective. The mother was loyal to her brood, tired and dispirited as she was.
>
> "But why do you have so many children," I asked bluntly.
>
> She shrugged her shoulders.
>
> "My husband not very bright, not make much money. But he do the best he can. . . . Too bad," [she said] apologetically, "some of the children not very bright too. . . ."
>
> Before the winter rains descended, the mother of five was again big with child.[130]

Despite her judgment that, among the myriad problems faced by this woman, lack of birth control was central, this caseworker was unable to offer contraception. She tried and failed to find a doctor to provide a diaphragm and fitting. She then tried to arrange a sterilization for her client but was disappointed to learn that the county hospital would not do it. All this apparently took place before any discussion with the woman about what *she* wanted. There is no report of offering condoms to the husband or of speaking to the husband at all—contraception was assumed to be exclusively a female responsibility.

Beyond her helplessness to offer concrete birth control assistance, the caseworker failed to try to understand her client's desires. She finds it somehow odd, or at least worth mentioning, that the woman loves her children; indeed, she describes their relationship in animal terms ("loyal to her brood"). The social worker's report that the woman said her husband was "not very bright" seems so unlikely, both in language and attitude, that one is inclined to question whether it was an accurate report at all or a projection of the social worker's own attitudes. A novice at her job, she was responding humanly and naturally to a circumstance that shocked her. Better education about the problems of poverty might have improved her sensitivity to the situation, but it was not available because the whole relief program was an emergency measure without long-range commitment to public responsibility for social welfare. Birth control fit this paradigm because it was considered a kind of emergency commodity rather than a matter of individual decision making. Some contraceptive information reached poor women, but its extent was small— the total amount spent by the federal government directly on birth control was $11,000, according to Sanger's confidential memo—and it was justified as an emergency measure, designed to help specific cases at the discretion of individual nurses and social workers. Hardly a program offering birth control as a right.

The depression did bring about one governmental attempt to introduce a massive birth control program, however, but not in the continental United States. There is no space here to examine fully the story of population control in Puerto Rico, which had been annexed to the United States in 1898, but the political debate about it raised issues that soon became of importance on the mainland. Since the early 1920s Margaret Sanger had visited third-world countries to explain the contribution that birth control could make toward alleviating poverty. In Japan, China, Korea, Hawaii, India, and Bermuda, among other places, she pushed for national birth control organizations. Liberal governments in several underdeveloped countries supported birth control programs, though lack of funds usually meant that their support was minimal. In the 1930s a major campaign was waged for the legalization of birth control in Puerto Rico, which succeeded in 1937, despite opposition from the Catholic Church. Federal government pressure was extremely important, if not defining, in this victory.[131] (That Catholic opposition could be defeated even in Puerto Rico, where there were no countervailing religious institutions, suggests that it might have been defeated on the mainland as well, given the right leadership.)

But in Puerto Rico, in addition to Catholic opposition based on antisexual and antiwoman attitudes, there was also nationalist resistance. Nationalists. perceived birth control as an imperialist weapon designed to weaken Puerto Rican independence aspirations and to deflect attention from the island's need for economic justice. One of the more moderate opponents of the pro–birth control legislation, J. Enamorado Cuesta, secretary of the Nationalist party, stated his position thus:

> There is no denying that overpopulation . . . is at present a problem to us. . . . [But] it is directly at the door of American capitalism that the blame must be laid for everything that is wrong in Porto Rico today. . . . when American in- tervention was started, while sanitary conditions were certainly not very good, still our people owned their land, the produce they exported. . . . in thirty-four years of American intervention . . . with the cooperation of American-made native and continental legislative bodies, the people have been dispossessed of their land and brought to the condition of paupers. . . .
>
> This does not mean that I am systematically opposed to birth control. But our real problem lies in the actual control by American capital of practically all our wealth. . . . We may, and we may not, enact birth control laws (I think we would) as soon as the American flag is lowered from our public buildings.[132]

Other internationalist critics of birth control have sometimes confused imperialist motives in birth control programs with the value of contraception as a technology and have minimized the value of birth control as an individu- al human right. Their confusion, however, was created in part by the birth con- trollers' relative silence on human and women's rights. Although this silence had begun to appear in domestic eugenic arguments for birth control in the 1920s and 1930s, it was carried much further in the discussions of birth con- trol as a cure for economic underdevelopment. For example, a committee of the American Child Health Association reported that Puerto Rico had 174,650 "too many" children.[133] Perhaps this was merely a clumsy formulation; but the mentality that leads demographers to calculate the number of "extra" children is one that is not particularly concerned with individual rights and human emotions and is likely to antagonize the parents of those children whom they probably do not regard as "extra."

In May 1939 President Roosevelt's Interdepartmental Committee on Puer- to Rico labeled overpopulation the basic cause of "the Puerto Rican problem." The committee proposed a mass campaign to reduce the birth rate at least to the level of the death rate. "All other endeavors to improve the health condi- tions of Puerto Rico must be organically tied to, and made contingent upon, effective birth-control work."[134] This Puerto Rican program was in many ways the embryo of later massive U.S. population control programs. Their common denominator was the treatment of birth control as a weapon in the arsenal of economic planners. It was almost a full reversal of the nineteenth-century conception of birth control—voluntary motherhood—in which technology followed the human and especially female desire for self-determination; now technology was leading and individual will was being molded, planners hoped, by powerful persuasive techniques. Birth control became a lever for the manipulation of the economy, much as advertising is used to stimulate consumption.

The Puerto Rican model extended on a smaller scale to the mainland. Although the United States was hardly a third-world country, the economic crisis of the 1930s had given it one of the characteristics of underdevelopment—namely, "overpopulation" in the form of massive and persistent unemployment. The depression was not a temporary collapse but the beginning of a permanent inability of private corporations to provide full employment without government assistance. The demographers began speaking of the danger of overpopulation in the 1940s, after decades of worrying about underpopulation, and their change of mind was stimulated as much by unemployment as by the birth rate. Even before they were postulating general overpopulation, however, while it was the differential birth rate that drew their attention, they began to suggest that birth control might alleviate or at least lessen the unemployment problem.

Some birth control professionals realized that the depression represented a major turning point for the economy and eagerly leaped at the opportunities it presented for birth control. Margaret Sanger, so often in the vanguard of new birth control arguments, asserted in a major speech in 1935 that unemployment was not a temporary but a permanent problem that only birth control could correct. She identified the cause as technology.[135] As the sociologist James Bossard observed: "The demand for unskilled labor has been declining . . . but it is in this group . . . that the reproductive rates are highest. . . . As the demand for unskilled, low intelligence labor decreases, corresponding readjustments must be made in the supply of this type of labor, if we are to avoid the crystallization of a large element in the population who are destined to become permanent public charges. This points again directly to birth control on a scale which we have not yet fully visioned."[136] Bossard, like so many professional eugenists before him, slipped from concern for the unemployment of the unskilled to the hereditary assumption that the "low-born" were only suited to unskilled jobs. But within the system set up by his assumptions, he had latched on to a new way to manipulate the employment market, a new variable open to social control: the supply of people.

This was a major factor behind birth control's ultimate achievement of respectability. The depression—capitalism's worst crisis to date—began the transformation of birth control into an official program for achieving economic improvement without redistribution. That program was encapsulated in the title of an article by Guy Burch, a leading eugenist and later population controller: "Birth Control vs. Class Suicide."[137] Four decades previously the cry had been that birth control *was* race suicide because its practice by educated, prosperous women challenged sex roles, sexual inequality, and the family structure within their class. In the 1930s birth control became the alternative to class suicide, a means of heading off the militancy of those at the economic bottom. Yet in both eras the impact of birth control was double. In the early 1900s race suicide represented not only a women's rebellion but also a deepening of class divisions among women. In the 1930s birth control not only represented an effort to prevent social explosion but, simultaneously, an explosion of new demands from and expectations among working-class and poor women. These complexities have been part of the history of birth control since its inception and continue today.

11 *Planned Parenthood*

In 1938, the birth control movement reunified, bringing Margaret Sanger's friends and enemies together in the Birth Control Federation of America, which became the Planned Parenthood Federation of America (PPFA) in 1942. It was the only national birth control organization until the abortion reform movement that began in the late 1960s, and its new name—usually shortened to Planned Parenthood—defined a new concept of birth control that dominated in the United States until then: family planning.

Planned Parenthood identified itself as apolitical. In confining itself to a single issue, it hoped to achieve a broad coalition, but in doing so it undercut the democratizing potential of birth control. Its primary claim was that family planning would strengthen the family. Planned Parenthood took the family, not the woman or the individual, as the unit for the application of reproductive control. The very concept of planned parenthood implicitly denied the feminist critique of inequality within the family. Whatever vestigial concern with social injustice remained in the PPFA, its leaders thought social instability a greater evil.

Reform to strengthen the family had been the earmark of all birth control campaigns, but the first two campaigns saw women's rights as the core of this reform. Planned Parenthood in the 1940s did not. It was continuing a move away from the feminist and leftist origins of the birth control fight that began in the 1920s with the influx of professional personnel and values into the American Birth Control League. Planned Parenthood expressed a distinct second stage in that progression: the incorporation of reproduction control into state programs as a form of social planning. The PPFA commitment to planning took in both child spacing and family size as well as governmental population planning. In the movement toward large-scale social planning of population, the 1940s was a midpoint between the seeds sown in the Great Depression and the harvest of the 1950s and 1960s, with its massive federal support for population control programs.

The PPFA in the 1940s did not yet call for population control; indeed, there was not yet agreement that overpopulation was a problem. Rather, the PPFA called for planning, not specifically reduction in numbers; and it was a planning that involved qualitative as well as quantitative views of what was a desirable population. It is this qualitative set of norms that provides the unity between the large-scale population planning and the small-scale planned families that the PPFA urged. Both rested on standards of excellence based on upper middle-class aspirations.

This was not a conservative but a reform program. Like the ABCL during the depression, the PPFA attracted the support of liberals in the government and the professions who welcomed and even fought for reforms to make the economic and social system more generous and tolerant. This was true not only of their desire to raise the standards of living of the poor through family planning but also of their increased recognition—at least among those aware of these issues—that women might be happier with more sexual fulfillment. Part of the PPFA program of family stability was the recognition of mutual sexual enjoyment as an important support for marriages and of women's sexual repression as a dangerous, explosive frustration. Their nineteenth-century voluntary motherhood predecessors thought sexual *control* led to family and social stability; planned parenthood advocates thought sexual *expression* led to stability.

The reforms promoted by Planned Parenthood were desperately needed by women, so many of whom were now coping with the double day—a waged job and an unwaged job. Nevertheless, Planned Parenthood both reflected and contributed to the decline of a popular birth control movement connected to a program of social justice. Under professional control, Planned Parenthood offered birth control wrapped in an ideological package that challenged neither the sexual inequities within the family nor the sexual or class inequities of the medical system.

Yet Planned Parenthood's impact was more radical than it intended. Its success in what it did do—making contraception more accessible and thereby freeing many women from unplanned pregnancies—helped create the conditions for a revived feminist movement, which in turn produced a second feminist birth control movement in the late 1960s . . . which by the 1980s had transformed Planned Parenthood into a feminist ally.

A New Name, a Clean Image

The radical associations of the term "birth control" seemed inescapable to many in the movement in the 1920s and 1930s. Opponents still called Sanger a free-lover, a revolutionary, an unwed mother. Some supporters tried to coin new names for the movement: "Children's Charter," "Better Families," "Child Spacing," "Family Planning" were a few of them. Many of these suggestions had a meaning similar to that which was finally victorious; they lacked only the catchy alliteration of "Planned Parenthood." All the names proposed took the focus away from women and placed it on families or children. All were designed to have as little sexual connotation as possible.

"Planned Parenthood" was proposed within the ABCL from at least 1938.[1] That it was not adopted until 1942 was due in part to opposition from Sanger. Within the birth control movement the name change was supported largely by the eugenists. But the victorious name was chosen by a public relations consultant, D. Kenneth Rose, originally hired by Sanger. In this language as well as policy, the switch to "Planned Parenthood" flowed, despite her objections, directly from Sanger's own policies.[2]

One of the arguments for the new name was that it connoted a positive program, unlike the negativism implicit in "birth control." This idea that birth control was negative reflected eugenic influence. Eugenists used a distinction between positive and negative eugenics and considered birth control a tool in the latter program; positive eugenics meant encouraging more reproduction among the "fit." In 1941 the medical director of the Birth Control Federation of America took this distinction, twisted it slightly, and applied it to birth control itself. He called for the addition of a positive birth control program, the "encouragement of a sound parenthood, in all economic classes, as a major means by which this nation can be maintained strong and free."[3] His implication was that birth control in itself was unpleasantly negative.

Beyond this the BCFA saw another kind of negativism in the tradition of birth control, especially one lingering from the voluntary motherhood tradition. Feminists had begun their birth control agitation by emphasizing the right of women to refuse their husbands sexually. Voluntary motherhood advocates interpreted this refusal in a political sense, understanding women's power of negation as the necessary condition for their winning the power of assertion; and they understood power relations within the family as a microcosm of the power relations of the whole society. Planned parenthood advocates, by contrast, sought to treat the family, and in particular the married couple within it, as a unit, capable of common decisions. They tried to de-emphasize the feminist connotations that still clung to birth control. Antifeminists have always seen women's complaints as negativism. The term "planned parenthood" was positive in the sense of being uncomplaining, positing no aggrieved parties seeking justice.

Planned parenthood seemed a more positive concept than birth control especially to those who liked the idea of planning. Presumably birth control left matters such as population size and quality to the anarchism of individual, arbitrary decision. But the propaganda of the birth control organizations from the late 1930s through the late 1940s increasingly emphasized the importance of social planning. A Birth Control Federation of America poster read: "'MODERN LIFE IS BASED ON CONTROL AND SCIENCE. We control the speed of our automobile. We control machines. We endeavor to control disease and death. Let us control the size of our family to insure health and happiness.'" Sanger used the planning rhetoric too. National economic and social planning, she argued in 1935, requires "family security through family planning."[4] In a CBS radio speech in 1935, Sanger pointed out, accurately enough, that "every good housewife accepts the idea of planning for the comfort of her household. She plans her budget. . . . She tries to plan for sickness and unemployment."[5] Thus, arguments for family planning took place on both the grandest and the smallest of scales. Common themes included planning the use of the nation's human resources; the waste of overpopulation, particularly "overproduction of people" among those families that could ill afford them; and the necessity to understand the consequences of population changes for economic problems.[6] "Haphazard childbirth" wastes resources, "planned childbirth" saves resources, wrote Woodbridge Morris, medical director of the BCFA.[7]

The respectability of planning had grown considerably since the inception of the birth control movement, and the New Deal brought an intensification of the state's intervention into people's lives. Nazi and Soviet state planning, including reproductive planning, generated opposition in the United States but also evoked admiration; even among its enemies, the Soviet Union commanded respect for its economic, and later military, achievements. The late 1930s produced a qualitative change, however, in the prestige of state planning. The response of reformers to myriad new issues was to demand the development of an overall governmental policy on each. The planned parenthood advocates, even before their organization adopted its new name, emphasized that contraception was a tool to achieve a goal greater than mere individual freedom.[8]

The application of planning to birth control helped transform it into a population control movement, a transformation nearly total by the early 1960s. In the 1940s PPFA leaders still saw large-scale population concerns as secondary to those of family health, but the two were converging. "Planned Parenthood is an invitation to apply a basic social and scientific concept to the improvement of the family unit—and thereby our whole population," read a PPFA pamphlet.[9] The social work leader Eduard Lindeman insisted as early as 1939 that population planning should "become an integral part of social and economic planning."[10] The birth control organizations demanded a "sound national population policy."[11] At the time, it was not at all clear what population planning meant, for almost all those who mentioned it were quick to denounce the "authoritarian" population planning used in Germany. They called for a "democratic population program" to "mobilize our human resources." The BCFA urged the development of a National Population Commission.[12] It was thinking in terms of demographic study and projection of long-range trends, moving toward recommendations about optimum growth rates and family sizes. In March 1943 a mass mailing from Planned Parenthood to lawyers and business owners spoke of the importance of population in planning for the postwar era: "Any sound peace plan must take into consideration population trends and natural resources, when we face such divergencies as the population of India. . . . Sound planning for business expansion on a national scale must also consider carefully not only the numerical growth of people, but their purchasing power."[13] The considerations necessary to population planning could never be strictly quantitative. What was overpopulation in one place might be good for business in another. Population control principles had rarely stayed in quantitative channels, and the dominant trends among the most recent demographers were eugenic.

To the extent that the government took official cognizance of population problems, it still did not consider birth controllers the relevant experts. The best birth controllers could do was to get pro–birth control eugenists to represent them. Henry Pratt Fairchild had been their spokesman during the Hoover administration, and as late as 1941, when Eleanor Roosevelt held a White House meeting on population, it was Fairchild and Frederick Osborn of the American Eugenics Society who argued the case for birth control.[14] The eugenists no longer used racial or ethnic identifications but often referred to income levels. "ONE HALF OF ALL BABIES ARE BORN TO THE LOWEST INCOME FAMILIES," proclaimed a BCFA poster. It did not, incidentally, compare this number of births to the percentage of low-income people in the population; the implication was that low-income people ought to have few children. As a Planned Parenthood pamphlet put it, parents should build families "commensurate with their abilities to provide for them adequately."[15] When a prospective parent says this to herself, it is common sense; when a birth control organization says it, with an explicit or implied "ought," it is urging different family sizes upon different classes.

World War II

As the emphasis on planning strengthened the population control and eugenics slant of birth control, so World War II further strengthened that orientation and de-emphasized contraception as a matter of individual and female rights. Civil liberties and individual rights are often weakened in militarily mobilized societies. During this war, domestic policies continued depression policies that made government planning and control easily accepted. The major PPFA pamphlet on birth control during the war declared:

PLANNING FOR VICTORY

> The American people today need no further evidence on the necessity for quality in man power and materials to win the war. It sees, at last, that victory cannot be won without planning. . . . Planned Parenthood, with your understanding and support can, in 1943, be made to mean that *more healthy children will be born* to maintain the kind of peace for which we fight.[16]

Nevertheless, despite its assimilation, now two decades old, to eugenics and population control, birth control still had a reputation as individualistic, selfish, and societally weakening. Birth controllers feared the impact of a "war psychology" upon their movement. They remembered the antiradicalism that had accompanied World War I as well as that war's cost in lives and the resultant concern for population growth; and they anticipated a reassertion of the logic that in a time of national crisis childbearing was a woman's contribution. Several years before the United States entered the war, the Birth Control Federation of America (and, after 1942, Planned Parenthood) began a propaganda offensive designed to counteract wartime anti–birth control sentiment.

The wartime slogans centered around birth control's contribution to national strength. They tried to squelch the lingering Malthusian association of national well-being with numbers, replacing it with a qualitative definition of strength. Sanger called for "national security through birth control."[17] She spoke of the national weakness created by the high birth rates among the poor and the international insecurity created by surplus population in Germany, Italy, and Japan.[18] After war broke out in Europe, the emphasis on national strength divided into three themes: birth control's contribution to the economy, to physical health, and to mental health. All were interrelated and all shared an emphasis on the good of the collective and a marked de-emphasis on individual rights.

Regarding the economy, BCFA and PPFA publicity argued that in modern war, as in industry, machines had come to be more important than men and that even in the infantry military strength was often a matter of quality rather than quantity. It argued that expenditures on "relief babies" were even more dangerous to the economy in wartime than before. One BCFA memo calculated costs, anticipating a hypothetical argument that five hundred birth control clinics could be closed at a yearly saving of approximately $2,500 each, creating a total of $1,250,000 that could be used for war work. "The average cost to the community of a baby born is $100. The average clinic serves 500 women. If 60 percent had unwanted babies, the cost to the community would total $15,000,000 annually. To save $1,250,000, we would saddle the United States with $15,000,000 additional expense. Rather than do this, we would redouble our efforts."[19] Another memo proposed arguing for birth control as a solution to the social disorders that might flow from economic disarray: the curtailment of world trade due to the war could be expected to deprive the United States of needed markets and raw materials, and these losses would in turn create unemployment and greater social unrest, for which a decline in the birth rate would be a helpful palliative.[20] This rather frank plea for birth control as a crutch for a weakened imperialism did not, however, find its way into public statements of the organizations.

Closely related to economic arguments was concern for supporting morale on the home front. Here, too, birth control could make a contribution: "A nation's strength does not depend upon armaments and man power alone; it depends also upon the contentment . . . of its people. To the extent that birth control contributes to the health and morale of our people, it makes them less receptive to subversive propaganda, more ready to defend our national system."[21] President Roosevelt had said the same thing in one of his fireside chats: that unless the social reforms of the New Deal were preserved, the people's morale would be weakened and they would be less resistant to foreign propaganda. The BCFA staff by this time saw themselves as an unofficial part of the New Deal. They were still worried about their radical image, however, especially in relation to wartime xenophobia. By May 1941 a BCFA fieldwork director wrote to a national staff member, "Can you think of a way to identify B.C. with 'Being an American?' . . . Out[side] of New York 'Being an American' is what folks are boasting about."[22]

World War II nationalism had a more liberal political content than that of the Theodore Roosevelt administration or World War I, two periods that had set back the birth control movement substantially. The view that World War II was a struggle of democracy against totalitarianism was especially appealing to the liberals and reformers of the birth control movement: birth control was a part of the fight for personal liberty against authoritarian governments, and in preparing for defense we should not sacrifice one of the rights we were defending.[23] The pronatalist, positive eugenics policies of the German and

Italian governments seemed the very essence of fascism to the birth controllers. "THE STORK IS THE BIRD OF WAR," headlined a 1938 article attacking the rewards given to prolific mothers in Germany and Italy.[24] This went beyond the argument that overpopulation caused belligerence; in fact, it was based on a distinction between authoritarian and democratic methods of population control. That birth control was an integral part of our democratic and free way of life became a basic theme in early wartime publications.[25] Sanger, for one, spoke out against the Soviet Union for its reintroduction of controls on birth control and abortion. Using her sharpest condemnation, she compared Mussolini, Hitler, and Stalin to the Catholic Church.[26] But interestingly enough, the birth controllers did not find it necessary to denounce fascist negative eugenics policies—for example, forced sterilization of Jews—though this may have been because such programs were less well publicized in the United States or because they had no supporters here.

If birth controllers had criticized fascist and communist suppression of women's rights, they might have found it harder to ignore discrimination against women in the democracies. When, for example, birth control organizations discussed women workers, whose numbers rose dramatically in the wartime economy, their concern was narrow and slanted toward serving the employers. A 1944 PPFA pamphlet asked plant managers to consider the "industrial loss incurred through the lessened efficiency of married women deprived of a normal sex life through fear of conception." The PPFA urged personnel managers to put Kotex- and Tampax-dispensing machines in the bathrooms and warned that women often used menstruation as an excuse for not working.[27] Elsewhere, they described women workers as expensive investments to be protected through proper care, including birth control.[28] Describing the general situation of birth control in wartime, Henry Pratt Fairchild's only comment about women workers was: "It needs no special argument to demonstrate the dangers of interruption and restriction of production if women are unable to exercise rational control over reproduction. It has been found in a few plants surveyed that absenteeism due to pregnancy or induced abortion is creating a problem which may increase as more women move into war industry."[29] Nowhere in BCFA or PPFA materials was there a suggestion that women were discriminated against, on the job or at home. If women were singled out in birth control propaganda, it was to suggest that contraception control was a woman's duty, not her right.

The contribution of birth control to health became another important argument in the general theme of building national strength. "Good health" replaced "good stock" as the measure of the quality of the U.S. population. From 1940 on, BCFA and PPFA spokespeople declared health the major immediate objective of birth control work.[30] The unfitness of many conscripted men brought the backwardness of U.S. public health standards to the fore, and the birth controllers argued that planned children would be healthier. The "waste of human resources" theme was applied to the 40 percent of men who were rejected by the armed forces. One PPFA leaflet calculated a total human "waste" of 37 percent, including 9 percent who died unnecessarily, 3 percent crippled, 1 percent with TB, 15 percent retarded, 8 percent "maladjusted," and 1.4 percent delinquent.[31] This dysgenic problem resulted from "lack of control of the size of family in relation to health and income."[32] Clearly, birth control could contribute to health. Planned Parenthood's emphasis, however, was not on individual welfare but on individuals as variables in social planning—"human resource management." During World War II social scientists analyzed the weaknesses and strengths of the human resources of the United States and its enemies—for example, national character studies—as well as workers' attitudes. They viewed people as instrumentalities, and the PPFA accepted that discourse in its health emphasis.

Furthermore, in its new emphasis on health, Planned Parenthood repeated its eugenic refrain. "Class," or income level, now replaced "stock" as the determining criterion, though many planned parenthood arguments continued to rest on the assumption that children of the poor would be less healthy than children of the rich; and since the PPFA did not suggest that better nutrition or medical care could change these health destinies, its arguments continued to reinforce hereditarian views. At least one PPFA staff member was perturbed enough about this content in birth control propaganda that she complained to the national director. She acknowledged that the propaganda was less elitist than it had once been, but she still thought that the tendency of the PPFA to make a family's economic status a "paramount criterion regarding desirability of reproduction" was a continuing problem. "We know too little about heredity," she wrote in 1943, "and certainly by implying that people without wealth have no right to have children, we are open to criticism. . . . True, we appeal to some people by expressing such views, but we can appeal to them on other, sounder grounds."[33]

Although the hereditarian assumptions of PPFA propaganda in the 1940s were expressed mainly in class terms, racial differentials in the birth rate were by no means ignored. World War II accelerated the migration of blacks to northern and western industrial cities. The incorporation of blacks, mainly men, into industry and then the armed forces created the conditions for a renewed civil rights struggle, just after New Deal programs had brought to the attention of white liberals and radicals the disproportionate poverty of blacks. For example, in 1940 the BCFA reported that half the black population of the United States was undernourished; that blacks had an infant mortality rate 60 percent higher than whites; that tuberculosis and syphilis were five to six times more prevalent among blacks; that black mothers had twice the rate of mortality in childbirth as white mothers.[34]

For both eugenic and social welfare motives, birth controllers tried to increase the availability of contraception in black communities. Birth control clinics included in public health programs in southern states had reached proportionally fewer blacks than whites, despite their intentions. In the North the clinics and organizations were primarily in white communities. In response, the American Birth Control League had begun in the 1930s a campaign specifically directed toward blacks. True to its overall orientation, the ABCL first courted the support of black professionals. Special "Negro Issues" of the *Birth Control Review* began to appear after June 1932, publishing testimony by black men of note (rarely women) supporting birth control. A Negro Advisory Council and a national Negro Sponsoring Committee were established; in 1944 the PPFA also hired a full-time "Negro Consultant."

In 1947 the PPFA promised a kind of affirmative action program for the organization, insisting that, beyond hiring staff and choosing board members on the basis of ability alone, there should be "qualified representation . . . for any racial group which is consistently represented in its geographic area" or "which constitutes a considerable clientele." Furthermore, "No staff member should be employed who does not possess the emotional acceptance and intellectual understanding of the problems represented in the minority groups of the Community."[35] The deeper aspects of the race problem, however, were not those of overt discrimination, severe as that might have been, but the structural aspects of racism and their impact on the significance of birth control. Throughout the 1930s and 1940s black resistance to birth control was reflected in the arguments of both black and white birth control advocates. They were continually countering charges that birth control was a policy designed to reduce the size of the black population, thus weakening it politically.[36]

That charge—in its extreme form a charge of genocide—must be taken seriously. It has been repeated up to the present time by many who suspect both the intentions and the consequences of birth control programs, and it is hardly odd that representatives of an extremely poor and exploited group might find some security in numbers. The opposing, pro–birth control view argued in response that a richer, healthier black population would be collectively (as well as individually) stronger and that numerical size was not the main source of political clout. This disagreement was based on the confusion—indeed, the virtual identification—of birth control with eugenics. De-emphasizing birth control as an individual right, birth controllers themselves had made their program safe only for those confident of being considered "superior stock."

Despite their suspicions, black women usually responded enthusiastically to contraception.[37] Their health was indeed worse than whites', and they welcomed increased control over reproduction. But the reasons for their poorer health were primarily environmental, not hereditary, and birth control could provide only a small improvement in that regard. A few birth control advocates, such as Joseph Folsom, argued for better overall health services to complement birth control. Some Planned Parenthood workers recommended that the PPFA call for better housing and expanded health programs.[38] PPFA statements not only failed to adopt this line but sometimes pointed out that birth control could make up for the inevitable curtailment of health and welfare programs due to war expenditures.[39] In an even more blunt acceptance of wartime cutbacks, one BCFA memo warned that the poor would need birth control in order to survive, since New Deal relief funds were likely to be cut.[40]

In failing to show the complexity of the relationship among family size, health, and class, Planned Parenthood was responsible for some misleading propaganda. A common example was the presentation of statistics on family size and/or child spacing and infant mortality. A BCFA poster that carried the headline "PROPER CHILD SPACING PREVENTS INFANT DEATHS" compared death rates for babies one year apart (146.7 per 1,000 live births) to those spaced two, three, and four years apart (98.6, 86.5, and 84.9 per 1,000, respectively). Such statistics imply that close births *cause* infant mortality. But closely spaced births are common among people with generally poor health care, nutrition, and housing, and it is the latter factors that more likely cause higher mortality rates. This confusion of symptom with cause, and the removal of birth control from the general health context, was becoming a hallmark of the modern birth control movement.

Although they did not wish to dilute their arguments for birth control by campaigning for improved general health care, Planned Parenthood workers knew they would gain through inclusion of birth control services in existing general health programs. A particular wartime problem that offered them such an opportunity was venereal disease. The armed forces quickly added V.D. prevention programs to their scope of work, but V.D. was also spreading among civilians, and it provided a wedge for increased governmental participation in birth control problems. A navy captain appointed by the White House to serve as liaison to Planned Parenthood forwarded recommendations that birth control work be done by the Public Health Service, the Children's Bureau through its maternal and child health programs, the Work Projects Administration through its V.D. prevention program, the Defense Health and Welfare Service of the Federal Security Agency, and the Food and Drug Administration (which was testing contraceptives). Captain Stephenson also recommended federal financing of a long-term research program and a test case against the Comstock law to be brought to the U.S. Supreme Court.[41] Little of this was initiated except direct anti-V.D. work, but the campaign won many supporters within the government, helped counteract fears of Catholic opposition, and brought closer the time when birth control would be eligible for federal support.

In general the emphasis on health was part of a BCFA and PPFA campaign to convince professionals in the health field that birth control should be included in health services, whether in governmental programs, private clinics, or individual practices. A second and more controversial aspect of that campaign argued that birth control was an important ingredient in mental health programs. This argument, too, was strengthened by war experiences, especially family instability. Social workers and sociologists were warning of the war-associated causes of the destabilization of family life: fatherless children, employed mothers, geographical mobility, "marry-and-run" weddings.[42] Their fears were borne out. Marriages, births, and divorces increased sharply. The marriage rate had gone up 5.7 percent by 1940 and another 20 percent by 1941; in the month after Pearl Harbor it climbed to 50 percent. The birth rate also went up steadily in the years 1940 to 1943 (from 17.9 to 18.9 to 20.5 to 22 percent).[43] Unwanted pregnancies probably increased even more than the birth rate, since the number of illegal abortions rose, especially in the large cities.[44] The attitude toward premarital relations between the sexes also changed rapidly during the war. "Dating" became the norm and the double standard in its practice was modified as women began sharing expenses and taking the initiative in proposing activities. Taboos against sex in dating relationships eroded.[45] The armed forces had given up preaching continence, and even those who advocated social purity in World War I had come to believe that soldiers' sexual indulgence was unstoppable.[46]

These changes in attitude and behavior punctured the ideal of an untroubled, abiding family life. The ideal had never existed in reality, but it was nonetheless powerful as an image, and the fear of social instability was intensified by anxieties produced by the depression and world war. If good morale on the home front was important to the war effort, it seemed that family stability should provide that morale. Birth controllers argued that unwanted conception and "excess children" threatened family stability.[47] They talked of "reinforcing family values"[48] and argued that birth control would produce "wholesome family life."[49] The journal of the National Conference on Family Relations, an organization whose leaders often also worked in the BCFA and PPFA, declared the potential erosion of family life a national problem of the greatest urgency, central to the national defense. Particularly concerned with cynical army morality, the editors called for inculcating members of the armed forces with attitudes compatible with healthy family life.[50]

This emphasis on the family was new to birth control. Yet it was the logical culmination of changes over the previous two decades that made of birth control a practice that would stabilize, rather than destabilize, society. The feminist orientation toward birth control had expected, even welcomed, a certain measure of destabilization, particularly of the family, as essential to women's liberation. The birth controllers' World War II propaganda avoided criticizing women's subordination and refrained from pointing out that birth control could expand women's opportunities and ease their workload. Planned Parenthood's wartime goals did not mention women's rights. Indeed, PPFA leaflets described women's appropriate family role in conventional, sexist terms. A cartoon pamphlet, *The Soldier Takes a Wife*, claiming to deromanticize marriage, prescribed what to look for in a wife: "She may be good at jive but a 'Sad Sack' at the skillet. She may be a dud at the piano but an ace with the needle. She may look like a angel at midnight but how about when she wakes up without her make up?"[51]

So the family stability they sought locked women into their conventional spheres. It is striking, but logical, that this image of the family persisted during a period when widespread employment of women and absence of men jolted many into creating new living situations, not in conventional nuclear families. Women showed remarkable ingenuity in finding alternative sources of stability, with roommates, collective living and eating situations, extended families, and the like. They also struggled for day care and equal treatment on the job, causes that Planned Parenthood did not enter. The official PPFA attitude toward women war workers was at best opportunist and at worst hostile: the birth controllers predicted that married women doing paid work would need birth control more than ever and that birth control organizations might thereby benefit from the war.[52] But nothing in their propaganda suggested that these work opportunities were desirable (though this was the view that predominated among the workers).[53]

Margaret Sanger, by now retired in Tucson, Arizona, and playing a diminishing role in Planned Parenthood affairs, seemed now an old-fashioned feminist by comparison to the new leadership. In 1942, for example, she protested a regulation of the Women's Army Corps against WACs having babies, there being no such regulation applied to army men.[54] The unfortunate WACs were in a double bind, for army men were issued contraceptives and the WACs were not. Sanger issued a statement attacking this discrimination as well, although PPFA public relations director Scull tried to prevent her from doing so and criticized her for not specifying each time that only married WACs should receive contraceptives (a requirement certainly not made of men).[55] Her speeches of the late 1930s and 1940s retained some of the feminist rhetoric of the past, calling for "rebellion" and "struggle." Sanger also held on to her grudges. Shown a proposal in 1940 for a National Marriage and Family Institute that was to include Dr. George Kosmak, the notorious antifeminist, as a charter member, she scribbled angrily in the margin, "Oh my god Why always honor the reactionary and keep him afloat. My interest would stop right at sight of his name."[56] By contrast, the orientation of the birth control organizations by this time was to make alliances and seek support from all influential, respectable people, no matter what their historical role or their overall politics, and required only the lowest common denominator of agreement.

Sanger's differences with the birth control organizations boiled down to an instinctive militance and residual feminism she could not shed. Birth control's success had only confirmed her conviction that gains were won and public opinion changed through confrontation and open conflict. To her, militancy and outspokenness did not necessitate political disagreements with the organizations that now harvested what she had cultivated. Her concern for women's problems had never appeared to her in any way antagonistic toward her growing commitment to eugenics and the social planning of population. If she was opportunistic, she never violated her own principles. She was eclectic, but consistent. As late as 1939 Sanger repeated what she had first said in 1919: that birth control could solve the key social problems through eugenic regulation if only "statisticians and population experts as well as members of the medical profession had courage enough to attack the basic problem at the roots":

> That is not asking or suggesting a cradle competition between the intelligent and the ignorant, but a drastic curtailment of the birth rate at the source of the unfit, the diseased and the incompetent. . . . The birth control clinics all over the country are doing their utmost to reach the lower strata of our population, but as we must depend upon people coming to the Clinics, we must realize that there are hundreds of thousands of women who never leave their own vicinity. . . . but the way to approach these people is through the social workers, visiting nurses and midwives.[57]

Sex and the Feminine Mystique

In one area Planned Parenthood continued a woman-centered orientation and that was in matters of sex. Although past birth control organizations and agitators had argued for the acceptance of women's sexuality, only the PPFA incorporated the goal of female sexual fulfillment into its program. Planned Parenthood led the way in bringing the medical, social work, and mental health establishments to support the sexual rights of women and thereby changing public opinion.

This contribution is even more impressive when seen in its social context. PPFA sex counseling and sex education were developed during the late 1940s and 1950s, a period of political reaction and great economic expansion. Wartime production finally brought the United States out of the depression. At home, the postwar era was prosperous if measured by the gross national product, disposable personal income, and purchases of consumer durables. However, a high rate of inflation and increasing productivity meant that the working class and the poor paid for the prosperity, gaining very little in real wages and losing on issues of working conditions. Despite some large strikes, many of them successful, organized labor lost ground to a sharp political attack. First communists were driven out of the unions, then the power of the unions themselves was restricted by federal legislation, and then the red scare was extended to liberals and leftists through the McCarthy investigations. The impact of all this on birth control was similar to that of political events in the post–World War I period: it created a political and cultural hysteria hostile to the liberalism of birth control.

Planned Parenthood was particularly affected by an aggressive cultural reassertion of a conservative femininity, later called by Betty Friedan the "feminine mystique." Communicated through the mass media, the schools, the psychiatric and medical establishments—indeed, through all the channels that create gender—the mystique resurrected some Victorian norms of femininity. Experts harped on physical differences between the sexes in a kind of biological determinism, the defiance of which could only lead to unhappiness, neurosis, failure, even sickness. Women's biological capacity for motherhood made it improper for them to attempt any other career. By contrast, a true woman, according to the mystique, would be able to make an important and fulfilling contribution to civilization through her "homemaking" and her edifying influence on her children and husband. The transformation of housework into routine, alienated janitorial services was attributed to women's own failings rather than to the process of industrialization; indeed, the manufacturers and advertisers of industrially manufactured goods argued to the housewife that their products could help her restore creativity to her housework, although it was the mass manufacture of those commodities that had stripped the creativity from housework in the first place. The source of the power of the feminine mystique was partly in the economic need of the manufacturing sector to raise consumption rates in order to prevent an economic downturn when war production ended. Simultaneously, demobilization presented serious unemployment potential unless women could be forced out of the industrial jobs they had taken during the war, and the "women belong in the home" credo helped justify depriving women workers of seniority rights and laying them off. Thus, the feminine mystique was not merely a typical postwar retrenchment response but an economic tool.[58]

The actual impact of the feminine mystique is difficult to evaluate. Certainly, women of all classes continued to function as profitable consumers for the manufacturers who needed their services in this respect. But all women were by no means imprisoned housewives as Friedan suggested. Many were community activists and many individually refused to conform to feminine-mystique womanliness. In addition, women were not so easily driven out of the labor market; other economic forces drew them in, and the proportion of women working for wages continued to rise in the 1950s. (Women driven out of better-paying industrial jobs by demobilized soldiers typically stepped back down into the low-wage, nonunionized jobs, particularly in the service sector, that they had held before the war.) Most of these working-class women, like men, took jobs out of economic necessity, not because of ideological influence. Some educated women may have been dissuaded from seeking professional employment by a sense of duty to family and self. However, for some women of all classes it seems certain that the feminine mystique created a sense of inadequacy and frustration as the promise of fulfillment failed to materialize.

One aspect of that frustration was sexual. Unlike the Victorian proper woman, the feminine mystique ideal was not asexual. On the contrary, her gender duty included seducing and satisfying her husband indefinitely. But the feminine mystique implicitly offered women ecstatic love as the reward for the surrender of their larger ambitions, and few husbands could meet the high standards of the fantasies engendered by the mystique. Furthermore, masculine gender constraints often rendered them incapable of loving or sexual generosity. Meanwhile, the commercial culture surrounded women with images of free, enchanting sexuality just around the corner. For the middle-class housewife, with household aids, servants and/or babysitters freeing her time somewhat, resentment of sexual deprivation was practically an inevitable response. Some sought sex outside their marriages, with a resulting high rate of adultery and divorce. Others sought psychiatric help. As Friedan wrote, "Sex is the only frontier open to women who have always lived within the confines of the feminine mystique."[59]

Many of these women were clients at Planned Parenthood clinics, and some brought their sexual frustrations to the attention of clinic staff. Reluctantly at first, but later with eagerness, the birth control clinics began to offer counseling. They did this with an implicit sexual program analogous to the overall politics of Planned Parenthood: a tendency to isolate the problem—whether it was unwanted pregnancies or lack of orgasm—from larger social structures, thus accepting the surrounding social circumstances as a given. In comparison to alternative analyses of sexual problems that had been available previously, the PPFA version of sexual liberation for women avoided the issues of women's rights and male dominance. This avoidance, however, made solutions difficult, for women's sexual problems were caused by a complex network of sexist patterns of behavior that pervaded marriages and even sexual affairs. In their attempts to treat sex as an isolated problem, the birth control counselors offered, despite their intentions, a therapy that perpetuated the feminine mystique.

In 1947 the PPFA introduced its Marriage Education and Counseling Program thus:

> Any descriptive account of the current marriage and family scene, if it is honest, will reflect the same insecurities and uncertainties that are part of the social and economic readjustment in postwar America. One would like to think of the family as a retreat from the chaos of day-to-day conflict and strain . . . but the family is not a thing apart. . . . The juvenile delinquency figures and the resurgence of "gangs" in our big cities are part of it; so also is the increase in venereal disease among civilian groups disproportionately higher for adolescents. Unmistakably part of it are the current divorce statistics . . . one out of three marriages. . . .
>
> Further, the challenge is a double one, for the forces of reaction are at work. Our concern is not just for the family; it is for a democratic family! Newspaper headlines to the effect that we must legislate divorce out of existence and keep women so busy having children that they won't have time to get into trouble, are not uncommon today.
>
> A more thoughtful approach rejects the current hysteria . . . deplores the authoritarian approach . . . recognizes that one can't enforce happy marriages by laws, by strangling personality development . . . [and] that indiscriminate fecundity is itself a fascist notion.[60]

This description of the threat to family values struck a progressive note, condemning both family instability and authoritarian solutions. In defining the nature of the counseling Planned Parenthood would offer, the statement also reflected the increased complexity of birth control thought after several decades of organization. Denying that contraception was a panacea, the statement attacked the assumption that "given a good contraceptive most marital difficulties would be solved." On the contrary, "sometimes the use, even the very decision to use a contraceptive, unwisely arrived at, introduces conflicts and anxieties." The statement placed sex at the center of many human problems. PPFA counseling would not be focused exclusively on sex, the statement said, but would not deny the basic importance of good sexual relationships and would accept sexual maladjustment as the point of departure for counseling.

From the beginning, then, PPFA counseling advocates were responding to two different problems: women's sexual discontent and their restlessness in their subordinate family and social position. The still somewhat controversial psychiatric appraisal of sex as central to human relationships provided them with a connection between these social and individual problems. An emphasis on individual adjustment as the key to stability pervaded the Planned Parenthood approach to both social and individual problems. While rejecting authoritarianism, PPFA publications and counselors did not encourage women to risk instability or "maladjustment" in order to develop. Two decades later a women's liberation movement suggested that instability and maladjustment, in some degree, are the temporary costs of social change. Without feminist movement to offer that analysis, the birth controllers sought to solve problems and ameliorate suffering without challenging the gender system.

Planned Parenthood approached these tasks in two ways: propaganda and counseling. Although similar assumptions underlay both approaches, counseling tended to focus on sexual problems whereas publications discussed family, economic, and social values more explicitly. Let us look first at some PPFA propaganda of the 1940s. A renewed effort to win support from Protestant and Jewish clergy centered around the preparation of a pamphlet, *The Clergyman Talks with the Bride and Groom about Family Planning*, designed for use in premarital interviews.[61] The pamphlet included lengthy excerpts from Hannah and Abraham Stone's forthright sex manual and was offered for criticism and final editing to prominent churchmen in order to win clerical endorsements—for example, the PPFA staff accepted one minister's suggestion to omit the word "sensuality" and another proposal to soften the Stones' assertion that a good sex relation is "essential" to a happy marriage, making it only "most desirable." In this as in most PPFA publications the policy was not to give actual birth control information but to argue the moral and social benefits of birth control and to refer those who wanted it to clinics and doctors.

The pamphlet argued that birth control and good mutual sexual adjustment were central to a happy marriage. The authors did not share the nineteenth-century feminist view that women should control sexual activity, a view intended to allow women to check what they considered to be excessive male lust. In the 1940s sex experts did not identify "male lust" as excessive or oppressive to women in any respect; on the contrary, they expected women to reach and express parallel levels of desire themselves. Still, the mutuality recommended in marriage did not extend beyond the sex act itself. The pamphlet offered no challenge to nonmutuality in matters of economics, housework, or child-raising.

Most Planned Parenthood publications assumed that all sex, and therefore all birth control, belonged inside marriage and that equality in sex could be achieved without a fundamental alteration of marriage itself. They implicitly opposed the sexual revolution of the post–World War I era, and they explained away the depressions and hostility of frustrated housewives as products of sexual maladjustment and refusal to accept the female role.

This area of PPFA ideology was publicized largely through the psychiatric profession. Beginning in the early 1940s a number of psychiatrists were recruited to speak out for birth control as conducive to mental health. They assumed that marriage must be primary and central in women's lives. Dr. Marynia Farnham, a notorious antifeminist psychiatrist, served on occasion as a public spokeswoman for PPFA and specifically attacked spinsters. In her 1947 book *Modern Woman: The Lost Sex* (coauthored with Ferdinand Lundberg), she demanded that single women should be barred by law from teaching since a "great many children have unquestionably been damaged psychologically by the spinster teacher, who cannot be an adequate model of a complete woman."[62] In a speech for Planned Parenthood in 1943 she attacked the single women who played men's roles (e.g., in employment and sex).[63] Behind these condemnations lay the assumption that single women had to be, or ought to be, celibate.[64] Planned Parenthood's policy of not serving unmarried women was carried at this time to the impractical extreme of refusing to send out the pamphlet *The Doctor Talks with the Bride,* designed for premarital sex education, to unmarried women.[65]

When most psychiatrists discussed the value of birth control within marriage, they did not mention the value of activities outside their homes for women's personal development. Rather, they emphasized the chilling effect of fear of unwanted pregnancy on the sex act itself.[66] Psychiatrists sometimes insisted on women's right to sexual fulfillment, but they did not acknowledge rights to other areas of fulfillment or recognize that women's frustrations in other areas might be expressed in sexual coldness toward the husbands and family situations that restricted them. Farnham argued, like a nineteenth-century feminist, that the problem of reproductive control lay at the root of women's position, but in her development of that theme she sounded more like an early twentieth-century race-suicide alarmist: Since reproduction is woman's "primary function," it should not be outside her control: ". . . one of the most morbid aspects of the so-called 'modern' woman's development . . . [is the] steadily increasing tendency on the part of intelligent and well-trained, as well as intellectually alert, women to assert their independence at the cost of abandoning the function for which they are inherently responsible and biologically fitted. This exhibits itself in a variety of forms . . . [including the spectacle of married women who want the] emotional and social prestige of marriage . . . [but are] unwilling to tolerate all the burdens of a woman's life and elect either to bear no children or at most one or two."[67]

Such views differed from the race-suicide hysteria in the observations offered by Farnham and other psychiatrists that women who wished to avoid motherhood would probably make poor mothers anyway. This analysis might seem sensible enough were it not for the vicious condemnation of these women: "the woman who cannot find satisfaction in adult relations in life, who is incapable of succeeding in living a woman's role, who is constantly in revolt against her submission and who is unable to achieve sexual gratification with her husband cannot possibly be a satisfactory parent. . . . She will only find it necessary to obtain gratification through an excessive attachment to her children, particularly her sons."[68]

These psychiatrists thought the value of birth control was to promote good sex, not to offer women options other than full-time motherhood. Not only did they think of sex as "the sex act," but they perceived good sex as inseparably connected to women's acceptance of their "true" roles. At a time when the ideology that woman's place was in the home was reclaiming dominance, Farnham postured as an iconoclast in arguing to remove the stigma from women who worked as full-time homemakers and child-rearers.[69]

Viewing sexual adjustment in isolation from women's general problems, as these psychiatrists did, led to blaming women, especially aberrant or rebellious women, for their own unhappiness and for family instability. This was evident, for example, in the birth controllers' opportunistic use of the widespread concern over juvenile delinquency in the 1940s. In 1947 Planned Parenthood leaders listed their four main enemies as death and disease, divorce, juvenile delinquency, and sterility.[70] They argued that "unwanted" children were more likely to be delinquent.[71] Attendees at the 1947 PPFA annual meeting heard Rhoda J. Milliken, director of the Women's Bureau of the Washington, D.C., Police Department, argued that unwanted children tended toward criminality.[72] David Loth, PPFA public information chief, claimed that "excess" children tended to become delinquent and produced marital conflict, sibling jealousy, and family instability.[73]

These themes were part of, and contributed to, the attack on working mothers, an aspect of the feminine mystique that peaked in the 1950s. The attacks were marked by a singular superficiality in analyzing the problem. They blamed women exclusively, removing from the spotlight the contributions of men, poverty, unemployment, and racism. The assumptions that there was such a thing as excess children and that unplanned children were "unwanted" were not supported by evidence of the feelings of the parents or children involved.

The educational work of Planned Parenthood ignored the frustrations experienced by women that had been the original source of the birth control movement. Moreover, it may have contributed to the view that individual women were to blame for their own unhappiness. In its clinical programs, however, the PPFA offered not only contraception but sex counseling, which proved a more subversive undertaking.

Experiences in providing contraception drew doctors and nurses into sex counseling. Social prudery seemed only to make women more anxious to spill out their sexual miseries once they were in a safe and sympathetic environment.[74] Routine questions at clinic intake procedures often revealed deep wells of pain and astonishing sexual ignorance, even among mothers of many children. Indeed, in their sex counseling there was little distinction between therapy and education. In the 1970s, the therapy offered in clinics such as Masters and Johnson's and the educational publications of the women's liberation movement, such as *Our Bodies, Ourselves,* owed much to the experience and experiments of birth control work.

From early in the movement, women whose names became publicized as birth control advocates began receiving appeals for help by mail—not only for contraceptives, but also for sexual advice. Many of these letters were appeals for abortions, such as this one, addressed to Rose Pastor Stokes: "Dear Benefactress—Would you be pleased to include our little family. . . . I am an elevator runner, in the Hotel Savoy, and am salaried at $25 monthly. . . . We are threatened with a possible newcomer to our fold—my wife is two months and no show. . . . if you could only benefit us with your kind advice. . . .—Helen and John Sweeney."[75] Others had nothing to do with birth control. Here one of Sanger's assistants summarizes a particularly thorny problem: "I am afraid to tackle this one without some advice. The girl is 20 years old, had had a terrible home life, so she says. . . . She finally met a man who as she says, ruined her. She became pregnant and was aborted. She now says that she is engaged to marry a man who has studied medicine two years. She is afraid he will know she has had another adventure and wants to know whether he can tell or not. She says she has told him there is nothing in her past etc. and wants to know whether she should marry him or give him up."[76]

With a good deal of assistance, Sanger attempted to answer these appeals. In the 1920s she wrote in her own name, but by the 1930s she had developed the Margaret Sanger Marriage Advice Bureau and used form letters to speed the work, generally by refusing to offer abortion help and referring writers to birth control clinics or doctors. In 1931 she described the bureau as a direct extension of her birth control clinic work, calling it "a unique undertaking—the first of its kind in this country."[77] That was not the case, of course, for advice bureaus of this type had long been in existence, and they, in turn, succeeded neighborhood wisewomen. Sanger's boasts were indicative of a desire to professionalize such counseling services without surrendering them to psychiatric control. For her, the professionalization of advice bureaus was a form of democratization, making a service available on a mass scale, which was quite different from the inclination of the psychiatric establishment. (And, indeed, the provision of counseling services through birth control clinics, opposed at first by the psychiatric establishment, eventually helped force an expansion of the limits of what was professionally reputable therapy.)

Sanger's responses to written appeals for help offer a faithful microcosm of her overall sexual views and a useful basis of comparison with later Planned Parenthood views. Her approach remained that of nineteenth-century free-love ideology, which asserted the spiritual, honorable qualities of sex and the simultaneous dangers of its degradation into something low. To the woman who worried about her past affair and abortion, Sanger replied with a free-love defense: "You must not think of yourself or your relations with Tom, whom you have loved, in the wrong light. If you loved him and he loved you, any relations between you were just as holy and as pure in the sight of God as if a marriage certificate had been given you. . . . It is love between two people that sanctifies marriage. There are many marriages today that are not so sanctified."[78] Yet Sanger was no exponent of unmarried love, arguing generally that "sex belongs to love and love belongs to marriage."[79] She also tried to dissuade a woman from bearing a child alone: "I can understand how a very honest, straightforward, independent woman must despise the necessity for deceit, but isn't that just giving vent to our own inward satisfaction. . . . My own suggestion would be if it were possible, to go away to England or some place, that last three or four months and have her baby, or . . . to say she is married."[80] She consistently opposed masturbation, insisting that will power could get rid of the habit: "If you are sincere in your statement that you wish to overcome the habit of masturbation which you acquired during childhood, . . . try to interest yourself in some social, athletic, or other group . . . and as you develop such interests . . . your impulses and thoughts will center less upon your own body and gradually they will be diverted to more important matters."[81]

Heavy as was the flow of written appeals to Sanger, it was small compared to the expression of sexual discontent encountered at the birth control clinics. Clinicians seeking to provide effective contraception would have been hard put to refuse at least to discuss problems so closely related to birth control. Dr. Hannah Stone, medical director of Sanger's Clinical Research Bureau (CRB) in New York, had kept careful data on "adjustment to marriage" that began to reveal the dimensions of the problem: only 60 percent of her patients had a "normal" attitude toward intercourse, 19 percent were indifferent, and 20 percent were hostile; and only 42 percent said they usually had an orgasm (indeed, the doctors frequently had to explain the meaning of that word).[82] In 1931, she and her husband, Dr. Abraham Stone, opened the Marriage Consultation Center under the auspices of the New York City Labor Temple, and women from the CRB clinic were referred there. The large numbers of women needing help, however, led Stone and her co-workers to try incorporating counseling into the clinic's services. From 1932 on, the Clinical Research Bureau provided consultations on marriage problems.[83] The service was free if the woman was a birth control client at the clinic; otherwise, the average fee was five dollars. Women with marital problems were often advised to come in for additional consultations with their husbands.

An equally important part of the program was premarital consultation, a form of individualized sex education. Discussing sexual topics with unmarried women was still a controversial matter, even in the medical profession, in the 1930s. The "premaritals" had been accepted at the CRB in part because of the support of eugenists, who viewed them as a necessary means for investigating possible hereditary taints that should halt the marriage or at least parenthood. Dr. Robert Latou Dickinson, advocate of premarital consultations, adopted the eugenists' view that these consultations should take place before the announcement of engagement and definitely before a wedding date had been set. But Dickinson himself realized that the demand for premarital interviews was mainly a demand for contraceptive information among engaged couples,[84] and the CRB received hundreds of requests for such consultations. The bureau developed a standard format of examination and consultation. Although it offered surgical dilation or rupture of the hymen if desired, it usually directed the woman to come back three to four weeks after her marriage to be fitted with a diaphragm.[85]

Counseling services were also being offered by many birth control clinics elsewhere in the country,[86] but with little publicity. Toward the end of the 1930s the recognition of the need for counseling became so great that it stimulated a public program, but creating this required the PPFA leadership to undertake years of careful negotiations with and reassurance of psychiatric and social work professional organizations. Both professions were anxious to preserve their control over the content as well as the personnel of counseling. Planned Parenthood's medical director, C. C. Pierce, was forced to overrule a psychiatrist called in for consultation who demanded that all counseling begin with a preliminary interview with a psychiatrist.[87] It was 1947 before the PPFA was able to produce a public statement on its marriage counseling program.[88]

Although the program was called "marriage counseling" and was intended to relate planned parenthood services to overall family life through homemaking and health services, sex education, mental hygiene, and child welfare, in fact the service offered was primarily sex counseling. (A proposal by one PPFA staff member to call for "child care" as a necessity for family health, included in an earlier draft of the counseling program description, was modified in the final version to "child welfare.") This restriction was perhaps unavoidable if the small, private clinics were to be able to help any one person sufficiently to have any impact. Most of the other kinds of services mentioned, such as homemaking or child welfare, required resources far beyond the capability of the shoestring clinics. Had the clinic workers been deeply committed to these causes, the most they could have done would have been to help organize and focus pressure on other institutions, particularly the government, to provide better services. To offer sex education on a public scale (as opposed to its integration into individual and small-group counseling) would have required political struggles against censorious authorities such as school boards, churches, and the police. The basis of the restriction of the program was that the clinics no longer wanted to be involved in adversarial relations with state or private institutions. Indeed, the majority of the clinics had not wanted to dilute their impact with any issues other than contraception at all. Their introduction of counseling was a capitulation to overwhelming pressure from their clients and those in direct contact with the clients.

Sex-centered marriage counseling was offered at many clinics, nationwide, by the early 1940s. The style and content of the counseling sessions varied, but certain generalizations held. The counseling was short-term, ranging from single consultations to occasional or regular sessions for a relatively brief time to "classes" with a specified number of meetings. The PPFA tried to enforce high standards for the counselors, including a graduate degree and job experience, in a concession to the opposition from psychiatrists and social workers, although physicians without counseling experience were often employed. Although great variation must have existed among clinics, I want to focus here on the experience at the Clinical Research Bureau in New York City, later called the Margaret Sanger Research Bureau.

For doctors Lena Levine and Abraham Stone, who directed them, these counseling services were not a minor addition to birth control work. Stone envisioned the clinics as expanding their definition so greatly that birth control would be just one of several functions. Levine argued that most people, not just the exceptional, might need counseling.[89] Levine and Stone were both convinced that for most couples being told to "do what comes naturally" would not produce mutual satisfaction. According to Stone: "It is generally taken for granted, for instance, that men and women know instinctively how to perform the sex act, yet this is often not the case. Among primates, the act of coitus is not an instinctive behavior pattern but a technique acquired through association, imitation, experimentation, and learning."[90] The problem, of course, was that modern culture had set up obstacles, in the form of censorship and guilt, to effective sexual learning. Thus, in Levine's and Stone's view, therapy resembled education, seeking to remedy the ignorance-creating aspects of society. Indeed, they believed that most sexual failure was due to ignorance.[91]

The importance of the basic education offered in these counseling sessions can hardly be overestimated. Levine and Stone used sculpted models of the genital and reproductive systems. They found frequent examples of debilitating ignorance. Few clients knew exactly what or where the clitoris was. A man married many years, unable to effect complete penetration, confessed that he was not entirely sure where the vagina was.[92] The two doctors' comfort with discussions of sexual physiology and technique was contagious, and both female and male clients heard themselves, often with some surprise, speaking about their own experiences in the same direct, specific manner.

To aid this educational work, these and other birth control doctors wrote a number of manuals on marriage and sexual technique. Perhaps the most important was *A Marriage Manual* by Stone and his wife, Hannah, also a doctor, first published in 1935. Nothing could better illustrate how much the approach to sexuality of the birth controllers had changed than a comparison of the Stones' work to Sanger's own *Happiness in Marriage,* published in 1926. Sanger wrote nothing at all on the technique of physical love, confining herself to romantic philosophy about courtship, honeymoon, and the marriage relationship itself. Women should maintain a playful elusiveness during courtship, she admonished, not surrender to a young man's more insistent sexual urges. She claimed that while youth's reaction against prudishness was good, there were severe dangers in too much intimacy, emotional as well as sexual, during engagement.[93] According to Sanger, the responsibility for a proper marital adjustment was primarily the woman's: "She must dominate the relation. . . . she must create the happiness of their life together. The future depends on the woman's attitude toward sex."[94] Looking at this from the vantage point of the Stones' work, less than ten years later, Sanger seems deep in the nineteenth-century tradition. She emphasized self-control and the need to spiritualize sexual relations; and she was uncomfortable with physiological discussion. At the same time her view of marital relations reflected the view of the sex radicals of 1910–20 that male lust was healthy and women's inhibitions neurotic. Sanger kept the romanticism but lost the hostility toward a male-defined sexual rhythm characteristic of nineteenth-century feminists.[95]

The Stones were doing something completely different. Not that theirs was an amoral, strictly technical manual; nor did they disagree with Sanger. But for them sex was not something that needed to be spiritualized, and their view of the nonsexual aspects of a good marriage emphasized different features: "I quite agree with you that sex alone does not make a marriage. . . . there must of course be present mutual love and affection, a community of ideas, of interests, of tastes, of standards, an adequate economic arrangement and a satisfactory adjustment in many personal, family and social relationships."[96] The Stone and Levine approach was down-to-earth, family-centered (emphasizing moral responsibility and stability), and reassuring. (*A Marriage Manual*'s message to lovers was similar to the message Dr. Benjamin Spock carried to new mothers: whatever you're inclined to do is probably all right.) The message was that sexual happiness lay within every individual's reach. Although battling the effects of a repressive culture, the Stones did not protest or criticize or attribute blame for this repression, nor did they encourage even the most unhappy men and women to vent their anger. Theirs was not the sex manual of a sex-radical movement or a feminist movement but of therapists: encouraging, supportive. Even in the midst of a great depression it assumed the possibility of a secure, stable, and, if not prosperous then at least hopeful, family life. One suspects that their happy, confident outlook made them remarkably successful as counselors. Certainly, clients were enthusiastic about their sessions, and many reported improvements in their sex lives.

One of the most influential aspects of such counseling, and the aspect about which we have today the greatest documentation, was group marriage counseling. This was an experiment that Abraham Stone and Lena Levine approached with some caution, aware, as they put it, that "marriage counseling has always been considered to require strict individualization. . . . In reviewing our histories, however, we were increasingly impressed with the fact that the problems presented by couples coming for marriage counseling fell into several specific categories."[97] Essentially, they recognized that these sex problems were not personal but social. They compiled a list of the common complaints of women coming to the clinic:

> Lack of desire.
> Difficulty in becoming aroused.
> Arousal only after much precoital play.
> Lack of any sensation in coitus.
> Orgasm only from external play, but not from coitus.
> Fear of intercourse.
> Fear of pregnancy.
> Infrequency of sex relations.
> Painful intercourse.
> Orgasm achieved only in certain positions.
> Husband's anxiety over wife's lack of response.
> Husband's objection to wife's need of precoital play.
> Husband's loss of sexual interest because of wife's frigidity or slowness of
>   response.[98]

Stone and Levine's primary motivation in trying group therapy was to save time and to help more people. Their women clients met three times at one-week intervals in groups of six to eight, then once six months later; their husbands met once and then once again six months later. Clients had to be married, of course. The therapists' assumption and prescription were that single women should have no sex life. The program was defined as a medical one. The women clients had been examined for gynecological problems and fitted with diaphragms. The official justification was that the groups were natural extensions of medical services into the field of mental health to promote good sexual adjustment in marriage. These limits were required to protect the sex education program from charges that it stimulated "promiscuity." Moreover, Levine, an experienced psychiatrist, was on guard against negative interactions that might take place among the clients. To avoid "possible conflicting attitudes," the doctors tried to choose couples of similar age, class, and cultural backgrounds. But neither doctor intended to create a general discussion or encounter group. They led each session strongly. The first two-hour session began with a fifteen-minute physiology lecture; at the second session the doctor reviewed the earlier session and then called for progress reports; at the third session the doctor lectured on the effects of early childhood socialization into sexual inhibitions.[99]

It is clear from the transcripts of these sessions that group discussions developed an intensity, energy, and openness far beyond what Levine and Stone had anticipated. Indeed, they were rather surprised at their own success and did not precisely understand it. The power of the groups lay in the fact that the doctors were not only contributing their significant knowledge and experience in a frank manner but also creating situations in which women and, to a lesser extent, men could learn from one another. Evidence of that mutual learning can be found in nearly every transcript. Its most basic form was abatement of a sense of inadequacy as woman after woman, man after man, expressed the same fears and failures. The men consistently revealed embarrassment that they could not maintain erections long enough and a pathetic relief when the doctors assured them that the average duration of an erection was two minutes.[100] Among the women the relief assuaged more generalized, even total, anxieties, for they blamed themselves for their own lack of satisfaction. On the average, two-thirds never had orgasms; others felt that they were failures, even perverts, because they could not have "vaginal" orgasms or any orgasms during intercourse; and almost all felt inadequate because they were sexually disinterested much of the time or else too tired to respond at the end of an evening. They were comforted not so much by the doctors, who frequently labeled these symptoms as neurotic, but by one another. Often this mutual support helped women transform their own self-hatred back to its origin—namely, resentment of their husbands for their insensitivity and sexual selfishness. The men occasionally expressed fear of this transformation (though on the whole their gratitude for the sexual honesty encouraged by the sessions dominated). One man remarked of his wife, "She came here and listening to other women and came to the conclusion she had no problem."[101]

The rapport and openness that developed among the women in just three meetings was remarkable. In their first meetings women frequently plunged immediately into frank and painful complaints: "'I have been married fifteen months, and have not gotten any satisfaction yet. I am aroused when my husband plays with me, but as soon as he enters I lose all feeling. I lose it and I don't get it back again, and I get disgusted. Often I start crying.'"[102] By the third session some women expressed a desire for the groups to continue: "It's not fair, giving us just a taste."[103] Although there is no evidence that women continued to meet without the doctors, they did in many ways take small measures of control over the group. One group criticized the CRB for not providing contraception for unmarried women.[104] Some clients assumed a counseling role toward others, sometimes taking positions sexually more radical than those of the doctors, as when one woman said to another, who had been valiantly trying to achieve a "vaginal" orgasm, that maybe she should not care about it, that perhaps not every woman needed to have a "vaginal" orgasm.[105] Often the women sought to employ the doctors for their own ends, asking them to give particular messages to their husbands during the men's sessions. Sometimes the women said they felt too timid to deliver the messages themselves; more frequently they used the weight of the doctors' status to make an impression upon their husbands.[106]

The women's eagerness to communicate with their husbands was due to the importance of what Stone and Levine were teaching them. The key messages were primarily technical: that it was normal for women to require long periods of foreplay to reach arousal; that the vagina was normally quite insensitive in young women; that stimulation of the clitoris was extremely important in achieving arousal and orgasm; that men and women should not be expected to sense what was sexually pleasing to the other but should be told; that honesty in describing responses was the only route to a mutually pleasing sexual relationship; and that a wide variety of sexual activities could be normal and pleasing. Some of these ideas were not new to the urban, predominantly Jewish couples who attended the sessions, though their repetition by a doctor was a source of great reassurance. For others, these ideas were totally new, particularly the sexual importance of the clitoris. For many, that message—that a woman's clitoris was her most sensitive sexual organ—gave them the courage to try making love in a new way, with remarkable results. "My wife and I have felt like newlyweds," said one man who had just learned what and where the clitoris was.[107]

The transcripts show that instruction about the clitoris was the most important message delivered in these sessions because it became a license for women to heed their own feelings and led most consistently to actual change. We should not oversimplify this, for clitoral sexuality had complex ramifications, many of them disturbing to women. Experiencing orgasm for the first time, many women felt badly that their orgasms were separated from their husbands' and took place outside of intercourse; many also recognized that expectations for simultaneous, "vaginal" orgasms were false and noticed how they had been created. Clitoral stimulation at least temporarily relieved women of the fear of conception and undoubtedly led to relaxation; by contrast, women were uneasy with the feeling that their bodily rhythms should determine the dynamic of lovemaking and felt unable to make the men "wait." The clitoris was not a magic button that miraculously created a new sexual experience. But the discovery of that small organ, its capacity for feeling so long feared and suppressed, was the main theme of these sessions.

The enthusiasm of both participants and leaders of these sessions leaves no doubt about their success, although we should not exaggerate their novelty. Women have often formed informal, supportive clubs. In the 1870s Elizabeth Cady Stanton and other voluntary motherhood advocates organized women-only discussion groups, and the degree of frankness in them seems to have been as great, relative to current definitions of propriety, as in consciousness-raising groups a century later. But Stanton's groups had a women's movement and a burgeoning feminist consciousness to bring them together. So did the consciousness-raising groups of the women's liberation movement of the 1970s. The Stone-Levine clients came together not as participants of a movement but as clients of experts. It is a tribute to the achievements of the planned parenthood clinics that they brought sexual conflicts and frustrations into the open. But at the same time the fact that the counseling groups grew out of a national birth control program set some limits on the discussion that might not have been present otherwise. This judgment must be tentative, since many of the limits were imposed by the experience and acculturation of the participants themselves. Still, in many areas the session leaders authoritatively defended sexual conventions that would be rejected a few decades later under the critique of a renewed feminist movement. The leaders maintained a narrow focus, preventing exploration of the interconnectedness of sex and the rest of life and locating the source of sexual problems in alterable social conditions.

A single example should suffice: Despite their emphasis on the importance of clitoral excitement, Stone and Levine taught the superiority of the so-called vaginal orgasm. Their psychoanalytic interpretation represented an attempt to combine what they had observed and heard in years of practice with the categories of female psychosexual development that had been laid down by Freud and, by the 1940s, dominated the U.S. psychiatric establishment. According to the Stone and Levine interpretation, there were two kinds of orgasms, clitoral and vaginal; the former was immature, the latter difficult to achieve partly because girls did not normally masturbate in the vagina—vaginal sensitivity had to be developed. Clitoral orgasms were better than none, to be sure, but both Stone and Levine urged a continual striving for "vaginal" orgasms during intercourse. The technique they suggested to accomplish this "transference of sensitivity to the vagina" was intercourse in positions that allowed simultaneous clitoral stimulation.[108]

It was several decades later, of course, that the Masters and Johnson studies showed that there was only one kind of orgasm and that it was brought on by stimulation of the clitoris. For decades previously doctors had observed and written that the clitoris was the seat of all observable female sexual stimulation.[109] In the face of that knowledge, continued belief in the "vaginal" orgasm had an ideological basis: the desire to maintain heterosexual intercourse, nearly certain to provide orgasm for the male, as the norm—indeed, the very definition—of the sex act. Thus, for Stone and Levine the emphasis on the achievement of "vaginal" orgasms had as a corollary that certain sexual practices were perversions. It is true that they had narrowed the area of perversity greatly, admitting as normal a frequency and breadth of sexual activity that would have been unacceptable to most nineteenth-century sexual reformers. In their efforts to encourage naturalness and self-expression, the Stones had come up with a definition of perversion based on intention: perversity was the absence of attempt at "normal" heterosexual relations. Thus clitoral stimulation was acceptable if it was preliminary to intercourse, and clitoral orgasms were acceptable if they were a stage in a woman's progress toward "vaginal" orgasms; but it was perverse for clitoral orgasms to become a woman's standard route to sexual satisfaction. In the abbreviated style used by the secretary who transcribed the sessions, Stone was quoted as follows: "If want to take in mouth and kiss and it is preliminary diversion, not perversion. If always becomes end in itself would be beyond normalcy."[110] This view further implied a rejection of all homosexual activity and a condemnation—if kindly and understanding—of masturbation. (Alfred Kinsey later criticized Stone for his inaccurate and conservative views on masturbation and the clitoral orgasm.)[111]

In supporting relatively conventional ideas of perversion and continuing to use the "vaginal" orgasm as the definition of female sexual maturity, Levine and Stone maintained a male definition of sexuality itself. Indeed, throughout the counseling sessions they worked to suppress or deflect challenges to male-defined sex that their own therapy had stimulated. When women ventured to express resentment at having to fit their husbands' rhythms, Levine advised them to accept their husbands' failings and counseled against nagging or trying to change them. The Stones and Levine tended toward psychological rather than physiological analyses of maladjustments. The Stones concluded in 1940 that "in most instances . . . the failure to reach an orgasm is psychological in origin. For one reason or another, the woman sets up a barrier against complete surrender and abandon during the sexual act."[112] When a woman complained during a counseling session about losing excitement when her husband stopped touching her clitoris, Levine retorted, "You lost it because you thought it would be gone."[113] "Do you feel a complete woman?" she asked an unhappy client. "Maybe if you were more of a woman . . ." she challenged another.[114] For those already capable of clitoral orgasms, she advised suppressing the orgasm since, in her view, the average woman could only achieve one orgasm during a single encounter and it was important to stop foreplay prior to a clitoral orgasm in an effort to make possible a "vaginal" orgasm.[115]

When it came to the men's sessions, the doctors did little to check their tendency to blame their wives for their problems, even though it was usually the women's lack of satisfaction that *was* the problem. "She is always tired." "She's trying to be normal."[116] The helpful specific advice offered to the men— to extend the time of foreplay, to try clitoral stimulation during intercourse, and so forth—did not alter the fundamental assumptions that intercourse was the core of the sex act and that a woman's inability to achieve orgasm during intercourse represented her maladjustment.

Levine and Stone clung inconsistently to this view as they also believed that male and female sexuality were essentially different. They emphasized the slowness of women's sexual arousal; the periodicity of women's sexual desire (as opposed to the putative constancy of men's); the complex psychosexual development of women that required them, as children, to transfer libidinous impulses from mother to father; and the necessity to develop sexual sensitivity in a naturally insensitive organ, the vagina. It was as if nature had set up every possible obstacle to mutual heterosexual satisfaction. A reasonable conclusion from these assumptions might have been that homosexual activity was more likely to prove satisfying to women or that lack of female satisfaction was a normal condition. That the Stones and Levine clung to the notion that some sort of adjustment was required to overcome such major obstacles must be attributed to their inability to discard conventional categories despite the lack of evidence for them.

Perhaps their identification with the birth control cause made it more difficult for them to look openly at women's sexual experiences. Since modern contraception was designed to make unlimited intercourse possible, it was not at all odd that they focused on intercourse itself as the center of sexual normality. The development of mechanical contraception had made the twentieth-century birth controllers less aware than the nineteenth-century voluntary motherhood advocates of the importance of other forms of sexual expression, both genital and nongenital. Stone and Levine noticed that it was necessary to distinguish between a woman's desire for what she called "lovemaking" and for intercourse.[117] But as far as the Stones were concerned, the former was an incomplete, immature impulse.[118]

As Stone and Levine focused on psychological, rather than physiological, explanations for women's sexual disinterest or frustration, so they also tended to discard environmental explanations. The most common of these among women was tiredness. Levine argued that tiredness was a psychological as well as a physical problem and that men were less tired when it came to sex because they more regularly got pleasure from it. Women clients usually instinctively understood the truth of this. As one woman put it, "I get tired when I even think of it."[119] Yet Levine's approach to this problem mixed a certain amount of blame with her advice for achieving an orgasm: Tiredness, she said, was just another alibi.[120] Yet there were so many "alibis": ill health, lack of privacy, lack of child care, money worries, feeling unloved and unappreciated, feeling angry. The exclusive focus on sexuality may well have been the most productive choice given the limits of what she and Stone, the CRB, or the whole birth control movement could offer; nevertheless, it was unrealistic about the particular women they saw, whose sexual problems could not be separated from other problems. Offering this kind of service outside a general social welfare program and without a larger political education about gender suggested that women's frustrations need not poison their sexual relations, that poverty and overwork need not sabotage sexual pleasure, and that sexism was not incompatible with sexual ecstasy.

This narrow approach to sexual problems meant that prosperous women were most likely to be helped by focused sex counseling. A subjective snobbery was also evident in the case reports of many counselors. Here is a typical entry from the Clinical Research Bureau records: "Consultation with Miss Lichtenstein and fiancé—to be married on Saturday—rather poor type—poorly educated—not very intelligent."[121] There was also a double standard in responding to the numerous appeals for abortions that came to the clinic. Abortions were, of course, illegal and dangerous; although therapeutic abortions were sometimes arranged, most applicants were rejected. However, the clinic workers would sometimes go out of their way to arrange a "therapeutic" abortion, even for nonmedical problems, if the candidate impressed them. For example: "Miss Eide is a Norwegian, without relatives, who is unmarried, and is five weeks pregnant. Expected to be married in March, but when her fiancé discovered her condition he deserted her. She is a woman of education, came here wanting termination. . . . Then arranged with Dr. Appel for a D&C. Patient is out of work and has only $100 in the bank. . . . We explained to her the confidential nature of our assistance and she promised not to violate our confidence. Was not charged for conference."[122]

Sexual problems were also entwined in power struggles between husbands and wives, even in the best of marriages. Women's resentment of husbands for imposing male sexual expectations and rhythms reflected many other causes of resentments: inability to get out of the house, the burden of housework and child care, lack of interesting work, husbands' lack of sensitivity and emotional generosity. Stone and Levine saw no place for a gender analysis of marital maladjustments, despite the fact that both of them, in their writing and sex therapy, paid more attention to women's own experiences than most other doctors who were offering marriage counseling. Levine was particularly quick to brand women's resentments and rebellions as signs of a desire to dominate. For example:

> Mrs. S: I try to be analytical about it. Had orgasm once and tried to think what was different. Allowed myself to kiss and be kissed without restraint. Not able to repeat it even though tried. I don't know why. I don't like his breath or his mouth open and prefer it closed. Always seem to find some petty reason. Always feel he gets ahead of me and I resent it and if he would let me get ahead of him even in kissing. It leads to inner resentments.
> Dr. Levine: Would you like to run the marriage?

In this case, Mrs. S. tried to defend herself: "There's always a slight competition between two people. He's quite outgoing person. Accomplishes a great deal. . . . I have to keep going to meet his standards. Subtly makes me feel badly if I don't keep up. . . . If I don't look at it too carefully, we really get on very well together. Sometimes find as a woman a lot is asked of me. Have to do everything to make a perfect wife and he, in turn, has to be a perfect husband" (referring to husband's standards).[123] Mrs. S. was walking a delicate line: relaxed and relatively open in the discussion, she was probing to understand the source of her sexual problem yet also reassuring herself of her marriage, keeping a lid on her resentment. Levine supported her in the suppression, not at all in the expression, of anger.

Under the circumstances, Levine's desire not to open these marriages up to thorough examination was probably considerate. The problem was not with the doctors but with the limitations of clinic-referred, very short-term therapy (and possibly of psychotherapy altogether). Many of these women had general marital problems, and many of those were created by their overall social circumstances as working-class and middle-class wives. Their opportunities limited by sex discrimination even in prosperous times, the depression had intensified the pressure on them. Postwar prosperity had not produced substantial benefits for these women, most of whom were unemployed. Many of their husbands had served in the war, and the wives had lived through wartime loneliness and hardship, expecting and hoping for a better life after the men returned. But the reunification of their families had not taken away their restlessness and disappointment.

Despite the warm and helping intentions of Levine and Stone, and no doubt of hundreds of other birth control marriage counselors, the objective limitations of what could be offered created a "blame the victim" effect. Other leaders of the counseling movement within Planned Parenthood were even less sympathetic to women's sexual problems. Consider the approach of Emily Mudd, a national leader of the marriage counseling profession. The women attending birth control clinics, she wrote, fell into three groups: those who use contraception successfully and easily, those who are failures as contraceptors, and those who try but return with dissatisfaction and complaints. "The majority of those who register dissatisfaction . . . are drawn from that group of women who, largely because of their childhood influences and training, are unable to relate themselves freely to the sexual aspect of life. For want of a better term we might call them 'the complainers.' Their inability to accept sex . . . or, in more technical terms, their 'frigidity' varies . . . (1) the self-centered, narcissistic type of woman; (2) the passive, accepting type; and (3) the woman who is resentful but desirous of change."[124]

Perhaps these categories were useful to clinic workers in helping to provide an initial approach to women with problems. Beyond a bare beginning, however, they could only have been barriers to understanding, for they condemned while obscuring the possible sources of resentment and unhappiness. Like Stone and Levine, Mudd was of the Freudian school and emphasized the importance of early childhood experiences. This may well have been a correct analysis of the root of a problem, but in situations providing short-term therapy it could not offer much help and tended to exclude even the consideration of current environmental factors contributing to women's feelings of resentment and imprisonment.

For women to assert as equals their desires in the bedroom required an equality in the kitchen, nursery, and study as well. It required throwing off centuries of socialization into women's place in the sex act. The power of that inheritance meant that even the most egalitarian-minded women and men reproduced inequalities in their sexual encounters.

How could the sex therapists of the 1940s have helped women achieve sexual freedom? Only a movement challenging the gender system could do that. The birth controllers had involved themselves in a contradictory task: to encourage women's sexual liberation but not their efforts toward equality. The more inhibited sex reformers of the pre–World War I era had a greater impact. Although they seldom discussed sexual anatomy or technique, they supported women in more daring sexual assertions because they were simultaneously challenging conventions of femininity and propriety that the birth controllers of the 1940s left uncontested.[125] The planned parenthood approach emphasized family stability—which in sexual relations usually meant not rocking the boat.

In its inability to support greater change in the relations between the sexes, the birth control movement had become self-limiting. If sexual liberation was dependent on women's general liberation, then so was birth control. Access to birth control did not affect family size to the extent that women's motivation to control their fertility did. This motivation was changing extremely rapidly at this time, although often unnoticed, as a result of large-scale changes in the economy and in gender relations, specifically as a result of women's needs and desires to live a greater part of their lives outside their homes. Ultimately these changes would give rise to a renewed women's movement, which would, in turn, give rise to sexual emancipation for women far in advance of what sex therapy has ever been able to accomplish.

The sexual help that birth controllers were offering in the 1940s was brave and useful to clients. But it also contributed, ironically, to frustration. The sexual focus reflected and encouraged an exclusive focus on domestic life. Planned Parenthood urged sexual fulfillment even as it encouraged mothers to stay at home, there to be responsible for better but smaller families. Sexual fulfillment became a national concern simultaneously with the feminine mystique, and this juxtaposition led to contradiction. Psychologists, the advertising industry, the schools—all the opinion-forming artillery of the nation condemned married women, especially mothers, who pursued employment or activity outside their homes. The ammunition included the charge that mothers who did not stay home caused juvenile delinquency, family maladjustment, and divorce. At the same time the gender experts broadcast the propaganda that single women were miserable, leaving women no legitimate way to pursue any interest beyond domesticity. The feminine mystique campaign failed due to women's resistance and to economic pressures making the two-income family a necessity. However, it succeeded in making many working-class and middle-class women feel conflicted and guilty.

Planned Parenthood's sex counseling was in some respects within a tradition of feminist-led sexual reform and in other respects outside that tradition. It continued the century-old feminist struggle against Victorian prudery. From the voluntary motherhood advocates of the 1870s to the birth controllers of the World War I era to the Planned Parenthood workers of the 1940s, there was a progression toward greater frankness about sex and greater acceptance of women's sex drives. Yet the earlier sex reformers were more radical in the breadth of their understanding of their task. The voluntary motherhood advocates challenged male tyranny in sexual and family life. The birth controllers questioned conventional marriage and family as institutions that replicated and reproduced the existing authoritarian class and sex relations of the society. Planned Parenthood's sex counselors did the opposite. As contributors to the pioneering social scientific collection of information on sexual behavior, they knew that the marital and sexual norms so deplored by the earlier sex radicals were indeed disintegrating, or at least rapidly changing, as evidenced by escalating rates of premarital sex, divorce, and adultery. But they worked blindly against these trends, unable to perceive in the pain and loneliness of disintegrating relationships signs of the inadequacy of the old models of marriage. Though they lacked a strategy to shore up permanent, monogamous, male-dominated marriage, they continued moralistically to reaffirm its value in the face of incontrovertible evidence of its weakening.

The defense of traditional marriage by Planned Parenthood was an understandable response to wartime anxiety about social instability. Sex and marriage counselors could see that the reaction against prudery, while necessary and, in their view, healthy, had been a strongly individualist reaction, leading toward atomization and social disintegration. What they did not see so clearly was that there could be countervailing forces to this disintegrative tendency. Among those were the several waves of feminism that offered alternative forms of partner relationships along with attacks on the old sexual and marital system. The feminism of the 1870s had sought to remake marriage in the image of its traditional claims: permanent and monogamous, with dignity and power for women within it, retaining the separate functions of the sexes but instituting a single sexual standard. In one sense the voluntary motherhood advocates were reactionary because they associated the empowerment of women with the restoration of a preindustrial, family-centered society. Yet at the same time they were driving wedges into the old patriarchal unity of the couple. Decrying rape within marriage, insisting on women's right to refuse, often recommending separate beds and even bedrooms, they were not sentimentalizing marital togetherness or the couple as an inseparable unit. Furthermore, they were building the women's organizations and solidarities that provided sources of alternative support to those of marriage.

By contrast, the feminist birth controllers of the second decade of the twentieth century actually looked forward to a weakening of the traditional family through the increasing socialization of work outside the home. They too insisted upon a single standard, but they sought it in the removal of repression, not in its equal distribution. They welcomed industrial society, with its class, generational, and sex conflicts. They experimented with alternatives to marriage and the family, seeing in those experiments part of a search for new power relations in the society. They tried to create space for satisfying sexual and social lives for single people and to create women's organizational forms that could supply some of the support that families had always given. Theirs was a revolutionary strategy, however, and they spurned halfway measures. Failing to create a revolution, they also failed to create organizational forms that could assume defensive postures, could dig in for a lasting struggle for birth control and women's rights. They left the birth control issue to the professional social planners.

These professionals, who directed Planned Parenthood, faced a difficult situation. The Victorian restrictive and hypocritical sexual and marriage system began to unravel quickly in the 1920s. A challenge originally fueled by women's unrest metamorphosed through commercialization and mass media into a packaged, consumptionist set of sexual standards, as conformist as the old. By the late 1940s these new standards had been incorporated into a theoretically unchanged marriage system, save for including the possibility of divorce and remarriage. Adultery and illegitimacy continued in secret. The assigned place of women in these sequential families remained the same—full-time housewife and mother—although the actual content and conditions of women's labor in the family changed greatly. The feminine mystique idealized love and marital intimacy and spurned forms of collective support—particularly among women—outside the family and heterosexual relationships. Lacking a women's movement to revalue it, sisterly love was to them an outdated, infantile sentimentality, possibly perverted.

Even the best Planned Parenthood workers oversimplified the sexual and reproductive problems they encountered. As a consequence, they tended to isolate sexual and reproductive problems from women's overall subordination. They offered no alternatives to current norms or even suggestions for modifying them. In this they were no more choosing freely than were their clients, for they had no feminist movement to question these norms or even to suggest that they were not natural. In this vacuum, Planned Parenthood contributed mightily, standing for the right to reproductive self-determination in a hostile climate. Organizationally, Planned Parenthood helped integrate birth control ideas into mainstream social planning and thereby further separated birth control from any remaining feminist orientation. Ironically, in the long run Planned Parenthood also contributed to the eventual rebirth of a feminist movement by making birth control widely acceptable.

12   *Birth Control Becomes*
       Public Policy

          After World War II, two developments—one political, one scien-
tific—radically changed the terrain of birth control. They were the campaign
for population control and the development of the Pill, the first hormonal
contraceptive. They mutually influenced each other: concern about overpopulation stimulated contraception research and development; the Pill was so
widely publicized that it introduced knowledge of the possibility of reproduction control to many hitherto unaware of it; the two together created more
legitimacy for birth control.

          Both stories, of population control and of the Pill, have been well covered
by other writers, and I will not repeat what their excellent books and articles
have discussed.[1] Rather, I want to set those developments into a long-term
historical perspective, to call attention to the way in which they altered the
very meanings of birth control.

Population Control

About 1950 a new perspective—population control—came to dominate birth
control organizations. Descended from Malthusianism and neo-Malthusianism, population control had roots distinctly separate from previous birth control campaigns, which had emphasized sexual freedom and women's rights.
The Planned Parenthood Federation of America (PPFA), organizational heir
to the birth control movement, united the two, and in the 1950s and 1960s

the birth control "wife" was subordinated to the population control "husband."
Planned Parenthood's earlier emphasis on family size as a factor that contributed to family prosperity and stability had foreshadowed the revived neo-
Malthusian emphasis on population size as central to prosperity and stability.
The eugenics of earlier decades created a basis for the population control view
that what was then known as third-world underdevelopment flowed from
overpopulation and that birth-rate reductions could solve this and many other social evils. This union was recognized by virtually all birth control advocates. The convergence was so total that, by the 1960s, most Americans used
the phrases "birth control," "family planning," and "population control" interchangeably.[2]

Here, I distinguish among these terms. "Population control" in this chapter refers, generically, to the attempt in modern history to lower birth rates
on national or regional scales for the purpose of improving the standards of
living of large groups. It also refers, more specifically, to the population control programs and policies advanced in the post–World War II period by the
United States government, international organizations such as the United
Nations, and large foundations, notably the Rockefeller Foundation, as well
as later, on a national basis, by countries such as China and India. There were,
of course, population control practices before this—in hunting-and-gathering
societies. But not until the 1950s did population control become an important
part of the foreign policy of the greatest world power.

Prior to 1945 the dominant population anxiety in the United States was
about *under*population (or race suicide, in its eugenic formulation), and government did not view other countries' population problems as demanding U.S.
action. This changed as the velocity of world population growth became known:
in the twentieth century, human numbers quadrupled, from about 1.6 billion
in 1900 to 6 billion in 2000. As overpopulation anxiety spread, its leading purveyors repeated on an international scale the motifs of the eugenics sensibility, notably, the distinction between the moderate, restrained "us" and the
teeming, profligate "them." At first neo-Malthusian solutions met resistance
from traditional prudery: President Eisenhower, for example, insisted as late
as 1959 that population questions were an "inappropriate area" for government
action.[3] Nevertheless, by this time professional demographers had already
persuaded private foundations that population *was* a problem requiring a
public response, and government support followed in the 1960s.

During the 1930s, 1940s, and 1950s academic eugenists transformed themselves into population controllers. Eugenic thinking, as we have seen, was
widespread among reformers of every political persuasion since the late nineteenth century. An application of hereditarian thought to social improvement,
eugenics was by no means an exclusively conservative or racist point of view.

Eugenists did not deny the importance of environmental influence and they did not consider hereditarian and environmental theories of human development to be in conflict. But in the 1890s eugenic activism took a distinctly conservative political turn, vivid in the anti-race-suicide campaign. After World War I eugenics as an academic discipline distanced itself decisively from social reform (see chapters 9 and 10), assimilated itself to a growing nativist and antifeminist conservative spirit, and condemned those aspects of birth control that promoted women's autonomy.

This eugenics establishment merged into—or, more precisely, took over—the population control campaign. In the late 1940s the Milbank Memorial Fund, one of the main backers of eugenics, began to support research about overpopulation in underdeveloped countries.[4] In 1952 Frederick Osborn, a leading eugenist, organized the Population Council.[5] Osborn later set up the Population Association of America, and his cousin Fairfield Osborn became a leader of Planned Parenthood–World Population. The Rockefeller Foundation, another key funder of eugenics research, joined Milbank in 1936 in giving Princeton University (Henry Fairfield Osborn's and John D. Rockefeller III's alma mater) an Office of Population Research (OPR). In the 1940s the OPR became a center for eugenist demographers. Kingsley Davis, Clyde Kiser, Frank Notestein, Dudley Kirk, and Frank Lorimer all worked there. When the Rockefeller Foundation financed the Population Council, these five men moved there. (The foundation had also sent its man Charles Edward Amory Winslow into Planned Parenthood at its inception.) Out of the ten men on the Population Council's demographic and medical advisory boards, six had been associated with eugenics.[6]

In 1955, in an attempt to shore up the declining popularity of eugenics, the Population Council undertook to support the *Eugenics Quarterly* for three years, provided matching grants could be found. The Population Reference Bureau, which had functioned since 1929 as a eugenics organization, was remade on the population control model. Its organizer, Guy Burch, had been active in the campaign for immigration restriction and was one of the most persevering and fervent in his views. In 1939 he had campaigned against the admittance of "non-Aryan" children, Jewish refugees from Nazism, into the United States.[7] Soon afterward the Population Reference Bureau received grants from the Rockefeller, Ford, Mellon, Du Pont, Sloan, Standard Oil, and Shell foundations, among others. Additional monies flowed into other organizations now devoted to population control, including the International Planned Parenthood Federation, Planned Parenthood–World Population, the Population Crisis Committee, and the Committee to Check the Population Explosion.[8]

This connection between eugenics and population control must be carefully and historically interpreted. The racism, vicious coercion, sadism, and

militarism of Nazi eugenics—none of these were characteristic of these demographers, most of whom were moderates and liberals.[9] Moreover, there
were large differences within the elite network that promoted population
control. Some supporters called for coercive action, others emphasized contraceptive education, while still others focused on research.[10] But only the rare
birth control advocate in this period continued the feminist, individual rights,
and sexual freedom agenda associated with earlier birth control thinking.

In the transition from eugenics to population control, Planned Parenthood
was virtually taken over by the new cause. In 1948, at Margaret Sanger's request, the Brush Foundation (its head, Dorothy Brush, had previously funded eugenics work) agreed to finance, along with the Osborns, the International
Planned Parenthood Federation (IPPF). Its headquarters, in London, were
provided free of charge by the English Eugenics Society.[11] But the IPPF's focus
on international population control did not mean that Planned Parenthood in
the United States could remain focused on "old-fashioned" birth control or
family planning; instead, in 1961 the PPFA launched a new division, Planned
Parenthood–World Population (PP-WP), which dominated its orientation for
the next decade.

The main objective of the PP-WP was to "sell" international population
control to the American public. Around 1960 the major backers of international
population control programs began working to shift this responsibility to the
U.S. government. President Kennedy balked, and it took until 1965 to insert
population control into U.S. foreign and domestic policy. To accomplish this
the population control establishment supported a public relations campaign to
convince voters and taxpayers to support the cause. The campaign also raised
concern about overpopulation inside the United States, thereby incorporating
eugenic thinking—that is, it emphasized the high fertility rates of poorer and
allegedly less desirable groups. A particularly lurid example comes from the
1969 mass advertising campaign of the Committee to Check the Population
Explosion: "How many people do you want in your country? Already the cities
are packed with youngsters. Thousands of idle victims of discontent and drug
addiction. You go out after dark at your peril. . . . Birth control is the answer. . . .
The ever-mounting tidal wave of humanity challenges us to control it, or be
submerged along with all of our civilized values."[12] This and similar ads referred
to "birth control," not "population control"—there was no longer a distinction
between the two—and included the suggestion that urban crime was related
to overcrowding. "Urban crime" was also a code, however unconscious, for racism. This ad typified overpopulation rhetoric in its apocalyptic predictions of
catastrophe unless strong, immediate action was taken.

Although the more academic Population Council and the Population Reference Bureau did not formally endorse these ads, many of their leaders did.

Eugene Black, a board member of Planned Parenthood and a former vice-president of Chase Manhattan Bank and head of the World Bank, signed the ads, as did Frank Abrams, former chairman of Rockefeller-owned Standard Oil of New Jersey and a director of the Population Reference Bureau. Of fifty-eight frequent signers of these ads, thirty-six were part of the population control establishment, fourteen others were closely associated with Planned Parenthood, and four of the remaining eight were close associates of the Rockefellers.[13]

By the mid-1960s, U.S. government experts considered population control a necessary condition for economic development in the Third World. Population control had become a high priority within U.S. nonmilitary foreign aid, partly an artifact of the inclusion of a great deal of foreign aid in the military budget. Soon receiving any nonmilitary foreign aid obligated most receiving nations to undertake population control programs in accordance with U.S. specifications. Although the United Nations was also pressured to take up population control, the campaigns that first reached third-world countries from outside were primarily U.S.-funded and identified by recipients as a part of U.S. foreign policy.

Population control thus meant, to many politically aware Asians and Latin Americans in particular, an aspect of imperialism and an attempt to draw their countries into the cold war. It seemed to them and to many U.S. critics as well to be based on a flawed and highly ideological theory, still basically neo-Malthusian. The population control premise is that population growth and size are primarily causal, rather than primarily symptomatic, of poverty, distress, and inequality.

Population control experts rewrote the history of contraceptive behavior in the "First World" so as to support their cause. They argued that contraception can be basic to economic growth, that people can use "family planning" to bootstrap themselves upward both economically and socially. By contrast, the historical record suggests that the causality runs primarily in the other direction: that is, social change causes birth control. Historically, birth-rate declines have been, by and large, consequences rather than causes of economic development. In most developed countries, birth rates fell after reductions in infant mortality, after industrialization made children less valuable and more expensive economically, and in consonance with women's increased employment outside their homes. The continuation of peasant agricultural production and social organization perpetuates the incentive for large families.[14] In the United States, it was, in the main, neither technological invention nor legalization that spurred birth control use but birth control demand that spurred technology and legal change. There is, of course, a mutual influence between the desire for small families and the availability of birth control technology. But that mutual influence is not symmetrical, not equal, either on the scale of individual decisions to contracept or on a vast societal scale. The availability of contraception is not as powerful an inducement to contracept as are a variety of overall social and economic incentives, such as cost of and opportunities for children, employment needs or opportunities for women, a welfare state that lessens elderly parents' dependence on their children, and high parental aspirations for their children.

Population controllers also offered an ideological reading of the process of development, assuming that the United States and Europe represented the paradigm of economic development and that similar processes could take place centuries later in the Third World. In Europe and the United States, for example, the conditions of the industrial labor market created an incentive for lower fertility rates. But in many third-world countries the impact of foreign capital had the opposite effect, investing profits outside the country, intensifying the demand for low-wage, unskilled labor, and maintaining the incentive for high fertility rates.

Born of the cold war, population control goals also included stopping communism; indeed, in the rhetoric directed to U.S. citizens this was the main reason that economic progress in the Third World was desirable, far more important than the welfare of third-world peoples. The target nations were referred to as "population powder kegs"—the feared explosion was, presumably, revolution or "going communist." (Of course communist countries, notably China, also pushed population control.) Consider the language of the original version of *The Population Bomb,* a pamphlet first published in 1954 by the Hugh Moore Fund and reprinted frequently until the mid-1960s: "There will be 300 million more mouths to feed in the world four years from now—most of them hungry. Hunger brings turmoil—and turmoil, as we have learned, creates the atmosphere in which the communists seek to conquer the earth."[15]

Ironically, it seems likely that one effect of the U.S.-sponsored population control programs was to *retard* the development of indigenous birth control movements. Here there is a parallel within the United States among people of color, particularly African Americans, many of whom grew understandably suspicious of birth control from the way in which it was offered to them: in a top-down manner, singling them out as a problem rather than people with problems, using it as an alternative to and buffer against structural social change and economic redistribution. White-dominated and white-originated birth control programs in the United States created, as we have seen, fears of racial genocide, which made it harder for nonwhite women to voice publicly their own interest in birth control.[16] Many of the third-world societies to which the United States and the United Nations were trying to promote population control were characterized by patriarchal families in which women had few rights. There is plenty of evidence that women throughout the Third World longed for the power to plan and limit their pregnancies and births. In the best of scenarios they experienced strong opposition to exercising such powers from husbands and other controlling kin. When the birth control impulses (and tools) emanated from imperial powers, who simultaneously subverted national autonomy and tried to replace husbandly authority with their own, there was a doubly negative reaction from men and increased ambivalence among women.

Adding still more to the negative reaction were the incentives used to encourage compliance.[17] Individuals were offered cash, transistor radios, blankets, and other commodities to accept sterilizations; at one time in Kerala, India, cash incentives were three times the average monthly wage.[18] Payments were made not only to patients but also to doctors and other population control workers, and individuals not employed by the clinics were offered finder's fees, veritable bounties, for bringing in patients who were willing to be sterilized or fitted with an intrauterine device. Women were known to have IUDs inserted and then to remove them themselves (a painful and risky procedure) in order to have another one inserted for another payment.

These incentives turned out to be insufficient. Basic preferences about family size did not change because population control could offer only an incomplete program of modernization. The prescribed smaller families would have created an important change in traditional family systems—reducing the number of offspring who could work in the family economy and provide for elderly parents—without compensatory economic change. U.S. foreign aid packages did not include old-age security programs for those who limited their families or land redistribution or free education. Nor did the U.S. programs include campaigns to change the gender bases of these family systems, which made boys more valued and thus encouraged repeated childbearing until one or more surviving sons could be counted on.

Population control enthusiasm subsided during the 1980s. One reason was the opposition it provoked among the new social conservatives in the United States, as we will see in chapters 13 and 14. Another reason is that the intensity of public fear of overpopulation could not be maintained, particularly since the doomsday predictions of many experts were not borne out. The continued development of ecological awareness changed the analysis of many environmentalist organizations, leading to a relative de-emphasis on population size per se and a greater emphasis on per capita consumption of natural resources as a greater threat to world survival than overpopulation. Academic demographers have also fallen away from their population control beliefs. Many now echo some of the criticisms first made by Marxists and feminists—that overpopulation and population growth can be problems but are rarely the major independent variables.

But in the 1960s, just before the rebirth of feminism and a woman-centered birth control movement, population control was the defining element in the politics of reproduction.[19] Moreover, the new social movements and the early 1960s counterculture did not at first criticize the population control analysis and its prophecies of doom. The reborn conservation movement supported an antigrowth sensibility that shuddered to think of geometric population expansion. The sexual revolution of the 1960s further reinforced the already commonplace practice of contraception and sterilization for birth control purposes, and abortion continued at least as frequently, probably more so, than at any time in the previous hundred years. But nothing in this development challenged the overpopulation analysis. When the New Left (e.g., civil rights, the leftist student movement, and the anti–Vietnam War movement) first challenged population control as an imperialist policy, it often slid into suspicion of all reproduction control because it too lumped together population control and birth control. The politics of reproduction control was associated entirely with population control. It took a revival of feminism to change that.

The Pill

From the marriage of birth control and population control came a robust child: the contraceptive pill. And its heritage came fully from both parents. The two women most responsible for the Pill, its two "mothers," literally represented the old, feminist birth control movement. Katharine McCormick had met Margaret Sanger in 1917, the year Sanger was arrested for opening her Brooklyn, N.Y., birth control clinic. Both were passionately unconventional at the time. Although McCormick did not share Sanger's leftist politics, she was one of the first two women to earn a science degree from MIT. She had a schizophrenic husband, an experience that convinced her never to have children and sparked her interest in birth control. She worked steadily with Sanger, even smuggling diaphragms into the United States for Sanger's clinics.[20] McCormick also happened to be fabulously rich and gave generously to the movement. In 1950 she asked Sanger what grand project she could fund to advance birth control and Sanger seized the opportunity. Eventually Sanger obtained $2 million from McCormick to fund research and development of a contraceptive pill.

By this time Sanger herself had become a population controller. She believed there was an overpopulation crisis, that it was impoverishing much of the world's population, and that it represented dangerous opportunities for communism. She also believed that the diaphragm was inadequate to solve the problem, as was proven in India, but that modern science ought to be able to do so. In 1946 she was already dreaming of a pill of some sort.[21] The rest of the story is well known: with McCormick's money she hired Gregory Pincus, who hired fellow scientists Chang Min-Chueh and John Rock, a Catholic physician who did the first human testing. Using just-developed synthetic progesterone (the natural kind had been prohibitively expensive), the two showed that it could suppress women's ovulation. The Population Council contributed no funding whatever, and neither did the government or the pharmaceutical companies, though all three would benefit greatly, albeit in different ways.

Ironically, the Pill was first tested by Rock for the opposite purpose: He was treating infertile women and hypothesized that if their ovaries were allowed to "rest" by suppressing ovulation for a number of months there might be a rebound effect, resulting in increased ovulation. In 1954 he reported success with a limited number of highly motivated patients. But testing the Pill on a larger group led to questionable practices, raising first ethical and then political issues. Initially, Pincus set up trials involving psychiatric hospital in-patients—noninformed, nonconsenting women who had nothing to gain from contraception since they were unable to engage in sex. Then, in the late 1950s, he turned to Puerto Rico for large-scale studies.

Pincus chose Puerto Rico because it had long been used for testing; because he thought working there would allow him to avoid the press and premature publicity; because overpopulation contributed to poverty in Puerto Rico; and because he believed Puerto Rican women to be tractable and unlikely to protest—in his words it was "'a prototype underdeveloped country on America's own doorstep.'"[22] But he also knew that Puerto Rico had a pre-existing network of birth control clinics and that Puerto Rican elites had been interested in population control since the 1940s, when Luis Muñoz Marín, the first elected governor, became a supporter of Margaret Sanger's work. In the early 1930s Puerto Rican nurses and social workers active in the birth control movement had opened clinics on the island, which failed due to lack of funding—until 1937, when Clarence Gamble's foundation (he was heir to the Proctor and Gamble fortune) began funding them. Although Puerto Rican women disproportionately relied on sterilization for birth control (see chapter 14), many were eager for contraception as well.[23]

Finding women to volunteer in Puerto Rico was easy. Women were so eager for reproduction control that, as the physician who directed the tests said, "'they couldn't get hold of it fast enough.'"[24] But getting them to continue taking the Pill long enough to make the tests valid was not easy. They complained about bloating, weight gain, nausea, vomiting, stomach pain, headaches, and rashes. (The early oral contraceptives had 100 times more progestin and 3 times more estrogen than later versions.) The Puerto Rican physician who ran the tests reported that there were too many side effects—17 percent of users voiced complaints—to be acceptable. But Pincus insisted that these reactions were merely psychological and that Puerto Ricans were more suggestible that mainland Americans: "'We have never seen it in any of *our* patients.'"[25] There were also side effects of another sort: The Puerto Rican press denounced the test as racist and imperialist, using people of color as guinea pigs for white medicine. Priests and husbands protested, no doubt for different reasons.[26] In Humacao, more than half the women dropped out out of the program.[27]

When the Pill hit the mainland, however, women responded with great enthusiasm. American Catholics believed by a 3:2 ratio that the Church should accept oral contraception; 78 percent of Catholic physicians prescribed it routinely. G. D. Searle, the drug company that marketed Enovid without competition for two years, reaped staggering profits, although it had invested nothing. Searle had at first declined to be associated with such a controversial drug but was persuaded by the response to the publicity of its early success—it received many unsolicited letters begging to participate in further trials—and by a chance to market Enovid first as a treatment for gynecological disorders. But this was soon as much a euphemism as marketing condoms "for prevention of disease only." Women made Enovid into a birth control pill well before the Food and Drug Administration approved it as such. By late 1959, six months before FDA approval, a half million women were already using the Pill. Women barraged doctors with demands for prescriptions. Physicians hesitated to refuse because they knew, or sensed, that female patients would only go elsewhere if they did.[28] In this sense the Pill anticipated the pharmaceutical companies' more recent practice of advertising prescription drugs directly to consumers—just one of the ways in which the Pill, without its producers' intentions, empowered wmen.

As the Pill became the "moral property"[29] of millions of women, it became clear that this child of the birth control–population control alliance took after its mother. Women made of it a tool for autonomy, freedom, and higher aspirations. The Pill had a greater impact on gender and sexual patterns in the United States than on overpopulation in poor countries. Indeed, it was always far more widely used in the United States than elsewhere; in 1967, for example, women in the United States consumed more than half the world's oral contraceptives. The Pill did not so much change women's lives as enable them to make changes they longed for. Their sex was more free, their educational plans more achievable, their wage-earning more stable, their domestic labor reduced. Married women thought it improved marital relationships, and so did many husbands. The Pill was harder for unmarried and poor women to get, but no less desirable.

Public Family Planning Clinics

The Pill's father had some influence too. In retrospect it seems inevitable that some population control ideas, especially programs to cut fertility rates as a means of alleviating poverty, would also be applied in the United States.

Roadblocks to contraception were falling, smoothing the route to public funding. In 1958 a ban on prescriptions for contraceptives in New York City municipal hospitals was challenged and defeated. In 1963 former president Eisenhower reversed his earlier dismissal of population control as not government business. In 1965 President Johnson emphasized the population explosion in his State of the Union speech. Also in 1965, in *Griswold v. Connecticut*, the U.S. Supreme Court struck down the last remaining state law against contraception.[30] That same year the executive branch became directly involved when the War on Poverty provided some federal funds for birth control, and in 1966 thirty states established family planning programs.[31] In 1967 the Child Health Act *required* 6 percent of maternal-child health grants to be set aside for family planning, and guidelines for Aid to Families with Dependent Children were amended to *require* that state welfare agencies provide family planning services to women receiving public assistance, with the federal government providing 75 percent of the cost of the program. The Department of Health, Education, and Welfare (predecessor of today's Health and Human Services) established a unit on population and family planning, and the Department of Defense provided contraception to military wives. Then, in 1970, with broad bipartisan support, Title X of the Public Health Service Act created for the first time a comprehensive federal program to provide family planning services on a national basis. The new federal commitment was dubbed "'Congress's blank check for birth control.'"[32]

We can gauge how far the political mood has shifted since then by considering the promise of a conservative Republican president, Richard Nixon, that "'no American woman should be denied access to family planning assistance because of her economic condition.'"[33] The birth controllers were finally winning public support.

But establishing these jointly state- and federally funded birth control clinics required getting state legislative support and appropriation. Here the politics was different than in Washington. Even the most progressive and antiracist of birth control advocates, such as the extraordinary Joseph Beasley of Louisiana, calculated that they needed to use the time-honored appeals to conservatives and racists that family planning would lower welfare costs as well as the birth rate among blacks. Beasley argued that every dollar spent on birth control would save $13.50 in other state expenses. Indeed, such appeals helped to overcome the religious and moral bias against birth control found among

Catholics and, especially, Bible Belt white Protestants. Beasley tried to play both sides of the issue by asking the governor to get the most vocally racist politicians, Joseph Singelmann and Leander Perez, to keep quiet about their reasons for supporting family planning in Louisiana. (Perez was notorious for saying, "'The best way to hate a nigger is to hate him before he is born.'")[34]

It did not require overtly racist statements, however, to raise the concerns of people of color about the purposes of these clinics. In general the public family planning programs were disproportionately located in communities of people of color. The first state to establish a tax-supported birth control program was Alabama. Several southern states tried to enact punitive sterilization laws aimed at reducing welfare costs, drawing back only when informed that if they did so they would lose federal AFDC funds.[35] In states so stingy with other forms of help for the poor and people of color, it was not surprising that there was suspicion of their generosity in dispensing birth control. Blacks took notice that clinics supposedly offering overall health care put a disproportionate share of their funding into birth control. Moreover, public clinics tended to promote the more long-lasting forms of birth control, from IUDs to implants to sterilization, rather than pills or diaphragms, thereby to some degree weakening rather than strengthening women's control. In a New Orleans program, the patients were initially 96 percent black; whites never topped 15 percent.[36]

This program coincided, of course, with increasing African American militancy and anger as the states conducted massive resistance to civil rights. Although African Americans in general, especially women, supported birth control, male nationalist leaders cried genocide. In Pittsburgh in 1968 black militants used bomb threats to close a clinic; in Cleveland they burned one. Martha Ward's splendid study of the Louisiana program shows that, contrary to the cliché that these leaders spoke for the "black community," African American women leaders stood up to them. Called a "'pill-pusher' and 'a traitor to her race,'" one birth control outreach worker replied, "'You can get numbers, if you want, in the cemetery, because that's where lots of mothers and black babies are.'"[37]

Despite tensions, publicly funded clinics showed that birth control brought results. Some $340 million in federal and state funds was being spent annually on birth control services, with 5 million women receiving help at 5,200 clinics. Many of those who could not qualify for Medicaid were able to obtain birth control and other reproductive health medical care through this program. Ward details its impressive accomplishments in Louisiana: between 1970 and 1974 birth rates dropped by 11.5 percent, infant mortality by 26 percent, and maternal mortality by a staggering 51.5 percent. These declines were greater than the national averages, although Louisiana's indicators were near the bottom and the black maternal death rate remained three-and-a-half times the rate among whites. The program also put women and black men into responsible jobs—78 percent of the management and professional positions. It demonstrated that the poor, when the barriers they usually faced were removed, were as enthusiastic about birth control as the prosperous. Equally important, the program raised its clients' expectations for medical care. As one black community leader said, "'It set a model for how services should and could be. People got used to quality services and began to demand them from Charity and welfare.'" In the clinics, many of the female and black employees worked to educate the doctors about how to treat patients respectfully. These patients assessed their experiences in the family planning clinics with statements such as, "'Health is my right, I don't just have to take anything'" and one, when asked about her future intentions in visiting doctors, said, "'I'm gonna make them treat me better.'"[38]

The loyalty and enthusiasm of so many poor women for the family planning clinics also demonstrated the success of including birth control in a broad program of medical care. The Louisiana clinic guidelines called for a full medical history of each patient, a general physical exam including four or five lab tests as standard and five others as indicated, treatment for vaginal infections and venereal disease as needed, and referrals for other medical problems. Clinics were also directed to provide a review of all contraceptive options and to prescribe the patient's choice of contraceptive, including surgical sterilization. Post-exam interviews were required, as were followup visits at three months and every six months thereafter, including a full annual physical exam. Clinics were also advised to offer infertility services when requested.[39]

By the mid-1970s, however, the federal government's support of family planning began to weaken and funds diminished even as clientele increased. Precisely when a strong women's movement was positioned to win major advances in reproduction control access, the federal government was reducing the funding that extended that access to the poor and others discriminated against. In some ways the funding cutbacks confirmed black nationalist suspicions of family planning programs: just as program staff and clients succeeded in expanding the offerings of birth control clinics to include general medical care, the whites in charge cut the budget.

PART 4

Birth Control in the Era of Second-Wave Feminism

13   *Abortion, the Mother Controversy*

So far we have seen three historical peaks in the movement for reproduction control, each with a differently defined goal—voluntary motherhood, birth control, and family planning. This last part of the book examines a fourth birth control conflict created by the renewal of feminism in the late 1960s and the backlash against it. This stage of the movement was more complex because it focused not only on contraception but also on abortion and sterilization and because the movement was broader. Although no single term has uniquely defined this period, the slogan that best captures its politics is "reproductive rights."

Reproductive rights struggles of the late twentieth century consumed more of the energies of the new women's movements than voluntary motherhood had in the 1870s or birth control in 1910–20. And reproductive rights struggles of the late twentieth century had a greater impact on the entire U.S. political context. Never before in the history of the birth control movement—not in its free-love associations, not in the race-suicide debates, not in the civil disobedience of the early twentieth-century campaign for the legalization of contraception—had birth control ever been so controversial. The major reason for the heightened passion about reproduction issues is precisely that they seemed to express the core aims of the women's liberation movement and thus became the major focus of the backlash against feminism. Birth control politics has become an arena for conflict between liberal and conservative ideas about family, personal freedom, state intervention, religion in politics, sexual morality, and social welfare.

Reproduction control issues were also disproportionately influential within the women's movement. This second wave of feminism campaigned not only for equal rights for women but also to give women the economic and social power to claim and use those rights. Reproduction controversies provided many examples of women's powerlessness to exercise their legal rights—due to sexism, poverty, racism, and violent intimidation; indeed, reproduction control has been influential in the development of feminist thought about what "rights" are or can be. In the relatively short period since its rebirth in the late 1960s, feminism's ideas shifted considerably, from an emphasis on personal freedom to a concern with the values that underlie our whole social order and an understanding that reproductive policy could not only provide individual rights but also promote social goals such as equality. Progressing from demanding reproductive rights in law to calling for the provisions that would make those rights usable by all, the contemporary women's movement was redefining the boundaries of freedom and welfare as well as leading the defense against conservative retrenchment on those issues.

The political contestation over these issues in the 1970s and 1980s was, as so often in the past, pre-eminently a contest of meanings, a competition for how birth control should be understood. This competition was never before so polarized. The various alternative historical meanings of birth control— women's rights, individual freedom, family planning, population control, eugenics—were narrowed to two major interpretations: a liberal vision in which birth control is an individual right, a woman's right, part of a society committed to sex equality and sexual freedom; and a conservative vision in which birth control is a modern convenience that must be closely restricted lest it become destructive of social cohesion and sexual and family morality.

The drive to restrict reproductive rights was directed above all at abortion, and political alignments with respect to abortion constructed the overall shape of the debate. But at the same time differences among birth control supporters, differences we have previously seen as containing important class and race as well as political fissures, and different alliances between groups—as, for example, between feminists and medical professionals—complicated the debate.

Although greater in intensity, the political debates of these two decades recapitulated in many ways the early history of the movement for birth control. There were several consecutive impulses—a feminist and civil libertarian sense that reproductive control should be an individual right; a conservative and primarily religious backlash; and a reproductive rights defense that relied on lowest-common-denominator points of unity. This pattern has been characteristic of many social movements and expresses fundamental dynamics of social change. The backward steps derive from the fact that new gains typically produce backlashes as well as new and often unforeseen problems.

The call for women's control of their reproduction, signaled by the slogan "control over our own bodies," once again identified a claim for reproductive rights that rested on a critique of male domination and a demand for women's liberation, and once again it differentiated this claim from family planning, population control, or eugenic motives. This wave of birth control agitation rested on a more grassroots and comprehensive feminist program than had the previous wave. It invented a new word—"sexism"—which condemned practices once not even reprehensible, and invented an analysis that challenged not only sexual inequality but gender itself, including the view that motherhood had to be women's primary identity.

A conservative response identified abortion and unlimited access to contraception with sexual permissiveness and subversion of tradition, the family, morality, and the word of God. Like previous antifeminist reactions, this one was by no means simply a men's movement but equally a movement of women who did not see their own interests in the dominant feminist imagery, who even saw feminism as antagonistic to women's interests. In the 1970s a new conservatism focused far more on these social/sexual issues and less on economic ones than had earlier conservative responses, and it made birth control issues, particularly abortion, far more prominent in the conservative political agenda. This new conservatism was deeply shaped by fundamentalist Christianity.

In response to the conservative attacks and the (inevitable) weakening of the feminist movement in the 1980s, the campaign for reproductive rights once again lost its exclusively feminist identity. But this loss was in part a gain, as it brought together a broad liberal coalition of feminist, mainstream birth control and population control organizations in favor of abortion and contraceptive rights. However, this retreat from a key slogan of the previous decade—"abortion on demand"—and reliance on a right to privacy and "choice" came at the cost of arguing for abortion rights as a *social* good, part of a larger group of reproductive rights that helped to create equality for women and social responsibility for children. Unlike coalitions of the period 1920–60, this new coalition was based on a feminist common denominator. Women's rights, equality, and opportunity have become values shared globally by promoters of birth control— a tremendous victory for the global women's liberation movements.

Abortion and the Women's Liberation Movement

The legalization of abortion was one of the most clear-cut and concrete among many women's rights gains of the 1970s. It resulted immediately from the campaigns of feminists and civil libertarian physicians and lawyers as well as

from long-term changes in society and the economy that produced those campaigns. The decline in woman-identified political activism between 1920 and
1960 coincided, paradoxically, with greater independence for American women,
sometimes chosen and sometimes forced upon them, sometimes advantageous
and sometimes disadvantageous. Increases in wage-earning responsibility,
education, legal rights, sexual activity, divorce—and therefore single-mother-
hood—produced the kind of contradiction that is often at the root of a social
movement: greater opportunity and raised aspirations met by continued discrimination and frustration. Then the flowering of social activism in the 1950s
and 1960s, especially in the civil rights, student, and anti–Vietnam War struggles, revived the women's movement. It was influenced by the critique of
"structural racism" that came out of the radical wing of the civil rights movement and the New Left critique of conformist culture. It was born of expanding opportunities, notably for educated women. But women of virtually all
social groups nurtured dreams of upward mobility, dignity, and autonomy. It
is not the case, as many have suggested, that the whole women's movement
was white and elite; rather, there were numerous women's movements, many
arising among working-class and nonwhite women.[1]

Among the obstacles to women's aspirations, lack of control of reproduction seemed most basic and, ironically, also most easily overcome. This was
the case precisely because among some groups contraceptive use had already
spread so widely, long before the feminist revival and not only among married
people but also among unmarried and sexually active women. Planned Parenthood in the 1960s refused to serve the unmarried, as did many doctors, but
young women often obtained contraception by claiming they were about to
be married or by borrowing a wedding ring. Still, many women had no access
to birth control. Contraception was illegal in several states into the 1960s.
Martha Ward's study of Louisiana shows that birth control was virtually unavailable there to anyone except a thin stratum of prosperous women who
could count on the discretion of private doctors,[2] a situation characteristic of
many southern and rural or small-town locations. Influential African American male political leaders condemned birth control as genocidal well into the
1970s. Nevertheless, the birth rate was dropping among all groups, including
blacks, matching its depression-era low by the early 1970s.

Although there can be no definitive figures on illegal abortions, several
scholars suspect that these increased during the 1950s and 1960s.[3] The story
of two illegal abortionists operating during that period may capture the state
of affairs. Lorraine Florio operated as a lay abortionist in the small industrial
city of Lawrence, Massachusetts, between 1958 and 1968, performing an estimated 5,000 abortions with a saline injection method and charging an average of $300 each. She never became prosperous, partly because what she did

was well known in the community and so she was forced to pay protection money to police and at least one lawyer. No client ever ratted on her, however. A retired Lawrence policewoman, interviewed about Florio's business, said, "We made a few arrests. . . . But the women—you couldn't get them to finger anybody." (After Florio stopped performing abortions she worked as a waitress.) Dr. Robert D. Spencer ran a very different kind of operation in Ashland, Pennsylvania. He estimated that he performed about 75,000 abortions, beginning in 1923 and continuing to his death in 1969. An intellectual and political descendant of free-thinking physicians (see chapter 7), he included as his heroes Tom Paine, Robert Ingersoll, and Clarence Darrow, and his instinct to trust and help women came from a kind of maverick individualism and anti-Puritanism. His name was known, at least among college students, throughout the mid-Atlantic states (he helped several personal friends of mine). He was arrested three times but never convicted; arresting officers themselves were often reluctant to go after him, convinced that abortion was a needed service and one of many "victimless crimes" they considered best left alone.[4]

But even the minority of women who had access to reliable abortionists such as Florio and Spencer often suffered from the fact that abortions were illegal, because fear led them to put off seeking help and because of delay in finding a provider. Their fear was debilitating and their delay made the procedure more risky. The majority of women seeking abortions had to rely on unknown practitioners who at best might cut safety corners and keep prices high and at worst might assault and humiliate them.

By the mid-twentieth century, women were becoming less willing to accept such treatment, accustomed as they were becoming to respectable medical contraception and sexual freedom. Neither the women's liberation movement nor the legalization of abortion caused the more positive attitudes toward and greater use of abortion and contraception; instead, they merely recognized and confirmed these changes.[5] Indeed, at the time of the 1973 U.S. Supreme Court decision in *Roe v. Wade,* there was no evidence of great polarization of public opinion about abortion.[6]

The pressure for abortion legalization came from two groups: professionals, particularly physicians, and feminists.[7] In fact, some types of abortions had gradually become legal during the twentieth century since physicians had the discretion to perform D&Cs for "therapeutic" reasons. Women with access to private doctors, primarily prosperous women, of course, kept up a heavy demand for therapeutic abortions; physicians often found the pressure on them uncomfortable and hard to refuse. In response, during the 1940s and 1950s some hospitals established review boards to make abortion decisions in order simultaneously to control and to take the pressure off individual doctors.[8] Popular approval of therapeutic abortion grew in 1962 as a result of an epidemic of rubella (which can cause deformities in fetuses) and the case of Sherri Fink-bine: after taking the drug thalidomide, she learned that her pregnancy was likely to result in a deformed infant, so she flew to Sweden to obtain an abortion. Scorned by many, she also received a great deal of sympathetic publicity.

The fact that abortion became intensely controversial only after it was legalized has produced the suggestions that abortion was legalized "prematurely," that is, before public opinion was fully supportive of the reform, or wrongly, in defiance of majority sentiment. The evidence does not support these conclusions. First, abortion was not legalized by the Supreme Court in 1973. Seventeen states had legalized or decriminalized it before that, often in response to active feminist reform campaigns. Rather, it was this kind of local change that conditioned the Court's decision that state statutes universally prohibiting abortion should not stand.[9] Second, abortion was widely practiced and provoked little public attention in these years.

A better explanation of the spread of intense antiabortion feeling was that abortion had changed its meaning through its reinterpretation by the revived women's movement. We have seen before that particular birth control practices or sets of practices took on different meanings in different political contexts. Regarding the 1970s, one might speculate that had there not been a feminist movement, abortion might have been decriminalized with less opposition—and one might equally speculate that had abortion remained illegal, the opposition to other aspects of the feminist program would have been that much more intense. What did happen was the spread of a feminist understanding of abortion as a right of self-determination to which all women were entitled, replacing the previously dominant view of abortion as, alternatively, a form of medical treatment or an unpleasant and risky but often necessary private solution to a personal problem. As we have seen, abortion was a widely practiced birth control method, available and legitimized in most societies; and even when it was prohibited, it was not widely condemned on moral grounds by the public, including the religious public. Only since the birth of the Right to Life movement has a substantial group of women, although distinctly a minority, reported feeling agonies of guilt in deciding upon abortion; a range of literary, oral history, and statistical sources suggest that previously abortion was an often difficult and unpleasant but nevertheless not greatly guilt-inducing practice.[10] The morality of abortion, often presented today as a basic, metaphysical, timeless, and universal question, has in fact been changed by historical experience and possibility.

Another reason that abortion became so controversial was that the challenge to its illegality disrupted the interpretation of it as a medical matter and foregrounded its political meanings. The early twentieth-century compromise had, in a sense, legalized both contraception and abortion by placing them at the discretion of doctors (who could not only dispense diaphragms but also abortions by articulating a "therapeutic" indication). The whole category "birth control" appeared medical by the 1960s, and the *Roe v. Wade* decision attempted to keep abortion thus defined. But both pro- and antiabortion activists were, by the late 1960s, challenging the discretionary power of physicians, arguing that abortion's status should be a moral and political, not a technical, matter best decided by the citizenry, not by professionals. In this sense pro– and anti–abortion rights advocates shared a perspective. But they diverged as feminists (both liberal and radical) became convinced that abortions need not be wretched or shameful or dangerous, that they had been constructed in that manner by a power structure, and that they could be offered in a context that respected women and promoted responsible decision making about reproduction and sexual behavior.

On the pro–abortion rights side, the most vivid of these challenges were collective projects to help women obtain underground abortions, projects operating in the spirit, style, and politics of the early women's liberation movement. Byllye Avery, executive director of the National Black Women's Health Project, began her health activism in Gainesville, Florida, by referring women to places as far away as New York to get safe abortions; after legalization, this project opened its own abortion facility in Gainesville.[11] Protestant clergy created a national abortion referral service.[12] The most developed project was the Chicago-based Jane, an underground women's collective that arranged and performed more than eleven thousand illegal abortions from 1969 to 1973. It began as a counseling and referral service, connecting women with illegal abortionists and helping to preserve the safety of both. In its second stage, the group hired its own doctor in order to gain control of the conditions of the abortions, to guarantee safety and respectful treatment for clients. Stage three developed in part from the dishonesty of the abortionist they had hired, who had falsely claimed to be a physician: "when people found out he wasn't a doctor, they said, 'Well, the hell with it. If he can do them, we can do them.'"[13] In fact, laywomen gradually began to perform abortions in response to increasing demand. The Jane abortionist had been asking his women assistants to do more and more of the procedures before the actual abortion, such as administering medication and inserting a speculum, so when a counselor found herself alone with a patient whose amniotic sac broke, she had no choice but to complete the abortion—which she did without incident. The result of Jane performing its own abortions was not only an exemplary safety record but also a 75 percent drop in prices, from $400 to $100.[14]

Jane's impetus toward a radical demedicalization of abortion did not continue. One impact of the 1973 *Roe v. Wade* decision was reconfirmation of medical control of abortion. The Court situated women's right to abortion within a right to privacy but did not create this as an absolute right; rather, it was limited by the doctor's discretion and by the state's "'justifiable interest'" in the health of the pregnant woman and in "'preserving the potentiality of human life'" in later pregnancy. To adjudicate conflicts between women's desires and state interests, the Court placed "'the right of the physician to administer medical treatment according to his professional judgment'" and categorized abortion as a medical decision.[15] (These developments raise a stimulating counterfactual speculation: Had the state courts been slower to legalize abortion, might the women's movement have moved further toward challenging medical control?) The right to an abortion has in fact been significantly limited not only by physicians' discretion but also by their availability. Doctors have been reluctant to perform abortions for a variety of reasons, such as religious scruples, embarrassment at being branded abortionists, fear of attack by antiabortion supporters.[16] Hospitals have been reluctant to offer second-trimester abortions, which are very few in number but nonetheless needed, and medical schools have been less than enthusiastic about training students in abortion technique.

Using the spirit and argumentation of the "privacy" defense of abortion rights, the dominant pro–abortion rights lobby fixed on "choice" as its slogan. This language evoked the emotional and political power of the idea of freedom—as in freedom of choice—in American political discourse. Moreover, "choice" evoked commitments to civil liberties and women's autonomous decision making and de-emphasized abortion itself. But it also revealed and reinforced some of the limitations of the pro–abortion rights case: the abstract right to privacy suggested that a procedure legalized was actually accessible, thus trivializing the effects of nonlegal barriers to reproductive self-determination, notably poverty. "Choice" could have been used for a campaign that highlighted access to reproductive free choice, but in fact the movement's most visible emphasis was on legal barriers (a legacy of civil rights). Moreover, the emphasis was on individual rights and implicitly denied the validity of any social regulation of reproduction. The notion of a reproduction policy that could be designed actively to promote other social goods—for example, the eradication of infant mortality or the improvement of sexual relations—was de-emphasized in relation to arguments based on individual liberty.[17]

Origins of the Right to Life Movement

Just as the decision in *Roe v. Wade* was based on an abstract and allegedly gender-neutral right—the claim to privacy—so the antiabortion movement introduced a new argument focused not on gender but on the rights of the fetus. There were other antiabortion themes, such as women's "selfishness" and "frivolity" in rejecting maternity (a theme familiar from the nineteenth century). But the fetal rights argument was to become steadily more prominent, not only legally but also in the popular consciousness. It worked to transform abortion from a traditional form of reproduction control into murder.

The movement was initiated by the Catholic hierarchy, which had been alarmed about familial and sexual liberalization throughout the 1960s and particularly its failure to prevent divorce and contraceptive use among Catholics.[18] Deciding to take a stand against abortion, in the late 1960s the Church began to organize right-to-life committees in response to state laws legalizing abortion and well before *Roe v. Wade*. After the Supreme Court decision, the Church launched a drive for a "human life amendment" to the U.S. Constitution. The National Right to Life Committee, dominated at that time by Catholic leaders, benefited from priests' contact with and authority over parishioners in raising money, recruiting activists, and building an antiabortion climate of opinion among Catholics.[19]

But Catholic sentiment was never unanimous. Clergy on the Left denounced the movement's selective commitment to "life"—favoring the unborn over the born—in supporting capital punishment and military aggression and opposing welfare provision.[20] Those on the Right denounced the support of the National Conference of Catholic Bishops for Senator Orrin Hatch's 1981 bill, which gave Congress and the state legislatures the power to decide the legality of abortion; they preferred Senator Jesse Helms's bill, which defined life as beginning at conception and gave embryos constitutional rights.[21] Meanwhile, Catholic pro-choice sentiment was organized and articulated, notably by Catholics for a Free Choice. The bravest resistance came from nuns, including twenty-four who signed a 1984 newspaper ad asserting that there was a "diversity of opinion" among Catholics about abortion. A 1972 study of New York State priests revealed that only 68 percent fully agreed with the Church's teaching on abortion and many nevertheless believed that abortion should not be criminalized.[22] The greatest Catholic resistance to antiabortion views came from the laity, who have voted with their feet. Catholics had higher rates of abortions than non-Catholics, some 30 percent higher than among Protestants.[23] Moreover, Catholics are only slightly less approving of abortion than Protestants and no more supportive of criminalizing it.[24]

Despite its Roman Catholic beginnings, the Right to Life movement did not remain a parochial enterprise. It attracted activists in large numbers, many of them extremely passionate and willing to give substantial time, money, and daring to the cause. It became one of the largest social movements in the late twentieth century, possibly the largest grassroots conservative movement.[25] Soon Protestants outnumbered Catholics in the movement, a shift closely related to the powerful religious revival of the late twentieth century. At the

turn of the twenty-first century, evangelicals constituted half of all white Protestants. The proliferation of these evangelicals was a major force in making
antiabortion the strongest of the various single-issue causes[26] that together
created a dramatic conservative revival. One could never have predicted in
the 1970s such an outpouring of concern for the fetus or such a symbolic load-
ing of abortion.

Only in seeing the Right to Life movement as saturated with antifeminism does its strength become understandable. Abortion came to represent
a multidimensional attack on the "traditional" family and gender system. One
dimension was, of course, sexuality. A step beyond contraception in separating sex from reproduction, abortion was made to appear as a license to sexual promiscuity, a reproduction control method that would allow women to
have nonmarital and even multiple sexual partners without the restraint of
childbearing. Indeed, the antiabortion discourse has a pungently punitive
aroma, often appearing in the notion that those who would enjoy sexual pleasure must be ready to accept their punishment. The sexual dimension is always inflected by a gendered difference in that the "punishment" is to be
experienced by women. Despite lip service to sexual equality, most opponents
of abortion believe that women must accept as inevitable a direct path from
sexual intercourse to motherhood. The more extreme, or forthright, antiabortion leaders extend their opposition to contraception because of their hostility toward sexual activity. "I think contraception is disgusting—people using
each other for pleasure," remarked Joseph Scheidler, head of the Pro-Life
Action League.[27] Father Paul Marx, president of Human Life International,
developed the connection more thoughtfully: "You can't stop abortion without fighting contraception: it is the gateway to abortion. Not one of the 81
countries I've worked in has 'clean' contraception without abortion—not one.
Once there's contraception—separating sexual activity from procreation and
teaching people to use each other's bodies for selfish pleasure—abortion is
always used as a backup."[28]

This antisex attitude is prudery in the Victorian mode, ordaining not only
a double standard for men and women but also the hypocrisy of many leaders. The sex scandals of various Christian Coalition ministers and their survival
as leaders remind us that the Christian sin-and-redemption narrative remains
more powerful in religious discourse than simpler stories of consistent virtue.[29]
But the hypocrisy does not mean that anxiety about abortion is inauthentic;
the longing for a stable gender system and for sexual constraints on women
expresses a drive to reduce sexual anxiety and gender uncertainty.

Another dimension of the anxiety provoked by legal abortion relates to
conflicts over how to manage child-raising and employment. Here antiabortion protestors express a material tension experienced by all but the most

wealthy parents. The protracted and stubborn refusal of U.S. domestic policy to recognize the economic necessity of wage-earning by so many mothers has deprived them of basic provisions to make their double job possible—such as a living wage and benefits, affordable day care, affordable housing, medical insurance, parental leave, sick leave when they or their children are ill, and flexible schedules. Behind this failure lies a weakened but still breathing loyalty to the family wage, that is, to the standard that husbands/fathers should single-handedly earn enough to support nonearning wives/mothers and children. This family-wage standard has never been possible for the majority of Americans, now less than ever. Right to Life advocates have correctly pointed to the formidable stresses on the majority of mothers who must also be wage earners. But in the fantasy nostalgia for the family wage, abortion opponents search for blame, ignoring structural economic change and defining a willful evil—feminism—as the guilty party. In that story there is a wicked siren who lures women from their only fulfilling destinies into the job market. In fact, feminism is but a small factor among the reasons, overwhelmingly economic, that women work for wages.

Closely related to the fear that feminism pulls women out of their homes is an anxiety about the loss of motherhood—a loss not only to children but to marriages and to society as a whole. The family values of late twentieth-century conservatives involved the construction of yet another fictive nostalgia, for a mother who was ever comforting, providing, self-sacrificing—in other words, the "perfect" mother. Motherhood became an expression of longing for a caring relationship in which one is an individual rather than one among many. After all, being mothered is for most people their earliest experience of being treated as a subject, not an object. Abortion became for its opponents a powerful antimotherhood symbol, indeed, the antithesis of motherliness. (This is not an accurate conclusion about the purpose of abortion, as virtually all seekers of abortion are women motivated by desire to mother and to mother well.) The redefinition of the fetus as a preborn child turns abortion into baby killing, thus positioning aborting women as murderers of their own children.

Indeed, focusing on the fetus played an essential role in this discourse. The first campaigns against abortion, in the mid-nineteenth century, focused primarily against women's rights, attacking the selfishness of those who would evade their maternal calling, and only secondarily on the "dysgenic" implications of "race suicide" (see chapter 6); the status of the fetus was a minor theme, and opponents of abortion did not attribute legal rights or personhood to the fetus.[30] But women's lives had changed so greatly by the 1970s that no campaign directly attacking a woman's option to delay or limit childbearing could have become mainstream. By shifting the focus away from women, women's rights, and reproduction control to the fetus (or even the embryo) and its postulated rights, the antiabortion movement was able to create a discourse sufficiently compatible with the late twentieth-century gender system to garner widespread support.[31]

Underlying all this discourse was religiosity—most antiabortion advocates are not just churchgoers but involved in a personal relationship with God. They are predominantly Christian but also include Jews and Muslims. Many have been "born again"—that is, they have experienced a rebirth of devotion in their own lives—and they deeply resent the way that the dominant culture has strayed. Others come from lifelong religious traditions. To the white born-agains, women's expanded public sphere activities and withdrawal from domesticity represent one of the aspects of secularism they most detest. The movement decries the separation of church and state, the teaching of (secular) science and social science, the legal and moral discourse of individual rights, the decline of parental authority, and the tolerance of homosexuality.[32] This hostility toward secularism also expresses a conservative populist class politics: born-agains associate secularism with liberal elites, much as the Ku Klux Klan did in the 1920s. Of course, there are other antiabortion religious positions that are considerably more complex and less conservative. African American and Mexican American religious people, for example, often consider abortion a serious sin without such hostility toward other aspects of secular culture.

Not surprisingly, the populist impulse of the antiabortion movement attracted national conservative leaders. In the late 1970s, observing the strength of rank-and-file support for the antiabortion cause, New Right leaders of various religious affiliations saw that the Right to Life movement could help them build a new conservative electoral bloc, winning for conservative Republican candidates those who would have voted Democratic, despite their resentments of liberalism, because of their economic interests. According to Paul Weyrich, founder of the Heritage Foundation and an important New Right leader, during the 1978 elections the New Right first experimented with electoral manipulation of "family issues." He had seen their importance in 1971, he wrote, but it had not been easy for him to convince fellow conservatives of the political validity of these issues: ". . . the Republican Party is, in many parts of the country, an elitist social club which does not take kindly to association with the lower middle class, with precisely those people . . . most concerned with family issues." He convinced his political allies that these social, or family, issues would help to bring nonelite people, usually repelled by conservative economic policies, into a new conservative political movement. He identified three key groups for this purpose: right-to-lifers, fundamentalist and evangelical Christians, and parents' rights (anti–sex education, antibusing) advocates.[33]

Prior to 1976, non-Catholic New Right propagandists and publications rarely mentioned abortion.[34] At the 1977 Houston International Women's Year conference, the New Right organized the Pro-Family Coalition to combat the "feminist agenda," in which abortion rights were prominent. Since then the antiabortion leadership has been increasingly composed of evangelicals prominent in the New Right coalition, and its leaders believe they have been able to mobilize those who oppose abortion to support conservative political candidates.[35] "ABORTION KNITS RELIGIOUS RIGHT INTO GOP FABRIC," headlined the *New York Times* in 1986.[36]

The political integration of antiabortion into right-wing politics does not mean that all antiabortion supporters are conservative or that antiabortion feelings are exclusively antifeminist.[37] But most antiabortion sentiment arose from reaction against the feminist movement. Two case studies of antiabortion women active in local campaigns showed that while many lacked a coherent conservative perspective, and some shared opinions with feminists on issues such as employment, education, and civil rights, they were mainly concerned to defend their positions as mothers and, as they put it, as "traditional" women. Kristin Luker's interviews with activists in California revealed that antiabortion women were propelled by their desire for respect for motherhood more than by any overweening conservative agenda. Faye Ginsburg's study of Fargo, North Dakota, scene of intense abortion battles in the early 1980s, demonstrated that women's antiabortion activity there was a true women's movement, reminiscent of nineteenth-century women's social purity movements, such as those described in chapter 5. Some of her interview subjects even supported comparable worth and contraception but saw abortion as breaking a link between sex and marriage upon which women's security depended. Legalized abortion thus represented to them a state-sponsored assault on women's culture of nurturance and women's power in the family.[38]

Antiabortion attitudes have been complicated by racial concerns. Politically aware people of color know that birth control and population control advocates had, at times, racist motives but also that antiabortion advocates were often the same people who cheered the dogs and water hoses directed against civil rights activists. Male clergy and nationalist leaders have been historically antiabortion (and often anticontraception as well). But as population control gave way to a woman-centered reproduction control agenda, as feminisms developed among women of color, and as antiabortion activism grew more strongly associated with the political Right, positions fluctuated. As one socially conservative African American minister wrote about antiabortion demonstrators, "I have never heard any of them say that they should have blocked the entrances to the jails where we were beaten and tortured. . . . over the past few years there have been only a few Southern, white, evangelical Christians who have asked our forgiveness and extended a hand in reconciliation. On the contrary, for every step we take in their direction, it seems that most take another step toward the suburbs."[39] Some leaders shifted their views because of pressure from below. For example, black congressman Floyd Flake of New York gave up his opposition to public funding for abortion after polls showed that his constituents mainly supported abortion rights.[40]

African American women in particular were generally pro-choice in the 1970s and 1980s and increasingly public about their views. But, as on so many other issues, many women of color felt alienated from the mainstream abortion rights movement. This was not only because the movement was overwhelmingly white—many black activists had a history of working closely with whites on issues of mutual concern—but, perhaps more important, because the movement has been white and middle-class in its priorities. Its single-minded focus on abortion rights did not meet the needs of women who were poor and/or discriminated against, who had equally strong needs for contraception funding, prenatal care, and pediatric care, for example.[41] As Loretta Ross said of the pro-choice movement, speaking for the Women of Color Program of NOW, "'Until you can hook up infant mortality and sterilization abuse, you're going to have ambivalence because it doesn't reach the issues that are immediate for us.'"[42] ("Hooking up" various reproductive health needs is exactly what the women's movement tried to do, with significant if temporary success, as will be seen in chapter 14.)

The antiabortion movement remains at the turn of the twenty-first century an unstable coalition with internal political differences. Nevertheless, national right-wing funding and leadership have been dominant, and women-centered rank-and-file sentiment has not been able to shift the overall political meanings and impact of antiabortion away from social and sexual conservatism. Liberal right-to-lifers have not been able to challenge conservative opposition to sex education, to easier access to contraception, to insurance funding of contraception, to emergency contraception, and to a safety net for poor children.

Antiabortion Activism

Given its generous funding base, the Right to Life movement has been able to conduct an effective publicity campaign—using billboards, print and TV advertisements, Web sites, counterfeit "cemeteries" for fetuses, counterfeit abortion services—coordinated by national and local paid leadership. Nevertheless, it was also a mass participatory movement. Its members picketed and obstructed abortion clinics, demonstrated at the homes of abortion providers and abortion rights spokespeople, and protested abortion rights candidates and events. They sat down at clinics, even chained themselves to fences, forcing the police to carry them off. Right-to-lifers approached women entering abortion clinics to try to change their minds and entered clinics posing as patients in order to condemn abortion to other patients. They grew fond of comparing their movement to the civil rights movement, calling attention to their civil disobedience, passive resistance to police orders, and willingness to create public disorder.

In the late 1980s antiabortion advocates developed a new tactic: fake abortion clinics that directed their advertisements especially to pregnant, distressed teenagers but offered neither abortion services nor open-minded counseling and information. Rather, they presented clients with gruesome slide shows, pictures of rooms allegedly piled high with fetuses, and misinformation about the supposed dangers of abortions. By 1988 there were an estimated 800–2,000 fake abortion clinics in operation, involving an estimated 480,000 consumers.[43] For a short time opponents of abortion also began to operate homes for unwed mothers, an attempt to revive institutions that were largely extinct.[44]

The Right to Life movement came to include those who rejected nonviolence and used arson, bombs, and guns, as well as rhetoric, to get their message across. Picketing abortion clinics—which in 1985 alone occurred at 80 percent of all clinics—inflicted anguish on abortion clients, turning some away and deterring those who could not bear the persecution. Harrassment included picketing the homes of staff members, tracing patients' license plates, jamming telephone lines, sending hate mail, vandalism, and mass scheduling of fake appointments. In 1984 there were 161 reported acts of violence against abortion clinics and their staff and 21 death threats; in 1985 and again in 1986 there were approximately 400 reported cases of antiabortion harassment or violence.[45] The overwhelmingly negative public response to clinic bombings[46] may have contributed to a decrease in the use of violence during the late 1980s, but it increased again in the 1990s. Comparing abortion to murder, even frequently to the Holocaust,[47] some opponents of abortion justified assassinating abortion providers. (Killing one to save the lives of many, they said.) From 1977 through 2001, 3 doctors, 2 clinic employees, 1 clinic escort, and 1 security guard were murdered. There were also 17 attempted murders, 41 bombings, 165 arson attacks, 82 attempted bombings or arson attacks, and 372 clinic invasions. Threats and acts of vandalism and assault numbered in the thousands. Anthrax threats have been coming in to clinics for years, including 480 between September 11, 2001, and the end of the year.[48]

The antiabortion movement was divided over the use of violence, with the majority condemning it.[49] But abortion rights advocates charged that the rhetoric condemning abortion as murder contributed directly to the violence and allowed assassins to consider themselves as agents of holy work—the essence of terrorism.[50] Revulsion against this violence and continued pro-choice resistance led to the Freedom of Access to Clinic Entrances Act (FACE) in 1994 (upheld by the U.S. Supreme Court in 2001), which prohibited intimidating, injuring, or interfering with a person engaged in "obtaining or providing reproductive health services." FACE, along with several judicial decisions, provided results: confrontations at abortion clinics dropped dramatically, with only 12 antiabortion demonstrators being arrested in 1998 compared to 12,000 in 1989.[51]

Still, threats and acts of violence continued. The FBI had to offer abortionists round-the-clock protection by federal marshals when the American Coalition of Life Activists distributed "wanted" posters targeting specific abortion providers.[52] Soon after came the "Nuremberg Files" Web site, which extended the Holocaust metaphor to label abortionists as guilty of crimes against humanity. Neal Horsley, a computer programmer, established the site in 1995 in an attempt "'to record the name of every person working in the baby slaughter business.'" The site lists names in six categories: baby butchers, clinic owners and workers, pro–abortion rights judges (called "shysters"), politicians ("mouthpieces"), law enforcement workers ("their bloodhounds"), and "Miscellaneous Spouses & Other Blood Flunkies." The names of those who have been murdered are crossed out. Visitors to the Web site are asked to provide additional names and detailed personal information for anyone who might fit into one of the six categories, including addresses and phone numbers, photos (of the individuals as well as their cars, houses, and friends), and any available civil suit records, including divorce files.[53] A lawsuit brought by Planned Parenthood of Columbia/Willamette (Portland, Oregon) against those who distributed the posters and created the Web site won in a federal district court but lost on appeal in the Ninth Circuit Court (244 F.3d [9th Cir. 2001]), which considered the materials protected speech.

The leading right-to-life strategy, however, was legal. For much of the 1970s, 1980s, and 1990s the movement pressured state and federal legislatures to ensnare abortion in a thicket of regulations and prohibitions. In the 1980s, for example, these included a waiting period between the request for and the performance of an abortion; birth and death certificates for fetuses; providing the patient with an oral description of the fetus and its physiological characteristics; informing the patient that "the unborn child is a human life"; limiting abortions to hospitals (thereby raising the cost); using extraordinary measures (such as compulsory cesarean sections) to allow "aborted" fetuses to survive; and requiring permission from minors' parents and women's husbands. In the 1990s further state restrictions were added: postviability abortions (i.e., those beyond the point at which a fetus might live outside the mother) now required the consent of a second physician; gestational age, weight, and lung maturity of fetuses prior to abortion must be determined by a physician; birth control clinics receiving public funding may not inform women of their legal right to an abortion; and detailed information about abortion providers *and patients* must be reported publicly. Given the different balances of political forces in each of fifty states and the District of Columbia, the record of these restrictions is complex and volatile, but the most common patterns as of 2001 can be summarized as follows:

—17 states require parental consent before a minor may obtain an abortion, 14 require parental notification
—22 states require state-directed counseling of pregnant woman
—14 states require a waiting period between state-directed counseling and abortion
—20 states prohibit abortion after viability unless life or health of woman is at risk
—29 states prohibit Medicaid funding of abortion unless life is at risk or pregnancy results from rape or incest
—28 states have attempted to ban "partial-birth" abortion.[54]

Jointly, the two sides in the abortion struggle have supported hundreds of lawyers over the course of three decades. Complicating the litigation was the fact that even before *Roe v. Wade,* some states that had legalized abortion were already restricting it. Thus, simultaneously with *Roe,* the Court invalidated a Georgia law that required abortions to be performed in a hospital, conditional on the approval of three physicians and a hospital committee.[55] Two years later it invalidated a Virginia law that prohibited the advertisement of abortion services.[56]

Contributing to these legal victories for abortion rights was the fact that, in contrast to the situation in the nineteenth and early twentieth centuries, mainstream physicians and the women's movement were usually in the same camp. In *Thornburgh v. Pennsylvania College of Obstetricians and Gynecologists* (476 U.S. 747 [1986]), for example, an amicus curiae brief filed by the American Medical Association, the American College of Obstetricians and Gynecologists, the American Academy of Pediatrics, and the Nurses Association of the Obstetrical College, as well as one filed by the American Public Health Association, asserted that the information required to be given to abortion clients was inaccurate. Clearly, the medicalization of birth control had strengthened, at least in the short run, the legal pro-choice case.

Conservative court appointments during the Reagan years shifted the balance of decisions. The greatest defeat for the pro-choice side came in several decisions between 1977 and 1980 that upheld state laws and the federal Hyde amendments prohibiting the use of public funds for abortion.[57] The Hyde amendments, attached annually since 1977 to appropriations bills for the Department of Labor and the Department of Health and Human Services, allow Medicaid funds to be used for an abortion only in the case of extreme danger to a woman's life. Prior to 1977, approximately 295,000 women per year had abortions paid for by Medicaid. Following the funding cutoff, 80 percent of poor women who wanted abortions either scraped together the money at great cost to themselves and their families or resorted to unsafe, nonmedical (including self-induced) abortions, while 20 percent of them gave birth.[58] The result has been to create a dual health care system with respect to reproduction in which government effectively deprives poor women of choice, placing a tax on abortion and offering financial incentives to carry pregnancies to term (but without any guarantee of support for the child after birth).[59] This policy is, of course, consistent with 1980s conservative economics and judicial thought, a return to a classical liberal view of freedom in which blindness to the material obstacles to choice results in a double standard of justice. The Reagan administration also tried to stop private organizations offering reproductive choice by attaching restrictions to the use of Title X funds (for family planning and research in reproduction and contraceptive development) by clinics that provided sex education and abortion counseling.

In other cases the Supreme Court compromised, upholding some restrictions and rejecting others. In 1983, for example, the Court invalidated requirements that physicians tell patients "the unborn child is a human life from the moment of conception" and mandating a twenty-four-hour waiting period, but it upheld parental consent and second-physician requirements.[60] Reproductive rights lawyers fought back with serious research and analysis. In 1986, attorney Lynn Paltrow filed an amicus curiae brief in *Thornburgh v. American College of Obstetricians and Gynecologists* on behalf of a large group of women's and liberal organizations; the brief not only argued that the restrictions in question interfered with women's legal rights but included many letters from women describing their actual experiences of illegal abortion and their need for abortion—a first-person women's "Brandeis brief," so to speak.[61] This kind of argumentation moved beyond an individual rights premise to advance the view that legal abortion is part of a social program for creating sex equality.

The balance of power on the Supreme Court had shifted by the late 1980s, as was evident in the *Webster v. Reproductive Health Services* (492 U.S. 490 [1989]) and *Planned Parenthood of Southeastern Pennsylvania v. Casey* (505 U.S. 833 [1992]) decisions. In these decisions, only a minority of the justices voted to reaffirm *Roe v. Wade* and in the *Casey* decision, the Court promulgated a lower standard of scrutiny of state restrictions on abortion.[62]

The most recent theme in antiabortion litigation concerns so-called partial-birth abortion. This term, coined by the antiabortion camp and not recognized by the medical profession, is intentionally ambiguous. Proponents of the ban on partial-birth abortions allege that they are targeting only late-term abortions in which the fetus is partially extracted from the uterus and then killed while still in the birth canal. But all human tissue taken from a living person is itself living. So a "living" embryo or fetus enters the birth canal in many early abortions—which means that, according to the Centers for Disease Control, 99 percent of all abortion procedures could fall under such a ban. The fact is that fewer than 0.01 percent of abortions are performed during the third trimester and these are usually precipitated by medical emergencies involving risks to the pregnant woman's health, severe damage to the fetus, or psychological denial of the pregnancy until too late for a typical abortion, a problem most common among poor teenagers with high levels of sexual ignorance and shame.

Even the conservative Supreme Court has been forced to overturn most partial-birth bans, in *Stenberg v. Carhart* in June 2000. Although thirty-one states had passed laws against partial-birth abortion, the Court ruled against them on several grounds: that their deliberately vague terminology left physicians without clarity as to what specific procedures were allowed—not to mention the disturbing precedent of allowing legislatures to dictate medical practice; that they fail to include an exception to preserve the health of the woman; that they impose an undue burden on a woman's ability to choose an abortion; and that they prevent women seeking abortions from benefiting from the medical procedure their doctors believe is best in the particular case.[63]

The story of the abortion drug mifepristone, commonly (but imprecisely) known as RU-486, demonstrates the power of the antiabortion forces but possibly also their ultimate defeat by the widespread need for reproduction control. In 1980 the Roussel-Uclaf S.A. pharmaceutical labs synthesized a drug that blocks progesterone, a hormone needed to sustain pregnancy. By 1983, European trials of the drug had been successful and the Population Council began testing it in the United States. A 1988 conflict in France illustrates how the issue might have been resolved in the United States with different political leadership. The French Ministry of Health approved the drug, but antiabortion protests led Roussel-Uclaf to suspend marketing it until the minister of health ordered it back on the market, calling it the "moral property of women."

Soon after mifepristone was ordered back on the market in France, it was approved by most European countries, including Austria, Belgium, Denmark, Finland, France, Germany, Great Britain, Greece, Israel, Luxembourg, the Netherlands, Norway, Russia, Spain, Sweden, Switzerland, and Ukraine. Meanwhile, in the United States the Clinton administration directed the Department of Health and Human Services to support development of the drug, and Roussel-Uclaf donated its U.S. rights to the Population Council, which licensed Danco Laboratories to produce mifepristone. But antiabortionists were able to delay approval through a variety of tactics—for example, by trying to amend the appropriations bill for the Department of Agriculture to prohibit the Food and Drug Administration from approving mifepristone. After a decade of delay, FDA approval came in September 2000, but then George W. Bush's ascent to the presidency gave antiabortionists renewed hope. They have tried to restrict the drug by introducing bills in at least twelve states and the U.S. Congress that would make it illegal to prescribe or use it or to provide funds for mifepristone. At this writing, however, mifepristone is being prescribed in the United States under the brand name Mifeprex and is expected to nudge the average timing of abortions to an earlier moment in pregnancy.[64]

Another abortion-related controversy—stem cell research—grabbed the headlines in 2001 and presented an explosive dilemma for President Bush. The conflict says much about the ways in which antiabortion passion reaches beyond the boundaries of reproduction control. The purpose of stem cell research—treating or even curing currently incurable diseases—is almost universally applauded, but the most useful and easily accessible stem cells come from embryos. The cells that make up very early embryos are not yet specialized and can develop into any of the 220 cell types that make up a human body—which is precisely what makes them so valuable. (Adults also have stem cells, but they multiply more slowly and may not be undifferentiated enough to be useful.) In theory, human stem cells, which multiply endlessly, could be transplanted into a patient and coaxed to replace damaged tissue of various kinds. This procedure has been successful in rats and mice, and researchers are confident that in the near future it will be successful in humans too.

The best source of human embryonic stem cells is not abortion clinics but fertility clinics, specifically, the embryos that are "left over" from laboratory fertilization attempts. Typically, once a successful pregnancy and birth are achieved, the unused embryos are discarded. Hard-line antiabortionists take the position that any use that requires destroying embryos is murder, and harvesting stem cells destroys embryos. Such fundamentalist views are uncompromisable, since those who hold them have become invested in the kind of all-or-nothing purity that so often accompanies faith-based ideologies. Other antiabortion leaders and loyalists have drawn a line between lab-created embryos (acceptable) and what is removed in an abortion (unacceptable). They speak of potential benefits to friends and relatives with incurable diseases and are perhaps sensitive to public opinion polls that run 3-to-1 in favor of stem cell research. Such compromise by antiabortionists may indicate that, at least when sexual and gender behavior are not at issue, their commitment to preserving all unborn life may be considerably less passionate. President Bush, having won office thanks in large measure to the support of Christian Coalition social conservatives and more secular economic conservatives, ordered in August 2001 that federal funds could be appropriated for research that used already created stem cells but not for research that required creating new ones. Tilted to avoid alienating social conservatives, his order is unlikely to satisfy those who favor a robust research program as well as those who long for better treatments or even cures for Alzheimer's, juvenile diabetes, Parkinson's, and other diseases. Moreover, nothing will stop privately funded research; and, inevitably, the absence of federal funding will make the research less well supervised and speed the creation of a market for body parts and physiological elements.

The Stalemate

Which side is winning the abortion controversy? It depends on what evidence is used. In the 1990s abortion rates were falling, from 26 per 1,000 pregnancies to 23 per 1,000 pregnancies among women aged fifteen to forty-four.[65] But what caused the decline? Antiabortion groups hail it as a victory, attributing it to a growing moral revulsion against abortion and increased abstinence, at least among unmarried women. Pro–abortion rights groups offer a more complex analysis of the decline, which they interpret as reflecting some gains and some losses. To the degree that the decline points to better contraceptive use and less sexual activity among young teenagers, it is a good thing. To the degree that it results from women's loss of access to abortion, it is not so good.

Several social scientists have attempted to disentangle the various causes of decline in the abortion rate, but the results are inconsistent and indefinite because pregnancy, birth, and abortion rates are all falling. One study estimated that the lower birth rate results not from abortion but from fewer pregnancies, which it attributes to less sexual activity (25 percent) and better contraceptive use (75 percent). One economist estimated that antiabortion demonstrations in particular lowered the abortion rate by 19 percent (by reducing both supply and demand) and raised the price of an abortion by 4.3 percent.[66] Others found a significant racial difference in the decline of access to abortion—namely, while the decrease in abortion providers served to increase by 2 percent the number of female-headed households, among blacks this increase was 20 percent. Still others found that decreased access to abortion actually reduced the number of unwanted births.[67]

Certainly the right-to-life side has been able to shift the meaning of abortion in its favor. The very concept "Right to Life," the focus on the rights of the unborn, the gory pictures, and the moral damnation of aborting women have enveloped abortion in shame and loathing even among many of those who support abortion rights. The notion of abortion as murder has created a great deal of guilt. No doubt many abortions were thereby prevented, but there has also been some resistance to this shame. Right-to-life advocates tried to construct an official abortion-induced pathology: the so-called postabortion trauma syndrome. The National Right to Life Committee and its ally, the American Rights Coalition, encouraged women who have had abortions to sue their doctors for malpractice and offered the services of lawyers to that end. This strategy aimed both to intensify trauma about abortion and to intensify the degree of trauma associated with abortion in public opinion. The strategy also sought to raise the cost of malpractice insurance in an attempt to put abortion clinics out of business. However, the right-to-lifers could not even convince the antiabortion surgeon general C. Everett Koop to support their claim as to the existence of a postabortion trauma syndrome, since hundreds of studies found no evidence of it. Studies did find that depression was far more common after childbirth than after abortion, and the most common postabortion emotional reaction is relief.[68]

With regard to public opinion, often a volatile and malleable construction, the most interesting news is how little has changed. A stubborn majority of U.S. residents continue to oppose the recriminalization of abortion. Statewide and national elections reflect this: between 1978 and 1988, of twenty-two referenda on a variety of abortion questions, twenty-one went to the pro–abortion rights side; in the 1988 presidential election, won by the senior George Bush, three referenda went against abortion rights, but two of the three concerned public funding, for which there is less support.

When it comes to abortion opinion, however, it is not just a matter of being for or against it. Most Americans do not support abortion in absolutely all circumstances. Many who favor women's right to abortion are opposed to third-trimester abortions; others oppose abortions sought for "frivolous" reasons. And poll responses always depend very much on what is asked. In June 2001, for example, Americans were deeply split, 52 percent identifying themselves as pro-choice and 43 percent as pro-life.[69] But when given four options from which to choose, the dividing line became less clear:

Abortion should be legal in all cases	21%
Abortion should be legal in most cases	38%
Abortion should be illegal in most cases	25%
Abortion should be illegal in all cases	14%[70]

Public opinion shifts still further when the questions are designed to find a middle ground:

A woman should be able to get an abortion if she decides she wants one no matter what the reason—35%

Abortion should only be legal in certain circumstances such as when a woman's health is endangered or when the pregnancy results from rape or incest—50%

Abortion should be illegal in all circumstances—12%[71]

Naturally, antiabortion-funded polls show different results than, for example, those funded by Planned Parenthood. But no poll has found a majority in favor of sharply limiting abortion rights, and support for abortion rights ranges from 40 to 90 percent depending on the circumstances described in the questions. Most polls agree that there has been no substantial change in aggregate attitudes about the legality of abortion, although since 1965 whites have become slightly more opposed and African Americans have become significantly more favorable.[72]

The various polls also offer some insight into correlations between beliefs about abortion and other issues. Opposition to abortion is correlated with religiosity (meaning the intensity of religious commitment) across all racial and ethnic groups, including African Americans and Latino/as. Among white Protestants, 63 percent of evangelicals believe that abortion should be illegal in all or most cases, while 66 percent of nonevangelicals believe that abortion should mainly be legal.[73] Yet 37 percent of women who have had abortions say religion is very important to them.[74] Latinas differ greatly on abortion, with Puerto Rican women being positive and Chicanas less so. Moreover, an early 1980s study of Mexican Americans in Los Angeles showed that religiosity correlated with antiabortion attitudes only among those raised in the United States, not among those raised in Mexico, which suggests that the influence of religion operate mainly through the activism of the U.S. Catholic Church and the political intensity of the abortion issue in the United States.[75] However, the Church's views do not represent those of U.S. Catholics, who are divided on abortion rights more or less like the public at large: 55 percent believe that abortion should generally be legal, and 43 percent believe that it should be illegal in all or most cases.[76]

African Americans are less likely to approve of abortion than whites, but this differential is declining and blacks have become steadily more positive toward abortion over the past two decades. The black/white difference in part reflects class differences: those who are more educated and more secular support abortion more strongly. But black attitudes are also independently formed, drawing from the legacy of racism in family planning programs (discussed earlier) and challenged by the traditions of independence and even feminism among black women. Moreover, despite somewhat more negative attitudes, adult black women are twice as likely to have abortions as adult white women.[77] By contrast, white teenagers are more likely than black teenagers to have abortions, though this differential is almost entirely a function of class or socioeconomic status rather than race—that is, the more prosperous the teenager, the more likely she is to terminate her pregnancy.

Arguably the greatest antiabortion success has been in reducing women's access to abortion. A variety of efforts contributed to this change, including violence, withdrawal of funding, lack of training for medical students, state restrictions, harassment, and shaming. Costs are a major obstacle. The legalization of abortion at first produced a remarkable dip in price. Just as prohibition always raises the cost of that which is prohibited, so legalization reduces the cost: typical abortion costs in 1996 were only half the costs in 1973. The ban on public funding inflated the costs for those who most needed the help. When compared to the national average, women with family incomes under $15,000 were twice as likely to seek abortions, while those with incomes above $60,000 were half as likely.[78] As of early 2002, only sixteen states allowed public funds for abortion in most circumstances. Funding prohibitions have also affected military employees, federal and many state and local employees, residents of the District of Columbia, members of the Peace Corps, prison inmates, Native Americans, and numerous other groups whose medical insurance is, by one restriction or another, prevented from paying for abortions. Defunding not only prevents access but causes delays—on average, women wait two to three weeks longer to obtain an abortion as they search for the money to pay for it. Such delays not only increase a woman's health risks but further increase the cost of an abortion, doubled at sixteen weeks and tripled at twenty weeks. Raising money for an abortion creates serious hardship among 60 percent of Medicaid recipients. In states where Medicaid pays for abortions, the abortion rate among covered women is 3.9 times higher. Where funding is banned, aproximately 20 percent more pregnancies are carried to term (in a poor state, North Carolina, this figure reached 37 percent). Among African Americans, defunding accounted for half of the decrease in abortions.[79]

Several factors have combined to reduce greatly the number of abortion providers, which fell by 14 percent in the 1990s.[80] Access became a particularly difficult problem for rural women: by the mid-1990s, 84 percent of all counties and 94 percent of rural counties had no abortion providers, and 43 percent of women had to travel outside their home county for abortions. Two percent of ob/gyn physicians provide the majority of abortions, and the numbers willing to perform second- and third-trimester abortions fell even further. Anti–abortion rights campaigns succeeded in putting abortion applicants in a vice, squeezing them between, on the one hand, state laws requiring that abortions be performed only in hospitals and, on the other hand, campaigns pressuring hospitals not to provide abortions. In 1997 there were 600 *fewer* hospitals offering abortion services than in 1979.[81] This reduction was accomplished in part through pressure exerted by right-to-life groups on hospital boards and in part by means of mergers that resulted in Catholic control over hospitals where abortions had been provided. Since 1990 a record number of secular community hospitals have merged with religious ones, and many, especially the Catholic hospitals, are extremely restrictive. In 2000, Catholics provided 15 percent of all hospital care, forbidding contraception and sterilization as well as abortion services; 82 percent of these hospitals forbid even emergency contraception in cases of rape. In 91 percent of rural counties, Catholics run the only hospital, although in 95 percent of these counties only a minority of residents are Catholic. Even medical schools caved in to anti-abortion intimidation, eliminating training in abortion procedures. In 1991 only 12 percent of medical schools routinely included such training, even for first-trimester procedures, 57 percent offered it as an elective, and 27 percent offered no training at all.[82]

Some trends suggest that the decline in access to abortion is being reversed by abortion rights advocacy. In 1996 the Accreditation Council for Graduate Medical Education required ob/gyn residency programs to include contraception and abortion training, with the result that, just two years later, 81 percent of residency programs offered training in first-trimester abortion procedures, and 74 percent included second-trimester training. But much of this training was elective: only 26 percent of these residency programs offered it routinely, a disturbing figure for the very specialists whose patients might need abortions.[83]

The balance, then, is a stalemate. Opponents of abortion have stigmatized the procedure and made access to it much more difficult, yet it remains a necessity for many American women and will continue as a widespread practice even if it is once again prohibited. The context, however, will never be the same as it was before the second wave of feminism. Under any form of prohibition, the underground networks for abortion services that will inevitably arise will likely include feminist nonprofit as well as for-profit enterprises. Meanwhile, the issue steadily divides economic from social conservatives. As we will see in chapter 14, many conservatives oppose public support for poor children more than they oppose abortion—which may lead to a rebirth of the population control–eugenics type of pro–abortion rights lobby. Those who are worried about the costs of public care for babies who suffer from the effects of poverty, parental alcohol or drug abuse, or disease and disability may weigh in again for the public funding of abortion.[84] Environmental and ecological concerns may also undercut the antiabortion movement. But the fundamental political alignments of the abortion controversy remain stable and tenacious. No one issue dramatizes the basic cultural/political fissures in the United States at this time more than abortion does—although there is competition from gay rights, gun control, and religion in the schools. The abortion debate is not only about abortion; it is also about deep differences in social values that spill over into a variety of other issues related to sex and reproduction.

14 Is Nothing Simple about Reproduction Control?

It has been the central argument of this book that everything about reproductive rights must be seen in a political context. Reproduction control brings into play not only the gender system but also the race and class system, the structure of medicine and prescription drug development and production, the welfare system, the educational system, foreign aid, and the question of gay rights and minors' rights. The list is not a rhetorical gesture; in this chapter I will show how each of these influences reproductive rights debates.

Major social and political conflicts intersected with these systems to revise the meanings of birth control at several points during its modern history. In the second half of the twentieth century, these conflicts were primarily oriented by the clash between the Left movements of the 1950s–1970s and the Right countermovements. Because the revival of feminism changed the social and political significance of reproduction control, the subject came to evoke basic ideologies about gender, family, and sex. The feminist/antifeminist contest focused most intensely on abortion, and for that reason the abortion controversy was discussed first in chapter 13. Although oral contraceptives predated the legalization of abortion by approximately a decade, by 1973 abortion discourse permeated debate about the Pill.

This chapter takes up those key reproduction control controversies of the last quarter of the twentieth century that are not directly about abortion. It examines the women's health movement, which most directly influenced concerns about contraception, and addresses teenage pregnancy and out-of-wed-

lock childbearing as an offshoot of the birth control debate. The chapter concludes with some brief thoughts on how HIV/AIDS has affected the story of
birth control.

When the women's movement was reborn in the late 1960s, it transformed
existing paradigms for understanding reproduction control. Rejecting the
notion that women's primary duty was mothering and unpaid domestic labor
as well as the Victorian premise that a proper woman was by her nature chaste,
young feminists redefined the purpose of birth control. They did not, of course,
reject the idea of family planning, but they did emphasize women's rights to
sexual freedom, which included the right to reject motherhood and to raise
children outside conventional nuclear families. As we have seen, this perspective powered the demand for the right to abortion, but it also entailed challenges to the dominant mainstream birth control arguments, namely, planned
parenthood and population control.

True to its New Left origins, the women's liberation movement (the dominant influence on the first edition of this book) criticized population control
for promoting the interests of the neocolonial superpowers. These feminists
were also usually environmentalists, and they thought it hypocritical that the
United States promoted population control when, with only 6 percent of the
world's people, it gobbled up 50 percent of the world's resources. They also
contested Planned Parenthood's silence on abortion, its refusal to serve unmarried people, and its failure to promote reproduction control as a woman's
right. Thus, the first impact of the women's liberation movement was to di-
vide feminist from mainstream birth control advocates—though the later result of that same movement was to reunite them. The women's movement
spread so rapidly and contagiously that it transformed women of all generations, classes, and political persuasions. That there were Republican feminists,
unthinkable in 1970, became unremarkable by 1980. Moreover, the antifeminist backlash was so fierce that it nudged feminists of various stripes closer
together, especially around abortion rights. With other reproduction control
issues, such as contraception, the differences among feminists also steadily
diminished.

The Women's Health Movement

Within the women's movement, perhaps the most important achievement of
reproductive rights activity was the establishment of an enduring women's
health movement. An estimated twelve hundred groups considered themselves
part of this movement by 1973.[1] The movement addressed a wide range of
health issues—notably, transforming conditions of childbirth—but it also grew
in large part out of birth control activism. (The popular health movement of
the 1830s and 1840s, discussed briefly in chapter 3, was also closely connect-

ed to the women's movement and to birth control proposals.) Equally important, it grew up simultaneously with a community health movement, centered
in the black, Chicano, Asian, and Puerto Rican neighborhoods of several big
cities, concerned with providing health services to the poor and with giving
health care consumers a voice in the policies of medical institutions. Three
organizations stand out as emblematic of the women's health movement: the
Boston Women's Health Book Collective (BWHBC), author of the now famous
Our Bodies, Ourselves; the National Women's Health Network (NWHN); and
the National Black Women's Health Project (NBWHP).

The story of the BWHBC might be told as a fairy tale, a rags-to-riches
adventure, and the collective's success might appear miraculous if we disregard the intense material needs and powerful social movement from which
the group arose. In 1969, at a women's liberation conference in Boston, a group
of women found themselves together in a discussion group focused on "women
and their bodies." Discovering their common anger at many frustrating and
humiliating experiences with physicians, they decided to continue meeting in
order to prepare a list of "good doctors." When they found that list too short
to be helpful, they decided to do their own research on women's health issues
and began to offer health courses for groups of women. The results of their
work, *Our Bodies, Ourselves* (first called *Women and Their Bodies*), was published by the New England Free Press, a small New Left publisher, in 1970.
The book was most important to birth control precisely because it was *not*
specialized on that topic but informed people about contraception and abortion in the overall context of health education. It encouraged its readers to
respect their own desires and to think critically.

Printed on the cheapest newsprint paper, sold for seventy-five cents, and
advertised primarily by word of mouth and in the burgeoning feminist underground press, the manual had sold 250,000 copies by 1973. Then the collective authors negotiated a publishing agreement with Simon and Schuster with
the understanding that they would have editorial and advertising control and
that clinics and other nonprofit health organizations could order the book at
a 70 percent discount. Thirty years after its origins, the BWHBC remains stable and has used its substantial profits from book sales (now more than two
million copies sold in the United States alone) to support the women's health
movement. It has revised the book at least five times, produced and distributed a Spanish-language version for Hispanic Americans, and produced a book
on health and sex education for teenagers and another for women entering
menopause. It also established a health information center in Boston that is
open to the public, subsidized free distribution of *Our Bodies, Ourselves*
among various groups, distributed health information packets to some seven
hundred women's groups, and saw *Our Bodies, Ourselves* translated into many
foreign languages.[2] Rarely has such a small group had so much influence.

The National Women's Health Network, which emerged in 1975, was originally conceived primarily to monitor federal agencies; since then it has become the dominant national coordinating group for women's health activities. It led in the campaign against dangerous high-dosage contraception pills and the lawsuit against A. H. Robins over the Dalkon Shield deaths and injuries; pressured the Centers for Disease Control to conduct research on toxic shock syndrome; developed a model law guaranteeing patients' access to their medical records; educated the public about women's risks of HIV/AIDS; and campaigned for the approval of the cervical cap. In 1993 NWHN activism forced a randomized clinical study of hormone replacement therapy for menopausal women, which reported in 2002 that the risks outweighed the benefits of taking the estrogen-progesterone combination prescribed by most gynecologists. The NWHN charged that pressure on menopausal women to remain sexually desirable and desiring had led the FDA to accept anecdotal evidence about these hormones. Cynthia Pearson, director of the NWHN, noted, "'You couldn't approve a drug for healthy men . . . even aspirin . . . without a randomized clinical trial.'"[3]

Meanwhile, providing a base of support for these national organizations were unaffiliated women's clinics and self-help groups throughout the United States. Starting with the same critique of the medical establishment that had stimulated the BWHBC, thousands of feminists sought to take medical care into their own hands, by opening clinics for which they could hire their own medical personnel and/or by training laywomen to provide some services previously offered only by medical personnel. Some were abortion clinics, but some were clinics offering a full range of gynecological and sometimes prenatal and obstetrical care. Indeed, the women's health movement criticized separating birth control services from comprehensive medical care, although clinics were not always financially able to avoid this. It was not easy to find competent, committed physicians to staff clinics, and the use of lay health care providers faced the major obstacle that health insurance programs would not pay for services rendered by nonmedical staff.

Also entering the field in the late 1960s and early 1970s were family planning clinics established in minority and low-income neighborhoods with federal antipoverty grants. Population control was one of the incentives to their development, producing resentment among many community members about the implicit racism and the strategy of dealing with poverty by reducing the number of poor people instead of helping them. Yet because of public funding these clinics were often able to offer a broad array of services, and in contrast to conventional health clinics they were usually supportive of women's reproductive choice. Where these clinics succeeded, it was largely because of the activism of community women and community organizations led by women.[4] (Success brought problems, of course, and many such clinics were used by hospitals as dumping grounds for problem patients and more labor-intensive primary care.)[5]

Although united on many fronts, the women's movement was divided about so-called self-help projects. Starting in the early 1970s, these featured cervical self-examinations with the aid of speculum and mirror and the provision of services by lay or paramedical staff, a continuation of the antiprofessional tradition of Jane (see chapter 13). In its condemnation of all things medical, the self-help movement ignored not only progress from which all women had benefited but especially the differences among women. It was one thing for prosperous young white women to dispense with physicians and another thing entirely for poor women who had never had access to basic medical care to do so. Nevertheless, the bravery and antiauthoritarianism of these groups inspired and energized the whole movement. One of their most controversial offerings was "menstrual extraction," a suction abortion performed very early in a pregnancy—even before the pregnancy was confirmed—with a flexible plastic cannula inserted into the uterus, a system developed by Carol Downer and Lorraine Rothman in California.[6] Ellen Frankfort, the author of *Vaginal Politics,* was at first among those feminists who were critical of self-help procedures and feared they might prove dangerous—until she got a flood of mail supporting her position from physicians who convinced her that they were not worried about hazards to patients but only about women's independence from organized medicine.[7] The confidence of 1970s women's liberation in self-help medicine seems naïve and risky three decades later.

Despite internal differences—or perhaps partly because of the differences, which created an openness to exploration and nonconformism—the women's health movement strongly influenced regular medicine, especially gynecology and obstetrics. Women-controlled abortion clinics forced down the price of abortions and introduced a permanent new category of worker: the abortion counselor, a medical worker whose client was a whole, complex subject rather than simply an unwanted pregnancy. Commercial abortion clinics competed successfully with one another, and some nonprofit clinics returned to traditional medical and hierarchical models of operation.[8] Feminist pressure reinforced a pre-existing "natural" childbirth demand and forced hospitals to respond with renewed obstetrical emphases on vaginal deliveries and avoidance of drugs, when possible, during parturition. The movement to reform childbirth facilitated the increased use of midwives. Physicians and medical schools began to change the condescending, information-withholding, authoritarian style that had been so dominant. Evidence of the power of the women's health lobby is visible in the rise of "women's centers" as units of hospitals. Medical marketers know that women consume 60 percent of health services in the United States, schedule one-third more office visits than men, and undergo 63 percent of all nonobstetric surgery. Moreover, since women usually organize health care for other family members, these others are likely to patronize places that women like.[9] The hospital-based women's clinics promise to create a supportive and respectful atmosphere and to use nurses in more prominent roles, but they do not usually alter the hierarchy of the medical establishment—indeed, they often fail to succeed in improving women's health care experience at all.[10]

At the beginning of the 1980s, the women's health movement remained overwhelmingly white and middle class and was often insensitive to minority and poor women's needs. Reproductive rights politics had been singularly influential in creating this segregation. Birth control and abortion advocates were often insensitive to black fears about population control—51 percent of black women surveyed in the early 1970s believed that the survival of black people depended on increasing black births, and 37 percent believed that birth control programs were genocidal in intent. (Black men were even more suspicious.)[11] Indeed, throughout the 1960s and 1970s fears of genocide were prominent in black commentary on birth control. Endorsements of family planning seemed to come only from conservative black sources and to recall the Booker T. Washington tradition of emphasis on self-improvement as opposed to that of challenging discrimination.[12] Indeed, black opposition to birth control, like white opposition, often arose from conservative sexual and gender attitudes.

But among African Americans, as in all groups, there was always female resistance to the anti–birth control perspective. Already in the late 1960s a powerful pro–birth control statement from the Black Women's Liberation Group of Mt. Vernon, New York, circulated throughout the women's movement:

> Black women are being asked by militant black brothers not to practice birth control because it's a form of Whitey committing genocide on black people. Well, true enough, but it takes two to practice genocide and black women are able to decide for themselves. . . . Poor black men won't support their families, won't stick by their women—all they think about is the street, dope and liquor, women, a piece of ass, and their cars. . . . Poor black women would be foolish to sit up in the house with a whole lot of children and eventually go crazy. . . . Middle-class white men have always done this to their women—only more sophisticated-like. . . . For us, birth control is the freedom to fight genocide of black women and children.[13]

Under the influence of the radical women's liberation movement, new groups began to define reproductive freedom so as to include the concerns of women across class and race lines, as we shall see. Unfortunately, the intensity of the antiabortion attack in the 1980s produced a double narrowing of the politics of abortion rights defense: first to abortion alone, ignoring the many other needs involved in reproductive choice; and second to legal, individual rights, treating the cutbacks in funding and other obstacles to making rights usable with much less intensity. But this exclusion was increasingly challenged as black feminists seized the initiative to criticize sexual conservatism and male dominance. As Dr. Dorothy Brown, a pioneering black physician and feminist, argued in 1983, genocide in the United States "'dates back to 1619 and continues today'" but not through abortion; the issue of abortion is choice.[14]

Women of color soon created their own health movements, which placed reproductive rights within a holistic context of women's health. In 1981 the NWHN began a pilot project on black women's health issues and in 1983 sponsored a national conference on this topic in Atlanta, out of which Byllye Avery created the National Black Women's Health Project, an autonomous but vital part of the women's health movement. The NBWHP developed many local chapters throughout the United States and later moved its headquarters from Atlanta to Washington, D.C. Its members and contributors number ten thousand. Neither a clinic nor a referral center, the NBWHP is an advocacy project, much like the NWHN. Its blackness is not merely an organizational preference but expressed in its educational strategy. Birth control and better health cannot be taught to black women, NBWHP leaders assert, outside the historical context of their lives. The context includes cervical cancer, depression, domestic violence, obesity, pregnancy-related illnesses and deaths, and breast cancer deaths, which occur at rates considerably higher for black women than for white women. The NBWHP argues that black women's health problems are inseparable from the racism and sexism they experience. It is difficult to talk "choice," Avery explains, among women who have, for the most part, extremely limited choices. To talk about control over one's body and reproduction without first questioning the larger context, she argues, is inauthentic.[15]

The NBWHP developed its political education from African American experience, yet it shares a basic approach with the white-dominated women's movement: it is a consciousness-raising as well as an instructional approach. Twenty years after it began, the project remains strong and growing. In 2000 the Centers for Disease Control and Prevention awarded the NBWHP an implementation grant for a four-year community action plan focused on reducing racial disparity in cardiovascular diseases among black women in metropolitan New Orleans, and the NBWHP awarded ten Grass-Roots Empowerment and Advocacy Training (GREAT) grants to local groups to develop local health advocates who can identify issues, articulate positions, establish partnerships with other reproductive rights organizations, and, most important, provide leadership.[16]

Despite its breadth, the NBWHP has retained a particular committment to reproductive rights. In 1986 a coalition of organizations including the NBWHP, the Religious Committee for Abortion Rights, the International Council of African Women, and the Women of Color Programs of NOW held a historic forum on reproductive freedom in the black community that challenged nationalist anti–birth control claims, called for a full spectrum of reproductive rights, and, most important, situated this demand in the history of the civil rights movement.[17] In April 1989, the local Atlanta chapter of the NBWHP sent eleven busloads of supporters to the massive abortion rights demonstration in Washington, D.C. Moreover, during the weekend of that march, a national conference of approximately one hundred, dominated by women of color, challenged the agenda of the pro-choice leadership. The conference called for going beyond *Roe.* As Sabrae Jenkins, director of the Women of Color Partnership Program of the Religious Coalition for Abortion Rights, put it, "'Abortion is not an issue that people of color look at in a vacuum. We look at it as a part of a range of comprehensive reproductive health care issues. . . . you have pro-choice organizations that are looking solely at the issue of abortion. They're not looking at issues as they relate to women of color.'"[18]

The NBWHP stimulated the creation of women's health organizations among other people of color, such as the Organizacíon de la Salud de la Mujer Latina, the National Asian Women's Health Organization, and the Native American Women's Health Education Resource Center. The last conducts programs on domestic violence, HIV/AIDS prevention, child development, environmental awareness and action, cancer prevention, fetal alcohol syndrome, diabetic nutrition, and reproductive health and rights. Programs such as these, however much they owe to talented leadership, rest on women's movements. From an early focus against sterilization abuse and population control or eugenics, health groups among women of color have moved to a broader emphasis on woman's reproductive rights, including access to birth control and abortion and HIV/AIDS prevention and treatment.[19]

Meanwhile, the Moral Majority's hostility toward reproductive rights, including population control, served to push Planned Parenthood closer to the NWHN. In 1987 Planned Parenthood produced a series of ads with pictures of impoverished third-world women and captions such as "The last thing she needs is a sermon from Jesse Helms." By the turn of the twenty-first century, Planned Parenthood workers and volunteers formed the heart of the resistance to attacks on reproductive freedom. The Alan Guttmacher Institute's journal *Family Planning Perspectives* began to provide excellent coverage of right-wing strategies and tactics along with its scholarly articles on birth control technology and usage. Planned Parenthood also worked to increase minority representation on its staff and board. At the 1987 national convention, Planned

Parenthood chair Anne Saunier gave an unprecedentedly challenging speech, pointing out that the organization still exhibited discomfort with sexuality and with teen sex in particular and still did too much apologizing for abortion and not enough assertive defense of it as an integral part of a family planning program.[20] Many Planned Parenthood volunteers and staff came to agree that the cause of birth control would best advance as part of overall campaigns against poverty and for racial and sex equality.

Significant influences in this direction came from abroad, notably, the rise of women's movements in virtually every region of the world. They arose even in countries frequently understood in the West as maximally dictatorial and patriarchal, such as Afghanistan, and in some of the most populous countries of the Third World, such as China, India, Nigeria, and Mexico, large grassroots movements began. International women's health movements were particularly strong, and within them reproductive rights often took center stage—the result being a transformation of birth control strategy and ideology. These global movements, and the responses of women in traditional societies when offered birth control, convinced advocates of population control that family planning was more a result than a cause of economic development. A new consensus developed in the population control establishment that the route to reducing fertility must be led by women and that women must have legal rights, education, political power, economic autonomy, and social respect if they are to lead. This shift intensified the New Right opposition to government funding of birth control programs, which was indicative of the difference in political alignments between the 1960s and the 1990s: in the earlier period, political elites supported foreign population control programs and faced criticism from the Left; in the 1990s, they were divided, with proponents of population control facing criticism from the Right.

The transformation within the population control establishment becomes evident through comparing the outcomes of a series of international population conferences organized by the United Nations—in 1974 (Bucharest), 1984 (Mexico City), and 1994 (Cairo). At the Cairo conference, the program of action, signed by 180 nations, made the empowerment of women and gender equality a "cornerstone of population and development-related programmes." It called for, among other things, eliminating violence against women (an enormous global problem previously considered outside the scope of population control efforts); equalizing women's property and inheritance rights with men's; and ending employment and educational discrimination. The program disappointed some feminists who had fought to include a call for the global legalization of abortion, which was blocked by an alliance of delegates from countries with fundamentalists in power and by the Vatican. Still, the program endorsed some distinctly controversial principles:

4.21. Governments should strictly enforce laws to ensure that marriage is entered into only with the free and full consent of the intending spouses.

4.22. Governments are urged to prohibit female genital mutilation wherever it exists and to give vigorous support to efforts . . . to eliminate such practices.

4.23. Governments are urged to take the necessary measures to prevent infanticide, prenatal sex selection, trafficking in girl children and use of girls in prostitution and pornography.

7.34. Human sexuality and gender relations are closely interrelated and together affect the ability of men and women to achieve and maintain sexual health and manage their reproductive lives. Equal relationships between men and women in matters of sexual relations and reproduction, including full respect for the physical integrity of the human body, require mutual respect and willingness to accept responsibility for the consequences of sexual behaviour. Responsible sexual behaviour, sensitivity and equity in gender relations, particularly when instilled during the formative years, enhance and promote respectful and harmonious partnerships between men and women.[21]

Such recommendations would have been discarded as irrelevant at previous population conferences.

In fact, birth control has made substantial progress internationally. In the 1960s an estimated 10 percent of couples worldwide used birth control; in 1995 the figure was 55 percent. The average number of children born to each woman has fallen from six to three. These gains correlate well with gains in the percentage of women enrolled in secondary school. Infant and maternal mortality rates also fell significantly.[22] Birth rates have fallen dramatically, and as a result some conservatives now strengthen their arguments against population control with the claim that there is no longer an overpopulation problem.[23] Even population control supporters report that the world population in 2050 will be half a billion less than previously thought.

Ideal population size is, of course, a debatable and indeterminate matter, but there can be no doubt about the need for better reproductive health. Almost 600,000 women die of pregnancy-related causes each year, mostly from postpartum hemorrhage. Of the 50 million abortions performed annually, 75,000 result in death of the patient, overwhelmingly from illegal abortions. Where abortion is legal, there is an average of just 0.2–1.2 deaths per 100,000 abortions; but in developing regions, where abortion is often illegal or highly restricted, mortality rates are hundreds of times higher, averaging 330 deaths per 100,000 abortions.[24]

The number of children desired by women fell considerably in the past thirty years, and most couples say they want smaller families than is traditional in their culture. Six of ten women worldwide either want no more children or want to delay their next birth at least two years.[25] Women's grievances against birth control are overwhelmingly about the means of delivery—coercion, disrespectful treatment, long hours of waiting in uncomfortable waiting rooms, and dismissive responses to their complaints of side effects.[26]

Despite these needs, U.S. birth control aid was drastically reduced starting in 1996. The omnipresent abortion conflict has further reduced the efficiency of the aid that is given. The population controllers who argue that family planning has become "wrongly embroiled in the divisive politics of abortion" are understandably trying to find a noncontroversial ground on which to stand, but their analysis is wrong.[27] Contraception and abortion will not stay separated, and those who oppose both increasingly dominate antiabortion policy. President Reagan imposed a "gag rule" in 1984 prohibiting U.S. funds from going to any birth control service abroad that provided abortions or even informed women about the availability of abortions elsewhere. President Clinton rescinded this rule as one of his first official acts, but his successor, George W. Bush, reinstated it on his first day in office. This policy not only conflicts with U.S. law (which makes abortion legal) and public opinion (which supports legalized abortion), it not only conflicts with the laws of thirty-nine of the countries receiving the aid, but it also deprives foreign beneficiaries of the very freedoms that we enjoy in the United States—the rights to legal abortion and to free speech.

Of particular relevance here is the fact that the gag rule policy undermines contraception as well as abortion because providing contraception and abortion in the same clinic is the most efficient practice. For example, one of the most successful occasions on which to instruct clients in contraception is immediately after an abortion. In other words, not only does contraception help reduce abortion, but abortion can be used to promote contraception and thereby reduce the number of future abortions. Moreover, the gag rule exclusively targets contraception: U.S. aid for other medical uses flows freely to hospitals and clinics providing abortions. It is only contraception that may not be provided in the same setting as abortion.[28] The policy also works to weaken a woman-centered approach to birth control because clinics run by women and oriented to serving women's needs are those most likely to provide both contraception and abortion services or information.

Contraception

Within the United States the polarization between feminist and antifeminist perspectives, so prominent in abortion struggles, has become muted with respect to contraception. Instead, contraceptive politics had its own peculiar dynamics. These arose, first, from the fact that contraception remained legitimate and not legally restricted, at least for married people, among most sectors of the U.S. population. While abortion politics rests on a dichotomy between social liberals and social conservatives, some of the major disagreements about contraceptive policy occurred among groups that shared a positive view of reproduction control and even of women's rights. Second, the system of development, testing, manufacture, and distribution of contraceptives in the United States pitted critics of particular contraceptives as consumers against big corporations and the Food and Drug Administration in a conflict not primarily defined by gender interests or sexual morality.

The first political battle about contraception concerned the safety of the Pill, and it aligned the new feminists of the late 1960s against the birth control establishment, the pharmaceutical companies, and even the federal government. The feminist challenge helped to create lasting improvements in drug safety and consumers' right to information.[29]

Soon after the Pill became available in the continental United States, women who took it began to complain in large numbers of the same side effects that had been reported in Puerto Rico, where it was first tested (see chapter 12): bloating, weight gain, nausea, vomiting, stomach pain, headaches, and rashes. As in the Puerto Rico trials, physicians, population controllers, and researchers trivialized or even discounted these complaints. Many women quit using the Pill, but many others started, so there was no economic incentive for Searle, the lone U.S. manufacturer, to question its product, and the population control establishment had no political incentive to do so.

In 1961 came the first reports of Pill-related deaths from pulmonary embolisms (blood clots traveling to the lungs). Then four more deaths were reported in the *British Medical Journal*. Norway banned the Pill. Searle, Gregory Pincus (who had conducted the Puerto Rico trials), and the Population Council responded, first by denying the connection between health dangers and the Pill and then by saying that if there was a connection it was a 1-in-500,000 event. The Food and Drug Administration accepted these responses. By the end of 1962 there had been 272 reported cases of blood clots, thrombophlebitis, or strokes among Pill users, a ratio at least 135 times greater than that which Searle had allowed. Still, it was not until 1969 that the FDA conducted a study and found that women using the Pill were more than four times as likely to develop blood clots as nonusers.

These suspicions and denials occured just as the women's movement was inspiring challenges rather than deference to professionals (overwhelmingly male) who claimed to be authorities on women. One of the first manifestos in that challenge was Barbara Seaman's book *The Doctors' Case against the Pill*, published in 1969. This journalist did such masterful research and so carefully scrutinized the scientific research that her case—confirming the severe risks of high-dose oral contraceptives—could not be impeached (although it is revealing of the still developing confidence of the new feminism that in her title she felt she had to draw on traditional expertise, the "doctors' case," to legitimate her findings). Seaman soon had a large social movement behind her, raising questions and demanding public answers.

The fight was in part a consumer rights struggle, and Seaman has been called the women's Ralph Nader. The public outcry led Wisconsin Democratic senator Gaylord Nelson, chairman of the Subcommittee on Monopoly of the Select Committee on Small Business, to hold hearings in 1970 on the dangers of the Pill and whether consumers were getting adequate information about those dangers. The hearings provided one of the first stages on which the new women's movement could command attention. Frustrated by Nelson's refusal to let even a single woman testify as a consumer of contraception, the Washington, D.C.–based Women's Liberation seized the floor and the attention of the media, disrupting the proceedings and demanding to be heard. One poll found that an astonishing 87 percent of American women between the ages of twenty-one and forty-five followed the hearings. They heard politicians such as Bob Dole, then a Republican senator from Kansas, joke that reporting the dangers of the Pill would make women so terrified they would need tranquilizers as well as birth control. "'We must not frighten millions of women into disregarding the considered judgments of their physicians about the use of oral contraceptives,'" he declaimed.[30] Still, the FDA stalled; and it did not agreed to require informative patient inserts in prescription drug packaging until 1978.

Debate about the Pill may have overemphasized the danger of death and illness but it underemphasized the discomforts. The "harmless" side effects such as nausea, rashes, weight gain, and bloating, belittled by physicians and researchers,[31] were more influential than long-term health risks in reducing oral contraceptive use. For example, the Pill "dropout" began in 1967, before there was much publicity about its dangers. Most women who had stopped using oral contraceptives by 1982 had done so on their own initiative—only one-third had been advised by a doctor to discontinue use.[32] Women were "saved" from the Pill's dangers not primarily by health professionals but mainly by their own feelings and the efforts of feminist organizations.

The next major contraceptive battle concerned intrauterine devices. Debate about the Pill ended by making it safer. Debate about IUDs began similarly but ended quite differently. IUDs were extremely promising when introduced in the early 1960s, but now only 1 percent of contracepting American women use them. This disappointment was not due to feminist and consumer pressure but to the faulty structure of contraceptive testing and marketing in the United States.

IUDs have been used since antiquity. But as with many modern contraceptives, the demand that made large-scale manufacture profitable developed only later, about the same time that the Pill came on the market. At first the FDA did not claim authority to regulate IUDs. By the early 1970s several hundred gynecologists had "carved and twisted various metals, plastics, and fibers" for use as IUDs, and at least three million U.S. women and seven million women abroad received inadequately tested devices.[33] The women's health movement, which had learned from its experience with the Pill, began to see miserable and dangerous reactions in many users, notably pain and bleeding, pelvic inflammatory disease, septic abortions, uterine perforations, anemia, embedding, and even fragmentation of the devices.[34] But the pharmaceutical companies that made and sold IUDs did no testing to learn whether these problems were inherent in the principle behind IUDs or the result of a particular shape or composition.

One model—the Dalkon Shield—emerged from the crowd as a major danger, correlated with five times as much pelvic inflammatory disease, for example, as other IUDs. The story of the Dalkon Shield, which caused at least twenty deaths in the United States (and unknown others abroad) and probably hundreds of thousands of severe infections and injuries, often leading to sterility and other permanent damage and long-lasting pain, has been well told elsewhere. It is a story not only of inadequate testing but, worse, a profit-motivated cover-up of known dangers. The judgment in the class-action lawsuit that resulted found that Hugh Davis, the shield's designer, lied under oath and that A. H. Robins, the pharmaceutical company to whom he sold the patent, had ignored warnings, including that from one of their own research directors, and undertook no adequate testing of the product. The company admitted that 4 percent (90,000—hardly a negligible number of women) of Dalkon Shield users had suffered injuries, but 334,863 claimants joined the suit and many injured users were not reached by the publicity. In December 1987 a $2,475,000 judgment against the now-bankrupt company was handed down.[35] In 1985 and 1986 the big pharmaceutical companies, fearing similar suits, took almost all IUDs off the U.S. market rather than pay for testing to determine which of them were safe. Feminists contributed to this resolution by organizing consumer grievances against unsafe IUDs, but they did not get what they wanted—which was better testing. Instead, most manufacturers looked to the bottom line and simply quit the IUD business altogether, depriving women of a useful contraceptive option.[36] Women appear to be leery of the few IUDs that remain on the market.[37] It should be noted that A. H. Robins did not destroy its supply of Dalkon Shields. Rather, as the awareness of dangers grew in the United States, it dumped thirty-five thousand shields on the international market. The company later refused to notify third-world users of the IUD's dangers, agreeing only to alert foreign embassies. Today many women still have Dalkon Shields inside their bodies.[38]

Feminist-organized consumer resistance also played watchdog, making up for what the FDA did not do, with respect to other hormonal contraceptives. One of the most controversial was Depo-Provera, an injected progesterone that prevents conception for up to three months. Although its manufacturer, Upjohn, had already successfully marketed it to more than ten million women in eighty countries, a growing third-world consciousness had made some governments and agencies reluctant to allow the importation of drugs that were not approved in the United States. For that reason Upjohn, supported by the U.S. Agency for International Development (USAID) and the International Planned Parenthood Federation, fought for FDA approval. It failed twice, in 1978 and 1984, due partly to the feminist-led consumer lobby which insisted on better data demonstrating the product's safety. Although in 1999 only 3 percent of contracepting women used Depo-Provera, which produces unpleasant side effects in many of them, usage is much higher among poor and very young women (15 percent).[39] An alternate hormonal delivery system relies on an implant, such as Norplant. Inserted beneath the skin of a woman's arm, its contraceptive effect reportedly lasts up to five years, and like Depo-Provera it has been disproportionately urged upon poor women. Norplant, which can produce both minor and serious complications, was supposed to be removable at any time, but there arose a number of cases in which removal caused complications and permanent scarring. (In their defense, drug companies charged that if it had not been for the insistence of the women's health movement that the contraceptive be removable, they would have developed biodegradable implants.) The result has been a dramatic decline in the use of Norplant.[40]

Pharmaceutical and other corporations call these complaints and lawsuits paranoid and argue that women are unreasonable—that they want the impossible, namely, a contraceptive with no risks at all. In fact, feminist mistrust of pharmaceutical development procedures and profit motives has stemmed in large part not from scientific mistakes but from cover-ups of the dangers involved. Feminist anger at physicians' and population controllers' arrogance has been a response not only to their disrespectful, noninformative approach to women but also to their distrust of women's capacity to use barrier methods.

These mutually distrustful groups were eventually forced together by the antiabortion movement. Historically, contraception had been legitimized in part at the cost of delegitimizing abortion: the campaign for the legalization of contraception in the early twentieth century had, for the first time, placed contraception and abortion into different moral categories. Throughout this process, many birth control experts and advocates have contrasted "bad" abortion with "good" contraception, and some have predicted that advances in contraception would reduce or even eliminate the need for abortion. (It was in part Planned Parenthood's anxiety about defending abortion rights that encouraged its emphasis on the most "effective" but often more dangerous and uncomfortable methods.)

As the antiabortion movement's target expanded to encompass contraception, the strategy of distinguishing abortion from contraception had to give way. The movement particularly opposed measures that spread *access* to contraception. Make contraception too easily available, right-to-lifers argued, and it would license sex outside of marriage, especially among the young. These antiabortion advocates have the same objection to "emergency contraception," a high dosage of birth control hormones that, if taken within seventy-two hours after intercourse, prevents pregnancy. Several reproductive rights organizations have called for making emergency contraception available without a prescription, important because of the short window of opportunity. (Several counties in Oregon already allow pharmacists to dispense emergency contraception over the counter.) Advocates insist that emergency contraception is completely different from the abortifacient RU-486, but that distinction is shaky: mifepristone, the drug in RU-486, can also be used as emergency contraception. Since the body's reproductive processes are all part of a continuum, positioning a line between abortion and contraception is arbitrary.[41]

Antiabortion forces in the 1980s and 1990s consistently worked to cut public funding for birth control. During the Reagan and Bush Sr. presidencies, Title X funding for birth control (in real dollars) fell by 72 percent and total public funding by 27 percent, while the costs of contraception grew faster than inflation.[42] New regulations to Title X proposed by the Reagan administration in 1987 and 1988 not only prohibited funding of family planning projects that offered abortion counseling, referrals, or services but no longer required that they offer a "broad range of acceptable and effective . . . family-planning methods" (the old requirement). Instead, they defined family planning as "natural family-planning methods, adoption, infertility services and general reproductive health care, abstinence and contraception"—in that order. "Clinics" that offered only abstinence as a form of "natural" birth control could be funded under these regulations.[43]

The forms of contraception available in the United States have been influenced strongly by international and national political and economic structures. What U.S. consumers can get has been partly determined by the priorities of marketing in the Third World, because of the potential profits there and because the testing of new methods is skewed by the funding priorities of the international population control agencies—which push long-term hormonal and/or physician-controlled contraception over the "old-fashioned" barrier methods because they doubt that women in poor countries have the necessary skills and conditions to use diaphragms. (Today, some population experts have joined feminists in support of barrier methods, calculating that diaphragms may be more "effective" than pills or IUDs because of their greater "continuation rate"—that is, women who do not stop using them because of the discomfort. Population experts are also beginning to interrogate their use of the concept of "effectiveness," which has usually been based only on laboratory or clinical test results rather than on the evidence of actual and prolonged experience.[44]) Moreover, the education of the U.S. public about oral contraceptives, and the successful pressure on drug companies to develop low-dosage pills, was a product of the intersection of the U.S. women's movement and the British National Health Service. Britain blew the whistle about the dangers of birth control pills because its medical system is less obligated to the large drug companies and directly responsible for women's medical bills. Had the United States had a public health insurance program, there might have been an incentive to develop safer pills more quickly. In other ways the internationalization of the contraceptive business by the multinational manufacturers pits the interests of women in the developed and undeveloped worlds against each other: for example, American women's victories at lowering hormonal doses in pills led to the dumping of the old high-dosage pills in third-world countries.

How governmental, economic, and professional structures have intersected with pressure from the women's movement is visible also in the case of the cervical cap. The cap, sometimes called a pessary, is like a small diaphragm, designed to fit exactly and snugly over the cervix. Caps had been promoted by various early birth control pioneers—for example, Emma Goldman, Margaret Sanger, Edward Bliss Foote, and Rachelle Yarros—and Ortho Pharmaceutical manufactured a cap from the 1920s through the 1940s, though the cap began losing popularity in the 1930s.[45] Why did the diaphragm became preferable to the cap? It may have been a result of medicalization: physicians, and the clinics that employed them, doubted that women could insert the caps correctly or at least found it unprofitable to spend the time necessary to teach women how to use them, preferring the larger diaphragms, which did not require such careful fitting. When feminist health clinics and networks began promoting cervical caps in the mid-1970s, they envisaged a system in which many birth control services could be rendered by nonmedical personnel, making it less expensive to allocate the estimated forty-five minutes per patient that it takes to fit a cap and teach a woman to use it.[46]

The caps provided in the 1970s were imported from England. Then in 1976 an amendment to the Food and Drug Act required that devices used inside the body have FDA approval, which depended on which of three categories of risk the devices were assigned to. This change was in part a product of feminist concerns about IUD dangers, and health activists approved the decision to regulate the cervical cap. But they did not approve the FDA's 1980 decision to categorize the cap in the high-risk group, along with IUDs and cardiac pacemakers.[47] The cap might have been approved (as diaphragms were) through a grandfather clause on the grounds that it had been used for so long, but since in the decades immediately before the new regulations caps had not been manufactured in the United States, they were classified as new devices. Human testing was delayed because the FDA refused to waive the requirement for animal testing, which usually serve to ensure the safety of *anticipated* human studies, despite the fact that there had already been decades of human use. The British manufacturer Lamberts refused to cover the high costs of what it considered unnecessary additional research. Finally, a representative of the National Women's Health Network brokered an agreement, persuading the FDA to accept shorter toxicity studies instead of longer carcinogenicity studies, finding a firm to do the animal studies and arranging for Lamberts to fund them.[48] The cap was approved in May 1988, but only for women with normal Pap smears because of concern over its effect on cervical tissue.[49]

Why did the FDA behave this way? Some argue that drug manufacturers pressured the FDA against the cap because its use would reduce the sale of profitable spermicides, used with sponges and diaphragms but not with caps.[50] Others say that the FDA had been so bitterly criticized by feminists for its laxness about oral contraceptives and IUDs that its insistence on testing the cap was overcompensation so as to avoid criticism—or as a means of revenge. Whatever the motives, the major problems encountered by the cap were institutional. The FDA can only approve a drug or device that has a private sponsor, who must pay for the testing; small companies are thus deterred from introducing new products, and consumers can take no initiatives unless they find corporate manufacturers to fund the necessary testing.

Contrasting the cervical cap's history with that of the Today vaginal sponge is instructive. An energetic venture capitalist, predicting that the sponge would be profitable, hired experienced lobbyists and obtained five million dollars from private investors and another two million dollars from the USAID for clinical testing.[51] In 1983 a ¾-by-2–inch sponge that released the spermicide nonoxynol-9 over a twenty-four-hour period became the first over-the-counter birth control device for women and was received enthusiastically—so much so that it was featured on an episode of of the popular TV show "Seinfeld." The FDA had accepted very limited testing because of claims that the polyurethane of the sponge is inert and the fact that the spermicide it contains had been on the market for twenty years (although the FDA had rejected an even stronger parallel claim about the cervical cap). But the NWHN was concerned that polyurethane tampons had proven carcinogenic and/or toxic in mice and rabbits, that the spermicide was being used in concentrations nearly ten times that in the average dose received with a diaphragm or foam, and that no research was done on possible interaction between polyurethane and dioxane, the active ingredient in the spermicide.[52] In 1995 the FDA, acting under pressure, found that the factory in which the Today sponge was being manufactured had excessive levels of bacteria in its water and air. American Home Products decided that the necessary cleanup would be too costly and instead took the sponge off the market. Another drug company promised in 1999 to manufacture it in a cleaner factory and petitioned for FDA approval, only to be stymied by an Associated Pharmacologists and Toxicologists report that the product was likely to cause vaginal irritation and tissue damage.[53]

Amid these frustrated hopes for the perfect contraceptive and an awareness of health hazards related to contraception was a growing interest in "natural" birth control—through improved means of identifying fertile periods. Some, especially Catholics, emphasized that "natural" birth control was a way to avoid contraception; others stressed its self-help and know-your-body content (such as "fertility consciousness" groups that trained women to detect changes in vaginal mucus).[54] The call for "natural" birth control is reminiscent of the voluntary motherhood movement, not only in its rejection of "artificial" contraception, but also in its emphasis on self-control within a women's reproductive culture. Such thinking was progressive and popular a century ago when women had many fewer options and did not demand contraception of such high reliability; today, the emphasis on the "natural" and the maternal seems unlikely to provide a solution for most women's birth control needs. Indeed, its major support appears to come from anticontraception conservatives who have managed to allocate millions of dollars in federal funds to largely ineffective "natural" family planning clinics.

Although feminist health experts have long argued for a greater emphasis on barrier methods of contraception, it took the HIV/AIDS epidemic to produce a major effect in that direction, emphasizing condoms, which are the only form of birth control that can also protect against sexually transmitted diseases. In the 1980s the proportion of unmarried people using condoms increased from 9 percent to 16 percent (though there was no apparent increase in use among married couples), while the proportion of those using diaphragms declined.[55] Through the mid-1990s, condom use rose to 19 percent among all women and to 34 percent among women not living with a partner. Encouraging but far from good enough, since 75 percent of women who had had sex with more than one partner in the previous year or whose partner had done likewise were not using condoms.[56]

Given the trade-offs, the diaphragm remains an excellent form of birth control, provided there is legal abortion as a backup. This relation between contraception and abortion must be emphasized, for it is inaccurate to see them as alternatives. No method of contraception yet developed can eliminate the need for legal abortion. Indeed, from a historical perspective, contraception at first may have increased the clientele for abortion because it accustoms people to planning reproduction and makes them unlikely to accept loss of control. Paradoxically, legalized abortion probably increased the use of contraception because most high-quality abortion services promote contraception among clients. For example, Planned Parenthood of New York City doubled its contraception caseload after the legalization of abortion because those who came in for abortions and those who proved not to be pregnant began using contraception.[57] The continued attack on abortion serves only to discourage the use of barrier methods and keep alive hopes for the perfect contraceptive.

As an example of different political perspectives on contraceptive history, consider how different groups explain the stalled contraceptive revolution, that is, the fact that the range of contraceptive choices is no greater now than it was forty years ago. Some blame feminists and consumer groups, accusing them of overreacting and causing panic about the dangers of the most "effective" contraceptives. In fact, the only case that might qualify as an example of overreaction to the fear of health hazard—the withdrawal of IUDs from the market (to be discussed later in this section)—was not a product of consumer pressure but of other market and legal forces. Others blamed government (i.e., FDA) overregulation, while still others pointed to inadequate research funds or insufficient economic incentives for drug companies.[58] These factors are, of course, interrelated: The long testing periods required for FDA approval increase the costs of research and development; consumers file lawsuits against manufacturers and others, which further increase costs. Pharmaceutical companies claim that the cost of developing new drugs is staggering (although in 2001 the organization Public Citizen charged that the companies were systematically inflating cost estimates and that most costs are covered by government). Drug companies want to minimize their obstacles and the cases in which they are never allowed to market their inventions and recover their investment.[59] The women's health movement retorts that the record hardly suggests FDA regulations have been adequate, let alone tough, at protecting consumers. The situation is even more complex because in past decades publicly supported organizations have joined pharmaceutical firms in sponsoring contraceptive research and development—agencies such as the International Committee for Contraception Research of the Population Council, the Contraceptive Development Branch of the National Institute of Child Health and Human Development's Center for Population Research, and the USAID. These politically vulnerable agencies face considerable pressure in setting development priorities, with antiabortion lobbying proving more powerful than pro-choice lobbying.[60] Certainly, the population control establishment recognizes that "the political and ideologic climate" in the United States—that is, antiabortion pressure—is a primary reason for delays in contraceptive development.[61]

The first explanations to come from the women's movement for this lack of progress blamed a rather simply conceived sexism, expressed in research priorities: Why weren't the experts developing a male contraceptive? Why wasn't there adequate safety testing? Wouldn't the safety of a product aimed at men have been more carefully policed? This last question cannot be answered, of course, because there have been no contraceptives marketed for men except the low-tech condom. Many feminists have noted that in developing male contraceptives, side effects like those women were asked to accept became grounds for rejection. Progestins and other steroid hormones were unacceptable because they dampened libido and caused breast swelling. Analogs, antagonists, and agonists of a gonadotropin-releasing hormone were not usable because they lowered testosterone production.

But the feminist questions go deeper, to an examination of the goals of contraceptive developers and the preconditions for contraceptive use. This also requires a self-critique, since many birth control advocates and users, including feminists, had vicariously joined the scientists' search for a "magic bullet"— a contraceptive that is 100 percent effective, safe, and comfortable: perfect control in one package.[62] Such thinking is an extension of the medical model that began to dominate contraceptive development in the 1920s. The term "magic bullet" was used to describe Paul Ehrlich's 1910 development of Salvarsan, the first effective treatment for syphilis, and later the antibiotic model, a chemotherapeutic agent that is deadly to specific micro-organisms. Not only is the image military, but the goal is cure rather than prevention, and the target is a disease. Yet pregnancy, however venereal, is not an illness. The fact that there may be an inverse association between clinical effectiveness, as measured in pregnancy rates, and troubling side effects should give us pause.[63]

This does not have to spell defeat. Like legal rights, effective contraception relies on preconditions that include not only motivation and access but also the expectation of being able to reap rewards from controlling one's destiny. In some respects recent patterns of contraceptive development actually discouraged the taking of personal responsibility—another drawback of "magic-bullet" thinking. The orientation toward a technological solution de-emphasized the reforms needed to create the economic and social preconditions for contraceptive use, reforms designed to ameliorate poverty, reduce power differentials between men and women, provide women with more educational and work opportunities, and lessen sexual shame. In recreating contraception not as a human action but as a commodity, the "magic bullet" approach also discouraged personal responsibility and led contraceptive users to think of themselves as consumers waiting for the perfect product. The mid-twentieth-century gangbusters approach to technological development, driven in the case of drugs by the scramble of multinational pharmaceutical companies for the huge markets that make their expensive research labs profitable, provided no incentive to consider the long-term health consequences and/or discomforts of new chemicals and devices, and these dangers in turn discouraged active contracepting. Finally, the female-only focus of high-tech contraception reinforced the view of birth control as women's responsibility and avoided the discussion and sharing of sexual as well as birth control planning that barrier methods encourage.

The development of the oral contraceptive created a giant leap in birth control technology but did little to alter the fundamentally political bases of birth control issues. In the 1970s, the debate about contraception differed from that about abortion by remaining, for the most part, immune from the conservative critique of sexual permissiveness and the subversion of the family. Contraception was still publicly defined as a marital aid, and political disputes focused on safety. Planned Parenthood's quiet conversion to providing contraceptive services to the unmarried occurred without major national opposition because opponents were so focused on abortion. This began to change in the 1980s, however, when epidemics of teenage pregnancy and HIV/AIDS stimulated more aggressive proposals for making contraceptives easily accessible, a conflict to be examined later in this chapter.

Sterilization and Its Abuses

Disappointment in high-tech contraception also promoted a turn to sterilization, which has been the most common form of birth control for U.S. women over the age of twenty-five since the late 1970s.[64] The women's health movement has not been a particularly strong proponent of sterilization, preferring temporary methods that allow women to change their minds about reproduction. Furthermore, widespread patterns of coercive sterilization provoked a strong movement against sterilization abuse.

Forcible sterilization is not new. The first eugenic sterilization programs, adopted by thirty states during the 1920s (see chapter 10), forcibly sterilized some 64,000 "feebleminded" or "genetically defective" people. Disproportionately used in southern states, sterilization was imposed on many blacks, American Indians, and poor whites whose alleged "feeblemindedness," if any symptoms of it actually existed, was more likely the result of poor health and little or no education. Yet even in these overtly, nakedly eugenical programs, some of the sterilized women were willing, even eager clients. As one study shows, among women deprived of access to other forms of birth control, often so poor that their existing children were malnourished, ill clothed, and uneducated, approximately 6 percent of those sterilized had requested the surgery. During the 1960s that figure rose to 20 percent.[65]

Even in the textbook case of sterilization abuse that occurred in Puerto Rico, it is not always easy to distinguish voluntary from forced sterilization. Starting in the 1920s, sterilization was heavily promoted in Puerto Rico as a primary form of birth control. By 1949, 18 percent of childbirths were followed by sterilization. Between the 1930s and the 1970s, one-third of Puerto Rican women of childbearing age had been sterilized.[66] Many women welcomed the opportunity to acquire a reliable form of birth control, but their choices were limited—by the availability of cheap or free sterilization in contrast to expensive contraception; by a creative rewriting of Catholic doctrine that treated contraception as a vice but blinked at sterilization; by the fact that sterilization required no cooperation from husbands and could even be hidden from men. One study showed that 22 percent of unmarried Puerto Rican women knew about *la operacíon* but only 1 percent had heard of the diaphragm and only 12 percent knew anything about condoms.[67] In Puerto Rico sterilization became legitimated more than contraception because it was medicalized—surgery performed in a hospital while under anesthesia. Conversely, contraception became associated with prostitutes and thus doubly immoral. But aren't all birth control choices constrained? Perhaps for the majority of the world's people, constraint is a matter of degree.

Many politicized Puerto Ricans denounced the sterilization campaign as a tool of colonialism. They saw it as a eugenics as well as a population control policy, a judgment difficult to contest. Prior to attaining commonwealth status and the right to elect its own governor, Puerto Rico was led by a governor appointed by the U.S. government. In 1932 he declared that Puerto Rico's population problem was a matter not only of high quantity but also of low quality.[68] No one could argue that the purpose of U.S. public and private investment in population control in Puerto Rico was to increase Puerto Rican women's reproductive autonomy.

Women of higher class, race, and national status faced paternalism of another kind. While impoverished Puerto Rican women were being pressured into sterilization, many prosperous white women in the United States were denied sterilization as a birth control option. Most doctors stuck to the indications for sterilization recommended by the American College of Obstetricians and Gynecologists (ACOG), which relied on a formula (the woman's age multiplied by the number of children she had) to determine whether a woman was a candidate for sterilization. If the result was 120 or more, she was approved, but only if two doctors plus a psychiatrist also recommended the surgery. Responding to pressure from women, ACOG liberalized its guidelines in 1969–70 and sterilizations increased substantially. Left unchallenged were the medical establishment's assumption of authority to decide when women could be sterilized and the refusal of most medical insurance providers to pay for elective sterilization. The liberalization also reflected the general cultural shifts of the post–World War II period toward a more positive view of small families and marital sexual activity, combined with the impact of population control arguments.[69] A 1982 study showed that 30 percent of former users of the Pill had turned to sterilization as their birth control alternative.[70]

Was the increase in surgical sterilization a net gain for reproductive and sexual freedom? Not necessarily, because even when the surgery was voluntary the context often constrained women's choices. Many women enjoyed being free from the hassle of using contraceptives, but they preferred contraception over sterilization because it left open the option of further childbearing.

The ambiguity of the meanings of sterilization can be seen in class, race, and sex differences. Overall, 11 percent of American men in the mid-1990s had chosen surgical sterilization compared to 28 percent of women. Among couples, approximately 5 percent relied on vasectomy for contraception, while 15 percent relied on female sterilization.[71] Female sterilization is a poor person's birth control, most commonly relied on by women with less than a high school education or a household income below 150 percent of the federal poverty level. Vasectomy, by contrast, is more common among middle- and higher-income men and twenty-nine times more common among whites than blacks. Among whites, the more education a woman has received, the less likely she is to be sterilized for contraceptive purposes; with men, the correlation with education is reversed.[72] Overall, female sterilizations are medically more complex, and class differences influence how invasive the sterilization surgery will be: poor women are more likely to have hysterectomies than tubal ligations.[73] Public funds can be used to cover most of the cost of sterilizations for the poor, while there is little public funding for abortion or contraception. These differentials raise troubling questions. Vasectomies are safer, simpler, and generally easier to reverse than tubal ligations, and certainly safer and simpler than hysterectomies, so why aren't they the dominant method? Does the preponderance of poor and less well educated women suggest that sterilization might not be their method of choice if they had full access to the information, training, medical care, and money that contraception and abortion require?

The civil rights and women's movements entered the debate in the early 1970s to challenge sterilization abuse. The campaign was jump-started by the Young Lords Party, a Puerto Rican civil rights group in New York City that questioned the high rate of sterilization not only on the island of Puerto Rico but also among Puerto Ricans in New York, where the sterilization rate was seven times that among Anglo-Americans and twice the rate among African

Americans.[74] Led by an unusually strong feminist group within the organization, the Young Lords exposed the blatant coercion behind the sterilization of Puerto Rican women. Coercive sterilization appears to have been growing in the 1960s, part of the conservative backlash against welfare and civil rights, and it was overwhelmingly a eugenic practice, considering that the victims were primarily poor, black, Hispanic, and especially Native American. What differentiated this practice from that in earlier decades was a greater attempt to hide the coercion, so that it required more ambitious investigation to develop the proof that soon began to emerge.

It is not surprising that the new feminism, which revived the distinction between individual reproductive rights and population control, actively opposed coercive sterilization. But women's liberation supporters, a predominantly white and prosperous group in the early 1970s, had to be taught about sterilization abuse by people of color.[75] Insensitivity to what constituted coercion was related to the individual rights, or choice, perspective of the women's movement, and it was the socialist feminist branch of the movement that initiated and led the campaign against sterilization abuse.

In 1973, civil rights activists helped bring a number of lawsuits against physicians charged with performing coerced sterilizations. These were almost all abuses of poor, nonwhite, or mentally retarded women; virtually no abuses against white or middle-class women were documented.[76] In 1974, responding to this pressure, the Department of Health, Education, and Welfare issued guidelines for all sterilization procedures paid for with federal funds that would ensure informed consent and prohibit the sterilization of women younger than twenty-one. Then public interest groups—the American Civil Liberties Union, the Public Citizen—and federal agencies—the Centers for Disease Control, the General Accounting Office—studied hospital compliance with the new standards. Their findings were cause for alarm: one report indicated that 76 percent of hospitals were disregarding the guidelines, while a second report placed the figure at 94 percent; another study found that 700 sterilizations had been illegally performed on underage patients.[77] The GAO report on Indian Health Service hospitals found not one of them to be in compliance.[78] Women were commonly approached during childbirth for their consent to be sterilized: "'I used to make my pitch while sewing up the episiotomy when the anesthesia started wearing off,'" said a medical resident to a *Los Angeles Times* reporter. Others were threatened shortly before delivery with losing their welfare payments, their Medicaid payments, or withdrawal of obstetrician's services unless they consented to sterilization.[79]

In the early 1970s sterilization abuse was mainly understood in civil rights, civil liberties, anti-imperialist, and class-conscious terms. Gender analysis was underdeveloped and many condemnations of sterilization entirely ignored

women's desire for reproduction control. Indeed, the opponents of sterilization abuse sometimes fell into the same conflation of all forms of reproduction control that had characterized both population control and anti–birth
control groups in earlier decades. For example, the radical health research
group Health/PAC criticized all federal funding of birth control services and
took the book *Our Bodies, Ourselves* to task for offering a positive view of
sterilization as a reproduction control option.[80] This unqualified condemnation of sterilization was in part provoked by the fact that the influential Association for Voluntary Sterilization opposed the federal guidelines, as did
Planned Parenthood, on the grounds that they were paternalistic, deprived
women of choice, and interfered with the doctor-patient relationship. With
this kind of political polarization, it is not surprising that the gendered meanings of sterilization were rendered invisible. Surveys did not point out that
vasectomies were never imposed on men or that nearly all Medicaid sterilizations were being performed on women.[81] By contrast, some feminist groups,
representing a more privileged group of women, had difficulty in understanding the problem. For example, at its 1978 national convention the National
Organization for Women (NOW), by a narrow majority to be sure, voted to
condemn the thirty-day waiting period.[82]

The left wing of the women's liberation movement began to organize
against sterilization abuse and was particularly active in New York City, where
it was able to build a coalition that included the National Black Feminist Organization, Health/PAC, the Puerto Rican Socialist party, the Lower East Side
Neighborhood Health Center, and the local branch of NOW. Pressure from
this coalition won tougher guidelines from the city's Health and Hospital
Corporation in 1977. In 1978, the Department of Health, Education, and
Welfare issued yet more regulations, extending the required waiting period
for federally funded sterilizations from three to thirty days, requiring transla-
tors where necessary, and banning the signing of consent forms during labor,
childbirth, or abortion. But noncompliance rates remained high: surveys of
hospitals done again in 1979 found that 70 percent were not even in compliance with the 1974 guidelines.[83]

Out of this struggle came a more complex analysis of sterilization abuse
and a new type of feminist reproductive rights group that extended its concerns to all forms of interference with reproductive autonomy. These groups
insisted that the right to have children safely and to be able to keep them in
good health was as much a reproductive right as the freedom not to bear children. They also pointed out that there could be no truly free choice as long as
either right was interfered with. The leading such group was New York's Committee for Abortion Rights and Against Sterilization Abuse (CARASA), which
led the fight against coercive sterilization to substantial victories. The National

Women's Health Network organized an even larger coalition in New York in 1979, uniting CARASA with the Committee to End Sterilization Abuse, the Mexican-American Women's National Association, the Center for Constitutional Rights, and the Chicana Nurses Association, among others, to monitor the compliance of New York City hospitals with the new city laws,[84] thus appropriating an aspect of state power.

The New York City coalition in turn became part of a national coalition, the Reproductive Rights National Network, known as R2N2, which was established in 1981 and came to include eighty member groups. This network further developed and communicated feminist thinking about reproductive rights, and its national newsletter was very influential. R2N2 was committed to a multi-issue approach, hoping to change the movement's primary identification as white, heterosexual, and middle class. It united not only abortion rights and prevention of sterilization abuse but also demands for better maternity and infant care for those who chose to give birth.

The campaign against sterilization abuse represented in some ways the high point of the reproductive rights work of the women's health movement. At the peak of feminist power, it succeeded in eliminating some of the worst abuses and raising the consciousness of medical workers about patients' rights to informed consent.

Teenage Pregnancy and Out-of-Wedlock Childbearing

In the 1980s a new reproductive issue moved to the center of political debate in the United States. The alarm about teenage pregnancy and out-of-wedlock childbearing supported the condemnation of welfare and an "underclass" who allegedly lacked good moral values and work ethic. The alarm demonstrated that contemporary sexual and reproductive assumptions, as in the nineteenth century, formed an important part of social definitions of respectability. Most directly relevant here were the parallel controversies about whether birth control or sexual abstinence, abortion or adoption, were better approaches to the problem, and this has remained a relatively dichotomous discussion between liberals and social conservatives even into the twenty-first century. A feminist approach, integrating the gendered experience of girls into the discussion of poverty and sex, remains rare.

Despite a great deal of research and publicity about teenage pregnancy, much of the popular discussion in the 1980s relied on the mistaken assumption that teenage fertility rates were rising. The fact is that these rates have been declining since 1960, nearing a record low in 1998 of 51 births per 1,000 females ages fifteen to nineteen. As of 1995, about one-fourth of the decline was due to increased abstinence and three-fourths to fewer pregnancies among those who were having sex.[85] Also contrary to widespread misimpression, the decline was steeper among blacks than among whites, although blacks started from a higher teenage fertility rate.[86]

So what prompted the 1980s panic that teenage pregnancies and childbearing were increasing? One reason is that adult births were falling even more than teenage births.[87] More significant, however, is that the same cluster of conservative political attitudes expressed in antiabortion campaigns, now applied to the issue of teenage pregnancy, led to an unnoticed misunderstanding. Accepting the rhetoric of Christian social conservatism, commentators fell into the mistake of not noticing teenage childbearing when the teenagers were *married*. In the 1950s, the birth rate for teenagers was higher than that of today, but those teenagers were much more often married. More recently, while teen births overall were decreasing, the proportion of teen births to the *unmarried* was increasing. The proportion of all teenage births that were out of wedlock increased about fivefold, from 17 percent in 1970 to 79 percent in 1998, while the proportion of all births that were out of wedlock rose eightfold, from 4 percent in 1940 to 33 percent in 1999.[88]

In other words, the discourse about teenage childbearing typically rests on the hidden assumption that pregnancy among married teenagers is not objectionable—or, rather, that marriage somehow instantly makes teenagers into grownups. In fact, most of the negative consequences of teenage pregnancy pertain equally to the married and unmarried: teenagers have more-difficult childbirths and less-healthy babies, are worse parents, create more-unstable marriages, and achieve less education and lower earning power and status. Ironically, during the 1960s both scholarly and popular writing identified teenage marriage as the problem; by the 1980s the focus was on teenage pregnancy, with early marriage no longer considered problematic. In fact, some conservative commentators recommend early marriage as a remedy, failing to recognize that for many poor young women marriage is unlikely to increase stability or standard of living.[89] It is worth considering that while the rise of nonmarital pregnancies creates problems, the decline in early marriage is not a bad thing.

The racial subtext in the concern with pregnancy among unwed teenagers also fosters misunderstandings. While the percentage of out-of-wedlock births among all black women was higher during this period than among white women, it was only slightly higher than among whites of the same poverty level. Furthermore, white rates of out-of-wedlock (not necessarily teenage) pregnancy were rising while black rates were falling, among adults and teenagers.[90] African American attitudes about teenage and out-of-wedlock pregnancies went through particularly noticeable changes between the 1960s and the 1980s. Following publication in 1965 of the notorious "Moynihan Report," which blamed black poverty on "pathological" family patterns, many African American leaders responded critically, emphasizing the strengths of black extended-family networks and intergenerational child-raising and criticizing the report for diverting attention away from basic racial discrimination. As Joyce Ladner put it, there was a "closing of the ranks" behind black families, making open discussion of teen pregnancy or single-mother families appear disloyal, much like exposing one's weaknesses to the enemy. Indeed, the anger created by Moynihan's report probably impeded examination of these problems.[91] Since then, however, more black organizations have campaigned against teenage pregnancy, although they are as divided about solutions as are white organizations.

We can understand more by examining teenage pregnancy in a global context. The United States has substantially higher levels of teenage pregnancy, childbearing, and abortion than any of twenty-seven other industrialized countries. Teenagers in the United States are less likely to use contraception than those in other comparable countries. Furthermore, teenage birth rates have declined less steeply in the United States—from 68.3 per 1,000 in 1970 to 48.7 per 1,000 in 2000—than in other developed countries over the last three decades. These high rates in the United States are most correlated with the high rates of poverty and inequality in the United States, which on the individual level means less hope for upward mobility among the poorest teenagers who have most of the babies.

Teenage pregnancy often became a rhetorical surrogate for a larger 1980s discourse about single (or lone)[92] mothers, welfare, and the "underclass." While aid to lone mothers had long been more stigmatized than most other forms of public provision, the hostility increased markedly after 1980. Spurred by conservative interpretations of poverty, high taxation, and illegal drugs, welfare recipients were associated with a vaguely defined "underclass," thought to be characterized by criminal activity, rejection of the work ethic, reproductive irresponsibility, and, if female, sexual immorality. Even if these characterizations were true, and they are open to criticism on many grounds, they were not applicable to lone mothers, who were rarely criminals, who tended to work exceedingly hard, who typically did their best as mothers, and who were much less reproductively and sexually irresponsible than men of their class.

Single motherhood, poverty, and welfare receipt created difficulties for both mothers and children, but the three factors must be distinguished. Some lone mothers were prosperous, some chose this kind of family, and many suffered negligibly if at all from lack of husbands. The children of these mothers generally do very well. Single motherhood in general was highly correlated with poverty—especially where single mothers were heads of household—and it is overwhelmingly because of poverty that female-headed households were correlated with lasting disadvantages for children.[93] Moreover, while early pregnancy certainly added to the mothers' problems, they were poor mainly because they started off poor. Few would have done much better even if they had avoided early pregnancy; besides, pregnancies did not occur randomly among teenagers but affected those with the fewest resources and hopes for the future. Moreover, poor girls of all races were more likely to carry out-of-wedlock pregnancies to term than were more-prosperous girls.[94] This should not be construed as minimizing the damages of teenage pregnancy and parenthood. Many girls may have "chosen" to bear children, either passively (by their lack of attention to birth control) or actively (as a means of gaining status), but their "choices" emerged from a very limited range. For example, a far higher proportion of teenage girls than of adults described their pregnancies as unwanted, and this was the case three times as often among blacks as among whites.[95]

Teenage pregnancy was unusual among reproduction control issues in that nearly everyone thought it was a bad idea. But this consensus did little to promote agreement on policy. Liberals argued for promoting contraception and increasing access to it, but social conservatives feared that contraception would encourage teenage sexual activity, which they considered immoral and harmful in itself. Since the 1960s teenagers' sexual behavior had become a symbol both of sexual immorality and of parents' feelings of powerlessness. Many parents supported repressive policies because they felt helpless to control the sexualization of mass media. The 1981 Adolescent Family Life Act (AFLA), sponsored by Title X opponents, inaugurated a family-centered approach to teenage pregnancy prevention that promoted "chastity and self-discipline" to teenagers rather than providing them with contraceptive services. A group of clergy and other individuals brought suit, charging that this constituted government endorsement of a particular religious point of view. In 1993 the Clinton administration brokered a settlement requiring that the program not promote religious dogma or provide medically inaccurate information. Conservatives charged that the settlement weakened the original thrust of the program. In 1994 a Republican-sponsored amendment to the Elementary and Secondary Education Act that would have censored sexuality and HIV education in local schools failed to win approval. In 1997 the Republican-controlled Congress increased the appropriation for abstinence-only education to $64 million a year and continued to prohibit communicating any information about birth control.[96]

Vociferous opposition to giving minors access to contraceptives prompted the Reagan administration in 1983 to order that clinics receiving Title X funds be required to notify, by registered mail, both parents or the legal guardian of patients under the age of eighteen within ten days of prescribing a contraceptive. Advocates maintained that family planning clinics had built a "Berlin Wall between the kid and the family" and that this "squeal rule" was a legitimate way to encourage family participation. They also argued that mandatory parental notification would protect minors from harmful side effects of contraceptives, deter some teenagers from having sex, and improve the "consistency" of contraceptive use by teenagers who were sexually active. The order never took effect—it was enjoined by court injunctions, and the Reagan administration chose not to appeal—a source of anger among social conservatives.[97]

But even conservative parents are ambivalent about some related issues. For example, one-third of parents believe that teenagers should be told to have sex only when they are married, but 86 percent and 71 percent, respectively, want them to be taught HIV prevention and how to use condoms.[98] Yet, although every evaluation has shown that abstinence education does not reduce sexual activity, it remains the dominant theme in sex education for teenagers. Among the 70 percent of public school districts that teach sex education, the vast majority (86 percent) require that abstinence be promoted, either as the preferred option for teenagers (51 percent) or as the only option outside of marriage (35 percent). Only 14 percent address abstinence in a broader educational program to prepare adolescents to become sexually responsible adults. In one-third of school districts, information about contraception is either prohibited entirely or limited to emphasizing its ineffectiveness in protecting against unplanned pregnancy and sexually transmitted diseases. Of the 1,135 school-based health clinics that existed in 1999, more than three-fourths were prohibited from dispensing contraceptives. The HIV/AIDS danger seems to have encouraged some of these clinics to make an exception for condoms, but this leaves girls dependent on boys for protection.[99]

By contrast, providing contraception in high schools does seem to work.[100] An evaluation of five different pregnancy prevention programs found that the two that showed results were the two that were most active in providing access to contraceptive services.[101] Moreover, there is wide public support for such programs, and twenty-three states have adopted legislation that gives minors the authority to consent to contraceptive services for themselves.

The welfare system has provided another potential weapon with which to fight teenage pregnancy and out-of-wedlock childbearing, but it does not seem to be effective, partly because teenagers account for only 5 percent of welfare caseloads. In fact, teenage pregnancy rates are lowest where welfare benefits are highest, which counters the myth that the welfare system encourages childbearing among teenagers and unmarried women. Twenty-one states and the District of Columbia have "family cap" policies that deny increases in benefits when additional children are born to families on welfare, but a New Jersey study for the period 1992–95 found that these policies had no impact whatsoever: rates of childbearing and abortion were identical among those who got benefit increases and those who were denied them.[102] Other studies have drawn similar conclusions—that financial incentives or disincentives have negligible effect on childbearing among poor women—possibly because the monthly increase for an additional child is so small (in 1997, it ranged from approximately $24 in Mississippi to $109 in California).[103]

The Welfare Reform Bill of 1996 mandated cutting off public assistance for a variety of infractions ranging from not having a child's immunizations up to date to giving birth to a child while on welfare. It also promoted abstinence education—and, unlike the Adolescent Family Life Act, which targeted pre-marital sex among youth, the 1996 bill funds education efforts that have as their "exclusive purpose" censuring *all sex* outside of marriage, no matter the age of the individuals. Programs that qualify for funding must adhere to strict re-quirements as to what can and cannot be taught and are prohibited from pro-viding any information about contraceptives except for their failure rates.[104] States are entitled, by law, to $50 million annually in federal funds and must spend $3 of every $4 they receive. Moreover, this piece of legislation gained "entitlement" status, meaning that these programs will be funded automati-cally and without debate during each year's appropriation process.[105]

Antiwelfare politics has exposed a fissure among conservatives that dates back to the formation of the New Right, which brought together economic and social conservatives. The latter fear that cutbacks in welfare will encour-age abortion. The debate cuts to the heart of sex and reproduction policy, to basic priorities, and reveals the different interests of conservatives. But anti-abortion advocates argue that the differences are superficial. The Family Research Council argues that in the long run the family caps must be part of the conservative platform:

> While a pro-life position must be part of the agenda for national renewal, op-position to abortion must be only one plank of the pro-life platform. A crisis as broad and deep as abortion on demand requires a transformation of the political and moral culture. . . . Reducing illegitimacy is the sine qua non of moral reconstruction, and right-to-life activists should realize that . . . the family cap not only serves their cause in the long run but deserves their active sup-port in the short term. . . . The real fault-line in the current welfare debate is not between pro-life social conservatives and economic libertarians. Rather, the crucial dispute pits those who think relimiting government is a prerequi-site for moral reform against those who believe that the size of government bears no relation to cultural decay. . . . If man is more than a material being, then it is not unreasonable to expect some individual moral decisions to over-ride the economic incentives that run against the grain of virtue.[106]

Yet traditional economic conservatives might answer, If we allow morality to trump economic incentives, will that not lead to interference with the market? Conservatives in the United States at the beginning of the twenty-first century include both libertarians and their opposite, that is, those who have no hesitation to use the state to enforce moral values. Those concerned with children might question whether impoverishing "born" children through welfare cutbacks is consistent with these moral values.

Another aspect of the debate over teenage pregnancy is the tendency to discuss it without thinking about gender. This silence about the actual conditions of femaleness has characterized liberal as well as conservative discourse. In fact, throughout the 1980s most of the discussion of teenage pregnancy was entirely silent regarding boys, as if these pregnancies arose from immaculate conceptions. Very little anti–teenage pregnancy work was directed at boys, and in practice those who lobbied for abstinence education were challenging the double standard that accepts boys' sexual adventures. Also, the liberal teenage pregnancy discourse usually ignored pressures on girls to submit sexually, even though it is known that the sexual partners of teenage girls are often significantly older and that coercion in sex can take many forms short of rape with a weapon.

Birth control worked, historically, under two conditions: when women could take charge of their own sexual activity, resisting sexual pressure or violence while honoring their own sexual feelings; and when women had realizable aspirations beyond motherhood. Yet very few discussions of teenage pregnancy have touched on these issues. One example of shallow and gender-blind thinking followed a 1986 National Academy of Sciences report on teenage pregnancy. Most of the news media covered only one of its conclusions, calling for increased teenage access to birth control and aggressive public education to promote contraception. Another conclusion was virtually ignored:

> . . . the sense of what and who one is, can be, and wants to be is at the heart of teen-agers' sexual decision-making. . . . an important aspect of self-perception among teen-agers is their educational, occupational and family formation expectations . . . [which are] significantly influenced by perceptions of opportunities. . . . Teenagers, especially girls, with a strong achievement orientation and clear future goals are less likely to become sexually involved at an early age, more likely to be regular and effective contraceptors if they are sexually active, and less likely to bear a child if they experienced an unintended pregnancy.[107]

The report contained no gender analysis beyond this, and teenagers appeared in it as neutered. But the findings fit what feminist scholars and service providers have learned: that girls with high aspirations are more likely to be able to resist boys' sexual aggression when they want to, more likely to insist on contraceptive use, and more likely to choose abortion over unwanted early pregnancy. They also support the views of those who see teenage pregnancy as rooted in poverty and inequality, suggesting that only fundamental economic change, including improvements in the living conditions, education, and hopes of poor teenagers, can instill in teenagers the desire to postpone parenthood. Teenage pregnancy, like many reproductive issues, is problematic largely because of the social inequalities it thrives upon and helps to reproduce, and solutions are unlikely to be found if sex inequality is ignored.

HIV/AIDS and Birth Control

The HIV/AIDS epidemic born in the 1980s exposed similar inequalities. At first labeled a "gay disease," it has now become overwhelmingly a disease of heterosexual poor people of color, disproportionately female, both in the United States and abroad. The politics of HIV/AIDS has shifted somewhat in accord with the progress of the epidemic, but only slightly, and its basic alignment continues to parallel that regarding abortion and teen pregnancy.

The impact of HIV/AIDS on birth control in the United States mirrors that of venereal disease in the World War I era (see chapters 2 and 8). Like V.D., HIV/AIDS led to increased condom use but also provoked a backlash. Moreover, after appearing initially as a men's problem, it soon began disproportionately victimizing women—an effect magnified by public policy. Men characteristically become HIV-positive through sex with other men and/or the use of tainted hypodermic needles; women characteristically become HIV-positive through sex with men and/or the use of tainted hypodermic needles. Female-to-male and female-to-female sexual transmission are both relatively rare. (As of December 1998, there were no confirmed cases of female-to-female transmission in the United States.)[108] In other words, women rarely infect but are often infected, a biological dynamic that unfortunately seems to replicate a stereotype of female passivity. By far the more effective anti-HIV/AIDS campaigns have been constructed by gay men and aimed at gay men, and the politicized structure of public HIV/AIDS policy has been least effective among poor, young heterosexual women of color, who are now the fastest-growing sector of Americans with HIV/AIDS.

Between 1985 and 1999, AIDS cases among women more than tripled, from 7 percent to 23 percent. The most dramatic increases occurred among women of color: African Americans and Hispanics together constituted 77 percent of AIDS cases among women, although they make up less than one-fourth of the female population in the United States. The most dramatic increase occurred among African American and Hispanic teenage girls, whose rate of HIV infection rose 117 percent between 1994 and 1998.[109] Among women in general, the most frequently reported cause of infection was heterosexual intercourse, followed by drug injection (approximately 27 percent). High proportions of infected women were unaware of the risks associated with their partners.

Poor young males, especially African Americans and Puerto Ricans, also had disproportionately high rates of infection. At the end of 1999, 56 percent of AIDS sufferers in the United States were people of color. In 1998, African Americans constituted 12 percent of the population but 30 percent of new AIDS cases. Hispanics constituted 13 percent of the population and 20 percent of new AIDS cases. HIV infection of Native Americans increased 25 percent between 1997 and 1999. (Asian Americans seem to have lower than average AIDS rates, but there are no systematic studies.)

Structures of economic and racial inequality create this disproportionate infection rate among poor, young people of color, who are less likely to have access to medical care and sex education and who, if they become infected, are more likely to die. People already afraid of the law because of their status as drug users, welfare recipients, or illegal immigrants have an incentive to avoid testing or any other contact with officials. But sex and gender are also front and center. Poor young women are more vulnerable to rape, less likely to get help from the police if they are threatened, and less able to resist the pressure to have sex with older men or to insist that they use condoms. That so many infected women report not knowing that their partners were putting them at risk points to the failure of education, women's intimidation by their partners, and/or their partners' dishonesty or irresponsibility. Among all groups homophobia leads men to engage in unsafe sex because safe sex requires accepting and taking responsibility for one's sexual activities. Unrealistic sexual moralism creates the same unsafe sexual activity among women.

The opposition to effective HIV/AIDS policy has been shaped by much the same ideologies and interests that oppose birth control. In the past, fear of veneral disease sometimes spurred birth control and sexual responsibility. Condoms gained their modern legitimacy as protection against gonorrhea, and their use has been widely approved since the HIV/AIDS epidemic began. In theory that approval should have advanced the cause of birth control. But conservative moralists have opposed wide distribution of condoms for much the same reason they did so during World War I, and for much the same reason they oppose wide distribution of any contraceptives—namely, in their view easy access to any contraceptive not only encourages but signals acceptance of nonmarital, nonreproductive sex. Moreover, condoms have seemed to many sexual conservatives to be one of the most objectionable contraceptives be-

cause they are so nonmedical, so easily procured and carried, so easy to use—
and so difficult to restrict because of their tradition as a male privilege. The
same logic infuses conservative opposition to the distribution of clean needles—namely, that doing so encourages drug use.

When HIV/AIDS seemed a "gay disease," it was easier for sexual conservatives to label it a punishment for, in their words, "the sin of homosexuality."
Opposing condom distribution carried the not-so-subtle message that gays
should be cast out of society, or worse. Some proponents of abstinence-only
approaches disguised their own murderous impulses by broadcasting the failure rate of condoms in order to scare people away from sex. It became politically riskier, however, even among homophobes, to maintain that HIV/AIDS
is deserved punishment once heterosexuals became infected in increasing
numbers—although the fact that many of them were drug users, poor, and
nonwhite made it easier to withhold sympathy.

Sexual conservatives now protest condom distribution more cautiously
because, at least when HIV/AIDS is the issue, they face overwhelming opposition. Even among Americans with conservative views about birth control, a
majority support promoting condoms for protection against disease. But Christian Coalition–type threats have cowed those who should be leading safe-sex
campaigns, and HIV/AIDS remains an issue about which private-sector ex-
ecutives are resisting what the public wants. A majority of Americans favor
placing condom ads on network as well as cable TV, for example.[110] Yet little
progress has been made since the first ads aired in 1996. Such ads are few and
are allowed only in very restricted time slots.[111]

Conclusion

Birth Control and Feminism

Trying to control reproduction has been a human activity from as far back as historians can trace it. Reproduction control efforts constitute part of the evidence that biology has never been destiny, that even those functions most often described as "natural," such as reproduction, have always been formed by cultural and social organizations. In the twentieth century there was rapid, if intermittent, progress in birth control but also some disappointment. Methods became safer and more efficient, and their use became more widespread. But many people have been excluded from this progress. Women continue to suffer, even die, from birth control efforts, especially abortion—casualties that are due more to prohibitions and criminalization than to necessary risks.

Birth control is an area of very uneven development. For example, a majority of births throughout the world remain unplanned and perhaps unintended. But these children are by no means necessarily unwanted; indeed, the equation of desire with planning, the assumption that unplanned means unwanted, is an ahistorical, ideological view of self-determination. The notion of "planned parenthood" is, from a historical perspective, relatively recent, a unique product of twentieth-century industrial civilization, small-family preference, individualism, women's employment, and the high cost of rearing children. The limitation of the population control vision was its failure to understand that birth control motivation is historically constructed. Similar misunderstandings support the continuing perception of the teenage pregnancy problem in the United States as an effect of immorality, pathology, or ignorance, when in fact it too is more deeply a matter of motivation. Yet unplanned pregnancies in the United States, as in India and elsewhere, are often misfortunes that signal resignation to limited futures.

The defects of contraception in advanced countries represent another kind of underdevelopment. This inadequacy is not only a matter of dangerous and uncomfortable methods and of serviceable methods made obsolete but also a lack of access to contraception resulting from poverty, despair, deprivation of opportunity, sexual prudery, and sexual coercion. Moreover, another feature of this uneven development is the expectation that a "magic bullet" is possible—a contraceptive medicine that will have no side effects, require no sexual responsibility, and produce 100 percent protection.

The birth control problem does not stem from an inevitable, tragic march toward an overly high-tech civilization. Rather, the problems are primarily political—which has been the major argument of this book. Access, motivation, and technological development are all shaped by political conflicts and negotiations, sometimes personal, sometimes so far out of individual control that most people are unaware that decisions are being made. In the first chapters of this book I discussed how ancient societies used birth control and how this practice was then constrained or even stopped by religious and other cultural prohibitions. Interconnecting forms of class and male domination privileged large families and women's subordination. Industrialization (and to some extent commercial capitalism before that) subverted many of those traditional agrarian patterns, making large families less advantageous for some, creating an individual wage-labor economy in place of a family economy, and sparking a decline in birth and death rates.

From industrialization arose a new kind of mass politics in which birth control was involved from very early on. In the early nineteenth-century British socialist and trade union movements, birth control was a topic of serious discussion. The reception of birth control as anti–working class by some labor radicals helped stimulate a women's critique of the male socialist vision.[1] In the United States in this period a variety of reform perspectives, many of them quite feminist, spoke positively about the use of birth control. These streams coalesced in the 1870s into the first major political defense of birth control in the United States, voluntary motherhood, which emphasized the dignity of motherhood and women's right to refuse sexual activity. In line with the dominant tendencies in women's rights movements at that time, voluntary motherhood thinking resisted the separation of heterosexual intercourse from reproduction. This position was conditioned in part by feminists' understanding of women's sexual subordination and their sources of social power and in part by the strong conservative opposition to birth control that had succeeded in criminalizing abortion in most states and in categorizing birth control information as obscene.

At the end of the nineteenth century the anti–birth control forces in the United States were ascendant, having created a moral panic about "race suicide" by combining nativism with a backlash against women's rights. Still, in influencing birth control practices, this reaction had but a minor effect as compared to the impact of the second big wave of pro–birth control sentiment in the World War I era. A broad-based feminist, Left, and liberal movement for the legalization of contraception defended the separation of sex from reproduction and supported women's sexual freedom as well as their reproductive self-determination.

In the middle of the twentieth century, contraceptive use grew steadily, and abortion, although illegal, remained a common occurrence. But the social movements pressing for reproductive freedom declined, and professionals—physicians and academics—increasingly became the arbiters of contraceptive use, helping it gain legitimacy. The public meaning of birth control shifted, and by the 1940s and 1950s two new concepts became dominant: family planning, which located birth control's appropriate use exclusively within marriage and defined its purpose as better parenthood (in this respect a return to voluntary motherhood justifications); and population control, which considered birth control primarily a foreign policy tool, directed against third-world poverty but also against radical calls for the redistribution of property.

By the end of the 1960s, overlapping new movements—feminism and anti-imperialism—again transformed the meanings of birth control. They reintroduced, as part of a general campaign for women's equality, the view of birth control as a reproductive right, as a tool for individual (not just family) self-determination and sexual freedom, with an emphasis on women's special need for reproduction control. Rejecting the exclusive emphasis on birth control as promoting better motherhood, the women's liberation movement insisted that motherhood should be only one of many choices for women. The movement envisaged a new kind of nurturant family, based on male/female equality and joint responsibility for child-raising. But this vision was not convincing or reassuring to defenders of traditional gender systems. Moreover, the most influential, mainstream pro–birth control organizations relied primarily on individual rights as the ground for the ethics of birth control and seemed, at least to social conservatives, to be undermining the communitarian and selfless values of family. The abortion conflict not only intensified but spilled over into conflicts about policing pregnant women's behavior, stem cell research, and welfare. In this process the distinction between contraception and abortion lost some of its precision, and it became obvious that the conflict was now about fundamental sex, family, and gender values.

Throughout history, birth control use has increased through two sets of dynamics: the impact on individuals, families, and gender systems of large-scale, structural economic and social changes, which served to lower mortality rates and made rearing children much more expensive; and rapid social and legal transformations resulting from major social movements such as feminism.

Until recently, the anti–birth control political movements were primarily elite causes, such as the nineteenth-century campaign to criminalize abortion and the anti-race-suicide propaganda at the turn of the twentieth century. Since the 1970s, however, the antiabortion effort has become a popular, part populist and part revivalist, movement, supported and funded by elites, to be sure, but also involving many grassroots activists.

In some periods, usually brief and intermittent, birth control has been presented successfully as a value-neutral, technical, or medical aid to whatever family or sexual forms then appear conventional. But more often, birth control has been embedded in ideological, political, and social conflicts. This remains the case today. Attempts to resolve these conflicts through empirical study or "objective" expertise are unlikely to succeed because fundamental value differences remain.

Throughout this book I have tried to show how even this most private act— using a contraceptive—carries historically constructed meanings and ethical implications that are influenced by class relations, racial formations, and gender systems. Other factors that I was not able to discuss fully are relevant as well, including the structures of religion and of care for the disabled. These meanings of birth control also shifted over time and under the influence of social movements—for example, at one historical moment feminists saw contraception as disempowering, while a century later they considered it liberating.

Still, one generalization seems to hold across these shifts: that birth control is inevitably about gender. A stable social consensus about reproductive rights will probably require a new social consensus about gender relations and women's rights. The three political campaigns for reproductive freedom—in the 1870s, the 1910s, and the 1970s and 1980s—coincided with peaks of women's rights agitation. (And opposition to reproduction control was in all cases strongly associated with the defense of traditional gender systems.) There was a fundamental commonality among the contributions of these waves of feminism to birth control, despite the fact that feminism itself has been an evolving, even contradictory, political formation. All three periods were marked by campaigns for sex education and against sexual obscurantism, particularly for women's sexual and reproductive self-knowledge as the basis for their self-control.

Cultural values and even physiological knowledge changed radically from the manuals of the popular health movement of the 1840s to the social purity writers of the 1890s to *Our Bodies, Ourselves* in 1969, but all sought to throw off a blanket of lies and silences about women's psychological and physiological sexuality. All three periods opposed women's sexual repression, although their critique changed: voluntary motherhood advocates sought to free women from enforced sexual submission in marriage (though their secondary theme, that women's capacity for sexual pleasure was being thereby suppressed, was hardly unimportant); the birth controllers of Emma Goldman's and Margaret Sanger's era, in a radical break with the Victorian past, asserted women's right to sexual enjoyment without fear of conception; and the women's liberation movement synthesized the understandings of both previous periods with a simultaneous rejection of women's sexual exploitation, in or out of marriage, and an encouragment to women to discover their own sources of sexual pleasure, both heterosexual and lesbian.

Since the 1870s, feminist groups have used forms of consciousness-raising as a tactic. They encouraged discussions among women that connected personal to political matters, with sex and reproductive choices important among them. The discoveries made possible by consciousness-raising then underlay feminist challenges to standards that had previously seemed apolitical. Feminists uncovered, for example, how conventional forms of dress acted to keep women constricted and decorative, lower their ambition, and, ironically, stunt their sexual development, for the purpose of keeping them eternal objects rather than subjects of desire. Feminists grasped (perhaps counterintuitively) that sexual subjecthood required breaking the exclusive association of the female body with sexuality. Simultaneously, feminists tried to reintegrate sexuality into free human relationships and opposed the commoditization of sex, through criticism of prostitution, demeaning advertisements, and rape, including marital rape. In all periods feminists dared to challenge views of men's sexuality, denying that men's needs were uncontrollable or could serve as excuses for violence or insensitivity.

Feminists also rejected the use of maternalism as a club with which to batter women. They sought to claim for motherhood the respect that it deserves, as a form of skilled, creative, necessary labor, but to dispense with the pedestal that functioned as a prison. As with their sexual ideas, feminists' attitudes toward maternity were naturally influenced by the range of options that women of their class and race could claim at different historical moments. Yet even when feminists most glorified maternity, they argued for it as "an incident"—to use Elizabeth Cady Stanton's phrase—not the whole of women's lives. And even when feminists most angrily rebelled against domesticity, few actually repudiated the heroism and satisfactions of women's love for and devotion to children.

In every historical period, one effect of feminism has been to widen the latitude of socially permissible activity for women. This effect had interconnected consequences for single and married women, childless women and mothers. By supporting the dignity of single and lesbian women, feminism helped married women change the power relations within their marriages (making them, among other things, less fearful of ending marriages).

Feminists did not invent these approaches in a vacuum. They were responding, albeit creatively, to changes far beyond their control. For example, it is not feminism but processes of economic development that have been responsible for bringing so many women into the wage-labor force. In turn, the rise of women's employment was one of the largest single factors contributing to demands for birth control, women's sexual freedom, and women's political rights. Moreover, feminism was fractured and weakened, even in its campaigns for sexual freedom and birth control, by increasingly sharp class and race divisions structured by these larger changes. For example, privileged women benefited from the low wages of domestic servants; and the sexual freedom claimed by bohemian women in the early twentieth century was not a realistic option for the vast majority of women who remained dependent on husbands and marriage. The feminist movement was at various times shaky from resentments between professional women with salaries and working women with wages, between women in the paid labor force and housewives.

Moreover, the story told in this book of the disruption and erosion of Victorian gender, sexual, and reproductive regulation has two sides: one of liberation and another of the reimposition of new forms of social control. Sexual freedom and small families have sometimes become new standards to which individuals are pressured to conform. They are imposed on us through a highly sexualized commercial sphere and the pressure for consumption. Perhaps these new standards will in turn become objects of rebellion. But such rebels should not expect to return us to an earlier set of gender and reproductive relations. Conservative prohibitions and cutbacks in reproduction control services and resources will not be able to shift long-term trends in family and sexual behavior because these are being driven not only by desire but also by the exigencies of survival—that is, women's employment, the high cost of rearing children, and the increased education necessary to survive and prosper in the twentieth-first century. The U.S. Supreme Court may allow state laws against abortion, but the need for abortion is unlikely to decline without an increase in contraceptive quality, access, and education. Abstinence education is unlikely to alter sexual activity significantly unless there is a corresponding development in women's autonomy and confidence and men's egalitarianism.

Each historical campaign for birth control tried to enact a vision of a more democratic society, including not only its gender system but also its class divisions. Each campaign achieved its goals only partially, although each succeeding campaign achieved more than the previous one. Heady with their camaraderie and their new understandings, each group of feminists underestimated the emotional and political grip of the then-dominant sex/gender system and how radical a change their vision appeared to be. This was, in each case, a vision of egalitarian, voluntary family without coercive, permanent marriage as its necessary core; of public responsibility for the general welfare and for equal

opportunity for children; of sexual experiences free of coercion; and of reproduction as a freely chosen human activity. It was foolish to think that such a
program would fail to produce an intense resistance.

But radical as that feminist vision may have been and still is, it was not
utopian; indeed, in the United States parts of that vision are being acted on,
even as inequalities of class and race grow. However distant this vision appears,
reproduction cannot be free of coercion without it. Throughout its history, the
cause of reproduction control has been sometimes more attached to, sometimes more detached from, a feminist vision of family and society. The historical evidence suggests that the cause did better, and individuals did better,
when birth control was sought after as part of an overall movement toward
social equality and women's rights.

Appendix

Selected Recent Scholarship on the History of Reproduction Control

Baxandall, Ros, and Linda Gordon, eds. *Dear Sisters: Dispatches from the Women's Liberation Movement.* New York: Basic Books, 2000.

Brodie, Janet Farrell. *Contraception and Abortion in Nineteenth-Century America.* Ithaca, N.Y.: Cornell University Press, 1994.

Chesler, Ellen. *Woman of Valor: Margaret Sanger and the Birth Control Movement in America.* New York: Simon and Schuster, 1992.

Critchlow, Donald T. *Intended Consequences: Birth Control, Abortion, and the Federal Government in Modern America.* New York: Oxford University Press, 1999.

Ginsburg, Faye. *Contested Lives: The Abortion Debate in an American Community.* Berkeley: University of California Press, 1988.

Grant, Nicole J. *The Selling of Contraception: The Dalkon Shield Case, Sexuality, and Women's Autonomy.* Columbus: Ohio State University Press, 1992.

Joffe, Carole. *The Regulation of Sexuality: Experiences of Family Planning Workers.* Philadelphia: Temple University Press, 1986.

Kaplan, Laura. *The Story of Jane: The Legendary Underground Feminist Abortion Service.* New York: Pantheon, 1995.

Luker, Kristin. *Abortion and the Politics of Motherhood.* Berkeley: University of California Press, 1984.

McCann, Carole R. *Birth Control Politics in the United States, 1916–45.* Ithaca, N.Y.: Cornell University Press, 1994.

Mintz, Morton. *At Any Cost: Corporate Greed, Women, and the Dalkon Shield.* New York: Pantheon, 1985.

Petchesky, Rosalind Pollak. *Abortion and Women's Choice: The State, Sexuality, and Reproductive Freedom.* White Plains, N.Y.: Longman, 1984.

———. "Fetal Images: The Power of Visual Culture in the Politics of Reproduction." *Feminist Studies* 13:2 (Summer 1987): 263–92.

Reagan, Leslie J. *When Abortion Was a Crime: Women, Medicine, and the Law in the United States, 1867–1973.* Berkeley: University of California Press, 1997.

Reed, James. *The Birth Control Movement and American Society: From Private Vice to Public Virtue.* 1978. Rpt., Princeton, N.J.: Princeton University Press, 1983.

Rodrique, Jessie M. "The Black Community and the Birth Control Movement." In *"We Specialize in the Wholly Impossible": A Reader in Black Women's History.* Ed. Darlene Clark Hine, Wilma King, and Linda Reed. Brooklyn, N.Y.: Carlson, 1995. 505–20.

Sobol, Richard B. *Bending the Law: The Story of the Dalkon Shield Bankruptcy.* Chicago: University of Chicago Press, 1991.

Solinger, Rickie, ed. *Abortion Wars: A Half Century of Struggle, 1950–2000.* Berkeley: University of California Press, 1998.

Tone, Andrea. *Devices and Desires: A History of Contraceptives in America.* New York: Hill and Wang, 2001.

Vaughan, Paul. *The Pill on Trial.* New York: Coward-McCann, 1970.

Ward, Martha C. *Poor Women, Powerful Men: America's Great Experiment in Family Planning.* Boulder, Colo.: Westview Press, 1986.

Watkins, Elizabeth Siegel. *On the Pill: A Social History of Oral Contraceptives, 1950–1970.* Baltimore: Johns Hopkins University Press, 1998.

Notes

Preface

1. See the reviews of *Woman's Body, Woman's Right* by Edward Shorter (*Journal of Social History* 11:2 [Fall 1977]: 269–73; and the replies by Sarah Elbert and Sander Kelman, ibid. 12:2 [Fall 1978]), David Kennedy (*Journal of American History* 64 [Dec. 1977]: 823–24), and J. Stanley Lemons (*American Historical Review* 82 [Oct. 1977]: 1095). These were so extreme in their red-baiting and hostility to feminism that an article about them by Elizabeth Fox-Genovese was published in *Signs* 4:4 (Summer 1979): 804–8. See also Harriet B. Presser, "Birth-Control and the Control of Motherhood," *Family Planning Perspectives* 10:6 (Nov.–Dec. 1978): 374–76.

2. A more bizarre example of shifting political connections is the use of a bit of my work by the New Right. In their attack on reproductive rights, Right-to-Lifers have used Margaret Sanger and her socialist feminist commitments as a particular target (illustrating, of course, how quickly they slide from opposition to abortion into opposition to all forms of birth control). Discovering *Woman's Body, Woman's Right,* they discovered also my criticism of Sanger's use of eugenic arguments for birth control and opportunistically condemned abortion as racist, citing my book as their documentation.

Introduction

1. "Feminism" originally referred to a specific tendency and period within the women's rights movement. I use it more generically, however, since there is no other generic, all-encompassing word to describe women's struggles for gender and sexual justice. The definition of "feminist" in this book is: sharing in an impulse to increase the power, equality, and autonomy of women in their families, communities, and/or society.

Chapter 1: The Prehistory of Birth Control

1. By contrast with the typical workplace-home of the seventeenth century, crowded, hectic, and noisy.

2. "Respectable" had originally meant not working with one's hands, which required, among other things, being able to keep servants. Thus, originally working-class people were not "respectable," by definition, in the European usage of the term. In the

United States, and in Europe in the nineteenth century, there emerged a new concept of respectability that included those of the working class who had adopted modern industrial social and moral standards, such as refraining from drunkenness and requiring female virginity until marriage.

3. Carl N. Degler, "What Ought to Be and What Was: Women's Sexuality in the Nineteenth Century," *American Historical Review* 79 (Winter 1974): 1467–90. For other evidence of women's resistance to prudery, see chapter 5.

4. I am, of course, well aware of the Foucauldian argument that Victorian prudery was not so much a silencing of sexual discourse but an alternative discourse. Within this discourse, however, there were elements that were simply and directly repressive, as when law or custom required that certain topics, such as birth control, not be discussed, and I am using "repression" in this narrower sense.

5. Nicola Kay Beisel, *Imperiled Innocents: Anthony Comstock and Family Reproduction in Victorian America* (Princeton, N.J.: Princeton University Press, 1997).

6. In addition to these deliberate birth control methods, all societies have social regulations that affect the birth rate. Late marriages, of course, produce a lower birth rate because there are more years between generations. Prestigious groups that require celibacy—such as monastics—are common in many societies. Preindustrial societies frequently have taboos on sexual intercourse for long periods after childbirth and sometimes even during lactation. There is no proof, however, that such customs are intended to have a population control function; and indeed they are usually described as having other purposes by the people who practice them. For the sake of clarity, therefore, I have omitted them from consideration in this survey, and I consider only methods with conscious birth control purpose.

7. Norman E. Himes, *Medical History of Contraception* (1936; rpt., New York: Gamut Press, 1963); and Linton letter to Himes, quoted in ibid., 52.

8. Thomas R. Malthus, *An Essay on Population* (London: J. M. Dent, 1960–61), 1:141–42; William Graham Sumner, *Folkways* (1906; rpt., New York: New American Library, 1940), 272; Himes, *Medical History of Contraception*, 79.

9. W. E. H. Lecky, *A History of European Morals from Augustus to Charlemagne* (1869; rpt., New York: Appleton, 1877), 2:27.

10. Malthus, *Essay on Population* 1:chaps. 13–14; John J. Noonan Jr., *Contraception: A History of Its Treatment by Catholic Theologians and Canonists* (Cambridge, Mass.: Harvard University Press, 1965), 85–86.

11. Lecky, *History of European Morals*, 2:23; Glanville Williams, *The Sanctity of Life and the Criminal Law* (New York: Knopf, 1957), 16.

12. David Bakan, *The Slaughter of the Innocents* (Boston: Beacon, 1972), 35–36; Edward Westermarck, *The Origin and Development of the Moral Ideas* (London: Macmillan and Co., 1906), 1:411–13.

13. Harry L. Shapiro, "An Anthropologist's View," in *Abortion in a Changing World*, ed. Robert E. Hall (New York: Columbia University Press, 1970), 1:183; Burton Benedict, "Population Regulation in Primitive Societies," in *Population Control*, ed. Anthony Allison (London: Penguin, 1970), 173, 184.

14. I use the term "home-remedy" here to include self-induced abortions and those performed by friends, relatives, and community abortionists or midwives who are not physicians.

15. Paul H. Gebhard, Wardell B. Pomeroy, Clyde E. Martin, and Cornelia V. Christenson, *Pregnancy, Birth, and Abortion* (New York: Harper Brothers, 1958), 193–96.

16. George Devereux, "A Typological Study of Abortion in 350 Primitive, Ancient, and Pre-Industrial Societies," in *Abortion in America,* ed. Harold Rosen (Boston: Beacon, 1967), 129.

17. Himes, *Medical History of Contraception,* 109–10, 116–17, 151. All the information on contraception that follows, unless otherwise indicated, is taken from Himes. His excellent index should help interested readers read more about any of the details mentioned here.

18. Ibid., 138.

19. This anthropologist did not understand women's anatomy and, therefore, the technique of abortion. Clearly the intention was not to puncture but to enter the uterus through the cervix.

20. Herbert Aptekar, *Anjea: Infanticide, Abortion, and Contraception in Savage Society* (New York: William Godwin, 1931), 142–43. This is also described in Devereux, "Typological Study of Abortion," 128.

21. Himes, *Medical History of Contraception,* 179; George Devereux, *A Study of Abortion in Primitive Societies* (New York: Julian Press, 1955), 129.

22. Devereux, *Study of Abortion,* 123–24; Himes, *Medical History of Contraception,* 138.

23. Devereux, *Study of Abortion,* 136–37.

24. See, for example, Marie E. Kopp, *Birth Control in Practice: Analysis of Ten Thousand Case Histories of the Birth Control Clinical Research Bureau* (New York: McBride, 1934), 133; Lella Secor Florence, *Birth Control on Trial* (London: Allen and Unwin, 1930), 91; Raymond Pearl, "Contraception and Fertility in 4,945 Married Women: A Second Report on a Study in Family Limitation," *Human Biology* 6 (1934): 355–401.

25. For example, Nicholas Culpeper, *Complete Herbal* (n.d.; rpt., London: W. Foulsham, n.d.), 39–41.

26. Quoted in Himes, *Medical History of Contraception,* 118.

27. *The United States Practical Receipt Book; or, Complete Book of Reference* (Philadelphia: Lindsay and Blakiston, 1844), 29.

28. Ibid.

29. Marie C. Stopes, "Positive and Negative Control of Conception in Its Various Technical Aspects," *Journal of State Medicine* (London) 39 (1931): 354–60.

30. Kopp, *Birth Control in Practice,* 133.

31. *U.S. Practical Receipt Book,* 87.

32. Aptekar, *Anjea,* 122–26.

Chapter 2: The Criminals

1. See <http://www.census.gov/main/www/cen2000.html>.

2. Daniel Scott Smith, "Family Limitation, Sexual Control, and Domestic Feminism in Victorian America," *Feminist Studies* 1:3–4 (Winter–Spring 1973): 5–6; Smith, "The Demographic History of Colonial New England," in *The American Family in Social Historical Perspective,* ed. Michael Gordon (New York: St. Martin's Press, 1973).

3. Wilson H. Grabill, Clyde V. Kiser, and Pascal K. Whelpton, "Demographic Trends: Marriage, Birth and Death," in *American Family,* ed. Gordon, 3/5.

4. Ibid., 379.

5. Smith, "Family Limitation," 2. Even at the period of the highest numbers of permanent spinsters (1865–75), still 90.4 percent of all women married, and the figure

has never dropped below that. See Wilson H. Grabill, Clyde V. Kiser, and Pascal K. Whelpton, *The Fertility of American Women* (New York: John Wiley, 1958), 46.

6. It bears repeating that "birth control," in this book, means any kind of action taken to prevent having children, including not only abortion and infanticide but also periodic or even sustained sexual abstinence if it is done with that intent. "Contraception," by contrast, refers to specific devices or chemicals or medicines used to prevent conception.

7. Julia Spruill, *Women's Life and Work in the Southern Colonies* (Chapel Hill: University of North Carolina Press, 1938), 323–25.

8. *A Sketch of the Proceedings and Trial of William Hardy, on an Indictment for the Murder of an Infant, November 27, 1806, Mass. Supreme Judicial Court* (Boston: Oliver and Munroe, 1807). Thanks again to Nancy Cott for calling this transcript to my attention.

9. Horatio Robinson Storer, *Why Not?: A Book for Every Woman* (Boston: Lee and Shepard, 1868), 16, 34–35. Also see, for example, *The Police Gazette,* May 28, 1892, for a story typical of its sensationalist reporting: Mary Wertheimer is indicted, along with her two boyfriends, for the death of her three-month-old baby.

10. Thomas Low Nichols, *Human Physiology: The Basis of Sanitary and Social Science* (London: Trübner, 1872), 21–27.

11. *New York Times,* Sept. 4, 1871, p. 8.

12. Storer, *Why Not?,* 67–68; Horatio Robinson Storer, *Criminal Abortion: Its Nature, Its Evidence, and Its Law* (Boston: Little, Brown, 1868), 58; H. S. Pomeroy, *The Ethics of Marriage* (New York: Funk and Wagnalls, 1888), 57.

13. Quoted in Ann Scott, *The Southern Lady: From Pedestal to Politics, 1830–1930* (Chicago: University of Chicago Press, 1970), 38.

14. Thanks to Joanne Preston for showing me this letter from her family collection.

15. Martin Luther Holbrook, *Parturition without Pain: A Code of Directions for Escaping from the Primal Curse* (New York: Wood and Holbrook, 1871), 16.

16. Quoted in Storer, *Criminal Abortion,* 57–58.

17. *New York Times,* Aug. 23, 1871, p. 6.

18. Benjamin Grant Jefferis and J. L. Nichols, *Light on Dark Corners: A Complete Sexual and Science Guide to Purity* (New York, 1894; rpt. in 1919 as *Search Lights on Health*), 138.

19. Cited in Leslie J. Reagan, *When Abortion Was a Crime: Women, Medicine, and Law in the United States, 1867–1973* (Berkeley: University of California Press, 1997), 23.

20. Jefferis and Nichols, *Light on Dark Corners,* 138; A. Lapthorn Smith, "Higher Education of Women and Race Suicide," *Popular Science Monthly,* Mar. 1905, p. 470.

21. Arthur William Meyers, "The Frequency and Cause of Abortion," *American Journal of Obstetrics and Gynecology* 2:2 (Aug. 1921).

22. Cited in Reagan, *When Abortion Was a Crime,* 23. The depressed economy may have increased abortions at this time.

23. Ibid., chap. 2.

24. Cited in ibid., 139.

25. Rachel Benson Gold, *Abortion and Women's Health* (New York: Alan Guttmacher Institute, 1990).

26. "Quickening" is not the same thing as "viability" but referred instead to the mo-

ment at which fetal movements were detected by the pregnant woman, a variable moment anywhere from three to five months of gestation. Classical experts set the time of quickening earlier for male than for female babies, thus in theory giving an advantage to the male population: Aristotle computed it at about forty days after conception for the male, ninety days for the female; Hippocrates put the figures at thirty and forty-two days respectively; the later Roman view was forty and eighty days. How the pregnant woman was to know the sex of her fetus is, however, not explained. The Catholic Church, in accordance with its concerns, identified quickening with the acquisition of a soul, and most Protestant groups went along with that definition. Thus, abortion before quickening was not only not a crime but not even a sin. See Glanville Williams, *The Sanctity of Life and the Criminal Law* (New York: Knopf, 1957), 148–52.

27. Ibid.

28. Reagan, *When Abortion Was a Crime*, 25, 109–10; Cornelia Hughes Dayton, "'Taking the Trade': Abortion and Gender Relations in an Eighteenth-Century New England Village," *William and Mary Quarterly* (3d ser.) 48:1 (1991): 19–49.

29. Quoted in Meade Minnigerode, *The Fabulous Forties* (New York: Putnam, 1924), 101–2.

30. *New York Times,* Aug. 23, 1871, p. 6.

31. For example, Adelaide Hechtlinger, *The Great Patent Medicine Era* (New York: Grosset and Dunlap, 1970), 76, 188.

32. Quoted in Minnigerode, *Fabulous Forties*, 103–4.

33. Quoted by Spruill, *Women's Life and Work*, 325–26.

34. Dr. E. N. Pendleton, "On the Susceptibility of the Caucasian and African Races to the Different Classes of Disease," *Southern Medical Reports* 1 (1849): 338.

35. *Examination of Dr. William Graves before the Lowell Police Court from September 25 to September 29, 1837, for the Murder of Mary Anne Wilson . . .* (n.d., n.p.).

36. Augustus St. Clair, "The Evil of the Age," *New York Times,* Aug. 23, 1871, p. 6.

37. Ibid.

38. Augustus St. Clair, "The Evil of the Age," *New York Times,* Feb. 27, 1872, p. 6.

39. Orson Squire Fowler, *Love and Parentage . . .* (New York: Fowler and Wells, 1844), 69.

40. *New York Times,* May 6, 1871, p. 8.

41. When she began to "see" a rich young man, Augustus Harrison, her sister kicked her out, and she went to live with another working girl, Sadie Traphagan. Later that year Annie moved to the boardinghouse of a Mrs. Collins on 127th Street but was thrown out when discovered to be pregnant (*New York Times,* Nov. 30, 1892, p. 10).

42. *New York Times,* July 28, 1892, p. 2.

43. Pomeroy, *Ethics of Marriage,* 84–85; Emma Frances Angell Drake, *What a Young Wife Ought to Know* (Philadelphia: Vir Publishing, 1901), 130.

44. For example, Mrs. R. B. Gleason, *Talks to My Patients* (New York: Wood and Holbrook, 1870)

45. *Medico-Pharmaceutical Critic and Guide* 9:2 (June 1907): 59–63.

46. Pomeroy, *Ethics of Marriage,* 62–65.

47. William Alcott, *The Physiology of Marriage* (Boston, 1856), 180; Arthur W. Calhoun, *A Social History of the American Family from Colonial Times to the Present* (Cleveland: Arthur H. Clark, 1917–19), 2:157–59, 2:209–10, 3:34–35, 3:238–45; Joseph J. Spengler, "Notes on Abortion, Birth Control, and Medical and Sociological Interpretations of the Decline of the Birth Rate in Nineteenth-Century America," *Marriage*

Hygiene (Bombay), Nov. 1935, pp. 159–60; Richard Shryock, *Medicine in America: Historical Essays* (Baltimore: Johns Hopkins University Press, 1966), 117n.

48. For example, H. B. McKelveen, "The Depopulation of Civilized Nations," American Medical Association, 46th Annual Meeting, May 7–10, 1895; Richard Shryock, "Sylvester Graham and the Popular Health Movement," *Mississippi Valley Historical Review* 18:2 (Sept. 1931): 176n.; George J. Engelmann, "The Increasing Sterility of American Women," *Journal of the American Medical Association* 37 (1901): 890, 1532. For more references, see Spengler, "Notes on Abortion," 166n.

49. Norman E. Himes, *Medical History of Contraception* (1936; rpt., New York: Gamut Press, 1963), 336–37; Marie E. Kopp, *Birth Control in Practice: Analysis of Ten Thousand Case Histories of the Birth Control Clinical Research Bureau* (New York: McBride, 1934), 133.

50. Himes, *Medical History of Contraception,* 335ff.; Kopp, *Birth Control in Practice,* 134.

51. Abbot Kinney, *The Conquest of Death* (New York, 1893), 99; Frederick Hollick, *The Marriage Guide; or, Natural History of Generations: A Private Instructor for Married Persons and Those About to Marry, Both Male and Female* (New York: C. W. Strong, 1860), 336; Augustus Gardner in *The Knickerbocker* 55 (1860): 49; George H. Napheys, *The Physical Life of Woman: Advice to the Maiden, Wife, and Mother,* 5th ed. (Philadelphia: George Maclean, 1870), 97–98; Eliza Barton Lyman, *The Coming Woman; or, The Royal Road to Physical Perfection* (Lansing, Mich.: W. S. George, 1880), 242–46. Lyman wrote that withdrawal would cause hardening of the uterus in women (ibid.).

52. For example, Alice Stockham, *Karezza: Ethics of Marriage* (Chicago: Stockham, 1898); John Humphrey Noyes, *Male Continence* (pamphlet), 2d ed. (Oneida, N.Y.: Office of the American Socialist, 1877).

53. Letter from Mrs. A. B. Saulsbury, Ridgely, Md., May 1917, to Margaret Sanger, in Sanger Papers, Library of Congress.

54. For example, Napheys, *Physical Life of Woman,* 96–97, put ovulation just before menstruation; Mrs. P. B. Saur, *Maternity: A Book for Every Wife and Mother* (Chicago: L. P. Miller, 1891), 151, put it during menstruation.

55. Andrea Tone, *Devices and Desires: A History of Contraceptives in America* (New York: Hill and Wang, 2001), chap. 3; Janet Farrell Brodie, *Contraception and Abortion in Nineteenth-Century America* (Ithaca, N.Y.: Cornell University Press, 1994), chap. 7.

56. Brodie, *Contraception and Abortion,* chap. 7.

57. Ibid., 210; Tone, *Devices and Desires,* 155.

58. Himes, *Medical History of Contraception,* 200–201; Tone, *Devices and Desires,* 193–94.

59. David E. Matteson in *Medical and Surgical Reporter* (Philadelphia) 59 (Dec. 15, 1888): 759; Brodie, *Contraception and Abortion,* 68.

60. Quoted in Minnigerode, *Fabulous Forties,* 103–4.

61. Hollick, *Marriage Guide,* 337–39.

62. D. M. Bennett, *Anthony Comstock: His Career of Cruelty and Crime* (New York: by the author, 1878), 1080.

63. Ibid., 1073–75.

64. Ezra Heywood, *Free Speech: Report of Ezra H. Heywood's Defense before the United States Court, in Boston, April 10, 11, and 12, 1883* (Princeton, Mass.: Cooperative Publishing, 1883), 16.

65. Ibid., 3–6.

66. Ibid., 17.

67. Advertisement from *The Laws of Health* (Wernersville, Pa.), May 1878.

68. "Leucorrhoea" was the term commonly used by nineteenth-century doctors to refer to vaginal discharges of any kind.

69. Bennett, *Anthony Comstock,* 1067.

70. It bears emphasis that this dependence on physicians was largely a matter of perception. Women in preindustrial societies had little difficulty in inventing for themselves various forms of pessaries, suppositories, spermicidal jellies, and so forth. Many women seem to have lost much of that ability and self-confidence by the early nineteenth century.

71. At this time the word "pessary" was used vaguely and could refer to any intravaginal device.

72. Extract from the address of Dr. W. D. Buck, Prest. [*sic*] of the New Hampshire State Medical Society for 1866, in "Varia," *New York Medical Journal* 5 (1867): 464–65.

73. Advertisement in Marie C. Fisher, *Ought Women to Be Punished for Having Too Many Children?* 2d ed. (London: R. Forder, 1890).

74. Notebooks of Josephine Herbst, Beinecke Library, Yale University. I am indebted to Elinor Langer for this reference.

75. Kopp, *Birth Control in Practice,* 133.

76. For example, ibid., 134.

77. *Sexual Hygiene* (Chicago: Clinic Publications, 1902), 186–90, quoted in James Reed, "Robert L. Dickinson and the Committee on Maternal Health," ms., chap. 2, p. 43.

78. John Cowan, *The Science of a New Life* (New York: Cowan, 1874), chap. 3.

79. Augustus Kinsley Gardner, *The Conjugal Relationships as Regards Personal Health and Hereditary Well-being, Practically Treated,* 9th ed. (London, 1923), 100–101.

80. Quoted in D. M. Bennett, *An Open Letter to Samuel Colgate Touching the Conduct of Anthony Comstock and the New York Society for Suppression of Vice* (New York: D. M. Bennett, 1879), 9.

81. "Regular" physicians were those with degrees from established medical schools, as opposed to members of traditional or sectarian schools of healing. Bennett, himself an "irregular" druggist, used this term in a derogatory sense, as he believed that the main distinction of the "regulars" was their arrogance and desire to drive others out of the profession. See chapter 7.

82. Bennett, *Open Letter,* 11.

83. For example, Robert S. and Helen M. Lynd's *Middletown* (New York: Harcourt, Brace, 1929), a study of Muncie, Indiana, in the 1920s, showed that birth control use was universal among the "business class," while fewer than half of working-class people used birth control, and of these fewer than 60 percent used "scientific" methods (123–25).

Chapter 3: Prudent Sex

1. A tendency among historians to oversimplify that controversy has lumped together all Malthus's supporters in one group and all his opponents in another. In reality, a complex set of responses made Malthusianism a tradition open to many different interpretations.

2. Malthus appears in history as doing battle chiefly with the Radicals in large part because his work on population has continued to be controversial. Yet in the first edition of Malthus's *Essay,* then a mere pamphlet, it is clear that the population issue was but one among many points on which Malthus disagreed with Godwin and other advocates of revolutionary utopianism.

3. Thomas Malthus, *An Essay on Population* (pamphlet), 1st ed. (1798; rpt., London: Macmillan, 1926), 95.

4. Thomas Malthus, *An Essay on Population,* 2d ed. (n.p.: n.p., 1803), 531–32.

5. Maurice Dobb, *Studies in the Development of Capitalism* (London: George Routledge and Sons, 1946), 274–75; Kenneth Smith, *The Malthusian Controversy* (London: Routledge and Kegan Paul, 1951), 297. These comments should not be construed to mean that Malthus supported only "official" bourgeois economics. He also, for example, defended the unproductive consumption of the aristocracy.

6. J. R. Poynter, *Society and Pauperism* (London: Routledge and Kegan Paul, 1969), 225–27, 324.

7. Ronald L. Meek, foreword to *Marx and Engels on Malthus* (London: Lawrence and Wishart, 1953).

8. Indeed, in a later edition of his *Essay,* Malthus was forced to acknowledge that deliberate reproductive restraint might be workable. See Gertrude Himmelfarb, "The Specter of Malthus," *Victorian Minds* (New York: Knopf, 1968), 102–5.

9. Thomas Malthus, *Principles of Political Economy* (London, 1836), 254.

10. Karl Marx, *Capital* (New York: Modern Library, n.d.), 1:696n.

11. Neo-Malthusianism itself had two distinct stages. The first, which could be labeled "Radical neo-Malthusianism," was a small propaganda campaign undertaken sporadically between 1820 and 1850 by men also active in other Radical causes, such as trade unionism and workers' education. The second, by far the better known neo-Malthusianism, flourished particularly after the 1870s and, in Britain, established a tradition that continued uninterrupted into modern population control movements. The earlier form of neo-Malthusianism affected American birth control thought, while the latter form had less influence in the United States. (Malthusian economics, of course, has been influential in the United States, but it did not arrive through the mediation of British neo-Malthusianism.) For that reason I examine the early, Radical neo-Malthusian ideas closely, whereas the late nineteenth-century version is beyond the scope of this book. An intelligent popular summary of later British neo-Malthusianism can be found in Peter Fryer, *The Birth Controllers* (London: Secker and Warburg, 1965).

12. Throughout this section my interpretation of Place and the Radical neo-Malthusians is primarily indebted to E. P. Thompson, *The Making of the English Working Class* (London: Victor Gollancz, 1965), esp. chap. 16. See also Norman E. Himes, "Jeremy Bentham and the Genesis of English Neo-Malthusianism," *Economic Journal* (Historical Supplement), Jan. 1936; Himes, "The Place of John Stuart Mill and Robert Owen in the History of English Neo-Malthusianism," *Quarterly Journal of Economics,* Aug. 1928; Himes, introduction to *Illustrations and Proofs of the Principle of Population* by Francis Place (1822; rpt., London: Allen and Unwin, 1930).

In considering why Radical neo-Malthusians rejected the prevalent sexual standards, we find a combination of two historical influences. John Stuart Mill, himself a second-generation Radical and supporter of contraception, criticized Victorian prudery from a principled and philosophical vantage point; a feminist, he understood the connections between sexual repression and the subordination of women. Francis Place, by contrast, a self-educated former artisan, had perhaps never been influenced as deeply by prudish sexual standards. Prudery, a bourgeois invention of the late eighteenth century, did not automatically, immediately, or universally convince the lower classes. European workers and peasants had strong autonomous cultural traditions that made them resistant to Victorian sexual ideology. This is not to suggest that Francis Place was an advocate or practitioner of a hedonistic life. Sexual freedom was not his concern, and he believed in the importance of discipline and sobriety. But he was no prude. He could easily call a thing, even a sexual thing, by its right name, and he did not share in the growing Victorian sensibility that sexual things were shameful. Thus, when neo-Malthusian theory came to his attention, Place wrote a leaflet with plain instructions for inserting a vaginal sponge. Jeremy Bentham, by contrast, also suggesting a contraceptive sponge, disguised his recommendation so that only the already initiated could have guessed his meaning.

13. From Place mss., British Museum, quoted in W. E. S. Thomas, "Francis Place and Working-Class History," *Historical Journal* 5:1 (1962): 62.

14. Ibid., 65.

15. For evidence regarding Place's authorship, see Norman E. Himes, "The Birth Control Handbills of 1823," *Lancet,* Aug. 6, 1927, pp. 313–23.

16. Ibid., 317.

17. Ibid., 316.

18. John Peel, "Birth Control and the British Working-Class Movement," *Bulletin of the Society for the Study of Labor History* 7 (1963): 16. On Cobbett, see Thompson, *Making of the English Working Class,* 620–21.

19. Quoted in Fryer, *Birth Controllers,* 79.

20. Norman E. Himes, "McCulloch's Relation to the Neo-Malthusian Propaganda of His Time: An Episode in the History of English Neo-Malthusianism," *Journal of Political Economy,* Feb. 1929, pp. 77, 75. See also Fryer, *Birth Controllers,* 82.

21. J. A. Banks, *Prosperity and Parenthood* (London: Routledge and Kegan Paul, 1954).

22. For example, *The Free Enquirer,* Oct. 16 and 30, 1830.

23. Ibid., July 22, 1829, and Mar. 5, 1831; William Randall Waterman, *Frances Wright,* Columbia University Studies in History, Economics, and Public Law 115:1 (1924): 158–59.

24. Robert Dale Owen, *Moral Physiology; or, A Brief and Plain Treatise on the Population Question* (New York: Wright and Owen, 1831); Charles Knowlton, *Fruits of Philosophy; or, The Private Companion of Young Married People* (Boston: A. Kneeland, 1833). See also Richard William Leopold, *Robert Dale Owen: A Biography* (Cambridge, Mass.: Harvard University Press, 1940).

25. John Humphrey Noyes, *Male Continence* (pamphlet), 2d ed. (Oneida, N.Y.: Office of the American Socialist, 1877); Raymond Muncy, *Sex and Marriage in Utopian Communities* (Bloomington: Indiana University Press, 1973), 168.

26. The physiological possibility of that practice has, incidentally, been confirmed by Alfred C. Kinsey, Wardell Pomeroy, and Clyde Martin in *Sexual Behavior in the Human Male* (Philadelphia: W. B. Saunders, 1949), 158–69.

27. For example, Alice Stockham, *Karezza: Ethics of Marriage* (Chicago: Stockham, 1898); R. D. Chapman, *Freelove a Law of Nature* (New York: by the author, 1881); Octavius Brooks Frothingham, *Elective Affinity* (New York: D. G. Francis, 1870).

28. Lois Waisbrooker, *From Generation to Regeneration; or, The Plain Guide to Naturalism* (Los Angeles, 1879).

29. Quoted in Margaret Sanger, "Magnetation Method of Birth Control," ms., Sanger Papers, Library of Congress.

30. Owen, *Moral Physiology*, 21–22.

31. Norman E. Himes, "Eugenic Thought in the American Birth Control Movement 100 Years Ago," *Eugenics* 2:5 (May 1929): 3–8.

32. Henry J. Seymour, *The Oneida Community: A Dialogue* (pamphlet; Oneida, N.Y., n.d.).

33. *The Free Enquirer,* Dec. 18, 1830, p. 61.

Chapter 4: Voluntary Motherhood

1. Major writings of the free-love cause include R. D. Chapman, *Freelove a Law of Nature* (New York: by the author, 1881); Tennessee Claflin, *The Ethics of Sexual Equality* (pamphlet; New York: Woodhull and Claflin, 1873); Claflin, *Virtue, What It Is and What It Isn't; Seduction, What It Is and What It Is Not* (New York: Woodhull and Claflin, 1872); Ezra Heywood, *Cupid's Yokes; or, The Binding Forces of Conjugal Life* (Princeton, Mass.: Co-operative Publishing, 1876); Heywood, *Uncivil Liberty: An Essay to Show the Injustice and Impolicy of Ruling Woman without Her Consent* (Princeton, Mass.: Co-operative Publishing, 1872); C. L. James, *The Future Relation of the Sexes* (St. Louis: by the author, 1872); Juliet Severance, *Marriage* (Chicago: M. Harman, 1901); Victoria Claflin Woodhull, *The Scare-Crows of Sexual Slavery* (New York: Woodhull and Claflin, 1874); Woodhull, *A Speech on the Principles of Social Freedom* (New York: Woodhull and Claflin, 1872); Woodhull, *Tried as by Fire; or, The True and the False Socially: An Oration* (pamphlet; New York: Woodhull and Claflin, 1874).

2. Heywood, *Cupid's Yokes*, 20.

3. Claflin, *Ethics of Sexual Equality*, 9–10.

4. *Woodhull and Claflin's Weekly* 1:6 (1870): 5.

5. Heywood, *Cupid's Yokes,* 17–18.

6. Letter to her daughter Alice, 1874, Isabella Beecher Hooker Collection, Harriet Beecher Stowe Center, Hartford, Conn. (hereafter cited as Hooker Collection). Thanks to Ellen DuBois for showing me this letter.

7. Alice Stockham, *Karezza: Ethics of Marriage* (Chicago: Stockham, 1898), 84, 91–92.

8. Diary entry of Sept. 6, 1883, in *Elizabeth Cady Stanton as Revealed in Her Letters, Diary, and Reminiscences,* ed. Theodore Stanton and Harriot Stanton Blatch (New York: Harper and Brothers, 1922), 2:210.

9. For a good summary of the medical literature, see Carroll Smith-Rosenberg and Charles Rosenberg, "The Female Animal: Medical and Biological Views of Woman and Her Role in Nineteenth-Century America," *Journal of American History* 60:2 (Sept. 1973): 332–56.

10. J. J. Rousseau, *Émile* (New York: Columbia University Teachers College, 1967), 132. Rousseau was a chief author of the Victorian revision of the image of woman.

11. Dora Forster, *Sex Radicalism as Seen by an Emancipated Woman of the New Time* (Chicago: M. Harman, 1905), 40.

12. Heywood, *Cupid's Yokes,* 19–20, 16.

13. Ibid., pp. 19–20; *Woodhull and Claflin's Weekly* 1:18 (Sept. 10, 1870): 5.

14. Heywood, *Cupid's Yokes*, 14–15.

15. Stockham, *Karezza*, 82–83, 53.

16. Ibid., 86.

17. Heywood, *Cupid's Yokes*, 19.

18. Charlotte Perkins Gilman, *Women and Economics* (New York: Harper Torchbooks, 1966), 38–39, 42, 43–44, 47–48, 209.

19. Ezra Heywood, *Free Speech: Report of Ezra H. Heywood's Defense before the United States Court in Boston April 10, 11, and 12, 1883* (Princeton, Mass.: Co-operative Publishing, 1883), 16.

20. *New York Tribune*, May 12 and July 20, 1871, quoted in Nelson Manfred Blake, *The Road to Reno: A History of Divorce in the United States* (New York: Macmillan, 1962), 108.

21. Letter of Aug. 29, 1869, Hooker Collection.

22. Elizabeth Cady Stanton mss. no. 11, Library of Congress, n.d. (hereafter cited as Stanton, LC). Thanks to Ellen DuBois for showing this to me.

23. See, for example, *Lucifer the Light-Bearer* (ed. Moses Harman, Valley Falls, Kans., 1894–1907), Oct. 1889, 3 (hereafter cited as *Lucifer*).

24. Woodhull, *Scare-Crows of Sexual Slavery*, 21. Her mention of the YMCA is in reference to the fact that Anthony Comstock, author and chief enforcer for the U.S. Post Office of the anti-obscenity laws, had begun his career in the YMCA.

25. *The Word* (Princeton, Mass.) 20:9 (Mar. 1893): 2–3.

26. See, for example, *The National Purity Congress, Its Papers, Addresses, Portraits: An Illustrated Record of the Papers and Addresses of the First National Purity Congress, Held under the Auspices of the American Purity Alliance . . . Baltimore, October 14, 15, and 16, 1895*, ed. Aaron M. Powell (New York: American Purity Alliance, 1896).

27. *Lucifer*, Apr. 26, 1890, pp. 1–2.

28. Ibid.

29. Ibid., 8–9.

30. *Lucifer*, Sept. 1886, p. 3.

31. Alice Stockham, *Tokology: A Book for Every Woman* (1883; rpt., New York: R. F. Fenno, 1911), 152–53.

32. *The Word* 20 (1892–93).

33. For example, *Lucifer*, Dec. 1889, p. 3, and Oct. 1889, p. 3.

34. *Lucifer*, Dec. 1889, p. 3.

35. Agreeing on voluntary motherhood, free-lovers and conservative moral reformers differed about censorship. The free-lovers and other radicals were united in opposition to the Comstock law. The National Liberal League, for example, formed in 1876 to promote secularism, mounted a petition campaign for repeal of the Comstock law and collected over fifty thousand signatures.

36. Heywood, *Free Speech*, 17.

37. Ibid., 3–6, 16. "Comstockism" is, again, a reference to Anthony Comstock. At this trial, Heywood's second, he was acquitted. At his first trial, in 1877, he had been convicted, sentenced to two years, and served six months; at his third, in 1890, he was sentenced to and served two years at hard labor, an ordeal that probably caused his death a year later.

38. *The Word* 22:9 (Mar. 1893): 2–3.

39. Ibid.

40. For example, Horatio Robinson Storer, *Why Not?: A Book for Every Woman* (Boston: Lee and Shepard, 1868). Note that this was the prize essay in a contest run by the AMA in 1865 for the best antiabortion tract.

41. Claflin, *Ethics of Sexual Equality;* Emanie Sachs, *The Terrible Siren, Victoria Woodhull, 1838–1927* (New York: Harper and Brothers, 1928), 139.

42. Elizabeth Cady Stanton, Susan Anthony, and Matilda Gage, eds., *History of Woman Suffrage* (New York, 1881–1922), 1:597–98.

43. Heywood, *Cupid's Yokes,* 20. See also *American Journal of Eugenics* (ed. M. Harman) 1:2 (Sept. 1907); *Lucifer,* Feb. 15, 1906, June 7, 1906, Mar. 28, 1907, and May 11, 1905.

44. Elizabeth Cady Stanton to Martha Wright, June 19, 1871, Stanton, LC. Thanks again to Ellen DuBois. See also Stanton, *Eight Years After: Reminiscences, 1815–1897* (New York: Schocken, 1971), 262, 297.

45. Stanton and Blatch, *Stanton as Revealed in Her Letters,* 132–33.

46. *Papers and Letters Presented at the First Woman's Congress of the Association for the Advancement of Women . . . October 1873* (New York: Mrs. Wm. Ballard, 1873). The AAW was a conservative group formed in opposition to the Stanton-Anthony tendency. Nevertheless, Chandler, a frequent contributor to free-love journals, spoke here against undesired maternity and the identification of woman with her maternal function.

47. Woodhull, *Tried as by Fire,* 37; Lillian Harman, *The Regeneration of Society* (speech before the Manhattan Liberal Club, Mar. 31, 1898) (pamphlet; Chicago: Light Bearer Library, 1900).

48. *Woodhull and Claflin's Weekly* 1:20 (Oct. 1, 1870): 10.

49. Ibid.

50. Harriot Stanton Blatch, "Voluntary Motherhood," in *Transactions of the National Council of Women, 1891,* ed. Rachel Foster Avery (Philadelphia: J. B. Lippincott, 1891), 280.

51. Rachel Campbell, *The Prodigal Daughter; or, The Price of Virtue* (essay read to the New England Free Love League, 1881) (pamphlet; Grass Valley, Calif., 1885), 3.

52. *Woodhull and Claflin's Weekly* 1:14 (Aug. 13, 1870): 4.

53. Forster, *Sex Radicalism,* 39–40.

54. From an advertisement for *Perfect Motherhood; or, Mabel Raymond's Resolve* (New York: Murray Hill, 1890), in *The Next Revolution; or, Woman's Emancipation from Sex Slavery* (pamphlet; Valley Falls, Kans.: Lucifer Publishing, [1890]), unsigned but probably by Moses Harman.

55. Helen Hamilton Gardener, *Pulpit, Pew, and Cradle* (New York: Truth Seeker Library, 1891), 22.

56. Even the most outspoken of the free-lovers had conventional, gender-differentiated images of sexual relations. For example, Angela Heywood wrote: "Men must not emasculate themselves for the sake of 'virtue,' they must, they will, recognize manliness and the life element of manliness as the fountain source of good manners. Women and girls demand strong, well-bred generative, vitalizing sex ability. Potency, virility, is the grand basic principle of man, and it holds him clean, sweet and elegant, to the delicacy of his counterpart" (*The Word* 14:2 [June 1885]: 3).

57. Woodhull, *Scare-Crows of Sexual Slavery;* Charlotte Perkins Gilman, *Concerning Children* (Boston: Small, Maynard, 1900).

58. See, for example, Blatch, "Voluntary Motherhood," 283–84.

59. *The Word* 20:8 (Feb. 1893): 3.

Chapter 5: Social Purity and Eugenics

1. I owe some of these general views to David Pivar's *Purity Crusade* (Westport, Conn.: Greenwood Press, 1973), but my overall interpretation is based on sources listed in the notes that follow. For the earlier roots of women's social-purity organization, see Carroll Smith-Rosenberg, "Beauty, the Beast, and the Militant Woman: A Case Study in Sex Roles and Social Stress in Jacksonian America," *American Quarterly* 23 (Oct. 1971).

2. The three groups were, of course, not all equally influential. The National Women's Christian Temperance Union was enormous, perhaps the largest women's organization in U.S. history. Free-lovers, by contrast, were a few tiny groups.

3. Clara Cleghorne Hoffman, speech in *Report of the International Council of Women* (Washington, D.C.: National Woman Suffrage Association, 1888), 283–84.

4. Pivar, *Purity Crusade,* 173; Pivar, "The New Abolitionism: The Quest for Social Purity" (Ph.D. diss., University of Pennsylvania, 1965), 127–45.

5. Unlike the free-love movement, where many of the most militant feminists were male.

6. Lady Henry Somerset, "The Unwelcome Child," *Arena* 12:1 (Mar. 1895): 42–49.

7. Belle Mix, *Marital Purity* (pamphlet no. 2) (Chicago: National Purity Association, n.d.), 3.

8. Ibid., 4.

9. Elizabeth Lisle Saxon, speech in *Report of the International Council of Women,* 249–50.

10. Norman E. Himes, "Eugenic Thought in the American Birth Control Movement 100 Years Ago," *Eugenics* 2:5 (May 1929): 3–8.

11. Benjamin Flower, "Wellsprings of Immorality," *Arena* 11:1 (Dec. 1894): 58–59.

12. Moses Harman, *The Right to Be Born Well* (pamphlet; Chicago: M. Harman, 1905).

13. Margaret Deland, "The Change in the Feminine Ideal," *Atlantic Monthly,* Mar. 1910. For other reflections of this idea, see Alice Stockham, "Controlled Parenthood: The Child," *Omega* (n.s.) 7 (Apr. 1899); Kate Austin in *Lucifer the Light-Bearer* (ed. Moses Harman, Valley Falls, Kans., 1894–1907), 23 (hereafter cited as *Lucifer*).

14. Lillian Harman, *Regeneration of Society* (speech before the Manhattan Liberal Club, Mar. 31, 1898) (pamphlet; Chicago: Light Bearer Library, 1900).

15. *Woodhull and Claflin's Weekly* 1:20 (Oct. 1, 1870): 10.

16. Tennessee Claflin, *The Ethics of Sexual Equality* (lecture delivered at the Academy of Music, New York City, Mar. 29, 1872) (pamphlet; New York: Woodhull and Claflin, 1873); Victoria Claflin Woodhull, *Tried as by Fire; or, The True and the False Socially: An Oration* (pamphlet; New York: Woodhull and Claflin, 1874), Moses Hull, *The General Judgment* (Boston: by the author, 1875), 32–33; Harman, *Regeneration of Society.*

17. For example, Mrs. P. B. Saur, *Maternity: A Book for Every Wife and Mother*

(Chicago: L. P. Miller, 1891), 164; Eliza Barton Lyman, *The Coming Woman; or, The Royal Road to Physical Perfection* (Lansing, Mich.: W. S. George, 1880), 207–8.

18. For explicit statements of this belief, see Charlotte Perkins Gilman, *Concerning Children* (Boston: Small, Maynard, 1900), 9–16; Helen Hamilton Gardener, "The Moral Responsibility of Woman in Heredity" (speech to the World Congress of Representative Women, Chicago, 1893), in *Facts and Fictions of Life* (Boston: Arena Publications, 1895)—the whole essay is dedicated to refuting Weissman's theory that acquired characteristics are not transmissible; and Gardener, speech at the National Purity Congress, Baltimore, 1895, in *The National Purity Congress, Its Papers, Addresses, Portraits: An Illustrated Record of the Papers and Addresses of the First National Purity Congress, Held under the Auspices of the American Purity Alliance . . . Baltimore, October 14, 15, and 16, 1895,* ed. Aaron M. Powell (New York: American Purity Alliance, 1896), 101–2.

19. George Napheys, *The Physical Life of Woman: Advice to the Maiden, Wife, and Mother* (Philadelphia: George MacLean, 1870), 75–77.

20. For example, Saur, *Maternity,* 164; Lyman, *Coming Woman,* 206–10; Georgiana B. Kirby, *Transmission; or, Variation of Character through the Mother,* rev. ed. (New York: Fowler and Wells, 1889), 11ff.; James C. Jackson, *How to Beget and Rear Beautiful Children* (Dansville, N.Y.: Sanatorium Publications, 1884); Jas. S. Cooley, "Prevention versus Cure," serialized in *Laws of Health* 1:4 (Aug. 1878).

21. Lyman, *Coming Woman,* 209–10; Alice Stockham, *Tokology: A Book for Every Woman* (New York: Fenno, 1883), 162; John H. Dye, *Painless Childbirth; or, Healthy Mothers and Healthy Children* (Silver Creek, N.Y.: Local Printing House, 1882), 72; Joseph H. Greer, *True Womanhood; or, Woman's Book of Knowledge* (Chicago: Columbia Publications, 1902), 206–7; Somerset, "Unwelcome Child"; Hoffman, speech in *Report of the International Council of Women;* Martin Luther Holbrook, *Stirpiculture; or, The Improvement of Offspring through Wiser Generation* (New York: by the author, 1897), chap. 2; Holbrook, *Marriage and Parentage and the Sanitary and Physiological Laws for the Production of Children of Finer Health and Greater Ability* (New York: M. L. Holbrook, 1882), 153; Holbrook, *Physical, Intellectual, and Moral Advantages of Chastity* (New York and London, 1894); John Harvey Kellogg, *Plain Facts about Sexual Life* (Battle Creek, Mich.: Office of the Health Reformer, 1877), 64–69.

22. Mary Gove Nichols, *Lectures on Anatomy and Physiology* (Boston: Saxon and Pierce, 1844), chap. 1; Nellie Smith, *The Three Gifts of Life: A Girl's Responsibility for Race Progress* (New York: Dodd, Mead, 1913), 98ff.; Benjamin Grant Jefferis and J. L. Nichols, *Light on Dark Corners: A Complete Sexual Science and Guide to Purity . . .* (New York, 1894; rpt. in 1919 as *Search Lights on Health*), 118. The moderation of Jefferis, who wrote that although habitual drunkenness would produce defective children, "a single glass of wine or brandy on the wedding night can have no possible effect on the sperms already formed" (118), was exceptional.

23. Andrew Sinclair, *Prohibition: Era of Excess* (Boston: Little, Brown, 1962), 47–49.

24. See, for example, Frances Willard, speech in *Report of the International Council of Women,* 111.

25. For example, Horatio Storer, *Why Not?: A Book for Every Woman* (Boston: Lee and Shepard, 1868).

26. For example, Augustus K. Gardner, *Conjugal Sins* (New York: J. S. Redfield, 1870).

27. Lois Waisbrooker, letter to the editor in *Lucifer,* Mar. 27, 1890.

28. Hoffman, speech in *Report of the International Council of Women,* 283–84.

29. Waisbrooker, letter to the editor in *Lucifer,* Mar. 27, 1890. Others who explained that sex during pregnancy would cause defective children include Lucinda Chandler, "Marriage Reform," speech in *Report of the International Council of Women,* 284–85; Stockham, *Tokology,* 150; Dye, *Painless Childbirth,* 72; Greer, *True Womanhood,* 206–7. Still others merely cautioned generally that sexual excess at any time would lead to defective offspring—see, for example, Holbrook, *Advantages of Chastity;* J. B. Caldwell (editor of *Christian Life*), in *Familyculture* 1:7 (Sept. 1896); Eliza Bisbee Duffey, *The Relations of the Sexes* (New York: Estill and Co., 1876).

30. Quoted in Greer, *True Womanhood,* 182–83.

31. Duffey, *Relations of the Sexes,* 214–15.

32. Elizabeth Blackwell, letter to the Brussels International Congress against the State Regulation of Vice, probably 1888, in Blackwell mss., Schlesinger Library, Radcliffe. See also Duffey, *Relations of the Sexes,* 203–7.

33. For example, Ezra Heywood, *Cupid's Yokes; or, The Binding Forces of Conjugal Life* (Princeton, Mass.: Cooperative Publishing, 1876).

34. Blackwell, letter to the Brussels International Congress.

35. For example, Charlotte Perkins Gilman, *The Man-made World; or, Our Androcentric Culture* (New York: Charlton, 1911); Clifford H. Scott, "Naturalistic Rationale for Women's Reform: Lester Frank Ward on the Evolution of Sexual Relations," *The Historian,* Nov. 1970.

36. Charlotte Perkins Gilman, "How to Make Better Men," ms., n.d. [probably 1890s], in Gilman mss., folder 179, Schlesinger Library, Radcliffe; Gilman, *Man-made World,* 29–31; Gilman, *His Religion and Hers* (New York: Century, 1923), 88–91; Gilman, "Sex and Race Progress," in *Sex in Civilization,* ed. V. F. Calverton and Samuel Schmalhausen (New York: Macaulay, 1929), 112; editorial in *The Humanitarian* (ed. Victoria Claflin Woodhull and Tennessee Claflin) 6 (1892): 88; Helen Hamilton Gardener, introduction to *A Thoughtless Yes,* 9th ed. (Boston: Arena Publications, 1890).

37. For example, Dr. Rosalie Slaughter Morton of the American Society for Sanitary and Moral Prophylaxis, in *History of Woman Suffrage,* ed. Stanton et al., 5:224–25; Rev. Mary Traffern Whitney, speech at the National Purity Congress, in *Papers, Addresses, Portraits,* ed. Powell, 107; Stockham, *Tokology,* 154–55; Rachel Campbell, *The Prodigal Daughter; or, The Price of Virtue* (essay read to the New England Free Love League, 1881) (pamphlet; Grass Valley, California, 1885), 10.

38. Lester Frank Ward, *Dynamic Sociology* (New York: Appleton, 1883), 1:633.

39. Gardener, "Moral Responsibility of Woman," 163.

40. Gardener, speech in *Papers, Addresses, Portraits,* ed. Powell, 104.

41. Whitney, speech in *Papers, Addresses, Portraits,* ed. Powell, 107.

42. Harriot Stanton Blatch, "Voluntary Motherhood," in *Transactions of the National Council of Women, 1891,* ed. Rachel Foster Avery (Philadelphia: J. B. Lippincott, 1891), 282–83. See also Susan Anthony, "Social Purity" (speech of 1875), in *Life and Work of Susan Anthony,* ed. Ida Husted Harper (Indianapolis, 1898), 2:1004–12.

43. From *The Next Revolution; or, Woman's Emancipation from Sex Slavery* (pamphlet; Valley Falls, Kans.: Lucifer Publishing, [1890]), 24, unsigned but probably by Moses Harman.

44. Moses Harman, "Our Drift towards Imperialism," *American Journal of Eugenics* 2 (Fall 1908): 8–9.

45. Harman, *Regeneration of Society*.

46. Blatch, "Voluntary Motherhood," 282–83.

47. For one clear exposition of sentimental crypto-feminism, see Gail Parker's introduction to *The Oven Birds* (New York: Doubleday Anchor, 1972).

48. The rare rejections of this view, such as the free-lover Mary Florence Johnson's recommendations that men as well as women should work in day-care centers (*Lucifer*, Nov. 8, 1906), merely emphasize by their scarcity how universal the view was.

49. For example, Julia Ward Howe, speech to the Association for the Advancement of Women, 1896, in *Julia Ward Howe and the Woman Suffrage Movement*, ed. Florence Ward Howe Hall (Boston: Dana Estes, 1913).

50. Gilman, *Concerning Children*, 261–65.

51. Willard, speech in *Report of the International Council of Women*, 47–48. See also Alice Stockham, *Karezza: Ethics of Marriage* (Chicago: Stockham, 1898), 49ff.; Julia Ward Howe, "The Future of American Women," undated speech in *Julia Ward Howe*, ed. Hall, 185–86.

52. Gilman, "Sex and Race Progress," 111–12; Gilman, "Prize Children," *The Forerunner* 2:7 (July 1911). See also Helen Gardener, speech in *Papers, Addresses, Portraits*, ed. Powell.

53. Helen Gardener, *Pulpit, Pew, and Cradle* (New York: Truth Seeker Library, 1891), 2.

54. Frederick Hinckley, *The New Life: Supposed Thoughts of a Young Mare* (pamphlet no. 3) (Chicago: National Purity Association, n.d. [probably 1897]), p. 8.

55. Gardener, introduction to *A Thoughtless Yes*, vii–viii. See also Gardener, "Moral Responsibility of Woman," 161–63.

56. Duffey, *Relations of the Sexes*, chap. 5.

57. Eliza Bisbee Duffey, *What Women Should Know . . .* (Philadelphia, 1873), 317. See similar ideas in Gardener, "Moral Responsibility of Woman," 161.

58. Gardener, *Pulpit, Pew, and Cradle*, 2–21; Saxon, speech in *Report of the International Council of Women*, 249–50; Willard, speech in ibid., 47–48.

59. *A Message to Girls* (pamphlet no. 2) (Chicago: National Purity Association, n.d.); Saxon, speech in *Report of the International Council of Women;* Chandler, "Marriage Reform"; Whitney, speech in *Papers, Addresses, Portraits*, ed. Powell; Frances Willard, in *Family Culture* 1 (June 1896): 4; Greer, *True Womanhood*, chap. 1; Ellen Martin Henrotin, "Psychology of Prostitution," ms., n.d., p. 8, Henrotin mss., Schlesinger Library, Radcliffe.

60. Duffey, *What Women Should Know . . .*, 316; Elizabeth Boynton Harbert (vice-president of NWSA for Illinois), speech in *Report of the International Council of Women*, 247.

61. For example, Julia Ward Howe Scrapbook, 5:117, Howe mss., Schlesinger Library, Radcliffe.

62. Anna Garlin Spencer, reply to E. A. Ross, "Western Civilization and the Birthrate," in *American Journal of Sociology* 12:5 (Mar. 1907): 622–23.

63. Elizabeth Blackwell, introduction to a pamphlet by Francis William Newman (London: Moral Reform Union, 1889), in Blackwell mss.

64. "Penelope" [Moses Harman], "The Woman Question, Number VI," in *Next Revolution*, 29–30.

65. Moses Harman, in *Lucifer*, May 11, 1905.

Chapter 6: Race Suicide

1. Theodore Roosevelt, *Presidential Addresses and State Papers* (New York: Review of Reviews, 1910), 3:282–91.

2. See a compendium of journalistic expressions of these fears in Arthur W. Calhoun, *A Social History of the American Family from Colonial Tames to the Present*, vol. 3 (Cleveland: Arthur H. Clark, 1919), chap. 11.

3. Nathan Allen, "The New England Family," *The New Englander* 145 (Mar. 1882): 147.

4. Abbot Kinney, *The Conquest of Death* (New York, 1893), v.

5. For example, James Foster Scott, *The Sexual Instinct: Its Use and Dangers as Affecting Heredity and Morals* (New York: E. B. Treat, 1899); Joseph Spengler, "Notes on Abortion, Birth Control, and Medical and Sociological Interpretations of the Decline of the Birth Rate in Nineteenth-Century America," in *Marriage Hygiene* (Bombay), Nov. 1935; William Goodell, "The Dangers and the Duty of the Hour," *Transactions of the Medical and Chirurgical Faculty of the State of Maryland*, 83d Annual Session, Apr. 1881, pp. 71–87; John P. Reynolds, "The Limiting of Child-bearing among the Married," *Transactions of the American Gynecological Society*, Sept. 1890.

6. Francis A. Walker, "Immigration and Degradation," *Forum* 11:6 (Aug. 1891): 634–44.

7. Robert Hunter, *Poverty*, ed. Peter d'A. Jones (1904; rpt., New York: Harper Torchbooks, 1965), 305, 310–11.

8. Edward A. Ross, "Western Civilization and the Birth-rate," *American Journal of Sociology* 12:5 (Mar. 1907): 616. For other references, see Calhoun, *Social History of the American Family*.

9. Edward M. East, *Mankind at the Crossroads* (1923; rpt., New York: Scribners, 1928), 297.

10. Mark Haller, *Eugenics: Hereditarian Attitudes in American Thought* (New Brunswick, N.J.: Rutgers University Press, 1963), 79.

11. Charles Franklin Emerick, "College Women and Race Suicide," *Political Science Quarterly*, June 1909, p. 270.

12. "An Alumna," "Alumna's Children," *Popular Science Monthly*, May 1904, pp. 45–46. The use of pseudonyms was frequent in this controversy and suggests women's fear of being seen to support "race suicide."

13. Quoted in David Kennedy, *Birth Control in America* (New Haven, Conn.: Yale University Press, 1970), 44.

14. U. G. Weatherly, "How Does the Access of Women to Industrial Occupations React on the Family?," *American Journal of Sociology* 14:6 (May 1909): 740–52; George J. Engelmann, "Education Not the Cause of Race Decline [Rather False Ambition Is]," *Popular Science Monthly*, June 1903; Frederick A. Bushee, "The Declining Birth Rate and Its Cause [Women's Employment]," *Popular Science Monthly*, Aug. 1903; Henry T. Finck, "Are Womanly Women Doomed?," *Independent*, Jan. 31, 1901, pp. 267–71; and Finck, "The Evolution of Sex in Mind," *Independent*, Dec. 26, 1901, pp. 3059–64.

15. Arthur Macdonald, "Susceptibility to Disease and Physical Development in College Women," *Philadelphia Medical Journal*, Apr. 20, 1901, p. 4; A. Lapthorn Smith, "Higher Education of Women and Race Suicide," *Popular Science Monthly*, Mar. 1905, pp. 466–73; Edward L. Thorndike, "The Decrease in the Size of American Families," *Popular Science Monthly*, May 1903, pp. 64–70.

16. Engelmann, "Education Not the Cause of Race Decline."

17. Theodore Roosevelt, introduction to *The Woman Who Toils,* by Mrs. John Van Vorst and Marie Van Vorst (New York: Doubleday, Page, 1903), vii.

18. Kinney, *Conquest of Death,* 13.

19. I am indebted for this perception to a fascinating article about race suicide in Australia (for it was indeed an international controversy), Rosemary Pringle's "Octavius Beale and the Ideology of the Birth-Rate: The Royal Commissions of 1904 and 1905," *Refractory Girl* (Sydney), Winter 1973, p. 24.

20. Theodore Roosevelt, "The Greatest American Problem," *The Delineator,* June 1907, pp. 966–67.

21. Theodore Roosevelt "Race Decadence," *Outlook,* Sept. 13, 1927, p. 111; and Roosevelt, "Birth Reform, from the Positive Not the Negative Side," in *The Works of Theodore Roosevelt,* National Edition, 20 vols. (New York: Charles Scribner's Sons, 1926), 19:156, 158.

22. William S. Rossiter, "The Pressure of Population," *Atlantic Monthly,* Dec. 1911, p. 840.

23. Quoted in Henry F. Pringle, *Theodore Roosevelt* (New York: Harcourt, Brace, 1913), 470.

24. Ibid., 470–71.

25. From a letter to Cecil Arthur Spring Rice, in *The Letters of Theodore Roosevelt,* ed. Elting Morison (Cambridge, Mass.: Harvard University Press, 1951–54), 13:620–21; and in Stephen Gwynn, ed., *The Letters and Friendships of Sir Cecil Spring Rice* (Boston: Houghton Mifflin, 1929), 1:293. I am indebted to Donald K. Pickens, *Eugenics and the Progressives* (Nashville, Tenn.: Vanderbilt University Press, 1968), 124, for this reference.

26. Quoted in Pringle, *Theodore Roosevelt,* 471.

27. *A Compilation of the Messages and Speeches of Theodore Roosevelt, 1901–1905,* ed. Alfred Henry Lewis, in *Supplement to Messages and Papers of the Presidents* (Washington, D.C.: Bureau of National Literature and Art, 1906), 548.

28. Roosevelt, "Race Decadence," 764–67.

29. *Compilation of Messages and Speeches of Roosevelt,* 548, 576–81.

30. Aileen Kraditor, *Ideas of the Woman Suffrage Movement* (New York: Columbia University Press, 1965), chap. 3.

31. McCulloch papers, Dillon mss., Schlesinger Library, Radcliffe.

32. For a good summary of birth rates and family sizes, see Wilson H. Grabill, Clyde V. Kiser, and Pascal K. Whelpton, "Demographic Trends: Marriages, Birth, and Death," in *The American Family in Social-Historical Perspective,* ed. Michael Gordon (New York: St. Martin's Press, 1973).

33. Julia Ward Howe, "Does the Big Decrease in the Birth Rate of Mass. Mean Race Suicide?," *Boston American,* Sept. 3, 1905, in Howe Scrapbook, 5:117, Howe mss., Schlesinger Library, Radcliffe.

34. Howe Scrapbook, 4, Howe mss.

35. Ida Husted Harper, "Small vs. Large Families," *Independent,* Dec. 26, 1901, pp. 3155–59.

36. Elsie Clews Parsons, "Penalizing Marriage and Children," *Independent,* Jan. 18, 1906, pp. 146–47.

37. Elsie Clews Parsons, *The Family* (New York: Putnam, 1906), 351. See also Lydia K. Commander, *The American Idea* (New York: A. S. Barnes, 1907); Commander,

"Has the Small Family Become an American Ideal?," *Independent*, Apr. 14, 1904, pp. 836–40; and "Why Do Americans Prefer Small Families?," *Independent*, Oct. 13, 1904, pp. 847–50.

38. Harper, "Small vs. Large Families."

39. For example, Anna Howard Shaw, address to National Suffrage Convention, Portland, Oreg., June 29, 1905, in *Woman's Journal*, July 15 and 22, 1905; Lady Florence Dixie, *President Roosevelt's Gospel of Doom* (pamphlet), reprinted from *Weekly Times* and *Echo* (London), Apr. 18, 1903.

40. Martha Bensley, "Are Large Families Useless?," *Harper's Weekly*, Apr. 15, 1905, pp. 534–36.

41. "An Alumna," "Alumna's Children."

42. For example, Helen La Reine Baker, in *National Woman's Daily* (St. Louis), Dec. 29, 1909; Helen Campbell, in "Why Race Suicide with Advancing Civilization?: A Symposium," *Arena* 41 (Feb. 1909): 192–94.

43. Ida Husted Harper, in *New York Sun*, Feb. 22, 1903, quoted in Kraditor, *Ideas of the Woman Suffrage Movement,* 117–18.

44. Discussed in Kraditor, *Ideas of the Woman Suffrage Movement.*

45. For example, Peter E. Burrowes, "Woman and Her Masters," *The Comrade* 3:8 (May 1904): 173; Jonathan Mayo Crane, in *Lucifer the Light-Bearer* (ed. Moses Harman, Valley Falls, Kans., 1894–1907), Mar. 28, 1907 (hereafter cited as *Lucifer*). If this argument failed to take into account that the race-suicide theory concerned a declining birth rate among the upper classes specifically, its authors can hardly be blamed, since the phrase "race suicide" was used in the popular media in many different ways, often as a slander on any form of birth limitation.

46. Susan B. Anthony, "Reply to President Roosevelt's Race Suicide Theory," *Socialist Woman* 2:16 (Sept. 1908): 6.

47. Charlotte Perkins Gilman, "Men's Babies," Gilman mss., Schlesinger Library, Radliffe. The paper is undated but probably written somewhat later, in consciousness of the Great War.

48. Quoted from a letter shown to me by Ellen DuBois, in her possession.

49. Ellen Key, "Motherliness," *Atlantic Monthly* 110 (Oct. 1912): 562–70.

50. Moses Harman, *Love in Freedom* (Chicago: Light Bearer Library, 1900), 42.

51. George Noyes Miller, *The Strike of a Sex* (London: W. H. Reynolds, 1891), 61–63.

52. Harper, "Small vs. Large Families."

53. "A Childless Wife," "Why I Have No Family," *Independent*, Mar. 23, 1905, pp. 654–59. However strongly this woman felt, she nevertheless voiced her opinion anonymously; indeed, I have found no signed articles that discuss the issue from a personal standpoint.

54. Miscellaneous letters to the *Independent* in response to "Why I Have No Family"—for example, in the issue of Apr. 13, 1905.

55. Ida Husted Harper, "Women Ought to Work," *Independent*, May 16, 1901, pp. 1123–27.

56. Kate O'Hare, *The Sorrows of Cupid* (St. Louis: National Rip-Saw Publications, 1912), chap. 13.

57. This view is corroborated by Mari Jo Buhle in "Women in the Socialist Party" (Ph.D. diss., University of Wisconsin, 1974).

58. *Universal Suffrage: Female Suffrage,* "by a Republican, (not a "Radical")" (Phil-

adelphia: J. B. Lippincott, 1867), 103–4. I am indebted to Ellen DuBois for this reference.

59. Catherine Beecher, *Woman Suffrage and Woman's Profession* (Boston, 1871), 3–4. Beecher's phrase "the family state" is perhaps significant in view of the later analysis by professional sociologists, a constant refrain in Roosevelt's speeches, that the family was a microcosm of the state and its logical and necessary training ground.

60. Daniel Scott Smith, "Family Limitation, Sexual Control, and Domestic Feminism in Victorian America," *Feminist Studies* 1:3–4 (Winter–Spring 1973–74).

61. Commander, "Why Do Americans Prefer Small Families?"; Harper, "Women Ought to Work"; Commander, *American Idea;* "Paterfamilias," "Race Suicide and Common Sense," *North American Review* 176:6 (June 1903): 892–900; "A Childless Wife," "Why I Have No Family"; "One of Them," "A Woman's Reason," *Independent*, Apr. 4, 1907, pp. 780–84; Howe, "Big Decrease in the Birth Rate"; John S. Billings, "The Diminishing Birth Rate in the United States," *Forum* 15:6 (June 1893): 467–77; Rev. John Holmes, "Why Race-Suicide with Advancing Civilization?," *Arena* 41:230 (Feb. 1909): 189–96; Ross, "Western Civilization and the Birth-rate"; I. M. Rubinow, reply to Ross, *American Journal of Sociology* 12:5 (Mar. 1907): 629.

62. Commander, "Why Do Americans Prefer Small Families?"

63. Ibid.; "One of Them," "A Woman's Reason."

64. Joseph Ambrose Banks and Olive Banks, *Feminism and Family Planning in Victorian England* (Liverpool: Liverpool University Press, 1964); Joseph Ambrose Banks, *Prosperity and Parenthood: A Study of Family Planning among the Victorian Middle Classes* (London: Routledge and Kegan Paul, 1954).

65. Robert Wiebe, *The Search for Order, 1877–1920* (New York: Hill and Wang, 1967), chaps. 5–6.

66. Emerick, "College Women and Race Suicide," 278–80.

67. Wiebe, *Search for Order,* chaps. 5–6.

68. Emerick, "College Women and Race Suicide," 281.

69. "Paterfamilias," "Race Suicide and Common Sense," 897–99.

70. *World's Work*, Sept. 1908, pp. 10639–40.

71. *Harper's Weekly*, Feb. 28, 1903, p. 349.

72. *Harper's Weekley,* June 6, 1903, p. 952.

73. Smith, "Family Limitation."

74. Charles Franklin Emerick, "Is the Diminishing Birth Rate Volitional?," *Popular Science Monthly,* Jan. 1911, pp. 71–80; Commander, *American Idea,* chap. 4.

75. For example, Rubinow, reply to Ross, 629.

76. For example, Billings, "Diminishing Birth-Rate."

77. Reported in Otey M. Scruggs, "The Economic and Racial Components of Jim Crow," in *Key Issues in the Afro-American Experience,* ed. Nathan Huggins et al. (New York: Harcourt Brace Jovanovich, 1971), 2:80–81. I am grateful to Judith Stein for this reference. See also Billings, "Diminishing Birth-Rate."

78. Grabill et al., "Demographic Trends," 386; Billings, "Diminishing Birth-Rate."

79. Spengler, "Notes on Abortion."

80. Roland Pressat, *Population* (Baltimore: Penguin, 1971), 73–74; Joseph Spengler, *The Fecundity of Native and Foreign-Born Women in New England,* Brookings Institution Pamphlet Series 2:1 (Washington, D.C., [1930]).

81. Scott Nearing, "Race Suicide vs. Overpopulation," *Popular Science Monthly,* Jan. 1911, pp. 81–83.

82. Joseph Lorren, in "Why Race-Suicide with Advancing Civilization?: A Symposium," *Arena* 41 (Feb. 1909): 194–95. Joseph Lorren was probably a pseudonym for Louis Brandeis.

83. Pearce Kintzing, letter to the *Philadelphia Medical Journal,* reprinted in *Current Literature* 35:2 (Aug. 1903): 219–20.

84. Goodell, "Dangers and the Duty of the Hour."

85. *Medico-Pharmaceutical Critics' Guide* 9:2 (June 1907): 71.

Chapter 7: Continence or Indulgence

1. G. L. Austin, *Perils of American Women; or, A Doctor's Talk with Maiden, Wife, and Mother* (Boston: Lee and Shepard, 1883); [David Goodman Croly], *The Truth about Love* (New York: David Wesley, 1872); P. C. Dunne and A. F. Derbois, *The Young Married Lady's Private Medical Guide,* 4th ed. (Boston: F. H. Doane, 1854); O. E. Herrick, "Abortion and Its Lessons," *Michigan Medical News,* Jan. 10, 1882.

2. Norman E. Himes, *Medical History of Contraception* (1936; rpt., New York: Gamut Press, 1963), 282.

3. Carroll Smith-Rosenberg and Charles Rosenberg, "The Female Animal: Medical and Biological Views of Woman and Her Role in Nineteenth-Century America," *Journal of American History* 60:2 (Sept. 1973): 332–56; Smith-Rosenberg, "The Hysterical Woman: Sex Roles and Role Conflict in 19th-Century America," *Social Research,* Winter 1972; Barbara Ehrenreich and Deirdre English, *Witches, Midwives, and Nurses* (New York: Feminist Press, 1973); Ehrenreich and English, *Female Disorders: Sick and Sickening Women in the 19th Century* (New York: Feminist Press, 1973); Ann Douglas Wood, "The Fashionable Diseases: Women's Complaints and Their Treatment in Nineteenth-Century America," *Journal of Interdisciplinary History,* Summer 1973.

4. H. S. Pomeroy, *The Ethics of Marriage* (New York: Funk and Wagnalls, 1888), 62.

5. For example, Abbot Kinney, *The Conquest of Death* (New York, 1893); Horatio Robinson Storer, *Is It I?: A Book for Every Woman* (Boston: Lee and Shepard, 1867); John Todd, *Serpents in the Doves' Nest* (Boston: Lee and Shepard, 1867).

6. Eliza Barton Lyman, *The Coming Woman; or, The Royal Road to Physical Perfection* (Lansing, Mich.: W. S. George, 1880), 242–46. Others who gave such warnings included Horatio Robinson Storer, *Criminal Abortion: Its Nature, Its Evidence, and Its Law* (Boston: Little, Brown, 1868); Webb J. Kelly, "One of the Abuses of Carbolic Acid," *Columbus Medical Journal,* 1883, pp. 433–36; Augustus Kinsley Gardner, *The Conjugal Relationships as Regards Personal Health and Hereditary Well-Being, Practically Treated* (Glasgow: Thomas D. Morison, 1905), 84–109 passim; Frederick J. McCann, "Birth Control (Contraception)," *The Medical Press,* 1926, p. 359. For the same pattern among European doctors, see Alex Comfort, *The Anxiety Makers* (London: Nelson, 1967).

7. Edward J. Ill, "The Rights of the Unborn: The Prevention of Conception," *American Journal of Obstetrics and Diseases of Women and Children,* 1899, pp. 577–84.

8. For example, Kinney, *Conquest of Death.*

9. Ill, "Rights of the Unborn."

10. Thomas E. McArdle, "The Physical Evils Arising from the Prevention of Conception," *American Journal of Obstetrics and Diseases of Women and Children,* 1888, pp. 934–39.

11. Kinney, *Conquest of Death,* 93–94.

12. Ibid., 22. See also Irenaeus P. Davis, *Hygiene for Girls* (New York, 1883).

13. For example, Kinney, *Conquest of Death*, 27, 65ff.

14. Joseph F. Kett, *The Formation of the American Medical Profession: The Role of Institutions, 1780–1860* (New Haven, Conn.: Yale University Press, 1968); Richard Harrison Shryock, *Medicine and Society in America, 1661–1860* (New York: New York University Press, 1960), 143–51.

15. For corroboration of this interpretation, see Richard Harrison Shryock, *Medicine in America: Historical Essays* (Baltimore: Johns Hopkins University Press, 1966), chap. 5.

16. Kett, *Formation of the American Medical Profession*, 108.

17. Shryock, *Medicine in America*, 116; Kett, *Formation of the American Medical Profession*, 117ff.

18. Reported in Kett, *Formation of the American Medical Profession*, 117.

19. Quoted in ibid., 121.

20. Ibid., 119.

21. A. M. Mauriceau, *The Married Woman's Private Medical Companion* (New York, 1847), iii.

22. *New York Times*, Aug. 23, 1871, p. 6.

23. Himes, *Medical History of Contraception*, 262–63.

24. Ibid., 263.

25. Frederick Hollick, *The Marriage Guide; or, Natural History of Generation: A Private Instructor for Married Persons and Those about to Marry, Both Male and Female* (New York: C. W. Strong, 1860), 4.

26. Ibid., 336–39.

27. Ibid., 215–18.

28. Edward Bliss Foote, *Medical Common Sense* (Philadelphia: Duane, 1859).

29. Edward Bliss Foote, *A Step Backward* (New York: Murray Hill, 1875), 7.

30. Ibid., 5.

31. Quoted in Adelaide Hechtlinger, *The Great Patent Medicine Era; or, Without Benefit of Doctor* (New York: Grosset and Dunlap, 1970), 108.

32. Foote, *Step Backward*, 13.

33. Edward Bond Foote, *The Radical Remedy in Social Science; or, Borning Better Babies through Regulating Reproduction by Controlling Conception* (New York: Murray Hill, 1886), 59–60.

34. Himes thought it was a rubber cervical cap (*Medical History of Contraception*, 279).

35. Quoted in Hechtlinger, *Great Patent Medicine Era*, 110–11.

36. D. R. M. Bennett, *Anthony Comstock: His Career of Cruelty and Crime* (New York: by the author, 1878), 1036ff.

37. *Medico-Pharmaceutical Critic and Guide* 8:5 (May 1906).

38. *Medico-Pharmaceutical Critic and Guide* 11:10 (Oct. 1908): 355–56.

39. Robert L. Dickinson, "Marital Maladjustment: The Business of Preventive Gynecology," *Long Island Medical Journal* 2 (1908): 1–5.

40. John Foster Scott, *The Sexual Instinct* (New York: E. B. Treat, 1899), 34. For this general interpretation, see also Smith-Rosenberg and Rosenberg, "Female Animal."

41. This phenomenon was noticed by Ian Watt in *The Rise of the Novel* and discussed by Nancy Cott in an unpublished paper, which she graciously shared with me.

42. Gardner, *Conjugal Relationships*, 107.

43. Comfort, *Anxiety Makers*, chap. 5.

44. See, for example, Adelyne More, *Uncontrolled Breeding* (New York: Critic and Guide, 1917), 87–88, 98; Max Hodann, *History of Modern Morals*, trans. Stella Browne (London: William Heinemann, 1937).

45. *Journal of the American Medical Association* 58:23 (June 8, 1942).

46. *Medico-Pharmaceutical Critic and Guide* 3:6 (June 1904): 189.

47. *Medico-Pharmaceutical Critic and Guide* 5:8 (Aug. 1905) and 12:1 (Jan. 1909).

48. For example, in *Medico-Pharmaceutical Critic and Guide* 15:10 (Oct. 1912): 364–65.

49. *Medico-Pharmaceutical Critic and Guide* 10:6 (Dec. 1907): 157.

50. William J. Robinson, *Dr. Robinson and Saint Peter* (New York: Eugenics Publications, 1931), 24–25.

51. *Medico-Pharmaceutical Critic and Guide* 8:1 (Jan. 1907): 2.

52. Edward Bliss Foote, *Reply to the Alphites* (New York: Murray Hill, 1882), 5, 15, 18–19.

53. *Medico-Pharmaceutical Critic and Guide* 7:1 (Jan. 1906): 7.

54. *Medico-Pharmaceutical Critic and Guide* 14:2 (Feb. 1911): 43–45 and 14:8 (Aug. 1911): 283–84.

55. Ibid.

56. *Medico-Pharmaceutical Critic and Guide* 14:8 (Aug. 1911): 304–7.

57. *Medico-Pharmaceutical Critic and Guide* 14:6 (June 1911): 201.

58. *Medico-Pharmaceutical Critic and Guide* 14:10 (Oct. 1911): 376.

59. For example, *Firebrand* (Portland, Oreg., 1895–97); *Soundview* (Olalla, Wash., 1902–8); *Free Society* (San Francisco, 1897–?).

60. *Medico-Pharmaceutical Critic and Guide* 14:11 (Nov. 1911): 403.

61. *Medico-Pharmaceutical Critic and Guide* 14:10 (Oct. 1911): 367.

62. Winfield S. Hall, *Developing into Manhood* (New York: Association Press, 1912), is one good example.

63. Max Joseph Exner, *The Physician's Answer* (New York: Association Press, 1913), 14.

64. *Medico-Pharmaceutical Critic and Guide* 14:6 (June 1911): 201–6.

65. Peter Cominos, "Late-Victorian Sexual Respectability and the Social System," *International Review of Social History* 7:1 (1963): 18–48 and 7:2 (1963): 216–50; Steven Marcus, *The Other Victorians* (London: Weidenfeld and Nicolson, 1966); Ben Barker-Benfield, "The Spermatic Economy," *Feminist Studies* 1:1 (Summer 1972).

66. For example, Charlotte Perkins Gilman, "Sex and Race Progress," in *Sex in Civilization*, ed. V. F. Calverton and Samuel Schmalhausen (New York: Macauley, 1929), 114–20.

67. A.E.K., in *Firebrand*, Apr. 25, 1897. See also, for example, Lucy Parsons, Sept. 27, 1896, and Shay Mayflower, Oct. 25, 1896, both in *Firebrand*.

68. Mrs. S. H. Pile, in *Medico-Pharmaceutical Critic and Guide* 15:1 (Jan. 1912): 26–29.

Chapter 8: Birth Control and Social Revolution

1. For a discussion of the influence and misinterpretation of Freud, see Russell Jacoby, *Social Amnesia* (Boston: Beacon, 1975), and Nathan Hale, *Freud and the Americans* (New York: Oxford University Press, 1971).

2. See, for example, Frederick Lewis Allen, *Only Yesterday: An Informal History of the Nineteen-Twenties* (New York: Blue Ribbon Books, 1932), 98.

3. Edward Carpenter, *Love's Coming-of-Age* (New York: Modern Library, 1911), 37.

4. Ibid., 60.

5. For example, Havelock Ellis, *The Task of Social Hygiene* (London: Constable, 1912), 63–65; Ellen Key, *Love and Marriage* (New York: Putnam, 1911), 227–28.

6. Havelock Ellis, "Leaves from a Diary," *Morals, Manners, and Men* (London: Watts, 1939), 124.

7. Anita Block, editorial, *New York Call,* Oct. 22, 1916; *Boston Evening Record,* Oct. 18, 1916.

8. See, for example, James McGovern, "The American Woman's Pre–World War I Freedom in Manners," *Journal of American History* 55:2 (Sept. 1968): 315–38.

9. Floyd Dell, *Love in Greenwich Village* (New York: George H. Doran, 1926), 18–20.

10. On black bohemians, see James Weldon Johnson, *Black Manhattan* (New York: Atheneum, 1930); Jervis Anderson, *This Was Harlem, 1900–1950* (New York: Farrar, Straus and Giroux, 1981); and Ann Douglas, *Terrible Honesty: Mongrel Manhattan in the 1920s* (New York: Noonday, 1995).

11. Josephine Herbst, "A Year of Disgrace," Herbst Papers, Beinecke Library, Yale University. I am indebted to Elinor Langer for this reference.

12. V. F. Calverton, *The Bankruptcy of Marriage* (New York: Macauley, 1928), 11; Samuel Schmalhausen, "The Sexual Revolution," in *Sex in Civilization,* ed. V. F. Calverton and Samuel Schmalhausen (New York: Macauley, 1929), 380.

13. Ben Lindsey, *The Revolt of Modern Youth* (New York: Boni and Liveright, 1925); William Trufant Foster, *The Social Emergency* (Boston: Houghton Mifflin, 1914), 5–19.

14. Lewis M. Terman, *Psychological Factors in Marital Happiness* (New York: McGraw-Hill, 1938), 323; Gilbert Van Tassel Hamilton and Kenneth MacGowan, *What Is Wrong with Marriage* (New York: A. and C. Boni, 1929), 244–47.

15. Daniel Scott Smith and Michael S. Hindus, "Premarital Pregnancy in America, 1640–1966: An Overview and Interpretation," paper presented at the American Historical Association meeting, New York City, Dec. 1971.

16. Gilbert Van Tassel Hamilton, *A Research in Marriage* (New York: A. and C. Boni, 1929).

17. Terman, *Psychological Factors,* 321.

18. Calculated from unpublished data from the Institute for Sex Research, quoted in Daniel Scott Smith, "The Dating of the American Sexual Revolution," in *The American Family in Social-Historical Perspective,* ed. Michael Gordon (New York: St. Martin's Press, 1973), 329.

19. Katherine Bement Davis, *Factors in the Sex Life of Twenty-two Hundred Women* (New York: Harper and Brothers, 1929), chaps. 10–11.

20. The most influential study of these close female relations is Carroll Smith-Rosenberg, "The Female World of Love and Ritual," *Signs* 1:1 (Sept. 1975).

21. Floyd Dell, *Homecoming* (New York: Farrar and Rinehart, 1933), 288.

22. Caroline Ware, *Greenwich Village, 1920–1990* (Boston: Houghton Mifflin, 1935), 258.

23. Personal interview, Mar. 17, 1974.

24. Schmalhausen, "Sexual Revolution," 397.

25. Hutchins Hapgood, *A Victorian in the Modern World* (New York: Harcourt, Brace, 1959), 408.

26. Ibid., 354; Reed's telegram is quoted in Dodge Luhan, *Movers and Shakers* (New York: Harcourt, Brace, 1936), chap. 10.

27. Max Eastman, *Enjoyment of Living* (New York: Harper and Brothers, 1948).

28. Floyd Dell, quoted in Gilman H. Ostrander, *American Civilization in the First Machine Age, 1890–1940* (New York: Harper and Row, 1970), 24–25. This view of the class basis of the bohemians is shared by Malcolm Cowley, *Exile's Return* (New York: Viking, 1951), 58.

29. Anderson, *This Was Harlem,* 107; Douglas, *Terrible Honesty,* 313–17.

30. Johnson, *Black Manhattan,* 232.

31. Jessie M. Rodrique, "The Black Community and the Birth Control Movement," in *"We Specialize in the Wholly Impossible": A Reader in Black Women's History,* ed. Darlene Clark Hine et al. (New York: Carlson, 1995), 508–9.

32. Hutchins Hapgood, quoted in Ostrander, *American Civilization,* 177.

33. Alba M. Edwards, *Comparative Occupation Statistics for the U.S., 1870–1940* (Washington, D.C.: U.S. Bureau of the Census, 1943), table 21.

34. Esther Packard, *A Study of Living Conditions of Self-Supporting Women in New York City* (New York: YWCA, 1915).

35. Ware, *Greenwich Village,* 256–57.

36. Margery Davies, "The Feminization of the Clerical Labor Force," *Radical America* 8:4 (July–Aug. 1974): table 2.

37. Ware, *Greenwich Village,* 256–57.

38. John C. Burnham, "The Progressive Era Revolution in American Attitudes toward Sex," *Journal of American History* 59:4 (Mar. 1973): 890–91.

39. T. A. Storey, *The Work of the U.S. Interdepartmental Social Hygiene Board* (New York: USISHB, 1920), 6.

40. Andrew Smith, as cited in Foster, *Social Emergency,* 33.

41. In the nineteenth century, when licensed and regulated prostitution was being tried in Europe, American feminists and social purity advocates had mounted an effective campaign against the system. They prevented its establishment here except in one case: St. Louis established an inspection and licensing system in 1870. But in 1874 the social purity forces succeeded in repealing it. See John C. Burnham, "The Social Evil Ordinance: A Social Experiment in Nineteenth-Century St. Louis," *Bulletin of the Missouri Historical Society,* Apr. 1971, pp. 203–17.

42. For example, Lavinia Dock, *Hygiene and Morality* (New York: Putnam, 1910); American Social Hygiene Association, *Keeping Fit to Fight* (New York, 1918), 15.

43. Walter Franklin Robie, *Rational Sex Ethics for Men in the Army and Navy* (Boston: R. G. Badger, 1918), 20–25.

44. ASHA, *Keeping Fit to Fight,* 15.

45. Andrea Tone, *Devices and Desires: A History of Contraceptives in America* (New York: Hill and Wang, 2001), chap. 5.

46. Calverton, *Bankruptcy of Marriage,* 13, 141.

47. Davis, *Factors in the Sex Life,* 19–20.

48. For example, Edward O. Sisson, "An Educational Emergency," *Atlantic Monthly,* July 1910, pp. 54–63; Foster, *Social Emergency.*

49. David A. Shannon, *The Socialist Party of America* (New York: Macmillan, 1955),

76; James Weinstein, *The Decline of Socialism in America* (New York: Monthly Review, 1967), 27.

50. Even suffragists acknowledged this support from the Socialist party. See, for example, Ida Husted Harper in *History of Woman Suffrage*, ed. Elizabeth Cady Stanton, Susan Anthony, Matilda Gage (New York, 1881–1922), 5:362.

51. Weinstein, *Decline of Socialism in America*, 58–59; Caroline Lowe (general correspondent, Woman's National Committee, Socialist party), "Socialist Women Did Much in 1911," *Chicago Evening World*, Feb. 23, 1912, p. 4.

52. Mrs. S. I. Jenson, in *Socialist Woman*, Sept. 1913; Helen Unterman, in *Socialist Woman*, Oct. 1913.

53. For example, Caroline Nelson, "Neo-Malthusianism," *International Socialist Review* 14:4 (Oct. 1913): 228. Nelson wrote for the *Socialist Woman* on other topics.

54. Virginia Butterfield, *Parental Rights and Economic Wrongs* (Chicago: Stockham, 1906), 87.

55. Although Butterfield's identification of reproduction with production is unique, several Socialist party women of this period were concerned with the social importance of other aspects of women's unpaid labor in the home. Party journals sometimes discussed the economic value of housework under capitalism, suggesting that it represented perhaps the most extreme form of exploitation. For example, Theresa Malkiel, "The Lowest Paid Workers," *Socialist Woman*, Sept. 1908; "Woman's Work and Pay," editorial, *Chicago Evening World* (a Socialist paper), June 11, 1912, p. 8.

56. For example, Jonathan Mayo Crane, in *Lucifer*, Mar. 28, 1907; Charlotte Perkins Gilman, "Men's Babies," n.d. (probably after 1914), Gilman mss., folder 176, Schlesinger Library, Radcliffe; Sam Atkinson, *Science and a Priest* (Seattle: Libertarian Press, [1910]).

57. Crane, in *Lucifer*, Mar. 28, 1907; Helen Keller, in *New York Call*, Nov. 26, 1915; Margaret Sanger, "Comstockery in America," *International Socialist Review* 16:1 (July 1915): 46; Peter E. Burrowes, "Woman and Her Masters," *The Comrade* 13:8 (May 1904): 172–74; Nelson, "Neo-Malthusianism."

58. William J. Robinson, "The Prevention of Conception," *The New Review* 3:4 (Apr. 1915): 196–99.

59. Adelyne More, *Uncontrolled Breeding or Fecundity versus Civilization* (New York: Critic and Guide, 1917), chaps. 7–8; Max Hodann, *History of Modern Morals*, trans. Stella Browne (London: William Heinemann, 1937); William J. Robinson, "The Birth Strike," *International Socialist Review* 14:7 (Jan. 1914): 404; William English Walling, in *The Masses*, Oct. 1913, p. 20.

60. For example, Winfield Scott Hall, *The Biology, Physiology, and Sociology of Reproduction* (1906; rpt.,Chicago: Wynnewood, 1913).

61. For example, Dr. Edith Belle Lowry, *Herself: Talks with Women Concerning Themselves* (Chicago: Forbes, 1911); Ida Craddock, *Advice to a Bridegroom* (Chicago, 1909); *Helps to Happy Wedlock* (Philadelphia, 1896); *Letter to a Prospective Bride* (Philadelphia, 1897); *Right Marital Living* (Chicago, 1899); *The Wedding Night* (Denver, 1900).

62. Diane Feelley, "Antoinette Konikow, Marxist and Feminist," *International Socialist Review* 33:1 (Jan. 1972): 42–46; Birth Control League of Massachusetts mss., passim, Schlesinger Library, Harvard Uniersity.

63. For example, June 1, 1913, and Aug. 16, 1914.

64. For example, William J. Robinson, in *New York Call*, Aug. 11, 1912, June 8 and 15, 1913; Antoinette Konikow, in *New York Call*, Aug. 16, 1914.

65. *Mother Earth* 6 (Apr. 1911): 2; Richard Drinnon, *Rebel in Paradise* (Boston: Beacon, 1961), 166–68.

66. Drinnon, *Rebel in Paradise*, 67, 166.

67. Hapgood, *Victorian in the Modern World*, 170.

68. This episode is described in James Reed, "Birth Control and the Americans, 1830–1970" (Ph.D. diss., Harvard University, 1974). I am grateful to him for allowing me to read it.

69. Margaret Sanger, *Autobiography* (New York: W. W. Norton, 1938), 80–83; *New York Call*, Feb. 18, 1912; Reed, "Birth Control and the Americans," 37–38.

70. For example, *New York Call*, Nov. 5, 19, and 26, Dec. 3 and 10, 1911.

71. *New York Call*, Nov. 7 and 27, Dec. 1, 8, 15, 22, and 29, 1912; Jan. 12, 19, and 26, 1913.

72. *New York Call*, Feb. 8, 1913.

73. Peter Fryer, *The Birth Controllers* (London: Secker and Warburg, 1965), 202.

74. William Haywood, *Bill Haywood's Book: Autobiography* (New York: International Publishers, 1929), 268.

75. Sanger, *Autobiography*, 103–4; Margaret Sanger, *My Fight for Birth Control* (New York: Farrar and Rinehart, 1913), 68–69, 72–75.

76. For example, in *Medico-Pharmaceutical Critic and Guide* 4:6 (Dec. 1904): 163–64.

77. Sanger, *Autobiography*, 89–92.

78. Ibid., 93–94.

79. Ibid., 96.

80. Elizabeth Gurley Flynn, *The Rebel Girl* (New York: International Publishers, 1973), 166.

81. If I seem to de-emphasize Sanger's role in this movement, it is only to correct a historical record that has left out so many others. At the height of the movement, between 1915 and 1918, many political activists worked on birth control. For example, in New York most of the Socialist suffrage leaders and a few non-Socialist suffragists joined in: Jessie Ashley, wealthy lawyer, former treasurer of the National American Woman Suffrage Association (NAWSA), and Socialist party member; Clara Gruening Stillman and Martha Gruening; Mary Ware Dennett, a right-wing Socialist and former secretary of the NAWSA; Martha Bensley Bruere, active in the Socialist party and the Women's Trade Union League (WTUL); Rose Pastor Stokes, an immigrant Jewish cigar maker active in the Socialist party and married to a Socialist millionaire railroad and mining magnate; Ida Rauh Eastman and Crystal Eastman, sisters-in-law and both Socialist feminists; Elsie Clews Parsons, Barnard professor; Dr. William J. Robinson, who brought many others from his profession into the movement; and Floyd Dell, Max Eastman, and other male prosuffragists. In San Francisco, Los Angeles, and Portland, Oregon, many IWW and Socialist party leaders organized birth control groups. In Michigan there was Agnes Inglis, a wealthy reformer. In Cleveland, Sanger found and recruited Frederick Blossom, a skilled Socialist administrator and fund-raiser. There were also full-time organizers who traveled, spoke, and often distributed illegal birth control literature: Emma Goldman, Dr. Ben Reitman, Elizabeth Gurley Flynn, and Ella Reeve Bloor.

82. Moses Harman, free-lover and anarchist from Kansas, was arrested and imprisoned for birth control advocacy.

83. Letter in Himes mss., Feb. 13, 1937, Countway Library, Harvard University Medical School. I am indebted to James Reed for this reference. Note that I have silently corrected spelling and punctuation in the letter but retained the odd (by today's standards) use of capital letters.

84. For example, Sanger to T. J. Meade, Sept. 11, 1929, in Sanger Papers, Library of Congress (hereafter cited as Sanger, LC); Sanger, *Autobiography;* and Sanger, *My Fight for Birth Control.*

85. Emma Goldman, "Marriage and Love," in *Red Emma Speaks,* ed. Alix Kates Shulman (New York: Vintage, 1972); Goldman, *Living My Life* (1931; rpt., Garden City, N.Y.: Garden City Publ., 1934), 556.

86. Mary Ware Dennett, *Birth Control Laws* (New York: F. H. Hitchcock, 1926), appendix 4. For more on Reitman, see Roger A. Bruns, *The Damndest Radical: The Life and World of Ben Reitman, Chicago's Celebrated Social Reformer, Hobo King, and Whorehouse Physician* (1987; rpt., Urbana: University of Illinois Press, 2001).

87. Note that this pamphlet was written before the term "birth control," coined by Sanger, was in use.

88. Eastman, *Enjoyment of Living,* 423–24.

89. Alice Groff, "The Marriage Bed," *The Woman Rebel* 5 (July 1914). Groff was also a contributor to Robinson's *Medico-Pharmaceutical Critic and Guide.*

90. *The Woman Rebel* 6 (Aug. 1914). See also Lily Gair Wilkinson, "Sisterhood," in ibid.; and the editorial in the first issue of *The Woman Rebel,* Mar. 1914.

91. "Watchful Waiting," *The Woman Rebel* 3 (May 1914). A similar combination of ultrarevolutionary rhetoric and feminism reappeared in the women's liberation movement at the end of the 1960s.

92. Herbert Thorpe, "A Defense of Assassination," *The Woman Rebel* 5 (July 1914). See news stories about the suppression in the *New York American,* Aug. 27, 1914, and the *New York Evening Globe,* Aug. 25, 1914, clippings in Sanger, LC. Sanger disingenuously implied that the censorship was strictly directed against the journal's advocacy of birth control (*Autobiography,* 110–11; *My Fight for Birth Control,* 86–87).

93. Sanger to Upton Sinclair, Sept. 23, 1914, in Sinclair, *My Lifetime in Letters* (New York: Columbia University Press, 1960), 148–49; Harold Hersey, "Margaret Sanger: The Biography of the Birth Control Pioneers," ms., pp. 122ff., New York Public Library.

94. Sanger, *Autobiography,* 108–17.

95. Sanger, *My Fight for Birth Control,* 87; Sanger Diary, 1914, Sanger, LC.

96. *Family Limitation,* 1914, in Sanger, LC.

97. Sanger, *Autobiography,* 119–22; Sanger, *My Fight for Birth Control,* 91ff.

98. Sanger, letter to "Friend," printed, Sept. 1914, Sanger, LC.

99. Sanger, *My Fight for Birth Control,* 102–3.

100. Ibid.; Sanger, *Autobiography,* 128ff.

101. Margaret Sanger, *Happiness in Marriage* (New York: Brentano's, 1926), 142–43. For other characteristic expressions of these sexual views by Sanger, see Sanger to Edward Carpenter, Apr. 13, 1918, Carpenter Collection, Sheffield Public Library, Great Britain (I am indebted to Sheila Rowbotham for this letter); Sanger, *English Methods of Birth Control,* pamphlet, Sanger, LC.

102. Alice Echols, *Daring to Be Bad: Radical Feminism in America, 1967–1975* (Minneapolis: University of Minnesota Press, 1989).

103. Margaret Sanger, *Woman and the New Race* (New York: Brentano's, 1920), 239–40.

104. For example, Charles Schultz, Secretary, Oakland IWW, Nov. 17, 1915; B. Greenberg, Devil's Lake, N.Dak., Feb. 10, 1916; unsigned from Washington, D.C., Aug. 23, 1915; and many other letters to Sanger, miscellaneous clippings, all in Sanger, LC.

105. Caroline Nelson, June 12, 1915, and Georgia Kotsch, Jan. 18, 1916, both to Sanger, Sanger, LC.

106. For example, Alvin Heckethorn, Portland, Oreg., Sept. 9, 1914, Emma Goldman, Dec. 16, 1915, and Caroline Nelson, June 12, 1915, all to Sanger, Sanger, LC.

107. Elizabeth Gurley Flynn to Sanger, Aug. 1915, Sanger, LC.

108. Eugene Debs to Sanger, Nov. 8, 1914, and Dec. 16, 1914, Sanger, LC.

109. Goldman to Sanger, from Columbus, Ohio, Dec. 8, 1915, Sanger, LC.

110. Various letters to Sanger, 1915, Sanger, LC.

111. For example, *The New Republic*, Mar. 16, 1915, Apr. 17, 1915, and Dec. 11, 1915.

112. *New York Tribune*, May 21, 1915, p. 7, clipping in Sanger, LC. Speakers included Dr. Rosalie Slaughter Morton, a professor at New York University; Dr. Emily Dunning Barringer, a surgeon; Lavinia Dock, a suffragist and secretary of the International Council of Nurses; Dr. Lydia Allen DeVilbiss, formerly of the State Board of Health; Dr. Abraham Jacobi, president of the AMA; and Dr. Ira Wile, a member of the Board of Education.

113. The original call of formation of the NBCL listed Jessie Ashley, Otto Bobsien, Mary Ware Dennett, Martha Gruening, Bolton Hall, Charles Hallman, Paul Kennaday, Helen Marot, James F. Morton, Lucy Sprague Mitchell, Lincoln Steffens, and Clara Gruening Stillman. This was published in the *Survey*, Apr. 1915, p. 5. The presence of socialists' names on this list, such as Ashley and Morton, suggests that a few liberals led the organizational move—probably Dennett among them—and got the support of others who did not share equally in defining the policies of the new organization.

114. James Waldo Fawcett, ed., *Jailed for Birth Control: The Trial of William Sanger, September 10, 1915* (pamphlet; New York: Birth Control Review, 1917); Sanger, *My Fight for Birth Control,* 119–21; Sanger, *Autobiography,* 177–78.

115. The handwritten petition is in Sanger, LC.

116. William to Margaret Sanger, Sept. 1915, Sanger, LC. In response to the trial, many suffragists previously silent on birth control now spoke out in Sanger's defense, such as Carrie Chapman Catt, Bela Neuman Zilberman, Mrs. Norman De R. Whitehouse, and Catherine Waugh McCulloch, all quoted in miscellaneous clippings from New York City newspapers, Sanger Scrapbook no. 1, Sanger, LC.

117. For example, James F. Morton, Sept. 24, 1914; Bolton Hall, Dec. 13, 1915; Max Eastman, Jan. 11, 1916; and James Warbasse, Dec. 7, 1915, all to Sanger, Sanger, LC.

118. Goldman to Sanger, Dec. 8 and 16, 1915, Sanger, LC. See also Alexander Berkman to Sanger, Dec. 18, 1915, Sanger, LC.

119. Warbasse to Sanger, Dec. 7, 1915, Sanger, LC. On Goldman's anger at Warbasse for his sexism, see Goldman to Sanger, Dec. 16, 1915, Sanger, LC.

120. Sanger, *My Fight for Birth Control*, 132–34; clippings about the dinner, Sanger, LC.

121. *New York Times*, Feb. 19, 1916.

122. Sanger, *My Fight for Birth Control*, 144–49; Sanger, *Autobiography*, chap. 16.

123. News item in the *Survey*, Oct. 21, 1916, pp. 60–61.

124. *St. Paul Dispatch*, June 12, 1916, in Sanger Scrapbook no. 3, Sanger, LC.

125. Inglis to Rose Pastor Stokes, June 2 and 24, 1916, in Stokes mss., Tamiment Library, New York University.

126. Ella Westcott to Stokes, Oct. 28, 1916, Stokes mss.

127. For example, H. P. Hough, from Fortress Monroe, Va., Dec. 3, 1916, Joseph Rothman, Poughkeepsie, N.Y., Jan. 6, 1917, and Carl Haessler, Urbana, Ill., May 25, 1916, all to Stokes, Stokes mss.; Robt. Peary, July 12, 1916, and B. Greenberg, Devil's Lake, N.Dak., Feb. 10, 1916, both to Sanger, Sanger, LC.

128. *Chicago Evening Journal*, Apr. 25, 1916, in Sanger, LC. See also Sanger, *My Fight for Birth Control*, 145.

129. Flynn to Sanger in London, Aug. 1915, Sanger, LC.

130. Cigar makers traditionally pooled their money to employ *lectors*, or readers, to entertain them as they worked.

131. Flynn, *The Rebel Girl*, 184–85.

132. Mrs. Elsie M. Humphries, Cincinnati, to Stokes, Jan. 9, 1917, Stokes mss.

133. Mrs. W. R. Stevens, Swampscott, Mass., to Stokes, Oct. 20, 1916, Stokes mss.

134. Reprinted in Margaret Sanger, ed., *Motherhood in Bondage* (New York: Brentano's, 1928), 34, 281.

135. Mrs. K.A.B. to NBCL, n.d. (probably 1921), Sanger, LC.

136. Letter to Sanger, Feb. 1, 1916, Sanger, LC.

137. Sanger, *My Fight for Birth Control*, 149.

138. Inglis to Stokes, June 2, 1916, Stokes mss.

139. *St. Paul Dispatch*, June 12, 1916, in Sanger Scrapbook no. 3, Sanger, LC.

140. Sanger, *My Fight for Birth Control*, 144.

141. Sanger, *Autobiography*, 215.

142. Ibid., 218–19.

143. Ibid., 220. Note that Sanger gives the figure as 488 in *My Fight for Birth Control*, 158.

144. Sanger, *Autobiography*, 234.

145. Ibid., 231, for example.

146. Ibid., 250.

147. James Reed, *From Private Vice to Public Virtue: The Birth Control Movement and American Society since 1830* (New York: Basic Books, 1978), 107.

148. Dennett, *Birth Control Laws*, appendix 4; Mary Ware Dennett, *Who's Obscene?* (New York: Vanguard Press, 1930), 236–42.

149. *New York Evening Sun*, May 6, 1916, clipping in Sanger, LC; F. M. Vreeland, "The Process of Reform with Especial Reference to Reform Groups in the Field of Population" (Ph.D. diss., University of Michigan, 1929).

150. Stokes disliked this discrimination in her favor. Ashley wrote, reassuring her: "they think you *want* to be arrested and they are loath to increase the notoriety of the b.c. propaganda. They think your trial would be as widely advertised as Margaret Sanger's or Emma Goldman's. In any case it seems to me to the advantage of all of us to keep you out of jail. While you are free you can go about doing your work, and yours

is now more effective than Ida Rauh's or mine. After all, everyone knows there *is* injustice and we don't have to demonstrate that, *that* is not what we are trying to accomplish" (Ashley to Stokes, June 17, 1916, Stokes mss).

151. Rave statement [1929], Alice Park mss., Stanford University. Carl Rave was not a representative longshoreman accidentally interested in birth control; he was married to Caroline Nelson, a birth control activist. See Nominations for ABCL General National Committee, May 11, 1918, American Birth Control League Papers, Houghton Library, Harvard University (hereafter cited as ABCL).

152. Agnes Smedley to Sanger, Nov. 1, 1918, Sanger, LC.

153. Ibid.

154. Vreeland, "Process of Reform," 274–75; Sanger, *Motherhood in Bondage,* 439.

155. Stokes, "Shall the Parents Decide?," Stokes mss.

156. Sanger, "The Unrecorded Battle," Sanger, LC.

157. Nelson to Sanger, June 12, 1915, Sanger, LC. I have silently corrected the spelling in this letter.

158. Nelson, "Neo-Malthusianism," 228.

159. Sanger, untitled speech, pp. 28–29, Sanger, LC; letter from Parsons in *New Republic,* Mar. 18, 1916, pp. 187–88.

160. Statement by Anna May Wood, Jan. 31, 1917, Sanger, LC.

161. Eliza Mosher, "A Protest against the Teaching of Birth Control," *Medical Woman's Journal,* Dec. 1925, p. 320.

162. Alice Park to Mary Ware Dennett, Dec. 30, 1920, Park mss.

163. Dennett to Park, June 26, 1922, Park mss.

164. Carrie Chapman Catt to Sanger and Juliet Rublee, Nov. 24, 1920, Sanger, LC.

165. Charlotte Perkins Gilman, "Sex and Race Progress," in *Sex in Civilization,* ed. Calverton and Schmalhausen, 114–20.

166. Charlotte Perkins Gilman, *His Religion and Hers: A Study of the Faith of Our Fathers and the Work of Our Mothers* (New York: Century, 1923), 164–65.

167. David Kennedy, *Birth Control in America: The Career of Margaret Sanger* (New Haven, Conn.: Yale University Press, 1970), 234; Charlotte Perkins Gilman, "Progress through Birth Control," *North American Review,* Dec. 1927, pp. 622–29; and Gilman, "Divorce and Birth Control," *Outlook,* Jan. 25, 1928.

168. Sanger, *Autobiography,* 93.

169. Konikow, in *New York Call,* June 1, 1913.

170. Stokes, draft letter to Sanger, Mar. 12, 1925, Stokes mss.

171. Victor Berger, "Socialism and the Home," *Vanguard,* Aug. 1904, p. 8. This and other socialist opinions are quoted in Mari Jo Buhle, "Women in the Socialist Party" (Ph.D. diss., University of Wisconsin, 1974), chap. 9, p. 16.

172. Sanger Diary, Apr. 8–9, 1919, Sanger, LC.

173. Mrs. and Hermann S. Weissmann to Stokes, June 30, 1916, Stokes mss.

174. Letter in *New York Call,* Dec. 19, 1912.

175. Nelson to Sanger, June 12, 1915, Sanger, LC.

176. Copy of this letter, without signature, received Feb. 6, 1925, in ABCL.

177. For example, in 1912 John Spargo devoted a great deal of his basic tract *Applied Socialism* to refuting any connection between socialist and free-love ideas or practice.

178. For example, Sanger to T. J. Meade, Sept. 11, 1929, and Meade to Sanger, Sept. 19, 1929, both in Sanger, LC.

179. For example, Floyd Dell, "Socialism and Feminism," *New Review*, June 1914, pp. 349–53.

180. For example, Josephine Conger-Kaneko, "Socialism and the Sex War," *Progressive Woman*, Aug. 1909, p. 9.

Chapter 9: Professionalization

1. Quoted in Clarence J. Karier, "Testing for Order and Control," in *Roots of Crisis: American Education in the Twentieth Century*, ed. Clarence J. Karier, Paul Violas, and Josel Spring (Chicago: Rand McNally, 1973), 122.

2. Henry Goddard, *Psychology of the Normal and Subnormal* (New York: Dodd, Mead, 1919), 234.

3. Karier, "Testing for Order and Control," 121.

4. C. Wright Mills, *White Collar* (New York: Oxford University Press, 1951), 113.

5. Quoted in Karier, "Testing for Order and Control," 122.

6. David Kennedy, *Birth Control in America: The Career of Margaret Sanger* (New Haven, Conn.: Yale University Press, 1970), 169. My understanding of the role of the churches in the birth control movement is indebted to Kennedy's excellent analysis.

7. For example, Charles F. Potter, "Why the Church Should Champion Birth Control," *Proceedings of the Sixth International Neo-Malthusian and Birth Control Conference* (New York: American Birth Control League, 1926), 4:18–19; Federal Council of the Churches of Christ, Committee on Marriage and the Home, *Moral Aspects of Birth Control* (pamphlet; New York, 1934).

8. Kennedy, *Birth Control in America*, 170. On the opposition of the Catholic Church to birth control, see, for example, Fr. Francis J. Connell, "Birth Control: The Case for the Catholic," *Atlantic Monthly*, Oct. 1939, p. 472; Fr. Gerald J. McMahon to Alice Hamilton, Jan. 6, 1935, Hamilton mss., Schlesinger Library, Radcliffe.

9. Alice Hamilton, *Poverty and Birth Control*, American Birth Control League pamphlet [1927], Hamilton mss.

10. Linda Gordon, *Pitied but Not Entitled: Single Mothers and the History of Welfare* (New York: Free Press, 1994).

11. Margaret Sanger, "Original Speech," in Sanger Papers, Library of Congress (hereafter cited as Sanger, LC); Lawrence Lader, *The Margaret Sanger Story* (Garden City, N.Y.: Doubleday, 1955), 99. Lader's is an "official" biography.

12. *Birth Control Review* (hereafter cited as *BCR*), July–Aug. 1932, p. 209.

13. Frederick Blossom to Rose Pastor Stokes, Nov. 11, 1916, Stokes mss., Tamiment Library, New York University.

14. Henry Fruchter to Elizabeth Gurley Flynn, report on Blossom, Sept. 16, 1922; Margaret Sanger to Flynn, Nov. 3, 1922, both in Sanger, LC.

15. Margaret Sanger, *Autobiography* (New York: W. W. Norton, 1938), 211–12; Sanger, *My Fight for Birth Control* (New York: Farrar and Rinehart, 1931), 110; Mary Ware Dennett, *Birth Control Laws* (New York: F. H. Hitchcock, 1926), 11.

16. Letter to members of the NBCL from its Executive Committee, Jan. 11, 1917, Stokes mss.; statement by Dennett, Nov. 18, 1921, Sanger, LC.

17. Morris Fishbein, *Medical Follies* (New York: Boni and Liveright, 1925), 142.

18. Frederick McCann, "Presidential Address to League of National Life," printed in *Medical Press and Circular*, Nov. 3, 1926, p. 359.

19. For this and subsequent quotations from Kosmak, see George Kosmak, in *Bulletin of the Lying-in Hospital of the City of New York*, Aug. 1917, pp. 181–92. For similar

views among other doctors, see, for example, Edward C. Podvin, "Birth Control," *New York Medical Journal,* Feb. 10, 1917, pp. 258–60; C. Henry Davis, "Birth Control and Sterility," *Surgery, Gynecology, and Obstetrics,* Mar. 1923, pp. 435–39; B. S. Talmey, in *New York Medical Journal,* June 23, 1917, pp. 1187–91.

20. Robert L. Dickinson, "Hypertrophies of the Labia Minora and Their Significance," *American Gynecology* 1 (1902): 225–54, in James Reed, "Birth Control and the Americans" (Ph.D. diss., Harvard University, 1974).

21. Robert L. Dickinson, "Bicycling for Women from the Standpoint of the Gynecologist," *American Journal of Obstetrics* 31 (1895): 24–37, in Reed, "Birth Control and the Americans," 51–52.

22. Robert L. Dickinson, "Marital Maladjustment: The Business of Preventive Gynecology," *Long Island Medical Journal* (1908): 1–5; and Reed, "Birth Control and the Americans," 58.

23. Kennedy, *Birth Control in America,* 179.

24. Dickinson to J. Bentley Squier, Nov. 10, 1925, Dickinson mss., Countway Library, Harvard University Medical School.

25. Kennedy, *Birth Control in America,* 191.

26. Reed, "Birth Control and the Americans," 77–82; Kennedy, *Birth Control in America,* 190; Lader, *Margaret Sanger Story,* 216.

27. ABCL files, in F. M. Vreeland, "The Process of Reform with Especial Reference to Reform Groups in the Field of Population" (Ph.D. diss., University of Michigan, 1929), 280.

28. Sanger to J. Noah Slee, Feb. 22, 1925, Sanger, LC. See also American Birth Control League Papers, boxes 4–6, Houghton Library, Harvard University (hereafter cited as ABCL Papers).

29. W. N. Wishard Sr., "Contraception: Are Our County Societies Being Used for the American Birth Control League Propaganda?," *Journal of the Indiana Medical Association,* May 1929, pp. 187–89.

30. *Proceedings of the Sixth International Neo-Malthusian and Birth Control Conference,* 3:19–30, 49–60.

31. Vreeland, "Process of Reform," 280.

32. Form letters in ABCL Papers.

33. American Birth Control League, *An Amendment to the Federal Law Dealing with Contraception* (pamphlet, n.d.), in ABCL Papers.

34. Mimeographed letter to VPL members from President Myra P. Gallert, Dec. 2, 1925, Alice Park mss., Stanford University.

35. Dennett, *Birth Control Laws,* 88.

36. Antoinette Konikow, "The Doctor's Dilemma in Massachusetts," *BCR,* Jan. 1931, pp. 21–22.

37. Kennedy, *Birth Control in America,* 222–23.

38. Sanger to James Field, June 5, 1923, box 2, ABCL Papers; Sanger to Dennett, Mar. 4, 1930, and unmailed draft of same, Feb. 25, 1930, Sanger mss., Sophia Smith Collection, Smith College Library (hereafter cited as Sanger, Smith). See also *Journal of the American Medical Association* 85 (1925): 1153–54; Sanger to Dennett, [1929], Park mss.

39. See Cerise Carman Jack in *BCR,* Apr. 1918, pp. 6–8.

40. Paul Blanshard, *Personal and Controversial* (Boston: Beacon, 1973), 34–35.

41. *Boston Post,* July 25, 1916, in Diane McCarrick Gieg, "The Birth Control League

of Massachusetts" (B.A. thesis, Simmons College, 1973), 21; Cerise Carman Jack in *Boston American,* July 21, 1916, in Gieg, "Birth Control League of Massachusetts," 21.

42. Richard Drinnon, *Rebel in Paradise* (Boston: Beacon, 1961), 141; *BCR,* Feb. 1917, p. 10.

43. Jack to Blanche Ames Ames, June 17, 1917, Ames mss., Sophia Smith Collection, Smith College Library.

44. Jack to Charles Birtwell, June 17, 1917, Ames mss.

45. Jack to Blanche Ames Ames, Jan. 7, 1918, Ames mss.

46. Birth Control League of Massachusetts mss., Schlesinger Library, Radcliffe (hereafter cited as BCLM mss.).

47. See, for example, Konikow to Mrs. Edward East, Jan. 20 and Oct. 7, 1929, in Planned Parenthood League of Massachusetts mss., Sophia Smith Collection, Smith College Library.

48. From the opinion of C. R. Clapp, May 10, 1929, BCLM mss.

49. Konikow, "Doctor's Dilemma," 21.

50. Konikow to Blanche Ames Ames, Mar. 29, 1931; VPL mimeographed letter, n.d., both in BCLM mss.

51. Statements from the *Boston Post,* Feb. 19, 1932, quoted in Gieg, "Birth Control League of Massachusetts," 77.

52. Dennett, *Birth Control Laws,* 72–93.

53. There were six in New York, seven in Los Angeles, three in San Francisco, four in the East Bay in California, three in Chicago, and others in Baltimore, Detroit, Cleveland, Buffalo, Philadelphia, Denver, Atlanta, Minneapolis, Newark, Cincinnati, San Antonio, and Charlottesville. See Lader, *Margaret Sanger Story,* 219 and appendix B, pp. 358–59.

54. *Birth Control and Public Policy, Decision of Judge Harry M. Fisher of the Circuit Court of Cook County, November 1923* (pamphlet; Chicago: Illinois Birth Control League, 1924).

55. For example, see Minutes of the Advisory Council, Harlem Clinical Research Bureau, May 20, 1931, in Sanger, Smith.

56. Sanger to Dr. Clarence Gamble, Feb. 4, 1940, Sanger, Smith.

57. Conference program, Sanger, LC.

58. Mimeographed letter to VPL members from Gallert. For Sanger's justification for this exclusion, see, for example, Sanger to Prof. James Field, Aug. 13, 1923, BCLM mss.

59. Caroline Nelson to Alice Park, Feb. 3, 1930, Park mss.

60. J. Mayone Stycos, "Problems of Fertility Control in Under-developed Areas," in *The Population Crisis and the Use of World Resources,* ed. Stuart Mudd (Bloomington: Indiana University Press, 1964), 103.

61. Sanger, *Autobiography,* 402–8.

62. For example, Clarence C. Little to Robert L. Dickinson, Oct. 28, 1925, Sanger, LC.

63. Sanger, *Autobiography,* 374.

64. The best general secondary work on twentieth-century eugenics in the United States is Mark Haller, *Eugenics: Hereditarian Attitudes in American Thought* (New Brunswick, N.J.: Rutgers University Press, 1963). See also Leonard Ellman, "The American Eugenics Movement, 1905–1925" (B.A. thesis, Harvard University, 1963);

Donald K. Pickens, *Eugenics and the Progressives* (Nashville, Tenn.: Vanderbilt University Press, 1968).

65. Mills, *White Collar,* 129–34.

66. Jesse B. Sears, *Philanthropy in the History of American Higher Education* (Washington, D.C.: GPO, 1922), 55.

67. For a sample textbook, see Michael F. Guyer, *Being Well-Born: An Introduction to Eugenics* (Indianapolis: Bobbs-Merrill, 1916).

68. Pickens, *Eugenics and the Progressives,* 51.

69. Haller, *Eugenics,* 174.

70. I use the term "assumptions" because nothing in the genetic theory they relied upon, even as it progressed to Mendel's mathematically sophisticated and predictive models, provided any basis for distinguishing the relative impact of heredity and environment in producing characteristics such as feeblemindedness, insanity, laziness, and other common eugenic bugaboos.

71. Paul Popenoe, *The Conservation of the Family* (Baltimore: Williams and Wilkins, 1926), 129–30.

72. Guyer, *Being Well-Born,* 296–98.

73. Lothrop Stoddard, *Revolt against Civilization: The Menace of the Under Man* (New York: Scribners, 1922), 21.

74. Eugenists were pushing immigration restriction as early as 1914. See, for example, articles by Stanley Gulick and Robert DeC. Ward in *Proceedings of the First National Conference on Race Betterment* (Battle Creek, Mich.: Race Betterment Foundation, 1914).

75. Fourth Report, Committee on Selective Immigration, American Eugenics Society, June 30, 1928, p. 16, in Anita Newcomb McGee mss., Library of Congress.

76. Paul Popenoe and Roswell Hill Johnson, *Applied Eugenics* (1918; rpt., New York: Macmillan, 1925), 294–97.

77. For example, the Virginia State Board of Health distributed among schoolchildren a pamphlet by Walter Ashby Plecker entitled *Eugenics in Relation to the New Family and the Law on Racial Integrity* (Richmond: Bureau of Vital Statistics, State Board of Health, 1924). It explained in eugenic terms the valiant and lonely effort of Virginia to preserve the race from the subversion planned by the nineteen states plus the District of Columbia, which permitted miscegenation. It concluded, "Let us turn a deaf ear to those who would interpret Christian brotherhood to mean racial equality."

78. For example, Eduard Bernstein, "Decline in the Birth-Rate, Nationality, and Civilization," and R. Manschke, "The Decline in the Birth-Rate," both in *Population and Birth-Control,* ed. Eden and Cedar Paul (New York: Critic and Guide, 1917); Frank Notestein, in *BCR,* Apr. 1938; Haller, *Eugenics,* 79; Frank Lorimer, Ellen Winston, and Louise K. Kiser, *Foundations of American Population Policy* (New York: Harper and Brothers, 1940), 12–15.

79. Lorimer et al., *Foundations of American Population Policy,* 15.

80. See, for example, National League for the Protection of the Family, *Annual Report for 1911* (Boston: Fort Hill Press, 1912).

81. For example, Scott and Nellie Nearing, *Woman and Social Progress* (New York: Macmillan, 1912), chap. 1.

82. S. H. Halford, "Dysgenic Tendencies of Birth-Control and of the Feminist Movement," in *Population and Birth-Control,* ed. Paul and Paul, 238.

83. Henry Bergen, in *BCR*, Apr.–May 1920, pp. 5–6, 15–17. For similar socialist critiques, see J. B. Eggen, "Rationalization and Eugenics," *Modern Quarterly*, May–July 1926; Eva Trew, "Sex Sterilization," *International Socialist Review*, May 1913.

84. Eden Paul, "Eugenics and Birth-Control," in *Population and Birth-Control*, ed. Paul and Paul, 134.

85. Caroline Nelson, in *BCR*, Apr. 1918, p. 13.

86. Bergen, in *BCR*, Apr.–May 1920.

87. Ludwig Quessel, "Race Suicide in the United States," in *Population and Birth Control*, ed. Paul and Paul, 118.

88. For an early example, see letter of Dec. 20, 1865, to Martha Wright, in *Elizabeth Cady Stanton as Revealed in Her Letters, Diary, and Reminiscences*, ed. Theodore Stanton and Harriot Stanton Blatch (New York: Harper and Brothers, 1922).

89. Margaret Sanger, "Why Not Birth Control in America?" *BCR*, May 1919, pp. 10–11.

90. For example, Margaret Sanger, *Woman and the New Race* (New York: Brentano's, 1920), 34.

91. Margaret Sanger, *The Pivot of Civilization* (New York: Brentano's, 1922), 177–78.

92. *Stenographic Record of the Proceedings of the First American Birth Control Conference, 1921* (New York: ABCL, 1921), 24.

93. Margaret Sanger, "The Necessity for Birth Control," Oakland speech, Dec. 19, 1928, stenographic record, Sanger, LC.

94. Margaret Sanger, "My Way to Peace," speech to New History Society, Jan. 17, 1932, Sanger, Smith.

95. Sanger, "Necessity for Birth Control."

96. *Report of the Fifth International Neo-Malthusian and Birth Control Conference*, ed. Raymond Pierpont (London: Heinemann, 1922).

97. Brochure in Sanger, Smith.

98. Paul Popenoe in *BCR*, Mar. 1917, p. 6.

99. For example, Warren Thompson, "Race Suicide in the U.S.," serialized in *BCR*, Aug. 1920, pp. 9–10; Sept. 1920, pp. 9–10; Oct. 1920, pp. 10–11; Jan. 1921, p. 16; Feb. 1921, pp. 9–12; Mar. 1921, pp. 11–13.

100. *BCR*, Sept. 1923, pp. 219–20.

101. M. Winsor, "The Cost to the State of the Socially Unfit," *BCR*, Sept. 1923, pp. 222–24.

102. Havelock Ellis, in *BCR*, Oct. 1920, pp. 14–16.

103. Clarence C. Little, "Unnatural Selection and Its Resulting Obligations," *BCR*, Aug. 1926, pp. 244–57.

104. From an unpublished letter, quoted in Kennedy, *Birth Control in America*, 119.

105. Vreeland, "Process of Reform," 232.

106. East to Sanger, May 15, 1925, ABCL Papers.

107. National Committee on Federal Legislation for Birth Control, *Newsletter* 9 (Apr. 1932).

108. Vreeland, "Process of Reform," 376, 383–84.

109. Ibid., 297.

110. Tour schedules in Sanger, LC.

111. Sanger, *Autobiography*, 385–86. She wrote a more polite version of this episode in *My Fight for Birth Control*, 302.

112. Kennedy, *Birth Control in America,* 200–202.

113. For example, Katherine Bement Davis, *Factors in the Sex Life of Twenty-two Hundred Women* (New York: Harper and Brothers, 1929); Lewis Terman, *Psychological Factors in Marital Happiness* (New York: McGraw-Hill, 1938); Gilbert Van Tassel Hamilton, *A Research in Marriage* (New York: A. and C. Boni, 1929).

114. Caroline Hadley Robinson, *Seventy Birth Control Clinics* (Baltimore: Williams and Wilkins, 1930), 44.

115. Kennedy, *Birth Control in America,* 200.

116. Edward East to Sanger, Dec. 20, 1929; Sanger to East, Dec. 31, 1929, both in Sanger, Smith.

117. Robinson, *Seventy Birth Control Clinics,* chap. 4.

118. Sanger, *Autobiography,* 374–75.

119. Robinson, *Seventy Birth Control Clinics,* 50–52.

120. For example, Sanger, *Autobiography,* 401; Margaret Sanger, *Motherhood in Bondage* (New York: Brentano's, 1928), passim.

121. Robinson, *Seventy Birth Control Clinics,* chap. 5.

122. For example, in *BCR,* 1938–39, passim.

123. Editorial, *Journal of Heredity* 24:4 (Apr. 1933): 143.

124. Henry Pratt Fairchild, speech, Planned Parenthood Federation of America Papers, Sophia Smith Collection, Smith College Library.

125. Vreeland, "Process of Reform," 154ff.

126. ABCL bylaws, n.d., ABCL Papers.

127. ABCL mss., passim.

128. *Birth Control Herald,* July 1922.

129. *The Prosecution of Mary Ware Dennett for Obscenity* (pamphlet; New York: ACLU, June 1929). A decision in Dennett's favor by a circuit court in 1930 was an important free-speech precedent. Holding that the Comstock law was not intended to interfere with serious sex instruction, it was later cited in court decisions allowing the distribution of two contraception books by Marie Stopes as well as James Joyce's *Ulysses.* See *U.S. v. Dennett,* 39 F. 2d 564 (1930), cited in Kennedy, *Birth Control in America,* 244.

130. For example, Mary Ware Dennett to Alice Park, Jan. 7, 1921, and June 26, 1922, Park mss.

131. Mary Ware Dennett, *The Sex Education of Children: A Book for Parents* (New York: Vanguard Press, 1931).

132. For example, Elizabeth Green to Anne Kennedy of ABCL, Mar. 29, 1926, ABCL Papers.

133. For example, ABCL to Mrs. Edmonds, Mar. 24, 1926, ABCL Papers.

134. For example, ABCL to board members, June 6, 1928, ABCL Papers.

135. The findings of this survey are presented in Vreeland, "Process of Reform," 154ff., and all the following information is taken from that source.

136. Fifty-five percent of men were Republicans, 19 percent were Democrats; the women's figures were 46 percent and 25 percent, respectively.

137. Sanger form letter and many responses are in ABCL Papers.

Chapter 10: Depression

1. This interpretation is based on William Ryan, *Blaming the Victim* (New York: Random House, 1971), and C. Wright Mills, "The Professional Ideology of Social Pa-

thologists," in *Power, Politics, and People*, ed. Irving Louis Horowitz (New York: Ballantine, n.d.), 525–52 (reprinted from *American Journal of Sociology* 49:2 [Sept. 1943]).

2. Dorothy Dunbar Bromley, "Birth Control and the Depression," *Harper's*, Oct. 1934, p. 563; James H. S. Bossard, letter to *New York Times*, Jan. 25, 1935.

3. For example, *Time*, Apr. 8, 1935, pp. 30–32; *Birth Control Review* (hereafter cited as *BCR*), May 1935, pp. 2–3.

4. Margaret Sanger, "Is Race Suicide Possible?," *Collier's*, Aug. 15, 1925, p. 25.

5. R. E. Baber and E. A. Ross, *Changes in the Size of American Families in One Generation*, University of Wisconsin Studies no. 10 (Madison, 1924).

6. Dr. Lydia Allen DeVilbiss to Francis Bangs, ABCL president, Apr. 26, 1935, in Planned Parenthood Federation of America Papers, Sophia Smith Collection, Smith College Library (hereafter cited as PPFA Papers).

7. Clarence C. Little, in *BCR*, Jan. 1933, p. 6.

8. *BCR*, May 1933, pp. 134–35.

9. *BCR*, June 1933, pp. 141–43.

10. James H. S. Bossard, "The New Public Relief and Birth Control," address at the American Conference on Birth Control and National Recovery, Jan. 1934, printed in *BCR*, May 1934, p. 1.

11. Eleanor Dwight Jones, in *BCR*, Feb. 1935, p. 1.

12. *BCR*, July–Aug. 1932, p. 209.

13. Bromley, "Birth Control and the Depression," 564.

14. Paul Popenoe and Ellen Morton Williams, "Fecundity of Families Dependent on Public Charity," *American Journal of Sociology*, Sept. 1934, p. 220. To obtain this "data," eugenist investigators actually subjected women on welfare to IQ tests at childbirth.

15. Edgar Sydenstricker and G. St. J. Perrott, "Sickness, Unemployment, and Differential Fertility," *Milbank Memorial Fund Quarterly*, Apr. 1934, quoted in Norman E. Himes, "The Birth Rate of Families on Relief: A Summary of Recent Studies in the U.S.A.," *Marriage Hygiene* (Bombay), Aug. 1935, p. 60.

16. James H. S. Bossard, *Marriage and the Child* (Philadelphia: University of Pennsylvania, 1940), chap. 8.

17. *New York Times*, Aug. 24, 1932.

18. Henry Fairfield Osborn, "Birth Selection vs. Birth Control," *Forum and Century*, Aug. 1932, pp. 79–83.

19. Editorial, *BCR*, Oct. 1932, pp. 227–28.

20. David Loth, "Planned Parenthood," *Annals of the American Academy of Political and Social Science*, Nov. 1950, p. 96.

21. *BCR*, 1930s, passim.

22. Frank Lorimer, in *BCR*, Oct. 1932, p. 230.

23. Edgar Sydenstricker and Frank Notestein, "Differential Fertility according to Social Class," *Journal of the American Statistical Association*, Mar. 1930, p. 25.

24. National Committee on Maternal Health, Round Table Discussion on Marriage and the Family, May 13, 1937, minutes, p. 4, in Himes mss., Countway Library, Harvard University Medical School (hereafter cited as NCMH Round Table).

25. Joseph Folsom, in *American Eugenics*, Proceedings of the Annual Meeting and Round Table Conferences of the American Eugenics Society (pamphlet), May 7, 1936, p. 46.

26. These alarms rested also on the fact that in the 1930s demographers finally be-

came convinced that contraception was the major cause of the birth-rate decline. Raymond Pearl, for example, long a skeptic about the impact of contraception, was convinced by his own research that without contraception there would be no birth-rate differential at all (*Natural History of Population* [New York: Oxford University Press, 1939], chaps. 4–5).

27. *Omaha World-Herald,* quoted in *BCR,* May 1935, p. 3.

28. Bossard, *Marriage and the Child,* chap. 8.

29. Raymond Pearl, *Biology of Population Growth* (New York: Knopf, 1925), 167.

30. For example, Dr. Raymond Squier's comments in NCMH Round Table, p. 10.

31. T. R. Robie, NCMH Round Table, p. 12.

32. Clarence Gamble, report on DeVilbiss method, 1937, in PPFA Papers.

33. For example, DeVilbiss to Francis Bangs, June 30, 1934, PPFA Papers.

34. For example, Bangs to DeVilbiss, July 6, 1934; Marguerite Benson, ABCL executive director, to DeVilbiss, June 21, 1935; both in PPFA Papers.

35. Dennis Smith, "Techniques of Conception Control," in *Readings in Family Planning,* ed. Donald McCalister, Victor Thiessen, and Margaret McDermott (St. Louis: C. V. Mosby, 1973), 31.

36. For example, Dr. Regine K. Stix and Frank Notestein, *Controlled Fertility: An Evaluation of Clinic Service* (Baltimore: Williams and Wilkins, 1940), chap. 9.

37. Ibid., 91–92; Bessie L. Moses, *Contraception as a Therapeutic Measure* (Baltimore: Williams and Wilkins, 1936); Ruth A. Robishaw, "A Study of 4,000 Patients Admitted for Contraceptive Advice and Treatment," *Journal of Obstetrics and Gynecology* 31:3 (Mar. 1936): 426–34.

38. For a contemporary corroboration of this judgment, see Robert L. Dickinson and Lura Beam, *A Thousand Marriages* (Baltimore: Williams and Wilkins, 1932), 217.

39. For example, Pearl, *Natural History of Population,* chap. 5.

40. Rabbi Sidney Goldstein, in *American Eugenics,* 40. See also Leon F. Whitney, *The Case for Sterilization* (New York: Frederick A. Stokes, 1934), 7.

41. For example, Margaret Sanger, "The Function of Sterilization," *BCR,* Oct. 1926, p. 299; C. O. McCormick, "Eugenic Sterilization," *BCR,* Oct. 1932, pp. 241–42.

42. J. H. Landman, *Human Sterilization* (New York: Macmillan, 1932), 48–49.

43. Paul Popenoe, "Number of Persons Needing Sterilization," *Journal of Heredity,* 1928, pp. 405–10.

44. Landman, *Human Sterilization,* 41–46. Who incurred this loss was not specified.

45. Both polls are reported in *BCR,* Jan. 1939, p. 155.

46. Frederick S. Jaffe and Steven Polgar, "Family Planning and Public Policy: Is the 'Culture of Poverty' the New Cop-Out?," in *Readings in Family Planning,* ed. McCalister et al., 169.

47. Caroline Hadley Robinson, *Seventy Birth Control Clinics* (Baltimore: Williams and Wilkins, 1930), 91–94; Raymond Pearl, *Statistical Report on the Fifth Year's Operations of the Bureau for Contraceptive Advice* (pamphlet; Baltimore, 1933).

48. For example, Regine K. Stix, "Birth Control in a Midwestern City," *Milbank Memorial Fund Quarterly* 17:1 (Jan. 1939), 17:2 (Apr. 1939), and 17:4 (Oct. 1939); Dorothy Dunbar Bromley, *Birth Control: Its Use and Misuse* (New York: Harper and Brothers, 1934), 4.

49. Lini Moerbeck Fuhr to Sanger, Jan. 12, 1936, Sanger, LC.

50. For example, Robinson, *Seventy Birth Control Clinics,* 103.

51. Ibid., 116–17.

52. *Time,* Apr. 8, 1935, pp. 30–32; *BCR,* Sept. 1935, p. 3.

53. Emily Vaughn, in *BCR,* Jan. 1933, p. 144.

54. *BCR,* Dec. 1935.

55. Frank H. Hankins, "Poverty and Birth Control," *BCR,* July–Aug. 1932, p. 199.

56. Eleanor Dwight Jones, in *BCR,* Jan. 1933, p. 6.

57. For example, Clarence C. Little, in *BCR,* 1934–36, passim.

58. Margaret Sanger, "National Security and Birth Control," *Forum,* Mar. 1935, pp. 139–41.

59. In his later life, Dublin became an equally passionate exponent of the overpopulation theory that dominated the demography of the 1950s and 1960s. See Louis I. Dublin, *After Eighty Years* (Gainesville: University of Florida Press, 1966), 140–41.

60. Arthur Schlesinger Jr., *The Crisis of the Old Order, 1919–33* (Boston: Houghton Mifflin, 1956), 425–26.

61. ABCL, 1934 Report, Sanger, LC.

62. "Survey of Policies of FERA Administrators," Feb. 25, 1935, Sanger, LC.

63. DeVilbiss to Bangs, Mar. 25, 1935, PPFA Papers.

64. Norman E. Himes, "Birth Control and Social Work," *Survey Midmonthly,* Mar. 1939, pp. 74–75.

65. James Rorty, "Let Power Speak," *BCR,* May 1932, p. 136.

66. David Kennedy, *Birth Control in America: The Career of Margaret Sanger* (New Haven, Conn.: Yale University Press, 1970), 269.

67. Report of the John Price Jones Corporation, Sept. 15, 1930; "Recommendations to the Joint Committee of ABCL and CRB," Oct. 10, 1938, both in Sanger, LC.

68. Henry Pratt Fairchild, memo on his interview with Dr. Ray Lyman Wilbur, May 5, 1930, Sanger, Smith.

69. DeVilbiss to Bangs, Mar. 25, 1935, PPFA Papers.

70. Ironically, the combination of these two arguments overlooked the fact that the foremost proponent of the underpopulation theory, Louis Dublin, opposed most eugenic fears about the birth-rate differential, considering them racist, elitist, and unfounded. See, for example, Dublin, "The Fallacious Propaganda for Birth Control," *Atlantic Monthly,* Feb. 1926, pp. 189–93.

71. Regine Stix, in NCMH Round Table, pp. 4–5.

72. Dorothy Dunbar Bromley and Florence Haxton Britten, *Youth and Sex: A Study of 1,300 College Students* (New York: Harper and Brothers, 1938), 13.

73. Elizabeth H. Garrett, "Birth Control's Business Baby," *New Republic,* Jan. 17, 1934, p. 270.

74. Bromley and Britten, *Youth and Sex,* 13.

75. Bromley, "Birth Control and the Depression," 104.

76. Quoted in Norman E. Himes, *Medical History of Contraception* (1936; rpt., New York: Gamut Press, 1963), 329.

77. *Health and Hygiene,* June 1935, p. 18; Bromley, "Birth Control and the Depression," 104.

78. Quoted in Rachel Lynn Palmer and Sarah K. Greenberg, *Facts and Frauds in Woman's Hygiene* (New York: Vanguard Press, 1936), 168.

79. Quoted in Garrett, "Birth Control's Business Baby," 270.

80. Quoted in Palmer and Greenberg, *Facts and Frauds in Woman's Hygiene,* 250–51.

81. Report on Contraceptive Industry, prepared by Foote, Cone and Belding of Chicago, ts., n.d., PPFA Papers.

82. Sanger, "National Security and Birth Control," 140.

83. Ibid. It is important to bear in mind, however, that legalization and medical control of contraception ultimately gave the large pharmaceutical houses exclusive control over the contraceptive market and ended all competition.

84. Garrett, "Birth Control's Business Baby," 271.

85. Kennedy, *Birth Control in America*, 241.

86. *Ladies' Home Journal* poll reported in Birth Control Clinical Research Bureau press release, Feb. 17, 1938, Sanger, Smith.

87. The history of this case and Sanger's legislative work is well told in Kennedy, *Birth Control in America*, chap. 8.

88. Unfortunately, very little research has been done on local community organizing during the depression, even less about women's activities and birth control agitation.

89. *National Birth Control News* (National Committee for Federal Legislation on Birth Control), Dec. 1936–Jan. 1937, p. 14.

90. Lini Moerbeck Fuhr, typed report, mid-1930s, Sanger, LC.

91. Lini Moerbeck Fuhr to Sanger, Jan. 12, 1936, Sanger, LC. Fuhr was especially impressed with the Paterson effort because she had worked in the mills there as a child. I found no documentation about the final outcome.

92. Quoted in *National Birth Control News*, Mar.–Apr. 1937, pp. 10–11.

93. Natalie Lamport, "Report on the Recreation Rooms and Settlement Birth Control Clinic," a branch of the Clinical Research Bureau at 84 1st Street in New York City, Sanger, Smith. See also Stix and Notestein, *Controlled Fertility*. The percentage of Catholic women who attended clinics, as compared to non-Catholics, was never calculated and probably could not have been calculated accurately because of variables such as the location of clinics.

94. *BCR*, Dec. 1937–Jan. 1938, p. 39.

95. *BCR*, May 1935, p. 3.

96. Himes, "Birth Control and Social Work," 75.

97. Hannah Stone in *BCR*, Nov. 1932, p. 261; Eve Garrett, letter to *New York Times*, Nov. 19, 1933, quoted in *BCR*, Dec. 1933, p. 3.

98. *Birth Control—Questions and Answers*, National Committee on Federal Legislation for Birth Control, pamphlet, 1937.

99. Nadina R. Kavinoky, *A Program for Family Health*, ABCL pamphlet, American Birth Control League Papers, Houghton Library, Harvard University (hereafter cited as ABCL Papers).

100. Report of John Price Jones Corporation.

101. See, for example, Sanger's address at the ABCL's 18th Annual Meeting, Jan. 19, 1939, ts., p. 2, PPFA Papers.

102. See, for example, documents concerning Sanger's formation of the Committee on Public Progress for Birth Control, established after the court victory, and its lobbying program, in Sanger, Smith.

103. Gretta Palmer, "Birth Control Goes Suave," *Today*, July 20, 1935, pp. 14–15.

104. Harry Hansen to Sanger, Oct. 10, 1931, Sanger, LC.

105. Sanger to Hansen, Oct. 13, 1931, Sanger, LC.

106. For example, Dorothy Dent to Sanger, Apr. 30, 1932, Sanger, Smith. See also many other personnel letters in Sanger, Smith.

107. Eleanor Dwight Jones, "A New Era in Social Service," *BCR*, July–Aug. 1932, p. 209; statement in *BCR*, Jan. 1933, p. 6.

108. Statement of policy as approved by BCFA Executive Committee, Sept. 16, 1941, in PPFA Papers.

109. Loth, "Planned Parenthood," 96.

110. *BCR*, Dec. 1938, p. 143.

111. Don Wharton, "Birth Control: The Case for the State," *Atlantic Monthly*, Oct. 1939, p. 465.

112. DeVilbiss to Wood of ABCL, Nov. 12, 1937; DeVilbiss to Moore of ABCL, July 26, 1937, both in PPFA Papers.

113. For example, see Ellen H. Smith, Chairman, Board of Directors, Virginia League for Planned Parenthood, to Marie S. Key, Consultant on Work with Negroes for the PPFA, June 10, 1946; Smith to D. Kenneth Rose, PPFA National Director, June 10, 1946, both in PPFA Papers.

114. For example, two pamphlets issued by the Virginia State Board of Health, Bureau of Vital Statistics: *Eugenics in Relation to the New Family and the Law on Racial Integrity* (1924) and *The New Family and Race Improvement* (1925), both in the Widener Library, Harvard University.

115. W. A. Plecker, M.D., State Registrar of Vital Statistics, Virginia State Board of Health, to Mrs. Anne Kennedy, ABCL, Feb. 10, 1926, in ABCL Papers.

116. Wharton, "Birth Control," 467.

117. "Relief or Cure," leaflet, Mothers Health Clinic, n.d., PPFA Papers.

118. Leaflet, Mothers Health Clubs, Inc., PPFA Papers.

119. "Birth Control and the Negro," Sanger, Smith. All further references to the project are from this proposal.

120. Sanger to Clarence Gamble, Oct. 19, 1939, Sanger, Smith.

121. Gamble memo, n.d. (probably Nov. or Dec. 1939), Sanger, Smith. See also issue 28 (Fall 2001) of the newsletter issued by the Margaret Sanger Papers Project, New York University (hereafter cited as Sanger newsletter).

122. Ibid.

123. Gamble to Sanger, Jan. 25, 1940, Sanger, Smith.

124. Johanna Schoen, "Fighting for Child Health: Race, Birth Control, and the State in the Jim Crow South," *Social Politics* 4 (Spring 1997): 90–113.

125. Sanger newsletter.

126. D. Kenneth Rose to Florence Rose, Nov. 25, 1940, Sanger, Smith.

127. Helen Countryman, "Conditions in Miami," ts., n.d. (undoubtedly late 1930s), in PPFA Papers.

128. Confidential Report of Governmental Projects in Cooperation with the Birth Control Clinical Research Bureau, n.d., unsigned, Sanger, Smith.

129. For example, Mildred Delp, R.N., "How Mrs. Joad Learned to Use a Doctor," *Medical Care* 4:2 (n.d.[1939 or later]): 115, in Sanger, Smith.

130. Pauline G. Shindler, "Tent Life in California," *BCR*, May 1932, p. 158.

131. For example, letter to Secretary of State from Dr. Adolphus Knopf, *BCR*, Feb. 1933, pp. 50–51.

132. J. Enamorado Cuesta to editor, *BCR*, May 1932, p. 157.

133. *National Birth Control News*, May 1937, p. 3.

134. Reported by the BCFA Information Service, May 1941, pp. 1, 4, in PPFA Papers.

135. Margaret Sanger, "Birth Control Comes of Age," speech, Mayflower Hotel, Washington, D.C., Feb. 13, 1925, ms., Sanger, Smith.

136. James H. S. Bossard, "Population and National Security," *BCR*, Sept. 1935, p. 4.

137. Guy Burch, "Birth Control vs. Class Suicide," *Survey Graphic,* Apr. 1932.

Chapter 11: Planned Parenthood

1. Lydia DeVilbiss to Dr. Eric Matsner, Jan. 31, 1938, in Planned Parenthood Federation of America Papers, Sophia Smith Collection, Smith College Library (hereafter cited as PPFA Papers).

2. Sanger to D. Kenneth Rose, Aug. 20, 1946; Sanger to P. B. P. Huse, Dec. 20, 1937; Summary of Recommendations to Joint Committee of ABCL and CRB, Oct. 10, 1938, all in Sanger mss., Sophia Smith Collection, Smith College Library (hereafter cited as Sanger, Smith). Rose was later hired away from his public relations firm to become PPFA national director.

3. Dr. Richard N. Pierson, speech, 1941 annual meeting, PPFA Papers.

4. The poster is reproduced in Margaret Sanger, "National Security and Birth Control," *Forum* 93 (Mar. 1935): 139–41.

5. Margaret Sanger, "Family Planning: A Radio Talk," CBS broadcast, Apr. 11, 1935, printed as a pamphlet by the National Committee on Federal Legislation for Birth Control.

6. Miscellaneous BCFA and PPFA leaflets and pamphlets in PPFA Papers.

7. Woodbridge Morris to Rose, June 4, 1940, PPFA Papers.

8. For example, Eduard Lindeman, "The Responsibilities of Birth Control," *Atlantic Monthly,* July 1939, p. 23.

9. *Planned Parenthood . . . Its Contribution to Family, Community and Nation,* PPFA pamphlet, n.d. (probably 1946), PPFA Papers.

10. Lindeman, "Responsibilities of Birth Control," 25.

11. For example, PPFA proposed policy statement, draft of Apr. 6, 1943, PPFA Papers.

12. BCFA Executive Committee resolution, Oct. 29, 1940, PPFA Papers. This was not a new demand; the ABCL had called for a national birth-rate commission in 1928. See the undated resolution in the American Birth Control League Papers, Houghton Library, Harvard University (hereafter cited as ABCL Papers).

13. Mimeographed form letter, Mar. 22, 1943, Sanger, Smith.

14. Unsigned memorandum, Mar. 5, 1941, Sanger, Smith.

15. The poster is reproduced in *Planned Parenthood . . . Its Contribution.*

16. *Planned Parenthood in Wartime,* PPFA pamphlet, 1942, PPFA Papers (emphasis added).

17. Sanger, "National Security and Birth Control."

18. Sanger, speech, ABCL 18th Annual Meeting, PPFA Papers.

19. D. Kenneth Rose, "War Psychology and Its Effect on the Birth Control Movement: Suggestions from Staff Members," memorandum to staff, June 7, 1940, PPFA Papers. See also memos from staff members to Rose on this subject.

20. L. Gill to Rose, [June 1, 1940], PPFA Papers.

21. "The Contribution of Birth Control to Preparedness," draft statement by C. M. Smith, June 11, 1940, PPFA Papers.

22. Kathryn Trent memorandum to Morris Lewis, May 19, 1941, PPFA Papers.

23. Helen K. Stevens memorandum to Rose, June 7, 1940, PPFA Papers; Rose, "War Psychology and Its Effect."

24. Eugene Lyons, "The Stork Is the Bird of War," *Commentator,* Feb. 1938, pp. 97–101.

25. For example, *Planned Parenthood and the War: A Statement of Policy,* leaflet, June 1942, PPFA Papers; "Contribution of Birth Control to Preparedness."

26. Sanger to P. B. P. Huse, Jan. 2, 1940, Sanger, Smith. See also Helen Keller to Margaret Sanger, Aug. 5, 1944, and Sanger to Keller, Aug. 24, 1944, both in Sanger, Smith. Sanger was nevertheless strongly antifascist and signed a message of support to a Soviet Women's Conference through the Communist party–sponsored American Council on Soviet Relations (Sept. 6, 1941, Sanger Papers, Library of Congress [hereafter cited as Sanger, LC]).

27. *Advanced Hygiene Protects Womanpower,* PPFA pamphlet reprinted from *Modern Industry,* June 1944, PPFA Papers.

28. *Employing the Married Woman Worker,* PPFA pamphlet reprinted from a publication of the Alabama State Health Department, [1943], PPFA Papers.

29. Henry Pratt Fairchild, "Family Limitation and the War," *Annals of the American Academy of Political and Social Science* 229 (Sept. 1943): 84.

30. BCFA national policies, May 10 and 15, 1940, PPFA Papers.

31. *Planned Parenthood USA,* [1942], pamphlet of the National Committee for Planned Parenthood of the BCFA, PPFA Papers.

32. Rose to Board of Directors, State Leagues, and so forth, "Birth Control's Opportunity to Strengthen Our Human Resources—Our Population," July 6, 1940, PPFA Papers.

33. Elmira Conrad to Rose, Feb. 8, 1943, PPFA Papers.

34. *Birth Control Federation of American Information Service,* Sept.–Oct. 1940, p. 2.

35. PPFA Program Policies, adopted by Board of Directors, Oct. 17, 1947, pp. 3–4, PPFA Papers. These pro–civil rights policies may have been adopted in response to problems of racism within the PPFA or its affiliates. For example, in 1946 the chairman of the board of the Virginia League of Planned Parenthood refused a request of the PPFA's "Negro Consultant" to come to Virginia to present a special program on work with blacks. Ellen Smith of the Virginia League wrote to the PPFA director: "I know you agree with the conservative approach we have had in Virginia which has brought such satisfactory results. I am sure that Mrs. Key [the consultant] understands that this had nothing to do with the racial problem, but is merely the continuation of our expressed policy since the League was organized." Doubtless Key and PPFA director Rose suspected that Virginia's refusal did indeed have to do with the "racial problem" and may have struggled to overcome these prejudices as much as was possible within the structure of the PPFA. See Ellen H. Smith to Rose, June 10, 1946, and Smith to Marie S. Key, June 10, 1946, both in PPFA Papers.

36. For example, Charles H. Garvin, "The Negro Doctor's Task," *Birth Control Review,* Nov. 1932, p. 269.

37. See, for example, annual reports of Harlem Branch, Clinical Research Bureau, 1930–32; Natalie Lamport, Report on the Recreation Rooms and Settlement Birth Control Clinic, both in Sanger, Smith; Jessie M. Rodrique, "The Black Community and the Birth Control Movement," in *Unequal Sisters,* ed. Darlene Clark Hine et al. (New York: Carlson, 1995).

38. For example, Jessup memorandum to Rose, June 4, 1940, PPFA Papers.

39. For example, "Contribution of Birth Control to Preparedness"; "Planned Parenthood in Relation to the War," memorandum to Board of Directors, State Leagues, Oct. 5, 1942, PPFA Papers.

40. Smith memorandum to Rose, June 3, 1940, PPFA Papers; "Contribution of Birth Control to Preparedness."

41. BCFA memorandum on meeting with Captain Stephenson, Oct. 22, 1941, Sanger Smith; Stephenson memorandum to Admiral McIntire, Oct. 22, 1941, PPFA Papers.

42. See, for example, James H. S. Bossard, speech at National Conference of Social Work, quoted in a BCFA press release, June 3, 1941, PPFA Papers.

43. William Fielding Ogburn, "Marriages, Births, and Divorces," *Annals of the American Academy of Political and Social Science* 229 (Sept. 1943): 20–29.

44. "Birth Control, Ten Eventful Years," speech, July 30 [probably 1946], signed "emc" [probably delivered by Sanger], Sanger, Smith.

45. John F. Cuber, "Changing Courtship and Marriage Customs," *Annals of the American Academy of Political and Social Science* 229 (Sept. 1943): 30–38.

46. For example, Fairchild, "Family Limitation and the War," 84.

47. David Loth (PPFA public relations director), "Planned Parenthood," *Annals of the American Academy of Political and Social Science* 272 (Nov. 1950): 97.

48. "Our Human Resources," report of the National Committee for Planned Parenthood Temporary Advisory Committee on Population Policy of the BCFA, Mar. 1941, PPFA Papers.

49. "Birth Control's Opportunity to Strengthen Our Human Resources: Our Population," July 6, 1940, PPFA Papers.

50. Willard Waller, Sidney Goldstein, and Lawrence Frank, "The Family and National Defense," *Living* 3:1 (Feb. 1941): 1–3.

51. "The Soldier Takes a Wife," pamphlet, PPFA Papers.

52. For example, Stevens memorandum to Rose, June 7, 1940, PPFA Papers.

53. See, for example, Sheila Tobias and Lisa Anderson, *What Really Happened to Rosie the Riveter* (module 9) (New York: MSS Modular Publications, 1974).

54. Margaret Sanger, letter of June 17, 1942, Sanger, LC.

55. Florence Rose to Sanger, [June 10, 1943], Sanger, Smith.

56. BCFA memorandum to Sanger, July 30, 1940, PPFA Papers. Kosmak was a die-hard opponent of birth control during the second and third decades of the twentieth century. For more on his role, see chapter 9.

57. Sanger to Frank G. Boudreau, director, Milbank Memorial Fund, Mar. 12, 1939, in Sanger, Smith.

58. Tobias and Anderson, *What Really Happened.*

59. Betty Friedan, *The Feminine Mystique* (1963; rpt., New York: Dell, 1970), 249.

60. Statement drafted by Janet Fowler Nelson, Ph.D., consultant on marriage and family-life education, accepted by the PPFA Board, Mar. 20, 1947, PPFA Papers. Subsequent quotes in the text are also from this draft statement.

61. Numerous drafts of this manual and correspondence about it are in the PPFA Papers.

62. Ferdinand Lundberg and Marynia F. Farnham, M.D., *Modern Woman: The Lost Sex* (New York: Harper and Brothers, 1947), 364–65.

63. Farnham, speech at the Association for the Advancement of Psychotherapy Forum, Apr. 28, 1943, PPFA Papers.

64. Note that the view that sexual continence was damaging for men and women was widespread at this time. See, for example, Mary Antoinette Cannon, professor of social work at Columbia University, *Outline for a Course in Planned Parenthood*, PPFA pamphlet, 1944–45, PPFA Papers.

65. See, for example, Jes. H. Scull memorandum to Mrs. C. Damon, June 25, 1945, criticizing this policy, PPFA Papers.

66. For example, Karl Menninger "Psychiatric Aspects of Contraception," PPFA reprint from the *Bulletin of the Menninger Clinic*, Jan. 1943; Harvie DeJ. Coghill, "Emotional Maladjustments from Unplanned Parenthood," speech at the annual conference of the Virginia League for Planned Parenthood, Sept. 26, 1941; Adrian Holt Van der Veer, "The Unwanted Child," speech at the annual meeting of the Illinois League for Planned Parenthood, Apr. 30, 1941, all in PPFA Papers.

67. Farnham speech to the AAP Forum, p. 8.

68. Ibid., p. 9. See also Coghill, "Emotional Maladjustments from Unplanned Parenthood," which offers an example of the prevalent view that resentful mothers "punish" their children.

69. Farnham speech to the AAP Forum, p. 15.

70. *Look* clipping, Apr. 1, 1947, PPFA Papers.

71. Cannon, *Outline for a Course*, 15. See also Van der Veer, "Unwanted Child"; Menninger, "Psychiatric Aspects of Conception"; Coghill, "Emotional Maladjustments from Unplanned Parenthood"; and Margaret Ribble, M.D., *The Rights of Infants* (New York: Columbia University Press, 1943), chap. 1.

72. Rhoda J. Milliken, speech of Jan. 22, 1947, PPFA Papers.

73. Loth, "Planned Parenthood," 97.

74. Personal interview with Dr. Regine Stix, Boston, Mass., May 5, 1975; Carl N. Degler, "What Ought to Be and What Was: Woman's Sexuality in the Nineteenth Century," *American Historical Review* 79 (Winter 1974): 1467–90.

75. Letter of June 14, 1916, in Stokes mss., Tamiment Library, New York University. There are many similar letters in this collection.

76. HHH memorandum to Sanger, Mar. 1924, Sanger, LC.

77. Draft description of Marriage Advice Bureau, Oct. 17, 1931, Sanger, Smith.

78. Sanger to Bobby Walls of Tarrant, Ala., Mar. 7, 1924, Sanger, LC.

79. Sanger to Lydia Wentworth of Brookline, Mass., Apr. 30, 1935, Sanger, Smith.

80. Sanger to Ethelwyn Martz of Bloomfield, N.J., Mar. 1, 1935, Sanger, LC.

81. Sanger to Sam Voyner of Alberta, Canada, June 1, 1937, Sanger, Smith.

82. Reported in Marie E. Kopp, *Birth Control in Practice: Analysis of Ten Thousand Case Histories of the Birth Control Clinical Research Bureau* (New York: McBride, 1934), 101–3.

83. For example, see the staff meeting minutes and case histories, Feb. 1932 and thereafter, Sanger, Smith.

84. Robert Latou Dickinson, "Premarital Consultation," *Journal of the American Medical Association* 117 (Nov. 15, 1941): 1687–92.

85. See assorted case histories, Sanger, Smith.

86. See, for example, Klein memorandum to Rose, Dec. 31, 1942; report of discussion at the ABCL annual meeting, Jan. 26, 1938 (report dated Feb. 21, 1938), both in PPFA Papers.

87. C. C. Pierce report on conference with Dr. John Favill, Feb. 16, 1943, PPFA Papers.

88. Numerous drafts and the final version of this statement are in box 41, PPFA Papers. All of the following comments on the program are taken from this statement.

89. Report on BCFA Postgraduate Institute on Clinic Procedures held at Margaret Sanger Research Bureau, Feb. 1940, PPFA Papers. Levine considered marriage counseling, premarital advice, sex education, and cancer detection all by-products of the birth control movement.

90. Abraham and Hannah M. Stone, *Marital Maladjustments,* PPFA pamphlet reprinted from *The Cyclopedia of Medicine, Surgery, and Specialties* (Philadelphia: E. A. Davis, 1940), 821.

91. Ibid.

92. Transcripts of group marriage counseling sessions are in Sanger, Smith. See especially the session of May 15, 1947.

93. Margaret Sanger, *Happiness in Marriage* (New York: Brentano's, 1926), 60–63.

94. Ibid., 99–100.

95. Ibid., passim.

96. Hannah and Abraham Stone, *A Marriage Manual* (1935; rpt., New York: Simon and Schuster, 1939), 203–4. Of the two Stones, Hannah was always the more deeply involved in birth control work, having joined the CRB in the 1920s, but she died in 1941.

97. Abraham Stone and Lena Levine, "Group Therapy in Sexual Maladjustment," draft, n.d., Sanger, Smith. These groups consisted of those with sexual problems, expressed during interviews at birth control clinics. There should be no inference here that these groups were necessarily representative of the general population.

98. Ibid., 3.

99. Ibid.

100. Transcript of group session, Feb. 6, 1947, Sanger, Smith.

101. Transcript of group session, May 15, 1947, Sanger, Smith.

102. Quoted in Stone and Levine, "Group Therapy in Sexual Maladjustment," p. 7.

103. Transcript of group session, Mar. 13, 1947, Sanger, Smith.

104. Transcript of group session, Jan. 30, 1947, Sanger, Smith.

105. Transcript of group session, Apr. 24, 1947, Sanger, Smith.

106. For example, transcript of group session, May 8, 1947, Sanger, Smith.

107. Transcript of group session, Mar. 20, 1947, Sanger, Smith.

108. For example, transcript of group session, Dec. 26, 1946, Sanger, Smith.

109. For example, Helena Wright, *The Sex Factor in Marriage* (New York: Vanguard Press, 1931), 91; H. W. Long, *Sane Sex Life and Sane Sex Living* (1919; rpt., New York: Eugenics Publications, 1937), chap. 8; William J. Fielding, *Sex and the Love-Life* (Garden City, N.Y.: Blue Ribbon Books, 1927), chap. 7.

110. Transcript of group session, Mar. 20, 1947, Sanger, Smith. See also, for example, transcripts of group sessions, Jan. 16, 1947, and Nov. 7, 1946, Sanger, Smith.

111. Reported in Wardell B. Pomeroy, *Dr. Kinsey and the Institute for Sex Research* (New York: Harper and Row, 1972), 169. Note that Kinsey and Stone were nevertheless warm acquaintances and that Stone gave Kinsey data from the birth control clinic.

112. Stone and Stone, *Marital Maladjustments,* 827.

113. Transcript of group session, Dec. 5, 1946, Sanger, Smith.

114. Transcripts of group sessions, Jan. 30, 1947, and Dec. 12, 1946, Sanger, Smith.

115. Transcript of group session, Oct. 24, 1946, Sanger, Smith.

116. Transcript of group session, Dec. 26, 1946, Sanger, Smith.

117. For example, transcript of group session, Oct. 24, 1946, Sanger, Smith.

118. Stone and Stone, *Marital Maladjustments,* 824. The Stones accepted the categorization suggested by Albert Moll and Havelock Ellis twenty years before: the contrectation (or tumescence) impulse, the desire to touch and caress, and the detumescence impulse, the desire for orgasm. These categories were based on an inadequate understanding of female orgasm and the assumption that, as in the male, female orgasm led to immediate detumescence, a sense of completion. Thus the doctors labeled women as sexually immature for not sharing a particular male impulse; by contrast, when women did actively seek orgasms, in the manner successful for the great majority of women, the doctors condemned that too, albeit gently, as not fully womanly.

119. Transcript of group session, Dec. 5, 1946, Sanger, Smith.

120. Transcript of group session, Feb. 27, 1947, Sanger, Smith.

121. CRB records, entry of Feb. 24, 1932, Sanger, Smith.

122. CRB records, entry of Feb. 10, 1932, Sanger, Smith.

123. Transcript of group session, Feb. 27, 1947, Sanger, Smith.

124. Emily Mudd, "Counseling in Relation to the Clinic Patient," paper presented at the Clinic Session, BCFA annual meeting, Jan. 30, 1942, mimeographed for the press, PPFA Papers.

125. For example, Katherine Bement Davis, *Factors in the Sex Life of Twenty-two Hundred Women* (New York: Harper and Brothers, 1929); Alfred C. Kinsey, Wardell B. Pomeroy, Clyde E. Martin, and Paul H. Gebhard, *Sexual Behavior in the Human Female* (Philadelphia: W. B. Saunders, 1953).

Chapter 12: Birth Control Becomes Public Policy

1. See the appendix for selected recent scholarship on the history of reproduction control.

2. For an example of professionals treating these concepts as identical, see Louis M. Hellman (Deputy Assistant Secretary for Population Affairs, Dept. of HEW), "Family Planning Comes of Age" (1971), reprinted in *Readings in Family Planning,* ed. Donald V. McCalister et al. (St. Louis: C. V. Mosby, 1973), 18–29, and passim in this collection.

3. For this and examples of pre–World War II fears of underpopulation, see James Reed, "Public Policy on Human Reproduction and the Historian," *Journal of Social History* 18:3 (1985): 383–98.

4. Milbank Memorial Fund, *International Approaches to Problems of Underdeveloped Areas* (New York: Milbank, 1948), which is the text of a 1947 roundtable conference.

5. This and all following information about the personnel and financing of population control groups are taken from the annual reports of these groups, which are readily available from the groups themselves, and from *Who's Who.* For a fuller discussion of eugenics/population control connections, see Linda Gordon, "The Politics of Population: Birth Control and the Eugenics Movement," *Radical America* 8:4 (July–Aug. 1974); and "The Politics of Birth Control, 1920–40: The Impact of Professionals," *International Journal of Health Services* 5:2 (Fall 1975), reprinted in *The Cultural Crisis of Modern Medicine,* ed. Barbara Ehrenreich (New York: Monthly Review Press, 1978).

6. Those six were Kingsley Davis, Clyde Kiser, Frank Notestein, Frank Lorimer,

P. K. Whelpton, and Alan Guttmacher. Dudley Kirk, demographic director, and Warren Nelson, medical director, also came from eugenics backgrounds.

7. Burch to Himes, June 30, 1930, and Burch letter in the *Washington Post,* May 1, 1939, both in Himes mss., Countway Library, Harvard University Medical School.

8. Steve Weissman, "Why the Population Bomb Is a Rockefeller Baby," *Ramparts,* May 1970, pp. 42–47.

9. This point has been missed in a number of historical discussions of genetics and eugenics, as in Germaine Greer's *Sex and Destiny: The Politics of Human Fertility* (New York: Harper and Row, 1984) and Bonnie Mass's *Population Target: The Political Economy of Population Control in Latin America* (Toronto: Women's Education Press, 1976). See my discussion of this problem in my review of Greer's book: Linda Gordon, "Bringing Back Baby," *The Nation,* May 26, 1984, pp. 645–46.

10. Donald T. Critchlow, *Intended Consequences: Birth Control, Abortion, and the Federal Government in Modern America* (New York: Oxford University Press, 1999).

11. Miscellaneous memos, Dorothy Brush mss., Sophia Smith Collection, Smith College Library.

12. *New York Times,* May 11, 1969.

13. See William Barclay, Joseph Enright, and Reid T. Reynolds, "The Social Context of U.S. Population Control Programs in the Third World," paper presented to the Population Association of America, Apr. 17, 1970.

14. For a discussion of this phenomenon in China, see Jan Myrdal, "The Reshaping of Chinese Society," in *Contemporary China,* ed. Ruth Adams (New York: Pantheon, 1966), 65–91.

15. *The Population Bomb* (pamphlet), 12th ed. (New York: Population Policy Panel of the Hugh Moore Fund, 1954), 3. Paul Erlich's book *The Population Bomb* (San Francisco: Sierra Club, 1969) took its title from this pamphlet.

16. Robert G. Weisbord, *Genocide?: Birth Control and the Black American* (Westport, Conn.: Greenwood, 1975).

17. The following generalizations about the use of incentive payments are taken from *Incentive Payments in Family Planning Programmes,* International Planned Parenthood Federation Working Paper No. 4 (London, 1969). This report covers the seven countries listed, but there are undoubtedly others that also used incentive payments in their population control programs.

18. *New York Times,* Oct. 24, 1971.

19. Donald Critchlow dates its hegemony at 1945–64.

20. Ellen Chesler, *Woman of Valor: Margaret Sanger and the Birth Control Movement in America* (New York: Simon and Schuster, 1992), 431.

21. Andrea Tone, *Devices and Desires: A History of Contraceptives in America* (New York: Hill and Wang, 2001), 208.

22. Gregory Pincus, quoted in Paul Vaughan, *The Pill on Trial* (New York: Coward-McCann, 1970), 39.

23. Laura Briggs, "Discourses of 'Forced Sterilization' in Puerto Rico: The Problem with the Speaking Subaltern," *differences* 10:2 (Summer 1998).

24. Quoted in Tone, *Devices and Desires,* 222. See also Elizabeth Siegel Watkins, *On the Pill: A Social History of Oral Contraceptives, 1950–1970* (Baltimore: Johns Hopkins University Press, 1998).

25. Quoted in Tone, *Devices and Desires,* 223–24.

26. Maria de Lourdes Lugo-Ortiz, "Sterilization, Birth Control, and Population

Control: The News Coverage of *El Mundo, El Imparcial,* and *Claridad*" (Ph.D. diss., University of Wisconsin, 1994).

27. Tone, *Devices and Desires,* 223.

28. Ibid., chaps. 9–10.

29. When antiabortionists tried to block the abortifacient mifepristone (RU-486) in France, the French minister of health responded that it was the "moral property" of women and ordered it onto the market.

30. Martha C. Ward, *Poor Women, Powerful Men: America's Great Experiment in Family Planning* (Boulder, Colo.: Westview, 1986), 38.

31. Critchlow, *Intended Consequences.*

32. Ward, *Poor Women, Powerful Men,* 40.

33. Quoted in ibid., 68.

34. Ibid., 24–25, 30–31, quote on 31.

35. Weisbord, *Genocide?,* chap. 10; Ward, *Poor Women, Powerful Men.*

36. Ward, *Poor Women, Powerful Men,* 59.

37. Ibid., 91ff., quotes on 93.

38. Ibid., 131–37, quotes on 137.

39. Medical Services Offered by the Louisiana Family Planning Program, in ibid., appendix B.

Chapter 13: Abortion, the Mother Controversy

1. Rosalyn Baxandall and Linda Gordon, eds., *Dear Sisters: Dispatches from the Women's Liberation Movement* (New York: Basic Books, 2000).

2. Martha C. Ward, *Poor Women, Powerful Men: America's Great Experiment in Family Planning* (Boulder, Colo.: Westview, 1986), chaps. 1–2.

3. See, for example, Rosalind Pollack Petchesky, *Abortion and Woman's Choice: The State, Sexuality, and Reproductive Freedom* (New York: Longman, 1984), chap. 3; Leslie J. Reagan, *When Abortion Was a Crime: Women, Medicine, and Law in the United States, 1867–1973* (Berkeley: University of California Press, 1997).

4. On Florio, see Eileen McNamara, "Out of the Shadow of Back-alley Days," *Boston Globe,* May 16, 1989, pp. 1, 4–5. On Spencer, see Michael T. Kaufman, in *Lear's,* July–Aug. 1989, pp. 84–87.

5. Petchesky, *Abortion and Woman's Choice;* Donald Granberg and Beth Wellman Granberg, "Abortion Attitudes, 1965–1980: Trends and Determinants," *Family Planning Perspectives* 12:5 (Sept.–Oct. 1980): 250–64.

6. Jerome S. Legge Jr., *Abortion Policy: An Evaluation of the Consequences for Maternal and Infant Health* (Albany: SUNY Press, 1985), 117; Helen Rose Fuchs Ebaugh and C. Allen Haney, "Shifts in Abortion Attitudes, 1972–1978," *Journal of Marriage and the Family* 42:3 (Aug. 1980): 491–99.

7. Petchesky, *Abortion and Woman's Choice,* chaps. 6–8. See also Aryeh Neier, *Only Judgment: The Limits of Litigation in Social Change* (Middletown, Conn.: Wesleyan University Press, 1982), chap. 7.

8. Reagan, *When Abortion Was a Crime,* chaps. 6–8.

9. Nancy Stearns, "Roe v. Wade," *Berkeley Women's Law Journal* 4 (1988–89): 1–11.

10. R. Sauer, "Attitudes to Abortion in America, 1800–1973," *Population Studies* 28:1 (Mar. 1974): 53–67.

11. Interview with Byllye Avery by Gail Hovey, in *Christianity and Crisis* 46:10 (July 14, 1986): 244.

12. Arlene Carmen and Howard Moody, *Abortion Counseling and Social Change from Illegal Act to Medical Practice: The Story of the Clergy Consultation Service on Abortion* (Valley Forge, Pa.: Judson Press, 1973).

13. Quoted in Diane Elze, "Underground Abortion Remembered," *Sojourner: The Women's Forum,* Apr. 1988, p. 14 and passim; ibid., May 1988, pp. 12–13.

14. Marilyn Katz, "Hello, Is Jane There?": Illegal Abortion Service Run by Chicago Women," *Reproductive Rights Newsletter,* Fall 1981, pp. 20–21. The first basic research about Jane was done by Pauline Bart. The most comprehensive work on Jane is Laura Kaplan's *The Story of Jane: The Legendary Underground Feminist Abortion Service* (New York: Pantheon, 1995).

15. Petchesky, *Abortion and Woman's Choice,* 291, quoting *Roe v. Wade.*

16. Jonathan B. Imber, *Abortion and the Private Practice of Medicine* (New Haven, Conn.: Yale University Press, 1986). On Catholic doctors' views, see, for example, Dena Kleiman, "For a Catholic Doctor, a Crisis of Conscience," *New York Times,* Apr. 22, 1987.

17. Petchesky, *Abortion and Woman's Choice.*

18. Marion K. Sanders, "Enemies of Abortion," *Harper's,* Mar. 1974, pp. 26–30.

19. In 1980 abortion rights activists brought an unsuccessful suit to end the Catholic Church's tax-exempt status on the grounds that it had "intervened in political campaigns to further its religious belief." See clippings, press releases, correspondence, and briefs concerning the case *Abortion Rights Mobilization v. Catholic Church and Internal Revenue Service,* folder "Abortion: Catholics," in the Boston Women's Health Book Collective Archives, Somerville, Mass. (hereafter cited as BWHBC Archives).

20. For example, see Very Reverend George G. Higgins of the National Conference of Catholic Bishops/United States Catholic Conference, "Two Abortion Views That Will Never Mix," *Boston Sunday Globe,* Sept. 28, 1980.

21. See Kenneth A. Briggs, "Bishops Debate Strategy in Fight to End Abortion," *New York Times* Nov. 17, 1981, p. 11; "Bishops Mend Rift on Abortion Plan," *New York Times,* Nov. 19, 1981, p. 11.

22. Frank J. Traina, "Catholic Clergy on Abortion: Preliminary Findings of a New York State Survey," *Family Planning Perspectives* 6:3 (Summer 1974): 151–56.

23. S. K. Henshaw and K. Kost, "Abortion Patients in 1994–95: Characteristics and Contraceptive Use," *Family Planning Perspectives* 28:4 (July–Aug. 1996), online at <http://www.agi-usa.org/pubs/journals/2814096.html>; Frederick S. Jaffe, Barbara L. Lindheim, and Philip R. Lee, *Abortion Politics: Private Morality and Public Policy* (New York: McGraw-Hill, 1981), 12. According to earlier studies, 8 percent of Catholic women and 7 percent of Protestant women had had abortions (Stanley K. Henshaw and Greg Martire, in *Family Planning Perspectives* 14:2 [Mar.–Apr. 1982]). See also press release from the Alan Guttmacher Institute, Apr. 30, 1982, BWHBC Archives, folder "Abortion: Catholics." For the 1988 statistics, see the *Capital Times* (Madison, Wis.), Oct. 6, 1988, p. 9.

24. The *Gallup Opinion Index* 153 (Apr. 1976): 25–29 and 166 (May 1979): 20–24 finds Catholic support for abortion averaging about 5 percent less than Protestant support. Granberg and Granberg, "Abortion Attitudes," 257, finds that the Protestant-Catholic difference accounts for only about 1 percent of abortion attitude differences. See also Lucky M. Tedrow and E. R. Mahoney, "Trends in Attitudes towards Abortion, 1972–1976," *Public Opinion Quarterly* 43:2 (Summer 1979): 181–89. By contrast, degree of religiosity and church attendance among all religions are strongly correlat-

ed with disapproval of abortion. See B. Krishna Singh, "Contextual and Ideological Dimensions of Attitudes toward Discretionary Abortion," *Demography* 15:3 (Aug. 1978): 381–88.

25. Keith Cassidy, "The Right to Life Movement: Sources, Development, and Strategies," *Journal of Policy History* 7:1 (1995): 128–59.

26. For example, antibusing, anti–gay rights, anti–Equal Rights Amendment, anti–sex education, and anti–affirmative action.

27. Online at <http://www.home.nycap.rr.com/deisley/quotes.html>.

28. Fr. Paul Marx, "Pro Life/Family Catalog," 1991, available online at <http://www.cs.unc.edu/allen/food.html>.

29. Susan Friend Harding, *The Book of Jerry Falwell: Fundamentalist Language and Politics* (Princeton, N.J.: Princeton University Press, 2000).

30. On the history of antiabortion arguments, see *Brief of 281 American Historians as Amici Curiae Supporting Appellees, Webster v. Reproductive Health Services,* 492 U.S. 490 (1989), no. 88-605.

31. The most eloquent spokesperson for this view has been Ellen Willis; see, for example, "Putting Women Back into the Abortion Debate," *The Village Voice,* July 16, 1985. For a brilliant and fuller argument, see Rosalind Pollack Petchesky, "Fetal Images: The Power of Visual Culture in the Politics of Reproduction," *Feminist Studies* 13:2 (Summer 1987): 263–92.

32. Michael A. Cavanaugh, "Secularization and the Politics of Traditionalism: The Case of the Right-to-Life Movement," *Sociological Forum* 1:2 (Spring 1986): 251–83.

33. Paul Weyrich, "Family Issues," in *The New Right at Harvard,* ed. Howard Phillips (Vienna, Va.: Conservative Caucus, 1983), 17–22.

34. Gary K. Clabaugh's scholarly study *Thunder on the Right: The Protestant Fundamentalists* (Chicago: Nelson-Hall, 1974) does not mention abortion. Tim and Beverly LaHaye's *The Act of Marriage: The Beauty of Sexual Love* (New York: Bantam, 1976/1978), a New Right sex manual, is tolerant of abortion. I am indebted to Allen Hunter's research on this point.

35. Allen Hunter, "Virtue with a Vengeance: The Pro-Family Politics of the New Right" (Ph.D. diss., Brandeis University, 1984). See also Paul Gottfried and Thomas Fleming, *The Conservative Movement* (Boston: Twayne, 1988), esp. 84–95. A 1980 postelection study by the National Conservative PAC found abortion the most effective single issue in bringing Democrats to vote Republican. See Flo Conway and Jim Siegelman, *Holy Terror: The Fundamentalist War on America's Freedoms in Religion, Politics, and Our Private Lives* (New York: Doubleday, 1982), 101. Whether or not antiabortion attitudes have actually shifted electoral patterns is not clear. Pro–abortion rights studies deny that antiabortion sentiment has tipped elections toward conservatives. See, for example, Jeannie I. Rosoff, "Is Support of Abortion Political Suicide?," *Family Planning Perspectives* 7:1 (Jan.–Feb. 1975): 13–22; Michael W. Traugott and Maris A. Vinovskis, "Abortion and the 1978 Congressional Elections," *Family Planning Perspectives* 12:5 (Sept.–Oct. 1980): 238–46; Donald Granberg and James Burlison, "The Abortion Issue in the 1980 Elections," *Family Planning Perspectives* 19:2 (Mar.–Apr. 1987): 59–62. There is general agreement that in the 1986 congressional elections, antiabortion sentiments did not motivate voters effectively. See Linda Greenhouse, "A Turning Point on the Abortion Issue?," *New York Times,* Nov. 13, 1986.

36. *New York Times,* June 19, 1986.

37. Indeed, there are a number of liberal and even feminist antiabortion groups. For

a summary of them, see Mary Meehan, "The Other Right-to-Lifers," *Commonweal,* Jan. 18, 1980, pp. 13–16.

38. Kristin Luker, *Abortion and the Politics of Motherhood* (Berkeley: University of California Press, 1984); Faye Ginsburg, *Contested Lives: The Abortion Debate in an American Community* (Berkeley: University of California Press, 1988). See also Allen Hunter, "In the Wings: New Right Organization and Ideology," *Radical America* 15:1–2 (Jan.–Apr. 1981): 113–38; Linda Gordon and Allen Hunter, "Sex, Family, and the New Right," *Radical America* 11:6/12:1 (Nov. 1977–Feb. 1978): 9–25.

39. Spencer Perkins, "The Prolife Credibility Gap," *Christianity Today,* Apr. 21, 1989, p. 22.

40. "Blacks Agonize over Abortion," *Newsweek,* Dec. 4, 1989, p. 63.

41. Loretta J. Ross, "African-American Women and Abortion," in *Abortion Wars: A Half Century of Struggle, 1950–2000,* ed. Rickie Solinger (Berkeley: University of California Press, 1998), 161–207.

42. Quoted in E. J. Dionne Jr., "Tepid Black Support Worries Advocates of Abortion Rights, *New York Times,* Apr. 16, 1989, p. 28.

43. Kathy Boardman, "BOGUS, the Consumer Scandal of the 1980s: Bogus Pregnancy Counseling Centers," book-length ms., n.d., p. 5; National Women's Health Network, *National News,* Mar.–Apr. 1988, p. 1. On practices of the clinics, see also *Newsweek,* Sept. 1, 1986, p. 20; *New York Times,* Dec. 17, 1986.

44. Jane Gross, "Anti-Abortion Revival: Homes for Unwed Mothers," *New York Times,* July 23, 1989, pp. 1, 13.

45. "Antiabortion Violence" (editorial), *Family Planning Perspectives* 17:1 (Jan.–Feb. 1985): 4; Patricia Donovan, "The Holy War," ibid., pp. 5–9; Boardman, "BOGUS," 3.

46. On the response to clinic bombings, see "Little or No Change in Attitudes on Abortion," *Family Planning Perspectives* 17:2 (Mar.–Apr. 1985): 76–78.

47. Roger Neustadter, "'Killing Babies': The Use of Image and Metaphor in the Right-to-Life Movement," *Michigan Sociological Review* 4 (1990): 76–83.

48. National Abortion Foundation, "NAF Violence and Disruption Statistics," online at <http://www.prochoice.org>. Between 1990 and 2000, bombings and arson attacks caused an estimated $8.5 million in damage. See also other online sources: <http://www.prochoice.org/Violence/Analysis1999.htm>, <http://www.naral.org/mediaresources/fact/terrorism.html>, and <http://www.rcrc.org/new/rollcallad1122001.html>.

49. For example, "Falwell Denounces Operation Rescue," *Christianity Today,* May 18, 1998.

50. Philip Jenkins, "Fighting Terrorism as If Women Mattered: Anti-Abortion Violence as Unconstructed Terrorism," in *Making Trouble: Cultural Construction of Crime, Deviance, and Control,* eds. Jeff Ferrell and Neil Websdale (New York: Aldine De Gruyter, 1999), 319–46.

51. Jeff Stein, "Has Violence Killed the Anti-abortion Movement?," Apr. 28, 1999, online at <http://www.salon.com/news/feature/1999/04/28/abortion/index.html>.

52. Online at <http://www.aclu-or.org/ppcase.htm> and <http://www.lektrik.com/PPvsACLA/home.htm>.

53. Neal Horsley, quoted in the *New York Times,* Oct. 26, 1998, p. 10B. The Web site was taken down for a while due to lawsuits, but as of the end of February 2002 it could still be viewed at <http://www.christiangallery.com/atrocity/aborts.html>.

54. Online at <http://www.agi-usa.org/pubs/abort_law_status.html>.

55. *Doe v. Bolton,* 410 U.S. 179 (1973).

56. *Bigelow v. Virginia,* 421 U.S. 809 (1975).

57. *Maher v. Roe,* 432 U.S. 464 (1977); *Beal v. Doe,* 432 U.S. 438 (1977); *Poelker v. Doe,* 432 U.S. 519 (1977); *Harris v. McRae,* 448 U.S. 297 (1980).

58. Susan E. Davis, ed., *Women under Attack: Victories, Backlash, and the Fight for Reproductive Freedom,* Committee for Abortion Rights and Against Sterilization pamphlet no. 7 (Boston: South End Press, 1988), 44. Studies on the impact of cutting off public funding for abortion in California estimated that 25–36 percent of women who once sought abortions would now give birth (Vicki Haddock, "Hidden Costs of Denying Abortions for Teens, Poor," *San Francisco Examiner,* Aug. 2, 1989).

59. See below for a discussion of sterilization. The irony of this policy with respect to a conservative eugenics perspective should not be lost, since it is a policy that encourages reproduction among the poor. It may also show that opponents of abortion are motivated more by gender-based anxieties than by class or race elitism; or that they are simply inconsistent.

60. *City of Akron v. Akron Center for Reproductive Health,* 462 U.S. 416 (1983); *Planned Parenthood Association of Kansas City, Mo. v. Ashcroft,* 462 U.S. 476 (1983).

61. See *Thornburgh v. Pennsylvania College of Obstetricians and Gynecologists,* 476 U.S. 747 (1986). The *Thornburgh* amicus curiae brief, with an introduction by Rosalind Petchesky, was published in *Women's Rights Law Reporter* 9:1 (Winter 1986): 324. The introduction is an excellent summary of the assumptions involved on both sides of the argument. A "Brandeis brief" refers to the use of sociological evidence to demonstrate the actual harms of existing policies, as opposed to legal arguments; the phrase comes from a brief entered by Louis Brandeis (although mainly written by women reform activists) in defense of an Oregon law limiting working hours to ten per day for women (see *Muller v. Oregon,* 208 U.S. 412 [1908]).

62. In *Roe v. Wade,* the Supreme Court required that any restrictions on a woman's decision would be subject to strict judicial scrutiny and recognized two "compelling state interests": (1) the promotion of women's health; and (2) protection of the fetus after viability if the abortion was not necessary to a woman's life or health. In *Planned Parenthood of Southeast Pennsylvania v. Casey,* 505 U.S. 833 (1992), the Court upheld any restrictions that did not create an "undue burden" for the pregnant woman.

63. The cases are 192 F.3d 1142 (8th Cir. 1999) and 120 S.Ct. 2597 (U.S. Supreme Court). Excerpts from the Supreme Court decision can be found online at <http://www.crlp.org/pub_fac_svcsum.html>.

64. Information on the current status of mifepristone can be obtained from <http://www.naral.org/issues/issues_ru486.html> and <http://www.naral.org/mediaresources/fact/pdfs/fight.pdf>.

65. Stanley K. Henshaw, "Abortion Incidence in the United States, 1995–1996," *Family Planning Perspectives* 30:6 (Nov.–Dec. 1998): 263–70.

66. Alan Guttmacher Institute, "Why Is Teenage Pregnancy Declining?," Occasional Report, Mar. 13, 2001, New York; S. B. Caudill and F. G. Mixon, "Anti-abortion Activities and the Market for Abortion Services: Protest as a Disincentive," *American Journal of Economics and Sociology* 59:3 (July 2000): 463–85.

67. Daniel T. Lichter, Diane K. McLaughlin, and David C. Ribar, "State Abortion Policy, Geographic Access to Abortion Provides, and Changing Family Formation," *Family Planning Perspectives* 30:6 (Nov.–Dec. 1998): 281–87; Lisa A. Gennetian, "The Supply of Infants Relinquished for Adoption: Did Access to Abortion Make a Differ-

ence?," *Economic Inquiry,* July 1999; Guttmacher Institute, "Why Is Teenage Pregnancy Declining?"

68. Maggie Garb, "Abortion Foes Give Birth to a 'Syndrome,'" *These Times,* Feb. 22–Mar. 1, 1989, pp. 3, 22; "Koop Challenged on Abortion Data," *New York Times,* Jan. 15, 1989, p. 1.

69. ABC News/Beliefnet poll, June 20–24, 2001.

70. ABC News/*Washington Post* poll, Jan. 2001.

71. CNN/*Time* poll, Jan. 2001.

72. "Average of 63% Approve of Legal Abortion," *Family Planning Perspectives* 19:5 (Sept.–Oct. 1987): 221; Elaine J. Hall and Myra Marx Ferree, "Race Differences in Abortion Attitudes," *Public Opinion Quarterly* 50:2 (Summer 1986): 193–207.

73. Clyde Wilcox, "Race, Religion, Region, and Abortion Attitudes," *Sociological Analysis* 53 (Spring 1992): 97–105; Ranjita Misra and Bhagabah Panigrahi, "Effect of Age, Gender, Race on Abortion Attitude," *International Journal of Sociology and Social Policy* 18 (1998): 94–118; ABC News/Beliefnet poll, June 20–24, 2001.

74. Susan L. Norman for the Christian Broadcasting Network, quoted by Courtney Leatherman, "Nearly 1 in 10 Female College Students Has Had Abortion," *Chronicle of Higher Education,* May 31, 1989, p. A23.

75. Sandra Rosenhouse-Persson and Georges Sabagh, "Attitudes toward Abortion among Catholic Mexican-American Women: The Effects of Religiosity and Education," *Demography* 20:1 (Feb. 1983): 87–98.

76. ABC News/Beliefnet poll, June 20–24, 2001.

77. Michael W. Combs and Susan Welch, "Blacks, Whites, and Attitudes toward Abortion," *Public Opinion Quarterly* 46 (1982): 510–20. See also Granberg and Granberg, "Abortion Attitudes"; Willard Cates Jr., "Abortion Attitudes of Black Women," *Women and Health* 2:3 (Nov.–Dec. 1977): 3–9. It is relevant in this regard to note that, in contrast to repeated scholarly assumptions that African Americans did not traditionally use birth control, new scholarship argues that birth control use is the best explanation for declining black fertility rates since the late nineteenth century (e.g., Joseph A. McFalls Jr. and George S. Masnick, "Birth Control and the Fertility of the U.S. Black Population," *Journal of Family History* 6:1 [Spring 1981]: 89–106).

78. Stanley K. Henshaw and Kathryn Kost, "Abortion Patients in 1994–95: Characteristics and Contraceptive Use," *Family Planning Perspectives* 28:4 (July–Aug. 1996): 140–47, 158.

79. National Abortion Federation, *Economics of Abortion Fact Sheet,* Jan. 1996, <http://www.naral.org/medicaresources/publications/2002/funding.pdf>. The North Carolina study covered the years 1981–94.

80. Henshaw, "Abortion Incidence in the United States;" Stanley K. Henshaw, "Factors Hindering Access to Abortion Services," *Family Planning Perspectives* 27:2 (Mar.–Apr. 1995): 54–59; Marlene Fried, "Abortion in the United States," *Health and Human Rights* 4 (2000): 174–94.

81. Henshaw and Kost, "Abortion Patients in 1994–95"; Abortion Access Project, *Fact Sheet,* online at <http://www.repro-activist.org>.

82. "Hospital Mergers: The Hidden Crisis," in *Religious Pro-Choice Americans Speak Out* (pamphlet; Washington, D.C.: Religious Coalition for Reproductive Choice, 2000), also at <http://www.rcrc.org/pubs/speakout/merge.html>; National Abortion Federation, *Fact Sheet,* Sept. 1997; Liz Bucar, *When Catholic and Non-Catholic Hospitals*

Merge: Reproductive Health Compromised (Washington, D.C.: Catholics for a Free Choice, 1998).

83. Rene Almeling, Laureen Tews, and Susan Dudley, "Abortion Training in U.S. Obstetrics and Gynecology Residency Programs, 1998," *Family Planning Perspectives* 32:6 (Nov.–Dec. 2000): 268–71, 320; M. A. Shanahan, W. P. Metheny, J. Star, and J. F. Peipert, "Induced Abortion: Physician Training and Practice Patterns," *Journal of Reproductive Medicine* 44:5 (May 1999): 428–32.

84. A California legislative report calculated the additional costs to all levels of government in welfare expenses, education, day care, foster care, adoption services, hospitalization not only for "normal" pregnancies but for the many cocaine- or alcohol-affected babies expected to be born, and help for children with learning disabilities, demonstrating *additional* costs of $86–126 million, should public funding for abortion be ended; $4.5 million more would be added if a parental consent law was passed. See Haddock, "Hidden Costs of Denying Abortions."

Chapter 14: Is Nothing Simple about Reproduction Control?

1. Helen I. Marieskind and Barbara Ehrenreich, "Toward Socialist Medicine: The Women's Health Movement," *Social Policy* 6:2 (Sept.–Oct. 1975): 34–42; Rachel Fruchter et al., "The Women's Health Movement: Where Are We Now?," *Healthright* 1:1 (1974): 4.

2. Barbara Beckwith, "Boston Women's Health Book Collective: Women Empowering Women," *Women and Health* 10:1 (Spring 1985): 1–7; interview with Norma Swenson, June 27, 1988.

3. Pearson is quoted in Gina Kolata, "Hormone Replacement Study a Shock to the Medical System," *New York Times,* July 1, 2002, pp. 1, 16. The NWHN also supported the campaign for mandatory standards on absorbency labeling for tampons, led by Esther Rome of the BWHBC.

4. Thanks to Dr. Vicki Alexander for this information.

5. Sheryl Burt Ruzek, *The Women's Health Movement: Feminist Alternatives to Medical Control* (New York: Praeger, 1978), 171.

6. Their equipment was a smaller version of the expensive vacuum aspiration equipment being used by physicians, and their claim to have invented this was challenged by Harvey Karman. See Ruzek, *Women's Health Movement,* 54ff., for this story.

7. This story is told by Elizabeth Fee, "Women and Health Care: A Comparison of Theories," in *Women and Health: The Politics of Sex and Medicine,* ed. Elizabeth Fee (Farmingdale, N.Y.: Baywood, 1983), 26.

8. Carole Joffe, *The Regulation of Sexuality: Experiences of Family Planning Workers* (Philadelphia: Temple University Press, 1986), 34–35. There have been several feminist-inspired strikes by abortion clinic workers objecting to speedups that made it impossible for them to counsel women with enough individual attention to assure that they were making careful choices.

9. Steven R. Steiber, "How to Plan to Tap into the Women's Health Market," *Health Care Marketer,* Apr. 14, 1986, p. 7; Sandy Lutz, "Hospitals Develop Satellite Clinics to Tap Emerging Women's Market," *Modern Healthcare,* Jan. 2, 1987, p. 76; Nancy Worcester and Marianne H. Whatley, "The Response of the Health Care System to the Women's Health Movement: The Selling of Women's Health Centers," in *Women's Health: Readings on Social, Economic, and Political Issues,* ed. Nancy Worcester and Marianne H. Whatley (Dubuque, Iowa: Kendall/Hunt, 1988), 17–24.

10. Similar conclusions were drawn in a study of birthing centers by Raymond G. DeVries, "The Alternative Birth Center: Option or Cooptation," *Women and Health* 5:3 (Fall 1980): 47–60.

11. Castellano B. Turner and William A. Darity, "Fears of Genocide among Black Americans as Related to Age, Sex, and Region," *American Journal of Public Health* 63:12 (Dec. 1973): 1029–34, quoted in Willard Cates Jr., "Abortion Attitudes of Black Women," *Women and Health* 2:3 (Nov.–Dec. 1977): 3; A. O. Harrison, "Family Planning Attitudes among Black Females," *Journal of Social and Behavior Sciences* 22:3 (Winter 1977): 136–45; interview with Dr. Vicki Alexander, Aug. 2, 1988. According to Harrison, black women's use of birth control, just like white women's, was highly correlated with urban and middle-class living conditions.

12. For example, Vernon Davies, "Fertility versus Welfare: The Negro American Dilemma," *Phylon* 27:3 (Fall 1966): 226–32; Loretta Ross, "African-American Women and Abortion," in *Abortion Wars: A Half Century of Struggle, 1950–2000*, ed. Rickie Solinger (Berkeley: University of California Press, 1998), 161–207.

13. Quoted in Ros Baxandall and Linda Gordon, eds., *Dear Sisters: Dispatches from the Women's Liberation Movement* (New York: Basic Books, 2000), 135.

14. Quoted in *Women Wise*, Fall 1983, p. 2.

15. Interview with Byllye Avery, Aug. 5, 1988.

16. The accomplishments of the NBWHP are detailed on their Web site, at <http://www.nationalblackwomenshealthproject.org>.

17. For accounts of this meeting, see *Off Our Backs*, Apr. 1986, pp. 1–5; *Options* 13:1 (Apr. 1986): 3; *AMSA News*, May 14, 1986, p. 7.

18. Quoted in Maria Erlien, "Beyond *Roe vs. Wade*: Redefining the Pro-Choice Agenda," *Radical America* 22:2–3 (June 1989): 14–24; Jenkins, in *Boston Globe*, Apr. 26, 1989, p. 40, is quoted in Erlien, "Beyond *Roe vs. Wade*," 20.

19. Vicki Alexander, "Black Women and Health," *On the Issues* 6 (1986); "Assault on Reproductive Rights," *Asian-Pacific Health News*, Sept. 1982, pp. 1–6.

20. Norma Swenson, notes on PPFA national meeting, Nov. 18–21, 1987, in the Boston Women's Health Book Collective Archives (hereafter cited as BWHBC Archives).

21. U.N. Department for Economic and Social Information and Policy Analysis, Population Division, *Population Consensus at Cairo, Mexico City, and Bucharest: An Analytical Comparison* (New York: United Nations, 1995); C. Alison McIntosh and Jason L. Finkle, "The Cairo Conference on Population and Development: A New Paradigm?," *Population and Development Review* 21:2 (June 1995): 223–60.

22. Alan Guttmacher Institute, "The Cairo Consensus" ("Issues in Brief"), Mar. 1995, New York; Family Health International, "Contraception Influences Quality of Life," *Network* 18:4 (Summer 1998); Rockefeller Foundation, *High Stakes: The United States, Global Population, and Our Common Future* (report; New York: Rockefeller Foundation, 1997).

23. Nicholas Eberstadt, "The Population Implosion," *Foreign Policy*, Mar.–Apr. 2001, pp. 42–53.

24. Online at <http://www.agi-usa.org/pubs/fb_0599.html>.

25. Alan Guttmacher Institute, *Sharing Responsibility: Women, Society, and Abortion Worldwide* (report; New York, 1999); Rockefeller Foundation, *High Stakes*.

26. Family Health International, "Contraception Influences Quality of Life," *Network* 18:4 (Summer 1998).

27. Rockefeller Foundation, *High Stakes*, 11.

28. Susan A. Cohen, "Global Gag Rule: Exporting Antiabortion Ideology at the Expense of American Values," *Guttmacher Report on Public Policy* 4:3 (June 2001).

29. My synopsis of the political battles over oral contraceptives is indebted to Andrea Tone, *Devices and Desires: A History of Contraceptives in America* (New York: Hill and Wang, 2001); Paul Vaughan, *The Pill on Trial* (New York: Coward-McCann, 1970); and Elizabeth Siegel Watkins, *On the Pill: A Social History of Oral Contraceptives, 1950–1970* (Baltimore: Johns Hopkins University Press, 1998).

30. Quoted in Tone, *Devices and Desires*, 249–50.

31. Judith Bruce, "User's Perspectives on Contraceptive Technology and Delivery Systems: Highlighting Some Feminist Issues," *Technology in Society: An International Journal* 9:3–4 (1987): 359–83. Bruce quotes Bernard Berelson, president of the Population Council in the 1960s: "'When uninformed women encountered minor difficulties they tended to discontinue. . . . dissatisfied women have spread adverse gossip and encouraged others to discontinue'" (359–60).

32. William F. Pratt and Christine A. Bachrach, "What Do Women Use When They Stop Using the Pill?," *Family Planning Perspectives* 19:6 (Nov.–Dec. 1987): 257–65; Rosalind Pollack Petchesky, *Abortion and Woman's Choice: The State, Sexuality, and Reproductive Freedom* (New York: Longman, 1984), 188. By contrast, Jacqueline Darroch Forrest and Stanley K. Henshaw, in "What U.S. Women Think and Do about Contraception," *Family Planning Perspectives* 15:4 (July–Aug. 1983): 157–66, attribute the decline of oral contraceptive use to the impact of "adverse propaganda." The situation was substantially different in the Third World, where high-dosage pills were urged and sometimes dumped upon women often lacking any other contraceptive alternatives.

33. Ruzek, *Women's Health Movement*, 43. Note that the FDA apparently could have claimed authority to screen IUDs, on the basis of Supreme Court decisions, but did not do so.

34. My synopsis of the conflicts about IUDs is indebted to Morton Mintz, *At Any Cost: Corporate Greed, Women, and the Dalkon Shield* (New York: Pantheon Books, 1985); Richard B. Sobol, *Bending the Law: The Story of the Dalkon Shield Bankruptcy* (Chicago: University of Chicago Press, 1991); and Nicole J. Grant, *The Selling of Contraception: The Dalkon Shield Case, Sexuality, and Women's Autonomy* (Columbus: Ohio State University Press, 1992). Like oral contraceptives, IUDs were tested on poor minority women, largely Chicanas. An excellent early summary of IUD problems is in Katherine Roberts, "The Intrauterine Device as a Health Risk," *Women and Health*, July–Aug. 1977, pp. 21–30.

35. *Network News* (NWHN), July–Aug. 1987; Catherine Breslin, "Day of Reckoning," *Ms.*, June 1989, pp. 46–52. Some of the ironies of the Dalkon Shield case are especially bitter. For example, when Davis began to promote his new IUD, he targeted young and childless women, including teenagers, because the device was more flexible than other IUDs. At the 1970 hearings, he testified that IUDs were superior because oral contraceptives were too dangerous.

36. As I write, only two IUDs are available in the United States: the ParaGard Copper T and Mirena, a progesterone-releasing IUD. Less than 1 percent of contracepting women in the United States use IUDs.

37. And no wonder, given the current understanding of how IUDs work: "All IUDs that have been tested . . . induce a local inflammatory reaction in the endometrium that

changes the cellular and humoral components of the fluid contents of the uterine cavity; in humans, the entire genital tract then appears to be affected by the inflammatory fluids from the uterine lumen" (Polly F. Harrison and Allan Rosenfield, eds., *Contraceptive Research and Development: Looking to the Future* [Washington, D.C.: National Academy Press, 1996], 104).

38. Thanks to Norma Swenson of the BWHBC for this information.

39. Online at <http://www.agi-usa.org/pubs/>.

40. Harrison and Rosenfield, *Contraceptive Research and Development*, 21; S. E. Samuels and M. D. Smith, eds., *Norplant and Poor Women* (Menlo Park, Calif.: Henry J. Kaiser Family Foundation, 1992).

41. Charlotte Ellertson, "History and Efficacy of Emergency Contraception: Beyond Coca-Cola," *Family Planning Perspectives* 22:2 (June 1996): 52–56; "NARAL Urges FDA to Make Emergency Contraceptive Pills Available Over-the-Counter," online at <http://www.naral.org/mediaresources/press/pro62900_ecp.html>; "In Seven Oregon counties . . . ," *Family Planning Perspectives* 31:5 (Sept. 1999): 211.

42. Harrison and Rosenfield, *Contraceptive Research and Development*, 227.

43. Jeannie I. Rosoff, "Taking Family Planning Out of Title X: The Impact of the Proposed New Regulations," *Family Planning Perspectives* 19:5 (Sept.–Oct. 1987): 222–26; *The U.S. International Family Planning Program under Siege*, PPFA pamphlet, 1987; Michael Klitsch, "Courts Sink New Title X Regulations," *Family Planning Perspectives* 20:2 (Mar.–Apr. 1988): 96–98.

44. Malcolm Potts and Robert Wheeler, "The Quest for a Magic Bullet," *Family Planning Perspectives* 13:6 (Nov.–Dec. 1981): 269.

45. For a brief historical discussion and general review of contemporary issues, see Rebecca Chalker, *The Complete Cervical Cap Guide* (New York: Harper and Row, 1987).

46. Barbara Seaman, testimony before the U.S. Senate Subcommittee on Health and Scientific Research, Aug. 1, 1970, mss., in BWHBC Archives. In 1982–83 a conflict arose between Washington Women's Self-Help, a women's clinic, and the Public Citizen, a consumer protection organization—two groups usually on the same side—because of the latter's critical view of the clinic's use of lay health workers. *ObGyn News* cited the fact that cervical caps took about forty-five minutes per patient to fit as an argument against them ("Current Cervical Caps Often Fail to Meet Expectations," *ObGyn News*, Jan. 1, 1981).

47. The NWHN considered a court challenge to this high-risk designation but rejected that option in order not to weaken these important new protections in general.

48. Amy Shapiro, "What Ever Happened to the Cervical Cap?," *Harvard Women's Law Journal* 10 (Spring 1987): 308–39; Erica Gollub, "The Cervical Cap: Test Case for U.S. Regulatory Politics," *Health/PAC Bulletin* 16:6 (Aug. 1986): 22–26; Chalker, *Complete Cervical Cap Guide*.

49. Michael Klitsch, "FDA Approval Ends Cervical Cap's Marathon," *Family Planning Perspectives* 20:3 (May June 1988): 137–38.

50. Shapiro, "What Ever Happened to the Cervical Cap?," 318.

51. Gollub, "Cervical Cap," 26n.

52. Kathryn S. Meier, "The Today Sponge," *Network News* (NWHN), Nov.–Dec. 1985, pp. 4–5.

53. The pertinent documents are available online at <http://www.verity.fda.gov/search97cgi/s97_cgi.exe>.

54. For a useful brief bibliography, see Susan E. Bell, "Feminist Self-Help: The Case of Fertility Consciousness/Women-Controlled Natural Birth Control Groups," *Radical Teacher* 19 (1982): 17–20.

55. Jacqueline Darroch Forrest and Richard R. Fordyce, "U.S. Women's Contraceptive Attitudes and Practice: How Have They Changed in the 1980s?," *Family Planning Perspectives* 20:3 (May–June 1988): 112–18.

56. Akinrinola Bankole, Jacqueline E. Darroch, and Susheela Singh, "Determinants of Trends in Condom Use in the United States, 1988–1995," *Family Planning Perspectives* 31:6 (Nov.–Dec. 1999): 264–71.

57. Bruce, "User's Perspectives on Contraceptive Technology."

58. Ellen Sweet, "A Failed Revolution," *Ms.*, Mar. 1988, pp. 75–79.

59. Linda Atkinson, "Two Decades of Contraceptive Research: Prospects for the 21st Century," ms., Oct. 1986, BWHBC Archives; Richard Lincoln and Lisa Kaeser, "Whatever Happened to the Contraceptive Revolution?," *International Family Planning Perspectives* 13:4 (Dec. 1987): 141–45, also published in *Family Planning Perspectives* 20:1 (Jan.–Feb. 1988): 20–24. Interestingly, Carl Djerassi, one of the original developers of the synthetic progesterone needed for oral contraceptives, in a prescient 1970 article called for relaxation of FDA testing requirements, urging a kind of interim conditional approval, and predicted that, failing this reform, we would be no further ahead by 1984 ("Birth Control after 1984," *Science* 169:3949 [Sept. 4, 1970]: 941–51).

60. Atkinson, "Two Decades of Contraceptive Research."

61. Harrison and Rosenfield, *Contraceptive Research and Development*, 36.

62. The term "magic bullet" was applied to high-tech contraception by Malcolm Potts and Robert Wheeler in "The Quest for a Magic Bullet," *Family Planning Perspectives* 13:6 (Nov.–Dec. 1981): 269. It is discussed also by Petchesky, *Abortion and Woman's Choice*, 189. Frank Furstenberg has referred to an "'ideology of inoculation,'" the view that short-term assistance will magically have long-term effects (quoted in Joffe, *Regulation of Sexuality*, 24). Joffe points out that critique of the technocratic approaches of the population control establishment was heard from Kingsley Davis in the 1960s and even from Joseph Califano, secretary of the Department of Health, Education, and Welfare, in the 1970s (ibid., 26).

63. For a critique of "magic bullet" thinking about venereal disease, see Allan M. Brandt, *No Magic Bullet: A Social History of Venereal Disease in the United States since 1880* (1985; rpt., New York: Oxford University Press, 1987); Potts and Wheeler, "Quest for a Magic Bullet."

64. Forrest and Fordyce, "U.S. Women's Contraceptive Attitudes and Practice"; Rosalind Pollack Petchesky, "'Reproductive Choice' in the Contemporary United States: A Social Analysis of Female Sterilization," in *And the Poor Get Children: Radical Perspectives on Population Dynamics*, ed. Karen Michaelson (New York: Monthly Review Press, 1981), 51; Forrest and Henshaw, "What U.S. Women Think and Do." Thanks to Susan Jew at the Alan Guttmacher Institute for information used in this discussion.

65. The figures are from a North Carolina study by Johanna Schoen, summarized in "Between Choice and Coercion: Women and the Politics of Sterilization in North Carolina, 1929–1975," *Journal of Women's History* 13:1 (Spring 2001): 132–56.

66. Annette B. Ramírez de Arellano and Conrad Seipp, *Colonialism, Catholicism, and Contraception: A History of Birth Control in Puerto Rico* (Chapel Hill: University of North Carolina Press, 1983).

67. Cited in Jennifer A. Nelson, "'Abortions under Community Control': Feminism, Nationalism, and the Politics of Reproduction among New York City's Young Lords," *Journal of Women's History* 13:1 (Spring 2001): 167.

68. Ibid., 168.

69. Some critics have suggested as a further incentive that gynecologists and obstetricians were short of work, and especially surgical work, as a result of the falling birth rate and that residents needed more surgical practice. See Robert E. McGarrah, "Voluntary Female Sterilization: Abuses, Risks, and Guidelines," *Hastings Center Report*, June 1974, p. 6, quoted in Barbara Caress, "Sterilization," *Health/PAC Bulletin* 62 (Jan.–Feb. 1975): 4.

70. Pratt and Bachrach, "What Do Women Use?," 263.

71. This information was found online at <http://www.nichd.nih.gov/publications/pubs/vasect.htm>.

72. Online at <http://www.agi-usa.org/pubs/teen_preg_sr_0699.html>.

73. Petchesky, "'Reproductive Choice' in the Contemporary United States."

74. Nelson, "'Abortions under Community Control,'" 169.

75. Helen Rodriguez-Trias, "The Women's Health Movement: Women Take Power," in *Reforming Medicine. Lessons of the Lost Quarter Century*, ed. Victor and Ruth Sidel (New York: Pantheon, 1984), 107–26.

76. The double standard here—forcing sterilization on poor women, barring prosperous women from sterilization—is reminiscent of that regarding employment—requiring it of poor mothers, condemning it in prosperous mothers.

77. Robert E. McGarrah, staff attorney for the Public Citizen, to Caspar Weinberger, Secretary of HEW, Jan. 20, 1975; Ted Bogue and Daniel W. Sigelman, Sterilization Report no. 3, *Public Citizen*, July 17, 1979; ACLU, Hospital Survey of Sterilization Policies, 1975, all in BWHBC Archives, folder "Sterilization Abuse."

78. "Sterilization Abuse," *Network News* (NWHN), Sept. 1979, BWHBC Archives.

79. Quoted in Caress, "Sterilization," 5; Claudia Dreifus, "Sterilizing the Poor," in *Seizing Our Bodies: The Politics of Women's Health*, ed. Claudia Dreifus (New York: Random House, 1977), 105–20.

80. Caress, "Sterilization," 11.

81. Petchesky, *Abortion and Woman's Choice*, 180.

82. Rebecca Staton and Meredith Tax for CARASA to Eleanor Smeal of NOW, Aug. 10, 1978; *CARASA News*, Nov. 2, 1978, pp. 3–5, both in BWHBC Archives.

83. Bogue and Sigelman, Sterilization Report no. 3; *Family Planning Perspectives* 11:6 (Nov.–Dec. 1979): 366–67.

84. NWHN, "Sterilization Abuse."

85. Alan Guttmacher Institute, *Why Is Teenage Pregnancy Declining?: The Roles of Abstinence, Sexual Activity, and Contraceptive Use* (New York, 1999), 4.

86. Stephanie J. Ventura, Sally C. Curtin, and T. J. Mathews, "Declines in Teenage Birth Rates, 1991–98," *National Vital Statistics Reports* (Atlanta: Centers for Disease Control and Prevention, Oct. 25, 1999); Children's Defense Fund, "Trends in Teen Births," data sheet, Sept. 1986, Washington, D.C.; Children's Defense Fund, Adolescent Pregnancy Prevention: Prenatal Care Campaign, *The Health of America's Children: Maternal and Child Health Data Book* (Washington, D.C., 1988), 27–29; *Family Planning Perspectives* 19:2 (Mar.–Apr. 1987): 83; *Contraceptive Technology Update*, May 1987, p. 63.

Births to those fourteen and under are so few that statistically significant trends cannot be identified. Such births constitute 0.1 percent of all white births and 0.8 percent of nonwhite births. Not all publicists respect this limitation. For example, the pamphlet *Teen Pregnancy in Milwaukee* issued by the Wisconsin Association of Family and Children's Agencies in 1988 reports a 200 percent increase in the birth rate among girls ten to fourteen between 1980 and 1985 but doesn't report the actual numbers. On rates of teenage sexual activity, see Sandra L. Hofferth, Joan R. Kahn, and Wendy Baldwin, "Premarital Sexual Activity among U.S. Teenage Women over the Past Three Decades," *Family Planning Perspectives* 19:2 (Mar.–Apr. 1987): 46–53; press release of June 5, 1987, BWHBC Archives.

87. Christopher Jencks, "What Is the Underclass—and Is It Growing?," *Focus* (University of Wisconsin Institute for Research on Poverty) 12:1 (Spring–Summer 1989): 14–26.

88. Ventura et al., "Declines in Teenage Birth Rates, 1991–98"; Alan Guttmacher Institute, "Welfare Law and the Drive to Reduce 'Illegitimacy,'" *Issues in Brief,* Mar. 13, 2001, online at <http://www.agi-usa.org/pubs/ib_welfare00.html>. See also two very different estimates in Children's Defense Fund, *Health of America's Children,* 27–29, and *Family Planning Perspectives* 19:2 (Mar.–Apr. 1987): 83–84.

89. For example, Douglas J. Besharov and Alison J. Quinn, "Not All Female-Headed Families Are Created Equal," *The Public Interest* 89 (Fall 1987): 48–56; Maris A. Vinovskis, "Teenage Pregnancy and the Underclass," *The Public Interest* 93 (Fall 1988): 87–96.

90. *Family Planning Perspectives* 19:2 (Mar.–Apr. 1987): 83–84; Joyce Ladner, "Teenage Pregnancy: The Implication for Black Americans," in *The State of Black America 1986* (New York: National Urban League, 1986), 70.

91. Ladner, "Teenage Pregnancy," 69. The "Moynihan Report" was officially titled *The Negro Family: The Case for National Action* but became best known by the name of its author, Daniel P. Moynihan, at the time an assistant secretary in the Office of Policy Planning and Research at the U.S. Department of Labor.

92. In this discussion I use "single" and "lone" mothers interchangeably to refer to all women parenting children without a partner, regardless of whether they are currently or have been married.

93. There is no space here even to begin to summarize the voluminous literature about single mothers and their children, but see, for example, Kristen Luker, *Abortion and the Politics of Motherhood* (Berkeley: University of California Press, 1984); Irwin Garfinkel and Sara S. McLanahan, *Single Mothers and Their Children: A New American Dilemma* (Washington, D.C.: Urban Institute Press, 1986). On single mothers and the underclass, see Jencks, "What Is the Underclass?," and Sara McLanahan and Irwin Garfinkel, "Single Mothers, the Underclass, and Social Policy," *Annals of the American Academy* 501 (Jan. 1989): 92–104.

94. According to a study published in 1994, 83 percent of teens who give birth are from poor families, compared to 61 percent of teens who have abortions and 38 percent of teens overall (Alan Guttmacher Institute, *Sex and America's Teenagers* [New York, 1994], 58). See also Petchesky, *Abortion and Woman's Choice,* 148–55. The claim that there is a "market" for adoptive babies is false when it comes to nonwhite babies.

95. W. C. Pratt and M. C. Horn, "Wanted and Unwanted Childbearing: United States, 1973–1982," *Advance Data from Vital and Health Statistics* 108 (1985), summarized in *Family Planning Perspectives* 17:6 (Nov.–Dec. 1985): 274–75.

96. Susan N. Wilson, "Politicians: Our New Sexuality Educators?," *Family Life*

Matters 2 (Winter 1997); Daniel Daley, "Exclusive Purpose: Abstinence-Only Proponents Create Federal Entitlement in Welfare Reform," *SIECUS Report* 25:4 (Apr. 1997): 3–5.

97. Alan Guttmacher Institute, *School-based Health Centers and the Birth Control Debate*, online at <http://www.agi-usa.org/pubs/ib_1200.html>.

98. Kaiser Family Foundation Briefing, "Sex Education in America: A View from Inside the Classroom," Sept. 25, 2000, online at <http://www.kaisernetwork.org/health_cast/hcast_index.cfm?display=detail&hc=38>.

99. See <http://www.agi-usa.org/pubs/archives/newsrelease697.html>; AGI, *School-based Health Center.*

100. Ladner, "Teenage Pregnancy," 80; Michelle Fine, "Sexuality, Schooling, and Adolescent Females: The Missing Discourse of Desire," *Harvard Education Review* 58:1 (Feb. 1983): 44; Neely Tucker, "Factions Spur Hodgepodge of Separately Funded Clinics," *Florida Today*, Oct. 26, 1986.

101. D. Kirby et al., "School-based Programs to Reduce Sexual Risk Behaviors: A Review of Effectiveness," *Public Health Reports* 109 (1994): 339–60; K. A. Moore et al., "Adolescent Pregnancy Prevention Programs: Interventions and Evaluations," *Child Trends* (Washington, D.C.), June 1995.

102. Patricia Donovan, "Does the Family Cap Influence Birthrates?: Two New Studies Say 'No,'" *Guttmacher Report on Public Policy* 1:1 (Feb. 1998).

103. Alan Guttmacher Institute, "Welfare Law and the Drive to Reduce 'Illegitimacy,'" *Issues in Brief*, Mar. 13, 2001, available online at <http://www.agi-usa.org/pubs/ib_welfare00.html>.

104. The definition is in P.L. 104-193, sec. 510(b)(2).

105. Daley, "Exclusive Purpose"; online at <http://www.agi-usa.org/pubs/journals/gr030201.html>.

106. Jennifer E. Marshall, "Welfare's Battle Lines," *Perspective* (Family Research Council), May 1995.

107. Compare the report itself—National Research Council, *Risking the Future: Adolescent Sexuality, Pregnancy, and Childbearing*, ed. Cheryl D. Hayes (Washington, D.C.: National Academy Press, 1987), 1:120 –to Leslie Maitland Werner's "U.S. Council Urges Birth Control to Combat Teen-Age Pregnancies," *New York Times*, Dec. 10, 1986, pp. 1, B13, and the Alan Guttmacher Institute's press release, BWHBC Archives.

108. All of the data I offer on HIV/AIDS, unless otherwise indicated, comes from the Centers for Disease Control, Division of HIV/AIDS Prevention, miscellaneous surveillance data, posted at <http://www.cdc.gov/hiv/dhap.htm> as of August 2001.

109. Reuters Health News, July, 20, 2001.

110. Three-fourths of those polled in 2001 said they would be comfortable with anti-HIV/AIDS condom ads on TV, while only 60 percent said they would support ads for contraceptives if HIV/AIDS was not mentioned. Moreover, when HIV/AIDS was mentioned in the poll, religious differences in support for contraceptive advertising diminished. without mention of the disease, there was a 25 percent difference between high levels of Jewish and lower levels of Protestant support, with Catholics in between; mentioning HIV/AIDS produced an 11 percent difference. (It is interesting that Catholics object less than Protestants to TV ads for contraceptives even though Catholics are 10 percent more likely to have religious objections to using contraceptives.) See Louis Harris and Associates, *Attitudes about Television, Sex, and Contraceptive Ad-*

vertising (New York: Planned Parenthood, 1987), 46–47 (tables 19a and 19b), 67–70 (tables 30b, 31a, and 31b). In evaluating these figures, it should be noted that the survey was contracted by Planned Parenthood in order to develop evidence to convince television networks and individual stations to accept contraceptive ads; it was hardly a disinterested inquiry. Still, a more recent—and disinterested—poll found the same thing (online at <http://dailynews.yahoo.com/h/nm/20010619/hl/ads-1.html>).

111. Associated Press, July 1, 2001.

Conclusion

1. Barbara Taylor, *Eve and the New Jerusalem: Socialism and Feminism in the Nineteenth Century* (London: Virago, 1983).

Index

ABCL. *See* American Birth Control League
abortifacient, 16–18, 26–27, 34, 35, 150
abortion, 13, 24–30, 113, 120, 295–320, 339;
  abortionists, 186, 318; African American
  opinions of, 298, 307–8, 317; attitudes
  toward, 316–17, 359; availability of, 302,
  311–12, 315, 318–19, 359; birth control
  clinics and, 262; class differences and,
  315, 317; clinics for, 308–9, 325; conservative response, 297, 302–15; contraception
  and, 30–31, 113, 311, 335, 339; criminalization, 26, 316, 357, 360; D&C abortion,
  273, 299; demand for, 262; demedicalization of, 300–301; early twentieth century,
  107, 150; economics and, 305; education
  about, 113; in eighteenth and nineteenth
  centuries, 7, 13, 24–30, 65; emergency
  contraception defined as, 336; eugenic
  reasons for, 307, 319; family and, 307; gag
  rule, 331; guilt and, 300, 315–16; ideology
  and, 300; illegal, 16, 25; infanticide instead of, 15, 23–24; international policy
  and, 329–31; Latino/as and, 317; legality
  of, 1, 65, 297–300, 311, 330–31; minors
  and, 310–11, 318, 347, 349; morality of,
  301; obstacles to, 302, 311, 318; "partial
  birth" abortion, 311–13; politicization of,
  300–301; politics of, 297; preindustrial
  society and, 13, 15–17; rates of, 315, 352;
  redefined, 300, 303, 316, 319; religiosity
  and, 7–9, 25, 26, 305, 317; reproductive
  rights and, 296–97, 318–20, 326; RU-486
  use defined as, 313, 336; safety of, 16–17,
  25–26, 330, 336, 357; second-trimester,

302; sexuality and, 304; social purity campaign and, 12; therapeutic, 273, 299–301;
  third-trimester, 311–13, 316. *See also*
  Jane; pro-choice movement; Right to Life
  movement
Abrams, Frank, 283
abstinence, 59–60, 105, 118, 347. *See also*
  continence
Accreditation Council for Graduate Medical
  Education, 319
ACLU. *See* American Civil Liberties Union
ACOG. *See* American College of Obstetri-
  cians and Gynecologists
Addams, Jane, 176
Adolescent Family Life Act, 350, 352
adoption, 347
adultery, 277–78
advertising, 128, 276
AFDC. *See* Aid to Families with Dependent
  Children
African Americans. *See* blacks
agricultural society, 8–9, 13–15
A. H. Robins, 324, 334
AIDS. *See* HIV/AIDS
Aid to Families with Dependent Children
  (AFDC), 289–90
Alan Guttmacher Institute, 328
alcohol, 77–78
Allison, Van Kleeck, 184, 198
AMA. *See* American Medical Association
American Academy of Pediatrics, 311
American Birth Control League (ABCL),
  162, 171, 181–83, 189, 197, 199, 203,
  205–10, 213–15, 220–23, 227, 229, 233–

Linda Gordon taught for seventeen years at the University of Wisconsin at Madison and is now a professor of history at New York University. She has specialized in examining the historical roots of contemporary social policy debates, particularly as they concern gender and family issues, and during the Clinton administration served on the Advisory Council on Violence against Women of the Departments of Justice and Health and Human Services. Her 1988 book, *Heroes of Their Own Lives: The History and Politics of Family Violence*, which won the Joan Kelly Prize for the best book in women's history and was reprinted in 2002 by the University of Illinois Press, looks at the history of policies toward child abuse and violence against women. *Pitied but Not Entitled: Single Mothers and the History of Welfare* (1994) won the Berkshire Prize and the Gustavus Myers Human Rights Award. *The Great Arizona Orphan Abduction* (1999) won the Bancroft Prize for the best book in U.S. history and the Beveridge Prize for the best book on the history of the Americas. Her current project is a biography of Dorothea Lange.

The University of Illinois Press
is a founding member of the
Association of American University Presses.

_____

Composed in 10/13 New Caledonia
with New Caledonia display
by Jim Proefrock
at the University of Illinois Press
Designed by Paula Newcomb
Manufactured by Thomson-Shore, Inc.

University of Illinois Press
1325 South Oak Street
Champaign, IL 61820-6903
www.press.uillinois.edu